"Mel Blanc is without question the greatest voice-man of all time. I'm not talking about impersonations, I'm talking about voice.*"*
RICH LITTLE

"One of the people in Hollywood I've been pleased and honored to call a friend is Mel Blanc. The number of times he's made me laugh with his countless vocal impersonations places him among my favorite friends."
VINCENT PRICE

"He pioneered a new concept of comedy and is considered a genius. But best of all, he's a dear and loyal friend."
LUCILLE BALL

"What else can I say? I love the guy. He's one of the funniest people around."
KIRK DOUGLAS

"You have brought more than 400 characters into the lives of children and adults the world over in the progress of brightening our spirits and making us laugh. Though we really don't see your face, we know you're there behind our favorite cartoon personalities."

PRESIDENT AND MRS. RONALD REAGAN

"Mel Blanc was truly the greatest voice talent the world has ever known. He really was the man of a thousand voices. He voiced some of the most incredible characters that we have grown up with, like Bugs, Foghorn Leghorn, Daffy Duck and Barney Rubble, just to name a few. Mel Blanc had a tremendous gift where he was able to give each creation their own personality. They were not just animated cartoon characters but more like little souls and no two were alike. More importantly, no two sounded alike. That's a real feat in the voiceover world and that's why Mel was in a league of his own. He was a great inspiration to all who loved his work."

JOHNNY B. OF THE JERKY BOYS

"Nyaaah. What's up, doc? What else can I say? Mel and me's been buddies for the last 50 years. And he's the only person I know who always has the last word with me."

BUGS BUNNY

THE MAN
OF A
THOUSAND
VOICES

Mel Blanc

BY BEN OHMART

Published in the USA by:
BearManor Media
PO Box 1129
Duncan, Oklahoma 73534-1129
www.bearmanormedia.com

ISBN 978-1-59393-259-6

Printed in the United States of America.
Cover Illustrations by Donald Pitchford.
Book design by Brian Pearce | Red Jacket Press.

Table of Contents

For My Lovely Wife, Mayu

and to

Noel Blanc
Walt Mitchell
Charles Stumpf
Mary Lou Wallace
without whom there would be no book

Foreword by Bugs Bunny*

Nyaaah, what's up, folks? What's this I hear about youse wantin' to know more about my old buddy Mel? Well, listen, you've come to the right guy. What I know about Mel would fill a book.

When Noel (that's Mel's kid) who — or it is that "whom?" — you'll meet later asked me to write an introduction to this book, what else could I say? You see, me and Mel go back a long time, maybe thirty, forty years, and let me tell you it ain't been easy, doc.

'Cause you see, I'm sort of an upfront type rabbit, and to be perfectly honest, I like to have my rest now and then. But Mel never lets me. You'd be surprised the number of things I've had to do. Sell War Bonds, entertain soldiers, be in movies, and all that sort of non-rabbit stuff. But the way I sees it, if you get my drift, is that there's probably no one better qualified to write this introduction.

For more than fifty years, Melvin Jerome Blanc (ain't that a mouthful?) has been making people crack up with a thousand or so voices that he has created. Some folks even call him the world's greatest babysitter since some 50 million kids a day hear his voice. By the way, if you ask me, a lot of those "kids" are almost in their eighties now, and still get a chuckle out of hearing any one of my good buddies — Porky, Daffy, Yosemite, Tweety Bird, Sylvester — speak through Mel's lips.

I been around enough to know that what you're really waiting for is to learn more about Mel — what it was liking growing up with all those characters inside him busting to get out, what it was like to be a literal show business legend through a career that has seen Hollywood introduce sound, color, television, the works. So like my good buddy Porky always says, "That's all, folks." Down with the introduction and on with the show.

---

* *(From Noel Blanc's unpublished biography)*

Noel and Mel Blanc.

Introduction

This book contains as much first hand material as I could find, the majority coming from Noel Blanc's partial biography on his father (sometimes written with the aid of Ron Smith, who had been hired to write commercials for Foto Foto Fun Fun for Blanc Associates), the raw material of which became Mel's autobiography. However, I've quoted Noel's original work as much as possible (in the style of Joan Benny's book about her father, Jack, which also included an unpublished autobiography, Noel's writings/voice will be in **bold,** since it gives a different eyewitness account to the Blanc legacy.) As Noel's prologue states:

This book is written about my dad, Mel. It is a conglomeration of so many memories I have about him, and many other stories that I have heard him tell. It is a story about a man whom I love and trust. A man who has been a marvelous father and loving husband to my mother, Estelle. It is a story about a man who barely escaped death and who lived entombed in a plaster-of-paris body cast for a year, yet never complained. It is a story of a man who has been loved and respected in the industry for nearly 50 years, and whose voices have been heard by nearly everyone on earth. It is estimated that over 75 million people a day hear Mel's voice.

His "notes on the book" concluded that a possible "voices of Mel Blanc" tape or record could be inserted into the biography. "Not only would the most famous characters be heard on the record, but also the odd sound effect creations Mel has vocalized such as Jack Benny's parrot, English horse, Maxwell, etc., etc."

All quotes you see are from Mel's own mouth unless noted, generously supplied by Noel Blanc. Some of Mel's words also come Walt Mitchell's extensive interviews, which have been generously donated to this book, as has the wonderfully in-depth discography which takes up so many pages. Walt, and partner-in-Blanc, Mary Lou Wallace, are the ones who should have written this book. I pleaded with Walt to do it — but I'm just grateful he took the hours and hours out of his life to provide me with so much detailed material.

This isn't an animation book. There are *plenty* of books on the history of cartoons, especially Warner Bros. animation, so I'm not going to waste space here replicating cartoon information readily available elsewhere. Read Leonard Maltin, Jerry Beck and Mark Evanier for the full story on animation history. This book isn't even about voice actors or the art of voicing in general. It's about Mel. Sadly, there aren't enough books on voice actors or the sound half of cartoons, so I've been trying to make up for it with my own books on Walter Tetley, Paul Frees, and Daws Butler, as well as publishing books on fantastic voices such as Verna Felton, June Foray, Jerry Colonna, Wally Cox, and others. Mel Blanc is of course the King of the Voice actors, and that's mostly why his story has taken the longest to write.

But the pioneer of voice men, the only name most people know even today, the only man to star in his own self-named radio series, has long needed a fat biography to showcase his many talents. Mel Blanc did write an autobiography — actually written by his son, Noel, for the most part — but, as fabulous as it was to have in greedy little fan hands like mine, it is an incomplete book that needs more insight, not to mention a credit list and index. Again Mel was a trailblazer, the first voice actor to write his story, and I hope this humble effort supplements what the great man wrote.

I was born in 1970 and weaned on rerun TV, with a single working mother gone a lot of the time. *Sesame Street, The Muppet Show, Rocky & Bullwinkle*, and Warner Bros. cartoons were my babysitters. Though Bugs Bunny is as recognizable to me as a tree, my first true memory of the zippy Carl Stalling fanfare that introduced me to that carrot-chomping wabbit atop the Warner Bros. logo was in high school. I watched cartoons and The Three Stooges (hoping it wasn't a Little Rascals morning) before racing off to school on my bike. It wasn't until years later that I realized why I liked Warner Bros. characters *so* much and never, ever, watched Tom & Jerry. It was the voices. They made the drawings come alive in such a huge, humorous way and invaded my thoughts throughout the day, whether or not I tried to imitate the dopey vulture, or Elmer Fudd killing the wabbit.

So many people made this book a reality. I'd like to thank Bill Baldwin, Jr., Bob Bergen, Allan Berland, Wayne Boenig, Ray Breen, Jackie Chan (for inspiring me), Stephen Cox, Theresa Danna, Lon Davis, Paul Fulton, Britt Henderson (for *all* the good times), Larry G. Jones, Elise Rosenbaum,

Dan Wildt, Ted Hering, David Mitchell (for showing me that arguing the truth can be hilarious), Gary Owens, Rick Payne, Donald Pitchford (for drawing the characters on this *wonderful* cover), Laura Wagner, Cathleen Watkins, and thank *you*, legion of Blanc fans.

Special thanks to Keith Scott, Walt Mitchell, Mary Lou Wallace, Martin Grams, Jr. and Randy Bonneville who have doubled the page count of this book by almost single-handedly assembling the towering credit list that Mel's own book was sorely lacking. It's the only book I've written where the end matter outweighs the biography, and indeed it does. My sincere thanks to these nostalgic soldiers for making this an even more *valuable* book.

An extra special thanks to my wife's parents, Yutaka and Yoshie Fukushima, two of the most generous and sparkling people I've ever had the pleasure of meeting. It is an honor to call you *family*.

My loving mom, Vickie. My lovely aunt, Arleen.

And to my wife, my life, my constant companion, Mayu. She listens, she understands, she is a wondrous beauty that makes all of this worthwhile.

1 | Early Days Yet

Mel's mother's parents — Nachum Katz and Leah Beyla — picked potatoes that were left to rot on unharvested plots of land so they could sell them for marriage money. They arrived in America in the late 19th century and settled in Bismarck, North Dakota. Hearing that warmer temperatures and more fertile land awaited them in California, they moved to Porterville, between Fresno and Bakersfield, where they lived many years before moving to the Bay Area and starting a family.

Frederick Blank was used to traveling. At age 15 he left his Brooklyn, New York home and headed for Alaska with thoughts of making it big as a gold miner. He did manage to dig up a goodly amount of the yellow stuff near Nome, the site of the famed 1899 gold rush, but thieves soon relieved him of it. Being a pretty sharp pool player, poverty did not slow the man down. Strolling into the nearest town's pool hall, he won himself two thousand bucks and the desire to go San Francisco, where he managed a "while you wait" shoe shop, selling and repairing any kind of shoe.

It was there that he met Nachum and Leah's pretty young daughter, Eva Katz. A few months later, after he'd journeyed to Tacoma, Washington to start up a new business, he called Eva to ask her to marry him. They opened up a ladies clothing store called the Factory Sample Shop in the Spanish Mission District of San Francisco. Frederick bought a wooden-frame house at the corner of Bush and Divisadero streets in the Western Addition District, one of the few residential neighborhoods not destroyed by the 1906 earthquake.

And on Memorial Day, May 30, 1908, Melvin Jerome Blank was born.

From there, the Blanks moved into a cream-colored, two-story house in Portland, Oregon, with a backyard of apple, cherry and pear trees. Young Melvin had only fond memories of sitting under the trees, munching every kind of fruit. It was in Portland that he began his eight-year study on the violin, with his father (who could switch from trumpet to piano), mother (who sang), and brother Henry (who played piano by ear) joining in on evening jam sessions. "I'm Just Wild about Harry" (which would wind up in several Bugs Bunny cartoons) and "Yes! We Have No Bananas" were just a few of the hot numbers the close-knit family would concentrate on. Mel appreciated the love and support he was given by his progressive parents, especially through music. They even tolerated his growing penchant for dialects, which was beginning to get him in trouble at school.

In a grammar school called Portland's Commerce, Mel won a lot of laughs and applause from the other kids in assemblies by telling jokes and stories in different voices. The teachers laughed too, but it didn't stop them giving the twelve-year-old sensation Cs and Ds on his report card. That didn't matter. The showbiz bug bit with all teeth.

Not all the teachers were fans, however — sour Ms. Washburn's comments would slightly influence cartoon history. After Mel gave her an answer in four different voices, she reprimanded, "You'll never amount to anything. You're just like your last name — blank." Mel remembered that comment, and when he was 16, he began spelling his last name to end with a c, not a k. He later changed it legally.

The principal was equally not enamored of Mel's frequent gags, and his running down the acoustically wonderful school hallway, shouting a shrill laugh that would later become the template for Woody Woodpecker's call. The echo was too good for a fourteen-year-old to pass up, and it almost got him kicked out of school.

The only course Mel seemed to like was music. He ducked many a science and history class by sneaking out the side door and hoofing it over to the movie house on Jefferson Street and Eighteenth Avenue. Kids got their nickels' worth back then — a full afternoon's entertainment with cartoon, short subject, newsreel, B-picture, and a full-length feature. Mel would sometimes join in with the wiseguys by filling in words for all the silent (often, there wasn't even music playing) entertainment.

To earn more of those nickels, Mel and brother Harry sold newspapers on the sidewalk. (Hank Blanc, aka Henry Charles, was an announcer on several radio series, including *Silver Theatre*. He died a few years before Mel did. Mel later stated, "He loved his booze and it eventually killed him.") Then it was over to the grand old Orpheum Theatre at Taylor Street and Broadway Avenue where for just twenty-five cents, Mel could sit way in the back and watch one of the two daily vaudeville shows. He saw "the Eccentric Juggler," also known as W.C. Fields, Milton Berle, and that blue-eyed comedian from Waukegan, Illinois, "Fiddle Funology," whose jokes about his lack of skill playing the violin would soon shoot him to superstardom as Jack Benny.

Around 1922, Mel and Henry (nicknamed Harry), older by four-and-a-half years and more athletic-minded than Mel, would sit around during the stiflingly hot summer until Henry ran out to join his friends, leaving Mel to his crystal radio set. It only cost a mere three dollars to purchase, but it probably saved Mel's life by lifting him out of boredom and into the throes of excitement by patching into music or comedy a whole nine miles away. He'd wear his headphones, desperately trying to hone in on KGW, the local station owned by Portland's first newspaper, *The Oregonian*. He'd listen to news, the ballgame, music, and in 1927 it would be KGW that also gave him first taste of radio work. Already something of a local storyteller and class comedian, someone in the programming department called and asked Mel to sing the hoot of a novelty song, "Wanita (Wanna Eat? Wanna Eat?)" on their Friday evening program, *The Hoot Owls*.

I'd be a wreck when I got the check
I prayed that she'd get indigestion
But such luck, it was out of the question
They say nanny goats can eat soda cans and such
My girl eats things nanny goats won't touch
I call her my sweet Wanita
Wanna eat? Wanna eat? Pay the check!

He was a hit, and was quickly asked to be a regular. There was little pay, as *The Hoot Owls* was a charity show sponsored by local businessmen. On that series he became part of the radio troupe called the Degree Team. Mel was "The Grand Snicker," ad-libbing discussions with others of the Team about current events in Portland. To make ends meet, Mel joined the KGW radio orchestra (led by Del Milne) as its tuba player (having traded in his violin for that instrument a few years before), and soon found union-scale work with another nine-man ensemble, Frank Vaughn's Columbians. 16-year-old Mel rarely trekked more than 75 miles from home with the boys, sometimes as far as Centralia and Chehalis, Washington. They carpooled together, careful not to wrinkle the black tuxedos in which they had to perform.

From beer joints to ballrooms they toured the area, bringing small big-band music to all. Mel even set his tuba down to sing a few tunes. Being that rare commodity — a tuba player — he was soon snatched up by Frank Fogelsong's band, The Bohemians. At least once he conducted the group when Frank fell ill to hepatitis. Unfortunately, it caused deep resentment in Frank's younger brother Wendell, the trombone player, who felt *he* should be heir to the baton. He would curse Mel with vigor during their loud number, "Salute to Prohibition," at the exact moment when the excited band stopped playing and called out "Whiskey!" and "Vodka." The band boys got their revenge one particular night by opening

An early portrait. PHOTO COURTESY OF STEPHEN COX.

their mouths, saying *nothing*. When Wendell's obscenities poured forth that night, appalling the dancers and audience, Wendell was cured of the cussing and working with Wendell became a bit easier from there on.

It was onwards and upwards for Mel Blanc. He found himself on station KPO as part of the NBC Trocaderans, a radio orchestra in San Francisco. One benefit to the gig was that it was an easy walk from his mother's parents' home. Unfortunately, the late hours he kept — he didn't get in 'til well after midnight most nights — made him feel exceptionally guilty about disturbing their sleep. So, when he was offered the job to conduct as a musical director at the Orpheum Theatre in Portland, Mel jumped at the freedom and the opportunity. He was only 22.

It was the era of sound. And Mel, like many in 1927, felt highly influenced by Al Jolson's *The Jazz Singer*, Hollywood's first talking film, and by the great opportunities that the film industry might give the burgeoning voice actor. His parents were supportive, big step though it was, and they promised him that if he didn't make it, he could always come back and work in the store.

Mel didn't quite make it to Hollywood, but he did return to San Francisco. Talent scout Cecil Underwood had heard Mel on KGW and offered him a job as the emcee of NBC's *The Road Show*, a Tuesday-night variety program. It wasn't much of a job, introducing the acts and making a few jokes, but the salary was better than before, giving him enough to rent a room just around the corner from the studio. And in that town of many immigrants — Chinese, Japanese, British, Irish, etc.—he learned a lot of new dialects walking around the hilly streets of San Francisco. It was Japanese that intrigued him most (though Yiddish was the first dialect he mastered), living near a small grocery store run by "my first and only acting coach," a friendly Japanese man.

He stayed with *The Road Show* long enough to save $670, with which he purchased an old 1920 Ford Model A convertible. Once the series ended for its summer hiatus, Mel and two vaudeville friends from Portland crammed together in the car in search of Hollywood and fame.

They shot down Route 101, baking in the hot sun, but eventually arrived, exhausted and with only a few dollars among them. It was the Depression and a tough time for anyone, never mind the unknown, nonworking actor. Mel was lucky; he ran across an old acquaintance, Hymie Breslau, a violinist with the Del Milne Orchestra, so the two of them pooled resources to afford a cheap room on hilly Hyperion Avenue. Dragging himself up a ton of steps after a long day of job searching was less than fun, but still Mel kept his sights set on radio. Cecil Underwood helped him land some bit work on NBC, but Hymie was having even worse luck, as he was not a member of any musicians union. Finally the roomies decided to take a break and go listen to some *real* working musicians, at the Ocean Park Ballroom on Santa Monica Beach. They loved the then-poular swing sound, so for the admission price of a nickel each they drove the ol' Model A over and cut some rugs.

It was here that Mel's life changed. He met "a very attractive blonde" who was fox-trotting with her younger brother, though Mel didn't know he was her brother at the time. He didn't have the gumption to ask the blonde to dance, but once he found the courage to slow dance with another girl, Vera, she quickly introduced him to her friend, that "very attractive blonde," Estelle Rosenbaum. They danced the rest of the dances together that night.

Estelle was a legal secretary and on the entertainment committee for Junior League, which was having a big dance the next Saturday. Impressed that Mel had been emcee for *The Road Show* (Mel being equally impressed that she'd even heard of the program), she asked if he would like to emcee that show. He said sure, "Can I have your phone number?" But when he didn't write it down, Estelle wrote in her diary:

> *"Dear Diary,*
>   *"I've met the most wonderful man. He's Italian, I think, with the cutest shoe-button eyes. I offered to help him with his career, but I don't think anything will come of it. When I gave him my phone number, he didn't write it down. Men!"*

He didn't need to. As Mel admitted in his autobiography, "When it's the right girl, you remember her number."

The emcee job petered out, but not the relationship. Mel was in love.

Unfortunately, he wasn't earning enough from radio jobs to support even a girlfriend by this point. He was making maybe $25 a week, if he was lucky.

Then, he *was* suddenly lucky. It wasn't long before he got an out-of-the-blue offer from NBC's Blue Network affiliate, KEX, to write, perform, and produce his own hour-long show, in Portland. Ecstatic, Mel raced to Estelle's house and proposed on the spot. She was 22 and he was 24 when they eloped on January 4, 1933. They didn't tell anyone, and drove up to Riverside, halfway between Los Angeles and Palm Springs, to get hitched, which they followed by splurging on two 65-cent blue plate specials at the local diner.

The job fell through at KEX, as the station manager hired a relation instead, but it only strengthened Mel's resolve to make it big and support a wife. After months of trying to get an audition on Al Pearce's comedy program, *The Happy-Go-Lucky Hour*, Pearce's talent agent finally relented. Mel took out a cornet his father had given him and, to showcase his versatility, he spoofed a nightly radio newscast, "The Richfield Reporter" in the character of a skid-row derelict, teeming with other accents from around the world. After the five-minute audition, the talent scout said, "Pretty good" and requested a repeat performance for Al Pearce himself. It went over big, and Al said, "Book him for next week."

It was a foot in the door. The pay was a mere $5 per show, and for a while there was nothing else on the radio horizon. It was worse at home;

Young Mr. Blanc.

with the lack of opportunities, Mr. and Mrs. Mel Blanc still hadn't told anyone about their marriage and they were therefore still living separately. A Jewish wedding was important for both sides of the family, so after consulting the Jewish calendar (they were then smack in the middle of Sefirah, a period of mourning in the Jewish religion), May 14th was chosen. A rabbi conducted the ceremony at the Rosenbaum house, where both families gathered. For the rest of their lives the Blancs celebrated both anniversaries — January 4th and May 14th.

Their honeymoon was nothing but a drive up the coast to Portland, because a mere two days after their "second marriage," Mel was offered that same one-man show job again at KEX, which this time dangled long enough for him to take.

They said goodbye to Estelle's parents and the Model A, which Mel had traded in for a smoky 1932 Ford (which required oil like a thirsty man needs water) and rented a "countrified" house eight miles outside Portland. Estelle joined Mel on their Monday-through-Saturday show called *Cobwebs and Nuts*, which took up 16 hours of each day to write, produce, and perform. KEX wasn't paying Estelle, but when Mel asked for an actress to help with the female roles, all the management suggested was to stop writing women characters into the comedy sketches. It was a break-neck job for $15 a week, but Mel enjoyed the artistic freedom, not to mention writing the scripts, which Estelle would help with and edit down to the best bits.

Once the show was prepared, they'd sometimes drive down to the Hollywood Theater for a late afternoon movie, and after dinner, at ten o'clock, they'd head to the studio for the broadcast in front of a live, non-paying audience. Skits, commentary, hourly, wacky time checks, and recorded music, that was *Cobwebs and Nuts*. There were comedy skits about traveling, Westerns, and murder mysteries (Estelle had a great scream), and both Blancs taxed themselves to come up with enough original material to keep an audience interested for six hours a week. It was great improvisational on-mic practice for Mel, and it even brought Estelle much local popularity due to several of her characters, like the snooty Mrs. McFloggpoople IV, which resulted in a lot of fan mail.

The show became so popular that it moved to sister station KGW for greater broadcast range. Being stopped on the street to sign autographs occasionally felt good, but the $60 a month they were earning didn't go very far. $30 for food, $8 for rent. There was nothing left for gas for the car, but at least Crouch's restaurant was within walking distance and it was cheap: 25 cents for dinner, and a dime more for the "deluxe plate." Soon

Mel had to sell the eight shares of Bank of America stock he'd bought for their future, and he began moonlighting during his 70-hour work week by hosting a talent show for KEX, as well as working on KGW's *Sunday Morning Breakfast Club*.

By 1935 Mel was seriously rethinking his showbiz future. *Cobwebs* had eleven sponsors, and in all this time Mel had only been awarded a $5 raise. He considered selling insurance for $50 a week, but Estelle talked him out of it. "I know you. You wouldn't be happy selling insurance. You're a voice man, and you belong on the air."

Finally, after nearly going crazy with the pace, she merely asked Mel one day: "Do you want to have a nervous breakdown, or do you want to go back to Los Angeles?"

As long as they were going to be broke, they thought they might as well suffer where they didn't have Oregon winters to contend with. They traded in their car for something cheaper and returned to California, sleeping in the old vehicle most nights as they didn't have the money for a hotel.

They stayed with Estelle's parents in their large, four-bedroom, two-bathroom house while Mel beat the pavement looking for radio work. The Rosenbaums were supportive people who had once worked for Fox Studios' commissary, so they commiserated with the plight of the non-working actor. Mel was old-fashioned and preferred Estelle to stay at home rather than take a job offered to her to become a theatrical agent. Instead, she fielded calls while Mel was out auditioning. No matter who called and what sort of voice they requested, she said, "Mel can do that."

His first break came with a call asking if he could do a German dialect, "like Lew Lehr." Well, the Blancs didn't know who he was, but it didn't stop Estelle from taking the job. That evening they hurried down to the Wiltern Theatre on Wilshire Blvd. to catch a Fox newsreel in which he was featured. Lew was famous for his phrase, "Monkeys iz de craziest peoples." Armed with this knowledge, Mel showed up the next day to do his couple of lines. It didn't directly lead to anything else, so it was back to pounding the pavement for a few more weeks.

He finally found a regular spot on *Johnny Murray Talks It Over*, after which he was scouted by producer Nate Tufts for the popular *The Baker's Broadcast*, auditioning for popular comic Joe Penner. Penner was ecstatic after Mel's audition, pumping his hand, saying, "Why the heck didn't you come to me before? I could have used you in so many sketches!" Mel supplied various voices, including for Joe's duck ("Wanna buy a duck?"), Goo-Goo.

From there came more radio offers, but Mel was keen to try to break into films, especially *animated* films. The first cartoon he recalled seeing was Felix the Cat in the silent *Felix Saves the Day*, when he was only 14. He had a special affinity for the Disney and Warner Bros. studios. Mel said he actually wanted to work for Warner Bros. because at that point the voices for its Looney Tunes and Merrie Melodies cartoons were the worst in the business. He knew there was vast room for improvement.

After 18 months of trying to get into the Warner's inner circle, he finally made it in 1936. The story goes that he would constantly bound up the steps of Warner's Bronson Avenue building, and walk slowly back after yet another "Sorry, we have all the voices we need" response came from the man behind the desk; the man never even looked up to say it. From the summer of 1935 through the winter of 1936, it was the same. Then suddenly one day there was a new face behind the desk. When Mel asked where the other guy was, Treg Brown responded, "He dropped dead last week." "Jeez, that's too bad," said Mel. "How about giving me an audition?"

"Sure, let's hear what you've got."

Another version of the famous meeting comes from animation expert Keith Scott, author of the forthcoming book, *Cartoon Voices*: "Blanc's older brother Henry (whose industry nickname was "Hank Blanc") was already a professional radio announcer, billing himself as Henry Charles. In late 1936, while working at KFWB, Charles put in a word for his comic sibling with Treg Brown, the recently appointed head of sound editing at Schlesinger's. Brown informed Friz Freleng, who was concerned about replacing Joe Dougherty. In December, 28-year-old Blanc auditioned for Brown, who felt an instant kindred spirit to the young voice-actor: both men were seasoned band novelty musicians, the type of creatures who bond like mothers in childbirth."

As Mel performed his "World News Report" audition piece for Treg, it was enough of a hit for the WB man to fetch Isadore "Friz" Freleng, Frank Tashlin, Bob Clampett, and Tex Avery from the in-progress Christmas party. These were the biggies, the now-famed directors of Warner Bros. animation. Tex Avery was especially taken with the audition, quickly asking if Mel could do a drunken bull. It was a cinch, and he did it immediately: "Well, a drunken bull *(hic!)* would sound a l'il *(hic!)* loaded, like he wuz lookin' *(hic!)* fer the sour mash! *HIC!*" The directors were instant fans, and Mel reported the following Tuesday for his first cartoon: *Picador Porky* (released March, 1937), directed by legendary artist Chuck Jones (creator of Wile E. Coyote and Road Runner, among other characters).

The story: Porky and his two pals dress up as a bull and a matador in order to win the $1000 prize, splitting the winnings between them. Of course his friends get drunk and Porky ends up fighting the real bull (voiced by Billy Bletcher). The phony bull finally gets into the ring, allowing Porky to win when it "drops dead," but in a fit of conscience, Porky splits the prize money with the real bull.

Noel joins Dad at work.

This slight role quickly led to Mel taking over the role of the stuttering Porky Pig, since Friz Freleng, Porky's creator, was having problems with Joe Dougherty, a real-life stutterer. Joe was good for the role, but not if you couldn't count on *when* the stutters would come. Many a take was ruined with Joe's stuttering at just the wrong moment. When Mel was offered the job, he hesitated just long enough to drive out to a pig farm near Saugus, north of San Fernando, so he could hear firsthand what pigs sounded like. He came back stinking, but with *h-h-his ma-ma-mouth* ready to *b-be* Porky Pig from then until his final theatrical short, *Corn on the Cob*, in 1965.

Mel and Estelle soon changed lodgings, moving in the summer of 1938 into half of a two-flat house at 625 Alta Vista Blvd. They needed the room: Estelle had given birth to their son Noel while Mel was at work at the studio. The labor was difficult, resulting in a cesarean section, but on October 19, 1938, the brown-eyed boy weighing seven pounds, fourteen ounces, was born. Noel, named after Mel's grandpa Nachum (written as Nolan on his immigration form when he came to America), and Noel Coward. Later they learned that in French, Noel Blanc means white Christmas. "It was a hell of a name for a Jewish boy," Mel said.

Mel loved his time at Warner Bros., working in the cartoon unit located in a shack-like cottage nicknamed Termite Terrace, on Fernwood Ave. But there was nearly complete artistic freedom with every cartoon, as long as they didn't go over budget. When first hired, Mel would record his dialogue in sequence, from beginning to end, which took about a day and a half, and which Mel thought rather unnecessarily time consuming. Also, going from voice to voice, as Mel would have to, doing most all of the voices by himself, would sometimes result in flubbing takes. Editing was the answer. Soon he was reading each separate character straight through, then the tape editor would assemble the character sequences cohesively together.

Mel thought that the most characters he recorded in a single cartoon was fourteen. "For these one-man recording sessions I stood alone at the microphone," he recalled, "with just an engineer and the director looking on from the control room. All I needed was a pitcher of water, a waste-basket, and my script, which I either held or propped on a music stand."

Recording female characters was also a strain on his vocal chords, so most times June Foray would handle the likes of Tweety's Granny, and the fun-loving Witch who thirsted for parts of Bugs Bunny. He also worked with Julie Bennett (Miss Prissy the hen, and sometimes as Granny), Bernice Hansen (Sniffles), Sara Berner (another member of Jack Benny's radio family), and Bea Benaderet (another Granny, and later, she was "married" to Mel as Betty Rubble).

Stan Freberg was one of the few male actors to play opposite Mel in his WB years. As he wrote in his autobiography, *It Only Hurts When I Laugh,* "Mel Blanc would stand on one side of the mike, while I would fill in various characters on the other side. As the Goofy Gophers, Mel would do one very polite gopher, and I did the other: 'After *you!*' 'No, after *you.* I insist!'"

As director Chuck Jones stated in *his* book, *Chuck Amuck,* "As Mel cannot be expected to talk convincingly to himself, we recorded one voice at time. On the first recording I would be Daffy to his Porky, and each line was repeated as many times as necessary to get the intonation needed by the director."

They called him "First-take Blanc" because he was a pro at getting his work done right the first time. Treg Brown, who discovered Mel, was the sound-effects man and Mel's favorite co-worker. The two shared a love of jazz and animation, and they even looked alike.

As Mel often stated in interviews, his favorite character was the wisecracking Bugs Bunny. Not only did he save Mel's life in 1961, but "I

Chuck Jones, June Foray and Mel. Photo by Treg Brown, who gave Mel his first WB audition.

employ the rabbit's name as my citizen's-band-radio handle, and his bewhiskered visage adorns my ties, tiepins, shirts, sweatshirts, cufflinks, even one of my watches." Putting on the rabbit voice even got him out of a speeding ticket once.

Although in his autobiography Mel took credit for naming Bugs after artist Ben "Bugs" Hardaway, the story wasn't exactly true. Animator Charlie Thorson is usually credited for inadvertently naming the rabbit after writing "Bugs' Bunny" at the top of his model sheet when he was drawing for Hardaway's short, *Hare-um Scare-um* (1939).

Keith Scott writes of Bugs' vocal origins: "In 1940 Mel Blanc performed as the still unnamed Bugs Bunny in Tex Avery's *A Wild Hare*. There had been several cartoons in the previous two years featuring a screwball rabbit, which had combinations of character traits by Ben Hardaway, Avery, and Clampett. The early rabbit voice was a (speeded) crazy, 'pixilated' goof-ball. It was slowed down for a Chuck Jones stab at the character in *Elmer's Candid Camera*, where Blanc was directed to voice the embryonic Bugs with a goofy 'bucktoothed' tone to emphasize the rabbit's pronounced overbite.

"But it's Avery's cartoon that is correctly acknowledged as the first true Bugs Bunny. Although the rabbit's voice would be modified over the next couple of years (actually sounding more like the fox in Avery's *Of Fox and Hounds*, released just a few months after *A Wild Hare*), this role was the one which guaranteed Blanc's motion picture immortality. When working on the final voice with Blanc, Avery directed as he always did: 'I usually had someone in mind — a radio personality, or an actor or actress — to give the guy a clue as to what we were after, and then [he could] vary it from there.' For the rabbit, he suggested a New York wiseacre approach along the lines of Warner character player Frank McHugh. Avery said, 'I would see a lot of movies, and I would remember voices.' Brooklyn accent or not, essentially Avery wanted a more human sound for the character, not a 'trick' voice like Donald Duck's."

Mel was responsible for giving the tough Bugs his Brooklyn accent, proving beyond doubt that a hare could be anything but timid. Bugs would say "woik" and "joik" instead of "work" and "jerk," and was afraid of *nuttin'*. Not even dressing up in women's clothes.

The only problem when Mel laid down the voice tracks was the carrot. Not only did Mel hate carrots, but chewing and swallowing the vile things made it difficult for him to come out with his next line on time. He tried apples, potatoes, celery, but nothing else seemed to create the same authentic sound of the good ol' stereotypical carrot. Finally the recording crew just decided to go with the carrot, stop the tape, let Mel spit the veg out into the wastebasket, and then continue on with the recording. The average Bugs Bunny session, according to Mel, resulted in several wastebaskets full of carrots.

"We kept it a secret for years," Mel explained. "It would have hurt Bugs' image if the public had found out. After all, who ever heard of rabbit that couldn't eat carrots?"

Noel Blanc explained that **of all the characters, Bug Bunny lives within Mel not only during performances, but all the time. Bugs is a rascal, but Mel is, too. Bugs is hip and bright…so is Mel. Bugs is always one step ahead of his buddies…so is Mel. Bugs is a wiseacre, Mel can be, too. Bugs is very lovable, so is Mel. Bugs always comes out a winner, so does**

Mel. Bugs loves carrots…Mel hates them. In fact, during the recording of Bugs' voice, Mel chews carrots, but only because celery or apples don't sound the same. Then he spits the carrots out and continues the dialogue.

The devilish Bugs often provokes Mel to pull practical jokes on his close friends. For instance, Mel had a friend that owned two Chinese restaurants in San Francisco's Chinatown. Now this friend was always

Noel joins Mel in the control room.

pulling stunts on Mel, so Bugs decided to get even. On the eve of the Chinese New Year, Mel, using the voice of a lady, telephoned both these Chinese restaurants and told them that in approximately one hour, the Department of Water and Power would be forced to cut off their water supply due to a broken water main. Mel, knowing that Chinese cuisine is prepared with enormous amounts of water, then drove down to Chinatown to watch the action.

There he found everybody who worked in the two restaurants going nuts, running around trying to find barrels, buckets, bottles, dishes… anything that would hold enough water to cook the overwhelming amount of dinners that must be served on a Chinese New Year's Eve. Mel's friend was a mess. He realized that no matter how hard he tried, he still wouldn't be able to store enough water.

After watching this hysterical sight for about 15 minutes, Mel calmly walked to a pay phone down the street and called the restaurants again. In the same woman's voice he said, 'I'm sorry to have inconvenienced you, but I've made a terrible mistake. The water will not be shut off until tomorrow night.' With that, he hung up the phone. It wasn't until two years later that Mel finally had the guts to tell his dear friend that it was he who pulled the stunt. Of course, Mel laid it off on the 'Bugs Bunny' in him.

In his autobiography, Chuck Jones wrote: "Bugs *is* what I would like to be: debonair, quick-witted, very fast on the comeback, a sort of male Dorothy Parkerish D'Artagnan."

The only major Warner Bros. character Mel Blanc did not voice was Bugs' arch-enemy: the portly, childlike Elmer Fudd, voiced by radio veteran Arthur Q. Bryan. (Blanc and Bryan also appeared together often on the *Major Hoople* radio series.) After Bryan died, Mel tried his hand at imitating the Fudd voice, but he really didn't like doing that. "It's stealing from another person," he said. Only when Warner couldn't find anyone else did Mel agree to do a few cartoons and later a series of American Airlines commercials as both Elmer and Bugs.

"Though Bugs always gains the upper hand, he is ultimately a pacifist," said Mel, "disarming the gun-toting Elmer with his wiles and appealing to underdog-rooting audiences." Fudd, daftly dressed in big hat, hunting coat and sporting a shotgun, was the perfect foil for Bugs and appeared against the 'wascawwy wabbit' in more Bugs Bunny cartoons than any other foe.

Some of the gags were very adult. The cross-dressing, the flings with suicide, the constant violence (a far cry from what Disney was doing), and often, two male characters kissing each other. Chuck Jones didn't like the constant rabbit-kissing-Fudd gag, but Freleng did. "It got laughs every time. That was a characteristic of Bugs. Bugs was an aggressive character and he embarrassed the little guy, Elmer Fudd, by kissing him. I don't remember how the gag started, but we thought it was funny. At that time, it was comedy. That's all I ever thought about it. Whoever thought of a 'homosexual' context at the time? It never even entered our minds."

However, it was the violence (with Bugs and the Roadrunner especially) that caused the most continuous controversy for WB cartoons over the years. Mel defended Warner Bros.' often-criticized cartoon violence by saying, "To me, there's a huge difference between the realism portrayed in today's cartoons and the slapstick we plied for laughs. The Warner animated films showed obvious *un*reality. Yosemite Sam gets flattened by a falling drawbridge, only to return in the next scene unscathed."

The challenger to Fudd's title of lead villain, and the one who gave the rabbit the biggest run for his money, was the short, red-haired villain with the larger-than-life voice: Sam. Yosemite Sam was Mel's least favorite character to voice. At first he tried a mild-mannered Western drawl, but that wasn't appealing to many, including director Freleng. So they went in the opposite direction, which was pretty much a pain for long recording sessions. "Imagine screaming at the top of your lungs for an hour and a half, and you have an idea what it's like," Mel said. The result, however, was one of Mel's funniest and most memorable characters.

Director Friz Freleng thought *this* was the perfect villain for Bugs; not some timid Fudd, but his little yellin', stompin', larger-than-life, huge red mustache-totin', two-fisted gunslinger who shouted and shooted first and asked questions later. Sam was a *tough* voice — utterly shouting. Even the rambunctious novelty song Mel recorded, "Yosemite Sam," never lets up, nearly causing a stripped throat just *listening* to the energy steaming from that tough little nut.

Keith Scott writes that "Mike Maltese and Friz Freleng developed Yosemite Sam's voice, basing its unparalleled loudness on a character Avery featured in 1939's *Dangerous Dan McFoo*. In that cartoon, Blanc played a Yukon stranger who yelled everything at ear-splitting volume ('Well, WHAT OF IT????'). It so amused Freleng that he remembered it six years later, requesting Blanc adapt it with a more Western dialect for a belligerent Sheriff. Thus, Sam's vocal origins combined the Avery character with the similar but not-quite-as-loud sheriff in the Bugs Bunny film *Stage Door Cartoon*; the latter voice, in turn, was based largely on Red Skelton's popular "Sheriff Dead Eye" radio character ("Aw c'mon, horsie, won'tcha please whoa?" which was first borrowed for Clampett's Western parody *Buckaroo Bugs*), combined with earlier vaudeville and radio comics Jack Kirkwood and Red Ingle, both of whom had a lot of Sam, and Skelton's Sheriff, in their deliveries. All these elements, along with input from writers Mike Maltese and Tedd Pierce, resulted in the ferocious Yosemite Sam. Understandably, Blanc came to dread Sam's throat-pounding recording sessions."

Even though he was smoking a pack of cigarettes a day during those glory years, Mel shouted as much as was required. (Ultimately, after having developed emphysema and requiring oxygen to breathe, he did quit cold turkey in the early 1980s.) Mel rarely caught colds and could run his voice for hours on end in the recording studio. Noel Blanc later told *TV Guide*, "Over the years, his voice never changed—I think it actually got better. Up until the day he went into the hospital, it seemed like he could do more with it. He had more highs and lows than anyone I've ever heard. He had perfect pitch, and the greatest ear for dialect. In fact, a larynx specialist came and measured his vocal chords. My father sat with a tube down his throat for half an hour while his vocal chords were being watched. The musculature was so enormous and there was so much muscle tissue that the specialist said the only other ones he had ever seen like them were singer Enrico Caruso's." Even on those rare occasions when Mel lost his voice, an hour later it would be back to full measure. He would mix a teaspoon of salt and baking soda with *very* hot tap water, and gargle. Tasted terrible, but it got Yosemite back chasing rabbits.

Daffy Duck was probably Mel's second most-voiced character — that selfish black duck with the orange bill who began his life with such a craaaaazy, volatile disposition, jumping around with a high-pitched "whoo hoo hoo hoo!" but who later turned into an articulate, attention-seeking, highly argumentative duck always looking for treasure or to save his own hide, often at the expense of his good "friend," Bugs.

Chuck Jones said, "Daffy is bright enough to understand how to be in control, but he never quite makes it. Both Bugs and Daffy are talkers, but Daffy talks too much. Bugs stands back from a situation, analyzes it, and makes his move. Daffy becomes emotionally involved, loses his distance, and blows it. He's stuck with a one-track mind. He gallantly and publicly represents all the character traits that the rest of us try to keep subdued." Perhaps his character can best be summed up by quoting the duck himself: "I'm different from other people — pain hurts me." And, "Honesty is the best policy — when everything else fails."

Some state that the duck's voice was based on producer Leon Schlesinger, who had a lisp, but after viewing the first cartoon, Leon jumped up and said, "Hey, fellowths, thath the funnieth voith I ever heard! Where did you get that voith?" Chuck Jones and the gang never told him.

Author Keith Scott writes, "Leon knew he had another potential star character in the insane little black mallard, and Blanc, guided by Avery

Mel, Sylvester and Tweety.

and gagman Ben Hardaway, refined the voice for Daffy's next appearance, *Daffy Duck and Egghead*. [Daffy's first appearance was as Porky's unnamed nemesis in *Porky's Duck Hunt*.] Blanc began using the juicy, zany delivery he had given the title character in Avery's 1937 cartoon *Egghead Rides Again*, a voice based closely on lisping vaudeville star comic Charlie Kemper."

Daffy had himself a spraying lisp not unlike Sylvester the cat, but the duck voice was altered in recording sessions just a little above Mel's normal range thanks to a variable-speed oscillator which engineers would use for his high-voice characters such as Porky Pig and Speedy Gonzales. Mel's lines were recorded at 18% below normal speed (though Daffy would sound a bit lower in later years), then played back at regular speed to achieve a clear, raised pitch. Tweety was recorded at 20%.

"They all sound a little higher," Mel told Walt Mitchell, "and do you know the reason for that? They're very small [characters]. So what I do is have them slow down the tape and then I speak or sing it nor-
mally to that slowed-down tape. Then they play the tape back 'normal' which raises the voice. It's not done with any trick in my mouth or anything. Many times we have to record it in a differ-ent key, because when it's sped up it'll be recorded a little slower in a little lower key. And then when it's played back, it'll fit in the same key as what the orchestra's playing."

Tweety Pie began as a very aggres-sive character. Created by animator/director Bob Clampett, there was an explosiveness hidden behind those soft, big innocent eyes that could wreak havoc with any cat in the picture. When Friz Freleng took over the character in *Life with Features* (1945), Sylvester became the true villain, with Tweety as helpless victim trapped in a cage, never

initializing an attack but merely defending himself against that bad ol' puddy tat.

Mel's favorite Sylvester/Tweety cartoon was *Birds Anonymous*, which won the 1957 Academy Award for Best Short Subject. Though the pro-ducer was always the person who brought home the Best Picture/Short award, (a tradition Mel was not keen on) producer Ed Selzer, who had five of the six Oscars that Blanc's cartoons had won, had Mel pick out the one he wanted when Ed was very ill. The Oscar for *Birds Anonymous* was given to Mel when Ed passed away, and he proudly displayed the award in his home.

Mel's favorite character was Bugs Bunny, but the easiest one for him to play was Sylvester, mostly, he said, because it was the character closest to his own voice — without the dethpicable lisp, of course. His Sylvester scripts would be so full of saliva at the end of the recording session that he usually suggested to June Foray that she wear a raincoat to the sessions. Mel took the famous "thufferin' thuccotash" line from his character Roscoe E. Wortle on *The Judy Canova Show.*

Mel is often wrongly given credit for the solitary "Beep! Beep!" of the racing Roadrunner, but it's just one of several myths revolving around the most famous voice actor in history. Paul Julian, who worked mostly as a background artist in Warner cartoons, is actually the voice behind those infamous two words. He would "Beep! Beep!" to make sure he didn't run into people when his hands were full of drawings and he was unable to see who was coming down the hall. Though Mel himself admitted to recording the famed single line once, "for the second Roadrunner-Wile E. Coyote short, *Beep Beep*" (1952), as well as putting it on his demo reel, the usual "Beep! Beep!" heard in most Roadrunner cartoons is *not* Mel Blanc.

There's also a bit of controversy among which came first, the blowhard Claghorn or the cartoon Foghorn. Beauregard Claghorn, as played by Kenny Delmar on radio's *The Fred Allen Show* in its "Allen's Alley" segments, was a proud loudmouth from the deeeep south. Foghorn Leghorn, that huge red-and-white rooster always tormenting the farmyard dawg or resisting Henery Hawk's bold hunting for chickens, was exactly, I say, exactly the same character, son.

Mel stated, "When I created Foghorn, I remembered something that had happened as a kid. I saw a vaudeville act [or *The Gilmore Circus*] with a deaf sheriff who would say, 'Pay attenshun, I'm talkin' to you, boy.' So I stored that in my head and when Foghorn came along, I used that style." Cartoon historian Keith Scott says, "Claghorn was on radio at least two years before the rooster was even a drawing on a storyboard. Warren Foster and Bob McKimson ended up agreeing that certain aspects of the Senator Claghorn voice would be used for Foghorn." Even the names were similar, as it was the practice (especially in WB cartoons) to use radio personalities, real or imitated, in cartoons. The Great Gildersleeve, Baby Snooks, and tons of supporting radio actors were characterized during WB's heyday. It gave audiences a thrill to see what they'd only been hearing all this time. Foghorn was just as loud and overbearing as the egocentric Senator.

Keith Scott, author of *The Moose That Roared* (the definitive history of Jay Ward's studios), gives a detailed history of this character in "The Origin of Foghorn Leghorn by Keith Scott" (first published in *Apatoons* #150 and reprinted here by kind permission of the author):

"In late 1944, story man Warren Foster came up with a rooster story for Bob McKimson, recently promoted to a directing position and getting ready to begin his fourth cartoon. This story, eventually titled *Walky Talky Hawky*, ostensibly starred Henery Hawk, a tough-kid character originally created by Tedd Pierce for Chuck Jones's 1942 release *The Squawkin' Hawk*. But it was obvious from the storyboard that Foster's funny rooster would 'steal' this cartoon.

"McKimson decided to base the loudmouth's voice on a hard-of-hearing West Coast-only radio character from the 1930s, known simply as The Sheriff. Rather than using Mel Blanc (McKimson recalled he didn't think Mel could do [that voice]), another actor was auditioned (Auth. note: frustratingly, I don't know who this person was). But when that performer didn't work out, Blanc came aboard and, McKimson recalled, 'did a real good job.'

"It is at this early point in the Foghorn saga that even Bob McKimson himself falls victim to the vagaries of recall, because by the time he began being interviewed in the mid-1970s (along with Clampett, Jones, and many other Warner veterans), his memory was clouded by both the passage of time and the enormous fame that another old-time radio character, one Senator Claghorn, had enjoyed from 1945-49 on the highly respected comedy program, *The Fred Allen Show*.

"McKimson recalled telling Foster that he was listening to the radio and had heard Claghorn. He also believed that 'Claghorn' had taken his vocal delivery from the old, deaf sheriff on the early variety show, *Blue Monday Jamboree*. The *Jamboree*, like much of early West Coast radio, came out of San Francisco before the show moved to Los Angeles in 1933, when network lines became operational in Los Angeles. At that point most of its cast began Hollywood acting careers, including character man Jack Clifford who originated The Sheriff. Clifford continued appearing as the Sheriff all through the 1930s on local LA programs like *Comedy Stars of Hollywood, Komedy Kapers,* and *The Gilmore Circus*. He also played bit parts in many films.

"The Sheriff — who would yell obnoxiously, talk over people, and repeat what he'd just said, prefacing each reiteration with 'I say...'— was indeed the inspiration for Foghorn. But, it must be emphasized, only for the first cartoon, *Walky Talky Hawky*. (Actually a major running gag for The Sheriff — bad puns based on mis-hearing what somebody was saying to him — was never a part of Foghorn

Leghorn's character.) But as McKimson mis-remembered it in his later years, he and Foster merged the two characters — the old sheriff and Senator Claghorn — and made them parts of the rooster.

"But the plain fact is that the dialogue-track for *Walky Talky Hawky* was recorded on January 13, 1945, a full ten months before the debut of Senator Claghorn on Fred Allen's New York-based show. A careful listen to this cartoon's track reveals that Blanc sounds totally unlike the Foggy voice of the 1950s. Here he sounds much more like Yosemite Sam — loud and very gruff, and incorporating the Sheriff's habit of starting a sentence and then re-starting with 'I say…,' such as when the rooster yells, 'Lose something — I say, didja lose something?' And the way he shouts, 'Pay attention, boy…'

Although a major influence on the cartoon, Jack Clifford's Sheriff was virtually a forgotten local LA radio character by the time the cartoon was released in late August of 1946. But Senator Claghorn, ironically just ten months old, was already a national sensation.

"Kenny Delmar (1910-84) was a highly successful New York-based radio actor and announcer. He began, like so many others of his era, performing in vaudeville (with his mother and aunt as The Delmar Sisters), before he broke into radio in 1936. An accomplished dialectician, he worked scores of East Coast shows like *The Shadow*, where he met Orson Welles. Welles hired him in 1938 for his famous *War of the Worlds* broadcast, where Delmar, although playing 'Secretary of the Interior,' imitated President Roosevelt's voice and added to the reality feel that Welles was after. In the 1940s Delmar got the job of announcer for the prestigious, intelligent comedian Fred Allen.

In his late teens Delmar had hitchhiked cross-country and was given a two-day ride in Texas by a real-life character that every actor dreams about meeting. A bombastic rancher, this man would suddenly turn to his passenger and shout, 'Son, I own five hundred head of cattle — five hundred, that is. I say, I own five hundred head of cattle.' He also insisted on finishing his wheezy gags with a hearty, 'That's a joke, son! Ah say, that's a joke!' Delmar stored this voice up in his mental computer and made him a party piece he called 'Dynamite Gus.' After doing the voice briefly (as Counsellor Cartonbranch) on *The Alan Young Show*, a season before Young moved to the Coast in 1946, actress Minerva Pious — a long-time Allen supporting player — suggested Fred try Kenny's windbag voice for the upcoming radio season.

"Since 1942, a popular feature of Fred Allen's radio show was Allen's Alley, wherein the star would wander down a make-believe street and meet a melting pot of Americana (Jewish housewife, a windy Irish-American, a New England farmer, and a loudmouth politician). Jack Smart had been playing a pompous politico named Senator Bloat, but Smart had departed the show and Allen had a hole to fill in his Alley. So when Fred Allen returned to the air for the 1945-46 fall season beginning October 5, 1945, his large national audience heard the Senator Claghorn voice for the first time.

The Senator's chauvinistic Southern jokes ('I refuse to drink unless it's in a Dixie cup!') and catchphrases ('That's a joke, son' and 'That is'), bolstered by the strong comedy scripts written by Allen and his co-writers, became national bywords by the end of his first month, and all across America entranced listeners began imitating the Senator's voice.

"While Claghorn was proving an instant success, the second Foghorn Leghorn picture, *Crowing Pains*, was underway by late 1945, and on November 24, its dialogue was recorded. This was a full eight weeks after Claghorn had made his bow, and already some borrowing of his mannerisms begins. As mentioned above, it was Claghorn, not The Sheriff, who used the catchphrase 'That's a joke, son,' and appended 'that is' to various sentences, such as, 'He was too short. Short, that is.' So it was in fact this second entry that McKimson was thinking of when he recalled telling Warren Foster about the Claghorn voice (as he noted, Foster became very excited about the verbal gag possibilities). In *Crowing Pains* Foggy says, 'That's a joke, boy — ya missed it, went right past you!' And, most importantly showing the marriage of both The Sheriff and Senator Claghorn: 'What's the gag — I say, what's the gag, son? Gag that is.' This cartoon was the start of Foster's excellent use of the radio influences for the dialogue in the Foghorn cartoons, dialogue that by the early 1950s entries was often downright hilarious.

"A third rooster cartoon, *Rootin' Tootin' Rooster* began production in the summer of 1946. Its eventual title was *The Foghorn Leghorn* (the bellicose rooster, until then an anonymous barnyard denizen, finally took his name from this cartoon's title). It was in this cartoon that the Senator Claghorn influence became truly blatant. Foggy says, 'Scram. Scram, that is,' 'Lookee here, son,' and employs the actual Senatorial standby, 'That's a joke, son…a flagwaver…'

"Meanwhile, following his first season with Fred Allen, Kenny Delmar was wooed to Hollywood to make a feature film starring the highly popular Senator. The movie was called — what else? — *It's a Joke, Son!* (It was filmed in mid-1946, while the Allen show was on summer hiatus, and released in early 1947. Interestingly, the third Foghorn cartoon's dialogue was recorded in late July and early August, while Delmar was shooting his movie nearby). Delmar remained with Fred Allen until Allen's final show in June 1949, at which point the Senator's fabled radio career ended after four very successful years. (Of course he continued doing the Senator for years in commercials, and even played a similar Southern politician on Broadway in a production of Texas, *Li'l Darlin'*).

"And as for Foghorn Leghorn, his character — refined a little more film by film — went on into the 1950s and early 60s in a highly successful series of cartoons. Interestingly, a new supporting hen, Miss Prissy, was also lifted virtually intact from another New York-originated radio character on *The Milton Berle Show*, that of a dizzy rich woman whose answer to everything was an imperious, vacuous "Yeeeesss" — she was played by Pert Kelton, an early TV foil of Jackie Gleason.

"I trust this clears up some misconceptions. The legend of Foggy's origins has been, at best, semi-accurate and clouded in vagueness, but the facts show a different story, and there is simply too much animation studio history that is only semi-accurate or, even worse, totally wrong."

Pepe Le Pew's voice was inspired by that smoothie Charles Boyer, and was one of Mel's favorites. It wasn't because he actually received fan mail from the ladies about this character, but because he relished in playing zee cool and romantic lead for a change.

The most controversial of all Mel's Warner Bros. characters was certainly "Speedy Gonzales, ze fastest mouse in *all* Me-hi-co." Friz Freling said that the character's name originated from a joke that Mel and WB writer Tedd Pierce shared about a little Mexican fella who was *so* fast, making love to *so* many women, they called him Speedy Gonzales. Bob McKimson began directing the popular Speedy cartoons, but Friz took it over for just one cartoon, the self-titled *Speedy Gonzales*, which won the Oscar for Best Short in 1956.

Mel considered the character rather one-dimensional since all he did was race after the cheese and away from the cat, but he was Warner's most prolific star during the cartoon studio's swan-song years (the mid-1960s). Those cartoons received several Oscar nominations, and Mel's same accent,

Harnessing the powers of *luuuuv* for Pepe Le Pew.

as the Frito Bandito, was used to sell Frito-Lay corn chips around this time. In 1969 the Mexican-American Anti-Defamation Committee complained of the character's racist stereotyping of Mexicans as lazy and sneaky and began to boycott the spots. No Frenchman ever complained about Pepe Le Pew, nor were any southerners upset with Foghorn Leghorn, Mel later said, so he saw the Bandito's treatment as unfair.

Mel Blanc, with his screen credit, was a Warner Bros. *star* who voiced hundreds of characters for them through the years. Jack L. Warner himself liked the Tasmanian Devil, that garbage disposal of an orator. Mel called Marvin the Martian his most unusual voice, "delivered as if he's suffering from sound-barrier-breaking motion sickness." Mel's count had it that he had played some 700 incidental and unnamed characters in his Warner years. And when doing the voice, Mel unconsciously looked like the character he played. "When performing Bugs Bunny, I jut out my front teeth, just like the rabbit." Pepe Le Pew: ze suave look comes over heem and he arches that one eyebrow jest a leetle beet. Sylvester: he puffs out his cheeks, spits through his talk and tries hard not to bite his tongue.

He never rehearsed or practiced at home, just in his head. And in the car when stuck in traffic. He would never attempt a voice until he met with the directors and writers, and even then *sometimes* it would take him months, even years to perfect what would be the character's permanent voice.

To be a good actor, Mel said it takes a versatile and elastic voice box, ears to reproduce the tones and textures, and a sensitive brain to shape the character's persona.

As Noel writes, **Bugs Bunny, Porky Pig, Tweety, Sylvester, Pepe Le Pew, Barney Rubble, Foghorn Leghorn, Yosemite Sam, Daffy Duck, and many more cartoon characters live not only within the voicebox of Mel, but actually are part of him. Each character represents a little part of Mel's personality, and his own personality had rubbed off onto all his creations. In Mel's everyday life, certain turns of events will produce portions of these characters; perhaps not vocally, but rather instinctively within his personality. At times Mel will draw on the sly perceptiveness of Bugs Bunny, or the comic forcefulness of Yosemite Sam, or the timid humility of Porky Pig. I really don't think Mel has ever realized this chameleonic ability to transform himself into a character, except when he is in front of a microphone or an audience. Then, during the performance, both he and the audience can graphically realize the characters emerging to the surface and actually supplanting Mel's own identity.**

Mel, in the true sense, could be called a method actor. Each of his characters has a history which actually exists. And each performance of these characters is not just words on paper, but a complete story. When Warner Bros. was creating a new character, Mel would be shown a drawing and the director would explain what the character would be doing. The character's temperament, size, attitude, everything was discussed. Sometimes Mel would come up with a voice on the spot. Other times, it would take research.

Around 1960, Mel sat down one day and started to list the voices he had done. He stopped when he got to 400. As he told one radio interviewer, "So when they say the man of a thousand voices, they ain't kiddin'."

"Compared to the staff at Walt Disney's production house, we were downright anarchists," Mel said of his WB glory years. He attributed Warner's timelessness (with Bugs Bunny still one of the top characters in the world, *always* played on *some* TV channel) to the fact that Bugs, Daffy, and the gang were full of human foibles, more like real people than Disney's goody-goodies. Some of the top animators, including Freleng and Jones, have said that they made these cartoons for adults, not children, but they happened to wind up as children's' programming. They also had no idea of the longevity of their work, thinking it would run for a week or two, perhaps a second or third run at the theater, and then disappear.

Even after he started working for Warner, he kept *trying* to work for Disney. But it took a while for the studio receptionist to warm up enough to fetch Mr. Disney one afternoon, so Mel could do his drunk routine for him. Walt Disney liked it so much he hired him on the spot. As he related to Walt Mitchell, "In *Pinocchio*, I was Gideon, the cat. I worked sixteen days, and all it paid was fifty dollars a day. It was low pay for that time. Disney was afraid that the hiccup voice I was doing would sound like a drunk, so it was cut out of the picture. But still there was one hiccup that remained in the picture. For that one hiccup I got eight hundred bucks!" It was the only Disney work he would do for years. (In 1964 he added brief sounds for Disneyland's *The Carousel of Progress*, an Audio-Animatronic attraction in which he voiced a parrot and lazy Cousin Orville who liked to relax from the heat in the bathtub with a large block of ice between the fan and himself.)

The wild gang at Warner were making cartoons for themselves more than for anyone else. Drunks, suicides, same-sex kissing — they'd throw everything in! The puns and sight gags and the huge number of radio references surely go above the heads of 21st century kids, but the zany fun the artists and writers had while creating them is baked right into every morsel.

Of course Mel did moonlight on his regular WB characters some-times. In April of 1941 he had signed an exclusive contract with Leon Schlesinger, head of the WB cartoon division, which barred him from doing voices for any other animation company. But it didn't stop him from voicing "Trigger Joe" training films for the Air Corps, produced by the First Motion Picture Unit at Fort Roach, and a health series for the

Mel, Lucille Ball and Alan Ladd doing an Armed Forces Radio Service broadcast.

Navy and Marine Corps. He also appeared on countless transcriptions for the Armed Forces Radio Service.

On *G. I. Journal* he once put Orson Welles in stitches with his stuttering performance, causing the great actor to trip over his words and "lose his intense concentration."

Bugs Bunny and Daffy Duck also fought the Japanese and Germans

Jerry Colonna, Mel, Frank Sinatra, Bob Hope and others entertain the troops.

hard with a plethora of positive, war-winning cartoons made between 1942 and 1945. "Obviously, subtlety was not our intent. Comedy was."

Keith Scott writes: "Blanc truly came into his own during World War Two, with highly inspired performances which he rarely matched in the decades that followed. His work for Clampett (who graduated to color cartoons when he took over the departing Avery's unit), was particularly brilliant, enabling Blanc to employ his powerful throat and innate music and comic skills to splendid advantage in roles like the foaming-mad Adolf Hitler of *Russian Rhapsody*, and Daffy Duck imitating Danny Kaye's Russian dialect and "git-gat-geetle" singing in *Book Revue*. This was indeed the ART of cartoon voice acting."

With his film and radio work for the Army, Navy and Air Corps, Mel was on the road between jobs a lot, and bought himself a scooter that he kept stashed in the trunk of his car, commuting between Playa Del Rey and Hollywood, flicking his headlights on at night just enough to see the road ahead of him to scoot home. He'd ride 8 miles in darkness sometimes. Getting gas in that rationing age was sometimes a problem, like the time he went to voice a freebie for the Navy at Walter Lantz's studio. *Enemy Bacteria* had a $100,000 budget but had given him no pay stub for gas.

Mel's most famous or infamous wartime character was Private Snafu (the military's acronym for 'Situation Normal: All Fucked Up'), created by director Frank Capra, then chairman of the U.S. Army Air Force First Motion Picture Unit. These black-and-white shorts (some written by Dr. Seuss) were made between 1943 and 1945 as training films for soldiers, all of which were approved by the Pentagon. The purpose was to save soldiers' lives, but also be consistently entertaining enough to grab hold of a tired, disinterested, and hungry attention span. One cartoon began with the then-racy, "Here, it is cold enough to freeze the nuts off a jeep," followed by the scene of nuts falling off a jeep. Everything from fighting weather conditions to malaria to VD was covered, with Mel as the doltish voice of the careless soldier who just never paid attention to his officers or safety rules. When Annapolis Anne and her swarm of young female mosquitoes are after the nude Snafu, who is bathing in a rank pool, one insect remarks upon seeing his butt, "It must be Snafu! I never forget a face," The government let Chuck Jones and company have a free hand with the toons, without censorship, except for the one on "How to Keep a Military Secret," which drew the atomic bomb just a little too closely to the secretive *real* bomb. Though the animators ran into trouble with the Secret Service, the plot did allow Mel some great double-talk as the jerk who blabs too much.

The most popular creation Mel voiced outside of Warner during this time was Woody Woodpecker, for Universal via Walter Lantz Productions. On November 25, 1940, *Knock! Knock!* was released. Originally an Andy Panda vehicle, the nutty little bird would soon over-shadow such a "nice" character. Woody's/Mel's first words were "Guess who?" which would forever be part of Woody's introduction before the credits of later cartoons, though these first words sounded different from the final voice. Mel voiced this screwball character (who had a lot in common with early Daffy Duck, including the variation of his manic "whoo! whoo!") for the first four Woody cartoons, but soon left to sign his exclusive Warner Bros. contract. Ben Hardaway would take over Woody's voice, but then later Grace Stafford, Lantz's soon-to-be wife, claimed the role forevermore.

The exclusive WB contract Mel had signed stated that he couldn't freelance with other production companies, which in hindsight was unfortunate. He particularly regretted having to give up Woody's voice, having come up with the bird's famous, high-pitched laugh while running through the halls of Lincoln High School in Portland. Personally, Mel hated the look of the character, calling it the ugliest thing he'd ever

NBC, 1952.

seen. And he was being polite with his opinion. Luckily, the Warner exclusion only had to do with cartoons, so he portrayed Woody on a Mutual Network radio show, and in the smash hit single, "The Woody Woodpecker Song" which sold over a million copies in 1948, hitting No. 2 in the singles charts. He then put his Woody voice on several 45s and 78s, such as "Woody Woodpecker and His Spaceship" in 1952.

But even after Mel had gone exclusively with Warner, Walter Lantz continued to use Mel's WW laugh in the continuing cartoon series, without a cent paid to him. Unfortunately — as Mel would often lament — there was and is no copyright on a voice, so imitators were free to use his creations whenever they wanted. But studios *weren't* free, Mel assumed, to use his *own* recorded voice in projects he wasn't paid for. Lantz continued to use Blanc's laugh, recorded as a stock sound effect, in subsequent non-Blanc-voiced Woody cartoons, which did not please the Man of a Thousand Voices. Only when his WW laugh was used in a record did he take legal action. It was a touchy subject with Mel (and indeed with Noel Blanc who several times went after companies who used Mel's recorded voice after his death). "I'd never been a terribly money-conscious person, but this struck me as enormously unfair," Mel stated. Lantz contended that he owned *everything* about Woody, including the voice. Even though Mel considered Lantz a friend before and after the fact, he took Lantz to court on July 13, 1948, filing damages in Superior Court for $520,000 against Walter Lantz Productions, Inc. (distributor), Castle Films (which reduced photoplays to 16-mm for home use), and Leeds Music for using his Woody Woodpecker laugh on subsequent records.

Mel lost the suit, Superior Judge Daniel N. Stevens ruling that since Mel had failed to copyright his musical crescendo, his exclusive right under common law gave him title only for the original publication. But when Mel filed an appeal, Lantz settled out of court for an undisclosed amount of money. It was a hollow victory for Mel, since even Warner Bros. continued to do whatever they liked with the recordings they owned and paid for. Until the 1960s when he renegotiated his contract, Mel barely made above $20,000 a year from Warner cartoons. Most of his earnings came from radio and TV work.

Even so, Mel later admitted to Walt Mitchell that he preferred cartoons to any other area of his career. "Because I can actually see what happens later, as I watch the cartoon, and it's a great satisfaction to me to be able to see these things that I do and then wonder when the heck did I do 'em, you know."

2 | War & Radio

Mel left most money matters in the hands of his wife, but when Noel came along, more household income was needed. He marched into Leon Schlesinger's office and demanded a raise. Schlesinger, known for his tightfistedness, listened politely to the pitch Mel had rehearsed with Estelle all morning, then leaned back in his chair to say that more money just meant paying more taxes. Mel persisted, finally arguing, "All right, if I can't get more money, then how about screen credit?" That was doable, though a first (and pretty much only) at the time, since voice men were notoriously uncredited when it came to cast lists.

Mel soon got his "Voice Characterizations by Mel Blanc" credit on every Warner cartoon. Even if Mel was joined by Stan Freberg or June Foray or someone else, his would be the only credited voice name on the screen. That prompted yet another controversy, still smoldering today, as no one else was given the same recognition. Mel himself thought this practice of anonymous voices "unconscionably unfair."

At the time, however, it was the best thing ever to happen to Mel Blanc. Suddenly the talent agents knew who was the brains behind Daffy, Porky, and the rest, and offers from other studios started pouring in, mostly from radio shows. By the mid-1940s Mel claimed to be on upwards of 18 radio shows a *week*. That plus his cartoon work shot his take-home pay to $2,000 a week, a monumental figure at the time.

Looking back, he didn't see how it was possible that he did so much every week. He recalled that during the 1944-45 season alone he performed on *The Jack Benny Program, The Great Gildersleeve, Baby Snooks*, and *Blondie* every Sunday, each of those requiring one or two weekly rehearsals. Monday nights it was *The Burns and Allen Show, Major Hoople*, and *Point Sublime*. Tuesdays: *The Chesterfield Supper Club*, and *Fibber McGee and Molly*. Wednesdays: *Camel Comedy Caravan, The Eddie Cantor Show*, and *Icebox Follies. The Abbott and Costello Show* on Thursdays, *Amos 'n' Andy* on

Fridays, and *The Judy Canova Show* on Saturdays. Of course Mel wasn't a regular on many of these, but his list also doesn't count the huge number of bit parts he played on other, more minor series.

Luckily for him most of the shows were performed at CBS and NBC, because the studios were just a couple blocks from each other: CBS on Sunset Blvd. between El Centro Ave. and Gower St., and NBC at the

Mel on *The Charlie McCarthy Show.*

corner of Sunset and Vine. The pace sometimes became so dizzying that he would forget what brand of cigarettes he was smoking where; a definite no-no where sponsors were concerned. Mel kept a pack of Lucky Strike (Jack Benny), Chesterfield (Bing Crosby), Camel (Abbott and Costello and Blondie) on the dashboard of his car so he could please the roaming brand inspectors hired by the tobacco companies who often snooped stars' pockets to make sure they were smoking the right things during the right shows. Mel didn't like it and thought it ridiculous, as well as their all-encompassing power when it came to giving recommendations on the script, cast members and everything else. "True, they were footing the bill, but a cigarette maker's dictating to seasoned actors and writers made about as much sense as us telling them how much tar and nicotine to put in their product."

Mel made a lot of longtime friends during his early radio days. When he joined *The Lifebuoy Program* in 1938 it was on the verge of cancellation. When cast morale was low, he and Martha Raye would joke around; they also warmed up the studio audience together before the program began.

One of his favorite voice people, and the one he felt closest to in radio, was Bea Benaderet (the original Betty Rubble on *The Flintstones*). "Bea wasn't exceptionally pretty, but someone so warm, generous, and funny

Mel on the CBS lot.

couldn't help but be attractive." He called Verna Felton, with whom he worked on *The Judy Canova Show*, "one of the most versatile of all radio actresses." His least favorite radio actor was the prolific Gale Gordon. Al Jolson came in a close second.

Since Mel often voiced several characters on the same show, he would underline different parts with different color pencils with a mechanical pencil he always carried with him. He loved radio work and hearing the laughter of a live audience, which balanced his hours of cartoon time in the Termite Terrace studio, where he usually performed for the director alone.

Mel loved doing the sound effects, too. He claimed that he created his famous vocal rendition of Jack Benny's 1924 Maxwell at a rehearsal show in Palm Springs, when he saw that one day the record turntable that held the usual car S/FX wasn't plugged in, so he quickly stepped in with his stuttering, wheezing, dying rendition of an old-fogey car on its last legs. (In truth, Mel was the second voice man to do the sound of Jack Benny's Maxwell jalopy, as we shall see in the next chapter.)

One of Mel's most memorable voices was as the Happy Postman on *The George Burns and Gracie Allen Show*. Here was the most miserable

Don Wilson, Rochester, Jack Benny and Mel in the radio years.
PHOTO COURTESY OF STEPHEN COX

of characters, groaning a high-pitched, tortured man's voice, who at any moment was sure to start bawling his head off every time he thought of his wife. The June 18, 1945 episode went like this:

POSTMAN: Good afternoon, Mrs. Burns.

GRACIE: Oh, hello, Mr. Postman.

POSTMAN: There's a frown on your pretty little face today. Are you unhappy?

GRACIE: George and I are both unhappy, Mr. Postman. Yesterday was Father's Day and some thoughtless person mistook George for my father. Isn't it the dickens the way one little chance remark can affect you?

POSTMAN: Oh, yes. A man once made a remark to my Mrs. and me. And I've been mad at him for 17 years.

GRACIE: Oh, my goodness. What did he say to you two?

POSTMAN: I now pronounce you man and wife.

GRACIE: Well, I've just gotta find some way to make George look younger. How do you manage to keep so young looking, Mr. Postman?

POSTMAN: Oh, I go in for athletics, Mrs. Burns. That's what accounts for my glowing skin, my springy step, and the lovely symmetrical lines of my magnificent torso.

GRACIE: Oh. Athletics, huh?

POSTMAN: Yes, baseball, in particular. Every Sunday I go down to the corner lot with the old bat.

GRACIE: Oh really?

POSTMAN: Yes, and she pitches to me.

GRACIE: Are you a very good baseball player, Mr. Postman?

POSTMAN: Oh, phenomenal. Mr. Bob Cobb, the owner of the Hollywood Baseball Club has asked me to play on his team.

GRACIE: Oh, my. And you must really be good to get such an offer.

POSTMAN: Oh, yes. My team won the championship back in college. I'll never forget that big game. It was the ninth inning. There were two out and the bases full. We were losing by a run and the crowd was going wild.

GRACIE: Oh, my!

POSTMAN: Even before I grabbed my bat, the crowd began to scream, "We want Herman! Put in Herman! Herman will win for us!! Put in Herman!!!"

GRACIE: Oh, how thrilling! What happened?

POSTMAN: They took me out and put in Herman.

Just the next week, June 25, 1945, poor Mr. Postman was becoming even more aggressive in his marital obsession:

GRACIE: My husband and I are leaving on a tour of service camps.

POSTMAN: Yes, so I hear. What sort of act are you going to do at the camp, Mrs. Burns?

GRACIE: Well — George is going to — oh! Sakes. I almost forgot. It's a military secret. And people who know military secrets aren't allowed to talk.

POSTMAN: My, if only my wife knew a few.

GRACIE: Um. Mr. Postman, what are you planning to do on your vacation?

POSTMAN: Oh, I think I'll just lie out in the yard in the sun and let its glorious rays turn my magnificent body into a gleaming bronze Apollo. Instead of a white one.

GRACIE: Oh, well that doesn't sound like much of a vacation. Have you ever tried fishing?

POSTMAN: Well. Last year I hired a boat and took my wife *way* out in the ocean.

GRACIE: Oh. Did you have any luck?

POSTMAN: No. She swims like a duck.

GRACIE: My goodness! You mean she fell overboard?

POSTMAN: Yes. And I didn't even notice it at first. Then when I spotted her in the water, I started to row like mad.

GRACIE: Oh…I should think so.

POSTMAN: It was no use. She caught up to me.

GRACIE: But how could you leave her in the water? A shark might've attacked her.

POSTMAN: Why should I worry what happens to a shark?

GRACIE: Oh, now look here, Mr. Postman, you have no right to talk about your wife that way. You told me time and time again how ugly and ill tempered she is. That's not nice. Remember, she's your wife.

POSTMAN: Well…

GRACIE: You even said you regret marrying her.

POSTMAN: Well…

GRACIE: And you're always talking about how *mean* she is to you.

POSTMAN: Yes, I guess you're right, Mrs. Burns.

GRACIE: Hmm.

POSTMAN: But I never said I hated her, did I?

GRACIE: Well, no.

POSTMAN: Then I'll say it now, I hate her…! Well. Goodbye, Mrs. Burns. And remember. Keep smiling…!

The New York Times in 1944 wrote, "The unhappy postman is an inspired character well above the general run of subordinate comics." Mel told the press, "I have to be constantly searching for new characters. Sometimes I find them in unexpected places. The voice of The Happy Postman on *The Burns & Allen Show*, for example, belongs to an old beachcomber who one day asked me for a nickel for a cup of coffee. I gave him enough for sandwich money. He said, 'God bless you, mister, and keep smiling.' His voice had a peculiar whine which I remembered and have made famous, even to the 'keep smiling' phrase."

Mel, like others, considered Gracie Allen to be one of the smartest women in showbiz, a far cry from the ditzy character she put over the airwaves. By the time B&A took to television, however, Mel was far too busy with other jobs, and so the Postman retired. (Mel did put the voice into the character of a sad, exhausted Easter Bunny in WB's hilarious 1947 "Easter Yeggs" cartoon.)

George Burns, Mr. Postman and Gracie Allen.

Abbott and Costello were great to work with, but unlike their radio/ screen personae, they didn't like each other offstage much (Lou was always trying to find someone to replace Bud, but he never could). Mel thought that Bud Abbott was the best straight man around. He liked both men, but felt sorry for "Hard Luck Lou," as some in the business called him. Mel said he was rehearsing with A&C on that fateful day in

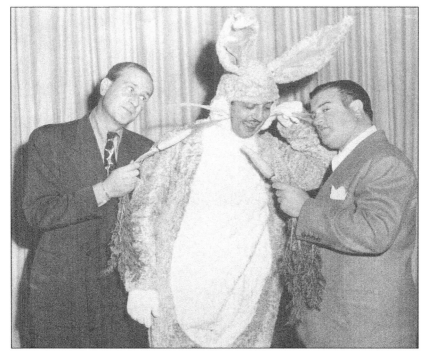

Abbott and Blanc and Costello.

1943 when Lou received the news that his eleven-month-old son, Butch, had drowned in their swimming pool. Lou had promised his son that he'd hear him on the broadcast, and he kept that promise, weeping only after the sign-off. Mel said that Lou was never the same after that day.

One of Mel's recurring characters on the show was Botsford Twink, a Scottish tenant in the boys' apartment building. He stereotyped the usual Scots cheapness with lines like "Get yer finger off th' buzzer! Yer usin' up th' electricity!" He also played a Russian movie director by the name of Cartoony Technicolorovitch. Mel learned a lot from the boys' timing, always watching Bud and Lou during his off-mic time.

Perhaps Mel's best radio series was *The Judy Canova Show*, as it gave him a wide array of characters to hoot and holler through. He was Paw to Judy's Maw, and together they...'d...tawk.... reeeelll.... slooooow. On the flipside was Roscoe E. Wortle (though that middle initial seemed to change), the loud, aggressive type — a traveling salesman who would often bellow, "Hello, girlie, remember me?!" He was like a combination of Yosemite Sam & Sylvester, but he was far more interested in laughing at his own jokes than in shooting varmints.

The Judy Canova Show.

WORTLE: Hello there, girlie, remember me? *(Big audience laughter)*

JUDY: Why sure! You're that travelin' salesman feller.

WORTLE: Yeeeep. Roscoe H. Wortle's the name.

JUDY: What's the H for?

WORTLE: Handkerchief. When I was born, my old man took one look at me and blew. *(Big audience laughter)* HAHAHAHAHA! Take off that saddle, grandma, this race is for two year olds! *(Big audience laughter)* Say girlie, did you know that when I was four years old my father took me to the zoo?

JUDY: What happened?

WORTLE: They rejected me! HAHAHAHA! *(Big audience laughter)* Ain't that a blockbuster? You tell 'em, Hershey Bar, you're a little nutty too! *(Big audience laughter)*

Though Wortle was married, it didn't stop him from hitting on Judy sometimes, because "ours is a football marriage. We're both waitin' for the other one to kick off!"

Seems like they met on a train in the December 1, 1945 episode:

WORTLE: My name is Roscoe Wortle, I'm a travelin' salesman. I got a line of fancy notions.

JUDY: Well, better change your line, fella. I got a notion it ain't goin' over so well. Say, ain't you rather old to be flirtin' with a girl like me?

WORTLE: Me? Old? Why, I'm just sneakin' up on 27.

JUDY: Well, you better turn around. You're sneakin' up on it from the wrong direction. Say, tell me somethin'. Are you married?

WORTLE: You tell 'em, chimney, I don't smoke! Ah hahaha, that's a killer! Hahaha! Yep, I'm married to the finest little woman you ever saw. Here's a picture of her.

JUDY: Say, she *is* mighty pretty!

WORTLE: You tell her, typewriter head, your neck's under wood! Whoo hooo! I'm *loaded* tonight!! Why, my little woman took first prize in a beauty contest back home.

JUDY: She took first prize?

WORTLE: You bet. But they made her put it back! Ha hahaha! Ain't that a piece of reno? I guess it ain't. Yes, sir! You know, she's the finest little woman that ever lived. She sure broke me up when she ran away with my best friend.

JUDY: Who is your best friend?

WORTLE: Whoever she ran away with! Ha haha! That ain't so bad. Well, so long, girlie!

Mel was also Sylvester, Judy's wet-lipped driver who was vocally and literally the spitting image of the cartoon cat of the same name. The audience was always primed and ready for this character, who usually came in somewhere after the first song. The writers penned many sloppy S-words for Mel's lines, and he often stole the biggest laughs of the show with his spraying impediment.

When Judy had a date with Mickey Rooney on the August 24, 1943 show and she needed the car, Mel turned in his "sufferin' succotash!" for "Shades of disappointment! Somethin's wrong with the mo-tor!" "Well, why won't it run?" Judy asks, and stands well back. "Well, the spark plugs are foul. The distributor's on the fritz. There's a leak in the cylinder head gasket. And oh yes! The starter's stuck!" The audience was howling.

Pedro the gardener was the biggest scene stealer, however, and after Judy Canova, he was certainly the most loved and most popular character on the show. This meek Mexican, the precursor to Speedy Gonzales, had a troubled private life but he always found time to shoot the breeze with his favorite employer. "Pardon me for talking een your face, senorita," he would always begin, at the most inappropriate time. And his goodbye was always a variation on: "Thirty days hacienda. April, June and sombrero. All the rest have thirty-one, except Gypsy Rose Lee. And everybody knows what she has, no?"

Poor little Pedro was always having tough luck with women, as illustrated on this February 5, 1952 episode:

PEDRO: Pardon me for talking in your face, senorita.

JUDY: Pedro, you look *awfully* unhappy. What's wrong?

PEDRO: Oh, senorita, yesterday my girl left town. And today I spend the whole morning just looking out a window.

JUDY: Oh, lonesome for her, huh?

PEDRO: No, I pull the string by the window and my nose got caught in the veniantion [sic] blind.

VERNA: Pedro, you're fond of your girl?

PEDRO: Oh, si, senor. The night before she went away we went to the movies. And we smooched a little. Hugged a little and keessed a little. Then we found out something.

JUDY: What?

PEDRO: We weren't even sitting together. I came home with a couple of black eyes.

JUDY: Your girl got angry with ya?

PEDRO: No, I was sitting between two sailors.

In a Happy Postman sort of way, it seemed like this guy was *always* sad. Even a few years earlier, on December 11, 1948:

JUDY: Oh, hello, Pedro. Say, you look kinda sad today.

PEDRO: Si, senorita. My cousin Gonzales got himself a broken leg from a cold in the head.

JUDY: Don't be silly, Pedro. Nobody gets a broken leg from a cold.

PEDRO: Gonzales did. He stopped to sneeze in front of a fire engine. Senorita, I have had bad luck all day.

JUDY: More bad luck?

PEDRO: Si. I was fixing the hot water pipes and I nearly tore my arm out of the socket.

JUDY: Oh my, how did that happen?

PEDRO: The instruction said to fix pipes, twist the elbow until it comes off. And senorita, my girl is glad I am such a handy man. Someday we might get married.

JUDY: Pedro, is your girl attractive?

PEDRO: Oh senorita, she has beautiful long hair growing down her back.

JUDY: She has?

PEDRO: Si. I wish more of it would grow on her head.

JUDY: Pedro, tell me, what do you do for entertainment when you have a date with your girl?

PEDRO: Senorita, sometimes when I am sitting alone with my girl in a parlor. The lights are low. Her little Airedale sits by her feet. Oh, it is so romantic. The parlor lights are soft and the radio is playing sweet music. And then she puts her head on my shoulder. Then I put my arm around her waist.

JUDY: Ooo, Pedro, then what do you do?

PEDRO: I feed dog biscuits to the Airedale. Well, I will go now, senorita, hasta la vista.

A few more of Pedro's greatest quips:

JUDY: What about that bloody nose, Pedro? Who gave it to you?

PEDRO: Nobody, Senorita. I had to fight for it.

PEDRO: Senorita, while you wuz a-way, I got a job as a lifeguard this summer.

JUDY: Why, Pedro, you only weigh 150 pounds. What if there was a woman out in the water and she weighed 300 pounds. How would you save her?

PEDRO: I would make two trips.

PEDRO: Every time I park my car. I put my arms around her. She whispers sweet nothing doings in my ear.

JUDY: Is your girl popular with the fellers?

PEDRO: Oh, she is very popular, senorita. I call her my soft drink girl.

JUDY: Your soft drink girl?

PEDRO: Si. She is interested in everything from 7 up.

Mel's Pedro was inspired by Jose, a talkative worker who helped build Mel's new home on a plot of land in Playa Del Rey in 1940. (With Noel growing up they were too big a family for their Alta Vista Blvd. apartment. The new place was several miles south of Ocean Park; beachfront property, and Charlie Chaplin lived nearby. However, it was far from the popular celebrity areas of Bel Air and Pacific Palisades.) But in one interview, Mel

gave a different origin: "The voice of Pedro on *The Judy Canova Show* I picked up from a Mexican waiter. On my own CBS show I use my real voice, which is the only time it is heard other than in everyday life."

Mel admitted to using the great Jose's voice for several other characters as well: the Frito Bandito, the Little Mexican on *The Jack Benny Program*, and Pan Pancho on *The Cisco Kid*. The latter he took over from Harry Lang for a spell after Lang had had a heart attack. Mel insisted that all the wages for the role be sent to Harry.

Radio was one of World War II's great heroes. Audiences needed their laughs, and Mel was right there to give them, along with a few other helpful services.

During the war he was an air raid warden who would belt out, "Turn out all your lights and shut your doors 'cause there's an air raid alert!" On the beach were what looked like a thousand protective barrage balloons to keep Japanese planes from flying under the radar. Just two blocks from the Blanc house a big fort with machine guns and cannons had been assembled to fortify the coast. "When it first started, a couple of hundred guys were stationed there, but the Army couldn't get any food for them for a couple of days, so Estelle and her mother and father went over there, bringing a bunch of hamburgers, beans, and a gigantic bowl of chili, which Noel toted in a little wagon he had. When they saw us bring it all, they shouted, 'Food!' These guys never stopped thanking us."

Blackouts were common during the war. "I had to drive from Culver City to Playa Del Ray with my lights off, turning them on just to see where I was, then off again. Seven or eight miles in almost total darkness." Mel once asked a high-ranking official about enlisting, but was told, "Mr. Blanc, I think you can probably serve your country better right here at home."

He did just that, along with the rest of Hollywood, by appearing on countless radio shows on the Armed Forces Radio Service, such as *Mail Call, Command Performance*, and *G.I. Journal*. They did more than boost morale and selling War Bonds: they gave hope.

Noel writes:

The air siren was loud and piercing. It would go off about two or three times a week. The year was 1944 and we lived in Playa Del Rey, which was only two miles from the largest Army airfield in Southern California. Anti-aircraft emplacements and Barrage Balloon facilities were peppered all over the hills near our home on Ellen Street. Infantry and artillery troops were spread out like a blanket throughout the area.

Mel, who was at that time working nearly every day for the Armed Service, was also an Air Raid Warden, and when that siren would go off, he'd put on his Air Raid Warden cap and go from house to house telling everyone to darken their windows during the "blackout" period.

After he had done his Air Raid Warden duties, he would head over to the Bivouac area for the troops and when the Air Raid warning was over,

Mel and Estelle.

he'd sit around and entertain the soldiers. Those who were lucky enough to be stationed in Playa Del Rey will never forget Mel and all the Warner Bros. characters who entertained them whenever there was an air raid.

Noel had started school in a kindergarten in Pico and Robertson where his grandmother lived, then attended a little school in Venice. One day a teacher called the Blancs to say, "Your son just sits there on the floor with the other kids. He says he can learn more at home." They asked Noel if he liked the school. "No, I hate it," he said. They took him to a school in El Segundo to which he would take a public bus. Mel would wait at the window and wave a handkerchief to him. It was one of the saddest parts of Noel's life, he said later, because "Dad, when you waved that handkerchief, I thought you were saying goodbye and I would never see you again." When El Segundo couldn't take him anymore, Estelle found out about a California military academy. She went and looked it over, and found a bunch of sharp-looking kids. There was bus service from home to school, so the Blancs decided to have Noel go there. He had to dress each day in his uniform before leaving. After that, he went to University High.

The Blancs moved to an apartment in Santa Monica on San Vicente Blvd., then into a house on 26th Street. They attended the Santa Monica Beth Sholom Temple, a Reform Synagogue where Noel later took his Bar Mitzvah lessons from Rabbi Bloch who was there teaching Hebrew. Noel explains his religious (via showbiz) upbringing:

"Boruch Atoh Adonoi…" My voice was shaky and scared, but it came out on key. "Alahanew Malach Heolum."

It was the night of my Bar Mitzvah. Dad and Mom had been planning it for months and no wonder I was scared. In the audience at the temple were Jack Benny, Dennis Day, Don Wilson, Phil Harris, the Jack Benny Show writers, the Sportsmen quartet, Hans Conried, Sheldon Leonard, and a variety of other show business personalities.

I was the star that night, but Mel was loving every moment of it. About midway through the service, he and my grandfather came up to the pulpit and read from the Torah with me. I don't think I've ever seen my dad so proud, and later at the reception, which lasted until four in the morning, he spent the night telling stories and exchanging jokes with all the Jack Benny gang.

Homelife was certainly interesting as the son of a famous voice. Noel:

"Wake up, it's seven o'clock," I heard my mom say. "It's time for breakfast."

When I was 3 or 4 I loved hearing those words because it meant another morning of my dad and the comic books. After breakfast my mom would say, "Mel, why don't you read Shakespeare to Noel?" Mel would laugh and then climb the stairs that led to his bathroom. I'd run to my room, grab some comic books, and meet him in the bathroom. Now that I look back, I didn't give the poor man a chance to go to the toilet, because as soon as he sat down, there I was on his knee holding a comic book in front of him. Jeez! I was a constipating little son of a bitch.

He'd never tell me to get out of the bathroom at any time, just picked up the comic book and started reading.

Can you imagine how sensational it was for the Man of 1000 Voices to read comics to you every morning? All the cartoon characters would literally come to life, and for a good solid one-half hour I would stay on his knee while he would read non-stop.

Each day of the week, Dad performed on three or four radio shows and as he finished shaving, he would give me the line-up of shows for the day and what characters he would be portraying on them.

It was a stormy afternoon at Big Bear Lake that July 12th, 1945, but Mom and I decided to take a bike ride anyway. After all, it was her birthday and my dad had just given her a new bike. We left the lovely smell of the C and S Cabins and headed down the road toward a place called Gilner Point. All of a sudden all hell broke loose and the skies opened up, drenching cold rain down upon us. We managed to find cover under a porch of an old cabin, and as the rain continued to pour down, my mom and I found ourselves gazing at one of the most beautiful areas we'd ever seen. Even though the wind was whipping at us where we stood, down below us and totally sheltered was a magnificent cove surrounded by a small pine forest.

We stayed under the porch until the rain let up, then hiked down to this lovely area. Mom said, "Let's go back to the cabin and bring Dad here right away." We pedaled like crazy back to the cabin — which, because of the smell, we could have found with our eyes shut — and insisted that Dad come right away to see this beautiful place. Dad, of course, agreed to come. He didn't need much of an excuse to leave the dreaded C and S Cabins.

Once at the cove, we all couldn't believe our eyes. Although the lake was rough and windy just 300 yards offshore, this cove was like glass with not a ripple in the water. The beautiful young pines grew all the way to the water's edge, and spectacular golden flowers blossomed everywhere.

I said, "Dad, why don't we come here tomorrow for a picnic?"

Well, not only did we come for a picnic that next day, but perhaps 20 or 30 picnics later Dad decided to contact someone about buying the property. The cove had become our meeting place, and all our friends knew where they could find us.

A few years later, Dad and Mom would build a cabin on that very spot, a cabin which they still loved and retreated to some 31 years later.

Mel always had a passion for the mountains, and when he and Mom discovered the small community of Big Bear Lake — I guess it was in the late Thirties — they never missed a year without a few weeks in the mountains.

As a child there are several times I remember vividly. It was August, 1945. We had spent the whole summer at Big Bear, boating, fishing, biking and hiking in the woods. There was, however, one major problem that summer, and the name of it was C and S Cabins where we stayed. It seems that the owner of C and S Cabins, in order to save money, would not drain the cesspool until it overflowed, and when it began to overflow, no one would come near the place. Our problem was we lived there, and every couple of days I would hear Mel on the telephone shouting at the landlord between gasps of breath. It was during one of these tirades that I heard him shout, "The water's running over, the water's running over!"

I ran inside and yelled, "Where?"

"Where what?" he said.

"The water," I replied. "Where is it running over?"

"No," he said, "the water's not running over, THE WAR IS OVER!!! The War is Over!"

He and my mom were dancing around the cabin with such glee that I thought I'd better join in. However, even the war's end didn't solve the problem of the memorable smell of the C and S Cabins.

And in 1950:

It was a real blizzard with driving rain that was coming down so heavily that you couldn't see 20 feet in front of you. And the wind was frightening as it caused high swells on the lake.

There I was out in the middle of Big Bear Lake with one of my friends with the outboard motor stalled and this incredible storm upon us. Just 10 minutes earlier it had been clear and sunny, so I asked Dad if we could take a ride in the dinghy. He said all right, as long as we wore life preservers, so off we went. However, we did forget one, or should I say, two things — the oars.

With the outboard out of gas and no oars we just floundered on the lake like a little cork. We tried paddling with our hands until we were about 300 yards from the shore, and then, out of nowhere, there he was. Bugs "the Hero" Bunny wading into the icy lake with most of his clothes on, shouting, "Don't worry, I'll drag you in." As the water got about neck deep, we were able to throw him a rope which he fastened around his waist. Then he began to swim ashore. With the rain still coming down in buckets, he finally managed to drag our dingy to a stretch of beach.

3 | Jack Benny Tortures Mel Blanc

Jack Benny was Mel's favorite comedian, and his best friend. Mel called him "the finest comedian ever to stand behind a microphone."

He joined Jack's show in 1939. He got a foot in the door due to the fact that Jack's mother-in-law, Mrs. Marks (Mary Livingston's mom), was an old friend of Estelle's mother. Jack politely refused an audition, but Mel wasn't about to give up during those lean years. He contacted Jack's secretary, Bert Scott, reminding him that he was the guy Mrs. Marks had mentioned. Before the end of the 1939 season, Scott called to say that Jack would give him a listen. He ran over to Hollywood Radio City and waited for the great man to arrive. Jack shook his hand and said, "Okay, Mel, let's see what you can do." Mel hit him with everything he had, ending with his then popular Porky Pig. "How did I *d-d-d-uh-d-d — uh, so how was I?*" Jack was hysterical!

He had the gig. (Although Mel appeared occasionally on Jack's show starting in 1939, it really wasn't until the 1943-44 season that he began appearing virtually every week. Actually, Mel had appeared once much earlier on Benny's show. Way back on June 7, 1936, Mel got a call to do the Benny show, but not from Jack personally. Although an undoubted thrill for the struggling actor, Mel was still establishing himself at the time. Any thoughts of confidently approaching the Benny production staff for more parts had to wait three more years, until Mel had built up some industry credibility via his growing cartoon career and other big-time radio shots. In this early appearance, Mel played a movie mogul named Gensler. Sadly, only a portion of this show is extant today, and Mel's role is missing)

In his autobiography, Jack wrote, "Everybody used his natural voice on the show — except one person. This person was a short, plump little person with a wispy mustache and big sad black eyes and a fantastic range of voices. They used to call Lon Chaney 'the man of a thousand faces.' Mel Blanc is the man of a thousand voices. He can play dialects — every kind — authentically. He can also play animals and birds."

Mel told Walt Mitchell, "He called me in and said, referring to his radio character and the script, 'I've got a bear down in my basement that's guarding my vault — he's already eaten the gas man!—but do you think you could do the growl of a bear?' And I thought for a moment and said, 'Yeah, I think I can.' He said, 'What would it sound like?' I said, 'Maybe like this…' (And at this point, Mel gave out with such a loud roar that even though Mary Lou and I were expecting it, we both gave a start. Naturally, Jack was impressed.) He said, 'Great, great! You're on next week!' So for six months, all I did was the growl of a bear. Finally I said to him, 'You know, Mr. Benny, I can also talk?' Well, Jack fell down, pounded the table and said, 'Good! I'll have the writers write something in for you.'

"So one of the first things they wrote in was the train caller at the Union Depot. You know, Jack always used to leave by train before planes were popular. And this train caller always said, 'Train leaving on Track Five for Anaheim, Azusa and Cuc — amonga!' [January 7, 1945 episode] Everybody beat me to Cucamonga." The writers kept making his pauses on that word so long — milking for laughs like a *very* contented cow — that on one episode, Mel stopped in the middle of the word to let the cast do few minutes of dialogue, and when he finally came back with "amonga" it brought the house down. The audience *knew* it was coming, but it was the antici — pation that killed 'em.

"But even when planes came in," Mel explained, "he had me as the plane caller on several programs. I was the guy who was supposed to be calling: 'Plane flying to Anaheim, Azusa…We don't stop at Cucamonga, so don't get off there!'

"Then he had a parrot which he couldn't get to come in on cue, so he said, 'Can you do a parrot?' I said, 'Yeah. (Squawking and whistling) Benny's a cheapskate! Benny's a cheapskate!' Well, he almost kicked me out for sayin' that, but I was his parrot."

It should be noted that a couple of voice men preceded Mel in this role, including cartoon voice actor and Spike Jones comic Purv Pullen, who specialized in many animal imitations. He did Polly back in 1940. Mel, however, became the voice of Jack's parrot once the bird became a weekly regular.

(Mel was so realistic as Jack's parrot Polly that he would use that talking bird voice many times on TV shows such as *Gilligan's Island* and *The Munsters*.)

That parrot got some of the biggest laughs in the show too, often repeating the insults he'd heard shouted at Jack. All that negativity took its toll, however, so in one radio episode, Jack took his depressed Polly to an animal psychiatrist. But it was Mary's idea, and Jack wasn't thrilled with doing it. "It doesn't seem right taking a parrot to a psychiatrist. The poor little thing will feel so silly lying on a couch on its back with its claws waving in the air." He had to wait in the doctor's waiting room with Bugs Bunny, but the two fought and Bugs left. When the doctor called the receptionist to send in both characters, she said, "I can't—Benny's here but Bunny's left." The line got big laughs.

Mel's most popular (and Jack's favorite) verbal duet with Jack was probably with the infamous precursor to Speedy Gonzales, done at slow speed: that poor, tired little soul by the name of Sy. This was a hilarious Mexican character created by the great Benny writer George Balzer. If Jack Benny didn't have the time for a full conversation, trust Sy to.

"Excuse me…Sir?" queries Jack.

"Si," replies the sad little Mexican.

"Is the train coming in on time?"

"Si."

"You're waiting for someone on the train?"

"Si."

"What's your name?"

"Sy."

"Sy?"

"Si."

"This person you're waiting for — is it a lady?"

"Si."

"A relative?"

"Si."

"Your sister!"

"Si."

"What's her name?"

"Sue."

"Sue?"

"Si." *(By this point, Jack is usually practically a broken man, doubled up in laughter)*

"Does your sister work for a living?"

"Si."

"What does she do?"

"Sew."

"Sew?"

"Si."

The routine altered a bit through the years — on radio *and* television — but the audience's reaction did *not*. They *roared* with laughter. The timing on this classic bit was always perfect, and it remained one of the staples of Jack's "sure fire" repertoire. Mel loved it because of the torture it would

Ask a silly question...

put Jack through to get to the end of it without cracking up. "That's what used to break Jack up, you know. At every rehearsal, 'cause I'd keep a sober face no matter what happened. I'd *always* keep a sober face, and he would break up every time. Then he'd say, 'I'm *not* gonna break up on the show, I'm *not* gonna break up on the show.' Come the show, he'd break up every time! He just couldn't control himself, he got such a kick out of

Mel on *The Tonight Show* with Johnny Carson.

it." Milt Josefsberg, one of Benny's writers, agreed that Jack just couldn't look at Mel's face as the sketch went on. In his book, *The Jack Benny Show*, Josefsberg wrote, "Mel played the little Mexican, and that was the only name we had for this character. In fact, most of his characters were nameless. We did endless variations [of the above routine], and we got huge laughs — usually the biggest ones from Jack."

When Johnny Carson was a senior at the University of Nebraska, he addressed his senior radio class thusly: "I was always interested in radio comedy, and I used the Jack Benny show as a prime example of fine comedy and comedy writing, especially in the way Jack and his writers played a running gag all the way through a program and then made it pay off at the end. I taped the 'Si-Sy' routine from Jack's satirical version of *The Treasure of Sierra Madre*, which was the first time it had ever been done, and I pointed it out as an example of a perfect comedy spot."

Television worried a lot of radio actors, including Mel Blanc. He hated it; the hot lights, the endless face makeup, the memorizing of lines, the constant interruption from the lighting crew informing you that you were standing in a shadow. Mel was terrified, and "thought it *stunk*."

Still, Mel endured it for the sake of his friend Jack Benny, who reluctantly began the transition from radio to TV in 1950 (though the radio

Mel undergoes the torture of make-up for his best friend.

series continued until 1955). Many on the show were worried about whether the radio characters would make a fair and believable transition to television. "I was in a daze for much of it, feeling out of my element," Mel said. Mel especially hated the makeup, always melting and running down his neck from the constant, searing lights. Some stars wore sunglasses right up until the moment of shooting.

But some of the best gags on radio just didn't work when it was all visual right in front of you. The vault, with all its laborious and time-consuming security, just couldn't be replicated. Jack's wheezing Maxwell just wasn't as funny; the mind could make that car *so* much worse, listening to Mel's deathbed utterances.

Noel wrote this, explaining the birth of one of Mel's most famous Benny "roles:"

It was hot, really hot, maybe 106 or 107 degrees in the shade. We were on our way to Palm Springs that summer of 1947 with the gang from the Jack Benny show. Dad, Mom, and I left L.A. early in the morning and after stopping for two date malts and a gallon jar of green olives, the car decided to boil over. So there we sat in the shade of a Coca-Cola billboard, waiting for the car's temperature to normalize. The Jack Benny Show rehearsal was scheduled to begin about 4 p.m., so we decided to give that maroon caddie another chance to hit the windy, sand-blown road to Palm Springs. The engine ignited and off we went eating fresh green olives and spitting the pits all over the highway, as we sped toward that overpriced oasis in the desert.

As we entered the city there was the banner that announced a welcome to all the Jack Benny gang. This particular week, Al Jolson was the special guest star on the show.

After checking into the motel, we were escorted to our room by the owner's halfwit son, who had a tough time finding cabin #3. We finally were able to convey to him that cabin 3 was most likely between cabins 2 and 4. As he opened the door to cabin 3, Mel gave an unnerving look at me and then at Mom.

"Where's the air conditioner?"

"There is none," said the halfwit son.

"Well, how the hell do we keep cool?"

The kid was obviously stuck for an answer and decided to exit quickly.

Mel then said, "I guess if all the bugs in this place beat their wings it should stay cool!"

At rehearsal:

"Mel!" came a roaring voice. "How the hell are you? Why aren't you staying at the Biltmore with Benny and me? Doesn't Jack give you enough bread to pay for a room at the Biltmore?" It was Al Jolson that was shouting the distance of the auditorium. Jeez, that man had the loudest damn voice I ever heard. "Well, Mel? Doesn't he pay you enough?"

"No!" Mel shouted. "Jack told us if we love him then we'd do the show for free!"

"That's what I thought," Jolson shouted. "He keeps all the cast's salary and gives it to Mary so she can buy two extra pairs of shoes." Everybody on stage roared with laughter, including Jack Benny, who was laughing so hard he was pounding on the floor. Jack always pounded something when he was laughing.

"Jolson's just pissed," Jack exclaimed. "Nobody recognizes him unless he has worked on his car engine or cleaned his chimney."

Mel jumped up on stage, grabbed a script and the rehearsal was on its way.

"What's all this air conditioning equipment doing here if the goddam stuff doesn't work?" shouted Jolson.

It was about 110 degrees outside the radio theater now, but inside it must have been 150 degrees. Most all of the cast was stripped to the

Mel and Al Jolson.

waist, except the ladies of course, and Mel looked as if he just climbed out of a pool. He was completely drenched with sweat and the script he was holding was nearly limp, but the rehearsal was still going smoothly. This was the last rehearsal before the show and I was permitted to watch. What a thrill to see Benny, Jolson and my dad on the same stage.

Near the end of the show, Jack was supposed to drive away with Rochester and Jolson in his Maxwell, but something went wrong with the sound effects turntable. The recording of the old automobile didn't work and the sound effects man was going crazy. Without blinking an eye, Mel was at the mike supplying the sounds of the Maxwell, which turned out to be so funny that Jack continued to use Mel as the motor of the Maxwell from that time on. According to writer Milt Josefsberg, after Jack told Rochester to start the engine (a line which alone got laughs for its anticipatory conditioning), "Mel would add his efforts to the mechanical sound effects, and Mel was a vocal virtuoso. From his mouth issued sounds never made by mortal man. He actually became the engine of that car, and his asthmatic wheezing and coughing would keep the audience, and of course Jack, in a state of continual laughter. He wheezed, whooped, coughed, choked, snorted, snuffled, and sneezed until we were all mentally praying for him to stop because he brought forth all of these unearthly sounds with one single deep breath, and as his air supply began to fade his face would start to change color, and we worried for his health." [It should be noted that Jack had done several Maxwell car gags back in the late 1930s, and therefore the actual first voice of Jack's wheezing, ancient lemon of a car was supplied by a cartoon voice man who was in the business earlier than Mel: his friend and fellow Oregonian Pinto Colvig (most famous as the voice of Walt Disney's Goofy).]

Josefsberg admitted that many characters written for Mel were "one shots," to try and see if a character would work for a longer series of jokes/shows or as a recurring character, but sadly most of them didn't gel.

There was another time on the Jack Benny show when the whole cast had supposedly traveled to England for the Upson Downs Horse Race [a joke on the actual racecourse at Epsom Downs in England]. It was the first rehearsal of the show, and like always, the writers were up to stumping Mel on sound effects. This time, they wrote on the script, "Mel does whinny of English horse." Again, Mel didn't hesitate. He began his horse whinny like a normal horse, but ended it with a typical old, stuffy English laugh. Everyone on the stage fell down with laughter, especially Jack, who had the habit of pounding the table, floor, or any flat surface when he laughed. Mel once credited Milt Josefsberg of instigating the dastardly deed. Another time, he was instructed to make the sound of a goldfish, so he walked up close to the mike and pursed his mouth open and closed. No one heard a thing, but the studio audience loved it.

Josefsberg did admit that one of life's little pleasures for the writers was trying to insert impossible parts for him. "In one bit we wrote we had Jack ask a man something on a street, and in the stage directions we had written the instructions: 'Mel answers, using the voice of a Colored, Jewish Fag.' Damned if he didn't do it, but it never got on the air."

Jack's show held a special place in Mel's heart, and was certainly different when it came to looking for laughs. "On the Benny show, we always used to do the rehearsals exactly as we were going to do the show 'cause Jack would time it…and he would see whether the rest of the cast laughed at the jokes that were in the script. If they didn't, he would take that out or change it. He was quite an editor that way. And he had a marvelous sense of humor…and great timing, which was so very important. I used to do The Cisco Kid [filling in for old friend Harry Lang in the role of Pancho opposite Jack Mather after Lang had a heart attack, Mel later said], and we'd kid through the rehearsal just to time it. I'd say, 'Ceesco, thee sheriff I theenk ees cuuumeeng!' You'd hear a lot of shots, then Cisco

Jack and Noel.

would say, 'Did he hitcha, Pancho?' I'd say, 'I dunno. Geeme a glassa water. I'll see eef I leeak." Mel had the checks sent to Harry until he died, then Mel continued the role for a few years.

Mel admitted to ad-libbing, especially at rehearsals where gags were being finalized. On the air, things were almost 100% as they were meant to be, but "once in a great while I'd throw in some crazy gag. Jack'd fall down laughing."

It's common knowledge that Jack was perhaps the greatest single-digit audience in all of Hollywood. Mel agreed. "He was. He was a marvelous audience. You know, the joke was always pulled on Jack, and he was the brunt of all the jokes. But you'd say something to another listener, you'd say, 'Gee, I thought that was a very funny gag!' The other guy would say, 'Where did you hear it?' 'On the Jack Benny Show.' No matter who did it, it was always 'on The Jack Benny Show.'"

As Joan Benny wrote in her book on Jack, "Mel Blanc in his many roles did look, I think, as one imagined. The fact that so much of the radio show could be duplicated was the major reason for Dad's long and successful sojourn on TV."

One character that made the transition to television *very* well was that semi-regular character, Professor LeBlanc, Jack's persecuted violin teacher. It was torture for the poor Prof. to have to teach such a tone-deaf no-talent like this Mr. Benny — but he desperately needed the money. If Jack would pay, that is. No matter how much sawing Jack Benny did on that violin, his incredibly crummy technique never raised above an untalented five-year-old's. And while Jack sawed away on his practice bars, poor Le Blanc would make up rotten verse to lament his plight:

> *"Make the notes a little thinner,*
> *I don't want to lose my dinner."*
> or
> *"My poor heart is nearly breaking.*
> *What an awful sound you're making."*
> or
> *"Make the bow strokes a little longer.*
> *How I wish my stomach were stronger."*
> or
> *"Shorter notes, make them littler.*
> *This should only happen to Hitler."*

When the alarm clock signaled the end of the lesson, the Prof. would sometimes be overjoyed with giddy pleasure as he shouted, "I'm FREE! FREE!! FREE!!!" as he ran off into the night.

The love-hate relationship of teacher and student is explored fully in an entire frantic 1964 TV episode dedicated to the frazzled Prof. when LeBlanc finds himself in a shrink's office. Mel stated, "Oui. We got loads of [fan] mail on that show. And Jack wore me out. I worked with heem. I *slaved* with heem! Finally at the end of the lesson I would say, 'Please, Monsieur Ben-nee! Take the ball and chain off my foot! The lesson is ovair! Let me go home!' I would sing to him while he was playing: 'Now please play it nice and classy. Hold your tongue in, you're not Lassie.' And 'What a tune your fiddle brings on. How I wish it had not strings on.'

"Well, Jack loved that show, and we both loved to work on it because we actually characterized the two as they should have been characterized.

And when I got through with the show, Jack said, 'Mel, you're not only a comedian, you're a great actor!' I said, 'What did I do?' He said, 'You acted a beautiful part.' And I said to Jack, 'Jack, this is the best thing I ever saw *you* do, too, because you are actually a real bad violin player — which I thought you were!'"

In this episode poor LeBlanc has finally cracked and is sitting on a psychiatrist's couch 'Blancly' staring into space while reaching out for a box of Kleenex, slowly putting them in his pocket one by one…A concerned Jack arrives and begins to relate the bittersweet history of their relationship through a series of flashbacks: as the men age, Jack's terrible playing does not sweeten. For some reason, the doctor assumes that his fine playing today would snap the Prof. out of it, so Jack races home to get his violin. Jack does indeed somehow play beautifully in front of LeBlanc, curing him instantly of his failure complex, giving an uplifting ending to the episode and the poor guy's life.

Mel admitted to improvising the Kleenex bit. The flashbacks were done for *that* episode, in different costumes, rather than a "greatest hits" collection from previous shows. The visual gags were great — each man wearing a selection of gradually diminishing toupees, while the frantic professor seemed to wear his one tuxedo out as the years wore on…"My shoes had holes in the bottom of 'em. Finally it got to the point where I said, 'I can't live on what I'm making. I owe the bank! My wife is gonna have a baby, and I haveta have more money!' So he raised me…gave me a quarter more."

Whether or not he got paid his $2 for the *long* hour-long lessons, when the alarm clock rang to signal the end of the hour, it was *the* most beautiful sound in the world. Once he even made his impassioned exit speech completely in French, singing the first four lines of the "Marseillaise" as he marched away.

Most people never realized that Mel could play the violin — a little — including Jack. Mel told Walt Mitchell, "When I was a kid I played violin just to practice the violin. I never was a *good* violinist, but I played a number of tunes, so I *could* read music.

"Jack didn't know I played the violin. He was rehearsing a duet with Gisele MacKenzie and on this one show, I took the violin away from him and I played along with her. Jack was flabbergasted! He said, 'Oh, my god! I didn't know you could play!

We're gonna keep that in the show!' So in the show, I came back with a bunch of visitors and I walked up to him, took the violin away from him and started playing with Gisele. And I had to join the union! I had belonged to the [musician's] union before in Portland, but I had to join the Los Angeles union to play on the show."

Mel did show up a few times on Jack's TV show as other characters, and his appearances were memorable. For one particular show, Jack drives Mel, a salesman at a busy department store, crazy (and to suicide) when Jack keeps wanting to exchange or rewrap a Christmas present for Don

Amazing Jack Benny.

Wilson. He didn't fare any better as a burglar another time when he tries to rob Jack's lethally-trapped bedroom.

Mel credited Jack for his learning of timing, and called him the best editor in comedy. "I have worked with practically every star in the business," Mel said, "but *none* can compare with Jack Benny. He was a wonderful man. He wasn't only my boss, but he was my best friend, too. And Jack was very considerate, very liberal, just the opposite of what he was on the program. And we never signed a contract. I never signed a contract with Jack. He just asked me at the end of the season, 'Say, you gonna be with me next year?' And I'd say, 'Well, if y' give me a raise an' buy me a drink!' 'Well,' he says, 'c'mon, then. I'll buy you a drink.' That's the way we worked for years since 1939."

Jack was one of the few Hollywood celebrities that Mel and Estelle socialized with after work hours. Mel didn't care for going to Hollywood parties where they talked about nothing but business; he got enough of that at work all day. Jack didn't mind the formal glamour, but he also liked getting away. During July and August, radio's vacation from the airwaves, Mel and family would spend many a year at their lakeside cabin on Big Bear Lake. Mel even recorded a song called "Big Bear Lake" for Capitol Records in 1949, and thought the song might have had something to do with the population explosion of the area sometime after its release.

One Big Bear Benny adventure that happened in 1952:

"Hello, Mel?" It was Jack Benny on the phone. I recognized his delivery immediately.

"No, Jack, this is Noel."

"Oh, Noel, what are you doing home from school?" Implying that I may be playing hooky.

"This is Saturday, Jack. Don't you think 5 times a week is enough?"

"Where's Mel?" he said, wearying of my conversation.

"Wait a minute. Hold the phone, I think he's in the dark room."

I ran down the two flights of stairs and shouted to Mel who was making eight-by-tens of some pictures he took in Canada last summer. "Jack's on the phone, Dad. Pick it up."

As Mel picked up the dark room phone, I ran back upstairs to listen in. It was unlike Jack to call so early on a Saturday morning. Evidently he knew Mel never slept later than 5:30 a.m.

"Mel, what do you think if I came up to Big Bear Lake with Joanie and her girlfriend for a few days?" Joanie was Jack's 14-year-old daughter, and her girlfriend turned out to be a knockout 15-year-old named Hanna.

Mel told Jack that we would be going up next weekend which turned out to be the end of the school semester and that we'd probably stay there most of the summer.

Big Bear Lake is a beautiful hideaway tucked into the San Bernadino Mountains about 120 miles from downtown Los Angeles. Because of the proximity, Mom and Dad had been spending summers there since 1938. They could get away and at the same time, have easy access to the radio studios in Hollywood.

Anyway, Jack had heard about Big Bear Lake many times from Mel and decided that his daughter would love it there. Arrangements were made and two days after we arrived at the lake, Jack, Joanie and Hanna drove up.

Jack stepped out of the black Caddie convertible and pretended his legs were made of rubber. "I've never taken that many hairpin curves before. It's worse than two weeks on the Queen Mary!"

Mel offered him some Dramamine, which he refused, and as he dizzily ambled into the cabin, Joan, Hanna, and I schlepped the suitcases into the guest house.

"How come I'm breathing so hard?" Jack asked. "I've only walked from the car to the cabin."

"Don't worry about it, Jack," Mel assured him, "we're over 7000 feet up and the air seems thin for the first couple of days."

"And I was going to swim across the lake today," Jack said wryly.

The first day was spent relaxing around the cabin with Mel telling stories of Big Bear's history…great legends of how Indians had happened upon the area hundreds of years ago, but were unable to camp in the area because of killer bears that stalked the woods. The legend goes that these killer bears were created by the Sun God to keep out evil spirits that had infested the area after a volcanic eruption. Mel had a lot of these stories, but I always knew why he told them. Knowing that the air was so thin for first-timers to the mountain, he would keep them entertained with stories the first day and let their systems acclimate to the thin air gradually, before they tried hiking, water skiing, or other exertive sports.

"Joanie is sensational. Don't you think so, Mel?" Jack asked. Mel nodded but kept his hand firmly on the steering wheel, ever so often glancing to the rear of the boat.

Joan Benny was water skiing on one ski with the rope and baton around the back of her head. She was one hell of a water skier and Jack loved being up at Big Bear Lake with her, her girlfriend Hanna, Mom, Dad, and myself. This time they had come for about a two-week stay so Joanie could really practice her water skiing.

Jack tended rope for her each time she skied, and little by little he gathered the courage to want to try his hand at the sport.

After a long ride to the dam and back with Joan doing all kinds of tricks, Jack asked Mel if he could be next. Mel said he thought it would be a great idea, but first he thought Jack should take a lesson on the dock, so Mel helped Jack on with the skis and gave him some first-class instruction.

Mel was a good skier himself but an even better teacher, having learned both how to ski and give instruction from the national champion, Elva Swaffor. Jack realized also that if we were going to ski, he'd better have a life jacket that would keep him afloat, so we looked around and found a whopper! It weighed about 12 pounds and looked as if it would keep Kate Smith afloat.

Getting into this battleship-gray Navy survival preserver was no easy chore. It took three of us to strap him in. Finally, Jack was ready. He sat at the end of the dock as the mahogany Chris Craft rumbled away from the slip. The rope played out easily. Joanie told Mel there was about 15 feet left, and that Jack should get into the water. Mel shouted, "Hey, Jack, get in!" Jack shouted back, "Bullshit! I'm not getting into that water, it'll freeze my ass off!"

And with that, he unstrapped the hulking life jacket and scampered quickly off the dock before any of us could question why he decided not to ski.

Fishing was more Jack Benny's style, so the next day we drove into Fred's Sporting Goods in Big Bear Village so Jack could obtain his fishing license.

Fred was a young mountain-born-and-raised fellow who we became friends with when he opened his tiny store in tinier downtown Big Bear, which incidentally is only two blocks long.

Jack, wearing dark sunglasses and a cap, was ushered into the store which could barely hold the four of us, and Fred began to ask the questions on the Fishing License form.

"Hair?" Fred asked.

"Brown," Jack replied.

"Eyes?"

"Robin's egg blue."

Fred didn't know what to make of this strange answer, but he wrote it down anyway. "Height?"

"5' 11."

"Weight?"

"145."

"Age?"

"39," Jack replied.

Now Fred began to catch on. Although he had not recognized Jack at first, the answers to the questions were beginning to turn Fred's mental wheels.

"Name?" Fred asked. Then answered his own question: "Jack Benny!" he shouted.

Jack took off his glasses and Fred blushed a crimson red. Never before had a star of such magnitude come to Big Bear, let alone to Fred's three-by-ten foot sporting goods store.

Once Jack had obtained his license, we all went to our favorite fishing cove, ready to catch our limit.

Mel had just purchased a small outboard motor, which he had attached to a 14-foot rowboat named "Bugs Bunny PTE #2." The PTE stood for "Pardon the Expression." This was the boat that we all climbed into. Joanie, Hanna, Mom, Dad, Jack and I. We barely had room for the life preservers and the fishing tackle, but at least it was larger than Fred's Sporting Goods Store.

Two hours went by and not even a nibble. Mel changed bait several times, Jack performed an old Indian fishing prayer and I chummed the water all around the boat, but to no avail. It seemed that all the fish had gone elsewhere.

At about 5 o'clock, just as we were about to pull the anchor and go home skunked, Jack's pole nearly bent in two. Jack didn't know what to do first. He started to crank his reel, but ended up turning it the wrong way. Now the fish had swum under the boat so Jack maneuvered past us and up to the bow where he dragged his line to the other side of the boat.

"What'll I do? What'll I do?" he shouted, suggesting that he may have latched onto a Marlin.

"Reel the damn thing in, Jack!" Mel shouted.

Jack was trying, but the fish was outsmarting him. Every time Jack reeled in a few feet, the fish would swim to the opposite side of the boat, causing Jack near hysteria.

To any other fisherman nearby, the whole situation must have looked like a Marx Brothers routine, but Jack wasn't about to let a mere trout get the best of him. Finally, he put the pole on the floor of the boat, grabbed the line, and yanked the fish up to the side of the boat where I netted it.

It wasn't a bad looking trout, as far as fish go, and Jack was ecstatic that he had caught the only one of the day.

The sun was now just setting behind the mountains and the water of the lake took on a deep purple glow. A chilly breeze drifted in across the lake and Mel decided that we had had enough fishing for one afternoon, so he gave the new outboard motor a tug on the starter rope…nothing. He pulled the rope again…still nothing. After 50 or 60 pulls, he gave up and asked me to try. About 20 times was all I was good for and nobody else volunteered so I took one oar and Dad took the other and we rowed the two or three miles back to our dock. This was not one of my favorite fishing experiences.

As darkness came, we began to barbecue a huge New York-cut steak on the charcoal grill just outside the kitchen on the front porch overlooking the water. Joan brought out her ukulele and began to sing, which prompted Mel and Jack to drag out their violins, and before dinner we had one hell of a jam session.

Mel was at best fair with his violin, but Jack was brilliant. He could play any song we would mention, and play it well.

The music pouring over the lake brought the neighbors out of their

The Jack Benny Show cast.

cabins and before we knew it, the porch was full of people, all of them requesting a different song.

"Sing 'I Taut I Taw a Puddy Tat,' Mel," he heard one of the group say. Dad didn't waste any time. Jack and Dad both played the song while Dad sang the song that was number one of the hit parade at that time, and remained #1 for nearly a year in England.

After we had finished the enormous steak dinner, Jack announced that he would like to show us a new game that he had learned from a few of his friends at the Friars Club. The game was called "Search" and it entailed hiding objects in plain view. The trick was to camouflage the object by blending their colors with the colors of where they were placed. For instance, if you had a cigarette, you'd place it on the piano's white keys, or if you had a piece of licorice, you'd place it on the black keys.

Two people would place up to 15 objects while everyone else left the room. Then, when the others came back after the objects were placed, as they found the objects, they would whisper where and what object to the two players. The person finding all the objects first would then be the winner and would become the placer.

Though Mel didn't care for appearing live on camera, he agreed to be on Jack's first two television shows, the first 45-minute episode on October 21, 1950, and then eight months later on May 20, 1951, since Jack was slowly testing the waters to make sure his formula would float in the new medium. Almost everything was kept the same, including characters and the commercial format. Unfortunately, the radio bits worked better in the listener's mind than laid out for them expensively on screen, and changes were quickly made to adapt to the new medium without going broke or boring the increasingly fickle audiences.

Mel recalled that after Jack Benny had seen Warner's Abbott and Costello cartoon, *A Tale of Two Kitties*, he wanted the Benny gang to voice a cartoon themselves. Mel was wary that Jack would do it, as it would be a substantial cut from his radio salary, but after agreeing to do it free of charge, *The Mouse That Jack Built* was built, and released on April 4, 1959. Mel again appeared as the sputtering, dying Maxwell.

4 | *The Mel Blanc Show*

"What brand of cigarettes do you have in your pocket, Mr. Blanc?" The man spoke with authority and definitely meant business. "Uh…Pall Mall," Mel said. "Damnit, Mel, this is the Lucky Strike show and you sure as hell better have that lucky green in your pocket next time I come around."

At that time in his career, Dad was performing on 18 radio shows a week, and six of them were sponsored by cigarettes…all different brands. Dad would keep a pack of each brand in the glove compartment of his '41 Packard and rarely would he forget to make the change for the next show, but today he had blundered, so we walked out to the parking lot behind NBC and exchanged the Pall Malls for Luckies. "Big deal," he said, "they're both made by the American Tobacco Company, what difference does it make?" But it did make a difference, a big difference, and that's why each of the radio shows had on salary a full-time cigarette inspector…ah…the heyday of radio.

Later that day, after Mel had exchanged brands about three times and the cigarette packs began to look a little ratty, he and I entered the stage of the Burns and Allen show.

As was common in those radio days, the cast would sit around a large table and read through the script for the new show. This time I was allowed to sit in even though I was only 6 years old. What a thrill to sit next to Gracie Allen, and I got really excited each time Dad said his lines. It always seemed that he got the loudest laughs of the show.

We went to one last show that day, The Chesterfield Supper Club, for a short rehearsal and there he was again, the cigarette inspector. This one didn't say anything, he just walked up to all the performers and crew one at a time and peeked inside their shirt pockets. This annoying fellow was not liked very much, and it seemed to me he really enjoyed being obtrusive. When he came up to Mel, and started for the shirt pocket, Dad beat him to the punch with the fastest draw in cigarette packages. Out came the Chesterfields and, of course, the inspector smirked and walked on. Incidentally, Mel hated Chesterfields, and I figured if he had to work that show every day, he would have quit smoking forever.

Later, when he was in charge of his own advertising company, Mel would voice and produce a series of anti-smoking ads for television.

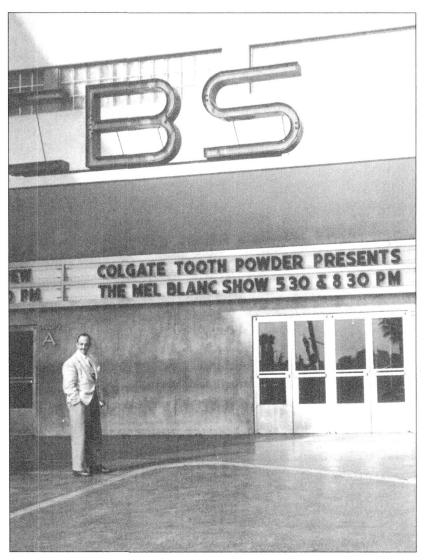

Mel gets his own show.

Mel more than likely caught the eye of a potential sponsor for his own radio show while stealing scenes on *The Judy Canova Show*. Colgate Tooth Powder thought Mel's repertoire was strong enough to launch him in a solo series. He had the name value from the cartoons, which was properly exploited in the show's opening credits.

The previous summer, Mel had purchased and opened a hardware store in Venice, California (just a few minutes from the Blanc home) for his

COLUMBIA BROADCASTING SYSTEM
COLUMBIA SQUARE PLAYHOUSE
6121 SUNSET BOULEVARD —— HOLLYWOOD

TUESDAY
DEC.

Nº 639

STUDIO
B
C B S

COLGATE TOOTHPOWDER
Presents
THE MEL BLANC SHOW

10
1 9 4 6
5:30-5:55 p.m.
Doors Close
at 5:25 p.m.

CHILDREN UNDER TWELVE WILL NOT BE ADMITTED

PHOTO COURTESY OF RICK PAYNE.

father-in-law. That was to be the autobiographical basis for *The Mel Blanc Show*. The store's name in Venice and on the show was The Fix-It Shop. Mel would put little ads in the paper: "come to the fix-it shop" and "if we haven't got it, we'll get it for you." There Mel sold fishing equipment whenever his schedule would permit, doing all of his own purchasing. He had even visited New York City to stock the place up before its grand opening. It didn't make much money, but it was good for some gags for the show, and provided his father-in-law with something to do as he was "losing his marbles trying to keep occupied."

The actual store lasted longer than the series, which only ran for a year. As Noel wrote:

Every odd hour that Mel wasn't on the air, he'd spend at the Fix-It Shop which he ran with my grandfather. Now, Mel didn't know the first thing about a retail operation, but he loved the shop and did all the buying for it. He had items that no one had even thought of buying and his rapport with the customers was marvelous.

One day a customer came in and wanted a certain type of small file called a "bastard." Mel said, "We don't have a little bastard, sir, but we do have this big son-of-a-bitch."

This is the type of dialogue that would come out of Mel's Fix-It Shop, and having a national radio program with the same name was a local merchant's dream. People would come from all over California to see the original Fix-It Shop and would usually end up buying one or two weird things which were literally hanging from the rafters.

In any given week, numerous Hollywood personalities would drive down for something to buy. Jack Benny would drop by for fishing tackle, Al Jolson for a hunting knife, Sheldon Leonard to ask Mel about aquarium supplies, Roy Rogers for toys for his kids. It was a never ending parade of Hollywood talent. In fact, if tourists really wanted to see stars, all they had to do was sit in front of the Fix-It Shop.

Many funny incidents that would occur at the real Fix-It Shop were told to the writers of Mel's show and they would incorporate some of them into the formats. It really gave the program a non-fictional quality, and the comedy was exceptional.

The premiere episode, "Birthday Card Promotion," began with announcer Bud Hiestand smilingly shouting, "From Hollywood! Colgate Tooth Powder, for a breath that's sweet and teeth that sparkle, presents The Mel Blanc Show!" Music. "Colgate Tooth Powder, for a breath that's sweet and teeth that sparkle, brings you The Mel Blanc Show, with Mary Jane Croft, Earle Ross, Bea Benaderet, Zookie, Victor Miller and his orchestra." Mel gives samples of his other characters, including The Happy Postman, Jack Benny's train caller, Judy Canova's Pedro, and "the lovable character, Zookie!" Zookie was Mel's second-in-command, a real Porky Pig-like character who would usually try hard to introduce himself to the audience: "Hello, *everyb-de-b-de-b-de-hello, everyb-de-b-de-b-be — huhuhuhuhuhuhaaa*, hi!"

Later, the show's intro was changed a bit, but still tied in to his cartoon work: "…and starring the creator of the voice of Bugs Bunny, Mel Blanc!" Mel gave a carrot-biting, "Eh…? What's up, doc?" Announcer: "And starring himself, in person, Mel Blanc!" Mel: "Hi, folks, ugga ugga boo ugga boo boo ugga." Then right away, the catchy sponsor's song shined out in glorious harmony:

> *Use Colgate Tooth Powder*
> *Keep smilin' just right*
> *Use it each morning and use it each night!*
> *Don't take a chance, with your romance*
> *Use Colgate—Tooth Powder!*
> *[and also:] It cleans your teeth, makes breath so sweet…*
> *Use Colgate Tooth Powder…!*

The opening program had Mel trying to drum up more business (so he can afford to marry the ever-faithful Betty) by buying birthday cards to send to all customers who had birthdays that month. Of course, helper Zookie messes up by buying cards that promise a free gift under separate cover, which is further complicated by his Uncle Rupert who tries to help out by buying a load of chocolate boxes from a friend that turn out to be

Outside the actual shop.

"Ace Novelty Company's #1 joker. Be the life of the party — treat your friends to sure-pucker Alum candy." The luck of the stupid stops Mel from being the most hated man in town when none of the boxes are delivered thanks to Zookie's mistakenly taking a list of deceased people from City Hall, rather than a list of customers.

At first, Mel, owner of Mel Blanc's Fix-It Shop ("You bend it, we mend it") had to put up with his loafing Uncle Rupert (Earle Ross) who was always after the rich old maid, Mrs. Longnecker (Bea Benaderet). Soon Longnecker was dropped, and Hans Conried was brought in as Mr. Snoop the postman, along with The Sportsmen harmony group from Jack Benny's show. But it was on November 5, 1946 that the show introduced Hans as lodge president Mr. Cushing and finally slipped the series into its regular formula.

The Mel Blanc Show hardly deviated from its original format, the plot of which invariably began with three couples doing the same thing, the last of which was Mel and girlfriend Betty, showing off what a loser or poor man he was. Betty's father, Mr. Colby (Joe Kearns), hated Mel, and most episodes had the poor shop owner trying to impress his would-be dad or improve his lot in life. At the start of the show the exasperated Colby would berate Mel for trying to fix something of his. On the May 13, 1947 episode it was:

COLBY: Mel Blanc, you idiot! What did you do to my sausage-making machine?
MEL: I fixed it, Mr. Colby. I was fixing the sewing machine and I may've got the parts mixed up.
COLBY: A sewing machine, so that's it!
MEL: Somethin' wrong?
COLBY: Plenty! All the frankfurters are coming out with belts in the back!

Still, it was hard for Mr. Colby to get angry with anyone that day — he was hoping to have the story of his life written by a journalist from *Supermarket Journal*. Mel sends Zookie to the library to stock up education books so he can bone up on egghead things to say about the great and brainy Mr. Colby.

While Mel's in his Shop getting ready, in walks the "town Beau Brummel," Hartley Benson (Jim Backus), who's always good for a few laughs. This time the egotistical, girl-crazy Ronald Colman-type idiot tells of his Cornell education:

HARTLEY: Look at the Cornell yearbook for 1938 and you will see "Hartley Benson voted the man most likely to succeed — at Vassar! Mel, old boy, they went wild over my student *body*. In fact, I was their star athlete.

MEL: What game?

HARTLEY: Tiddlywinks. I played left tiddly. In fact, a beautiful girl was my downfall. I was out to score one for our side when…she looked at me.

MEL: What did you do?

HARTLEY: I winked when I should've tiddled!

Hartley never had anything to do with the plot, but then in walked the Mighty Potentate (Hans Conried), with his usual, guttural, Loyal Order of Benevolent Zebras (a prelude to Fred & Barney's Loyal Order of Water Buffalos) greeting:

MP: Hello, Mel, ugga ugga boo ugga boo boo ugga…!

MEL: Greetings, great zebra!

MP: Mel. You look down at the mouth.

MEL: Oh, I wish I was dead. I can't get married.

MP: I wish I was dead, I *got* married! The other day my wife and I had an argument and she said, "John, you drive me to my grave."

MEL: What did you do?

MP: I had the car out of the garage in two minutes.

But as much as he hates his sweetie, the Mighty Potentate is happy to give Mel some misplaced advice on how to save the day. Usually — and this time as well — it's to disguise his face and voice to solve the problem. Now he urges the poor sap to imitate a foreign professor to laud over Colby's academic accomplishments. Of course the scheme backfires when the reporter is more interested in Colby because he's a self-made man, never pampered by foreign schools. With no way to warn Mel beforehand, Colby tries to keep Mel out and shut him up, but Mel is determined to do well for his prospective father-in-law, and does. The poor lug never did get married.

One of the biggest laugh-getters on the series was certainly Hans Conried (vocally most famous as Captain Hook in Disney's *Peter Pan*), whom Mel had urged to be a part of his series. Mel thought that Hans was so serious about acting that he became the funniest man he'd ever met, though he had true doubts about doing comedy.

The show's main catchphrase, "Ugga-ugga-boo, ugga-boo-boo-ugga," became so popular that Mel co-wrote (with Eddie Maxwell, Mac Benoff and Irving Miller) a song by that name which was recorded by Spike Jones and His City Slickers for RCA Records. (Note: Mel did not do the vocal for this Spike Jones song; it was sung by sax player Eugene Walla, as "Ding Bell" on the label.)

...and inside.

Unfortunately, reviewers didn't think the show itself was so exceptional. *The New York Times'* September 15, 1946 review cried over "the deplorable waste of Mr. Blanc's indisputable talents. [His] writers have not grasped the first essentials of farce. The boff gags needed to keep it in motion were omitted, leaving only disconnected fragments of awkward and forced humor…[the show] has a long way to go before it hits the Big Time." *Variety* said almost the same thing: "Mel Blanc and producer Joe Rines did a swell job with the material at hand, but had nothing to work with. Blanc is okay as himself — his first straight role. Supporting players, all hand-picked by Rines, and showing it, did good jobs, too, especially Bea Benadaret in the Billie Burke-ism part of the wealthy 'Mrs. Longnecker.' Possibility of building Blanc into a top-rating ether draw is definitely there. Colgate gave signs of recognizing that when they signed him up for five years. But ouch, that writing job."

Noel Blanc agreed with the general consensus that *The Mel Blanc Show* wasn't the best thing on the airwaves: **Dad was disappointed about the radio show but it really suffered from bad writing, chiefly from Mac Benoff who also directed it. He kinda knew it didn't stand a chance with Mac at the helm.**

Though disappointed when his series was canceled after only a single season, Mel was also relieved that he didn't need to succumb to the pressures of being a star, and developed even greater respect for the likes of Jack Benny, et al. He, like Paul Frees and other famed voice actors, liked the fact that he could walk down the street and go anywhere and not have to worry about living "a star's fishbowl existence."

By the way, Mel Blanc's real Fix-It Shop was located in Venice Ca. on Market Street, number 39, about half a block from the beach. However as Noel Blanc also points out, Mel was *not* a Mr. Fix-It in real life: **Sylvester the cat and Wile E. Coyote have a lot in common. Both, no matter how hard they try to catch their respective adversaries, always seem to bungle the job. Sylvester is always trying to build some type of hair-brained trap to capture Tweety, and Wyle E., with the help of Acme accessories, creates everything from rocket-powered roller skates to electrically-operated Roadrunner look-alike bombs. However, one thing always seems to plague both Wyle E. and Sylvester, and that's the fact that whatever they build to stop Tweety or the Roadrunner goes sour after it's constructed. Nothing ever works right, no matter how carefully it's built. And, strangely enough, nothing Mel had ever tried to build or even fix has ever worked right.**

The first evidence of this, I can remember, is when I was almost three years old. I recall my mom asking Mel to go out to his workbench in

the garage and fix a table leg, which had broken off her favorite small mahogany end table. Now this looked like an easy job…a little glue and one nail. Mel smeared the leg with glue, withdrew a large nail from a glass mason jar, and took his professional-looking leather-handled hammer from its place on the wall. Then with one precision strike of the hammer, he calmly broke his thumb. 'Son of a bitch, son of a bitch!!' he shouted.

But being only 2 1/2, I didn't know what the hell he was saying, so I copied what I thought I heard: 'Some bitch…some bitch!' 'No!' he said. 'Don't ever say that word!' 'Some bitch…some bitch!' I shouted again. He ran into the house for some ice for his finger, and from that day on, I knew my Pop wasn't your basic fix-it man.

Three weeks later, this particular incident was to haunt both my mom and Mel. It was the holiday season, and our family was invited to attend a Christmas party at the home of Mrs. Cecil B. DeMille. Now, this was quite an honor for my mom and dad, since we were fairly new in the neighborhood, and Mrs. DeMille was considered to be on the top stratum of the social pecking list.

My mom and dad had no babysitter, so, knowing I was a pretty even-tempered child, they decided to bring me along. The lunch was beautiful, and while the adults chatted, I sat in my tailor-tot next to my folks, playing with my mother's key chain. Suddenly, I caught my finger in the key ring. It hurt like hell, and I belted out, 'Some bitch…some bitch!' knowing that's the thing to say when one hurts his finger. After all, that's what Dad said in the garage that day.

My mother, red faced, and my father, stuttering more than Porky Pig, fired off twenty or thirty excuses for my salty language…everything from, 'Oh, he learned it from the workmen across the street" to "He probably heard it at the garage this morning when the mechanic touched a spark plug wire." Even at three years old, I could see that nobody bought the excuses, and I don't believe that my folks were invited back for the delicious annual Christmas brunch at the DeMille's ever again.

Mel often brought Noel to radio work with him and the ladies (Sara Berner, Gracie Allen, Judy Canova, etc.) would fawn over the beautiful boy who would sit in the sponsor's soundproof booth and listen to the shows. From the age of four, "Jack Benny virtually became the kid's uncle." Mel and Estelle were careful not to heap too much fuss on the kid. He'd seen how big heads could be made out of Hollywood offspring. Noel went to kindergarten at Nightingale Elementary School in Venice, but he wasn't happy. The pace was too slow. It wasn't until his teacher suggested that Noel would be at an advantage elsewhere that his parents changed him to a more challenging school, where Noel was content, going to school with the sons and daughters of Tony Martin, Harry James, and others.

"If we were fated to have but one child," Mel stated, "we couldn't have been blessed with a better son than Noel. He was, and still is, my pride and joy."

In 1940 Mel's father died following a short illness, and his mother moved into Los Angeles to live with her sister. (In November of 1956 Mel lost his mother, Eva Blanc, to a heart attack in a Gardena poker club.) It was wonderful being close to family again. Though his circle of close friends was limited, Mel and Estelle did socialize with the Jack Bennys, Mr. and Mrs. Friz Freleng, Mr. and Mrs. Carl Stalling (Warner Bros. cartoon composer), and Mr. and Mrs. Milt Franklyn (who orchestrated and would take over for Stalling as composer).

Sometimes Mel would instruct Warner Bros. leading men on dialects: Clark Gable for New Yawk, Alan Ladd for a Texas twang, singer Ezio Pinza to soften his Italian accent. As his circle of acquaintances grew, so too did Mel's radio work.

In early 1946 Mel Blanc was named honorary mayor of Anaheim, Azusa, and Cucamonga. The character of his that was receiving the most fan mail at the time was Judy Canova's Pedro, and at this time Mel was netting about $75,000 a year from radio alone. As *Liberty* magazine wrote: "Being around Mel is never dull. Ask Estelle, who never knows whether he'll turn up at the end of the day with a new voice, a new fishing rod, or a new watch. His watch collection is the envy of all Hollywood. His favorite, a solid gold timepiece which his wife gave him last Christmas, practically sits up and talks. Once, when an unsuspecting stranger on a bus asked him for the correct time, Mel jerked it out of his pocket, pushed a button, and let loose a miniature carillon concert that ended in a beautiful friendship. The stranger missed his stop in order to find out how the gadget worked, and Mel took him home for dinner."

Much of Mel's press — and he got a lot of it — revolved (and still revolves) around his prolific cartoon output. As a 1947 *Citizen News* headline proclaimed: "Today you're going to meet a man with 57 voices!" He explained that before it would take him anywhere from 8 to 12 hours to complete a cartoon voice session in the studio, but now he can get through it in 30 to 90 minutes. "That was due to my lack of experience. Now I have all the tricks of the trade down so thoroughly that I can run through an assignment in 90 minutes or less." Once the voice is recorded it takes 9 months to a year for animators, etc. to finish a cartoon. Mel does his voice first, before the 10,000 required drawings and inkings for a cartoon short. "I start an assignment by listening to the story of the cartoon. Then I learn the dialogue and rehearse it carefully, adding touches here and there in conformity with the characters–possibly a gag or characterization emphasis–and then the recordings of my voice begin. Each line is separately recorded, and two different versions are made for a choice of a better take." He will record all of one character's lines first, then move to another character. The two recordings are then matched together. The animators gather together to listen to the finished soundtrack and start the long chore of drawing the pictures that they would synchronize from it.

5 | Recording Star

Except for Walt Mitchell's impressive discography (reprinted here and in the Credit List with the author's kind permission) and his expansive article written for *The World of Yesterday* magazine, little has been written of the many records, singles and albums both, that Mel recorded through the years, at least in comparison with his overshadowing cartoon and radio work. Mel began this new career with a January 12, 1942 session with Spike Jones and His City Slickers which produced the hit single, "Clink, Clink, Another Drink" (later rereleased as "The Clink Clink Polka"). Mel inserted his drunken hiccups over Spike's manic band, even repeating the feat on camera in *Clink-Clink! Another Drink*, a Soundies short from that same year.

Singing "Clink, Clink, Another Drink" for Spike Jones.

Spike also worked with Mel to record the song based on the catch-phrase of Mel's radio show, "Ugga Ugga Boo Ugga Boo Boo Ugga," but Mel had no vocal input. He was merely the songwriter this time. According to him, the City Slickers arranged it and "Del Porter and everybody put their name on it — didn't even write it! They all wanted a piece of it." Mel also wrote "Big Bear Lake" (after the area in which he would spend much of his off-hours), "Okmnx," and one to capitalize on another of his radio characters: Pedro, singing "Pancho's Christmas" (written with Marve Fisher and using the famous "La Cucaracha" melody).

On December 2nd, 1946, he signed with Capitol Records as part of their stable of talent to conquer the as-yet-unmined field of children's records. With the cooperation of Warner Bros., he made Bugs Bunny and friends available to kids everywhere. Though Mel was signed to Warner in an exclusive cartoon contract, it left him wide open for voicing anything, including Woody Woodpecker, on record. With Jack Benny's Sportsmen Quartet, in 1948 he recorded the million-selling single, "The Woody Woodpecker Song." (There was no orchestra on this record, due to a musicians' union strike against the record companies that was going on at the time.)

Though he did many other singles, including a parody of Al Jolson singing "Toot, Toot, Tootsie (Goodbye)," it was possibly the cartoon records, with their colorful covers and funny voices, that made kids ask mom for more pocket money. Warner's cartoon writer Warren Foster, with Alan Livingston and Billy May, wrote Mel's biggest hit — a musical version of Tweety's catchphrase, "I Taut I Taw a Puddy Tat" in 1950. A duet for Sylvester and the bird, it became almost a standard in children's recordings, though on its original release, it was on the second record of the two-disc set of character songs called *Bugs Bunny Sings*. By the time the single climbed to #9, it had been on the charts for 11 weeks (and in its third Capitol issue) in 1951, also scoring a success in England. When a British DJ played "Puddy Tat" a few days straight as a novelty, the day he decided to give the audience a rest from it was the day a slew of calls came in wondering what happened to the puddy tat! By the time the furor was over, that song had topped 2 million copies sold — incredible for a children's novelty record in 1951…and that's not counting the reissues through the decades.

A lesser known single was a promotional release which Capitol periodically sent out to make record dealers happy, with the thematic message that they were very important in the success of Capitol Records. "I Taut I Taw a Record Dealer" was mainly a Baby Snooks & Daddy release, but featured Sylvester also — as he put it, "What'm I doin' here?! I'm makin' a personal appearance — that's what I'm doin'!" Jealous of all the attention Tweety's getting in the shop, he and Snooks hatch a plan to get the bird out of that cage, but of course it doesn't work. At least Sylvester gets a plate of liver and recognition out of the situation before joining the bird to sing "Jingle Bells." Bugs Bunny and Bozo the Clown (voiced by Pinto Colvig, Disney's Goofy) pop in for a line, too.

Once Warner Bros. started their own record division in the late 1950s, Mel supplemented his cartoon work even further. In 1959 he was heard on the *Drink Along with Irving* LP with several other comedians, on tracks "Separate Bar Stools" (using a tiny, meek voice) and a monologue, "Liquor Is Our Business," in which he uses his normal voice to play the owner of a package store on a stormy night. The next year he donned a British accent for both sides of a 45: "Blimey"/"I Can't Fool My Heart."

Mel was also heard on a fair number of reissues, including many albums of radio show excerpts through the years, one of the earliest being the 1960 RCA Camden release of recreated *Judy Canova Show* bits (in front of a live audience) on *Judy Canova Comedy in Person!* Also around then, to cash in on the name recognition, LP "soundtracks" of *The Flintstones* and *The Jetsons* were released, with Mel doing his usual characters.

Released in 1973, the Peter Pan LP *The New Adventures of Bugs Bunny* was so popular it was followed by *Four More Adventures of Bugs Bunny* the following year. And to complete the Peter Pan trilogy there was *Holly-Daze*, a 1974 Christmas release.

Mel described his recording of the records to Walt Mitchell: "We run through it maybe two, three, or four times and make little changes as we rehearse it, then we do it. It's very simple. It is for me, anyway, 'cause I do that voice [speaking of the "Yosemite Sam" single]. I *created* that voice, and it's easy for me to do. We'd always do it once and then if they like that take, then we'd do it again for safety's sake. This is something we didn't *have* to do, but we just wanted to, to play safe." At that speed, they could record three or four songs in a standard 3-hour union musician session.

One of Mel's funniest LPs was *Capitol Presents Bugs Bunny, Daffy Duck, Porky Pig, Elmer Fudd in Warner Bros. Looney Tunes and Merrie Melodies, featuring Mel Blanc.* Music by Billy May. (This LP is actually a 1977 repackaging of Mel's very first Capitol children's record set, recorded 30 years earlier.) Mel's positive narration begins, "Well, here we are, deep in the wild wood where Bugs Bunny, the famous rabbit, lives.

He's just about the smartest rabbit in the world. He should be around here someplace. I wonder where he is…" Bugs introduces himself, but hides back in the hollow log when little Elmer Fudd gets too close. Elmer's looking for wabbits, of course, but can't seem to see the powder puff tail and long ears in front of him, so Bugs helps him out by taking him to visit the other animals of the forest for directions on finding the bunny. The trouble is, the hoot owl doesn't give a hoot, the dim turtle can't figure out just what he is, and the mocking bird mocks, tricked into calling himself a bad little bird. So the bird tells on Bugs, but, out of character, Elmer only wants "a wabbit for dinner" because he hates to eat alone. The two friends go off for a good meal of woast beef, macawoni sawad and pwenty of cawwots.

To the quacking of Mel-ducks begins the second story: "My name is Daffy Duck. People say I'm looney. I'm like an old piano, a little out of tuney." After the song, Daffy (sounding a bit like Sylvester) is preparing to fly south for the winter, warming up his wings as if he's Jack Benny's Maxwell. After getting official permission to take off, he flies into a chimney, flies through a storm of pea soup, finally making a three-point landing on his knees and nose in Backwards Land. He meets a backwards-walking native, a cow that goes "oom," and a schoolhouse filled with kids singing "Clothes Our Wash We Way the Is This." He has to take off backwards to get out of the place, but, because everything's backwards-screwy, winds up in the cold north where he started.

The third story, beginning to the strains of May's jungle music, finds Porky Pig leading an *exp-p-p-p*-dition into darkest Africa. He meets an elephant who tells the secret of why elephants never forget — they write everything down in a little notebook…which he's forgotten to bring. Next, a crane (in a Marvin Martian voice) tells Porky that his legs *have* to be this long, otherwise they'd never be able to touch the ground. He meets a leopard trying desperately to wipe off his spots with cleaning fluid, harmonic ants singing "We've Been Working on the Railroad," a strong ape with a weak cough, and a rhino who blows his own horn, before signing off with "*th-th-th-th*-that's all, folks!"

The Records of Mel Blanc
A Discography/Commentary
Compiled and written by Walt Mitchell

In addition to his thousands of performances in the other media of show business, Mel Blanc somehow found time over the years to be a recording artist on numerous occasions. This facet of his career began shortly after the USA entered World War II (one month and four days after Congress' declaration of war, to be exact). Mel made approximately one hundred different records. The word "approximately" really fits the situation here, for two reasons. First of all, even though this is being written in April of 2008, it appears that there are still a tiny number of Mel Blanc records made which are unknown to me. And second, there was an oddball Little Golden Records recording session which would have produced six of the small yellow 78 rpm discs to be sold individually and as a boxed set. Twelve tracks were recorded. Subsequently, the idea of issuing them as a boxed set was abandoned. But two of the tracks were issued on one disc. Five years later, all twelve tracks were put out on one side of a Golden Records Bugs Bunny LP. With circumstances like this, how could I determine how many records Mel made?

To illustrate the above point about some of Mel's records remaining undiscovered decades after they were recorded, let me say that in 1984 I was told of a record dealer in California who was offering two 78 rpm records by Mel in the Capitol series. They were *Bugs Bunny and Rabbit Seasoning*, and *Bugs Bunny and the Pirate*. I was delighted that these copies had turned up 30 and 31 years after they were recorded. In all that time, I never knew that they existed.

Despite the aforementioned missing data, I am grateful for the fact that most of Mel's records are in my collection. It is an honor for me to describe their contents here.

The one-hundred-or-so records in this discography include each originally-released disc made to be sold to the public. The reference is a literal one. To cite an example: while the 78 rpm storybook set *Bugs Bunny in Storyland* is indeed all one story, it is counted as two records in the above estimate, since it took two discs to go through the whole adventure.

Also included in that figure are the promotional or demonstration records which Mel made from time to time. I chose to include them partly because of the fascinating performances which they contain. Another reason is that, while it is true that the promo discs were not intended to be sold commercially, they do turn up in private collections. Mailing lists, mail auction catalogs and internet sites such as eBay sometimes offer one or more of them. So I thought it was appropriate to call attention to the existence of these special, rare records, even though they were made in smaller quantities.

The estimated figure cited does not count the many repackagings and reissues of Mel's commercial releases. They are included here, though, in a separate section. Also, no attempt has been made to include the radio transcriptions which Mel made mostly in the 1940s. They *are* records in the most literal sense. But at 16 inches in diameter (as the vast majority of those wartime discs were), they're so large that they can only be played on machines designed for radio stations. (Though at least one company is now manufacturing turntable decks for audiophiles to play those giant discs at home.)

Another reason for not including transcriptions: Mel was heard on so many of them the data for which is virtually nonexistent, that a complete list of them by him would be just about impossible to assemble.

Mel's First Records

Although the majority of Mel's records were made for Capitol, he did make a few others before signing with that label.

His first one was for RCA Victor, guesting with Spike Jones and His City Slickers. Mel was never formally a member of this wacky comedy band, but Del Porter was a friend of Mel's from their Portland, Oregon days. Now, as singer-composer-musician- arranger, Del was Spike's right-hand man. Del realized that Mel would be perfect for one of the songs which the band was scheduled to cut on January 12, 1942. So Mel was booked for the session. "Clink, Clink, Another Drink" was the song, part of the band's second session. Victor released the performance (along with Spike's other records of that year) on their bargain-priced Bluebird label. All Bluebird singles sold for only 35 cents.

On "Clink, Clink" Mel sang an inebriated chorus and also provided bar-filling hiccups. But on the label, he received credit only for his hiccup effect. When RCA reissued "Clink, Clink, Another Drink" on a regular-priced Victor record in 1949 (under the title "The Clink Clink Polka"), this time he got credit for his singing, but not for the hiccups. Worst of all, when RCA's British division released the performance as part of a Spike Jones LP in 1975, Mel received no label or cover credit whatsoever. And neither did any of Spike's other vocalists.

For the next few years, as far as I know, Mel made no more records after his hilarious debut. Then in 1947, he suddenly began to make up for lost time in a big way. Arrangements were made in that year by a record company for a truly ambitious undertaking: the stars and supporting casts of seven comedy radio shows were engaged to make a special series of 78 rpm album sets. These were recorded by the Apollo record company

Clark Gable, Gracie Allen, Mel Blanc and George Burns.

for issue on the Monitor Top Ten label. The company even hired the orchestra from each show to play the music cues. This was *serious* money budgeting, especially for a smaller record company.

Each show was featured in its own special set of four 10-inch 78s (the standard size). Each set's playing time totaled about half an hour. For the set made by George Burns and Gracie Allen, Mel reprised his most famous role as the Happy Postman, an intentionally hilarious misnomer. He was featured throughout one side of the eight-side set. He was featured more prominently on *The Jack Benny Program*. It naturally followed that he was given more to do on Jack's record set. Professor LeBlanc, Jack's long-suffering violin teacher, can be heard on three of the eight sides of this set. In one sketch, he arrives at Jack's home to give him a lesson. Upon his early arrival, he finds Rochester in the middle of giving Jack a shave. The other two sides are erroneously listed as "The

Violin Lesson" in two parts, but each of the two is a complete violin lesson sketch in itself.

In a separate deal, Mel recreated another of his radio characters early that same year. Judy Canova was singing for Majestic Records at the time. Mel was signed for one performance with her in which they performed as the lazy hillbillies, Maw and Paw, a popular feature on Judy's radio show. Interestingly, the performance was recorded at the very end of Majestic Records' activities. This means the firm could have gone bankrupt before the sketch could be issued on the label.

Fortunately, "Maw and Paw" did not remain unissued for long. Majestic's master plates from which the records were made were eventually sold to another firm. The result was that "Maw and Paw" was issued on a 78 rpm Varsity record, probably in 1950. (My copy of this issue is vinyl, or maybe plastic, unlike most Varsity 78s which were breakable shellac.) A cherry-red vinyl 45 rpm edition was issued perhaps a year or so later on Varsity's sister label, Royale.

Mel's name does not appear on the label of either issue. When I visited Mel and Estelle Blanc in their home in 1987, I brought along a tape of this performance so that they could hear it before we recorded a conversation. I said to Mel that his name was not on the label and he didn't seem at all surprised. His dry response was, "Judy wasn't much for giving other people credit."

Glory Days at Capitol

It was also in the spring of 1947 that Mel made his first Capitol records. Alan Livingston was in charge of Capitol's children's marketing division at the time. Late in 1946, he had signed Mel to an exclusive contract, the first step in Mr. Livingston's plan. Next stop: Warner Bros. An agreement was reached to allow production of records featuring Warner Bros.' would-famous cartoon characters. In many cases, the stories were written by the same people who wrote the cartoons, and Mel did most of the voice work. He was often assisted by Arthur Q. Bryan, who was a popular actor on radio. Bryan performed on Mel's records as Elmer Fudd, as he did in cartoons for the last two decades of his life. June Foray, best known as Rocky the Flying Squirrel on the *Bullwinkle* show, also assisted on Mel's Capitol records.

In a separate deal, arrangements were made with Walter Lantz for characters from his Woody Woodpecker "cartune" family to be released on Capitol. Mel had created the voice for Woody in 1941, and had given

Woody the laugh for which Woody was famous. Mel's later exclusive contract with Warner Bros. cartoons ended his availability to continue doing
Woody's voice for the rival cartoon studio. However, that Warner Bros.
contract applied only to *films*. Thus, Mel was free to do Woody's voice
for Capitol. His first record performance in this role was "The Woody
Woodpecker Song." This was recorded with The Sportsmen, the quartet
which sang regularly on *The Jack Benny Program*. The great popularity of
this song resulted in record sales totaling over a million copies — another
first for Mel. Between 1948 and 1955, he performed as Woody 13 times,
including 11 commercially-released titles and two promos, "Sneak
Preview" and another disc pitching the Woody Woodpecker radio show.

In addition, Mel had a big hit with the popular "I Taut I Taw a Puddy
Tat." The song was recorded and released in 1950 on the second record of
a two-disc set for children called *Bugs Bunny Sings*. "I Taut I Taw a Puddy
Tat" was a duet for Tweety and Sylvester. Word eventually reached Capitol
from the record dealers that the public was paying particular attention to
the Tweety/Sylvester number, so Capitol obliged by repackaging "Puddy
Tat" (with its original flipside, "Yosemite Sam") on a single disc still in the
children's series. A new cartoon picture cover was created for this issue,
showing all three cartoon stars.

Much to Capitol's amazement, adults were buying this children's
record themselves. The result was that Tweety and Sylvester were now
climbing up the pop charts. Capitol responded to this happy news by
issuing the disc in yet a *third* edition, this time in the adult popular series.
By now it was 1951, and the runaway success of "I Taut I Taw a Puddy
Tat" made it the biggest novelty hit of the year. By the time the record's
popularity had subsided, it had sold over two million copies, making it
Mel Blanc's all-time best-selling record.

When Mary Lou Wallace and I were interviewing Mel for the first
time (in 1978), he told us that at the time that "Puddy Tat" was on the
charts in the USA, it was also a tremendous hit in England. A British
disc jockey named Sam Costa came across the record, not recognizing
the content by the label information. Curious, he played it on the air and
was immediately sold on it. So much so, in fact, that he played it several
times the first day. On his next program, he did the same thing. On the
program after that, he decided that he'd better not repeat it again, lest his
listeners demand that he be shipped off to the nearest boobyhatch. So he
deleted it from his schedule — and phone calls from all over came in from
his listeners. They all wanted to know what had happened to the puddy
tat! So he gleefully played it over and over. Costa was very influential, so

more and more attention was paid to the cute duet. The result was that it caught on like wildfire with the British public, just as it had over here.

When the sheet music for "Puddy Tat" hit the music stores, the lyrics were different from the way that Mel sang the song. Since Mel was the voice of the characters, he sang the lyrics in the first person. The commercial version was rewritten in the third person. It thus became a song sung *about* the characters, not *as* the characters. But on the back cover of the British printing of the sheet music, the words alone are printed just exactly as Mel sang and spoke them on the record. The front cover, in addition to Tweety and Sylvester, also shows a photo of a jovial-looking Sam Costa, plus credits for his radio show and the British Capitol Record catalog number.

In addition to his famous cartoon character records, Mel had some releases on Capitol which were comedy performances intended primarily for the adult trade. Whether they were new novelty tunes or dressed up revivals of silly songs from the vaudeville era, Mel chose just the right voice or voices in each case and provided just the right sound to make each record a joy to listen to. His burlesque of his good friend Al Jolson on Mel's record of "Toot, Toot, Tootsie (Goodbye)" is an outstanding example of the wild side of comedy of which he was capable. "There's a Hole in the Iron Curtain" is a satire of the Cold War which Mel and comedy bandleader Mickey Katz wrote and recorded together.

Mel's other songwriting stints include "Okmnx" and "Big Bear Lake," both of which he recorded, and "Ugga Ugga Boo Ugga Boo Boo Ugga," which he didn't sing. This was initially a password on his radio series, *The Mel Blanc Show*. When he composed and wrote the song around the phrase, it was given appropriately wacky treatment on an RCA Victor record by Spike Jones and His City Slickers, who recorded it on February 11, 1947. While Mel did indeed write and compose the basic song, apparently it wasn't quite long enough to fill a record side. So three other songwriters seem to have added the words and music of the verse part, then arranged the whole thing in Spike's unique style.

Capitol's Backstory — and Mel's Part In It

Among the many children's records made by Mel for Capitol, standout performances can be heard. They utilize highly entertaining stories and songs featuring familiar cartoon characters in most cases. The fun is enhanced by full-orchestra backup. Billy May's orchestra usually backed Mel on these records, but on some sessions Van Alexander's orchestra was used. In certain other cases, the orchestra of Dave Cavanaugh did the music honors.

This all came about because Capitol got a late start in the record business. Entertainment genius Johnny Mercer was one of the founders of

Capitol Records, which began recording sessions in the spring of 1942. At the time, most of the top stars of the day were already signed up by the Big Three (Victor, Columbia and Decca). This meant that Capitol had to develop their own stars. It also meant that Capitol had to discover other record areas not already covered adequately by the competition. Having this thought in mind, the people at Capitol soon noticed that there was a definite lack of good, high-quality records for children. Alan Livingston (who would later become Capitol's president) was given the assignment to take an entire division of the company and go to work in this area. Under his direction, the children's division became one of the most important in the company, both artistically and financially. Moreover, Capitol's success in this field forced the Big Three to compete for the dollars in a market that they didn't realize was there. Adding to this were new companies which made nothing *but* children's records. The result was what I call "The Golden Age of Children's Records." This spans roughly the years between 1945 and 1960 inclusive. And from *Bugs Bunny in Storyland* to *Woody Woodpecker and His Talent Show*, Mel Blanc's gifts for comedy and voice creations served him well in this field, just as in his other performing venues.

Capitol's management in those days felt that their dealers played such an all-important part in the success of the company that a special "thank you" should be extended periodically to their buyers. Therefore, records containing sketches were distributed to dealers sometimes during the Christmas season or some other time of the year. Each sketch, usually humorous and with music, gave Capitol artists the opportunity to greet the dealers and sales force alike. As far as I know, Mel made seven of these special discs. The first one, a cardboard 78, *eight* inches in diameter, showed Bugs Bunny in a Santa outfit. The title was *Greetings and Here's Good Wishes for a 14 Carrot Christmas from Capitol Records*. This was mailed to dealers during the 1947 holiday season. It was recorded only on one side. The other six were pressed on plastic, vinyl, or a mysterious compound called Superflex. Unlike the cardboard disc, these six were all two-parters.

The cardboard disc referred to above is set in a record store on Christmas Eve. The dealer (played by Alan Livingston himself) is just about to close up shop when Bugs Bunny pops in to greet him. Soon, Johnny Mercer joins in the fun. It's a short sketch, but it's great.

Mel's second promo record was a 7-inch 78 which was recorded and distributed in 1948. He was joined in the recording studio by Vance D. "Pinto" Colvig who had a long career as the voice of Goofy for Walt Disney. At this time, he was also the voice of Capitol's Bozo the Clown. Here they take turns telling each other about all the new Capitol children's records that are coming out. The disc has some gags but it's basically a pitch for the product, called *Bozo and Bugs Talk Big Business.*

Next comes *Season's Greetings from Capitol 1949.* On this one, Bugs Bunny is knocking on various doors at Capitol. He invites performers of different types of records to greet the dealer. Bugs finally winds up by talking to the Vice-President in Charge of Speeds (played by Mel). The Veep's voice is slowed down when he mentions the two new slower record speeds, for a hilarious finish. This is also a 7-inch 78.

In 1950, Capitol produced three separate 45 rpm promo records in which Mel was involved. The first of these is what I believe to be the rarest promo that Mel Blanc ever made. I have been collecting pre-owned records for five decades. Nevertheless, it was just weeks ago that I learned of the existence of this promo. It remains the only copy known to still exist as of this writing.

The title is *Any Friend of Bozo Is a Friend of Mine!* The format is like the book-and-record combination known as the Capitol Record-Reader. Indeed, this item is described at the bottom of the front cover as "A Capitol Record-Reader FOR DEALERS ONLY" *(sic).* But there are distinct differences which relate only to this promo. First of all, it is the same size as a commercially released Record-Reader which would contain two regular 10-inch 78 rpm records in pockets in the back. But instead, this promo contains *one 45 rpm* disc with corresponding material on it.

The pages of the book are different as well. Normally, (except for the last few Record-Readers) the left-side pages of the open book would have the records' narration and dialog printed out in play form. In this instance, however, all that appears on those pages is a drawing of a cash register. The right-side pages feature pictures of Bozo, Glenn Wallichs (Capitol's president at that time), and Bugs Bunny with his cartoon friends. The item was heralding a Capitol children's record promotion whereby new releases would have a seal of approval from Bozo the Clown.

I have one example in which a gummed and shaped paper seal was actually attached to a previously manufactured issue made before the promotion began. But in nearly all cases, the "seal" was actually a graphic image worked into the artwork on each issue's front cover. It showed Bozo's smiling face along with the words "Bozo Approved." On the record, Mel sings a ditty about "Bozo Approved" as Bugs Bunny.

The next promo is titled *Sneak Preview.* Although it was not connected to the previously discussed disc, the two records' master numbers are consecutive: 6301 to 6304. This indicates that they were most likely recorded on the same day. The exact date is unknown as of this writing, and indeed, may never be known. We do know that both promos were pressed in July of 1950, and were probably recorded early that same month.

Sneak Preview spotlights the many records that Capitol was releasing for children during the Fall and holiday seasons of that year. The disc — a fine fantasy — finds Bugs Bunny, Woody Woodpecker, and Bozo the Clown sneaking into an after-hours party in the office of a Capitol executive. They feel that they deserve this treat following a busy day of record-making. While "Pinto" Colvig is back as Bozo, Mel does triple duty as Bugs, Woody, and a record dealer who drops in on them. The dealer is invited to join them in listening to acetate playback samples of Capitol's latest children's issues. It's a good thing that this record is a 45. It plays for 5 minutes or more — on each side. Unless *Any Friend* is longer (I haven't heard it yet), *Sneak Preview* is the longest Capitol promo that Mel ever made.

Next: recorded sometime in mid-November (again, the exact date is not known at this time), the outstanding disc *I Taut I Taw a Record Dealer* was pressed in December. It looks as though this Christmas-themed disc must have been shipped to the dealers via Air Mail in order to reach them in time.

The scene is a record store. Radio's famed Baby Snooks and her ever-present Daddy (played as always by the great star Fanny Brice and her straight man, Hanley Stafford) have just entered the crowded shop. They encounter Sylvester on the floor and Daddy asks him what's he's doing in the store. "What'm I doin'!" snaps Sylvester. "I'm makin' a personal appearance — that's what I'm doin'!" He goes on to say that he's irritated by the fact that Tweety Pie, in his cage on the counter, is getting all the attention from the crowd. As Daddy joins the autograph line, Sylvester goes into a huddle with Snooks and hatches a plan. Snooks is to coax Tweety out of his cage, whereupon Sylvester will sneak up behind him and solve the personality clash in his own barbaric way:

> "Jingle Bells, Jingle Bells, for everyone but me
> Until I get that Tweety Pie into a fricassee!
> Jingle Bells, Jingle Bells, for Baby Snooks a cheer!
> She'll help me make this '51 a Tweety Pie-less year!"

The plan fails, of course, and Sylvester eventually gets his much, much-wanted recognition (and a plate of liver!) from a clerk in the shop. At that point Snooks pays tribute to the record dealers. Then Sylvester rather begrudgingly agrees to sing a duet of "Jingle Bells"—the right way — with Tweety. Bugs Bunny pops in with one line and Bozo for two. Everything ends on a happy note with the whole gang calling out, "Merry Christmas!" Music for this disc was provided by Buddy Cole at the electric organ.

This concludes the special records Mel made to promote the sale of his Capitol records. But there was one more promo: a 10-inch, two-part 78 rpm record made in 1953 to herald a brand new project—*The Woody Woodpecker Show*. This is not to be confused with the later television show of the same name. This was a children's radio show, co-hosted by Woody and Mel.

On the demo, Woody and Mel talk about what will happen on this show. I have never heard one of the actual broadcasts. I don't even know whether or not any exist in any format today, but I once had an opportunity to look at one of the scripts. Besides the talking, Woody and Mel would play children's records on the show. As I recall from seeing the script, it was only Capitol children's records that were played. And the scripts even showed the records' catalog numbers in parentheses. Could Capitol have had a hand in this show? Although the Capitol logo does not appear on the labels, they definitely manufactured the demo. The show itself aired over the Mutual Broadcasting System on Saturday mornings beginning in the Fall of 1953. The show ran for one season.

Records that Mel *Didn't* Make

There have been a number of records made over the years which feature Warner Bros. and Hanna-Barbera cartoon characters that were not recorded by Mel Blanc. The records in question were all authorized editions manufactured with the cartoon studios' consent and studio-drawn illustrations. But for any of several reasons (most notably, his exclusive contract with Capitol), Mel was unavailable to make these records. Most of them were recorded anonymously, with the imitators given label credit in only a couple of instances. I call attention to these records so that people who happen to come across them will understand that they are *not* anonymous performances by Mel.

Before Mel was free to record birthday songs as Daffy and others for Little Golden Records, this company had released at least ten issues of songs featuring the Warner Bros. characters. There are two bizarre facts concerning the imitations on these records. One is that some of the labels and covers for these records actually state that the records contain the *original voices* of the characters. The second odd fact is that one of these little discs has a cover credit to the Elmer Fudd man, Arthur Q. Bryan. But this is a Bugs Bunny record with an Easter tie-in, and Elmer is nowhere to be heard. Bryan's name is followed on the cover by that of

Dave Barry who was a comedian and mimic in that era, not to be confused with the present-day author/humorist of the same name. I surmise that it was this mimic who did his best to copy Mel's characters on all of the paper label issues. This record contained "Bugs Bunny's Easter Song" and "Mr. Easter Rabbit." Both songs are clever, so it would have been nice if Mel had been free to do them himself.

In 1973, an LP was released in England on the MFP (Music For Pleasure) label called *Bugs Bunny Goes to London*. Here, the voice of the imitator was speeded up somewhat, and for all his tough-guy demeanor, he spoke in proper British tones. To top if off, he "proves" he's the real Bugs when challenged by saying, "What's up, Doc?" without so much as an "Ehhh..." in front of it.

Warner Bros. Records in France issued the song "What's Up, Doc?" on a 45 rpm record. The song was composed for Bugs by Warner cartoon conductor Carl Stalling many years before. This 45 featured a Bugs imitator singing a French translation of the lyrics. Again, the voice sounds nothing like Bugs but, at least for his enthusiastic rendition, I'll give him some credit.

Sometime in the 1980s, there were Bugs Bunny LPs (picture discs, in this case) on the Kid Stuff label. The imitations here are better than most, but again, these aren't Mel.

Back to Little Golden Records. One of the company's small 78 rpm discs was a real jaw-dropper. Record number R250 was recorded and released in 1956 and was yet another Warner Bros. cartoon character record with imitation voice work. The song titles were "Daffy Duck Cowboy," and "Kangaroo Hop." What's shocking about this issue is that Mel Blanc's name appears on both of the record labels, despite the fact that he had nothing at all to do with the recordings.

The oddest circumstance involving this company concerns the idea they had, to have each of 12 Warner Brothers characters sing a birthday song to children born in a given month. By this time (a little later in 1956), Mel's exclusive contract with Capitol Records was ended. He was thus available to Little Golden Records to do the project. When decision-makers at LGR changed their minds about issuing the six records as a boxed set after Mel's recording session was completed, the boxed set was never released in that form. For some who-knows-why reason, the company decided to issue two tracks on one LGR from this session. The birthday song for kids born in March was sung by Daffy Duck. The song for April was sung by a new Warner Bros. cartoon character, Ollie Owl, which never became famous. Both record sides credit Mel Blanc on the ink-stamp type of label in use at the time. Mel does indeed sing Daffy's song. But on the flip side, Ollie Owl's song is actually sung by an *imitator*. When I played a tape of the record for Mel, he agreed that the Ollie track was not him, despite what the label credit claimed. He remembered the obscure character and noted that he had given Ollie a slightly British accent, which was missing from this record.

Six years after the (mostly shelved) recording session, LGR put out an LP called *Bugs Bunny Songfest*. Side One was a reissue of those imitator tracks, with the twelve birthday tracks on the other side, all of them by Mel.

Even when Mel was past his Capitol-exclusive contract days, his characters were not always recorded by him. In the 1960s, he performed frequently on records as Barney Rubble with the other Flintstones characters. These were issued on Golden Records, Colpix Records, and later on the cartoon producers' own Hanna-Barbera Records (HBR). A few of these HBR discs, without Mel's name on them, contain Barney Rubble imitations by someone else. These may have been done by Daws Butler who was actually credited on the back cover of at least one HBR Flintstones LP as Barney Rubble. Some confusion results from the fact that for those HBR records where Mel performed as Barney, he received the usual label and/or cover credit on some issues, but not on others. All HBR records listened in the discography have been verified as being genuine Mel Blanc performances.

The Peter Pan LPs of cartoon character stories recorded in the 1970s make for an interesting contrast. When the stories are about Bugs Bunny and other WB characters, the Peter Pan LPs (7-inch and the regular 12-inch) are by Mel and nearly all are credited as such. But any Peter Pan records from the same period which feature Flintstones characters are not Mel's. Either Barney is done by an imitator on these, or the character doesn't speak or is missing entirely.

More About the
Post-Capitol-Contract Years

During personal interviews with Alan Livingston (1994 and 1995), it was stated that there were no more Mel Blanc Capitol children's records after 1956. After nine years as an exclusive Capitol artist, Mel was able to freelance again in the record industry.

Capitol wanted Mel to come back for a one-shot engagement in late 1956. Mel's dear friend Jack Benny was going to make a fantasy LP for children. Jack's narration was augmented by Isaac Stern's violin soli. Mel was needed for two brief character voices in the LP that was issued as *Jack Benny Plays the Bee Ably Assisted by Isaac Stern.* (When it was reissued 22 years later, the title was changed to the shorter and funnier *Jack Benny Fiddles with the Classics.)* Whether on records, radio, or television, Mel was always very happy to be working with Jack.

He recorded two Woody Woodpecker records for Decca following his Capitol years, but this time not as Woody. Walter Lantz's wife, Grace Stafford, had been performing Woody's voice in cartoons for the previous several years. She did it again on the Decca 45 and LP which were recorded in 1957. Mel was engaged to voice several supporting characters, including Santa Claus on the flip side of the 45. With other performers

Noel works with Jack Benny.

being Gloria Wood and a female vocal group dubbed The Woodyettes, Mel found himself the only male vocal performer at the session. Originally issued as a standard black vinyl LP, the material on it was reissued more than twenty years later by MCA as a picture disc.

Also in 1957 Mel made his last Capitol record, using his Mexican voice. Released for the holiday season, it included "The Hat I Got For Christmas Is Too Beeg" and "Pancho's Christmas" (the latter co-written by Mel).

The last time that Mel was involved with a record that made it onto the charts came in 1962. Pat Boone recorded the novelty song "Speedy Gonzales," enhanced by having Mel speaking as the title character. The disc went to No. 13.

In the late 1950s, Mel also made three Warner Bros. 45 rpm records. He also participated in a comedy LP made by comedy writer Irving Taylor. One of the two speaking tracks he did was repackaged in another Taylor LP.

Mel was quite busy during this period. He was continuing his performances in a variety of roles on *The Jack Benny Program* (TV). He was also wanted for a variety of one-shots on TV shows such as *Dennis the Menace*, *The Many Loves of Dobie Gillis*, *Angel*, *The Beverly Hillbillies* (as a frustrated cab driver in "Granny Learns to Drive"), and Ann Sothern's *Private Secretary*. And many others.

But on top of that, Mel spent a lot of time in various recording studios. He recorded public service radio spots for everything from fighting cancer to preventing forest fires. He recorded audio narration 45s as Warner cartoon characters to accompany children's toy slide-projector shows.

Another project of particular interest was a series of greeting cards with clear plastic sound sheets laminated inside the cards, one per card. These were 6 inches square, and by tearing the perforated spine of the card and punching out the cardboard center circle to form the hole, the user could then play the record by hand (they weren't quite large enough to be played using an automatic changer mechanism) on any 33 1/3-speed record player. These were produced by American Telecard, Inc., a Los Angeles company.

Some of these cards feature Bugs Bunny and other Warner Bros. cartoon characters, with Warner copyright credit on the full-color card fronts. Others feature the monster characters from Universal Studios. Mel did his usual voices on the cards that feature the Warner Bros. characters, of course. All (or most) of these undated cards were made in 1964. On the cards which included Elmer Fudd, his voice was now done by Hal Smith, as the original voice, Arthur Q. Bryan, had died in 1959.

As for the cards featuring Universal's monster characters, Mel recorded the sketches for those as well. In these instances, he was teamed with Lennie Weinrib, another comedian of the era.

RCA Victor issued a comedy album starring Judy Canova in 1960. Although no mention was made of this on the album, the material was obviously taken from radio shows of some years earlier. Mel performed regularly on that show in a variety of roles, which included the lazy hillbilly referred to earlier and an old cowpoke, both of which are heard prominently on this album. Judy herself bankrolled the reissue.

Reissue vs. Repackaging

Some people might say that there is no difference between reissuing and repackaging previously recorded material. To my way of thinking, there is a distinct difference. The *Judy Canova* RCA Camden LP described in the previous paragraph, and her own reissue of it, form the perfect segue to a general discussion of this topic. Regarding the Judy material here, it should also be noted that RCA itself reissued one track ("Ma and Paw") in 1972. This was included in their Vintage series LP *The Golden Age of Comedy*.

In my view, "reissue" refers to a recorded performance issued again after the original release has ended its run. I contend that the term "repackaging" means bringing out a recording again in a different form while the original issue is still available from the original source. In Mel's case, a good example of this would be the Capitol Record-Reader of *Bugs Bunny and the Tortoise*. This set was recorded late in 1947 and released in 1948 on 78 rpm. It continued to be sold as such into the 1950s. But by that time, it had been repackaged in the newer 45 rpm format and (briefly) in the also newer 33 1/3 ten-inch LP format. This latter format, which was introduced in 1950, sold very poorly. This is very strongly suggested by the evidence at hand today. I refer to a Capitol children's record flyer. It is undated, but I have determined that it must have been distributed in late summer or early fall of 1952. Mel had made three Record-Readers in the late 1940s. All three were also made available on 45 rpm in 1949 and on the 10-inch LP format in 1950. The 10-inch LP versions of the Record-Readers had catalog numbers in the HX3000 series. All three numbers are missing from the 1952 flyer. All of the other Record-Readers by other artists in this format were deleted from the catalog as well.

On top of that, Mel's fourth and final Record-Reader (*Tweety's Puddy Tat Twouble*), recorded early in 1951, was never even issued in the 10-inch LP format at all. This in turn suggests that this format, as a venue for children's records, was abandoned only a year or less after it was introduced. So, collectors who find these HX3000s-numbered Record-Readers have very rare issues. In these instances, however, "very rare" does not automatically mean "very valuable." Since these stories were sold in the millions of copies on 78 and 45 rpm, even the HX3000s issues should not command a high premium.

By 1960 Capitol was no longer marketing the children's records which had sold so well since the late 1940s. Then in 1963, Capitol came out with regular 12-inch LP reissues of much of this popular material. Naturally, this included some of Mel's best-sellers from a decade or more earlier.

For this series of LPs Capitol would assemble several single-disc stories and/or songs into the new (for that material) 12-inch LP format. Others in this series could not be simply put on an LP and sold in a regular LP cover. In these cases, a gatefold cover was needed. Gatefold was a 12-inch-square of cardboard, printed in the same manner as a standard LP cover, attached to the left edge of the LP cover. The record buyer would thus be able to open the cover like opening a book. The inside would show pictures and/or liner notes about what was on the record itself.

The gatefold covers in this series were the new version of the old Record-Readers. And Capitol continued to refer to them by that name. Instead of interior pages, the new version showed all of the illustrations reduced in size and spread out within the gatefold interior. It ended with the last of the illustrations on the back cover. On the newer variations of the illustrations, a number in a circle was added onto each picture so that the child listening to the record would know which illustration was the next picture to look at as the story progressed.

As a fascinating fact: a snippet of each record in the gatefold group had to be re-recorded and inserted into the newer issue. On the original recording, whoever was narrating the story instructed the kids to "turn the page" when they heard a certain sound. This, of course, meant that the children's viewing of each page was in perfect coordination with what they were hearing at that point on the record. The newer version had to reflect the change in the picture format by eliminating the records' references to turning pages. So the narrators of the Record-Readers (including Mel) were hired to return to Capitol. There, each man recorded just a sentence or two for each Record-Reader that he had narrated. In Mel's case, he was only doing this for one story, *Woody Woodpecker and His Talent Show*. That's how "turn the page" was changed to "That sound means you should look at the *next* picture."

The one man who could not return to Capitol, of course, was Arthur Q. Bryan. Neither Mel nor Hal Smith had taken over as Elmer at this time, so Capitol had no choice but to release both LPs in this series with no Record-Reader pictures. The tapes were copied and the copies were then edited down. This was a somewhat tricky job. The audio engineer had to remove not only the initial spoken announcements about turning the page when the sound was heard, but also the sound itself whenever it was heard throughout the stories. Then the new tapes were ready to use.

The next go-around for the great Capitol children's records came in 1972. This time, the series as a whole was given a name: The Capitol Children's Book & Record Library. Like the first 12-inch reissue series, some of these discs were 78 rpm single-disc transfers to LP in a standard cover. Others were in the gatefold Record-Reader format, but with two dramatic differences. This time, each gatefold issue contained not one but *two* Record-Reader stories. And inside the gatefold cover were paper booklet reproductions of the original Record-Reader pages showing the two stories on the LP. The last page of one booklet was glued to the top half of the right side of the open gatefold. The other was glued to the bottom half. In order to make the booklets fit into that packaging format, it was naturally necessary that the booklets be a version that was reduced in size. The original white borders of the pictures were cropped, along with the outer edges of the pictures themselves. The end result was that these booklets measured slightly smaller than the pages for the 1950s 45 rpm editions.

Even more importantly, since the children were now back to the "turn the page" format, that meant that the original unedited tracks could be used on the new LPs. Thus, for the first time in over ten years, children could again experience *Bugs Bunny and the Tortoise* and *Bugs Bunny in Storyland* as they were intended originally to be heard *and seen*.

In 1975, Ziv International Corp. expressed interest in reviving this material. I believe that this was the last reissue by anybody of this material on vinyl. When Capitol agreed to enter into this new business arrangement, Ziv apparently bankrolled the project. Certainly the Ziv logo appears on the covers of these issues along with the Capitol logo.

The 1963 series sold for $1.98. The ones with the Record-Reader gatefold cover sold for $2.98. There were no gatefold issues in the Ziv group, and the list price was $4.98. This group usually sold for less when found in the discount houses.

For the benefit of record collectors who want to buy the Mel Blanc LPs from the issues just described, it is easy to identify which group an LP is from when buying from record dealers' lists or off the internet. The key, of course, is the catalog number. The 1963 group is numbered in the J 3200s for LP-only release. The JAO 3200s of the same group refer to those which are the Record-Reader gatefold type. The 1972 group are in the L6800s, with the suffix "-RR" for the ones with the Record-Reader pages inside. The Ziv group (1975-1978), the one with no Record-Readers, is in the L6900s.

Of all of Capitol's various repackagings and reissues, their repackaging of Mel's adult novelty singles ranks up there among the harder-to-find discs by him these days. *Party Panic!* was issued in 1953 in two formats. The eight songs were released on a 10-inch LP and also as a 2-disc 45 rpm extended-play set in a two-pocket gatefold cover.

Since the advent of CDs, it wasn't until 2005 that EMI, Capitol's ownership successor, dug into Capitol's vaults and produced the 25-track

CD called *The Best of Mel Blanc—Man of a Thousand Voices*. This was done at the behest of Collectors' Choice Music, whose mail order catalog distributed the disc under their own name. In the case of this CD, however, much credit is given in print to the actual manufacturer. And the street address given for EMI Music Special Markets is indeed the location of the famous round Capitol Tower building which was constructed for the company in the 1950s. Two years later a second compilation CD (entitled *Mel Blanc: The Man of 1,000 Voices*) was released on the Remember label. It, too, contained a mix of Mel's Capitol titles, both adult and children's numbers. Both CDs are worth purchasing as each contains rare titles, and there are only a few songs that appear on both discs.

In addition to the songs familiar to collectors of Mel's records, this EMI CD contains two never-before-released bonus tracks. On one, Mel sings yet another comedy hit from the vaudeville era, "Barney Google," in which he goes from stock voice to stock voice through several verses. The other was a then-newly-written item called "Grandfather's Will" and was probably the weirdest track that Mel ever recorded.

Inside Mel Blanc's Capitol Recording Sessions

Having interviewed Mel extensively, I was most curious about the recording side of his career. I wanted to know how they were made, whether the more complicated performances were more difficult and more time-consuming, etc.

To begin with, I mentioned the Yosemite Sam song because of its simplicity of composition and the fact that it requires only the voice of Sam himself, with no tricky tape work. I wanted to know what work was involved with rehearsing such records. Although quick to answer most of my questions, Mel spoke slowly and very carefully on this one.

"Well, uh, we run through it maybe two, three, or four times, and make little changes as we rehearse it, and then we do it. It's very simple. It is for *me*, anyway, 'cause I do that voice — I *created* that voice — and it's easy for me to do."

"Were the more complex sides harder to do since they involved several voices, music cues, etc.?" I asked.

"No," he said, "but just in case, we'd always do it once 'n' then if they like that take, then we'd do it again for safety's sake. This is just something we didn't *have* to do, but we just wanted to, to play safe."

But this was not the way later Capitol records were made. Alan Livingston decided to take advantage of what could be done with tape mixing. Recording performances on large reels of tape before transferring to disc masters was the new process. It was gaining in popularity by the late 1940s. The result was that it was possible at that point to record the orchestra part of a song or story separately from the voice or voices of the finished product. Then Mel or other voice performers would come into the studio at a later date and record the voice track(s). This resulted in recordings that were absolutely flawless by the time they reached the record stores.

Alan told me that each recording session lasted for three hours. All voice performers were paid a flat fee of $100 per session. Most of them were paid that instead of a royalty payment based on the number of copies sold. Even Capitol children's records' own star, "Pinto" Colvig, was paid the same flat $100 fee each time he made records as Bozo the Clown (owned jointly by Alan and Capitol).

But Mel Blanc's participation was a different story. In the first place, he was already a star on his own, outside of Capitol. In the second place, Alan wanted Mel's services exclusively, so that he could not make records as his famous cartoon characters for the competition.

A royalty contract was necessary not only due to Mel's participation, but also due to Warner Bros. That company's permission to use their copyrighted characters was essential to the success of Capitol's intended projects. Capitol also wanted the services of the artists under Warner Bros.' employ, to provide specifically-designated artwork for Capitol's Record-Readers, record covers, and advertising.

On top of those considerations, some of the men who wrote the Warner Bros. cartoons (mainly Warren Foster and Tedd Pierce) were brought in to write the record stories as well. Indeed, some of the record stories were the same as the cartoon stories, often modified to suit the record format and given different titles from their cartoon counterparts.

Capitol executives knew that if they were to succeed in their goal to produce top-selling children's records, it would serve them to put really serious money into production and promotion of these records. Alan Livingston said that Capitol had earmarked five percent of the money expected from the sales of this series of records for royalty payments. The money was divided on a percentage basis between Mel and Warner Bros. It was not an even split.

I have never seen a copy of the formal contract between Mel and Capitol, but its information was later rewritten in text form in conjunction with Mel's performance sheets, which contained a somewhat condensed version of the contract. Mel Blanc signed the agreement on December 2, 1946. The contract was Number 246 and was to run for a period of two years. It called for the "exclusive right to record voices of cartoon characters 'Bugs Bunny' 'Daffy Duck' 'Porky Pig' etc. as may be mutually agreed upon and cartoon story material relating to such characters and art work as requested for albums or adv.

"Capitol may produce records which do not embody performance by Artist [Mel] and pay Warner all royalties for Warner & Artist. Warner pays replacement for Blanc. Payment to Warner & Artist individually upon acceptance of masters for one album. Capitol pays musicians and may use Warner's (arrangements) without additional payment. Artist & Warner Bros. to receive credit in each album. Albums may contain recordings by other artists. Capitol to give Warner six sets. Periods of suspension for any reason to be added to current year of term. Artist and Warner may terminate after four months suspension of operation by Capitol unless suspension beyond control of Capitol."

Capitol and other record companies had not forgotten the strike against them earlier in the decade by the musicians' union. So that ominous clause had to be included for Capitol's protection in case this should happen again. Sure enough, it did. And it happened during the second year of Mel's initial Capitol contract. Musicians were barred by their union from making commercially released records through nearly all of 1948. Mel's only released track for the whole year was "The Woody Woodpecker Song." Since no instrument musicians were allowed, Jack Benny's quartet (The Sportsmen) backed Mel. Besides vocalizing the notes the musicians would have played, the boys also sang lyrics along with Mel.

As noted above, Mel and Warner Bros. were not required to wait until the money from record sales came in before receiving their pay. Capitol paid them in advance, after first giving full approval of the recorded performances and the accompanying artwork for mass manufacture and release. The advance figure was $5,000. The 5% split was divided as Warner Bros. receiving 3.33% and Mel receiving 1.66%, so $3,333 of the advance went to Warner Bros. and $1,667 to Mel. Not bad for 1947.

A handwritten notation on Mel's performance sheet stated that the $5,000 advance was per *album*. Maintaining complete control over its operations, Capitol's contract stipulated that during the course of each contract year, Mel was required to record a minimum of six sides/tracks with a maximum of twelve. Mel fulfilled his obligation by recording two album sets in 1947 which totaled ten tracks.

The contract was reactivated on the same terms effective May 28, 1949 for one year. Another handwritten notation authorized the extension of the contract for a fourth year as of May 28, 1950. This contract extension ended in the spring of 1951, but Mel soon found himself signing on to his unprecedented five-year deal with Capitol commencing from April 1, 1951 through March 31, 1956.

The last record that Mel was scheduled to make under the terms of this long contract was "Save Up Your Pennies" and its B-side, "Day Dreaming Danny." The two instrumental tracks were recorded by Van Alexander's orchestra on February 8th, but for whatever reason, Mel did not go to Capitol to add his voice tracks until April 25th. This, of course, was more than three weeks after his Capitol contract had ended. "Save Up Your Pennies" inspired the wholesome cover graphic: two children running along and rolling giant pennies as if they were hoops.

Warner Bros. actually got more money from Capitol than had been cited in the contract since the $3,333 was for the use of its characters and incidentals, and did *not* include the accompanying album artwork. Artwork was ordered from Warner Bros. on an album-by-album basis, depending on what was needed at any given time.

It was a complicated process, but it all resulted in one of the biggest success stories in the record industry at that time. At its height, 40% of Capitol's income was from the sales of their children's records.

Mel told me that the man behind his Capitol Records success was Alan Livingston, for whom he had high praise. It is true that Alan built up Capitol's children's division during his first year there. The Bozo and Sparky record sets were his own creations and were best-sellers from the get go. But adding the genius of Mel Blanc's voice creations to the roster resulted in even more millions of Capitol records being sold.

Bugs Bunny
and the Grow-Small Juice

During the interview we did with Mel for my article in *The World of Yesterday*, he volunteered some information about the actual recording of the tracks. In some cases, he said, his voice was sped up on tape before the recorded performance was transferred to the master disc. But this process was done only slightly. Mel's voices were not raised as high as double speed, like The Chipmunks created by "David Seville" (the late Ross Bagdasarian, Sr.). Mel explained it this way:

"You notice that there are several characters each of whose voice sounds higher, like Tweety, Porky, Daffy, and Speedy Gonzales. They all sound a little higher, and y' know the reason for that? They're very small, so what I have (the recording engineers) do is have them slow down the tape and then I sing it normally to that slowed-down tape. Then they play the tape back 'normal,' which raises the voice. It's not done with any trick in my mouth or anything. It's all done normally, and they just have the speed of the tape a little slower when I'm recording it. Many times we have to record it in a different key, because when it's sped up it'll be recorded a little slower in a little lower key. And then when it's played back, why, it'll fit in — the same key as what the orchestra's playing." It might have been just one half-tone off, but a minor adjustment in the speed of the tape would correct the problem.

There was at least one instance in which the gradual change of tape speed could actually be heard on the finished record. It was "Bugs Bunny and the Grow-Small Juice," recorded in 1952 with June Foray. In the story, as the juice takes effect, Bugs and Daffy Duck shrink in size. "You crazy duck!" Bugs scolds. "Look what ya've done ta both of us! Ya made us as small as ants! Foist ting ya know, someone'll step on us!" Their plight is doubly emphasized through the dialog and the tape of their voices.

As Mel explained, "As we were recording it, they slowed down the tape. Then they played the whole thing back 'normal' (when dubbing from tape to disc) and it made the voices higher."

45 to 78

Mel's first four adult single releases were most probably not issued on 45 rpm single counterparts. Beginning with Mel's collaboration with Mickey Katz on Capitol number 869, the rest of Mel's adult novelty singles were issued on 45 rpm.

Though "Tootsie," "Big Bear Lake" and "Animal Crackers" were not released as 45 rpm singles, they were reissued in 1953 as part of the 45 extended play (EP) record set, *Party Panic!*, as well as on the ten-inch LP version of the release.

Mel's first Capitol release, the album set called *Bugs Bunny*, was issued in three 78 rpm editions. Recorded in April of 1947, the set was first released on breakable shellac discs. About a year later, Capitol developed and began manufacturing a stronger, better quality children's record. This new compound was called Superflex, even though these discs were really not flexible. Shortly after Capitol's Superflex records went into production, the *Bugs Bunny* set was repackaged, using the newer manufacturing process. This was Mel's only 78 rpm set to make such a transition intact.

Addenda and Conclusion

The Best of Mel Blanc, a CD compilation of (mainly) adult novelty songs directly from Capitol's vaults, was released in 2005 by Collectors' Choice Music. This contained two bonus tracks: "Barney Google" and "Grandfather's Will," released for the first time since they were recorded 50 years earlier. These two tracks were not the only adult-market novelties which were not issued at the time that Mel recorded them. During those exclusive-contract Capitol years, Mel cut several other sides which were shelved at the time. They remain unissued to this day:

> Old Gamblers Never Die
> Honey
> Who, Me? Yeah, You
> Mother Dixie and You
> If You Knew Susie
> Buzzy Bazoo
> Cub Scouts

Other unknown gems are possible.

According to Noel Blanc, Mel also wrote "Old Gamblers Never Die." Since Capitol chose not to issue it, Mel asked for a copy of his song, so the company obliged by making a single copy for him in the form of a ten-inch 78 rpm disc (on an acetate — a metal disc, usually aluminum, on which the groove is cut into the metal via a record-cutting machine). Noel still has that disc today.

In 1954, Capitol's president, Glenn E. Wallichs, broke ground to start construction on the company's new office building: The Capitol Tower. A day was named in his honor, and a luncheon featured guest speakers praising Mr. Wallichs' accomplishments.

Also present at the luncheon were just about all of Capitol's top recording artists, there to salute the boss. Most of the stars were not among the speakers, but the emcee was Dean Martin. He gave a funny monologue, then mentioned each of his performing colleagues, pausing while each presumably stood and took a bow to a round of applause. One of the last was Mel Blanc.

Capitol recorded the celebration and preserved portions of it, including the luncheon, on a pair of ten-inch LPs which were preserved in a special two-pocket gatefold cover with photos, etc. This was most likely an in-house project and was not sold commercially. True, Mel does not speak on it, but if collectors of Mel's records are completely fanatical about getting every Capitol record with which Mel was at all involved, this pressing is truly the last word.

Anyone who has heard a fair number of Mel Blanc's records knows that he successfully converted the fun of animated cartoons onto phonograph records. In a career that spanned 62 years and thousands of performances, I don't know how he found the time to make records, but I'm very glad he did.

If you have other records of Mel that were put out which I have not listed in my discography, I'd like very much to hear from you with a description of what you have. Other comments or questions are also encouraged. You can write to me directly at P O Box 201, Oriskany, NY 13424-0201, or c/o this publisher, or email me at *wm62676@yahoo.com*.

I'd like to acknowledge with grateful appreciation the following people for their help in assembling the above information and discography: Fred DeHut, "Dr. Demento" (Barry Hansen), Tom Holbrook, Alan Livingston, Jack Mirtle, Randy Morris, and Peter Muldavin. Special thanks go to Mary Lou Wallace, my best friend for 36 years, who shares a loyalty and love for all things Mel! To Mel himself for carefully answering all my questions — he was far more than the awesome talent that everyone knew — he was kind, generous, and helpful to many people over the years. The friendship of Mel, his wife Estelle, and their son Noel, is something that will remain with Mary Lou and me forever. Lastly, a heartfelt thank you to Ben Ohmart, who wanted to include this labor of love in his Mel Blanc biography — his dedication to accuracy in the life stories of both the famous and obscure performers of the 20th century is outstanding.

6 | Warner Bros., Continued

Having conquered radio and cartoons, the next step was invariably films. However, Mel Blanc only made a handful of films in his long career, and not always playing himself. In *My Dream is Yours*, a 1949 Doris Day film, he shows up in the verbal guise of Bugs, and Tweety (saying his most famous line), but only in a dream sequence.

This was also the year Mel made one of his rare on-screen film appearances, as Pancho, Jose O'Rourke's (Ricardo Montalban) helpful stable lad, in *Neptune's Daughter*. In a high-pitched Mexican accent, obviously gleaned straight from Judy Canova's show, Pancho helps his boss woo the girl of his dreams (Esther Williams) by leading a small band and playing the violin. He also tries to assist her sister (Betty Garrett) when she asks for directions to the find Jose. He points to every available road, giving partial directions, but finally just has to say, "Gee, I don't think you can get there from here."

For the most part, Mel stayed off camera, enjoying the anonymity of stardom, with a star-type paycheck (plus royalties, for the commercials, the recordings, etc.). Mel (along with contemporaries June Foray and Daws Butler) enjoyed this aspect, preferring to separate his professional life from his private life, seeking the solace of a good meal with Estelle at home or in any restaurant without fear of autograph hounds. The few Jack Benny TV shows he appeared on didn't do much to make him "walking around famous."

During the late '40s, Mel, Mom and I would take long driving trips all over the United States and Canada, but a particular trip in 1950 to New York and Washington D.C. will be long remembered by all of us.

It was a hot, muggy night in D.C. We had been sightseeing all day, and the memory of the millions of fresh dollars we had just seen counted at the Bureau of Printing and Engraving was etched in our minds. The hotel air conditioner was on the blink so Mel suggested that we walk over to the Statler Hilton and maybe look around the shops. The Hilton was known to have a better air conditioning system than our hotel, so off we went.

Red Skelton and Mel in *Neptune's Daughter*, 1949. PHOTO COURTESY OF STEPHEN COX.

The Hilton drugstore was our first stop and there Mel bought some rubbing alcohol and a paperback. The druggist put these items in a brown paper bag and handed it back to Mel.

As we left the drugstore and entered the cool lobby of the Hilton, there was quite a commotion going on. Asking a bellman what's up (doc), we learned that President Harry Truman was on the Mezzanine and about to come downstairs into the main lobby, so we decided to wait and maybe get a chance to see the President.

Mom asked Mel if she should hold the drugstore package, but Mel said that he would just put it under his arm…that was a mistake to be sure, because Mel decided to relocate the package from his left hand to under his right arm at the exact moment Harry Truman appeared in the doorway.

Instantly, secret service men were at Mel's side grabbing the square brown package and looking inside just to find the rubbing alcohol and a paperback. Mel didn't realize what was happening when four large gorilla-like men pinned his arms at his side and grabbed the bag, but with the usual glint in his eye, he just looked up at them and said, "What's up, Doc?" The secret service men immediately recognized him and apolo-

Mel and Betty in *Neptune's Daughter*, 1949.

gized and Harry Truman was most happy to shake his hand, as was Mel to shake the President's.

The 1950s was a transitory era for Mel. Radio was dying, being replaced by television, which was also the ultimate downfall of theatrical cartoons. But they weren't quite dead yet. Mel made some of his most memorable WB cartoons very late in that career. On July 22, 1953, *Duck Dodgers in the 24 1/2th Century* was released, one of Warner's best shorts, pitting confident/cowardly Daffy Duck against Marvin the Martian, intent on claiming the Planet X in the name of Mars (the Duck is trying to claim it for Earth). George Lucas later said that after having seen the original screening of that, it made him want to make films. He even wanted a new one made to precede his 1980 classic sequel, *The Empire Strikes Back*, but Warner had ceased its cartoon shorts in the '60s. It finally showed up as part of NBC's 1980 TV special, *Daffy Duck's Thanks-For-Giving Special*, in which Daffy tries to interest the studio in a Dodgers sequel by showing them some of his greatest past films.

Keith Scott writes: "This was the period where Blanc honed Warner's distinctive stable of postwar regulars like Foghorn Leghorn and Yosemite Sam to pinpoint vocal hilarity, and added highly eccentric voices like Jones's Commander X-2 from the planet Mars (more recently named Marvin Martian for the inevitable merchandising reasons). In fact it is Blanc's 1950s work, even with previously established stars like Bugs, Porky, and Daffy, that has entered the popular consciousness as the benchmark of how these famous characters should sound for all time. Blanc's work for Freleng was often spectacularly good, his readings of Warren Foster's sharp dialogue defining the art of comic acting. His portrayals of blustery Sam in *Ballot Box Bunny* and *Hare Trimmed*, and the harried Sylvester in *Canned Feud* and *Birds Anonymous*, remain unequalled for energy and comic flair."

One of Warner Bros.' most memorable and oddest characters also came late in the studio's canon. The Tasmanian Devil grunted, burped, snarled and whirled like a blender in search of his prey, usually after the old grey bunny. When Mel first saw the image of the character "I asked if anyone had ever heard a Tasmanian Devil, and they hadn't. So I created this crazy ongoing growling that sort of sounds like words, and I defy anyone to tell me that's not the way a Tasmanian Devil sounds."

Mel's appetite for food was ravenous and perhaps this is where the Tasmanian Devil first appeared in Mel, eating everything that came within his reach.

A typical meal for him was to start off with a large portion of herring and sour cream, followed closely by an immense salad, inundated with plenty of creamy Thousand Island Dressing, and then a bowl of soup or a glass of tomato juice. The entrée was a thick pound-and-a-half steak with a baked potato, sour cream, and chives, and a sizable portion of "Sufferin' Succotash," which, incidentally, he loves. After pie a la mode for dessert, he'd settle down in front of the radio with me and Mom to listen to his favorite shows. Then, about midnight, he would wander back into the kitchen again and devour two large boxes of chocolate covered marshmallow cookies with a quart of milk. Believe me, the Tasmanian Devil had nothing on Mel's appetite.

One of Bugs' most enduring and influential cartoons was *What's Opera, Doc?* (1957), the musical short which killed Wagner's Ring Cycle for all time. And made "kill the wabbit" as famous a line as anything from

Casablanca. As Chuck Jones stated, "For sheer production quality, magnificent music, and wonderful animation, this is probably our most elaborate and satisfying production."

By now Mel was one of Hollywood's elite. This was the era of the TV/ radio commercial and its lucrative bounty. No one made a bigger splash in this tiny but ripe medium more than Mel Blanc. In a November 1958 newspaper article, Mel's voice was claimed to make as much as $1,400 per word; one pen commercial only had a $55 performance fee, but by the time the ad played for a year, his residuals on that spot alone came to $7,000. He only said five words in the commercial. The pen company was Paper-Mate. The end of the commercial was a live shot of a pen posed vertically. Superimposed over the image was an animated cartoon of two pigs, one above the other, clinging to the pen. In the two different voices of the pigs, Mel's five words were: *(First pig)* "With the" *(Second pig)* "Piggy back" *(First pig)* "Refill!"

In 1960-61, the Clark Oil and Refining Corporation, a Midwestern oil company, ran a two-year radio ad campaign for Clark gasoline featuring two characters named "The Chief," a true blowhard who was always coming up with impossible schemes for promoting Clark gas, and his meek, low-key employee, Fizbee, who would always have to save the Chief from himself. Mel Blanc voiced both characters. These would often air during Milwaukee Braves games, and the cartoon characters appeared on Braves' scorecards, schedules and on most of Clark's promotional items (maps, calendars, trading stamp booklets, etc.).

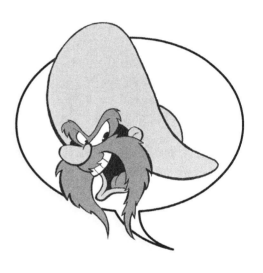

7 | Time Off

With the kind of recording hours Mel was putting in with cartoon and commercial work, he needed something that *wouldn't* keep him busy. One of his *(most expensive)* hobbies was cars.

The shiny, green Aston Martin literally ignited the long driveway that led to our home in the Pacific Palisades. It was 1960 and nobody on the block had ever seen such a racy looking car. Kids came from all over the neighborhood to see Bugs', or should I say the Roadrunner's, new automobile.

Yeah, Mel is a car buff, to say the least. Even to this day, he's always testing new automobiles to see which he likes best.

But that summer day in 1960 it was the prize Aston Martin DB3 that held his fancy. During the years from 1940 till 1960, I could remember each and every car he took so much pride in. There was a green '38 DeSoto, which puffed great billows of black smoke into the air each time it was started. Then there was his tan '41 Packard, which during the war years must have made him think he was driving a tank. There was a lipstick red '41 Pontiac convertible that he bought my mom, but he used to love to drive it himself on hot, sunny days. Then, in 1947, he became the *first* owner in our neighborhood of a brand new Cadillac. Nobody had ever seen such a car. It was burgundy with a long fastback and he would stop people in their tracks with it. Jeez, I loved riding in it with him and watching all the people turn and look. Almost every year after that he bought a Cadillac, and each one he bought had more gadgets on it. Then in 1957, he bought a full race T-bird, again to the amazement of everyone on the block.

Yes, Mel was the car buff and I loved every minute of it, but little did he realize that the Aston Martin he loved so dearly in 1960 would nearly become his coffin on wheels.

He also invested wisely, combining his hobby of collecting watches into a lifelong venture. When Mel turned 38, Estelle gave him an antique

Patek Phillipe minute-repeater watch, made in Switzerland, which chimed on the minute when you pushed a lever. When he decided to buy a watch like it for Bud Abbott's birthday, Mel was astounded to hear from Tiffany in Manhattan that they had the same one for $2,040. That was the day Mel officially became a watch collector. First as an investment, then as a true collector, fascinated by the intricate detail and loving craftsmanship,

and relaxing to examine after a hard day at the studio. They were historic. "Not merely a timepiece, but a piece of time," he said.

As of 1988 Mel owned close to 400 watches, some true rarities, including what collectors said was the first watch ever made: a 1510 carrying timepiece handmade by Peter Henlein, a young locksmith in Nuremberg, Germany. It was drum shaped, with only one hand to mark the hours

The Blanc family.

and no crystal covering the dial. "A mob which unjustly accused him of murder and thievery chased him to a cathedral," Mel told the press, "where he sought sanctuary. There, with the aid of an abbot, he went to work on what was the first watch a person could carry. It took him two years. He probably made but 15 during his lifetime." Of course the coiled iron spring that made it go made the watch run fast when fully wound, so that it often gained an hour or two.

He bought the Henlein piece for $300 in the 1950s from an employee of the Swiss Eturnamatic Watch Company who was in sore need of cash. When Noel had it appraised in London 15 years later the Blancs were astonished to learn that it was worth over $200,000. "I'd never sell it, though, for its historical value it is priceless."

Another favorite in his collection was an enameled pocket watch made circa 1790 by Julian LeRoy for Louis XVI of France. "The face depicts a pastoral scene and three tiny gold figures: one strumming a mandolin, the second a lute, and another walking a tightrope. Their limbs actually move! Wind the watch with a key, and the musicians 'play' a delicate tune. In addition, it strikes time on the hour and quarter hour." He also loved his character watches of Mickey Mouse, Bugs Bunny, Ronald Reagan, Mel Blanc, Little Lulu, and the Richard Nixon with the shifty eyes which moved back and forth.

Noel and Mel with just a few of the watches.

He kept the valuable ones in a bank vault and others, like the ones which melodically chime, at home. "One watch has a nine-foot mainspring that takes a half-hour to set."

He joined the National Association of Watch and Clock Collectors and got Noel ultimately and ravenously involved in the hobby, though at first the kid just wasn't interested. Among Mel's collection were timepieces from England, Switzerland, Germany, Russia, and Italy, from the 16th through 19th centuries. The variety was incredible: one watch was encased in a hollowed-out $20 gold piece; another was a copy of a watch that belonged to Mary Queen of Scots *(in a skull-like case)*; another was shaped like a fan on which the hands go to 12, then fold back again; plus watches with detailed portraits and sylvan scenes painted on their enamel cases, and watches with figurines tolling the hours with tiny hammers.

"It's an unusual hobby, but I love it as much as a kid loves a mechanical toy."

Mel's favorite was a Rolex called a Swiss Oyster, which he wore every day on his wrist. "The salesmen used to demonstrate that they are waterproof by stirring drinks with them. The watch is mounted in a bar of solid gold. It cost a bundle." And he worked hard for them.

8 | *The Flintstones* and Dead Man's Curve

In 1955 Mel was a regular panelist, along with Rose Marie and Johnny Mercer, on *Musical Chairs*, a game show hosted by the ever-popular Bill Leyden that had people writing in with music questions which were supposed to stump the panel. For every question used, that person at home would receive "this beautiful RCA Victor Slumber King," a clock radio that changes stations while you sleep. If you stump the panel, "you get this beautiful RCA Victor 21-inch mahogany console — a big change in TV styling!" A bit more complex than *Name That Tune*, questions could be anything from figuring out a famous quote sung by the in-house harmony singers *(The Cheerleaders),* to the popular "Song on the Spot," in which the panel makes up a song instantly, based on a suggestion sent in.

By the 1950s, television had gutted the theatrical cartoon short. Staying at home to keep entertained was the way of the world now, and it was closing down many a cartoon studio unit, including MGM's in 1957. Bill Hanna and Joe Barbera, creators of Tom and Jerry, escaped the bread line by beginning their own limited animation company which fed the always-hungry TV programming schedule. After *Yogi Bear, Huckleberry Hound,* and other hits, they were thinking of something different. They wanted to conquer prime-time with a sitcom formula, and so *The Flagstones*, soon to be *The Flintstones*, was born. Based on *The Honeymooners'* formula of best friends getting into trouble *(usually at Fred's suggestion, to better their lives)* as their long-suffering wives stand by, the cleverness of putting the show in a stone-age setting was what captured the imaginations and staggering viewing figures of children and adults both.

When director Joe Barbera called to ask Mel about doing the voice of Barney Rubble, he said he wanted a prehistoric Art Carney. Mel didn't want to imitate Art; he preferred doing original creations. Joe relented once Mel started improvising as they talked about the character. The compromise was giving Barney the same vocal characteristics and low tone that Norton had. Mel liked Joe, but not his way of directing takes from the top each time rather than just redoing the mistake. Otherwise Mel loved working with old acquaintances from the studios, now that

A promotional photo for *Musical Chairs*.

most of the talent had moved to television. Joe Barbera described Mel as "a quiet man, who would come into a studio, do his job with spectacular skill, then leave."

As Bill Hanna wrote in his autobiography, *A Cast of Friends*, casting the voices for Betty Rubble *(Bea Benaderet)* and Wilma Flintstone *(Jean Vander Pyl)* had been easy. Fred and Barney were the hard rocks. "The actors first selected for the roles proved to be dismally miscast and had to be replaced at the cost of a considerably expensive settlement. Fortunately, this made way for the recruitment of two veteran talents, Alan Reed and Mel Blanc, who respectively breathed vocal life into Fred Flintstone and Barney Rubble that seemed inspired by the cartoon gods themselves."

Like many animation fans, Mel didn't care for the instant flash of screen credit that was so common in HB shows. "You drop your hat and you never see who did it." Still, it was a living. Mel spent some of the money he was making on cars, but "I was frugal. Cars were my lone self-indulgence. *Fast* cars." The collecting also became an investment; the opposite of how he began with watches. He bought Estelle

The Flintstones family. COPYRIGHT HANNA-BARBERA PRODUCTIONS

a new 1941 Pontiac convertible and spent more time driving it than she did. Then he moved on to Cadillacs, Rolls-Royces, and Lincoln Continentals. One of his prizes was a 1957 Ford Thunderbird. "What a machine. I loved racing it up and down the Pacific Coast Highway, listening to its hopped-up V-8 hum as I watched the waves lap against the coastline."

Betty & Barney and Mel Blanc & Bea Benaderet. PHOTO COURTESY OF STEPHEN COX. COPYRIGHT HANNA-BARBERA PRODUCTIONS

Little did he realize that this passion for fast cars would almost take him out of the picture completely.

After years of getting his own work, in 1959 Mel took on Jack Wormser, former radio sound effects man, as his agent. Jack thought having Mel Blanc on his roster would help attract other clients.

Wormser had booked Mel for a nine o'clock commercial taping session on Tuesday, the night of January 24, 1961. It is not known exactly what time Mel left his home to go to that commercial recording session.

On rounding Sunset Blvd. and Groverton Place, known more infamously as Dead Man's Curve, he was hit by Arthur Ralston, an 18-year-old Menlo Junior College student driving his father's Oldsmobile 98. Ralston's power steering had failed while rounding a turn on the dangerously winding stretch of Sunset, causing him to lose control of the car and cross the dividing line, directly into Mel's expensive 1959 Aston-Martin. Both cars were demolished.

It happened at 8:29 p.m. The reason that the exact minute of the accident is known is that the impact stopped Mel's watch at that instant.

Within minutes traffic officers P. C. Weir and L. J. Blunt arrived on Sunset Blvd. The head-on collision only caused knee and forehead lacerations on the kid, who crouched by the side of the road, but it had just about destroyed Mel Blanc. Peering through the Aston Martin's shattered windshield they spied the unconscious Mel, trapped by his steering wheel. "The vehicle's lightweight aluminum body had crumpled like a wad of tinfoil upon impact." It took a special unit of the California Highway Patrol more than 30 minutes to pull him out. A fireman at the scene said, "We should have just put him in a sack."

Both men were rushed to the UCLA Medical Center, Ralston with minor injuries, but Mel suffered compound fractures of both legs *(the right leg alone had 39 fractures)*, a fracture of the right arm and pelvis, severe head injuries, a brain concussion, and internal injuries. His head struck the steering wheel and windshield, causing a concussion and the loss of nine pints of blood. By late the next morning, Mel still hadn't regained consciousness.

As Noel explains:

He was on his way into Hollywood to do a commercial but he hadn't shown up at the studio, and his agent, Jack Wormser, had called my mom to ask where Mel was. Finally, by calling the police, she was able to ascertain that Dad had been in an accident, but she had no idea of the extent of the damage.

My mom and I arrived at the UCLA hospital together although we had come from different directions. I had learned of the accident from friends who had heard about his accident on a TV bulletin. As Mom pulled into the long, circular UCLA Medical Center delivery, I jumped out of the car I was in and ran to hers. "The police said that a green Aston Martin was involved in an accident, so it must be Mel," she exclaimed. We walked together toward the emergency waiting room and at the very moment the glass doors swung open it seemed like a hundred flash guns went off. This put Mom and myself into a semi-state of shock, for it made us realize the severity of the situation. Why all the people and all the reporters?

Jack Wormser came quickly up to us and made us sit down while he told us that Mel had been in a terrible head-on collision and that he was critical. Mom and I were taken to a private waiting room to await the surgeon who was performing the orthopedic operation on Dad. Finally, the doctor came into the room and told us that he had done all he could orthopedically. Now he had to wait to see if the neurosurgeon would have to operate. It seemed that pressure was building in Mel's skull and if it remained, an operation to repair what damage had been done when Mel had struck the dashboard and windshield was imminent.

We waited up all night and finally at 4 p.m. the neurosurgeon said the pressure was relieving itself, but he also stated that Mel's injuries could be distributed equally among four healthy young men each of whom could succumb. In other words, he had about a thousand to one chance of living.

My mother and I kept the long vigil and along with our many friends and relatives we waited to see each day if Mel would live or die. Many newspapers and radio stations had already given his obituary.

Third day — there were so many baskets of flowers for him that my mom asked the nurses to distribute them throughout the hospital.

Sixth day — Mel still hadn't regained consciousness and the doctors began to worry that this prolonged unconsciousness might cause permanent brain damage.

At 4 in the morning UCLA's Dr. Tracy Putnam and Mel's own physician, Dr. Ralph Dilly, informed Estelle, Noel, Jack Wormser, and Noel's friend Richard Clorfene that the swelling in Mel's skull had abated, but that it still didn't look good. It would be a few days before they would even know if he would live. Dr. Dilly said, "His recovery is in God's hands. I suggest everyone pray for Mel."

Mel was never a very religious man, but he was certain that the positive wishes and constant prayers of friends, relatives and strangers did much to keep him going. "Even though I was enveloped in blackness, people's kind thoughts somehow reached me."

"Calling Dr. Bainfield. Calling Dr. Bainfield." The PA system cracked sharply but it didn't seem to disturb the almost lifeless figure of my dad, who had been unconscious for six days.

"Calling Dr. Bainfield." They were calling for the doctor to bring a coagulator into Mel's room so he could breathe better, and it made me remember the many times I had watched him in children's hospitals all over the country, entertaining the children in small groups, large groups, bed to bed. Once I remembered him doing his character into these mirrors so the kids in the iron lungs could see the face that went with the voice. Now Mel himself was barely able to breathe. Day after day I would sit by his bed waiting for him to say something — anything. The team of doctors had given him only one chance in a thousand to live the night of the accident, and now, eight days later, the odds were not much better.

Then, on the morning of the 9th day, he started to become conscious. But his loss of memory prevented him from knowing anything about his surroundings or why he was in the hospital.

From the very first night of the accident, hundreds of phone calls poured into the hospital switchboards. They even asked our relatives and friends to help on the switchboards. Calls for Mel's condition were overloading the hospital administrative staff. Friends and family kept pouring in all night to keep my mom and me company, and telegrams arrived every couple of minutes from all his show business friends. They all prayed for Mel to fight for his life. Radio stations all over the country had given his obituary and all five of the L.A. papers the next morning had front page headlines about his impending death. Christ, they already had him buried. But he'd show them.

Letters and telegrams were coming in from all over the world, some of them just addressed to Bugs Bunny, Hollywood. To pass the agonizing time away, my mother and I would open these letters and to our amazement, kids had sent Mel get well carrots wrapped in tinfoil and large crayon pictures of the cartoon characters done by all the members of their class. Many elementary schools had spent days organizing their classes to paint get-well posters which they brought over to the hospital, but still no response from the near-lifeless Mel.

The closeness of the Blanc family was amazing. Never were my mother and myself without relatives who would congregate in the lobby of the UCLA Medical Center and remain there to keep our spirits up. Dad's brother and sister-in-law had driven down from San Francisco to see if they could spark some memory out of Mel, who still had total amnesia. No one was allowed to see Mel except his immediate family until the 10th day after the accident.

At that time, a few close friends and relatives were able to see Mel and try to stimulate his memory, but it wasn't until the 11th morning that a spark of memory came to Mel.

We had turned on the television set to pass the time when all of a sudden, who should appear on the tube but Bugs Bunny! After about 4 or 5 minutes of the Bugs Bunny show, Mel's eyes began to focus on the TV. Then when the doctor walked in, Mel looked at him and with a twinkle in his eye said, "What's up, Doc?" Yes, Bugs Bunny had sparked the memory of Mel and we knew that finally the amnesia was only temporary.

On the 16th day, Jack Benny, who would call every morning, was finally permitted to come over to the hospital and see Mel. When I

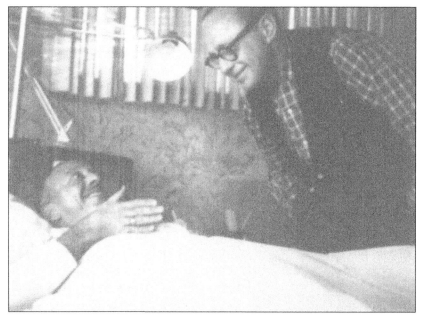

Jack Benny visits Mel at home.

picked him up in front of his office on Santa Monica Blvd., he was quite excited to get the chance to see my dad. Once in the lobby of the Medical Center, he went to the gift shop and bought a funny card and a candy bar which he broke in half, saying, "I don't think Mel is in shape to eat the whole thing, so why waste it?"

By this, the 16th day, Mel was beginning to recognize people like Mom, Henry, his brother, me, and when Jack walked into the room, Dad's eyes lit up. Jack walked in, kissed Dad on the forehead and handed him two ping pong balls painted pink, along with the funny card and the half candy bar. With the ping pong balls was a short note that said, "Noel told me that your voice was a bit higher in register and thought that these might be the reason. I found them near the scene of the accident." It was the first time that Dad had really laughed since the accident and it made me feel so good to see him coming around.

During his unconsciousness, newspapers shouted Mel's accident globally, while the *Honolulu Herald* had already printed his obituary. Telegrams and flowers flooded Mel's room from all his friends and associates, including Mickey Rooney, Judy Canova, George Burns, and Jerry Lewis, plus 15,000 cards and letters sent from children around the world. Though, as Noel stated, some were merely addressed to "Bugs Bunny, Hollywood, USA," they all found Mel. Drawings of Bugs Bunny, handwritten cards, the carrots wrapped in tinfoil, Estelle and Noel opened many of them to read to the unconscious Mel. When he was able to read them himself, Mel was terribly grateful for all the fan mail, telling the *Los Angeles Mirror*, "These people I didn't even know offered me their prayers, and they were Protestant, Catholic, Jewish, Mohammad, and even Buddhist. I am sure their prayers helped."

The newspapers made a lot of Mel's recovery via Bugs Bunny, and as usual, there were slightly varying reports. Another went thusly:

Mel's strong vital signs were encouraging to the doctors. Estelle stayed at his beside as much as she could, though Noel had to report to enter the Army Signal Corps on February 3, 1961. It wasn't until Valentine's Day that Mel spoke for the first time, thanks to Bugs Bunny. Dr. Louis Conway asked, "How are you feeling today, Bugs Bunny?"

Mel's broken but audible reply was, "Eh, just fine, Doc. How're you?" He followed it up with Porky Pig, causing Dr. Conway to rush to the nurse's station to phone Estelle, then at home. Mel had no memory of the event at the time, but was skeptical no more when Dr. Conway repeated the story on *This Is Your Life*, when Mel was honored. "From then on, his health improved each day," he told the TV audience.

Testing his voice was traumatic — would he be able to continue in his profession? The pipes were fine, but the thought of being without gainful employment for the next three months made him glum. Luckily he was visited by the country's top comedians, including Jack Benny who had called every morning for fifteen days to ask if he could come and try to cheer him up. After the pink ping-pong balls visit, Jack sent Mel funny telegrams over the next two months whenever he was out of town, such as:

"Dear Mel:

"How could you have done such an idiotic thing? You could have taken Wilshire, Olympic, or even Pico Boulevard. Why Sunset? You're fired, and I should remind you that this will not only cost you your salary, but also all of your hospital benefits."

During the recovery, Shep Menkin offered to do Mel's voices for him, to give the money to his family, but Mel preferred not to. Daws Butler did, however, briefly fill in for Mel as Barney Rubble. There was *quite* a recognizable difference in the voices of the two Barneys, so Mel was back doing Barney just as soon as possible. *(Keith Scott writes that "Blanc told Mark Evanier that Butler was the first voice-man he truly regarded as competition.")*

As Joe Barbera stated in his autobiography, his reaction when he heard the special bulletin on TV about Mel's accident was his realization that "I hadn't been working with Mel for long, but long enough to realize that he was indispensable as the voice of Barney and Dino on *The Flintstones* and, even more importantly, long enough to come to the conclusion that he was not only a genius but a great guy who was rapidly becoming a good friend."

On March 20, 1961 Mel filed a $350,000 suit against 18-year-old Arthur L. Ralston and his parents. He also asked for $100,000 for medical expenses and loss of earnings. Mel then filed a $500,000 claim against the city of Los Angeles on March 24th, citing that the city had failed to correct "Dead Man's Curve" *(at Sunset Blvd. near Groverton Place)*. Mel charged that city officials had known for years that the curve was hazardous and dangerous, and indeed it had been the scene of three fatal accidents before that; not counting serious injuries given to yet more motorists. The City Council settled by paying him $25,000.

Something good came of the tragedy. The city hastened to eliminate hazards from that particular stretch of Sunset Blvd. by planning to recon-struct the curve by raising the outside lanes of the roadway which would permit a safer driving speed. The safe and posted speed there was 45 miles an hour — now it would be 25. City Engineer Lyall A. Pardee reported to the Board of Public Works that 26 accidents had occurred at that intersection in the past two years, resulting in three fatalities and 15 persons injured. Work was to be completed by July 1st, at a cost of $78,000.

Finally, Mel was taken home to Pacific Palisades in an ambulance, with more than a hundred friends and neighbors spilling out onto Toyopa Drive and next-door neighbor Walter Matthau's front lawn to welcome him home. Below the "Hi Mel!" banner a neighborhood pickup band *(including trumpet, violin and bongo drums, and led by Councilman Karl Rundberg)* sang an original song, "Welcome Home Mel" as his hospital bed was lifted out of the ambulance.

Mel was moved in another way too — he cried. So did Estelle. They were speechless.

His most frequent home visitor was Jack Benny, who always asked, "Is Mel home?" like a little school friend. There was also ample time for a reunion with Mel's older brother Henry who had flown down from San Francisco and who would die of alcoholism in 1979. "I never quite knew what to say to him about his drinking," Mel admitted. "But I never stopped loving him."

Antsy in bed, Mel was eager to get back to work and began voice work on *The Bugs Bunny Show*, which had debuted the previous September on ABC. Freleng was glad to have the "original" voice back, and the day after they agreed for Mel to continue:

The giant Warner Bros. television trucks pulled up in front of Mel's house in Pacific Palisades. Two 18-wheelers loaded to the gills with all kinds of magnetic film equipment.

Mel had gotten out of the hospital only the day before. The ambulance had brought him home, and four men had lifted him into the hospital bed in his room. Now Mel was asked to record 7 or 8 different Warner Bros. cartoon voices in order to keep 185 animators working.

Friz Freleng, one of the cartoon directors, had come to the hospital three weeks previously to obtain a "scratch track" so the animators could start work, but now they were ready for the final voice recording.

Warner Bros. had called in several top voice people to imitate Mel, but the voices were not close enough, so Mel was asked to do this favor for them.

There he was, flat on his back, but the voices were as clear and concise as ever. *The Bugs Bunny Show* had to go on. After all, it was a prime time show, and doing very well back in 1961. This first recording session at his house gave him the courage and incentive to want to work even harder. The recording studio that I had installed with an engineer by the name of George Travell was about to get a real workout. A little program by the name of *The Flintstones* was number one nationally, and for the next 42 shows, all of the recording sessions would be done in Mel's bedroom with all the cast — Alan Reed, Bea Benaderet, Jean Vander Pyl, John Stephenson, Don Messick, and Mel flat on his back with a microphone suspended over his bed.

These were no ordinary recording sessions. Sometimes they would begin at 3 or 4 in the afternoon and last until midnight with Mel never complaining. Joe Barbera would produce the show listening to a huge speaker suspended from the ceiling in a room on the other side of the house, while Alan Dineheart would direct it from the bedroom in a fashion reminiscent of Leonard Bernstein directing a 120-piece orchestra.

After nine months of doing *The Flintstones* on his back, the doctors finally permitted Mel to work from a semi-sitting position. He said it was great seeing the people he was working with between takes, rather than the ceiling.

In the first recordings, an engineer held the microphone to Mel's mouth while Noel held the script and noiselessly turned the pages. "I realized my mouth and throat were undamaged and I could talk. I know it is a miracle that I am still alive. That's why I thank God every day for his help. I'd always taken my talent for granted before, but as I sat talking in Sylvester's voice to a darling little girl in the hospital, I thanked

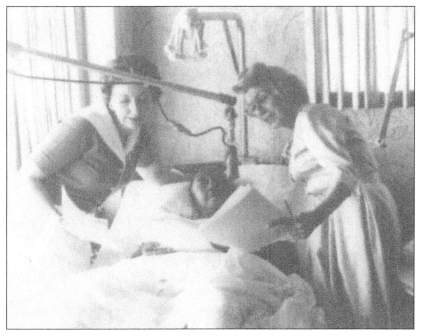

Mel recording at home with Jean Vander Pyl *(left)* and Bea Benaderet *(right).*

God for not revoking this undeserved gift."

Mel didn't want a penny — he was just happy to be back working. That is, until Lloyd's of London refused to honor his long-standing disability policy *(which he promptly canceled)*, claiming that he was "fit for work," since he was recording again.

Now that necessity coupled with desire, Noel and an engineer friend of his, George Travell, built Mel a mini home studio for cartoon work. The bedroom was now a full-fledged recording studio, with the room next door converted into a control room with speakers, tape machines, console, the works. A boom stand — extended microphone — had been fixed directly over Mel's bed, right in front of his mouth, where soon he could grip a script in his own two hands and really go to work.

But the first recording of *The Flintstones* was chaotic: "tangles of wires were scattered all over the floor, and chairs and microphone stands were arranged around my hospital bed." A speaker on the wall allowed producer Joe Barbera and Noel to communicate with the actors. "Director Alan Dineheart cued us from across the room, gesturing frantically as if he were Leonard Bernstein conducting the New York Philharmonic."

That first session lasted from seven in the evening until two in the morning. Barbera kept asking Mel if he was too tired, and Mel kept on to the end. During the episodes they recorded like that, Mel was relieved a bit by having a pulley-cable system let him sit up more by the time September 1961 came around. Alan Reed, seeing Mel's bravery, admitted to him that in past, perhaps because Mel had had his own radio show *(on which Reed played a few times)*, he thought Mel a "conceited little jerk." But the accident brought "Fred and Barney" closer together like never before. "From that day on," said Reed, "we became better pals than even Fred and Barney."

"Mel was swathed in bandages from head to toe," said Barbera. "There were openings for ears, nose, and mouth — but that's it. He could look straight up only, and his legs were held apart and immobile by an iron bar. No one who would see the finished cartoon could possibly have guessed that Barney's words were emanating from a living mummy. To say he was a trouper is the understatement of the century, but, maybe even more important, I am convinced that getting back to the show, getting back to being Barney, helped Mel recover sooner than he might have otherwise."

It did, though reviews for the series weren't optimistic. *Variety* complained about its lack of staying power, *The New York Times* complained that Fred and Barney were gruff, coarse and unattractive. But the Emmy nomination and Golden Globe *The Flintstones* received after its first season refuted the power of the critics. The show was a hit with viewers and therefore with sponsors, which was all that truly mattered in TV terms. That caused Hanna-Barbera to keep thinking up new shows, like the flipside to *The Flintstones*...

In 1962 *The Jetsons* was born, a futuristic tour de force spouting sci-fi gags with the same abandon that bronto burgers and animal slaves had in Fred and Barney's prehistoric world. George Jetson worked for Cosmo C. Spacely *(voiced by Mel as a toned-down Yosemite Sam)* in his career as "digital index operator," pushing buttons to help make Spacely Space Sprockets. He rockets into work after dropping his son and daughter off at school, and his wife *(who takes most of his cash)* at the beauty parlor, before folding his "car" into a briefcase and taking the conveyor belt into the office. The post-modern, ultra-modern jokes were just as clever as *The Flintstones*. Even the names of people and places were adapted in the same way — Dean Martian might be crooning at the Flamoongo Hotel in Las Venus one week, etc., etc.

Unfortunately, though focus group tests were highly optimistic for *The Jetsons'* success, ABC in its death wish wisdom put the show up against two top dogs: *Walt Disney's Wonderful World of Color (which could and did destroy any competition)* and *Dennis the Menace*. The show died quickly, though its ratings were equal to *Dennis* for that year. But 'good enough' wasn't good enough, and after only 24 episodes, the series was canned. It did return in 1985 for 41 additional shows, then 10 shows and two feature-length specials in 1987.

In 1966 a feature *Flintstones* film was released to cash in on the current craze of spy/James Bond movies, putting Fred in the unlikely role of secret agent in *The Man Called Flintstone*. Just because he looks just like Rock Slag *(voiced by Paul Frees)*, Fred is sent to Paris, then Rome, in order to pretend to be Slag *(in the hospital after an attack by the bad guys)* and have the villainous Green Goose *(also Frees)* pointed out to him by a sexy spy. It's actually a trap to catch Slag, but Fred and Barney save the day — and the world — by tricking the evil gang into a rocket ship which was invented to blow up the earth. Instead the boys launch it into outer space, and the Flintstones and Rubbles head back to Bedrock for a hero's welcome.

Paul Frees and Alan Reed had much more to do in this feature than Mel, but Mel could be heard in various bit characters, such as the poor cabbie who takes the villains from Paris to Rome, foolishly expecting his $1 million Francs fare.

During his time at Hanna-Barbera, Mel stated, "Because of my deep affection for animated films, I have to say that I am saddened by the execrable quality of most of today's cartoons. I'm not referring so much to the limited animation as I am to the limited imagination exhibited by their directors, writers and actors." He called many of the voices "characterless," especially the fact that many voices at the time were simply impressions of famous voices or personalities rather than original voices. It also steamed him up that there was *(and is)* no legal protection for an original voice. "Others can blatantly plagiarize Bugs Bunny or Woody Woodpecker, and there's nothing I can do about it. Unfortunately there are so many thieves in this business, it's laughable."

Mel admitted that his residuals on commercial and cartoon work kept him going for the seemingly unending time he was laid up in the hospital. He'd been insured by the Screen Actors Guild *(SAG)* and the American Federation of Television and Radio Artists *(AFTRA)*, each of which paid him $5000, but his bill for the first two months in the hospital was $18,000. Eventually he was able to become mobile via a wheelchair, occasionally going to the studios to work, and that helped both physically and financially.

At the end of November 1961, he was slated to return to his beloved Jack Benny program to film the Christmas Eve telecast. Jack had visited Mel at least once every 10 days of his convalescence, with the exception of his command performance in England. If he was going to miss a week, Jack would call Mel first to explain his absence. "I don't know how I got along without him," Jack said. Mel played himself *(in a wheelchair)* on the Christmas show, broadcast on December 24th. In Benny's gift boxes was nothing but fresh air. The gag being, "Well, in Los Angeles, that's *something!*"

Even with the work to take his mind off his plight, recovering at home was slow and painful. Mel had 21 breaks in his right leg from the knee to the foot. One of them was compound. The left leg had the knee cap torn off, but it was somehow sewn back on. Breaks to his ribs, six vertebrae, both sides of his pelvis, and three skull fractures were among his healing injuries. "When I asked my doctor what bones I had broken, he told me, 'If someone tells you he broke a bone, you can say you broke the same one, unless it's a left arm.'"

(12 years later he again broke the leg that had been broken in 21 places. The Blancs were at their Big Bear Lake cabin for the 4th of July. The leg still had six silver screws in it to keep the bones in place. An ambulance again took him to the same orthopedic surgeon, Dr. Lynn, at the UCLA Medical Center. He was in traction for another 2 months, and Noel set up another mini-studio, this time in his hospital room.)

12 months after his accident and two months after he appeared on Jack Benny's annual Christmas show, a roast was given in his honor, during which Jack said, "I can't love you more than everybody else in this room, but I certainly do as much."

Mel said to the audience, "You know, a year ago I was fighting for my life. I was in terrible pain. I didn't think I was going to live, and at times I didn't want to. I'm touched tonight, deeply. I'm blessed to have so many friends."

The near-death experience made Mel a more demonstrative person. *Imagine all the things that would have been left unsaid if I had died,* he thought to himself. "I found that saying 'I love you' felt every bit as fulfilling as hearing it." It also caused him to upgrade his number of performances at various Masonic and Shriners children's hospitals. Mel had been a Mason since 1931 in Portland, and a Shrine Mason from 1951. The kids loved being able to ask The Man himself to do Bugs Bunny and Tweety. "There isn't a time that I walk out of their rooms without tears in my eyes. Honestly, sometimes I don't know how I manage to blink them back until I'm out the door."

In November of 1961 Mel was given a "14-carat award" by the Thalians for his Bugs Bunny work for the youngsters of the Hathaway Home for Children. It was presented by Connie Stevens and Elmer Bernstein at a studio party.

In March of the following year he was honored again by the United Jewish Welfare Fund as their Man of the Year. He'd been a member of UJWF *(which helps overseas refugees)* since 1948, and now was cited for his "philanthropic service to the community at a Sunday breakfast in the Beverly Hills Hotel.

9 | MBA

While recovering, Mel announced to the press the forming of Mel Blanc Associates, which would "work creatively with advertising agencies in devising, developing, and producing humorous TV and radio commercials," much as Stan Freberg did with great success. Mel planned to record his voices on tape from his recuperative bed until he was able to get to a proper recording studio. Headquarters were set up in the Taft Building in Hollywood. Noel Blanc would produce, Henry Marx and Richard Clorfene would write, and Johnny Burton would be animation consultant. He teamed up with Johnny Burton, former executive producer at Warner Bros., since Mel had no knowledge of business whatsoever, just a large list of contacts and "a cheesy brochure" that the Blancs sent to every top ad exec. in the country. Noel thought the flyer looked like it was from a used-car dealership.

One thing the company would later produce was a five-minute syndicated radio series called *Hollywood Flashback*, narrated by Mel, which contained amusing and informative anecdotes about film personalities. The narration was straight, but dialects were used when situations called for it. At least 260 shows were recorded, with titles like "Greta Garbo, The Lady that Oscar Forgot" and "Curse of the Dreaded Autograph Seeker."

An offshoot of MBA and the crash was that Noel was urged to go into the family voice business. He would set off for Warner Bros. studios during this time and do a lot of material for Bugs, Tweety, Sylvester, etc. Porky was his favorite character "because he's inherently funny. He knows what he wants to say, but he has a hard time getting it out."

According to one report, Noel, by then a fair imitator of his father's characters, was asked by Warner Bros. to loop a series of cartoons, ones which needed an extra phrase or word redone. He would still pinch-hit for Mel later on occasion too, but "about 99% of what the public hears is my dad. My voice is basically used in public service announcements and on Armed Forces broadcasts."

Noel had graduated from UCLA's Theatre Arts program in 1961. He wanted to make movies, part of this influenced by working with Sheldon Leonard on Danny Thomas' TV show while Noel was still in college. (Leonard had produced and directed a variety of hit TV shows, most

Jack Benny works for Mel Blanc Associates.

notably *The Andy Griffith Show* and *The Dick Van Dyke Show*.) "I learned a great deal from Sheldon. He taught me the fundamentals of good directing, as only an accomplished artist could do." Noel also enlisted in the United States Army Reserves that year just after recording a single for Acclaim Records, "No Man Walks Alone," which he and Mel had written with Earl Lawrence.

While dividing his time between being Photo Officer at Fort Lewis, Washington, and commuting to Los Angeles to help his father record Bugs Bunny and *Flintstones* television shows from the studio at Mel's home, Noel pushed his dream of producing movies into the background. However, in November 1961, the dream came closer, in a way. Lieutenant Noel B. Blanc, 23, was assigned to head the Motion Picture Unit of the U.S. Army Signal Corps at Ford Ord. It had been announced in the *Santa Monica Evening Outlook* on November 27, 1961, along with the surprise announcement that Mel would make an appearance on Jack Benny's December 24th television show.

After producing dozens of movies on such topics as "How to Write Checks" and "How to Clean Your Weapon," Noel returned to Los Angeles to plunge into advertising full time with his father. The emphasis was on using humor to sell. Mel stated, "Humor is particularly effective if you are producing a new product or moving into a new market with an established product. Another area where humor is beneficial is the promotion of the impulse item. Also, humor can be strong when the product has built-in consumer resistance. Of course, even the finest comedy in a commercial might miss its mark if the timing and the product situation are wrong."

In 1964 he told *Variety*, "Comedy has been my career, but yet there are admen who try to tell me what I'm doing is wrong. How many laughs have they gotten since they left college? I'm not criticizing the lot of them. There are some very good ones who respect our ability to help them sell their product and that's where the re-orders are coming from."

The gag approach served well for clients like Ford, Pontiac, Kowalski Sausage, Chevrolet, and Rolls-Royce. According to *Variety*, by 1964 the company was billing close to a half-million dollars a year. That was also the year that Warner Bros. closed down its cartoon division, with a few more theatricals being released by the DePatie-Freleng company, but the end was nigh. Porky Pig gave his farewell performance just the next year in *Corn on the Cop*, and Sylvester's was in *The Wild Chase*. Now the Blancs' dual ambition was put full force into the ad agency.

On February 3, 1964 *Broadcasting Magazine* reported that Mel was making a radio show for syndication: *Inside Show Business with Mel Blanc*, consisting of anecdotes, vignettes, and behind-the-scenes looks into the entertainment world. Scripted by Richard Clorfene, Noel produced the shows with Mel serving as narrator and executive producer.

Funny man and *Laugh-In* announcer Gary Owens was also an integral part of MBA. "I owned a company with Mel Blanc and his son for about 25 years. We syndicated radio shows together. When my kids were small he recorded a tape for each of them, using every voice from Bugs Bunny to Tweety, singing "Happy Birthday."

"Mel bought oil wells and so did Jack Benny, but only Mel's paid off. Noel and I do voices for art galleries around the country. Mel was a beautiful man, a very nice man.

I worked with him every week for 20-some years. He loved clown paintings. He had a Rolls-Royce that had a license plate that read 'KMIT,' which meant 'kiss my ass' in yiddish."

Keeping busy was incredibly important to keeping his mind off his pain. Mel put down his recovery — as he told columnist Hedda Hopper — to "courage, patience, and a wonderful wife," though in retrospect he wanted Estelle to get top billing. The ordeal had been just as hard on her.

Johnny Burton had taken over the daily running of the MBA operation, but he was "nervous and insecure," Mel explained. "Certainly not cut out

Noel Blanc, Pat Bailey, Gary Owens, Mel Blanc and Bill Baldwin *(writer).* PHOTO COURTESY OF GARY OWENS

for the business world. Whenever Noel visited our Taft Building office, poor frazzled Johnny could usually be found at his desk in one of two standard positions: shouting hoarsely into the telephone, with his hands covering his face, or staring wishfully out his seventh-floor window as if ready to jump." Operating costs so far were two full-time, "incurably eccentric" copy writers on salary.

Noel took over as production manager. Mel had never actively encouraged his son to go into the touchy business of entertainment, telling him at a young age, "Be whatever you want, except a bank robber." Noel in his early years had toyed with the notion of being a doctor, but once he started taking piano lessons, the performance bug had bitten hard.

In 1962, Johnny Burton asked to leave MBA. It was just too much work. Noel took over in December as general manager, and Estelle joined the family unit as supervisor to all its secretarial and legal work. She also listened to the guys' pitch gags for commercials, giving her take on the good, the bad, and the ugly. In just four short months, their clientele rose 25%. MBA was producing over 100 consumer and general-industry spots, specializing in the comical commercial, which was more of a novelty 50 years ago. "I always stress that our commercials are entertaining, not

Gary Owens and Mel at a celebrity basketball game in Beverly Hills. PHOTO COURTESY OF GARY OWENS

funny," Mel told the press, "a crucial difference." Mel worried about the reliance of punch lines, claiming that if that's all audiences were listening for, "you will lose them after several hearings."

Their first major account was a radio ad campaign for the Midwestern Clark Oil and Refining Corp. MBA and Tatham-Laird Advertising devised the clever series of "Fisby and the Chief" characters, which became popular and spiked Clark Oil's stock considerably.

An absurd 10-second radio spot for Pepsodent grabbed listeners' attention. "The makers of Pepsodent, in an effort to promote dental hygiene, will now demonstrate the right way and the wrong way to brush your teeth. (Sound of teeth brushing) That is the wrong way. (More brushing) And that is the right way."

In just a few years MBA became a major player in the field, list-ing Volkswagen, Ford, Pontiac, Avis Rent-a-Car, and others as clients. Mel gave speeches at advertising seminars around the country, including an American Association of Advertising convention on the quality and cleverness of using humorous commercials. Mel was walking without a cane now — finally. After several years of physical therapy (underwater exercises, weightlifting, walking with a walker, then crutches, then a cane), "I can't even begin to describe the exhilaration I felt the first time I took a stroll without any support."

Mel stood before a crowd and you could hear a pin drop. The 800 or so people that had gathered in the Convention Hall were awaiting the keynote address of the American Association of Advertising Convention in Omaha. The year, 1964.

"Believe this or not," Mel quipped, "the first advertising was done by a horny caveman. He stood outside his cave and hollered, 'I want a woman, I gotta have a woman.'" The crowd began to laugh. "When he found that this brought him no action, he picked up a rock and gave the first woman he saw a knock on the head. Then he dragged her to his cave and fulfilled his desires." Mel took a long pause as the trickles of laughter trailed off. "It has been said that advertising has changed very little since that time,"…more laughter…"for even now it often ends up with a client getting screwed…"…thunderous applause! (For his entire speech, please see the Appendix.)

Advertising ideas had always been a hobby with Mel and in the fall of 1960, he and the executive producer of Warner Bros. Cartoons, Johnny Burton, decided to open a small office in Hollywood to do comedy radio and TV commercials. They rented a tiny room in the Taft Building on the corner of Hollywood and Vine and went into business. Only one problem…neither one of them had ever done anything like this before. They didn't know who to contact or which direction to go…so, in the winter of 1960, with no business prospects in sight, they decided to mail out a brochure to the top ad agency execs in the country.

It took Mel and Johnny a month to design the brochure and on January 21, 1961, they mailed 1500 of the clever print pieces. However there was one small problem to follow. On January 24, 1961 Mel was driving along Sunset Blvd. near UCLA at a place called "Dead Man's Curve." Suddenly from out of the blackness a car swerved across the double line and hit him head on…the result, nearly every bone in his body broken, a triple skull fracture, and six surgeons nearly gave him up for dead.

A Honolulu paper printed his obituary on January 25, 1961 at the exact same time most of the brochures telling about the formation of Mel Blanc Associates reached the desks of the intended advertising executives. A dead man had just opened his new company!

Mel and Noel working with Jesse White.

Noel was now VP of MBA as they moved further into radio territory with a popular series of one-liners for radio disc jockeys, called *Superfun*. Albert Brooks, Bob Einstein, John Rappaport (later producer of *M*A*S*H*), George Balzer *(The Jack Benny Program),* and 20 others were among the writers of these 4,000 "brief vignettes" Mel would record for playing between songs. Also recording were Don Knotts, Hans Conried, Lenny Weinrib, Joan Gerber, Joe Sirola, Henry Corden, Bob Crane, June Foray, Sid Melton, Ed Prentiss, John Stephenson, Lee Zimmer, Lou Horn, Byron Kane, Daws Butler, Howard Morris, Jesse White, Dave Ketchum, Hazel Shermut, Pat Carroll, Naomi Lewis, Leo Delyon, Rudy Hoffman, Arte Johnson, Gary Owens, and many others.

Variety stated that the prices for this "comedy ad-lib library" they were leasing and mailing to stations were set according to the population of the area that leased it. Min. $50 a month, max. $250 a month, with exclusivity guaranteed within a 100-mile radius. The initial library contained

60 different voices doing spots of everything from the weather to time signals to lead-ins for commercials. There were also running gags, vocal sound effects, and other material. The initial disc sent to DJs contained approximately 200 drop-in lines, 30 short running gags on various subjects, 20 intros to commercials, 20 time signals, 20 station breaks, 20 miscelanneous one-minute bits, 15 vocal sound effects, and 10 "man in the back alley" bits. The library was supplied on a series of 12-inch 33 1/3 microgroove records, with an accompanying written index of lengths and short descriptions. Stations were to receive new material every 45 days.

Within 5 years, MBA had accounts exceeding $10 million annually from the likes of Chrysler, Hancock Oil, Kool Aid, Winchell's Frozen Doughnuts, Delta Airlines, Raid, and thought-provoking anti-smoking commercials for the American Cancer Society.

"This is the most challenging assignment we've ever been given," Noel told *Variety* in 1967. Though he was set to go on his honeymoon the following week, the American Cancer Society had just approached him to do an anti-smoking campaign for radio. "What we're called on to do is to give a light touch and the right touch to the evil of smoking and the deleterious effects on the health of the addicts. We realize that the campaign must not be in questionable taste and still have shock value and there we will have to split hairs." This came about from the FCC's ruling that equal time be given to anti-cigarette commercials if cigarette companies were still to be allowed to advertise.

In one of the latter motivational spots, a man is tortured to death by being forced cigarettes, one after another. Mel said at the time, "We're telling the truth. We believe our campaign will be effective because it will force the listener to have involvement through humor."

A few forceful lines in their national campaign that really socked audiences with memorable, favorable response included: "The next time you have to give something to someone you don't like, give him a carton of cigarettes. And if you really hate him, give him two cartons!" Mel firmly believed that the stronger the message, the more important humor was. It was longer-lasting, more memorable. "The next time you think you're dying for a cigarette, you might be right," wasn't too funny, but it worked.

Vice-president in charge of production Harry O'Connor stated, "There may be eight different commercials used in one campaign. By bicycling them in and out, four spots can be spread over 32 weeks. By that time, they have served their purposes."

Mel himself quit smoking years later. He had smoked a pack of cigarettes a day from age 9 to 77, at which time he was diagnosed with emphysema. Even that almost wasn't enough to make him give up the habit. As Noel recalls, "I finally made him quit smoking when he was about 77 by telling his heart doctor to tell him that he should be on oxygen most of the time, and if he lit up he would blow up....that did it when nothing else worked."

December 9, 1966's *Variety* article on Mel Blanc called him one of the richest performers in radio or TV. Mel Blanc Associates was indeed going strong, accomplishing about half-a-million dollars' worth of business for clients like Ford, Wilson Packing, Dodge, Quaker Oaks, Avis, and General Electric. Their "Superfun" campaign had been such a success that a Broadcast Service Division of MBA, employing 16 workers, had to be set up. Noel rightly predicted that by the end of next year these comedy vignettes would gross $750,000 for the company.

Of course it wasn't all ad work, not by a long shot.

From 1964 to 1966 Mel squawked for *The Munsters'* pet raven on that cult-hit TV program, in a variation from his Jack Benny parrot. Sometimes Bob (*McHale's Navy*) Hastings would pinch hit, but never doing an imitation, so it's easier to spot Mel on the DVD sets today.

Mel worked on *The Monkees, The Jack Benny Program, The Lucy Show, Gilligan's Island, The Beverly Hillbillies, Burke's Law, The Many Loves of Dobie Gillis, The Flying Nun,* and *The Mothers-In-Law;* putting voices to these and hundreds of other shows proved that Mel had to be one of the busiest men in show business. The count goes to hundreds when you couple them with the many shorts he was still doing for WB, plus the plethora of cartoon series TV had to offer: *Lippy the Lion and Hardy Har Har* (1962), *The Bugs Bunny Show* (1960-62), *The Magilla Gorilla Show* (1964), *The Peter Potamus Show* (1964), *The Porky Pig Show* (1964), *Sinbad, Jr.* (1965), *The Atom Ant/Secret Squirrel Show* (1967-68), *The Bugs Bunny/ Road Runner Hour* (1968), and more.

In print ads for the 1969 Oscar-winning *Midnight Cowboy,* a *New York Times* article was often quoted, which included the line: "[Dustin] Hoffman looks like a sly, defeated rat and talks with a voice that might have been created by Mel Blanc for a despondent Bugs Bunny."

That was the year everyone turned out to honor Mel at a dinner event in the Sportsmen's Lodge for Pacific Pioneers (a group for radio professionals), including Jim "Fibber McGee" Jordan, Eddie "Rochester" Anderson, Janet Waldo, Paul Winchell, and Alan "Fred Flintstone" Reed. Reed introduced him. Mel began by doing his cartoon voices, then gave an overview of his career, and finished on a couple of jokes: A Catholic church and Jewish synagogue were both being built at the same time close together, but the synagogue was finished first. A Catholic priest came over and said, "You Jews are lucky to have the money to finish building. We Catholics have to scrape together a dime here and a dollar there. We still need $300 to finish our urinal." The little Jewish rabbi said, "Listen, I want there to be good relations between us Jews and Catholics, so I'll give you the $300 to finish your urinal out of my own pocket." He went home and told his wife who asked, "What's a urinal?" The little Jewish man said, "How the hell should I know, I'm a Catholic?"

Mel was a great collector of jokes, even keeping a collection of punch lines in his wallet to go with the 2000 jokes he had written down and mostly memorized. He took great delight in telling jokes at any occasion.

10 | School's In

After successfully producing more than 4,000 commercials and grabbing 187 national and international broadcast awards, the Blancs had decided to share their working knowledge with the public. Aside from Daws Butler, who had a continuous workshop who had a continuous workshop for voice students (which included Nancy Cartwright, later the voice of Bart Simpson), there were few opportunities to learn from the masters at that point.

In 1972 the Mel Blanc School of Commercials briefly opened its doors in the posh Westwood United Methodist Church, to offer six courses to all wannabes eager to learn commercial acting from the masters.

Noel Blanc was director of the school, while Mel supervised the course in cartoon, dialects, and character voices, assisted by Larry Moss, expert in phonetics and the diction coach for Barbra Streisand in *Funny Girl*, who now taught at Long Beach State College and led the dialect class. Stanley Ralph Ross, who received an Emmy nomination for a script for *All in the Family*, taught the class in on-camera techniques, assisted by Steve Carlson. Lurene Tuttle, who taught radio-TV communication at USC for 6 years, gave the class on radio and television voice-overs. She was mostly concerned with how to read the script, and would give the pupils 103 pages of material and coach them on the proper verbal moves to "get it off the page." Industry lecturer and narrator Marjorie Lyte taught public speaking (for non-performing purposes). The Blancs used their professional connections to construct a volunteer "talent-review board" to give would-be actors instant and professional feedback from talent agents, directors, producers, casting officials, studio/talent scouts, ad executives, and actors such as Kirk Douglas, Jack Palance, and Vincent Price. Other school officials included administrative director Lee Hansen, vice president Pat Bailey, assistant administrator in charge of enrollment Stanley Gibben, and

creative director Cliff Einstein. The school was a subsidiary of the Noel
Blanc Broadcast Organization.

There were also frequent guest speakers, such as Monty Hall, Sheldon
Leonard, Gary Owens, and Walter Lantz. Mel claimed it to be an *unact-*
ing school, to unlearn all of the usual traits of self-consciousness that many
actors suffer from, in order to appear completely natural as a *commercial*

Jack Palance with Noel.

actor. Depending on the course, each pupil put his "final exam" on audio or video which were then distributed to the board to be graded. Undergrads sometimes received job offers.

The Hollywood Reporter wrote that Mel began his school because he thought most acting in commercials was lousy. The need for Stanislavskian teaching in commercial acting was needed, he said. "They don't know where the hell to look, what the hell to say properly, how to use the right inflection to bring out the product. They hem and haw. They look like they're being followed by a camera because they know they are being followed by a camera."

Likewise he told one magazine, "You'd be surprised how many actors and actresses with years of experience do not know how to act in a commercial. It's an art in itself. The idea is to sell the product, not the performer. One of the big secrets is to be natural, and not to make the audience conscious that you are being filmed."

Classes began on February 7th. All applicants were screened prior to enrollment "to establish legitimate potential." Out of an interviewed 400 applicants, 92 students (4 men to every woman) were chosen to attend the opening classes. Students could choose from four classes: on-camera techniques; voice-over for beginners; voice-overs for the more advanced; and cartoon dialects and character voices. The classes cost $300 each to attend, and were given every Monday for 6 weeks.

Thus began the Mel Blanc School of Voice and Commercials. MBA PR man Bill Baldwin, Jr. wrote the following article which appeared in the *Los Angeles Times*:

A Day at The Mel Blanc School

I'm seated in an auditorium in Beverly Hills. Mel Blanc is standing near the front of the stage. It's now a few minutes past seven and Noel Blanc, Mel's son and the president of the Mel Blanc School of Commercials, walks to a podium mike on stage and says hello.

Noel is 33 years old and he knows the commercial business well. Yet his youthful looks sometimes fool people. Seated at the piano, stage left, is what looks like a happy-go-lucky grizzly bear. His name is Stanley Ralph Ross. One of three instructors in the On-Camera class. Stanley has 13 years of producing, directing, acting and writing commercials in his background, including an Emmy nomination for an *All in the Family* episode.

The other two teachers are Steve Carlson, a multi-talented actor and Dan Vinokur, one of the town's top young executives. Dan is VP at Asher-Gould.

Noel is speaking: "This semester each class will have guest speakers. Again Gary Owens and Jesse White and perhaps Sheldon Leonard or Walter Lantz will be coming over to speak, and your instructors have lined up special guests."

I'm told Monty Hall of *Let's Make a Deal* sat and talked with Rowland Barber's creative writing class the previous week. Rowland Barber is a Pulitzer Prize nominee, contributing writer to *West Magazine* and *TV Guide*, and is now writing a book and screenplay on the life of Erik Von Stroheim.

The auditorium meeting breaks up with students and instructors moving toward their individual classrooms. Sitting next to me is Pat Bailey, VP of the school and of Mel Blanc Audiomedia, the school director, Lee Hansen, and associate director John St. John.

"Come on, I'll take you around to the classes and you can watch what goes on," says Pat. Stopping in front of Room 200, the sign reads VO I, Lurene Tuttle. The students in Voice-Over I are for the most part beginners and are here to learn projection, pronunciation and how to read a piece of advertising or film copy. In short, how to use their voice. They have come to the right place. For Lurene Tuttle, an Emmy nominee for *Julia*, knows her business. She left the telecommunications department at USC to join the Mel Blanc School. After spending a half-hour watching Lurene with her students, Pat said, "Let's drop in on Peter's class."

Peter is Peter Leeds, another veteran. A Bob Hope regular with 1,000 shows, 25 movies, over 500 commercials behind him, Peter Leeds, like all of the teachers at the Mel Blanc School, doesn't have to teach. He doesn't need the money. I ask him why then is he here? His answer echoes the feelings of every instructor I talk to. "I'm excited about the whole concept of the school. The teachers are all tops in their respective fields. And the students excite me. No one made them come to the Mel Blanc School, they paid their money and they're here to learn." [Leeds taught the "use of the five senses: concentration, imagination, freedom from inhibition, sight-reading and microphone techniques."]

Peter and Cliff Einstein, creative director and senior VP of Dailey and Associates, are the instructors for Voice-Over II, the extension of Lurene's beginners class. As I cross the hall to Cliff's section, he's busy going over the taped reading of a spot. Seated behind a mike is a pleasant looking man in his mid-thirties.

"What you have to do here, Don, is to smile while you're reading this spot. Talk to it as if you're telling your brother about his new car. Be honest. That's the key to this spot." Cliff flips on the tape machine and Don begins again, and reads it perfectly. Cliff smiles, "That was very good. Excellent."

Mel Blanc is the driving force behind the school. Along with Larry Moss, he teaches cartoon dialects and character voices. Just think, Bugs Bunny, Porky Pig, Daffy Duck, Sylvester and Tweety, Speedy Gonzales, Yosemite Sam, Foghorn Leghorn, and as he says, about 390 other original voices, are all the creation of one man, Mel Blanc. And now I find myself sharing coffee and donuts with this talented man.

"Honesty and naturalness are the keys to commercial acting, plus of course, talent. The agencies are using real people in commercials these days. We teach our students to be themselves, be natural."

"Well, what about honesty and your school?" I ask.

"You mean, do we promise our students jobs as a come-on for enrollment?" Mel asks. "No, we're not one of those schools. We don't promise any student a job after graduation, they earn their jobs. Our talent review board is made up of many of the top agents, casting directors and producers in the business, and the final work of each student is critiqued by them. Fifteen of our first semester students have gotten jobs through their exposure to the talent review board."

Students Train for Producing Commercials

In the news of late there have been countless stories concerning phony talent schools and agencies being busted throughout California. Some weeks ago I did an article on one of the legitimate schools in the business, the Mel Blanc School of Communications. Why not, I asked myself, return for the closing night of the semester and try to evaluate the progress made and lessons learned by the students? Therefore, here I am, once again ensconced within the confines of "Bugs Bunny Tech."

No caps and gowns, not a trace of pomp and circumstance do I see, yet leading off the evening's agenda is the presentation of diplomas. Sitting with me is Noel Blanc, Mel's son.

"After this, all the students will be moving on to their classes, and we'll be getting right down to the final taping sessions," says Noel. "Saturday is the talent review board session, where the board will listen to and critique the final work of each student. That's why it's nervous time tonight. Everyone wants to do his best in the taping sessions."

Before I can ask anything more, Noel is off to see to final arrangements in one of the voice-over classes. I intend to find out a lot more about the review board from Noel later, as its membership is comprised of many of the town's top agents, casting directors, producers, directors, and performers.

I'm told that some journalistic colleagues have appeared. Writers and photographers have come tonight to interview some of the first semester students — students who have since gone on to get commercial work and/or been signed by talent agents. I've been sitting in the back of the auditorium people watching. Rowland Barber of the Writer's Workshop deviates from the norm by not giving diplomas.

"They'll be presented at a later date," he says. "Writers begin their careers by writing and stop by not writing." Rowland smiles and sits down. "Most of the workshop projects won't be finished until midsummer," he tells me later. "After all, we know writers hardly ever get things done on time." (An editor said that to him once.) "Most writers do not agree with editors." (He said that to an editor, once.)

Hanging around the auditorium to watch some of the on-camera taping, I notice that although the pressure is on, the students aren't being rushed into accepting a "take" as final.

"We've got all night, kids," says Steve Carlson, "so relax and take your time." Steve, being a busy commercial actor, knows that some people need more time and rehearsal than others and if you rush things, they may blow the whole spot.

Ironically, the lead-off student does her first spot in one take. Nicely done, and quite natural. The girl's second commercial goes in two takes, and although she's not completely satisfied, she sits down very pleased and relieved. She has done well and might be signed by an agent in a few weeks. I say might, because in this business, nobody ever knows for sure.

I've decided to wander upstairs to watch some of the voice-over classes at work. Coming upon Mel Blanc in the hallway, I decide to visit his class. Mel has just arrived after an 11-hour taping session for a new commercial. Eleven hours!

"Cartoon dialects and character voices" is perhaps the toughest class at the Mel Blanc School. Tough, in that you have to work to perfect a character voice and/or dialect, and the same time, act.

In the 20 minutes or so I spend with the instructors, Mel Blanc and Larry Moss, four students are taped. Doing original character voices and using accents, I find myself amazed at their improvement over the past seven weeks. These four have become professionals, and I can only assume that the rest of the class has improved as much.

The majority of Mel Blanc School graduates have reached the point where they can now be called professionals. But the commercial business is an extremely competitive one, demanding an incredible amount of dedication. For some, the jobs will come almost immediately. For others, that first job may be six months off, or a year, or maybe never. Nobody said it would be easy. Yet from what I've seen here at the school, there's a great deal of personal confidence shown by most of the students. And confidence, next to talent and drive, is the most important quality a performer can have.

In March the school had been renamed the Noel Blanc Broadcast Organization when Noel took over the four-part class. Special advisors to aid and monitor student progress on the creative review board were Joe Barbera, Walter Lantz, and Friz Freleng.

Noel wrote of the School:

"No! Open your mouth wider and let your tongue roll down the cheek," Mel said. He was teaching some students what he thought a giant hippopotamus should sound like if it could talk. The students tried again, this time with even greater voice dynamics. Mel smiled, "That's it, now you're getting closer!"

This particular class was called Cartoon Voices and Dialects and was headed by Larry Moss, the finest of all dialect coaches, and Mel, who taught the creation of cartoon voices. It was just one of the classes being taught at the Mel Blanc School of Commercials.

In the On-Camera class, which was taught by many of the top Hollywood directors, videotape recorders would whirr all night, sometimes till 2:30 in the morning, as the actor or actress tried take after take until he/she got the commercial down letter-perfect. Mel would stop by all the classes each school night and delighted in seeing his students grow more professional.

This school was a dream Mel had always had…where a school could be established to teach and train students who really wanted to learn the ins and outs of the commercial business. It was the first really big commercial-oriented school, and it had one thing that no school before or since has had: a Talent Review Board, made up of just about every major agent, casting director, and agency producer in town. We had 95 people on the board who saw and/or heard final examples of each student's work. Depending on the class, either On Camera or Voice-Over, we used both videotape and audio tape to present each student's talent in the best light during Review Board Critique sessions. These Final Exams, if you will, were graded by each Review Board member and then returned to the student. It was constructive criticism of the best sort, where aspiring actors and actresses were given honest opinions about their commercial abilities and potentials. I'm proud to say that many of our students were signed by commercial talent agencies and are now working.

As you can imagine, a school like this eventually proved to be a very costly means of finding new talent. Even though tuitions were high, we still lost about $300,000 every 8 weeks, and for this reason we reluctantly had to discontinue the school which had been Mel's dream. "Someday," Mel said, "the industry will have this type of school and review board again, but it will only happen if the talent unions support it financially, or maybe the state could help with tuition." Mel's office staff was paid nothing by the school. Everyone first volunteered, but the teaching and coaching staff, the rest, the food, etc. soon became too much and in the winter of 1973 the Mel Blanc School of Communication closed its doors.

Mel later told *Film Collector's World* that part of the reason they gave up the school was because they didn't have time for their own commercial work. Also, it seemed that the Blancs were inundated with requests from states and big cities to open up voice schools. "And I could have made myself a million bucks in six months if I'd wanted to, but I didn't want to fool the people into thinking it was my school and not one of those crazy schools like they have had out here where they just collected money and went out of business. And promised them work, which I didn't do in my school."

11 | Cartoons, Commercials, Awards

It was a hot, muggy 4th of July weekend and Mom and Dad were up at Big Bear Lake to find some cool air.

The phone at the cabin rang and rang, but no answer. That's strange, they usually stayed around the house. It was right then and there that I felt something strange. I knew all was not right. I couldn't put my finger on it, but the feeling was there.

Then a half hour later, the phone rang. It was Mom telling me that Dad was en route to St. John's Hospital. "Dad fell down and broke his leg," she said. It was the same leg that had been shattered in 1961 and still contained six silver screws to keep the bones in place.

They were at the Big Bear Lake emergency hospital waiting for an ambulance to transfer him to Santa Monica's St. John's Hospital where the orthopedic surgeon that had put him back together in 1961 was waiting.

When Mel arrived at St. John's, he looked terrible. Mom had ridden down with him in the ambulance and going around all those hairpin curves down the mountain had made him ill and dizzy. Theodore Lynn, the orthopedic surgeon, took him to X-ray immediately. Mom and I both thought it was a simple break, but an hour later when Dr. Lynn came out of X-ray he explained that the very leg that had been broken in 1961 was broken again. This time in five places, including the knee.

Dr. Lynn spent three hours in the operating room and told me and Mom that Dad would walk again, but he needed to be in a cast for at least two months and off his feet for seven weeks or so, so we set up a temporary recording studio in his hospital room so he wouldn't lose a day's work.

Mel again took the accident in stride and with good nature. Just as he had done 12 years previously when he was laid up for over a year, we heard no complaints. Even when he was in pain, we never knew about it.

It was July of 1972 and Mel was out of commission again, this time from a loose rock in Big Bear. Earlier that year, on February 15th, Mel was given the Shalom Award at an Israel Dinner of State sponsored by the Irving Thalberg Lodge of B'Nai B'Rith. The event was on behalf of Israel Bonds, in celebration of Israel's 25th anniversary of statehood, at the Marquis Restaurant on Sunset Blvd.

To keep busy again, Mel refused to let up on his workload. He voiced a football special, *Son of Football Follies*, a sequel to the popular *Football Follies*, which collected up some of the weirdest mistakes and funny moments from games, setting documentary-style music behind it, and laden with most of his Warner Bros. catalog, including a few he didn't do. Roadrunner's "beep, beep!", Elmer Fudd's lisping as a "wefawee," and even a brief and able impression of Donald Duck in the mouth of a football player having a tantrum at the ref — it was an amusing, spirited performance for TV audiences, and now available on DVD.

(Speaking of Elmer, *et al*, when the famous "What's Up, Doc?" was sung by Bugs and Elmer at the end of Barbra Streisand's 1972 film of the same name, Mel didn't receive compensation until he complained to Warner Bros.)

On January 24, 1974, *The Hollywood Reporter* wrote that Mel Blanc Audiomedia had changed its name to Blanc Communications Corp. when it expanded its operations to include consumer motivation work, campaign creation, production, and full placement services. New international accounts were taken on in addition to their national ones. The muscle of the new company included President Noel Blanc, Executive Vice-President Patrick Bailey, Vice-President of Production Bill Baldwin, Jr., sales director Joe Parenzan, and media director Mary Callahan. The new accounts would require a bit of European travel.

It was June, 1975. Dad and I were on the non-stop TWA flight to London. After a terrific dinner of whatever it was and two packs of Rolaids each, we landed at Heathrow airport at about 8:20 a.m. Someone was supposed to meet us, but his alarm had failed to go off and there we were at the end of the "queue" line waiting for a taxi. Two hours later, we arrived at the Inn on the Park, exhausted, but there was work to do. We were on a 5-day trip, and during the 5 days we had to record 95 five-minute radio shows, 25 promos, and 13 television commercials for the American Forces

Radio and TV network. The reason for doing them in London was because Vincent Price, who was co-starring in the commercials with Mel, couldn't come to the United States since his wife, Coral, had a hit play in London.

After checking in we called Vincent, who told us he was ready and waiting to record, so I called the recording studio to double check the times we had booked.

Vincent and Mel.

The studio security told us that they had had several bomb threats that day and wondered if we still wanted to record. We said yes, not realizing that the IRA really meant business with these bomb threats.

Two weeks prior they had blown up a café, and just three days before our landing, they had threatened the hotel across the street from where we were staying.

Presuming that we were invincible to danger, we said the hell with it and went to record Vincent and Mel. Once inside the confines of the studio we were told of another bomb threat just minutes before we had arrived, but Vincent wanted to get the work done. So, we began to record. It seemed strange that the engineer wanted me to run the control board. He said he wanted to get some lunch. Then when Vince took a break, I walked around the halls and found nobody. Everybody had gone...

To where…I don't know, but it must have been the bomb threat. I opened a few doors and shouted in them, but to no avail. Then I walked down to the cafeteria and no one was there. Were we the only people left in the building? Were Mel Blanc and Vincent Price going to be the next unknowing victims of an IRA attack?

All of a sudden we heard the ground tremble. It seemed as if an earthquake had struck but the shock was not really intense. I knew if the bomb were in the studio building, the walls were soon to be coming apart, but they didn't. Then what the hell was that rumble?

As it turned out, the rumble was that of a bomb totally destroying the first floor of the Hilton Hotel, which happened to be located right next to the hotel in which we were staying. A number of people were killed and 30 to 40 more were seriously hurt. Debris was hurled out into the street and most of the windows of the surrounding buildings were blown in. Human body fragments were everywhere and the smell of death was pungent in the air.

Dad, Vincent, and I were scared shitless, to say the least. Vince wanted to get back to his flat, and Dad and I didn't know where the hell to go. Our hotel had also received a bomb threat. The streets around our hotel were cordoned off, and the bomb squads were everywhere.

In August of 1975 Mel toured (not in London) to promote Warner Bros.' new Bugs Bunny Birthday Call kit. For $5 parents could buy it, fill in a postcard with the child's name and birthdate, and mail it at least a week ahead of time to prompt a call from Bugs on the child's birthday. The prerecorded message was one of 2,500 voices Mel had taped the previous summer to be matched up with the birthday names. All names — including Jose and Jesus — were thought up as well. But just in case a wild card like Topperbody crept in, a non-personalized message could be sent. The test market showed it to be popular, with 35% of the patrons being *adults*.

One story from Ron Smith's part of Noel's book told more of the story:

Looking back through my journals while preparing this book, I ran across three entries which when combined tell quite accurately the answer to the question, "What is Mel Blanc really like?"

The first happened in Kansas City. In a hotel suite prior to a VIP cocktail party promoting the Bugs Bunny Birthday Call, Mel and several Warner executives are looking over the guest list. One of the executives mutters, "What the hell is this? There's not one really *important* person on this list." Mel slammed down the list and looked the young man in the eye. "Son, you'll never go anywhere until you realized that every person is important."

The second happened in St. Paul, Minnesota. After a grueling two days in which he had made fourteen radio appearances, five television shows, and visited three hospitals, we arrived at the offices of the Mayor of St. Paul. He was a bright, energetic shirt-sleeve type of guy who had worshipped Mel forever. As Mel and the Mayor chatted, secretaries and other workers gathered outside the office. "Mel," said the Mayor, "the whole city's out of commission right now until you sign some autographs. Can they come in?"

Mel said sure and soon the office was filled with workers getting his signature. I kept looking at my watch since the plane was leaving shortly and we were due at another reception in another city.

The Mayor noticed my agitation, and when I explained the situation, he got on the phone to the Chief of Police. "Get me a black and white to get Bugs Bunny to the airport." As we raced through rush hour traffic, Mel continued chatting about how nice the Major had been. All I could think of was whether or not we would miss the plane.

Arriving at the airport with six minutes to go, I was frantically racing to get the luggage checked through and discovered to my horror that Mel was nowhere to be found. After a quick search, we found him at the police car, talking with the two officers who had escorted us. "I wanted to thank them," he said, "they didn't have to do that for us. That was really nice." I wondered how many other world-famous celebrities would do that.

The final entry occurred in Salt Lake City. As a 32nd degree Mason and a Shriner, Mel throws a lot of support behind the Shriner Children's Hospitals. Mel, several grizzled reporters and myself made an appearance on a Saturday afternoon at the terminally ill ward in Salt Lake City. Walking into the ward, the stench of death mixed with the hospital smells as fourteen young children lay dying. I watched for a few moments as Mel walked to each of the beds, chatting briefly with the children. One I recall in particular, a lad named Bobby who was 10. Lymphatic cancer was ravaging his young body, and this 64-pound wreck lay motionless with tubes running from his nose and mouth.

"Nyaaahhh, what's up, doc?" Mel asked Bobby. Instantly the pain seemed to leave his face as Mel stood by his bed, doing Yosemite and Daffy and Porky and Barney Rubble. I couldn't take it, and excused myself rather than cry in front of the kids. In the hall I found three reporters also overcome by the scene we had just witnessed.

At last Mel came out of the ward, with the voices of the kids yelling, "Goodbye, Bugs" after him. "How can you do that?" I asked in the limousine. "Doesn't it get to you?"

"Hell yes, it does," he answered. "But those kids need it. And as far as I'm concerned, laughter helps make the pain go away."

Kids would often ask Mel for his autograph. Occasionally the adults accompanying them would say, "Don't you ever get tired of doing that?" Mel admitted that he would only get tired if they *stopped* asking. As of 1970, Mel said six to ten kids a day would ring his doorbell for an autograph. He had a pad of Bugs Bunny cartoons saying "What's up, doc?" which he would sign for anyone; some fans were barely old enough to speak.

Apart from his impressive career, one of the reasons the name Mel Blanc is remembered still to this day is that Mel was much more of a performer off camera than any of the other top voice men. Daws Butler and Paul Frees were happy to make their top money and keep out of the spotlight, doing the occasional interview when asked. Mel sought the limelight and, because of his advertising company also, continued to put himself in a starring role. Press releases, TV & radio interviews, public appearances, speeches — it was no wonder his fame never waned beyond WB screen credit.

Such personal appearances included:

Halloween, 1975. From 10:30 to 11:30 a.m. Mel joined Dodgers first baseman Steve Garvey and other speakers for a student-sponsored United Way fund drive at El Camino Real School in Woodland Hills, California.

Two years later, *Variety* announced that Mel had been brought in to Appleton, Minnesota on Saturday September 20th to help a Doctor Procurement Committee raise funds to help lure in a new M.D. to help the town's current doctor who had spread himself too thin with the 1,800 town and 3,200 rural residents. A $15 a plate dinner was given at the Appleton Gold Club at which he was the featured guest. He also did a show at the Swift County fairgrounds.

A live costumed cast featuring the main Warner Brothers' characters entitled *The Bugs Bunny Follies* was performed at the Coliseum on Wednesday April 14, 1975 through Sunday the 18th. Not quite a personal appearance for Mel, but he had recorded the show's soundtrack. This was

Bugs' first time on stage, according to the papers. A feature-length collection of cartoons, *Bugs Bunny Superstar* was also screened around Easter time at the World East and World West. The manager of the theatre, Frank Hurley, ordered carrots with green tops to be given away on Friday's opening night. Mel was a bit busy at the time, currently working with Chuck Jones on the half-hour television cartoon, *Carnival of the Animals*.

The New York Times reviewed *Bugs Bunny Superstar* by stating, "Children, brought up on TV, should be dazzled by the slam-bang wit and the excellence of the animation technique," though they did not care for Orson Welles' "facetious" narration or the directors' (Avery, Freleng, Jones) too-long commentary on "how great it was in the old days on the Warner Bros. lot."

As of the mid-1970s Mel was lamenting the "short" radio program (i.e. funny bits for morning shows), but he still had a wealth of properties in development. Blanc Communications Corporation's division of Mel Blanc Automedia was expanding with even more accounts, with Noel as company president and Mel as CEO. Noel himself had received more than 240 awards for his commercial productions, while Mel became a "name celebrity" again to fans when he appeared on camera for an American Express commercial in 1975. Filmed in a restaurant, Mel states, "Do you know me? Would you believe I'm Bugs Bunny? I'm also the voice of many other cartoon characters. But in here, they don't care if I'm Elmer Fudd. So I carry an American Express card. The one card I need for travel and entertainment, for business and pleasure. Why, without this (shows AE card), the only way I'd get any attention is by saying *th-th-th-th*-that's all folks! Huhuhuhuhuh!" After Mel's name is typed on the card and the announcer tells America where to apply for a card, Mel returns to say, "The American Express card. Don't leave home without it."

Mel said that that 30-second commercial resulted in more public recognition and autograph requests than in his entire career during cartoons. He was constantly stopped on the street and asked if he had his AE card with him. And, as was his lifelong policy, he never refused an autograph request. It was an important point with him: "If people come up to me and tell me they like my work, the least I can do is give them an autograph!"

There was only one occasion when it was announced that Mel would not be signing autographs. This was the day that Bugs Bunny's star was laid on Hollywood Boulevard (December, 1985) in front of C.C. Brown's ice cream parlor (a business now defunct). Since the ceremony was just three months after Mel collapsed at St. John's Medical Center in Santa Monica, his health was still quite fragile. On top of that, signing autographs for the thousand Bugs Bunny fans there that day would have been a serious strain on his 78-year-old body.

1975 was also the year Mel got a new toy, as Noel explains:

"Ten-four there, 'Yellow Bird' and pass the good numbers to your family for me. This is Bugs Bunny KLS 1839 going ten-ten and ten-eight."

"Breaker for the Bugs Bunny," a child's voice rang over the CB speaker.

"You got the Bugs Bunny. What's your handle, Doc?" Mel said in the character's voice.

"The Silver Streak," came the small, scared voice back, "and my twenty is in my dad's boat."

"10-4. What can I do for you, Silver Streak?" asked Mel.

"Well, we're out of gas and drifting toward the rocks off of Malibu, can you call the Coast Guard?"

Mel did, and a few minutes later Silver Streak got back on the radio and told him that everything was okay.

Silver Streak is only one of the nearly 70 breakers a day for the Bugs Bunny, Citizen Band base station in the Pacific Palisades. Children of all ages and their folks grab their microphones when nearing the Santa Monica area and switch to Channel 21, knowing they'll hear one of Mel's many characters coming over the radio to humor or help them.

I gave Dad the CB rig for Christmas, but he said that he probably wouldn't use it. "After all," he said, "what the hell am I going to say to someone I don't know?" I told him to answer any "breaker" with one of his cartoon voices, and then ask me the same question.

Mel's been into CB for about a year and has enjoyed it as much as the kids have. Incidentally, there are several times when Dad has helped people out in emergencies and once, he saved a little girl's life by reacting fast with the citizen's band radio in his automobile.

In 1976 a group of made-for-TV specials starring Bugs Bunny began the lucrative resurgence of Warner Bros. re-releases to new audiences. Usually packaging new material around old shorts, the first, Chuck Jones' *Carnival of the Animals*, was actually a half-hour of original Bugs and Daffy animation. It was more likely an easy sell after Bugs' first feature, *Bugs Bunny Superstar*, went to the big screen the previous year. Just like Snoopy, Bugs found himself in all of the holidays, plus thematic specials such as *Bugs Bunny in Space* (1977; incorporating the popular Duck Dodgers short) and *The Bugs Bunny Mystery Special* (1980; Bugs is Public Rabbit #1 being tracked by Special Agent Elmer Fudd, with Mel supplying Fudd's voice in this all-new animation). One of the strangest entries came in 1982 when *Bugs Bunny's Mad World of Television*, in which Bugs is sought after to be its new president, despite the back-stabbing antics of Yosemite Sam, turned its gentle satire on the QTTV network. This one, though mostly made up of old cartoons, was all voiced by Mel Blanc. For these specials it was usually Mel and June Foray or just Mel alone.

The following year saw the same formula being used for the Flintstones, beginning with *A Flintstone Christmas* which has Fred taking over for Santa who has sprained an ankle after falling off Fred's roof. Holidays weren't used so much as fads and classic ideas: *The Flintstones: Jogging Fever* explored the jogging craze (1981) that had hit Bedrock, while *The Flinstones Meet Rockula and Frankenstone* (1980) was a Halloween release in which Fred and Wilma have won a romantic trip to Rocksylvania in Count Rockula's castle. As usual, Mel Blanc supplied the voice of Barney and sometimes Dino and the odd misc. character. Henry Corden had taken over as Fred's voice after Alan Reed's passing on June 14, 1977.

Mel and Henry also did a *lot* of commercials for their very lucrative Fruity Pebbles cereal, and Flintstones Vitamins (both products are still around today). Mel figured he had also made $40,000 from all the airplay his Fritos commercial received, plus $50,000 in residuals as the voice of the Frito Bandito.

Cartoons may have been the fun part, but commercials grabbed the real money. In the mid-70s, Mel's firm produced another *Superfun* project which was again marketed towards radio stations to liven up their then mostly-music formats. It was a record of blackouts, one-liners, and two-minute comedy routines that was picked up by more than 50 radio stations across the country in its first six months in release. They also recorded a soap opera spoof in 65 parts called *Return to Paper Plates*. In this clever spoof, Carl Morgan and Julia Fairholme go through a wacky series of adventures ranging from being lost in a goldmine in Brazil to Carl overthrowing the Czar of Russia, with spoofing stops in Hollywood and the rest of the country along the way.

Superfun, a set of 12 LPs, was actually a revamp of their 1963 Ad Lib Library, featuring most of Mel's "1000 voices." One example:

ANNOUNCER: And now, it's time for *Sea Hunt*. (Piano hits E flat)
VOICE: Is that it?
VOICE 2: Nope. (D sharp sounds)
VOICE: How about that?
VOICE 2: Nope.
VOICE: I give up. I can't find it.
ANNOUNCER: You've been listening to *C Hunt*.

After the great popularity of *Superfun*, the guys decided to pitch *The Gary Owens Special Report* to stations, which in a way was even more hilarious than *Superfun*, trading on Gary's perfect deadpan humor that's so serious it makes one wonder why he was never in an *Airplane* movie.

Mel Blanc Audiomedia was making enough money to move to "a silly looking building" on Hollywood Blvd. called "Crossroads of the

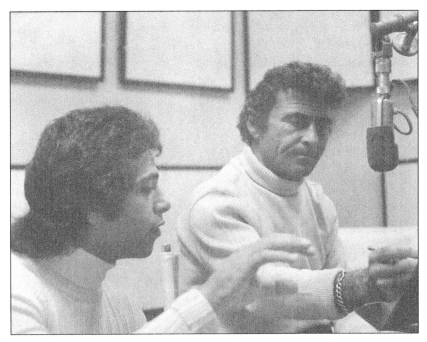

Noel working with Rod Serling.

World." The complex, designed to look like a large ship, housed a series of small boutiques, advertising agencies, and professional offices. With their ever-growing success, the Crossroads office proved too small, so the firm made their big move into Beverly Hills, taking a suite of offices in the Glendale Federal Building at 9454 Wilshire Blvd. After seeing the sign on the building, "Glendale Federal Savings, Assets $25 Billion," Mel quipped, "Well, now we can tell everyone we meet that Mel Blanc Audiomedia's ass sits on $25 billion."

Shortly after the move, Mel and Noel developed another radio advertising concept called "Shock Media." Noel explained at the time, "It is a new direction. Very little is said about the product in our 'shock impact' commercials. The listener, left dangling, conjures images which must be explained by going to the location of the particular product." And writer Patrick Bailey, who had joined MBA in 1970 as director/producer of the bulk of MBA's TV projects, told a Minneapolis reporter, "What we're using is psychological techniques that embrace the idea that the strongest motivation the consumer has is the consumer himself. If we can cause the consumer to excite himself about a product or a service by implication rather than direct statement, then the consumer will be phenomenal." For the Foto Foto Fun Fun quick photo processing booths which were located in 63 Super Valu stores in Minneapolis, "we created a series of spots using Rod Serling and Gary Owens which never mentioned photo processing, but which set up intriguing images that something is happening at Super Valu that will change the picture of things to come." Foot traffic increased by 15% the first week from curious customers.

When the developers of a new shopping center underneath Arco called "The Plaza" were desperate for 25,000 people to show up for their grand opening, MBA conceived a series of dramatic commercials that featured a great deal of mystery. "Something is happening...underground," said the voice of John Dehner. "Beneath the streets of Los Angeles a miracle is happening. When Jules Verne traveled to the center of the earth, he found an incredible world of mystery, but nothing to compare with this. The Plaza." Without any newspaper/magazine support, these commercials ran on seven Los Angeles radio stations and gathered 58,000 people to the site on opening day.

In September of 1976 Mel lent his Bugs and Daffy voices to ten important radio Public Service Announcements for the Office of Emergency Services in California to instruct kids how to act during earthquakes. "What do I do when the shaking stops?" asks Bugs. "Stay away from damaged structures and power lines and remember to stay calm," Daffy instructs. In another PSA, Bugs advises schoolchildren to dive under their desks if caught at school during an earthquake, and "not to watch the action." Mel also did a few on-camera PSAs for kitchen safety (be careful with hot bath water, and keep dangling cords out of reach!) for the Shriners Hospital for Crippled Children.

Bugs and Daffy even once sang a minute-long commercial to show how great our Constitution is that we can constantly amend it.

On the opposite side, Bugs and the gang were often seen touting a wealth of commercial products such as Tang, Kool-Aid, Ziploc Storage Bags, and Bugs Bunny sugar-free chewable vitamins; Bugs even once plotted with the "silly rabbit" to get some of those deliciously fruity Trix.

In between *all* of this, Mel was still doing his college talk tour, inspiring young'uns on the excitement and hard work that a career in voices entails. Luckily, during one of these tours in April of 1978, Mel met Walt Mitchell at Onondaga Community College in Syracuse, NY, which would begin what was to become the most extensive collection of interviews the voice man had ever given. Nearly 7 hours were ultimately recorded

thanks to Walt's perseverance, helped ably by old-time radio buff Mary Lou Wallace, giving many details on the whole of his professional and personal life with emphasis on Mel's relatively undocumented recording career. How he treated these two fans was a tribute to Mel's generosity: knowing the two couldn't make it to an 11 a.m. talk, Mel invited the couple to his hotel room where he signed some records Walt brought, gave them both already specially signed 8x10s of himself, and spoke for an hour into Walt's portable Sony recorder (the same kind Mel had at home). It was the beginning of a friendship both sides would relish for the final decade of Mel's life.

"Every so often he'd catch us off guard with a funny ad-lib," says Walt, "and we'd all have a good laugh. That was one of the nicest things about the interviews. Although we were there to learn as much from Mr. Blanc as we could, Mary Lou and I also had a lot of fun before and during the interview. And we didn't have to ask him if he would do his famous voices for us while we were taping. The voices just came rolling out of him quite naturally in the course of the conversation.

"On one of these talks, after we'd spoken into his reel-to-reel tape recorder for 48 minutes (at my request; I always taped our talks), he later confessed that his doctor had given him holy heck (or words to that effect). Mel had emphysema at the time. What I did *not* know was that his doctor had given him strict orders that he was therefore not to speak continuously for more than 30 minutes at a time. Mel had truly gone above and beyond, far more than anybody should expect from a friend."

The three became great friends over the years, trading calls, visits, and letters. Walt described Mel's stationery as "…unique. His name is printed in large blue capital letters near the upper left-hand corner of the sheet, at an angle, and underneath his handwriting there is a large light-gray-and-white drawing of Bugs Bunny's head."

In the December 21, 1979 edition of the *Los Angeles Times*, Cathleen Watkins gave the following description of one of Mel's talks to college audiences. "Mel Blanc steps onto the stage. He is calm, relaxed. The near-capacity audience greets him with eager applause and he smiles warmly. On a screen flash slides of Bugs Bunny, Porky Pig, and Daffy Duck, and Blanc, who provides the voices for these and others, tells the story of each figure." After explaining more, such as the seldom-done Wile E. Coyote, he draws applause and questions from the audience. And of course at the end of all speaking engagements he would give Porky Pig's final closing line, "*Th-th-th*-that's all, folks!"

Mel told Walt Mitchell in 1978, "I love my work. I love to entertain people, and tomorrow I'm speaking at the 59th college in a little over a year. I've broken the attendance record at every college I've spoken at, so the kids must be cartoon freaks!"

Mel's legacy was burning brighter than it ever did. In 1978 the Road Runner was added to the title of Bugs' long-running TV series to produce *The Bugs Bunny/Road Runner Show* which ran until 1985. The catchy "This Is It" song by the award-winning Jerry Livingston and Mack David is still recalled to this day:

> *Overture, curtain, lights*
> *This is it. We'll hit the heights*
> *And oh what heights we'll hit*
> *On with the show, this is it!*

Plus, Mel kept going strong in other markets. In that same 1978 his Talk-To-Me Books were being advertised. They were small (supposedly break-proof) records that were laminated right onto the book pages, put out by Fisher Price for about $20 for a player and book, and $4 for other books. *The New York Times* was hesitant about the device, couching its comments with "The nice thing about it all is that although a lazy child

Mel and Twiki.

can just listen, the printed word is still there for those who care." At least one Blanc/Bugs record was done for the series.

Mel was also part of the occasional live-action feature, one of the most successful being *Buck Rogers in the 25th Century*. The TV pilot was first released as a feature and then as a series which ran for two years (32 episodes). *The New York Times'* March 30, 1979 review of the film was mixed, but wrote that "they've added a relentlessly cute drone, Twiki (voice by Mel Blanc), who's approximately the size of your extra gasoline can and who carries around his neck a computer named Theo, who looks like the headlight off a Cadillac and talks like a doctor in a commercial about stomach distress." Though Buck's lines were charged with flippancy, it was usually Mel's very, very sparse comments as Twiki which stole the scenes. Indeed, the little droid even received the last line in the pilot of this *Star Wars* clone: "Buck, you're my kinda guy."

12 | All, Folks

On October 16, 1980 *The Hollywood Reporter* announced that Mel would be creating the title role of Heathcliff for a Saturday morning cartoon series of the same name for Filmways, to be broadcast on ABC.

It was the beginning of Mel's final decade — a decade that would see him with more honors and tributes than any other.

A Salute to Mel Blanc was given on February 9, 1981, at the Samuel Goldwyn Theatre of the Academy of Motion Picture Arts & Sciences. Mel provided a slide show illustrating how he accomplished the voices of his famous characters, plus the Oscar-winning short cartoons "Knighty Knight Bugs," "Speedy Gonzales" and "Birds Anonymous" were also screened. (This was basically the same talk that Mel had given at the colleges and universities during the previous four years.) Chuck Jones was the master of ceremonies, with tributes given by old friends Kirk Douglas, Walter Lantz, and June Foray.

The Pacific Pioneer Broadcasters also honored Mel at their January 15, 1982 luncheon at the Sportsmen's Lodge in Studio City. At this event, Mel was especially surprised and gratified when a certain telegram was read congratulating him on that occasion. It was from President Ronald Reagan. Mel was so proud of that, he subsequently read it aloud into a microphone while recording one of his conversations with Mary Lou and Walt.

Dear Mel:

Nancy and I are delighted to join your family, friends, and colleagues in this very special tribute to you.

In awarding you their Carbon Mike Award, The Pacific Pioneer Broadcasters recognize one of the most amazing and unique show business careers. You have brought more than 400 different characters into the lives of children and adults the world over in the process of brightening our spirits and making us laugh.

Though we usually don't see your face, we know you're there — behind our favorite cartoon personalities.

You have our best wishes for a very successful program and for continued health and happiness in the years ahead.

Sincerely,
Ronald Reagan

Meantime, rereleases of earlier cartoons packaged into new stories were all in vogue. *The New York Times* wrote of *The Looney, Looney, Looney Bugs Bunny Movie* (1981): "Bugs and his friends have legions of admirers already. Here's a film to win them a generation of new ones." Their favorite bit was Bugs against the dragon in "Knighty Knight Bugs" and its groaning puns of characters like Sir Osis of Liver and Sir Loin of Beef.

The following year, upon release of *Bugs Bunny's 3rd Movie: 1001 Rabbit Tales, The New York Times* again praised, "The movie effortless interweaves what seems to be two dozen old cartoons into a comparatively coherent entity that is always something of a lark and, occasionally, as hilarious as one remembers the shorts to have been years ago." As usual, Mel was mentioned right after Friz Freleng as one of the creators of the cartoons.

Mel and WB were/are inseparable. In 1982 he and Noel began a massive recording project at JEL Recording Studios in which Mel recorded the audio for fifty automated stage shows featuring Bugs, Daffy, and the gang, full of dialogue and song. It stemmed from a long-term contract between Warner-Blanc Audio Associates and JEL, under the direction of Noel and Bill Baldwin, Jr. For years, on a weekly basis, these new recordings of Mel's voices were also given to a variety of toys, watches, video games, websites, etc.

Mel continued to keep busy with charity work as well. In 1982, he made a public service film for the Shriners Hospitals about burn prevention. According to Theresa Danna, who worked on the film, "there were two versions: a shorter one (24 minutes) of live action and animation with Mel and his Warner Bros. characters, and a longer one with that same footage plus documentary-type footage of patients at one of the Shriners hospitals specializing in treatment of burns.

The short version of the 'Ounce of Prevention' video shows Mel in a TV production control room with Bugs, Daffy, Tweety, and Sylvester. Then they go into a home with two kids, where Bugs shows them burn hazards in the kitchen. For example, the pot on the stove changes to animation and shows how the handle should be turned inward so kids don't pull on it. Then in the garage, Sylvester gives the kids magic glasses, which allows them to see gas fumes — which take the form of an animated snake. Tweety helps the kids in the bathroom, where the tub becomes an animated caldron to teach about water getting too hot. In the bedroom, Daffy shows the kids how to burnproof the room. The smoke detector turns to animation, as well as the door (when they say to feel if it's hot before opening it). Mel does all

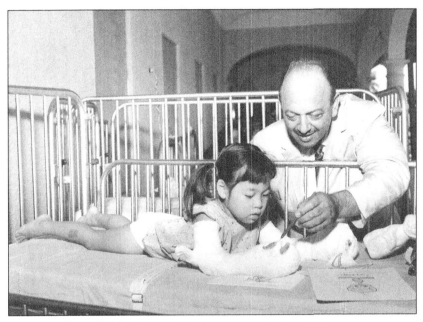

Shriners Hospitals' children's burn center in the 1970s.

the voices for the animated burn hazards. Then it goes back to the control room with Mel and the four characters to wrap it up.

"I was told that it was the only film (at least at that time) in which Mel appeared on camera with his animated characters. I think he had also done some short PSAs for Shriners Hospitals. Mel was a member of the Al Malaikah Shrine Temple in Los Angeles." It was co-produced by Joel Douglas (Kirk's oldest son) and Bill Baldwin, Jr., with Noel serving as executive producer.

As of 1982, as a long feature in *Entrepreneur* magazine stated, Mel had given 137 lectures to college students in the last 3 years. After showing stills of his characters and how he creates the voice, and showing the three Oscar-winning cartoons he made, the kids eat it up. After the hour-long talk, a half-hour's worth of questions follow.

Ron Smith biographer wrote, "After each performance, many of the 'broadcast junkies' (who want to break into TV or radio) gather around Mel in the same manner as moths to a flame. They want books autographed. They want to know what kind of mikes Mel used. They want to hear more about taping on wire before magnetic tape was invented. And many of them want jobs. Could Mel give them a recommendation? If they came to Hollywood, could he help get them work?

A *Variety* ad congratulation Mel on 50 years in show business.

CHARACTERS COPYRIGHT HANNA-BARBERA PRODUCTIONS

"Each one he answers patiently, giving the best advice he can. 'No one can help you out. You have to make your own breaks. Learn as much as you can, then go out in the world and tough it out.'

"There are times when it's tough being a celebrity. Watching Mel on the road in between appearances proves this. All smiles as the flashbulbs go off, and then as he climbs into the limousine he will slump into an exhausted rest. Very seldom does he talk, resting for the next appearance. After a fifteen-minute drive, he's at the next television station, listening to the program director praise him and of course he's smiling graciously. Then with a quick make-up touch-up, the lights come on and yet another talk show host in yet another city says, 'Bugs Bunny, Porky Pig, Daffy Duck. Those people we all know and love are all done by our next guest, Mel Blanc.' Once again, he launches into the story about Porky and the pig farm, he chats about what it was like being with Jack Benny, he talks about Hollywood."

This was around the time that Noel and Blanc Communications staff writer Ron Smith began collaborating on a book on Mel to be entitled *Mel Blanc: Fifty Years of Magical Voices* (copyright SUPDOC, Inc.). The book was never published. *Variety* did, however, publish an excerpt from the book in their April 29, 1983 "Tribute to Mel Blanc."

Entertainment Weekly ran a feature article on Mel in their May-June, 1983 issue, telling of the Blancs' work on Warner's new franchise of family restaurants featuring their characters, called Gadgets Restaurants. Two had been opened by this point, with 80 more planned. Noel and Mel provided WB voices for the large robots (Robotic Animatoons) inhabiting each Gadgets. They also recorded about 1400 different popular songs ("in 10-minute musicals") from the past 25 years done (Elvis, Beatles, etc.) on every conceivable subject. Mel loved the place. "They are the most beautiful things I've ever seen. In addition to the shows, there's a game room for the kids, a lounge for the adults, and plenty of supervision. And their food is terrific. We were there for one of the openings and the lines started at eleven in the morning and continued well past midnight."

The Gadgets musical shows (which ran about ten minutes each) had a theme for each program. One theme might be vaudeville songs, while another show would feature songs by The Beatles or The Rolling Stones, or music from the 1940s. Once, Mel was asked if he ever in his life imagined that the day would come when Yosemite Sam would be singing a Rolling Stones song. Chuckling at the recollection, Mel replied, "Never!" The song assigned to Sam was certainly appropriate, however: "(I Can't Get No) Satisfaction!"

And the tributes continued.

Mel received the first Life Achievement Award given by the Show Business Shrine Club at the Sportsmen Lodge in Studio City on October 23, 1983. Mel had been a past president of the Shrine's only show business club. It was Mel's 57th year as a performer.

That was the same day that Los Angeles Mayor Bradley proclaimed

Something you don't see every day.

"Mel Blanc Day" in LA to celebrate his 57th anniversary in show business.

Then, March 28, 1984 saw the introduction of a permanent Mel Blanc memorabilia exhibit — "50 years in the making" — on display in the Smithsonian Institute's Museum of American History in Washington D.C. Included were magazine and newspaper articles from the '40s, photos, videos, movie posters and a Bugs Bunny alarm clock that speaks on the hour. It was dedicated in the Presidential Suite of the MAH, followed by a discussion of his voices and their evolutions, plus a slide show of his characters, voicing them at the same time. The performance also again featured screenings of three of his Oscar-winning cartoons: "Knighty Knight Bugs," "Speedy Gonzales," and "Birds Anonymous." Tickets for the event sold out almost immediately.

While in D.C., the White House invited Mel and Estelle to meet Ronald Reagan — the first time the two had met in 40 years; way back, Reagan (a Democrat then) had once asked Mel to entertain with him at the Boys Club of Brentwood.

At a noontime news briefing, Mel was introduced to the press by Deputy Press Secretary Larry Speakes as "Mr. Pierre Lapin [French for

Mel addresses the Smithsonian.

rabbit], visiting from France. He's a renowned scholar in the field of cybernetic cellulose performance, a subject the President himself has increasingly had great interest in." In a heavy Gallic accent Mel apologized for his poor English, saying, "In this country, I talk like a rabbit." And went right into Bugs Bunny, at which point the press got the early April Fool's Day joke and began tearing up their notes.

Mel Blanc's star on the Hollywood Walk of Fame. PHOTO COURTESY OF STEPHEN COX.

The honors continued.

Though Mel had received his star at 6385 Hollywood Blvd. on the Walk of Fame on February 8, 1960, his best friend Bugs also got one 25 years later, on December 21, 1985. Later that year, at a gala in New York's Museum of Modern Art in September, celebrities gave their take on Warner Bros. characters at a showing of the studio's animation art. Bill Murray said, "Bugs never did anything for anybody that didn't serve Bugs Bunny — that's why he's a star." Jeff Goldblum, Jeremy Irons, Cher, Steve Martin, and others were also there for the sold out screening.

Mary Lou Wallace states, "Mel was bothered by an eye infection over Labor Day weekend in 1985 and was going to wait until after the holiday to have it treated. Estelle insisted that he go to the Emergency Room at St. John's Medical Center in Santa Monica but when either

Mel or Estelle spoke with Mel's doctor on the phone, he told them to go to the UCLA Medical Center instead. While they were waiting at the hospital, Mel got up to walk across the hall and collapsed….his heart had stopped! They rushed him into a nearby room to work on him and Estelle was told later on that if Mel had been anywhere else, he would have died. I seem to recall that there was a problem with a heart valve and Mel had surgery in June 1986 (we visited with him about 2 weeks after the surgery)."

To some voice actors, Mel Blanc seemed arrogant. To others, he was utterly accessible. In 1986 famed cartoon writer Mark Evanier hired him (at considerable cost) for a TV special and found him the most gracious professional in the world when asked to re-read his Bugs Bunny lines. "But Blanc didn't object," Mark recalled, "not a peep." As they continued, a crowd began to gather outside from the adjoining studio. "Mel looked through the glass and I'm sure it wasn't the first time he'd seen those expressions. He turned back to his microphone and launched into a dialogue of Porky and Yosemite Sam having an argument. Then came Sylvester announcing he was going to eat Tweety, then Tweety saying he taut he taw a puddy tat, then Daffy, then Foghorn…As he wound up a three-minute impromptu concert, the spectators broke into wild, loving applause. Mel came out of the booth with a fistful of color photo handouts of himself and signed one for each of them. As each dancer said his or her name, Mel greeted them in the voice of Porky or Daffy, while scribbling out, 'To (name), Best wishes, Mel Blanc' on a picture. The dancers scampered back to their rehearsal with their treasures and I walked Mel out to his car" where they talked for an hour about cartoons and Mel regaled the young man with stories of the radio and Jack Benny.

(One such non sequitur occurs in Irving A. Fein's book on Jack Benny, in which he relates an interesting later "meeting" between Mel and Jack Benny after Jack had decided to sneak into a viewing of America's first porn movie, *Deep Throat*. Too embarrassed to buy tickets or even be seen there, he and Fein "parked that day on a side street, and as we approached the theater, Jack with his hat pulled low to cover his face, the earlier show broke, and the audience streamed out. Who was exciting but Mel Blanc, and when he spotted us, he yelled, 'Hi, Jack, you'll love it!'")

Obviously, Mel Blanc had no desire to retire. He was having too much fun, even if it was just recording original linking material for new WB compilation films. On November 26, 1986 *The New York Times* reported the release of one such film, *Porky Pig in Hollywood*, writing that "this 1 3/4 hour collection should fascinate anyone interested in the history of animation." And the money was good. Until the mid-1960s Mel admitted to never making more than $20,000 total at Warner Bros., but now, with 20-something Noel Blanc as his business manager, Mel could command $50,000 to $100,000 for saying a single sentence in a TV commercial, or

just providing linking dialogue for new episodes of cartoons, because even newer directors knew he was worth it.

While working on "The Duxorcist" (his next to last short), Mel said, "If I said to them [writers/directors], 'I'm sorry, but Daffy wouldn't say something like this,' it was changed without debate."

Mel wanted Noel to take over voicing his main stable of characters for him, which Noel was reluctant to do at first. "After much persuasion I finally convinced him, and we began practicing together. It didn't require much, though. My son picked them up as if he'd been doing them all his life." And "It's true. Noel performs my characters so well, I could sue him."

When Mel had his 80th birthday party at Warner Bros. on the Burbank lot, he kept getting asked that age-old question: "Mel, when are you going to retire?" "The day I drop," Mel replied. He considered Duffy and Bugs and the rest as his other children, as were the countless children who laughed at them. Why give all that up just to sit around the house? "I feel blessed, which is why I continue to record three or four days a week in my sixteen-track home studio."

His philosophy for a happy life was simple: enjoy yourself. Pick a career you love, not just for the financial satisfaction, and believe in yourself. Keep trying.

On June 1, 1988, Warner Brothers celebrated Mel's 80th birthday with a special luncheon hosted by WB chairman Robert A. Daly and Noel. The special present: a turquoise Edsel driven by a life-size Bugs Bunny dressed in a tux. *The Los Angeles Times* was on hand to snap pictures and write up the story. Mel said at the time he'd wanted an Edsel for at least 20 years because there were so few of them and they were hard to find. Noel paid about $20,000 for it from a collector in Texas. It was transported (not driven) so it would arrive in pristine condition.

That September Mel's final short subject cartoon, "Night of the Living Duck," was released. It was, according to Warner Bros., the first Hollywood cartoon ever selected to be part of the New York Film Festival. The new, 7-minute cartoon had comic-book-loving Daffy singing "Monsters Lead Such Interesting Lives (They Don't Live 9 to 5)" in a nightmare sequence, in a Mel Torme voice, in front of classic movie monsters — everything from the Bride of Frankenstein to the Blob.

On November 23rd, Mel was interviewed by *The New York Times* on his just-published autobiography, *That's Not All, Folks*. In it, he gave a joyful overview of his career and mused a bit on his favorite characters, his favorite of course being Bugs Bunny.

Mel celebrated Christmas two days early that year by donning a Santa cap and handing out pieces of carrot cake to local children and doing voices in front of Warner Bros. Studios to inaugurate a new Looney Tunes holiday billboard. As the new sign lit up in neon, fans could watch a mechanical Wyle E. Coyote chasing the Road Runner amidst lights and "Seasons Greetings." A duplicate was raised on the Sunset Strip. It was to be his last public appearance.

On May 19, 1989, Mel and Noel Blanc finished voicing an Oldsmobile TV commercial. Mel's last words on it had been, "That's all, folks." The next day, complaining of chest pains, Mel entered the Cedars-Sinai Medical Center in Los Angeles. While he was in the hospital he fell from his bed and broke his hip, complicating his treatment. Mel Blanc died there of heart disease and emphysema on July 10, 1989 at 2:30 p.m. He was 81 years old.

"I guess everybody in the world loved him," said Noel at the time. "What more is there than that?"

Variety began its lengthy obituary: "A silence has fallen over Toontown — and everywhere that cartoons thrive." Laurence Olivier died the day after Mel. As one dual-obituary reported, "Olivier was indisputably Britain's most famous actor, one of the best-known in the world. But his audience was only a fraction of Mel Blanc's."

At the funeral on July 13th hundreds of fans and celebrities turned out for the sad event. Mel was buried at a private ceremony in Beth Olam Cemetery. It is located within Hollywood Forever Cemetery, which can be found at 6000 Santa Monica Boulevard in Hollywood.

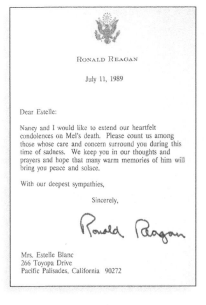

RONALD REAGAN

July 11, 1989

Dear Estelle:

Nancy and I would like to extend our heartfelt condolences on Mel's death. Please count us among those whose care and concern surround you during this time of sadness. We keep you in our thoughts and prayers and hope that many warm memories of him will bring you peace and solace.

With our deepest sympathies,

Sincerely,

Ronald Reagan

Mrs. Estelle Blanc
266 Toyopa Drive
Pacific Palisades, California 90272

Timing wasn't necessarily good for Warner Bros., as the *Los Angeles Times* on that same day carried a huge write-up of the planned "Bugs Bunny at 50" celebration that was set to kick off soon, including a Hollywood party and parade. Mel was to have been a centerpiece of the festivities. Noel, as usual, was there to pinch-hit. Also, Oldsmobile was worried whether it might be considered in questionable taste to air Mel's commercial as part of their "this is not your father's Oldsmobile" ad campaign. The concern was for the fact that Mel had died before the commercial's tech work was completed. It was feared that the car company's intent could be misinterpreted by the public as being crass. The end result was that Noel reshot the commercial, doing a few of the cartoon voices himself on camera. The original version in which Mel appeared was never aired.

Warner had also scheduled a six-story high Bugs, costing $300,000, to fly as one of the balloons in Macy's Thanksgiving Day parade. Everyone wanted a piece of Bugs in 1990 when the *Bugs at 50* logo was set to stamp everything from home videos to records. Six Flags and Brock's Candy had recently signed with Warner as corporate sponsors, and lots of tie-ins with soft drinks and snack foods were lined up, not forgetting retail chains like Macy's, Sears, and others. Bugs was second only to Mickey Mouse as far as icons go — ranking dead even with Snoopy, in fact. (When Mickey turned 60 two years earlier, Disney cleaned up at least $100 million in

additional sales.) Warner also planned several black-tie Bugs Bunny birthday parties, more TV specials, and *lots* more book tie-ins, plus everything
from T-shirts, watches, and stuffed animals to mugs and lunch boxes, all
sporting the 50th anniversary logo.

On August 4, 1989, a giant tribute was paid to Mel at The Directors'
Guild of America headquarters in Los Angeles by 400 friends, animators,

Kirk Douglas and Noel.

and Warner Brothers executives. The speakers included Noel Blanc, long-
time friend Kirk Douglas, animation director Friz Freleng, June Foray,
Gary Owens, Walter Matthau, and Sheldon Leonard. Estelle was ill and
did not attend. Ed Bleier was the emcee, screening short clips of Warner
cartoons, early appearances on Jack Benny, and the recent Oldsmobile ad
done with Noel that had originally been scheduled to air later that month.
Owens said, "He was the soundtrack of our lives. It's impossible not to
hear Mel's voice in your head." June Foray read a letter from George Bush:
"Mel left this world a happier place."

Fritz Freleng (reportedly the model for Mel's rip-roaring, half-pint
Yosemite Sam) said, "He will never die. He will live on through the
voices of these characters for eternity." In another letter read by June
Foray, Chuck Jones wrote of Mel's "virtuosity, his almost limitless ability
to understand the essence of a character and to invest himself into its

being." A letter from Ronald Reagan was also quoted: "He is the standard by which all who follow in his path will be judged."

Walter Matthau had been Mel's neighbor for 20 years. He spoke of only seeing him 5 times during that time, but described him as a "quiet, gentle, cordial, and pleasant man" who would delight the neighborhood children with his voices when they would stop by on Halloween. He told of Mel's license plate — KMIT ("kiss my backside" in Yiddish). Gary Owens played tapes of Mel cracking up his co-workers with Serbian and Yiddish expressions while doing radio spots. Sheldon Leonard recalled Jack Benny's writers who would say, of a dubious line, "Let's protect it, let's give it to Mel." Kirk Douglas spoke of Mel's phonetically written letters to him. Bill Hanna and Joe Barbera sent their Head of Recording Operations, Gordon Hunt, to read their message: "He did much to build our company. He was many things to both of us, but most of all he was our friend."

The Oldsmobile spot, and sales reel made to accompany it, was unveiled: father and son bantering back and forth as Bugs Bunny and Yosemite Sam. Noel also read from Wordsworth's "Intimations of Immortality"...

> *"What though the radiance which was once so bright*
> *Be now for ever taken from my sight,*
> *Though nothing can bring back the hour*
> *Of splendour in the grass, or glory in the flower;*
> *We will grieve not, rather find*
> *Strength in what remains behind..."*

Noel said, "That says it all because a lot's going to remain behind, and we're going to hear his voice forever and ever."

Warner had purchased double page spreads in *Daily Variety* and *The Hollywood Reporter* on July 13th to run a special "Speechless" cartoon in tribute to Mel by artists Darrell Van Citters and Chris Buck from their animation department. It was a beautifully poignant drawing of a microphone in a yellow spotlight, with all WB characters bowing, off to the side, in silent respect. *THR* sold out of their issue, and *Variety* received many calls requesting unstapled copies of the poster for framing. The image was so powerful that Warner itself ran more than a hundred extra copies just for execs and others in their offices who were so touched by the tribute.

On October 7, 1989 at the Mill Valley Film Festival, a 90-minute Salute to Mel Blanc was given, including the screening of cartoon classics and Oscar-winners, with Noel Blanc in attendance. Noel quoted Rich Little: "The big question is, was the cartoon invented for Mel Blanc, or was Mel Blanc invented for the cartoon?"

At the time, Noel told Dr. Demento on his radio show that he was now doing Mel's voices, but he couldn't duplicate *what* he did. "With 1500 voices, it's going to take an army," Noel said. He was there to discuss

This ad ran in *Daily Variety* and *The Hollywood Reporter* in tribute to Mel. CHARACTERS © WARNER BROS. ALL RIGHTS RESERVED

Bugs' coming 50th birthday, plus the new pay number, 1-900-VIP-BUGS. For $6.95 a minute you could get a very personalized birthday greeting, whenever you want the phone to ring, calling up anyone. Congratulations, Happy Anniversary, Get Well and other "audio cards" were also available. 1400 names had been recorded by Noel, sitting in a database, waiting for orders.

On the first anniversary of Mel's death a five-foot white marble headstone with the inscription, "That's All Folks — Man of 1000 Voices — Beloved Husband and Father" was set upon his grave.

In August of 1992 Mel's 4,000 square-foot ranch-style home came on the market for a $1,575,000 asking price. Estelle decided the house was just too big for her by herself, so she moved closer to Noel. Of course she missed the Bugs Bunny spa, with its mosaic of Bugs in the bottom.

Later, an ad appeared in *The Hollywood Reporter* on January 26, 1993 to report that the 2nd portion of Mel's estate — the animation art collection — was to be auctioned off at Superior Galleries in Beverly Hills in June. In a November 17, 1992 letter quoted in the ad from Noel regarding the first estate auction, he wrote, "Since my father's collection was so personal to my mother and me, I hesitated at first to

call you, Ira, because you had never auctioned animation material, but knowing your reputation in the coin and manuscript fields, I felt that you might be the perfect choice." The letter continued to commend Superior Galleries' Ira Goldberg for his previous work, and the second sale was an even bigger success. Over 250 animation cells, many signed, had been collected by Mel through the years, and sold to collectors for a small fortune.

Though Mel was gone, his legacy continued, sparked at times with some controversy. One of the most public events came on July 24, 1994 when Noel filed suit against MCA/Universal Studios for using Mel's original Dino voice in the new big-budget movie, *The Flintstones*. Though California Civil Code section 990 permitted the use of a deceased person's image and voice in a film without compensation, the Dino bark was sampled from the original *Flintstones* TV show. An attorney for the

Blanc estate was quoted in *Variety* as saying, "Hanna-Barbera still pays the estate when they use his voice in cartoons, why shouldn't Universal?" When MCA made a very low settlement offer, Blanc attorney Jonathan Weiss rightly claimed, "That's not even close to the ballpark, not even in the same city." Their main concern was lack of screen credit, and that the Blanc family should have a share of the licensing profits, estimated at $1 billion.

The suit sought $1 million in damages for "commercial misappropriation, breach of contract and civil conspiracy." A hearing was set for October 17th, and an undisclosed settlement was reached. The part of the settlement that became the most visible was significant, and an important victory for Noel on behalf of his illustrious father: MCA/Universal agreed to place Mel's name in the cast list appearing at the film's end when the movie would eventually be released on home video. There, Mel is credited as the voice of Dino. (The original theatrical prints contained an attempt at humor by listing the credit to read, "Dino as Dino.")

Things were still fine, and continue to be, with Warner Studios. Soon after, the Blanc estate and Warner Bros. forged a new alliance — the Warner-Blanc Audio Library which consisted of approximately 550 songs and voices of every character in Mel's repertoire which he had begun setting down at his multi-track studio in 1958 amid fears of a future when he'd be around no longer to record. 15 hours of new tapes of Mel's material had been discovered in 1996, and Noel expected to find more soon.

In August of 1997 Mel's expensive, expansive car collection went under the hammer in a Christie's auction. Combined with a Rolls-Royce from Frank Sinatra and the Ferrari Mille Miglia Spyder which won the 1953 Daily Express trophy, the autos were expected to raise up to $12 million. Kept in a specially-built showroom with a dust-free, temperature-controlled environment (and also containing high security and specially-commissioned automotive art), three of the cars alone were expected to go for a million dollars. Miles Morris of Christie's told the press, "The condition of the best of three Ferrari Daytonas, a black 1973 365 GTS/4, is quite unbelievable. It's the best Christie's has ever seen. It's almost certainly better than when Enzo Ferrari sold the car."

 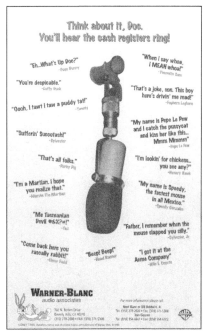

The Warner-Blanc Audio Library included new material recorded by Mel in the years before his death.

Noel had caught the car bug from Mel. One day in Beverly Hills a Daytona Spyder (Ferrari) caught his eye and he followed the owner home, asking him to name his price. Money changed hands on the spot. Now it was worth between $375,000 and $475,000. But as Noel told Christie's, Noel "has turned his attention to hot rods and admits these cars no longer get the attention and driving they deserve. Because he's a perfectionist he's decided to sell them now while they are still in pristine condition." Even the Daytona Spyder had a mere 3,427 miles on the odometer.

In 1999, Mel's 1957 Edsel Citation was part of another stable of celebrity cars (Frank Sinatra, Greta Garbo, Disney's Herbie, etc.) which went on display in the Hollywood Gallery at the Petersen Automotive Museum in Los Angeles. Completely restored by Warner Bros., it was also filled with stuffed animals of their characters and a photo of Mel being presented with the keys by Bugs from Mel's 80th birthday celebration. The car had been sitting in front of Noel's Rodeo Drive home since Mel's passing.

Of course Mel's death never did diminish his impact on society as a cult icon. New technology has made him fresh for each generation. Around 1998 a line of talking watches featuring Warner characters were released under a joint venture from Warner-Blanc, digitizing some of Mel's vast back catalog to use in new items. The Mel Blanc Voice Watch Collection by Armitron was produced to celebrate what would have been his 90th birthday. Daffy spitting, "You're dethpicable," Tweety chirping, "I taut I taw a puddy cat," and the ever-popular Bugs asking the eternal question, "What's up, doc?" were a few choices emanating for 10 or 15 seconds from a small computer chip and miniature speaker at the press of a button. The price for each: under $50.

Noel Blanc, married one day after Mel's 90th birthday, began a tour of the country to promote the watches, and Mel. Always Mel.

That's All Folks!

Tributes

Bob Bergen The modern voice of Porky Pig

I wanted to be Porky Pig since I was 5 years old. My folks were a bit baffled. Plus, it's not the kinda thing a Jewish mother wishes for her kid, let me tell you. I grew up in the Midwest 'til I was 14, when my Dad moved the family to Los Angeles. I was thrilled since I knew LA is where cartoons were produced. Being that I wanted to be Porky I figured the best way to get the gig was to contact Mel Blanc. So, I turned to the phone book. LA is a huge place and has dozens of phone books. So my Dad traveled the city, gathering phone books from Pasadena, to Beverly Hills, Culver City, etc. I searched the books for Mel Blanc. Being from the Midwest I didn't know the concept of unlisted numbers.

I found an "E. Blanc" listing in the Pacific Palisades book. I remembered seeing Mel on a show called *Wonderama* when I was a kid where he mentioned his wife's name was Estelle. So I called the number, and sure enough this was his residence. Once he got through "How did you get my number??" he was very nice. He gave me some sound advice regarding the importance of original characters rather than impressions, as well as the necessity of an agent. Incidentally, I taped the conversation. I listened to this tape endlessly for a week. Unfortunately, I listened too much because the tape broke. I was devastated and threw it away.

Fortunately my mother retrieved it and threw it in the back of a drawer. About two years ago she told me she was cleaning out a drawer and found a tape labeled "conversation with Mel Blanc." I instantly knew what it was, of course. I took the tape to a buddy at a studio and he spliced it back together and digitally enhanced the recording. I have that conversation up on my website, bobbergen.com, on the page labeled "cool clips." Sadly, much of the conversation was lost when it was broken. This was the part of our conversation where I asked Mel if he was still doing cartoons today.

He told me that WB had closed down their cartoon shorts department in the '60s. But he said he was still recording projects with the Looney Tunes. That week, he said, he was finishing up recording the soundtrack for an "Ice Capades" type show with the Looney Tunes. He mentioned the name of the studio where he was booked but not the date or time. So, being the ballsy 14 year old that I was, I called the studio and pretended to be one of Mel Blanc's "people" confirming his recording session for that week. I was able to find out an exact day and time he was going to be there. I told my mother that I was skipping school and she was going to take me to see Mel Blanc work. Mom was cool and said, "OK!"

When we arrived at the studio, I told the receptionist we were guests of Mel Blanc. When we walked into the recording booth I told the producer we were friends of the receptionist. I learned that a li'l bullshit goes a long way in show biz!! Through the glass I could see Mel, sitting in a chair, dressed in a brown suit and tie. As he went from voice to voice in between puffs from a cigarette I was in heaven. He physically took on the persona of each character. This was one of the most important lessons I ever learned as an actor. In fact, to this day one of the things I teach my own voice-over students is "if you physically play the character, the voice will follow." I owe this bit of wisdom to Mr. Blanc.

What surprised me at the session was that he didn't sound as much like the characters as he used to. He did Tweety and it just wasn't right. I figured it was due to the fact he was older. Not to mention the car accident several years earlier that must have taken a toll on him. But when they played it back it sounded great! I asked the producer what they did to make his voice sound more in character in the playback? She told me they sped up his voice. I asked her when did they start speeding up his voice? She told me when he first got the part of Porky in the '30s. Years later I learned from a producer, who worked at WB in the early days, that Mel wasn't the original voice of Porky. A man named Joe Dougherty, who really stuttered, originated the character. But due to his stutter the cartoons came in too long. So they sped him up to get them in at the appropriate length. Those were the days before tape, and cartoons were recorded onto film. The budgets for film stock were so huge that the powers that be at WB asked the animation department to find someone who could control the stutter so as to not use as much film stock. They'd hired Mel to voice a drunk in a bull costume for a cartoon and were so thrilled with his work (Bob Clampett *loved* his hiccups!!) they hired him to voice Porky. Incidentally, he played that drunken bull in the only Porky cartoon in which he worked but did not play Porky.

At the end of that "Ice Capades" session, when he finished, Mel gave me an autograph. I have it framed on a wall in my office.

I only met him one other time, at a bookstore years later where he was autographing his autobiography. I reminded him of the phone conversation and recording session, and he politely acknowledged he remembered, though I'm sure he didn't. But he was sweet to fake it.

After Mel passed away I found out that his family was having an estate sale, which I attended. I saw his home recording set up, his pool with what looked like a tiled Bugs Bunny at the bottom, and tons of memorabilia. I purchased a large brass key that says, "Mel Blanc, honorary mayor of Pacific Palisades," along with tiny Porky and Tweety figures. About a year later I recorded my first gig for Warner Brothers, playing Porky and Tweety in *Tiny Toons*. Those tiny figures were my good luck charms.

I'm honored to be one of a handful of actors who voice the classic Looney Tunes today. But I'll be the first to tell you that none of us can replace Mel. I believe him to be one of the great actors of our time, up there with Olivier and Barrymore. I don't think I come close to being as good as, or sounding exactly like Mel. I'm often asked if I "do" Mel Blanc when I record the Looney Tunes? The answer is, no. I do can't "do" Mel. None of us can, in my humble opinion. But I do my damnedest to uphold the integrity and dignity of Porky, Tweety, etc. As do many others who also voice the Looney Tunes today. But there will only be one Mel Blanc.

Stephen Cox Author of books on *The Beverly Hillbillies, The Addams Family* and *The Munsters*

I was fourteen or fifteen when I sat down and plunked out a letter to Mel Blanc on my mom's Smith Corona typewriter. Somehow, I had gotten the address of Hanna Barbera Studios on Cahuenga Blvd. in Hollywood, and I thought I'd send this interesting man a letter. Not really following his career with any conscious drive, I noticed that I was able to pick his voice out of a variety of characters while watching cartoons. As versatile as he was behind the microphone, I knew I could pick him out. I might have been inspired by the popular American Express commercial he had done, one where he was actually shown — as a human being, not an animated character. I knew I loved Bugs Bunny on Saturday mornings, and I also loved *The Flintstones* on afternoons on my local station. (Back then it was an absolute treat to catch any cartoons outside of the weekend mornings.)

I knew that I wanted to write this man and hopefully obtain his autograph. My letter was received and astonishingly, I received a personal, handwritten reply on his Bugs Bunny stationery along with a beautiful color-inscribed photograph. What followed was a very nice correspondence and eventually Mel supplied to me his phone numbers at home and work. Naturally, I wanted to talk with this singular genius; that was only a natural progression. While other kids my age were spending their hard-earned cash on arcades, better bicycles, and stereos, I was shelling out for long distance calls…which was fine with me. I ended up recording some of those conversations and I'm glad I did. I would call Mel on weekends, because it was less expensive and I never wanted to keep him long. I really tried to be polite, but I think he sensed my pleasure in it all and he was patient with me.

Mel and I struck up a friendship, although I'm not sure why he would pay such kind attention to a kid out in the Midwest. I was truly interested in his career and he always had patience to answer my questions and, on the phone, near the end of the conversation, I couldn't help but ask him to do a few voices. My favorites weren't Bugs Bunny or Daffy Duck. I wanted to hear Barney Rubble and Dino. Loved it! He always obliged. I can only imagine what his home life was like when that phone rang. I'm sure his wife, Estelle, was quite used to seeing him sitting on the sofa in the evenings barking into the telephone and doing voices for friends. It must've been a sight.

Mel was an extremely generous and kind friend and pen pal, almost always sending out handwritten replies and sometimes including an extra photo or maybe a poster or unusual Warner Bros. item. Years later, when I graduated from high school, I remember him sending me a beautiful Bugs Bunny tie and gold tie tack as a surprise.

I had the opportunity to see Mel give one of his popular college lectures at the University of Missouri Columbia. I'd never seen something like this. It was standing room only, with a crowd of people lined up to get in the auditorium and sadly many who were left out due to capacity. Mel had set aside seats for my sister and I, front row, and we watched in awe. Although he walked with a cane at that time, he left that in his dressing room. When he was introduced, he walked from behind the curtain over to the podium as the crowd rose to their feet with monstrous applause. This was no ordinary speaker, not a politician, not a motivational speaker. This was an icon of the entertainment industry, a man who every one of us in the audience could relate to because we'd all adored these cartoons he helped create, we'd all loved these characters he literally breathed life into. The audience went wild and burst with laughs at just the right moments in his speech, his delivery impeccable. He showed a few Warner Brothers shorts, and then took questions from the audience and amazed us with more vocals. No one wanted him to leave the stage. It was beautiful.

The first time I met Mel was in 1979 when my father took me on a little father/son trip to Los Angeles to finally meet a few of the people I'd been corresponding with and do a little of the tourism thing around Hollywood. I was in heaven. And to meet Mel Blanc at his home was quite extraordinary. I remember when we pulled up in his driveway in our rental car, Mel was at the door and said to us, "It looks like the Coxes have arrived." He and his wife were beautiful hosts. They showed us their house, his office, and even the new big screen television that was installed in their bedroom. It was a monstrosity, something like I'd never seen before. It had a three-color picture tube-like projection system right in front of the screen and Mel turned it on to demonstrate the state of the art television.

Mel was so great with me as I got my little tape recorder set up and conducted an "interview" with him. He helped me set it up so the microphone was just at the right placement to capture the best audio. Of course, he sent flying all kinds of samples of the voices and he answered my questions that I had written out and those I hadn't. That tape is one of those things I hate listening to today — and not because of Mel, but because I hadn't quite hit puberty yet and my voice was squeaking and I tried desperately to sound and appear grown up.

And over the years I did grow up and my relationship with Mel evolved into a nice guy-to-guy friendship and we talked about so many things: showbiz, women, life, work, all that stuff.

I recall visiting Mel at his ranch-style house in Pacific Palisades back in the late 1980s and stopping by one afternoon when he was just lounging around, taking it easy. He opened his door and greeted me and welcomed me in the house. He was taking it easy that day, just wearing a nice robe. We walked back into his day room where you could see the pool and the Jacuzzi outside the window. (His custom-built Jacuzzi had beautifully inlaid tile and at the bottom of the Jacuzzi was a large colorful tiled image of Bugs Bunny's face…the coolest thing I'd ever seen.)

I remember talking with Mel about many things that day and spent a couple of nice afternoon hours with him. What struck me at the time were the massive scars on his legs. He sat on a couch opposite me and I couldn't help but notice these large, Frankenstein-like scars and stitch marks running up his legs — certainly the aftermath of the major accident he'd been in a few decades prior. I never mentioned the scars, but it was something I remember. And probably for that reason, the conversation turned toward that accident. I was curious about the young kid who had recklessly hit him head-on. I asked Mel, "What would you do if this kid came up to you today and said, 'I'm the one that hit you in the car'… What would you say to him?"

Mel and Steve Cox in 1988, as Mel prepares to receive an honorary college degree. PHOTO COURTESY OF STEPHEN COX.

Mel paused for a few seconds and said, "I guess I'd call him an asshole," and then laughed a little bit.

I don't think anyone had ever asked him that and I'm not sure the thought ever crossed his mind. I remember him showing me the very bedroom and studio set up they'd arranged when he was recuperating from the accident and recording a season of *The Flintstones* while in bed. One of the large walk-in closets had been converted to a sound booth which housed the equipment and all. The cast would gather around Mel's hospital bed for the recording session. I asked him what would happen if he had to go to the restroom and he said, "I'd tell everyone, 'Okay folks, you'll have to leave for a few minutes' and then I'd use the bed pan because I couldn't get out of bed, I was in nearly a full body cast." It was amazing to stand there right in the room where Bea Benaderet, Alan Reed,

Mel, and Jean Vander Pyl recorded *The Flintstones* — albeit in the most uncommon of circumstances and manner. But right there in that room they were creating a cartoon classic.

One thing that I'm proud of is that I was instrumental in getting Mel his only honorary degree from an institution of higher learning. He couldn't believe it. An honorary college degree? As a guy who hadn't

finished high school, I think that receiving the honorary degree was a highlight for him near the end of his life. Yes, despite his lack of education, Mel had made a huge success of his life, but I also recall him advising me, around the time that I finished high school, that a college education was so important.

I was in my senior year at Park College (now Park University) in Kansas City, Missouri. I was finishing my four years and having the time of my life at this fantastic old liberal arts college with its beautiful, picturesque campus built into rolling hills with a river at its feet. The old buildings, with a majestic towering main hall, looked like an Ivy League school. The education was, and still is, parallel to none. I was closing in on my journalism / communication arts degree and something gave me the idea one day to nominate Mel for the honorary degree that year. Probably a long shot, at best. Secretly, I hoped and envisioned he would be there to accept the degree and I thought it would be quite an event for the college that year. Over the decades, just a few celebrities in the entertainment industry had been selected for this honor at Park, so I was determined to submit all the right paperwork and secure his nomination. After all, this guy was a pioneer in the industry who deserved the recognition. And this was Kansas City, the land where Walt Disney began his own animation empire.

Park accepted and approved this nomination and Mel was invited to the graduation ceremony by the President of the college, however, at this time, we learned that Mel's health was diminishing. He was having heart problems, was on a strict diet, and really was unable to travel. In a letter from his wife, Estelle, she mentioned to me that she was concerned that Mel might insist on attending and traveling out of town despite the physician's warnings. So, a way to still bestow this honor was devised. With another Communication Arts student, Les Bradley, I flew out to Los Angeles for a weekend and together we videotaped Mel's acceptance — in his cap and gown and all — and Mel Blanc received his Doctorate in Humane Letters in 1988. In his acceptance speech he naturally provided voices and related what an honor and surprise it was. He added, "Now I can say, 'What's up, doc?…Doc.'"

Joe Alaskey The current voice of Bugs Bunny, Daffy Duck, Sylvester, and Tweety

We all admire and revere Mel Blanc for his amazingly versatile and impressive acting abilities.

But, as a humble successor to his Looney Tunes workload, what strikes me as the most outstanding aspect of Mel's performances is not his talent itself. The true secret of Mel's success is the *power* of his delivery.

As we all know, Mel wasn't just a very good voice actor. No matter what character he's playing, his voice always grabs you. How and why was this guy so *driven* to entertain us? I believe Mel Blanc was determined to prove himself as the absolute best in the vocal media. Well, eventually, he did, didn't he?

Surely Mel recognized that his unique talents were as flexible and outrageous as the imaginative fields of radio and cartoons themselves. Once ensconced, he enhanced his vocal primacy by locking onto whatever qualities worked best for any given character (e.g.: a lisp, a cowardly quiver, sheer volume). Consciously or not, Mel used his skills to highlight himself as strongly as possible. This not only served the material best, of course, but also established that every voice he delivered, everywhere he worked, was his and his alone. The result was that we all know when we're hearing him; it could be nobody else.

Was it a conscious decision on his part to transcend his characters and emerge as the best in the business? I think so. I think his specific plan was to become indispensible, and he was, almost wherever he worked. Does this seem accidental to you?

"Aha!! I know that voice!! It's him!!"

Mel's powerful delivery instantly alerts the ear. And we know this will be good. And we instinctively know his power will work on any level: as a shockingly versatile comic actor, natural vocalist, sound effect, etc. So "Who will he be? What will he do? Where will he take us this time?!" If you've heard as much of Mel Blanc on OTR (old-time radio) as I have, you even begin to wonder *how* — not *if* — he'll earn real applause as he exits. And all this is based on performance alone.

But he didn't just wing it, all that genius. Mel was a very thoughtful performer. He did his homework. He wouldn't allow a single utterance — not even a gasp — slip by without endowing the moment with the most perfect approach he could find on the best (emotionally humorous) level, in all roles, great and small; from the wildest shout to the tiniest, most vulnerable utterance of "Mother!"

Who else could bellow like Mel in his heyday of Foghorn or Yosemite Sam? Who else could enact a laughing or crying fit like him? His drunks were the drunkest, but always with razor-sharp timing. His dynamism comes through even in the voice placements he found for key characters. Consider the switch made for Bugs Bunny with "A Wild Hare:" Gone was the toothy, "dumb"-sounding madcap, replaced by a sharp, nasal, New Yawk wiseacre. Sure, we know what he sounds like now, but can you remember the first time you heard it? It was an arresting improvement, making Bugs funnier and more lovable, and vocally designed to be exactly that.

If you think about it, though, a tough New Yorker seems an unlikely choice for such a casual character. The genius of that choice is that it's the voice of a tough little survivor *at leisure,* the flip side of all those WB gangster stars trying to survive their movie plots. Bugs' insouciance only enhances the material, as it puts him in control of any situation. And of course, it is unmistakably Mel's voice.

"What's up, Doc?" was Tex Avery's contribution, but Bugs Bunny's new voice, new attitude, the very essence of this redesigned character, was

Mel's. I wonder if even the best cartoon directors could have, or would have, suggested any specific vocal attributes for the myriad characters they handed Mel to play. Unless they knew every inch of his surprisingly versatile range as well as he did, the many choices for the many voices were probably mostly his, with some directorial fine-tuning.

Lucky that my pipes approximate his in the first place, I've found that in trying to preserve Mel's Looney Tunes characters, his highly concentrated work ethic has been the hardest characteristic for me to recreate. Mel's very healthy actor's ego, his pride in being the best, was part of that. (Daffy remains the cornerstone character for the direct expression of this tricky human trait.) I've sometimes said that, in trying to continue his work with new material, I've tried to think like Mel.

So how did Mel think? To give you some idea, this was an actor who asked himself questions like "How fast can I hiccup? And make it sound *real?* Which is the best way to make it sound funny?" and "What's the most annoying laugh I can do? And make *that* funny?" (Answer: Woody Woodpecker.) When Jack Benny's writers asked him to provide the voice of a British horse, he did his regular whinny, then added a polite, perfectly-timed "uh-haw!" Mel *thought* funny.

The primary example: At the outset of his WB career, in taking over Porky Pig, Mel instinctively realized that the funniest thing about having a stutter is not the stutter itself. The humor comes from the final choice made by the speaker, providing a surprise punch line every time, e.g.: "Oh, that mean little *m-m-mou* — Oh, the little rat!"

Meanwhile, many, many other voice actors were merely trying to *sound* funny (which is still true today). But the best voice actors, like Mel, Jack Mercer, and Paul Frees, were also skilled comedy writers, as good at seeing the big picture as they were at adlibbing.

Add to that the incredible, operatic range of his instrument and the effortless control of his acting talent, and there you have Mel Blanc's magic: unusual talent, self-taught skills, a funny mindset, and hard, hard work. Not to mention luck, in being in the right places at the right times during the Golden Age of American Entertainment.

Of course, luck can be fickle. It's well-known that, having become indispensible at Termite Terrace, Mel began receiving screen credit in lieu of a much-needed and much-wanted raise. I wish he'd gotten both. But I'm glad for him, because not only was he the first voice actor to get his name up there, he was very arguably the first to deserve it. And historically, of course, anybody who works at WB automatically deserves a raise. (That was a joke…Hadda be there, I guess.)

I believe Mel Blanc matched his amazing talents with the sheer personal force of his strategy to excel, not only establishing but maintaining his well-earned above-and-beyond status for most of his half-century career.

I think he took himself very seriously as an actor because he knew his work would last. No wonder he thought himself entitled to name his own successor, though WB has always held the legal rights to the Looney Tunes characters. I think that, professionally, Mel thought he'd earned that right. And maybe he was right.

Pat Fraley Voice-over Talent

I'm old enough to have had the opportunity of working with Mel Blanc. The first time I worked with him, I was a guest on the Hanna Barbara animated series, *Captain Caveman*, in the early Eighties. I walked into the booth and sat down to the left of Ken Mars, a fine character actor who people might remember for his performance as the Nazi writer in Mel Brooks' original movie, *The Producers*. I was star struck. I turned to say something stupid, I'm sure, about his wonderful abilities. Just as I began to speak, he turned away to his right and said, "Mr. Blanc. What an honor. Would you be so kind as to say those great words, 'You're despicable!'" (A favorite Daffy Duck line to all). I looked beyond Ken, and saw an old guy smoking a Salem 100, sitting on the lowest stool I've ever seen. Mel Blanc. Mel did not hesitate, and delighted both me and Ken with his wet and wonderful duck. There we were, two generations of voice actors, lined up to pay homage. That was over 25 years ago. When a young voice talent asks me to do any line from anything I've done, I never hesitate, as I learned from the best.

Walt Mitchell Discographer and Mel's friend

Mary Lou Wallace (my best friend for the last 36 years and counting) and I met Mel Blanc for the first time in his hotel room in Syracuse, New York, on the evening of April 20, 1978. The meeting was easily obtained by writing to Mel in advance, for he was glad to make himself available for interviews. Short magazine and newspaper articles had appeared before, focusing on one aspect of his career or another, but nobody had yet combined all of them together in one place. I was determined, with this opportunity, to get an interview with Mel (for the magazine *The World of Yesterday*) that would be in greater depth. He talked extensively about all of his careers that night, and the result was my 50-page piece in that issue. When I sent him the finished product, he liked it so much that he bought two more copies from the editors! The other result was that we were privileged to become his close friends, a friendship that continued for his remaining eleven years.

In addition to his other performances at the time, Mel put together a program designed for personal appearances at colleges and universities throughout the country, beginning probably sometime in early 1977. These were, of course, highly successful. He did not go on tour — each event was engaged individually. But the engagements were grouped together whenever possible, to cut down on Mel's travelling as much as could be arranged, especially since they had to be arranged within his otherwise busy schedule.

On subsequent visits to colleges in central New York State, Mel would let us know in advance when and where we could attend his talks. These were usually scheduled in the evening. On the morning of that day, Mel would have a sort of run through with college personnel, since he needed someone to run a slide projector and a movie projector during his talk. (He brought slides of his cartoon characters and a reel of three Oscar-winning cartoons to show.)

The result of all of that was that his afternoons were free, and when we were going to see his show, he welcomed us to visit with him at that time wherever he was staying near the college. That dear man treated us like visiting royalty. He had told the committee that had engaged him to give us reserved seating in the front row! He stopped in the middle of his talk, acknowledging our presence to the audience, and inviting us to stand and take a bow! We also knew that we were to go backstage afterward while he relaxed as he talked with the committee. On one of those occasions as we stood off to the side, silently watching him, a member of the committee asked him about those two strangers standing over there. Mel explained that we were his friends, and added pointedly, "They know more about my career than I do!" What a compliment — we were so grateful to overhear that.

Mel's two trips to Washington have been referred to earlier in this book. But there is more to tell about the latter one — on a very personal level, as far as Mary Lou and I are concerned.

One day in early February of 1984, Mel told us during a telephone call from his home that he had been surprised by being the honoree on a taping of *This Is Your Life*, telling us to watch out for it when it was aired, since the show was syndicated by that time. He also told us that he would be doing the talk that he usually did privately at colleges, but this was to be a public performance in Washington, D.C., under the auspices of the Smithsonian Institution. The occasion was to mark a special ceremony (separate from the public event) where Mel was to donate some of his career memorabilia to the Institute.

Of course, Mary Lou and I were in no position to fly all over the country to be at his other college talks. But this talk would be so very special that I told Mel that Mary Lou and I wanted to be there for that one! Mel was glad that we could plan on it. We immediately made plans for the flight and the hotel, planning to stay a few extra days to see our nation's Capital.

All of this Washington business had been scheduled for the last week in March. By the day of our flight down there, we were hit with horrible weather! It was storming heavily all up and down the East Coast. Where it wasn't snowing, it was raining! But we were determined not to let that stop us, and our flight landed safely in Washington, on Tuesday morning, I believe. Mel's talk was scheduled for Wednesday night. But something amazing happened in the middle of all of this.

The Smithsonian had made arrangements for Mel to give his talk that night in a 500-seat theater. This appearance, of course, was announced and promoted far in advance. By the time the Blancs arrived with their press agent in Washington, all 550 tickets were sold — the first sellout. Oops. That's right — the Smithsonian had accidentally printed and sold 50 more tickets than there were seats for them. Luckily, the mistake was discovered far enough in advance so that no calamity ensued.

Mel's appearance was hastily — within days, if I remember correctly — relocated to a different auditorium nearby. That auditorium had a seating capacity for 1,000 patrons. The people who had bought the 550 tickets were told that they would be honored at the other location. Meanwhile, even more tickets were sold for that location, and by the time Mel walked out on that stage, that auditorium had sold out as well! So, in a rather convoluted way, that was how Mel managed to sell out a single performance twice.

Once we arrived in Washington and had checked into our modest accommodations, we called Mel in his hotel suite to let him know that we had arrived safely. He gave us the location and time of the event and also gave us instructions. We were to report to the auditorium at least an hour ahead of time, hunt up the lady in charge, and tell her that we were Mel's special guests — we were again to be given special seats. Another tradition would continue: Mel told us that after his performance, there was to be a press event in the room that was next to the left wall beyond the stage, and he was inviting us to be there to watch the proceedings.

The show came off without a hitch. Mel usually did his college appearances travelling alone. So I know that it was a great source of pride when he stopped in the middle of his presentation to tell the audience that his wife Estelle was there, and he invited her to take a bow, which she did to a nice round of applause. Then Mel said, "And we have a little boy whose name is Noel. Would you stand up, little boy?" And Noel stood up — all six feet of him — laughing as he waved to the laughing audience. And then Mel mentioned that his two good friends had flown here from Syracuse. He called us by name and we took a bow to Mel's big audience! What a thrill!

When the show was over, the audience filed out and we headed for the door next to the stage. It was ajar, and a woman was standing in the doorway. She saw us heading toward her, and when we got there, she said to us, "I'm sorry, but this is only for the press!" Before I could say a word to explain who we were, up stepped Mel's press agent from inside the room. She didn't know us, so she said, "Are you Mel's friends?" and we replied that we were. She turned to the other lady and said, "It's okay — let them in." And in we went.

This was not a regular press conference in the normal sense. Mel was not giving a speech in front of rows of seated reporters. There was no podium and there were no chairs. Instead, the reporters were gathered in perhaps eight or ten clusters of a handful of people each, and the small groups were spread out around the room. Mel talked to one of these groups for a few minutes. When he was through, that group continued to talk quietly among themselves, checking their notes or whatever, while Mel walked across the room to speak with another group. That was the way it went the entire time, with Mel crisscrossing the room over and over.

We stood by and watched all of this. We knew instinctively not to approach Mel nor speak to him. He was engaging in promotion or, as the saying goes, "taking care of business!" Besides, we knew that our time would come: When Mel was giving us our instructions from his hotel suite, he also said that we could come there for our customary visit with him on the morning after the event, which we did. While this was going on, we did speak quietly with both Estelle and with the press agent. At one point as Mel made yet another crossing of the room, he saw me looking at him. He didn't stop. He didn't speak. He didn't even turn his head. But at the same time, he wanted us to know that he knew we were there — so he gave me a wink. I immediately turned to Mary Lou and said, "Mary Lou! Did you see that? He winked at me!" Mary Lou deadpanned, "Well, don't worry about it, Walt—I don't think he was flirting." Estelle was standing nearby at that moment. When she overheard that, she burst out in a raucous laugh!

We also visited with Mel, Estelle, and Noel when we were taking vacation trips to Hollywood. When he was in our area, it was our custom to take my reel-to-reel tape recorder along to the private meetings, where we would ask Mel more questions, swap jokes, and engage in general conversation. In Hollywood, we did the same thing at Mel's house. For that, I didn't have to bring my tape recorder clear across the country. I'd simply bring along a reel of tape and Mel would thread it onto his own machine and we'd go at it for a little while.

In 1987, due to scheduling, Mary Lou and I went on our Hollywood vacations at separate times that year. That's how Mel and I were talking alone on the tape (with occasional comments from Estelle). A couple of days later, I called from where I was staying, to tell Mel goodbye as I was about to leave for home. During that phone call, I got the shock of my life. Mel told me words to the effect that his doctor had given him holy heck for talking too long with me on that tape. Mel had actually risked his health — for me!

The way Mel explained it, because his respiratory condition was so fragile, his doctor had given him strict orders that he was not to talk continuously for more than half an hour at a time. Of course, I knew that Mel had emphysema, but I did not know about that doctor's restriction.

By that time, I knew him well enough that I was able to chastise the great man. In a stern voice, I said, "Mel! Why did you go against your doctor's orders like that?" In a kind voice, he replied, "Well, you came so far to see me, I made an exception in your case." I thanked him warmly — and assured him that I wasn't going to let him get away with that again!

And what of the tape? Well, I didn't know at that moment how long we had talked, but I did realize that it had to be more than half an hour. When I got home, I played the tape and timed it. 48 minutes!

Our last visit with Mel was unique. We didn't go to his home in Pacific Palisades, nor did we connect with him and Noel at Noel's home in Beverly Hills. When we called Mel to set up our meeting, he told us that, rather than our coming there, he would come to see us at our digs in the Hollywood Best Western — a four-block zigzag walk from the corner of Hollywood and Vine. Mel also explained that these days, he was no longer driving and had a regular driver on call to take him wherever he wanted to go. So, for the only time in our lives, we played host to him, pleasant driver and all. At the end of the visit, Mel announced that it was time for us all to go to lunch. I thanked him and added, "But you've treated us to lunch so many times, this time we'll treat you and him (the driver) as well." Mel replied, "Well, we'll see."

During the meal, Mel was recognized by a couple seated nearby with their young daughter. They must have told her that that man was the voice of Bugs Bunny and they sent the child over to our table to say hello to him. Mel was ready! He asked her first name and chatted with her briefly in a few voices, saying her name as the characters. Of course she was thrilled! Then, Mel reached inside his jacket pocket, pulled out an oblong card with his photo on it, autographed it to her and sent her on her happy way.

Then eventually the meal was ending. Mel must have seen the waiter approaching with the check. At that moment, he spoke, enunciating distinctly and in a low, somber tone of voice: "Now, I don't want anybody to say a word!" And out came his credit card to pay the check. By golly, he did it again!

But I saved the best part of this story for last, even though it happened before we set foot in the restaurant. The driver was cruising, looking for a parking space. He found a space right around the corner from the restaurant and asked Mel if we should park there. Mel looked at the sign and replied, "Seventy-five cents to park for twenty minutes? I should say NOT!!!" The three of us got out and the driver looked for a parking rate that wasn't highway robbery, then he walked to the restaurant to join us.

Mary Lou and I looked at each other when Mel said those words. The irony! This was the same man who, only a half hour beforehand at our hotel, had given each of us a one hundred dollar bill to help us with our travel expenses. He did that for us each time we saw him in Hollywood.

I don't call Mel Blanc a miracle man because of his awesome voice talent. I don't call him that because of the supremely kind way in which he treated his family, his friends, and his fans. Rather, I call him that because that man cheated death three times over a period of 28 years, the last time continuously for nine months. This has been referred to at appropriate places in the timeline throughout the text, but I underscore it here, all in one place, because the events are so dramatic, and they all deal with his survival.

The first, of course, was the head-on collision that night in January, 1961, that put him in a coma for three weeks, until the doctor got Mel to speak as Bugs Bunny. The second was when he was suffering from the eye infection over Labor Day weekend. Mel planned to wait until Tuesday to have it taken care of when the doctors would be back in their offices. But by Sunday, poor Mel was in such agony with it that Estelle called their doctor, who told her which hospital to take him to. And while he was in the ER waiting for treatment, he got up to walk across the room and collapsed right there! He received help immediately, but the word was that if he had been anywhere but in a hospital, EMTs could not have gotten to him in time.

And then there were the nine months that followed. Mel was fixed up temporarily, but he needed a delicate new procedure that a doctor had just developed. But he was the only doctor doing the procedure and he was a European doctor. Mel's family had to wait nine months until the doctor came to America. Mel was one of the first five people in California that the doctor operated on.

During those nine months, Mel's health was so fragile that nobody told him how sick he really was, for fear that the stress of knowing that might do him in. If he had been doing no voice work during those months, he might have caught on to the reason that he wasn't working. So, though there was surely some degree of risk, Noel gave his dad a very light schedule of voice work, to keep him in the dark. And Mel survived until that doctor arrived and did his lifesaving work.

So that why I reiterate it in capital letters. Because he was indeed,

MEL BLANC: MIRACLE MAN!

Appendix

A speech given by Mel to the American Association of Advertising Convention in Omaha. The year, 1964.

Believe this or not, the first advertising was done by a horny caveman. He stood outside his cave and hollered, "I want a woman, I gotta have a woman." When he found that this brought him no action, he picked up a rock and gave the first woman he saw a knock on the head. Then he dragged her to his cave and fulfilled his desires. It has been said that advertising has changed very little since that time…for even now it often ends up with a client getting screwed…

The next noteworthy man to come along in the development of creative advertising was Moses. Moses figured he'd have to do some pretty fancy promoting if he wanted Pharaoh to let his people go. So for his first presentation, he turned his staff into a snake. But Pharaoh was unimpressed. Because he knew that most advertising staff turned into snakes every Monday morning. But Moses kept plaguing Pharaoh so long that he finally agreed to free his people. Of course, Moses had some pretty good help, like Cecil B. DeMille, Charlton Heston, and God. And besides, his methods would be obsolete today. I mean, how would it be if today an agency created a spot that went, "Smoke Winston or we'll kill your first unborn child!"

In the early years of this century, another important step in creative advertising was taken. This time it was by the Commonwealth Edison Company. It was the very first demonstration commercial. The commercial showed a step by step account of Thomas Edison in his Menlo Park laboratory in the midst of one of his important inventions. It showed Edison blowing glass into a pear-shaped bulb. He carefully inserted a thin tungsten filament into the glass bulb and sucked all the air out of it. Next, he attached a strip of copper to the bottom of the bulb and plugged the whole thing into an electrical outlet. Finally, he picked up the bulb and said, "Hellloooo…"

Soon, two new media were introduced — radio and television. At the same time, music began to emerge as an advertising device. The first jingle I can remember was sung by a group called the Cherry Sisters. The product was Manischewitz Wine. The jingle accomplished a great deal. Not only did Manischewitz's sales go up, but the Cherry Sisters changed their names and became *big* stars. You now know them as Ronald Reagan and Vincent Price.

Advertising quickly saw the development of entertainment devices in commercials, and then took the logical progression from music to humor. Humor is now functioning as an important part of advertising, and has brought us a long way from the shouting caveman. Several elements are needed before a humorous advertising campaign will succeed on a large scale. The first thing you need is a product. For convenience, we'll invent one. A new toothpaste called Scrap. Next, we need an advertising agency. If the agency wants to kick off a promotion for a new product, they'll often call in a psychologist to interview people. This psychologist told the agency that the Scrap commercial should be designed to appeal to children. This piece of news was well received by the agency who've always geared their commercials to children. Particularly their beer commercials. But *how* does one appeal to children? Humor. Here's the first commercial:

"Oh, hello there. This is Milton Flirt for Scrap. We're at the home of Mr. and Mrs. Suckthumb and this is their son, Homer. Homer was in a group that used new blue Scrap for three years. Will you tell us about it, Homer?"

"Yes, yes, yes, yes, I will!"

"Alright, Homer, what happened after three years of brushing with Scrap?"

"Oh, oh, I had to have my teeth capped."

"Oh ho, you are making a funny, are you not, Homer?"

"N-yes, yes, I am."

"Alright, seriously, Homer, tell us what Scrap taught you."

"It taught me that grown up people are *bad*. And if I brush my teeth with new blue Scrap, grown up people will be afraid of me."

"Oh, you hear that, kiddies? Now, why will grown up people be afraid of you if you use new blue Scrap, Homer?"

"Oh, because I'll have new blue teeth!"

"Oh ho ho ho…But seriously, friends. Pick up new blue Scrap at your drugstore. If your druggist doesn't carry it, do something clever like throw up on his prescription counter! *(Laughs)* Oh my…"

Well, the Scrap people decide that it's too way out. And the commercial is rewritten and rerecorded:

> "Homer, why aren't you using new blue Scrap?"
> "Scrap?"
> "Scrap."
> "Scrap?"
> "Yes, Scrap toothpaste. Scrap is great."
> "Scrap is great? Scrap?"
> "Right! Scrap! S-C-R-A-P. Scrap."
> "Oh, Scrap!"
> "That's right — Scrap!"
> "What was that name?"
> "Scrap!"
> "Scrap?
> "That's right, Scrap! Scrap!"

Just as everything seems perfect, you read in the trades that the agency has lost the Scrap account. And their psychologist has been arrested for appealing to children. Well, Scrap appoints a new agency which immediately calls Mel Blanc Associates. The agency is Shlunt, Shlunt, Shlunt and Gundlefinger. Gundlefinger is, of course, married to a Shlunt. Shlunt, Shlunt, Shlunt and Gundlefinger want to go the humor route. And realizing their lack of experience in the field, has called us to help. Clifton Shlunt, the account exec, after rambling on for twenty minutes about how he's always been a fan of mine, announces that he would like us to work out a campaign for him. On spec. Perhaps I should define spec. Spec is what someone does now for nothing on the promise that he will get more than he deserves later on. It's also a small piece of dirt.

Well, in spite of my feelings about spec jobs, I agree to a meeting. As I enter the agency's conference room, I am introduced. The agency's principals are seated around the table. At the head of the table is the chairman of the board, Fairfax Shlunt. Fairfax is 124 years old. Every now and then he wanders into a broom closet and starts giggling. He makes the big decisions! He talks a little like this: "My name is Fairfax Shlunt and I make all the big decisions, hahahaha…! Who da hell is Mel Blanc?" To the right is Clifton Shlunt, the one who called us. He is Fairfax's great grandson and the account executive for Scrap.

Clifton has always wanted to be a radio announcer, but he *"t-t-t-t-t-*talks *l-l-l-l-l-*like *t-t-t-t-t-t-*this. *S-*so he's *n-n-n-*never *b-b-*been ab-*b*-ble *t*-*t*-to *b*-*b*-*b*-*b*-become an an-*n*-*n*-*n*-nouncer." He just sits there cursing Ed Rhymers. Next to him is Marcel Gundlefinger, the agency's art director. *(Camp)* He's very sensitive and he wins just *gobs* of awards. *(Normal)* Clifton introduces me: "P-*p*-*p*-*p*-people? You've all *m*-*m*-*m*-*m*-met *m*-*m*-*m*-*m*-Mel *b*-*b*-*b*-Blanc from *m*-*m*-Mel *b*-Blanc Associates. *T*-*t*-they're *g*-*g*-going to *c*-*c*-*c*-create a *h*-*h*-humorous *r*-*r*-*r*-radio *c*-*c*-campaign for our *Sc*-*sc*-scrap account." And Marcel says, *(Camp)* "I resent him. I have my own ideas about handling Scrap. I want to take a full page ad in *Strength* and *Health*. Four-color job showing a tube of Scrap nestling in a seashell on the beach. Surrounded by four strapping men clad only in seaweed. Might even throw in a flounder or two."

Sitting next to Marcel is Hans Huberman, the creative director, who looks at me and says *(German accent)*, "In the first place, I do not believe in humor. Dere is nothing funny about advertising. Advertising is the conquering of minds and overcoming de public's vill — by force, if necessary! Und if we did vant humor, ve wouldn't go outside. Ve go outside for nutting. Occasionally ve go outside for a cheese danish, but that's all. I know as much about humor as de next guy. I happen to know several very, very dirty jokes. Vhy, vhen I used to vork in this Argentina agency, I was known as the Pinky Lee of the Pompas. But mine is basically a scientific mind! Und my idea for Scrap vould be the first campaign ever created strictly from scientific research! Achtung! I vill now play you my campaign idea!" *(Previous caveman voice)* "I want a woman! I've gotta have a woman!"

Well, this brings us to the present. What I like to call the age of confusion in radio. It's appalling to me to find that most advertising on radio is created and produced without the slightest understanding of the medium. I'd now like to show you several approaches to radio advertising that we have worked with successfully, and I demonstrate them for one purpose only. To show you the variety of creative approaches that can be utilized when you set out to entertain as you sell.

Heading up the list of creative platforms which we avoid like the plague, are singing jingles, followed closely by hard sell, straight copy, slice of life, fantasy, and demonstration. That is, we avoid these garden variety approaches unless they can be used with tongue in cheek, as we did for Pepsodent Toothbrushes on this demonstration commercial:

(Announcer) "In the interest of dental hygiene, the Pepsodent Toothbrush people will now demonstrate the wrong way and the right way to brush your teeth. *(Sound of brushing)* That is the wrong way. *(Same sound)* And that is the right way."

It's the slice of life commercials that really confuse me. I always thought slice of life meant a believable segment of everyday experience. Well, I don't believe anything in those Proctor & Gamble commercials. I mean, I had a grandmother. But she absolutely never worried about bad breath. She had bad breath, but she never worried about it.

Did you ever notice that in every Prell commercial, someone drops a tube of it on the floor? If that's a slice of life, it only shows that Prell cleans your hair but louses up your coordination.

Anyway, we've created the one *true* slice of life. A slice of human dialogue for Fidelity Philadelphia Bank:

MAN'S VOICE: Yes, that's right, headaches. Terrible headaches. They would start in my knees, you know, and go all the way up to my face.

MEL: Didn't aspirin help you?

MAN'S VOICE: Aspirin, are you kidding? The only thing that helped me was screaming.

MEL: Screaming?

MAN'S VOICE: Right. If you scream loud enough, your neighbor would punch you in the mouth and make you forget your headache. But then I found a product that worked.

MEL: Yeah, what was that?

MAN'S VOICE: Fidelity Philadelphia Trust. I opened a checking account up there.

MEL: You mean a checking account at Fidelity helped your headaches?

MAN'S VOICE: You see, the reason I had these headaches was, you know, I was broke all the time.

MEL: Ha ha, you mean you were kind of a spendthrift.

MAN'S VOICE: Yeah, yeah, yeah, I'd see an offer on kidney beans, and I'd buy 40 pounds. That's wasteful, you know what I mean. And when my bills came in for rent and water, I didn't have any money left.

MEL: But with a checking account at Fidelity you could keep track of your expenses.

MAN'S VOICE: Yeah, it's like having your own bookkeeper, for instance, and it gives me a great sense of identity.

MEL: How's that?

MAN'S VOICE: Well, my name's printed right there on the checks, see?

MEL: Oh, so you suggest…

MAN'S VOICE: That all people with headaches should go to Fidelity and open up a checking account, it's better than taking aspirin. I mean, you could crumple up a couple of checks, I guess, and take 'em with a glass of water maybe, and they could cure the common cold for instance.

MEL: Swallow the checks?

MAN'S VOICE: Well, you'd have to mark them void first, for instance.

I love satire and regard it as the most sophisticated form of humorous advertising. But it has value alone when the satire puts forth an effective advertising concept. I believe we achieved this successfully in a campaign created for a major Eastern dairy, Martin Century Farms. *(Plays commercial)*

"The sun is high in the sky when Senor Valdez come down the mountainside with his burro, down into the town. Senor Valdez is go into restaurant and say hello to all his friends. 'Hello, all my friends.' Senor Valdez is tired and thirsty from trip down mountainside, so orders something to drink, a nice 'glass of Martin Century Farms milks, please.' Hey, wait a minute, hold on, what's with this milks business? 'It's richer with that straight from the farm quality.' Listen, Valdez, you not supposed to drink milk. 'Oh, but dis is different. Martin Century Farms milk is milk that people who don't drink milk drink.' I don't care. 'Look, I am the one what schlepped heavy bags down the mountain, right?' Right. 'Twelve times a week down the mountain, up and down de mountain, de rain, de snow or de dark of night.' Okay, okay. 'You drink what you want, and I drink what I want, and I want Martin Century Farms milk.' Okay. 'By de way, what's in dose heavy bags I carry down the mountain?' I don't know. 'Me too.'"

The next commercial I'd like to play is one of a series we created for Avis Rent-A-Car. Most of you probably didn't know that *we* are directly responsible for Avis's advertising campaign. Well, it's the truth. Until they hired us, Avis was #1.

"On a main highway, counting the passing cars in front of us. The results promise to be exciting, because of Avis' vacation travel plan. For $99 you can leave your car at home and travel in the new Plymouth or other new late model car from Avis. There is no charge for mileage and the price includes a tank full of gas and dependable insurance. And here are the final figures…The figures are in! 30,283 cars were not rented from Avis. 694 cars were rented from Avis. Avis has done it again. A solid 2%."

The argument we all hear against humorous advertising is that it isn't compatible with the serious image. We feel our campaign for the 1966

Cancer Crusade puts this argument to rest neatly. We used Jack Benny, George Burns, Lucille Ball and a dozen other stars as our performers. And we used humor. The American Cancer Society has informed us that the campaign has motivated a greater percentage of the public to take cancer checkups than in any previous year. What humor does is remove the public's fear of a serious image, but it does not damage the image itself. A graphic demonstration of this is a series of commercials we just completed introducing the First Bank card, Seattle's First National Bank credit card. The job was to eliminate the public's reluctance to use the card to its full potential. Imagination, humor, and the able help of Don Knotts' performance has accomplished this with a flourish. *(Plays commercial)*

"We've asked you 500,000 people to meet here at the summit of Mount Rainier because you're all First Bank card holders. Now, to make sure we have no non-holders here, I want you to take out your cards and wave them. (Crowd sounds) You, you there in the plaid mackinaw, you can show snapshots of your children at a later date, please. (Sound of something hitting) Now, I don't know who threw that snowball, but that sort of levity is uncalled for. Now, the First Bank card is an all-purpose charge card. With it, you can charge almost anything you need in thousands of stores all over the state. Also, you can get an immediate cash loan of up to $350 at any First branch. Now. How many plan to get out there and put their First Bank cards to use? (Large cheer) And how many don't plan to? (Something else is thrown) Putting a rock in the middle of a snowball is about as low a trick as I know."

This year my company will create several million dollars in new radio budgets by exciting advertisers to the use of this medium. A typical example is Bachman Jax. We were hired to create four radio spots by this Eastern manufacturer of snack food items and their original air budget was $100,000. By the time we completed the campaign, the number of spots had grown to eight, and the budget to $400,000. *(Plays commercial)*

(Train sounds)
WOMAN: Pardon me, is this seat taken?
MAN: No, help yourself.
WOMAN: Thank you. *(Thinks)* Hmmm…he's eating Bachman Pretzel Rods.

MAN: *(Thinks)* Look at her, pretending not to notice my Bachman Pretzel Rods. I think I'll take a big bite outa one. *(Crunch)*

WOMAN: Do you have to make so much noise when you eat? I've got a terrible headache.

MAN: Sorry. *(Thinks)* She's just dyin' for me to offer one of those big jumbo pretzel rods.

WOMAN: Do you live around here?

MAN: No, matter of fact, I don't. You?

WOMAN: Oh, I was born and raised in Pretzelvanian.

MAN: *(Laughs)* Little bit of a Freudian slip there, huh?

WOMAN: *(Thinks)* Oh, I could kick myself. Now he knows I want him to offer me one of his Bachman Pretzel Rods.

MAN: *(Thinks)* Well, there's one of these jumbo pretzel rods left in the bag. I'll hold it out, let the sunlight play off it, that ought to drive her out of her mind.

WOMAN: Listen, I — I can't stand it anymore, would you please — *(Loud train whistle)*

ANNOUNCER: Should the gentleman offer the lady a Bachman Pretzel Rod? This gentleman didn't. Bachman Pretzel Rods are too good to share. But, maybe, someday...

If we have a pet project, it's our campaign for Hebrew National Meats. This product has a lot going *against* it. First of all, it sells for nearly *twice* the price of the competition. Our campaign had two goals. The first was to play down the ethnic aspect of the product. The second was to play the high quality for all it was worth. With pompous self-satire. Our first idea for handling the ethnic problem was simple. Change the name to Gentile National. A year later we got another crack at the account. Here's the result.

(Chinese voices)

ANNOUNCER: The representative's lounge at the United Nations has seen some of the world's most influential people. Important discussions are said to be held here 24 hours a day. Let's eavesdrop for a moment.

(More foreign voices. "Yum yum," "frankfurter" and "Hebrew National Salami" are among the discernible words)

ANNOUNCER: People who have tasted life have tasted Hebrew National Salami, franks and knockwurst. Available at leading markets, everywhere.

Well, in closing, I wish you all my very best and in the words of Clifton Schlunt, "*Th-th-th*-that's all f — *th-th-th*-that's all f — *w*-who the hell is Mel Blanc?"

(Laughter, applause)

Credits

Radio
Contributed by Martin Grams, Jr.

1933 to 1935 KGW, Portland, Oregon
Mel Blanc was writing, acting and starring on his own show.

Circa 1936 NBC, San Francisco radio broadcasts

September 29, 1935 to June 21, 1936 *The Jell-O Program*
Weekly regular: Jack Benny. Mel Blanc played a variety of supporting comedic roles. Sponsored by Jell-O. NBC.

October 4, 1936 to June 27, 1937 *Park Avenue Penners*
Weekly regular: Joe Penner. Joe Penner was a standup rooted in vaudeville and built around one line: "Wanna buy a duck?" The role of his Duck, sometimes nicknamed "Goo Goo II," was played by Mel Blanc. Blanc also played other supporting roles on the series. Sponsored by Cocomalt. CBS.

October 3, 1937 to June 26, 1938 *Park Avenue Penners*
Weekly regular: Joe Penner. Joe Penner was a standup rooted in vaudeville and built around one line: "Wanna buy a duck?" The role of his Duck, sometimes nicknamed "Goo Goo II," was played by Mel Blanc. Blanc also played other supporting roles on the series. Sponsored by Cocomalt. CBS.

January to May 1938 *The Mickey Mouse Theatre*
Mel Blanc was in all 20 editions doing his "hiccupping man" character, which Walt Disney was going to use as the voice of Gideon the Cat in *Pinocchio*. NBC.

April 20, 1938 *Town Hall Tonight*
Weekly regular: Fred Allen. Comedy series with various skits and songs. Mel Blanc appears on rare occasion in a comedic supporting role. Sponsored by Ipana-Sal Hepatica. NBC.

September 6, 1938 to June 27, 1939 *The Johnsons Wax Program*
Weekly regulars: Fibber McGee and Molly. Situation comedy series starring Jim and Marion Jordan. Recurring characters visit the residents of Wistful Vista to exchange jabs, funny lines and aid Fibber in his comical exploits. Mel Blanc, on occasion, supplied the voice of a comical character. Sponsored by the S.C. Johnson Company. NBC.

September 27, 1938 to June 20, 1939 *The Pepsodent Show*
Weekly regular: Bob Hope. Comedy/variety series with Mel Blanc appearing every few weeks in a comedic supporting role. Sponsored by Pepsodent. NBC.

October 2, 1938 to June 25, 1939 *The Jell-O Program*
Weekly regular: Jack Benny. Situation comedy program with occasional comedy skits. Series supporting cast included Eddie "Rochester" Anderson, Don Wilson and Dennis Day. Mel Blanc appeared on an almost regular basis through most of the series in supporting roles from disgruntled store clerks, train announcers, Carmichael the polar bear (especially through this season), a Mexican who cannot speak English, and Benny's untrustworthy Maxwell. Sponsored by Jell-O. NBC.

October 8, 1939 to June 16, 1940 *The Jell-O Program*
Weekly regular: Jack Benny. Situation comedy program with occasional comedy skits. Series supporting cast included Eddie "Rochester" Anderson, Don Wilson, Dennis Day and Mel Blanc. Sponsored by Jell-O. NBC.

November 11, 1939 to April 3, 1940 *Al Pearce and His Gang*
Weekly regular: Al Pearce. Comedy/variety series. Mel Blanc played the recurring role of Elmer Burt, "the low pressure salesman," always trying to sell some merchandise that no one wants to buy. Sponsored by Dole. CBS.

Circa 1939-1940 *Community Mobilization for Human Needs*
Sponsored by the Community Chest Fund Appeal. Mel Blanc plays the role of Elmer, a cousin of Joe E. Brown, who tries to inherit an English castle and finds love instead. This recording was syndicated to radio stations across the country in the hopes that radio listeners would be reminded of making an annual donation to their local Community Chest.

September 5, 1939 to June 25, 1940 *The Johnsons Wax Program*
Weekly regulars: Fibber McGee and Molly. Situation comedy series starring Jim and Marion Jordan. Recurring characters visit the residents of Wistful Vista to exchange jabs, funny lines and aid Fibber in his comical exploits. Mel Blanc, on occasion, supplied the voice of a comical character. Sponsored by the S.C. Johnson Company. NBC.

October 1, 1940 to June 24, 1941 *The Johnsons Wax Program*
Weekly regulars: Fibber McGee and Molly. Situation comedy series starring Jim and Marion Jordan. Recurring characters visit the residents of Wistful Vista to exchange jabs, funny lines and aid Fibber in his comical exploits. Mel Blanc, on occasion, supplied the voice of a comical character. Sponsored by the S.C. Johnson Company. NBC.

October 2, 1940 to June 25, 1941 *Texaco Star Theater*
Weekly regular: Fred Allen. Comedy/variety series with short skits and songs. Mel Blanc appeared in supporting comedic roles for a number of episodes. At least two episodes from May 1941 have been confirmed, but more than likely Blanc was on much of the season. Sponsored by Texaco. CBS.

October 6, 1940 to June 1, 1941 *The Jell-O Program*
Weekly regular: Jack Benny. Situation comedy program with occasional comedy skits. Series supporting cast included Eddie "Rochester" Anderson, Don Wilson and Dennis Day. Mel Blanc appeared on an almost regular basis in supporting roles. Sponsored by Jell-O. NBC.

September 30, 1941 to June 23, 1942 *The Johnsons Wax Program*
Weekly regulars: Fibber McGee and Molly. Situation comedy series starring Jim and Marion Jordan. Recurring characters visit the residents of Wistful Vista to exchange jabs, funny lines and aid Fibber in his comical exploits. Mel Blanc, on occasion, supplied the voice of a comical character. Sponsored by the S.C. Johnson Company. N B C.

October 5, 1941 to May 31, 1942 *The Jell-O Program*
Weekly regular: Jack Benny. Situation comedy program with occasional comedy skits. Series supporting cast included Eddie "Rochester" Anderson, Don Wilson and Dennis Day. Mel Blanc appeared on an almost regular basis in supporting roles. Sponsored by Jell-O. N B C.

Circa 1942 *Are You a Genius?*
"On this AFRS 15-minute program, Mel entertained the troops with a quiz show where the emphasis was on fun! He would pose each quiz question to the G.I.s. A little music would follow to give the listeners time to think of — and write down — the answer. Then Mel would reveal the correct response. Each question was announced as having a certain point value, which varied from question to question. The point values for each show totaled 100 points. Anyone who got a perfect score at the end of the show was facetiously declared by Mel to be a genius. To keep the show lively, Mel would tell a joke and/or do one of his funny voices after revealing an answer before going on to the next question. An uncredited pianist played the theme song at the beginning ("School Days") in the breakneck pace of Spike Jones. The pianist also played the bridge music between the questions, accompanied by a hokey violinist. At signoff, the pianist played the theme again to fill out the time, but this time in a straight jazz version. In 1980, Mel was asked who that pianist was, but he couldn't remember. He was also asked if that was he playing the violin every now and then. He replied, "I don't remember, but if it was pretty bad, it was probably me!" The earliest known transcription disc was waxed in 1943, but it has such a high show number that the first ones were almost certainly done some time in 1942. The exact number of shows is unknown, but it is a fact that Mel recorded over 150 of them." *(Walt Mitchell)*

April 26, 1942 *The Great Gildersleeve*
Situation comedy series starring Harold Peary in the leading role. Mel Blanc is known to have appeared on the program only twice during the series' long run. This was his first and Blanc plays the role of "Horace the Goat," a phrase Gildersleeve commented to his friend Horace repeatedly through the series.

June 21, 1942 *The Great Gildersleeve*
Situation comedy series starring Harold Peary in the leading role. Mel Blanc is known to have appeared on the program only twice during the series' long run. This was Blanc's second appearance.

June 18, 1942 *Command Performance*
(Program #18) The date listed is the recording date, not broadcast date. This radio program was syndicated to troops overseas for their enjoyment and was not broadcast in the U.S. Mel Blanc plays a comedic supporting role with guests Martha Tilton, Judy Garland, William Powell and Gene Autry.

September 29, 1942 to June 22, 1943 *The Johnsons Wax Program*
Weekly regulars: Fibber McGee and Molly. Situation comedy series starring Jim and Marion Jordan. Recurring characters visit the residents of Wistful Vista to exchange jabs, funny lines and help Fibber in his comical exploits. Mel Blanc, on occasion, supplied the voice of a comical character. Sponsored by the S.C. Johnson Company. NBC.

October 4, 1942 to May 30, 1943 *The Grape Nuts Program*
Weekly regular: Jack Benny. Situation comedy program with occasional comedy skits. Series supporting cast included Eddie "Rochester" Anderson, Don Wilson and Dennis Day. Mel Blanc appeared on an almost regular basis in supporting roles. Sponsored by Grape Nuts. NBC.

October 6, 1942 to June 29, 1943 *The Al Jolson Program*
Weekly regular: Al Jolson. Comedy/variety series with weekly guests and short comedy skits. Mel Blanc played supporting roles in a number of episodes throughout the season. Sponsored by Colgate. CBS.

October 6, 1942 to June 29, 1943 *The George Burns and Gracie Allen Show*
Weekly regulars: George Burns and Gracie Allen. Situation comedy with
Mel Blanc as the recurring role of the mailman who exchanged witty
one-liners and reminded Gracie to "keep smiling." Sponsored by Swan
Soap. CBS.

October 8, 1942 to March 18, 1943 *The Abbott and Costello Show*
Weekly regulars: Bud Abbott and Lou Costello. Comedy/variety series.
Supporting cast included Connie Haines, Billy Gray and Mel Blanc,
who frequently supplied comedic roles for various skits, including
the recurring role of The Scotchman. Sponsored by Reynolds (Camel
Cigarettes). NBC.

October 9, 1942 to October 1, 1943 *Tommy Riggs and Betty Lou*
Weekly regular: Tommy Riggs. Variety program with occasional comedy
skits. Mel Blanc played the recurring roles of Uncle Petey and Rover
the dog. Sponsored by Lever Brothers. NBC.

February 27, 1943 *Command Performance*
(Program #55) The date listed is the recording date, not broadcast date.
This radio program was syndicated to troops overseas for their enjoyment and was not broadcast in the U.S. Mel Blanc plays a comedic
supporting role with guests Betty Grable and Margaret Whiting.

March 27, 1943 *Command Performance*
(Program #59) The date listed is the recording date, not broadcast date.
This radio program was syndicated to troops overseas for their enjoyment
and was not broadcast in the U.S. Mel Blanc plays a comedic supporting
role with guests Spike Jones and the City Slickers, and Hedda Hopper.

April 14, 1943 *G.I. Journal*
(Program #5) The date listed is the recording date, not broadcast date.
This radio program was syndicated to troops overseas for their enjoyment
and was not broadcast in the U.S. Mel Blanc plays a comedic supporting
role with guests Ken Christy and Eddie "Rochester" Anderson.

April 19, 1943 *The Lux Radio Theatre*
Hosted by Cecil B. DeMille. A dramatization of "A Night to
Remember" with Ann Sothern and Robert Young. Also in the cast is
Mel Blanc, who makes his first of only two appearances on the series.

May 8, 1943 *Command Performance*
(*Program #66*) The date listed is the recording date, not broadcast date. This radio program was syndicated to troops overseas for their enjoyment and was not broadcast in the U.S. Mel Blanc plays a comedic supporting role with guests Martha Raye, and Rudy Vallee and his Coast Guard Band.

May 19, 1943 *This is My Story*
Produced by the American Red Cross, this series was syndicated across the country. The broadcast date originates from the New York airing over CBS, sponsored by Forty-Two Hair Oil. Gracie Allen guests in "Mrs. Laura Graham." Mel Blanc is among the supporting cast.

June 2, 1943 to June 13, 1945 *The Camel Comedy Caravan*
Weekly regular: Jack Carson. Comedy/variety series with short skits and music. Supporting cast included Billy Gray, Arthur Treacher, Mel Blanc and Herb Shriner. Each week's episode featured a different Hollywood guest. Music supplied by Freddy Martin and his Orchestra. Sponsored by Campbell Soups. CBS.

June 19, 1943 *Command Performance (Dedicated to the British Commonwealth)*
(*Program #71*) The date listed is the recording date, not broadcast date. This radio program was syndicated to troops overseas for their enjoyment and was not broadcast in the U.S. Mel Blanc plays a comedic supporting role with guests Bing Crosby, Dinah Shore, Fanny Brice, Hanley Stafford, Ziggy Talent, the Murphy Sisters and Vaughn Monroe's orchestra.

July 6, 1943 to June 27, 1944 *Rancho Canova*
Weekly regular: Judy Canova. Comedy series featuring short skits and songs. Ruby Dandridge and Mel Blanc are weekly regulars. Eddie Dean supplies additional music for the series. Blanc plays a variety of recurring characters including Pedro, salesman Roscoe Wortle, and the chronic hiccough. Sponsored by Palmolive and Colgate. CBS.

July 12, 1943 *The Lux Radio Theatre*
Hosted by Cecil B. DeMille. A dramatization of "Air Force" with Harry Carey and George Raft. Also in the cast is Mel Blanc, who makes his second of only two appearances on the series.

August 21, 1943 *Command Performance*
(*Program #80)* The date listed is the recording date, not broadcast date. This radio program was syndicated to troops overseas for their enjoyment and was not broadcast in the U.S. Mel Blanc plays a comedic supporting role with guests Ed Gardner, Frank Sinatra, Ginger Rogers and Alice Faye.

August 31, 1943 to June 13, 1944 *The George Burns and Gracie Allen Show*
Weekly regulars: George Burns and Gracie Allen. Situation comedy with Mel Blanc as the recurring role of the mailman who exchanged witty one-liners and reminded Gracie to "keep smiling." Sponsored by Swan Soap. CBS.

October 9, 1943 *G.I. Journal*
(*Program #12)* The date listed is the recording date, not broadcast date. This radio program was syndicated to troops overseas for their enjoyment and was not broadcast in the U.S. Mel Blanc plays the mailman in a comedic supporting role with guests George Burns and Gracie Allen.

October 10, 1943 to June 4, 1944 *The Grape Nuts Program*
Weekly regular: Jack Benny. Situation comedy program with occasional comedy skits. Series supporting cast included Eddie "Rochester" Anderson, Don Wilson and Dennis Day. Mel Blanc appeared on an almost regular basis in supporting roles. Sponsored by Grape Nuts. NBC.

October 22, 1943 *G.I. Journal*
(*Program #14)* The date listed is the recording date, not broadcast date. This radio program was syndicated to troops overseas for their enjoyment and was not broadcast in the U.S. Mel Blanc plays the role of "Private Sad Sack" with guests Bob Hope, Jimmy Durante and Linda Darnell.

November 4, 1943 to June 8, 1944 *The Abbott and Costello Show*
Weekly regulars: Bud Abbott and Lou Costello. Comedy/variety series. Supporting cast included Connie Haines, Billy Gray and Mel Blanc, who frequently supplied comedic roles for various skits, including the recurring role of The Scotchman. According to files at the Library of Congress, Mel Blanc played the role of Bugs Bunny a number of times. Sponsored by Reynolds (Camel Cigarettes). NBC.

November 5, 1943 *G.I. Journal*
(Program #16) The date listed is the recording date, not broadcast date. This radio program was syndicated to troops overseas for their enjoyment and was not broadcast in the U.S. Mel Blanc plays the role of "Private Sad Sack" with guests Linda Darnell, and Kay Kyser and his Orchestra.

November 19, 1943 *G.I. Journal*
(Program #17) The date listed is the recording date, not broadcast date. This radio program was syndicated to troops overseas for their enjoyment and was not broadcast in the U.S. Mel Blanc plays the role of "Private Sad Sack" with guests Red Skelton and Eddie "Rochester" Anderson.

November 26, 1943 *G.I. Journal*
(Program #18) The date listed is the recording date, not broadcast date. This radio program was syndicated to troops overseas for their enjoyment and was not broadcast in the U.S. Mel Blanc plays a supporting role in a spoof of horror radio programs called "The Inner Stinckum," with guests Linda Darnell and Jack Carson.

December 9, 1943 *The Lifebuoy Show*
Weekly regulars: Spike Jones and the City Slickers. Sponsored by Lifebuoy Soap. NBC.

January 14, 1944 *G.I. Journal*
(Program #24) The date listed is the recording date, not broadcast date. This radio program was syndicated to troops overseas for their enjoyment and was not broadcast in the U.S. Mel Blanc plays the role of "Private Sad Sack" with guests Ransom Sherman, Bob Hope and Eddie "Rochester" Anderson.

February 1944 *G.I. Journal*
(Program #28) The date listed is the recording date, not broadcast date. This radio program was syndicated to troops overseas for their enjoyment and was not broadcast in the U.S. Mel Blanc plays the role of "Private Sad Sack" with guests Ransom Sherman and Kay Kyser.

February 2, 1944 *Orson Welles' Radio Almanac*
Weekly regular: Orson Welles. Guest Lionel Barrymore conducts a "Kiddies' Corner" and Mel Blanc appears as a talking groundhog. Sponsored by Mobil Oil. CBS.

February 11, 1944 *G.I. Journal*
(Program #30) The date listed is the recording date, not broadcast date. This radio program was syndicated to troops overseas for their enjoyment and was not broadcast in the U.S. Mel Blanc plays the role of "Private Sad Sack" with guests Jerry Colonna and Harry Babbitt.

February 18, 1944 *G.I. Journal*
(Show #31) Mel (probably as "Pvt. Sad Sack") shares the time with Bing Crosby, the Music Maids, Ransom Sherman, Linda Darnell, Eddie "Rochester" Anderson, Gloria De Haven and John Scott Trotter's orchestra.

March 3, 1944 *G.I. Journal*
(Show #33) Mel (probably as "Pvt. Sad Sack") performs with Bing Crosby, the Music Maids, the Charioteers, Ransom Sherman, Arthur Q. Bryan, Anita Ellis, Linda Darnell, Andy Devine, Hedda Hopper and John Scott Trotter's orchestra.

March 12, 1944 *The Radio Hall of Fame*
Variety series with music and dramas. Groucho Marx appears as Dr. Hackenbush, reprised from one of the Marx Bros. movies. Also in the cast is Audrey Christie, Kenny Baker and Mel Blanc. Paul Whiteman and his Orchestra supplied the music. Sponsored by Philco Radio. Blue Network.

March 24, 1944 *G.I. Journal*
(Program #36) The date listed is the recording date, not broadcast date. This radio program was syndicated to troops overseas for their enjoyment and was not broadcast in the U.S. Mel Blanc plays the role of "Private Sad Sack" with guests Kay Kyser and Eddie "Rochester" Anderson.

April 21, 1944 *G.I. Journal*
(Program #40) The date listed is the recording date, not broadcast date. This radio program was syndicated to troops overseas for their enjoyment and was not broadcast in the U.S. Mel Blanc plays the role of "Private Sad Sack" with guests Ransom Sherman, Carol Landis, Jack Carson and Jerry Colonna.

April 28, 1944 *G.I. Journal*
(Show #41) Mel (most likely as "Pvt. Sad Sack") works with Bing Crosby, the Moon Maids, the Charioteers, Arthur Q. Bryan, Ransom Sherman, Phyllis Brooks, Anita Ellis, Jerry Colonna and John Scott Trotter's orchestra.

April 29, 1944 *G.I. Journal*
(Program #42) The date listed is the recording date, not broadcast date. This radio program was syndicated to troops overseas for their enjoyment and was not broadcast in the U.S. Mel Blanc plays the role of "Private Sad Sack" with guests Ransom Sherman, Jerry Colonna and Betty Grable.

May 19, 1944 *G. I. Journal*
(Show #44) Mel (most likely as "Pvt. Sad Sack") shares the spotlight with Bing Crosby, the Moon Maids, Ransom Sherman, Arthur Q. Bryan, Phyllis Brooks, Anita Owen, Jerry Colonna and John Scott Trotter's orchestra.

June 2, 1944 *Mail Call*
(Program #94) The date listed is the recording date, not broadcast date. This radio program was syndicated to troops overseas for their enjoyment and was not broadcast in the U.S. Mel Blanc appears in the cast, along with Dinah Shore, Bob Hope, Maria Montez and Bob Hope.

June 2, 1944 *G.I. Journal*
(Program #46) The date listed is the recording date, not broadcast date. This radio program was syndicated to troops overseas for their enjoyment and was not broadcast in the U.S. Mel Blanc plays the role of "Private Sad Sack" with guests Ransom Sherman, Laraine Day, Jack Carson and Eddie "Rochester" Anderson.

June 9, 1944 *G.I. Journal*
(Program #47) The date listed is the recording date, not broadcast date. This radio program was syndicated to troops overseas for their enjoyment and was not broadcast in the U.S. Mel Blanc plays the role of "Private Sad Sack" with guests Harry Babbitt, Frank Morgan, Jinx Falkenburg, and Kay Kyser.

June 16, 1944 *G.I. Journal*
(Show #48) Mel (as usual, probably as "Pvt. Sad Sack") shares the mikes with Bing Crosby, the Music Maids & Men, Ransom Sherman, Lena Horne, Henny Youngman and John Scott Trotter's orchestra.

June 23, 1944 *G.I. Journal*
(Program #49) The date listed is the recording date, not broadcast date. This radio program was syndicated to troops overseas for their enjoyment and was not broadcast in the U.S. Mel Blanc plays the role of "Private Sad Sack" with guests Dorothy lamour, Bob Hope and Jerry Colonna.

July 7, 1944 *G.I. Journal*
(Program #51) The date listed is the recording date, not broadcast date. This radio program was syndicated to troops overseas for their enjoyment and was not broadcast in the U.S. Mel Blanc plays the role of "Private Sad Sack" with guests Ransom Sherman, Jack Carson and Jimmy Durante.

July 14, 1944 *G.I. Journal*
(Show #52) Mel (as usual, probably as "Pvt. Sad Sack") takes to the mikes with Bing Crosby, the Music Maids & Men, Ransom Sherman, Linda Darnell, Andy Devine, Helen Forrest and John Scott Trotter's orchestra.

July 21, 1944 *G.I. Journal*
(Show #53) Mel (again probably as "Pvt. Sad Sack") works with Bing Crosby, the Music Maids & Men, Ransom Sherman, Jo Stafford, Lynn Bari, Peter Lorre and John Scott Trotter's orchestra.

July 28, 1944 *G.I. Journal*

(Program #54) The date listed is the recording date, not broadcast date. This radio program was syndicated to troops overseas for their enjoyment and was not broadcast in the U.S. Mel Blanc plays the role of "Private Sad Sack" with guests George Murphy, Linda Darnell and Jimmy Durante.

August 2, 1944 *Mail Call*

(Program #103) The date listed is the recording date, not broadcast date. This radio program was syndicated to troops overseas for their enjoyment and was not broadcast in the U.S. Mel Blanc plays the role of Bugs Bunny in this episode. Mel is joined with guests Jack Carson, Nelson Eddy and Ann Rutherford.

August 4, 1944 *G.I. Journal*

(Program #55) The date listed is the recording date, not broadcast date. This radio program was syndicated to troops overseas for their enjoyment and was not broadcast in the U.S. Mel Blanc plays the role of "Private Sad Sack" with guests Connie Haines, Jack Carson and Ransom Sherman.

August 15, 1944 to June 25, 1945 *The George Burns and Gracie Allen Show*
Weekly regulars: George Burns and Gracie Allen. Situation comedy with Mel Blanc in the recurring role of the mailman who exchanged witty one-liners and reminded Gracie to "keep smiling." Sponsored by Swan Soap. CBS.

August 25, 1944 *G.I. Journal*

(Program #58) The date listed is the recording date, not broadcast date. This radio program was syndicated to troops overseas for their enjoyment and was not broadcast in the U.S. Mel Blanc plays the role of "Private Sad Sack" with guests Ransom Sherman, Connie Haines, Jimmy Durante and Jack Carson.

September 1, 1944 *G.I. Journal*

(Program #59) The date listed is the recording date, not broadcast date. This radio program was syndicated to troops overseas for their enjoyment and was not broadcast in the U.S. Mel Blanc plays the role of "Private Sad Sack" with guests Lucille Ball, Joe E. Brown and Connie Haines.

September 8, 1944 *G.I. Journal*
(Program #60) The date listed is the recording date, not broadcast date. This radio program was syndicated to troops overseas for their enjoyment and was not broadcast in the U.S. Mel Blanc plays the role of "Private Sad Sack" with guests George Murphy, Jane Wyman, Connie Haines and Jerry Colonna.

September 15, 1944 *G.I. Journal*
(Program #61) The date listed is the recording date, not broadcast date. This radio program was syndicated to troops overseas for their enjoyment and was not broadcast in the U.S. Mel Blanc plays the role of "Private Sad Sack" with guests Verna Felton, Jane Wyman, and Abbott and Costello.

October 1, 1944 to May 27, 1945 *The Lucky Strike Program*
Weekly regular: Jack Benny. Situation comedy program with occasional comedy skits. Series supporting cast included Eddie "Rochester" Anderson, Don Wilson and Dennis Day. Mel Blanc appeared on an almost regular basis in supporting roles. Sponsored by American Tobacco (Lucky Strike Cigarettes). N B C.

October 5, 1944 to June 28, 1945 *The Abbott and Costello Show*
Weekly regulars: Bud Abbott and Lou Costello. Comedy/variety series. Supporting cast included Connie Haines, Billy Gray and Mel Blanc, who frequently supplied comedic roles for various skits, including the recurring role of The Scotchman. According to files at the Library of Congress, Mel Blanc played the role of Bugs Bunny a number of times. Sponsored by Reynolds (Camel Cigarettes). N B C.

October 27, 1944 *G.I. Journal*
(Program #66) The date listed is the recording date, not broadcast date. This radio program was syndicated to troops overseas for their enjoyment and was not broadcast in the U.S. Mel Blanc plays the role of "Private Sad Sack" with guests Jane Wyman, Jerry Colonna and Bob Hope.

November 17, 1944 *G. I. Journal*
(Show #69) Mel (probably as "Pvt. Sad Sack") joins Bing Crosby, the Charioteers, Pat Friday, Joan Blondell, Jimmy Durante and John Scott Trotter's orchestra.

November 24, 1944 *G.I. Journal*

(Program #71) The date listed is the recording date, not broadcast date. This radio program was syndicated to troops overseas for their enjoyment and was not broadcast in the U.S. Mel Blanc plays the role of "Private Sad Sack" with guests Robert Benchley, Arthur Treacher and Bonita Granville.

December 15, 1944 *G.I. Journal*

(Program #73) The date listed is the recording date, not broadcast date. This radio program was syndicated to troops overseas for their enjoyment and was not broadcast in the U.S. Mel Blanc plays the role of "Private Sad Sack" with guests Orson Welles, Connie Haines, Ziggy Elman and Victor Moore.

December 22, 1944 *G.I. Journal*

(Program #74) The date listed is the recording date, not broadcast date. This radio program was syndicated to troops overseas for their enjoyment and was not broadcast in the U.S. Mel Blanc plays the role of "Private Sad Sack" with guests Louella Parsons, Bob Hope, Dorothy Lamour and The Andrews Sisters.

December 24, 1944 *The Electric Hour*

Weekly regular: Nelson Eddy. Music and variety program. Mel Blanc plays the role of Bugs Bunny in a brief scene. Sponsored by 160 Business-Managed Independent Light and Power Companies. CBS.

December 29, 1944 *G.I. Journal*

(Program #75) The date listed is the recording date, not broadcast date. This radio program was syndicated to troops overseas for their enjoyment and was not broadcast in the U.S. Mel Blanc plays the role of "Private Sad Sack" with guests Kay Kyser, Jerry Colonna, Ann Miller and Connie Haines.

January 5, 1945 *G.I. Journal*

(Program #76) The date listed is the recording date, not broadcast date. This radio program was syndicated to troops overseas for their enjoyment and was not broadcast in the U.S. Mel Blanc plays "Private Sad Sack" on a skit, sharing time with guests Connie Haines, Lucille Ball and Jack Carson.

January 13, 1945 to June 30, 1945 *The Judy Canova Show*
Weekly regular: Judy Canova. Comedy series featuring short skits and songs. Verna Felton, Joseph Kearns and Mel Blanc are weekly regulars. Opie Cates and his Orchestra supplies additional music for the series. Blanc plays a variety of recurring characters including Pedro, salesman Roscoe Wortle, and the chronic hiccough. The series was intended to premiere on January 6, but President Roosevelt's special address to Congress caused the program to premiere January 13. Sponsored by Colgate. CBS.

January 12, 1945 *G.I. Journal*
(Program #77) The date listed is the recording date, not broadcast date. This radio program was syndicated to troops overseas for their enjoyment and was not broadcast in the U.S. Mel Blanc plays "Private Sad Sack" on a skit, sharing time with guests Jim and Marian Jordan, Ginger Rogers and Frank Sinatra.

March 9, 1945 *G.I. Journal*
(Program #85) The date listed is the recording date, not broadcast date. This radio program was syndicated to troops overseas for their enjoyment and was not broadcast in the U.S. Mel Blanc plays "Private Sad Sack" on a skit, sharing time with guests Connie Haines, Lucille Ball, Johnny Weissmuller and Groucho Marx.

March 16, 1945 *G. I. Journal*
(Show #86) Mel (most likely as "Pvt. Sad Sack") joins forces with Bing Crosby, Leo Cleary, Marilyn Maxwell and Allen Jenkins. Orchestra unknown.

April 1, 1945 *The Electric Hour*
Weekly regular: Nelson Eddy. Music and variety program. Mel Blanc plays the role of Bugs Bunny in a brief scene. Sponsored by 160 Business-Managed Independent Light and Power Companies. CBS.

May 3, 1945 *Command Performance*
(Program #173) The date listed is the recording date, not broadcast date. This radio program was syndicated to troops overseas for their enjoyment and was not broadcast in the U.S. Mel Blanc plays the role of Bugs Bunny in a tribute to Walt Disney and his animated friends!

May 4, 1945 *G.I. Journal*
(Program #93) The date listed is the recording date, not broadcast date. This radio program was syndicated to troops overseas for their enjoyment and was not broadcast in the U.S. Mel Blanc plays a comedic supporting role with guests Bob Hope, Lucille Ball and Eddie "Rochester" Anderson.

May 10, 1945 *Command Performance*
(Program #174) The date listed is the recording date, not broadcast date. This radio program was syndicated to troops overseas for their enjoyment and was not broadcast in the U.S. Mel Blanc plays a comedic supporting role with guests Paulette Goddard and Jack Benny.

May 11, 1945 *G. I. Journal*
(Show #94) Mel (probably as "Pvt. Sad Sack") performs with Bing Crosby, Chili Williams, Elvia Allman, Andy Devine and the AFRS Orchestra, conducted by Dick Aurant.

May 14, 1945 *Jubilee*
(Program #133) The date listed is the recording date, not broadcast date. This radio program was syndicated to troops overseas for their enjoyment and was not broadcast in the U.S. Mel Blanc is among the guests for this episode, which include Lena Horne, Ernest Whitman, and The Nat King Cole Trio.

May 18, 1945 *G.I. Journal*
(Program #95) The date listed is the recording date, not broadcast date. This radio program was syndicated to troops overseas for their enjoyment and was not broadcast in the U.S. Mel Blanc plays "Private Sad Sack" on a skit, sharing time with guests Connie Haines and Sidney Greenstreet.

June 8, 1945 *G.I. Journal*
(Program #98) The date listed is the recording date, not broadcast date. This radio program was syndicated to troops overseas for their enjoyment and was not broadcast in the U.S. Mel Blanc plays "Private Sad Sack" on a skit, sharing time with guests Arthur Treacher, Gloria Blondell and Robert Benchley.

June 15, 1945 *G.I. Journal*
(Program #99) The date listed is the recording date, not broadcast date. This radio program was syndicated to troops overseas for their enjoyment and was not broadcast in the U.S. Mel Blanc plays "Private Sad Sack" on a skit, sharing time with guests Connie Haines, Victor Borge and Kay Kyser.

June 29, 1945 *G.I. Journal*
(Program #101) The date listed is the recording date, not broadcast date. This radio program was syndicated to troops overseas for their enjoyment and was not broadcast in the U.S. Mel Blanc plays "Private Sad Sack" on a skit, sharing time with guests J. Carrol Naish, Lucille Ball, Sterling Holloway and Alan Ladd.

July 13, 1945 *G.I. Journal*
(Program #103) The date listed is the recording date, not broadcast date. This radio program was syndicated to troops overseas for their enjoyment and was not broadcast in the U.S. Mel Blanc plays "Private Sad Sack" on a skit, sharing time with guests Mel Torme, Connie Haines and Rita Hayworth.

August 31, 1945 *G.I. Journal*
(Program #108) The date listed is the recording date, not broadcast date. This radio program was syndicated to troops overseas for their enjoyment and was not broadcast in the U.S. Mel Blanc plays "Private Sad Sack" on a skit, sharing time with guests Robert Young, Ann Rutherford and Lionel Stander.

September 1, 1945 to June 22, 1946 *The Judy Canova Show*
Weekly regular: Judy Canova. Comedy series featuring short skits and songs. Ruby Dandridge, Verna Felton, Joseph Kearns and Mel Blanc are weekly regulars. Opie Cates and his Orchestra supplies additional music for the series. Roy Acuff appeared in a number of episodes. Blanc plays a variety of recurring characters including Pedro, salesman Roscoe Wortle, and the chronic hiccough. Sponsored by Colgate. CBS.

September 11, 1945 to June 11, 1946 *The Pepsodent Show*
Weekly regular: Bob Hope. Comedy/variety series with Mel Blanc appearing every few weeks in a comedic supporting role. Sponsored by Pepsodent. NBC.

September 14, 1945 *G.I. Journal*
(Program #110) The date listed is the recording date, not broadcast date. This radio program was syndicated to troops overseas for their enjoyment and was not broadcast in the U.S. Mel Blanc plays "Private Sad Sack" on a skit, sharing time with guests Bing Crosby, Allen Jenkins and Marilyn Maxwell.

September 15, 1945 to July 6, 1946 *The Life of Riley*
Weekly regular: William Bendix. Situation comedy about Chester A. Riley and his comedic situations involving the family, work and his friend Gillis. Throughout the season, Blanc played the role of Mr. Johnson, plus other comedic roles such as the September 15 episode, when Riley and Gillis feud over a pet goat, Mel Blanc takes command by voicing the animal effects. Sponsored by Ivory Soap. NBC.

September 20, 1945 to May 30, 1946 *The Maxwell House Coffee Time*
Weekly regulars: George Burns and Gracie Allen. Situation comedy with Mel Blanc in the recurring role of the mailman who exchanged witty one-liners and reminded Gracie to "keep smiling." Sponsored by Swan Soap. CBS.

September 21, 1945 *G.I. Journal*
(Program #111) The date listed is the recording date, not broadcast date. This radio program was syndicated to troops overseas for their enjoyment and was not broadcast in the U.S. Mel Blanc plays "Private Sad Sack" on a skit, sharing time with guests Fred MacMurray, Bob Hope and Olga San Juan.

September 30, 1945 to May 26, 1946 *The Lucky Strike Program*
Weekly regular: Jack Benny. Situation comedy program with occasional comedy skits. Series supporting cast included Eddie "Rochester" Anderson, Don Wilson and Dennis Day. Mel Blanc appeared on an almost regular basis in supporting roles. Sponsored by American Tobacco (Lucky Strike Cigarettes). NBC.

October 4, 1945 to June 27, 1946 *The Abbott and Costello Show*
Weekly regulars: Bud Abbott and Lou Costello. Comedy/variety series. Supporting cast included Connie Haines, Billy Gray and Mel Blanc, who frequently supplied comedic roles for various skits, including the recurring role of The Scotchman. According to files at the Library of Congress, Mel Blanc played the role of Bugs Bunny a number of times. Sponsored by Reynolds (Camel Cigarettes). NBC.

October 5, 1945 *G.I. Journal*
(Program #113) The date listed is the recording date, not broadcast date. This radio program was syndicated to troops overseas for their enjoyment and was not broadcast in the U.S. Mel Blanc plays "Private Sad Sack" on a skit, sharing time with guests Jack Haley, Sara Berner and Lucille Ball.

October 7, 1945 *Request Performance*
Variety program answering listener requests. Music, drama and comedy sketches. The actors changed every week. Mel Blanc was among the cast on this broadcast, the first episode of the series. Sponsored by Campbell Soups. CBS.

October 12, 1945 *G.I. Journal*
(Program #114) The date listed is the recording date, not broadcast date. This radio program was syndicated to troops overseas for their enjoyment and was not broadcast in the U.S. Mel Blanc plays "Private Sad Sack" on a skit, sharing time with guests Jack Carson, Bonita Granville and Connie Haines.

October 26, 1945 *Pabst Blue Ribbon Town*
Weekly regular: Danny Kaye. This particular broadcast was different from the rest of the season's episodes. Danny Kaye was away on a U.S.O. tour so the cast of *The Jack Benny Program* substituted for him. Mel Blanc was among the cast. Sponsored by Pabst. CBS.

November 3, 1945 *G.I. Journal*
(Program #117) The date listed is the recording date, not broadcast date. This radio program was syndicated to troops overseas for their enjoyment and was not broadcast in the U.S. Mel Blanc plays "Private Sad Sack" on a skit, sharing time with guests Lucille Ball, Cass Daley and Joe E. Brown.

November 6, 1945 *The Bob Hope Show*
Weekly regular: Bob Hope. This particular broadcast was broadcast from the Glove Theater in San Diego. Mel Blanc was among the cast. Sponsored by Pepsodent. NBC.

November 17, 1945 *G.I. Journal*
(Program #119) The date listed is the recording date, not broadcast date. This radio program was syndicated to troops overseas for their enjoyment and was not broadcast in the U.S. Mel Blanc plays "Private Sad Sack" on a skit, sharing time with guests Jack Haley, Arthur Treacher and Diana Lewis.

November 24, 1945 *G.I. Journal*
(Program #120) The date listed is the recording date, not broadcast date. This radio program was syndicated to troops overseas for their enjoyment and was not broadcast in the U.S. Mel Blanc plays "Private Sad Sack" on a skit, sharing time with guests Kay Kyser, Jerry Colonna and Lynn Bari.

December 25, 1945 *Command Performance*
The date may not be accurate, but this broadcast certainly represents Christmas of 1945. It was recorded in September 1945. This radio program was syndicated to troops overseas for their enjoyment and was not broadcast in the U.S. Mel Blanc shares comedic duties with guests Bob Hope, Jimmy Durante, Dinah Shore, Bing Crosby, Kay Kyser, Ed Gardner, Frances Langford and Frank Sinatra.

Circa 1945 *1945 Christmas Seal Campaign*
Produced by the Los Angeles Country Tuberculosis Association, with the cast of the Judy Canova Show, without Judy Canova. Ruby Dandridge, Verna Felton, Joseph Kearns and Mel Blanc are in the cast. The Sportsmen perform. Music supplies by Opie Cates and his Orchestra.

Circa 1946 to 1947 *To The Rear, March*
Produced by the Armed Forces Radio Service, this 30-minute series was created to entertain troops stationed overseas. Each episode featured excerpts from three programs including *The Adventures of Ozzie and Harriet, Blondie, The Charlie McCarthy Show, The Pepsodent Show, The Victor Borge Show,* and many others. Mel Blanc was the host of this program.

January 1946 *G.I. Journal*
(Program #128) The date listed is the recording date, not broadcast date. This radio program was syndicated to troops overseas for their enjoyment and was not broadcast in the U.S. Mel Blanc plays "Private Sad Sack" on a skit, sharing time with guests Monty Woolley, William Bendix and Ginny Simms.

January 1946 *G.I. Journal*
(Program #129) The date listed is the recording date, not broadcast date. This radio program was syndicated to troops overseas for their enjoyment and was not broadcast in the U.S. Mel Blanc plays "Private Sad Sack" on a skit, sharing time with guests Jack Carson, Claire Trevor and Charlie Ruggles.

January 31, 1946 *Command Performance*
(Program #209) The date listed is the recording date, not broadcast date. This radio program was syndicated to troops overseas for their enjoyment and was not broadcast in the U.S. Mel Blanc shares comedic duties with guests Chico Marx, Lena Romay, Robert Young and Jack Benny.

May 1946 *Command Performance*
Celebrating the fourth anniversary of the Armed Forces Radio Service. This radio program was syndicated to troops overseas for their enjoyment and was not broadcast in the U.S. Mel Blanc shares comedic duties with guests Fred MacMurray, Edgar Bergen, Frances Langford, Bob Hope, Janet Blair and The King Sisters.

May 2, 1946 *Bird's Eye Open House*
Weekly regular: Dinah Shore. Musical/comedy series featuring short skits and songs. Mel Blanc was among the cast on a special one-hour show combining the George Burns and Gracie Allen show with the Dinah Show program. Sponsored by Colgate. CBS.

August 31, 1946 to June 28, 1947 *The Judy Canova Show*
Weekly regular: Judy Canova. Comedy series featuring short skits and songs. Ruth Perrott, Joseph Kearns and Mel Blanc are weekly regulars. Charles Dant and his Orchestra supplies additional music for the series. The Sportsmen sung songs. Blanc plays a variety of recurring characters including Pedro, salesman Roscoe Wortle, and the chronic hiccough. Sponsored by Colgate. CBS.

September 3, 1946 to June 24, 1947 *Mel Blanc's Fix-It-Shop*
Also known as "The Mel Blanc Show." Situation comedy series with Mel Blanc as the weekly star. Supporting cast included Mary Jane Croft, Hans Conried, Jerry Hausner. The Sportsmen supplied musical vocals. A total of 41 episodes were produced and broadcast. Sponsored by Colgate. CBS.

Circa 1946 *G.I. Journal*
(Program #139) The date listed is the recording date, not broadcast date. This radio program was syndicated to troops overseas for their enjoyment and was not broadcast in the U.S. Mel Blanc plays "Private Sad Sack" on a skit, sharing time with guests Peggy Lee, Linda Darnell and Garry Moore.

September 5, 1946 to May 29, 1947 *The Maxwell House Coffee Time*
Weekly regulars: George Burns and Gracie Allen. Situation comedy with Mel Blanc as the recurring role of the mailman who exchanged witty one-liners and reminded Gracie to "keep smiling." Sponsored by Swan Soap. CBS.

September 29, 1946 *Stars in the Afternoon*
A special 90-minute CBS preview of the new 1946-47 season. Guests heard during the broadcasts include Ozzie and Harriet, Gene Autry, Fanny Brice, Meredith Willson, Joan Davis, Wally Brown, Agnes Moorehead, Lionel Barrymore, Arthur Treacher and Mel Blanc.

September 29, 1946 *Command Performance*
(Program #234) This radio program was syndicated to troops overseas for their enjoyment and was not broadcast in the U.S. Mel Blanc plays three roles in this episode: Private Sad Sack, The Postman who "keeps smiling" and Bugs Bunny. Other guests on this broadcast: Mary Pickford and Dave Barry.

September 29, 1946 to May 25, 1947 *The Lucky Strike Program*
Weekly regular: Jack Benny. Situation comedy program with occasional comedy skits. Series supporting cast included Eddie "Rochester" Anderson, Don Wilson and Dennis Day. Mel Blanc appeared on an almost regular basis in supporting roles. Sponsored by American Tobacco (Lucky Strike Cigarettes). NBC.

October 3, 1946 to June 26, 1947 *The Abbott and Costello Show*
Weekly regulars: Bud Abbott and Lou Costello. Comedy/variety series. Supporting cast included Connie Haines, Billy Gray and Mel Blanc, who frequently supplied comedic roles for various skits, including the recurring role of The Scotchman. Sponsored by Reynolds (Camel Cigarettes). NBC.

November 22, 1946 *Santa Claus Parade*
Special program originating from Hollywood. Mel Blanc appears in the role of Pedro, from *The Judy Canova Show.* Sponsor unknown. NBC.

January 30, 1947 *Chesterfield Supper Club*
Weekly regulars: Perry Como and Jo Stafford. Musical/variety program. Michael Ayers and his Orchestra supplied the music. Mel Blanc was the guest. Sponsored by Leggett & Myers (Chesterfield Cigarettes). NBC

February 11, 1947 *Boston Blackie*
(Program #96) Detective program with Richard Kollmar in the title role, as an ex-safe cracker who often finds himself involved in capers and tries to clear his name with Detective Faraday. This series was a ZIV syndication so the broadcast date is not accurate, depending on what part of the country you lived. Mel Blanc plays a supporting role in this episode.

August 5, 1947 *Command Performance*
(Program #284) The date listed is the recording date, not broadcast date. This radio program was syndicated to troops overseas for their enjoyment and was not broadcast in the U.S. Mel Blanc shares comedic duties with guests Judy Canova and David Street.

October 6, 1947 to May 31, 1948 *Point Sublime*
Weekly regulars: Cliff Arquette and Mel Blanc. Blanc plays the stuttering railway clerk August Moon in this situation comedy about life in a small seaport village. Blanc reprises his Porky Pig voice for the role of Moon.

August 30, 1947 to June 26, 1948 *The Judy Canova Show*
Weekly regular: Judy Canova. Comedy series featuring short skits and
songs. Ruby Dandridge, Joseph Kearns, Ruth Perrott, Gerald Mohr
and Mel Blanc are weekly regulars. Charles Dant and his Orchestra
supplies additional music for the series. The Sportsmen sung songs.
Blanc plays a variety of recurring characters including Pedro, salesman
Roscoe Wortle, and the chronic hiccough. Sponsored by Colgate. CBS.

September 4, 1947 to June 10, 1948 *The Maxwell House Coffee Time*
Weekly regulars: George Burns and Gracie Allen. Situation comedy with
Mel Blanc as the recurring role of the mailman who exchanged witty
one-liners and reminded Gracie to "keep smiling." Sponsored by Swan
Soap. CBS.

September 26, 1947 *Community Chest Program*
"Mobilization For Human Needs" was the title of this special four-
network broadcast, originating from Hollywood, inaugurating
Community Chest Drives. President Truman speaks on behalf of
Community Chests of America. Guests include Jack Benny, Bob Hope,
Dorothy Lamour, Jimmy Durante, Edgar Bergen, Margaret O'Brien
and Mel Blanc. NBC.

October 5, 1947 to June 27, 1948 *The Lucky Strike Program*
Weekly regular: Jack Benny. Situation comedy program with occasional
comedy skits. Series supporting cast included Eddie "Rochester"
Anderson, Don Wilson and Dennis Day. Mel Blanc appeared on
an almost regular basis in supporting roles. Sponsored by American
Tobacco (Lucky Strike Cigarettes). NBC.

January 22, 1948 to July 8, 1948 *The New Sealtest Village Store*
Weekly regulars: Jack Carson and Even Arden. Comedy/variety program
with Mel Blanc in various roles, but not on every program. Sponsored
by Sealtest. NBC.

April 22, 1948 *The Adventures of Ellery Queen*
Stars Howard Culver in the title role. Mel Blanc is featured as a
contestant determined to solve the mystery dramatized, "Murder
by Installments." Blanc correctly guesses and wins the prize money.
Sustaining. ABC.

May 9, 1948 *Guest Star*
(*Program #59*) Syndicated by the U.S. Treasury Department. George Burns and Gracie Allen go door to door to sell bonds. Mel Blanc is featured in the supporting cast.

September 30, 1948 to June 23, 1949 *The Maxwell House Coffee Time*
Weekly regulars: George Burns and Gracie Allen. Situation comedy with Mel Blanc as the recurring role of the mailman who exchanged witty one-liners and reminded Gracie to "keep smiling." Sponsored by Swan Soap. CBS.

October 2, 1948 to June 25, 1949 *The Judy Canova Show*
Weekly regular: Judy Canova. Comedy series featuring short skits and songs. Ruby Dandridge, Joseph Kearns, Ruth Perrott, Gale Gordon, Hans Conried, and Mel Blanc are weekly regulars. Charles Dant and his Orchestra supplies additional music for the series. The Sportsmen sung songs. Blanc plays a variety of recurring characters including Pedro, salesman Roscoe Wortle, and the chronic hiccough. Sponsored by Colgate. CBS.

October 3, 1948 to December 26, 1948 *The Lucky Strike Program*
Weekly regular: Jack Benny. Situation comedy program with occasional comedy skits. Series supporting cast included Eddie "Rochester" Anderson, Don Wilson and Dennis Day. Mel Blanc appeared on an almost regular basis in supporting roles. Sponsored by American Tobacco (Lucky Strike Cigarettes). NBC.

December 1948 *Command Performance*
One of two annual Christmas programs for 1948. This radio program was syndicated to troops overseas for their enjoyment and was not broadcast in the U.S. Mel Blanc plays the role of "Private Sad Sack" in this episode. Also guest on this broadcast: Jack Benny, Bob Hope, Jimmy Durante, Jimmy Durante, Jack Benny and Edgar Bergen.

December 1948 *Command Performance*
One of two annual Christmas programs for 1948. This radio program was syndicated to troops overseas for their enjoyment and was not broadcast in the U.S. Mel Blanc shares comedic duties with guests Gene Autry, Bing Crosby, Ann Sothern, Lum and Abner, Jerry Colonna and Francis X. Bushman.

Circa 1949 *Here's to Veterans*
(Program #100) Produced by the U.S. Veterans Administration. This 15-minute broadcast was created for the troops overseas. This episode features an excerpt from a prior broadcast of *The Judy Canova Show*. Mel Blanc is in the supporting cast. Broadcast in New York on NBC.

January 2, 1949 to May 29, 1949 *The Lucky Strike Program*
Weekly regular: Jack Benny. Situation comedy program with occasional comedy skits. Series supporting cast included Eddie "Rochester" Anderson, Don Wilson and Dennis Day. Mel Blanc appeared on an almost regular basis in supporting roles. Sponsored by American Tobacco (Lucky Strike Cigarettes). CBS.

May 8, 1949 *Amos 'n' Andy*
Weekly regulars: Freeman Gosden and Charles Correll. Situation comedy involving the con artist methods of The Kingfish, and the gullible Andy. Mel Blanc is featured in the supporting cast. Sponsored by Rinso Soap. CBS.

September 11, 1949 to May 28, 1950 *The Lucky Strike Program*
Weekly regular: Jack Benny. Situation comedy program with occasional comedy skits. Series supporting cast included Eddie "Rochester" Anderson, Don Wilson and Dennis Day. Mel Blanc appeared on an almost regular basis in supporting roles. Sponsored by American Tobacco (Lucky Strike Cigarettes). CBS.

October 1949 *The Challenge of the Yukon*
Adventure series for children from the producers of *The Lone Ranger* and *Ned Jordan, Secret Agent.* During this month, Mel Blanc appeared on a number of broadcasts in the Quaker Oats commercials, supplying the voice of Bugs Bunny to help promote the Bugs Bunny comic books.

October 1, 1949 to July 1, 1950 *The Judy Canova Show*
Weekly regular: Judy Canova. Comedy series featuring short skits and songs. Ruby Dandridge, Joseph Kearns, Ruth Perrott, Hans Conried, and Mel Blanc are weekly regulars. Charles Dant and his Orchestra supplies additional music for the series. The Sportsmen sung songs. Blanc plays a variety of recurring characters including Pedro, salesman Roscoe Wortle, and the chronic hiccough. Sponsored by Colgate. CBS.

April 9, 1950 *The Phil Harris–Alice Faye Show*
Weekly regulars: Phil Harris and Alice Faye. Situation comedy about a
zany, egotistical bandleader of questionable musical ability and wife,
a glamorous film star. Mel Blanc plays the role of a six-foot Easter
Bunny after Phil Harris claims he saw two large rabbits. Sponsored
by Rexall Drugs. NBC.

September 10, 1950 to June 3, 1951 *The Lucky Strike Program*
Weekly regular: Jack Benny. Situation comedy program with occasional
comedy skits. Series supporting cast included Eddie "Rochester"
Anderson, Don Wilson and Dennis Day. Mel Blanc appeared on
an almost regular basis in supporting roles. Sponsored by American
Tobacco (Lucky Strike Cigarettes). CBS.

October 7, 1950 to June 30, 1951 *The Judy Canova Show*
Weekly regular: Judy Canova. Comedy series featuring short skits and
songs. Ruby Dandridge, Joseph Kearns, Ruth Perrott, Hans Conried,
and Mel Blanc are weekly regulars. Charles Dant and his Orchestra
supplies additional music for the series. The Sportsmen sung songs.
Blanc plays a variety of recurring characters including Pedro, salesman Roscoe Wortle, and the chronic hiccough. Sponsored by Colgate.
CBS.

December 3, 1950 *The Phil Harris–Alice Faye Show*
Weekly regulars: Phil Harris and Alice Faye. Situation comedy about a
zany, egotistical bandleader of questionable musical ability and wife, a
glamorous film star. Mel Blanc plays a supporting role in this episode.
Sponsored by Rexall Drugs. NBC.

Circa 1951 *Hollywood Flashback*
An Armed Forces Radio Service production. Very little is known about
this program.

January 17, 1951 *The Family Theater*
Anthology program with various guest stars every week. A retelling of
the King Midas story, "The Golden Touch," was dramatized with Jack
Benny, Alan Reed and Mel Blanc in the cast. Sustaining. MUTUAL.

January 31, 1951 *The Family Theater*
Anthology program with various guest stars every week. Mel Blanc supplies a number of voices for this broadcast, a retelling of "The Adventures of Pinocchio." Sustaining. MUTUAL.

September 16, 1951 to June 1, 1952 *The Lucky Strike Program*
Weekly regular: Jack Benny. Situation comedy program with occasional comedy skits. Series supporting cast included Eddie "Rochester" Anderson, Don Wilson and Dennis Day. Mel Blanc appeared on an almost regular basis in supporting roles. Sponsored by American Tobacco (Lucky Strike Cigarettes). CBS.

October 14, 1951 *Amos 'n' Andy*
Weekly regulars: Freeman Gosden and Charles Correll. Situation comedy involving the con artist methods of The Kingfish, and the gullible Andy. This same radio script would later be adapted for an episode of the television series, but only the radio version featured Mel Blanc in the supporting cast. Sponsored by Rexall Drugs. CBS.

December 2, 1951 *Amos 'n' Andy*
Weekly regulars: Freeman Gosden and Charles Correll. Situation comedy involving the con artist methods of The Kingfish, and the gullible Andy. This episode is supposedly titled "Good Neighbors," but the new neighbors that moved in next door are anything but good. Mel Blanc is among the supporting cast. Sponsored by Rexall Drugs. CBS.

December 15, 1951 to June 28, 1952 *The Judy Canova Show*
Weekly regular: Judy Canova. Comedy series featuring short skits and songs. Ruby Dandridge, Joseph Kearns, Ruth Perrott, Hans Conried, and Mel Blanc are weekly regulars. Charles Dant and his Orchestra supplies additional music for the series. The Sportsmen sung songs. Blanc plays a variety of recurring characters including Pedro, salesman Roscoe Wortle, and the chronic hiccough. Sustained. NBC.

Circa 1952 *Mel Blanc with Billy May and his Orchestra*
An Armed Forces Radio Service production. Part of the AFRS Music Transcription Library. Many of the commercial musical albums with Mel Blanc's voice is featured.

February 9, 1952 *Boy Scouts of America*
Originating from Hollywood and broadcast only along the West Coast, Mel Blanc participated on the first half of this special. NBC.

March 23, 1952 *Portland 620*
Broadcast from Hollywood, this special radio broadcast commemorated the 30th Anniversary of Station KGW. The entire broadcast was pre-recorded via electrical transcription and broadcast on March 23. Mel Blanc participated. Broadcast only on the West Coast over selected NBC stations.

August 10, 1952 *The Jack Arthur Show*
Talk and interview program with Mel Blanc as guest by recording. NBC.

September 14, 1952 to June 7, 1953 *The Lucky Strike Program*
Weekly regular: Jack Benny. Situation comedy program with occasional comedy skits. Series supporting cast included Eddie "Rochester" Anderson, Don Wilson and Dennis Day. Mel Blanc appeared on an almost regular basis in supporting roles. Sponsored by American Tobacco (Lucky Strike Cigarettes). CBS.

October 23, 1952 to September 10, 1953 *The Judy Canova Show*
Weekly regular: Judy Canova. Comedy series featuring short skits and songs. Ruby Dandridge, Joseph Kearns, Ruth Perrott, Hans Conried, and Mel Blanc are weekly regulars. Charles Dant and his Orchestra supplies additional music for the series. The Sportsmen sung songs. Blanc plays a variety of recurring characters including Pedro, salesman Roscoe Wortle, and the chronic hiccough. Sustained. NBC.

January 28, 1953 *The Family Theater*
Anthology program with various guest stars every week. Mel Blanc plays the role of a talking dog in "Spunky," a story scripted by Monte Masters. Jeffrey Hunter and Barbara Rush appear in the cast. Sustaining. MUTUAL.

September 13, 1953 to June 6, 1954 *The Lucky Strike Program*
Weekly regular: Jack Benny. Situation comedy program with occasional comedy skits. Series supporting cast included Eddie "Rochester" Anderson, Don Wilson and Dennis Day. Mel Blanc appeared on an almost regular basis in supporting roles. Sponsored by American Tobacco (Lucky Strike Cigarettes). CBS.

December 11, 1953 *The Phil Harris-Alice Faye Show*
Weekly regulars: Phil Harris and Alice Faye. Situation comedy about a zany, egotistical bandleader of questionable musical ability and wife, a glamorous film star. Mel Blanc plays a supporting role in this episode. Sponsored by Rexall Drugs. NBC.

Circa 1954 *The Jack Benny Show*
Excerpts from the April 12, 1953 broadcast of *The Lucky Strike Program*, syndicated by the American Red Cross for charity relief.

Spring of 1954 *Salute to the 1954 Easter Seal Campaign*
Syndicated transcription sponsored by the Easter Seal Campaign. Jack Benny suffers from the effects of buying a new television set, and is forced to make a visit to his vault. Features the usual supporting cast: Dennis Day, Don Wilson and Mel Blanc.

April 26, 1954 *Second Chance*
Weekly regular: Johnny Olsen. Olsen interviews people having success, having received a second chance at the career they have. Mel Blanc was the guest this week. Multiple sponsors. NBC.

September 26, 1954 to May 22, 1955 *The Lucky Strike Program*
Weekly regular: Jack Benny. Situation comedy program with occasional comedy skits. Series supporting cast included Eddie "Rochester" Anderson, Don Wilson and Dennis Day. Mel Blanc appeared on an almost regular basis in supporting roles. Sponsored by American Tobacco (Lucky Strike Cigarettes). CBS.

November 7, 1954 *The Nutrilite Show*
Sponsored by Mytinger & Casselberry. NBC.

Circa 1955 - 1956 *The Cisco Kid*
Adventures series for children, syndicated by Ziv. Jack Mather plays the title role and Mel Blanc as Pancho (replacing Harry Lang who played the role for years) sometime near episode 700. The series was long-running with at least 750 transcriptions created since the mid-forties.

January 9, 1955 *Amos 'n' Andy*
Weekly regulars: Freeman Gosden and Charles Correll. Situation comedy involving the con artist methods of The Kingfish, and the gullible Andy. Mel Blanc is among the supporting cast. Sustained. CBS.

February 20, 1955 *The Dennis Day Show*
Weekly regulars: Dennis Day. This situation comedy was formerly titled *A Day in the Life of Dennis Day.* Mel Blanc was among the cast. Sustained. NBC.

March 1955 *The Dennis Day Show*
Weekly regulars: Dennis Day. This situation comedy was formerly titled *A Day in the Life of Dennis Day.* The cast spoofs the *Dragnet* radio program and Mel Blanc and Dennis Day perform the "Sy, Si" routine. Blanc reprises his Woody Woodpecker voice. Sustained. NBC.

April 1955 *The Dennis Day Show*
Weekly regulars: Dennis Day. This situation comedy was formerly titled *A Day in the Life of Dennis Day.* Mel Blanc does several of his cartoon voices and sings "The Pussycat Parade." Sustained. NBC.

October 28, 1956 to July 7, 1957 *The Best of Benny*
Weekly regular: Jack Benny. Recordings of prior Jack Benny broadcasts are repeated on this "best of" series. Series supporting cast included Eddie "Rochester" Anderson, Don Wilson, Dennis Day and Mel Blanc. CBS.

September 29, 1957 to June 22, 1958 *The Best of Benny*
Weekly regular: Jack Benny. Recordings of prior Jack Benny broadcasts are repeated on this "best of" series. Series supporting cast included Eddie "Rochester" Anderson, Don Wilson, Dennis Day and Mel Blanc. Sponsored by Home Insurance. CBS.

Spring 1967 *Superfun*

A comedy series developed by Mel Blanc Associates, featuring a different week-long adventure every week with "Meyer, the Spyer." There is a recorded demo dated 1968 with contemporary drop-ins: Gary Owens (KMPC, Los Angeles), Jack Palvino (WBBF, Rochester, New York), Don Munson (WJBC, Bloomington, Illinois), and J. Aku Papuli (KGMB, Honolulu).

Circa 1974 *Visual Radio*

The Southern California Broadcasters Association Luncheon on creative radio commercials. Mel Blanc tells the funny history of advertising. His son Noel Blanc is featured in the recording.

Cartoons and Short Subjects
Contributed by Randy Bonneville with Keith Scott

PORKY'S ROAD RACE (1937) D: Frank Tash[lin].
VOICES: *Joe Dougherty, Tedd Pierce, Elvia Allman, Billy Bletcher, Mel Blanc.*
Porky Pig (Dougherty) gets into an auto race with a batch of Hollywood caricatures, but must watch out for villainous 'Borax Karoff'. Animated cartoon with Blanc as 'Hiccups'. Entry in the LOONEY TUNES series. Other filmland notables represented: George Arliss, John Barrymore, Freddie Bartholomew, Charles Chaplin, W.C. Fields, Clark Gable, Greta Garbo, Leslie Howard, Charles Laughton, Stan Laurel & Oliver Hardy, Edna May Oliver.
SONGS: "Love And War" *(Harry Warren),* "Shave And A Haircut" *(traditional, composer unknown).*
MUSIC BY Carl W. Stalling.
Released on February 6
(7 min./Vitaphone Sound/DVD)
Leon Schlesinger Studios/Warner Bros.

PICADOR PORKY (1937) D: Fred [Tex] Avery.
VOICES: *Joe Dougherty, Billy Bletcher, Mel Blanc.*
Porky Pig (Dougherty) plans to fleece the local Mexicans by staging a fake bullfight, however he accidentally ends up in the ring with a real bull. Blanc voices the drunk. Entry in the LOONEY TUNES series.
SONGS: "La Cucaracha" *(traditional, composer unknown; sung by Blanc as the drunk),* "In Caliente" *(Allie Wrubel; Mort Dixon),* "Muchacha" *(Harry Warren).*
MUSIC BY Carl W. Stalling.
Released on February 27
(7 min./Vitaphone Sound)
Leon Schlesinger Studios/Warner Bros.

THE FELLA WITH THE FIDDLE (1937) D: I. [Isadore][Friz] Freleng.
VOICES: *Billy Bletcher, Bernice Hansen, Mel Blanc.*
An old mouse tells a tale describing the woes of avarice to his greedy
'grandmice.' Blanc is the fiddling mouse. Entry in the MERRIE MELO-
DIES series.
SONGS: "Fella With The Fiddle" *(Charlie Abbott)*, "All's Fair In Love And
War" *(Harry Warren; Al Dubin).*
MUSIC BY Carl W. Stalling.
Released on March 27
(7 min./Vitaphone Sound/Technicolor)
Leon Schlesinger Studios/Warner Bros.

PORKY'S ROMANCE (1937) D: Frank Tash[lin].
VOICES: *Joe Dougherty, Bernice Hansen, Shirley Reed, Mel Blanc, Teddy
Bergman [Alan Reed].*
Porky Pig (Dougherty) proposes to his girlfriend Petunia and is promptly
turned down. When he attempts suicide and is knocked out, Porky has a
nightmare about so-called 'wedded bliss.' Blanc plays an undetermined
character. Entry in the LOONEY TUNES series.
SONGS: "I Wanna Woo" *(Mabel Wayne; Arthur Swanstrom)*, "The Little
Things You Used To Do" *(Harry Warren; Al Dubin).*
MUSIC BY Carl W. Stalling.
Released on April 3
(8 min./Vitaphone Sound/DVD)
Leon Schlesinger Studios/Warner Bros.

SHE WAS AN ACROBAT'S DAUGHTER (1937) D: I. [Isadore][Friz]
Freleng.
VOICES: *Mel Blanc, Dave Weber.*
On tonight's theater program: 'Goofy-Tone News' — The bite of a mad
dog has people running around on all fours; a caricature of Adolf Hitler;
'The Petrified Florist' — Additional caricatures of Leslie Howard and
Bette Davis; a singalong. Blanc plays Dole Promise (a parody of the
broadcaster Lowell Thomas), Who Dehr (a spoof of comic Lou Lehr) and
Stickoutski (a parody of the conductor Stokowski). Entry in the MERRIE
MELODIES series.
SONG: "She Was An Acrobat's Daughter" *(Harry Ruby; Bert Kalmar).*
MUSIC BY Carl W. Stalling.
Released on April 10
(8 min./Vitaphone Sound/Technicolor/DVD)

Leon Schlesinger Studios/Warner Bros.
PORKY'S DUCK HUNT (1937) D: Fred [Tex] Avery.
VOICES: *Mel Blanc, Billy Bletcher, Dave Weber, The Sportsmen Quartet.*
Daffy Duck makes his first appearance when Porky Pig goes on a duck hunt and encounters the wacky fowl. Blanc voices both Porky and Daffy. Entry in the LOONEY TUNES series.
SONGS: "Moonlight Bay" *(Percy Wenrich; Edward Madden)*, "I Only Have Eyes For You" *(Harry Warren; Al Dubin)*, "Streamlined Greta Green" *(Fred Rose; T. Berwyck).*
MUSIC BY Carl W. Stalling.
Released on April 17
(9 min./Vitaphone Sound)
Leon Schlesinger Studios/Warner Bros.

PORKY AND GABBY (1937) D: Ub Iwerks.
VOICES: *Mel Blanc, Cal Howard.*
It's an arduous drive for Porky Pig and his pal Gabby Goat as they journey to their campsite, pitch a tent and have a run-in with a runaway outboard motor. Blanc is Porky, Gabby and the truck driver. Entry in the LOONEY TUNES series.
SONGS: "Who Is My Baby Gonna Love All Winter (Now That Summer Is Gone)" *(Seymour Simons)*, "Speaking Of The Weather" *(Harold Arlen; E.Y. Harburg).*
MUSIC BY Carl W. Stalling.
Released on May 15
(8 min./Vitaphone Sound)
Leon Schlesinger Studios/Warner Bros.

THE FOXY PUPS (1937) D: Ub Iwerks.
VOICES: *Mel Blanc, Robert Winkler.*
Dad Hound (Blanc) has trouble trying to teach his sons how to catch a fox. Entry in the COLOR RHAPSODY series.
MUSIC BY Eddie Kilfeather, Joe de Nat.
Released on May 21
(6½ min./RCA Sound/Technicolor)
Cartoon Films Limited/Charles Mintz Productions/Columbia

UNCLE TOM'S BUNGALOW (1937) D: Fred [Tex] Avery.
VOICES: *Billy Bletcher, Mel Blanc, Bernice Hansen, Kenneth Spencer, Tedd Pierce, Fred [Tex] Avery.*
The Termite Terrace version of the 'Uncle Tom' story, with our hero using dice skills to get away from the influence of evil Simon-Simon LeGree. Blanc voices undetermined characters. Entry in the MERRIE MELODIES series.
SONG: "The Old Folks At Home" *(Stephen Foster).*
MUSIC BY Carl W. Stalling.
Released on June 5
(8 min./Vitaphone Sound/Technicolor)
Leon Schlesinger Productions/Warner Brothers

PORKY'S BUILDING (1937) D: Frank Tash[lin].
VOICES: *Mel Blanc, Billy Bletcher, Bernice Hansen, Tedd Pierce.*
Porky Pig (Blanc) and his animal construction crew compete with no-good Dirty Diggs to win a city-hall building contract. Entry in the LOONEY TUNES series.
SONGS: "Organ Grinder's Swing" *(Will Hudson; Irving Mills)*, "Let's Put Our Heads Together" *(Harold Arlen; E.Y. Harburg)*, "The World is Full of Cuckoos (and My Heart is Full of Love)" *(J. Fred Coots; Charles Newman).*
MUSIC BY Carl W. Stalling.
Released on June 19
(8 min./Vitaphone Sound)
Leon Schlesinger Studios/Warner Bros.

STREAMLINED GRETA GREEN (1937) D: I. [Friz] Freleng.
VOICES: *Bernice Hansen, Mel Blanc, The Basin Street Boys.*
Humanoid automobiles with a story of life: A young car dreams of being a taxi, but ends up playing in traffic and getting smashed by a train. Blanc is various characters. Entry in the MERRIE MELODIES series.
SONGS: "Streamlined Greta Green" *(Fred Rose; T. Berwyck)*, "Little Man You've Had A Busy Day" *(Mabel Wayne; Maurice Siglar; Al Hoffman).*
MUSIC BY Carl W. Stalling.
Released on June 19
(8 min./Vitaphone Sound/Technicolor)
Leon Schlesinger Studios/Warner Bros.

SWEET SIOUX (1937) D: Frank Tash[lin].
VOICES: *Mel Blanc, Billy Bletcher.*
Some offbeat Indians are depicted as they prepare to attack a wagon train. Blanc is various characters. Caricature of Martha Raye. Entry in the MERRIE MELODIES series.
SONGS: "Oh, Susanna" *(Stephen Foster),* "Goombay Drum" *(Charles Lofthouse; Schuyler Knowlton; Stanley Adams).*
MUSIC BY Carl W. Stalling.
Released on June 26
(8 min./Vitaphone Sound/Technicolor)
Leon Schlesinger Studios/Warner Bros.

PORKY'S SUPER SERVICE (1937) D: Ub Iwerks.
VOICES: *Mel Blanc, Elvia Allman, Dave Weber.*
Gas-station attendant Porky Pig (Blanc) sees some odd customers, including an obnoxious brat who wreaks havoc and destruction. Entry in the LOONEY TUNES series.
SONG: "Swing For Sale" *(Saul Chaplin; Sammy Cahn).*
MUSIC BY Carl W. Stalling.
Released on July 3
(7 min./Vitaphone Sound)
Leon Schlesinger Studios/Warner Bros.

EGGHEAD RIDES AGAIN (1937) D: Fred [Tex] Avery.
VOICES: *Mel Blanc, Billy Bletcher, Fred [Tex] Avery, The Sons of the Pioneers.*
Inept Egghead (Blanc) dreams of being a cowboy and goes West to become one; but first he must pass some tests — which include a troublesome calf. Entry in the MERRIE MELODIES series.
SONG: "That's My Western Home" *(composer unknown).*
MUSIC BY Carl W. Stalling.
Released on July 17
(8 min./Vitaphone Sound/Technicolor)
Leon Schlesinger Studios/Warner Bros.

PORKY'S BADTIME STORY (1937) D: Robert [Bob] Clampett.
VOICES: *Mel Blanc.*
In order not to lose their jobs, Porky Pig and Gabby Goat need to get a good night's rest so they can awaken on time and not be late. However, some pesky obstacles hinder their slumber. Blanc is Porky, Gabby and the Boss. Entry in the LOONEY TUNES series.
SONGS: "How Could You?" *(Harry Warren; Al Dubin)*, "By The Light Of The Silvery Moon" *(Gus Edwards; Edward Madden).*
MUSIC BY Carl W. Stalling.
Released on July 24
(7 min./Vitaphone Sound)
Leon Schlesinger Studios/Warner Bros.

PLENTY OF MONEY AND YOU (1937) D: I. [Friz] Freleng.
VOICES: *Mel Blanc, Dave Weber.*
A hen unexpectedly hatches a baby ostrich (Blanc), who immediately begins to devour every odd item in sight. Trouble looms in the form of a hungry weasel — out to make the ostrich his next dinner. Entry in the MERRIE MELODIES series.
SONG: "Plenty Of Gravy On You" *(sung to the tune of "Plenty Of Money And You" as composed by Harry Warren and Al Dubin).*
MUSIC BY Carl W. Stalling.
Released on July 3
(7 min./Vitaphone Sound/Technicolor)
Leon Schlesinger Studios/Warner Bros.

SPRING FESTIVAL (1937) D: *(no director credited)*
VOICES: *Mel Blanc.*
A cartoon version of spring's arrival, as seen by a groundhog. Blanc is various characters. Entry in the COLOR RHAPSODY series.
MUSIC BY Joe DeNat.
Released on August 6
(7 min./RCA Sound/Technicolor)
Charles Mintz Productions/Columbia

PORKY'S RAILROAD (1937) D: Frank Tashlin.
VOICES: *Mel Blanc, Billy Bletcher, Dave Weber.*
Porky Pig (Blanc) is the engineer of an old locomotive whose existence is
threatened by a new streamlined super train. A race will determine which
is better. Entry in the LOONEY TUNES series.
MUSIC BY Carl W. Stalling.
Released on August 7
(7 min./Vitaphone Sound/DVD)
Leon Schlesinger Studios/Warner Bros.

A SUNBONNET BLUE (1937) D: Fred [Tex] Avery.
VOICES: *Bernice Hansen, Tommy Bond, Mel Blanc, Fred [Tex] Avery, The
Sportsmen Quartet.*
Mice in a hat shop come together when a villainous rat kidnaps a mouse's
girlfriend. Blanc is various characters. Entry in the MERRIE MELODIES
series.
SONGS: "A Sunbonnet Blue (And A Yellow Straw Hat)" *(Sammy Fain;
Irving Kahal),* "I Haven't Got A Hat" *(Robert D. Emmerich; Buddy Bernier),*
"Japanese Sandman" *(Richard A. Whiting; Raymond B.Egan).*
MUSIC BY Carl W. Stalling.
Released on August 21
(7 min./Vitaphone Sound/Technicolor)
Leon Schlesinger Studios/Warner Bros.

GET RICH QUICK PORKY (1937) D: Robert [Bob] Clampett.
VOICES: *Mel Blanc, Earle Hodgins, Cal Howard.*
Porky Pig (Blanc) and Gabby Goat buy a city lot which is reputed to have
oil. They toil to strike the gusher without success — until a dog wanders
in to bury a bone. Entry in the LOONEY TUNES series.
MUSIC BY Carl W. Stalling.
Released on August 28
(7 min./Vitaphone Sound)
Leon Schlesinger Studios/Warner Bros.

SPEAKING OF THE WEATHER (1937) D: Frank Tashlin.
VOICES: *Billy Bletcher, Mel Blanc, Fred [Tex] Avery, Dave Weber.*
A crime-and-chase playlet is enacted across the covers of noted magazines. Blanc is the 'scatting' caricature of Leopold Stokowski, Cholly Jam (a caricature of Warner Oland as Charlie Chan) and Walter Snitchall (caricature of Walter Winchell). Other caricatures: Bob Burns, Clark Gable, Greta Garbo, Hugh Herbert, Ted Lewis, William Powell, Ned Sparks, and Johnny Weissmuller as Tarzan. Entry in the MERRIE MELODIES series.
SONGS: "Storm Movement" from "William Tell" *(Gioacchino Rossini),* "Speaking Of The Weather" *(Harold Arlen; E.Y. Harburg),* "Organ Grinder's Swing" *(Will Hudson; Irving Mills),* "All's Fair In Love And War" *(Harry Warren; Al Dubin),* "Summer Night" *(Warren; Dubin).*
MUSIC BY Carl W. Stalling.
Released on September 4
(7 min./Vitaphone Sound/Technicolor/DVD)
Leon Schlesinger Studios/Warner Bros.

PORKY'S GARDEN (1937) D: Fred [Tex] Avery.
VOICES: *Mel Blanc, Earle Hodgins, Charles Judels.*
Porky Pig (Blanc) hopes to win a cash prize for his vegetables, but his neighbor and some overgrown chickens reduce our hero's garden to one lowly pumpkin. Entry in the LOONEY TUNES series.
SONG: "The Farmer In The Dell" *(traditional, composer unknown).*
MUSIC BY Carl W. Stalling.
Released on September 11
(7 min./Vitaphone Sound)
Leon Schlesinger Studios/Warner Bros.

DOG DAZE (1937) D: I. [Friz] Freleng.
VOICES: *Bernice Hansen, Billy Bletcher, Mel Blanc, The Sons of the Pioneers.*
Comical canines offer us puns, gags and a vaudeville show. Blanc is the Police Dog, Spitz, the Russian Wolf Hounds and Prairie Dog.
SONG: "My Little Buckaroo" *(M.K. Jerome, Jack Scholl; sung by Blanc as Prairie Dog).*
MUSIC BY Carl W. Stalling.
Released on September 18
(7 min./Vitaphone Sound/Technicolor)
Leon Schlesinger Studios/Warner Bros.

ROVER'S RIVAL (1937) D: Robert [Bob] Clampett.
VOICES: *Mel Blanc, Robert C. Bruce.*
Porky Pig has a slate of new tricks to teach his old hound, but Rover is not up to the task. When Porky turns his attention to a young pup, Rover has to prove his worth. Blanc is Porky and the puppy. Entry in the LOONEY TUNES series.
MUSIC BY Carl W. Stalling.
Released on October 9
(7 min./Vitaphone Sound)
Leon Schlesinger Studios/Warner Bros.

THE LYIN' MOUSE (1937) D: I. [Friz] Freleng.
VOICES: *Bernice Hansen, Mel Blanc, Billy Bletcher.*
When a hungry cat (Blanc) catches a little mouse, the squeaky prey spins a tale of heroism that will hopefully inspire the cat to set him free. Entry in the MERRIE MELODIES series.
SONGS: "How Could You?" *(Harry Warren; Al Dubin)*, "Too Marvelous For Words" *(Richard A. Whiting; Johnny Mercer)*, "Old King Cole" *(Whiting; Mercer)*.
MUSIC BY Carl W. Stalling.
Released on October 16
(7 min./Vitaphone Sound/Technicolor)
Leon Schlesinger Studios/Warner Bros.

THE CASE OF THE STUTTERING PIG (1937) D: Frank Tashlin.
VOICES: *Mel Blanc, Billy Bletcher, Shirley Reed.*
Porky Pig (Blanc) and his relatives are bequeathed a fortune — unless something happens to them. Since lawyer Goodwill is next in line to inherit, he plots the porcine family's demise with help from a 'Jekyll & Hyde' potion. Entry in the LOONEY TUNES series.
SONGS: "Half Of Me (Wants To Be Good)" *(Peter DeRose; Sam Lewis)*, "Fate" *(John S. Zamecnik)*.
MUSIC BY Carl W. Stalling.
Exhibitors Award *(Cartoon of the Year)* Leon Schlesinger.
Released on October 30
(7 min./Vitaphone Sound/DVD)
Leon Schlesinger Studios/Warner Bros.

LITTLE RED WALKING HOOD (1937) D: Fred [Tex] Avery.
VOICES: *Tedd Pierce, Arthur Q. Bryan, Elvia Allman, Mel Blanc.*
A pool-hall wolf spots a strolling Red and tries to 'pick her up' in his hot
rod. When he literally gets the cold shoulder, the Wolf follows her to
Grandma's house. Blanc voices undetermined characters. Entry in the
MERRIE MELODIES series.
SONGS: "Liebestraum No. 3" *(Franz Liszt),* "Have You Got Any Castles,
Baby?" *(Richard A. Whiting; Johnny Mercer).*
MUSIC BY Carl W. Stalling.
Released on November 6
(7 min./Vitaphone Sound/Technicolor/DVD)
Leon Schlesinger Studios/Warner Bros.

PORKY'S DOUBLE TROUBLE (1937) D: Frank Tashlin.
VOICES: *Mel Blanc, Frederick Lindsley, Shirley Reed, Dave Weber.*
An escaped 'Killer' notices the resemblance between himself and bank
teller Porky Pig, so he hatches a plot to kidnap Porky and assume his
identity. Blanc is Porky and Killer. Entry in the LOONEY TUNES series.
MUSIC BY Carl W. Stalling.
Released on November 13
(7 min./Vitaphone Sound/DVD)
Leon Schlesinger Studios/Warner Bros.

RAILROAD RHYTHM (1937) D: Manny Gould, Ben Harrison.
VOICES: *Mel Blanc, Leone LeDoux, Dave Webber.*
Krazy Kat (Blanc) is engineer of Locomotive #77 and becomes a hero
when he saves Winsome Winnie from being tied to the track.
MUSIC BY Joe DeNat.
Released on November 20
(6 min./RCA Sound/Technicolor)
Charles Mintz Productions/Columbia

PORKY'S HERO AGENCY (1937) D: Robert [Bob] Clampett.
VOICES: *Mel Blanc, Bernice Hansen, Tedd Pierce.*
Caught up in Greek legends, Porky Pig (Blanc) falls asleep and dreams
he's an ancient Grecian hero out to stop the Gorgon — a female monster
who turns people to stone. Entry in the LOONEY TUNES series.
SONGS: "Am I In Love?" *(Harry Warren; Al Dubin),* "Have You Got Any
Castles, Baby?" *(Richard A. Whiting; Johnny Mercer).*
MUSIC BY Carl W. Stalling.
Released on December 4
(7 min./Vitaphone Sound/DVD)
Leon Schlesinger Studios/Warner Bros.

THE WOODS ARE FULL OF CUCKOOS (1937) D: Frank Tashlin.
VOICES: *Mel Blanc, Tedd Pierce, Fred [Tex] Avery.*
A radio revue using microphone personalities of the day grafted onto
animal characters. Blanc is Mr. Growlin. Entry in the MERRIE MELO-
DIES series. Radio stars parodied: Fred Allen, Portland Hoffa, Jack Benny,
Milton Berle, Ben Bernie, Eddie Cantor, Irvin S. Cobb, Bing Crosby,
Andy Devine, Deanna Durbin, W.C. Fields, Wendell Hall, The Happiness
Boys (Ernie Jones & Billy Hare), Al Jolson, Ruby Keeler, Tizzie Lish (Bill
Comstock), Fred MacMurray, Haven MacQuarrie, Grace Moore, Louella
Parsons, Joe Penner, Lily Pons, Dick Powell, Martha Raye, Lanny Ross,
Sophie Tucker, Walter Winchell, Alexander Woolcott.
SONGS: "The Woods Are Full Of Cuckoos *(And My Heart Is Full Of
Love; J. Fred Coots; Charles Newman),* "My Green Fedora" *(Joseph Meyer;
Al Lewis; Al Sherman),* "How Could You?" *(Harry Warren; Al Dubin),* "Old
Folks At Home (Swanee River)" *(Stephen Foster; performed by Blanc as
Mr. Growlin),* "Shine On, Harvest Moon" *(Nora Bayes; Jack Norworth),*
"The Lady Who Couldn't Be Kissed" *(Harry Warren; Al Dubin),* "Here
Comes The Sandman" *(Harry Warren; Al Dubin),* "Oh, How Do You Do,
And How Are You" *(to the tune of "On The Rue De La Paix", as composed
by Werner R. Heymann and Ted Koehler).*
MUSIC BY Carl W. Stalling.
Released on December 4
(7 min./Vitaphone Sound/Technicolor/DVD)
Leon Schlesinger Studios/Warner Bros.

DAFFY DUCK & EGGHEAD (1938) D: Fred [Tex] Avery.
VOICES: *Mel Blanc, Cliff Nazarro, Dave Weber.*
Egghead takes his turn at hunting the crazy loon, but the lake-hopping duck proves to have more (half) wits. Blanc is Daffy, Turtle Referee and Nut House Duck. Entry in the MERRIE MELODIES series.
SONGS: "The Merry-Go-Round Broke Down" *(Cliff Friend; Dave Franklin; performed by Blanc as Daffy),* "Dawn" from "William Tell" *(Gioacchino Rossini),* "Song Of The Volga Boatman" *(traditional, composer unknown).*
MUSIC BY Carl W. Stalling.
Released on January 1
(7 min./Vitaphone Sound/Technicolor/Video/DVD),
Leon Schlesinger Studios/Warner Bros.

PORKY'S POPPA (1938) D: Robert [Bob] Clampett.
VOICES: *Mel Blanc, Russ Powell.*
Porky Pig's debt-ridden farmer-father buys a mechanical cow to out-produce his Bessie. Porky endeavors to help old Bessie win a competition between her and the mechanized bovine. Blanc is Porky, Poppa Pig and the duck. Entry in the LOONEY TUNES series.
MUSIC BY Carl W. Stalling.
Released on January 15
(7 min./Vitaphone Sound)
Leon Schlesinger Studios/Warner Bros.

MY LITTLE BUCKAROO (1938) D: I. [Friz] Freleng.
VOICES: *Frederick Lindsley, Mel Blanc, Charlie Lung, Fred [Tex] Avery.*
In this cartoon western, Porky Pig (Blanc) goes in pursuit of the Terror, a notorious border bandit. Entry in the MERRIE MELODIES series.
SONGS: "My Little Buckaroo" *(M.K. Jerome; Jack Scholl),* "Oh, Susanna" *(Stephen Foster).*
MUSIC BY Carl W. Stalling.
Released on January 29
(7 min./Vitaphone Sound/Technicolor)
Leon Schlesinger Studios/Warner Bros.

PORKY AT THE CROCADERO (1938) D: Frank Tashlin.
VOICES: *Mel Blanc, Dave Weber.*
Porky Pig (Blanc) is a washing dishes at a nightclub when he is called upon to perform when all the acts fail to show up. He imitates various bandleaders (including Cab Calloway, Benny Goodman, Guy Lombardo, Rudy Vallee and Paul Whiteman). Entry in the LOONEY TUNES series.
SONGS: "Summer Night" *(Harry Warren; Al Dubin)*, "Chinatown, My Chinatown" *(Jean Schwartz; William Jerome; performed by Blanc as Porky imitating Cab Calloway)*, "Remember Me?" *(Warren; Dubin)*, "Little Man You've Had A Busy Day" *(Mabel Wayne; Maurice Siglar; Al Hoffman)*, "Avalon" *(Al Jolson; B.G. DeSylva; Vincent Rose)*, "Sentimental And Melancholy" *(Richard A. Whiting; Johnny Mercer)*, "You Can't Stop Me From Dreaming" *(Cliff Friend; Dave Franklin)*, "Rhapsody In Blue" *(George Gershwin)*.
MUSIC BY Carl W. Stalling.
Released on February 5
(7 min./Vitaphone Sound)
Leon Schlesinger Studios/Warner Bros.

MAN HUNT (1938) D: Walter Lantz.
VOICES: *Mel Blanc, Shirley Reed.*
Oswald the Lucky Rabbit tries to shield his animal friends from deadly hunters. Blanc provides his vocal talent.
MUSIC BY Frank Marsales.
Released on February 7
(10 min./Western Electric Sound)
Walter Lantz Productions/Universal

JUNGLE JITTERS (1938) D: I. [Friz] Freleng.
VOICES: *Mel Blanc, Tedd Pierce.*
A door-to-door salesman finds himself in Africa trying to sell items to a tribe of cannibals. He's about to get stewed (literally) until their homely queen falls in love with him. Blanc is the natives, the guard and the preacher. Entry in the MERRIE MELODIES series.
SONGS: "Too Marvelous For Words" *(Richard A. Whiting; Johnny Mercer)*, "Goombay Drum" *(Charles Lofthouse; Schuyler Knowlton; Stanley Adams)*, "Jitterbug Jamboree" *(M.K. Jerome)*.
MUSIC BY Carl W. Stalling.
Released on February 19
(7 min./Vitaphone Sound/Technicolor)
Leon Schlesinger Studios/Warner Bros.

WHAT PRICE PORKY (1938) D: Robert [Bob] Clampett.
VOICE: Mel Blanc
Porky Pig's farm becomes a battle zone when a flock of ducks use war tactics to steal his corn. Blanc stars as Porky. Entry in the LOONEY TUNES series.
SONGS: "Mademoiselle From Armentieres" *(composer unknown),* "Reveille" *(traditional, composer unknown).*
MUSIC BY Carl W. Stalling.
Released on February 26
(7 min./Vitaphone Sound/DVD)
Leon Schlesinger Studios/Warner Bros.

FEED THE KITTY (1938) D: Alex Lovy.
VOICES: *Mel Blanc, Shirley Reed.*
A Great Dane named Elmer (Blanc) almost kills a mother cat and decides to tend her kittens while she recuperates.
MUSIC BY Frank Churchill.
Released on March 14
(7 min./Western Electric Sound)
Walter Lantz Productions/Universal

PORKY'S PHONEY EXPRESS (1938) D: Cal Howard, Cal Dalton.
VOICES: *Mel Blanc, Billy Bletcher, Fred [Tex] Avery.*
In the Old West, lowly Porky Pig (Blanc) gets his chance to ride the Pony Express mail into Red Gulch — but he has to get through a band of marauding Indians. Entry in the LOONEY TUNES series.
SONG: "San Antonio" *(Egbert Van Alstyne; Harry Williams).*
MUSIC BY Carl W. Stalling.
Released on March 19
(7 min./Vitaphone Sound)
Leon Schlesinger Studios/Warner Bros.

NELLIE THE SEWING MACHINE GIRL
OR HONEST HEARTS AND WILLING HANDS (1938) D: Alex Lovy.
VOICES: *Billy Bletcher, Shirley Reed, Mel Blanc.*
Nellie is in peril when tied to a buzz-saw as our hero searches for a can of spinach (if it works for Popeye…). Blanc provides his vocal talents.
MUSIC BY Frank Marsales, Frank Churchill.
Released on April 11
(6 min./Western Electric Sound)
Walter Lantz Productions/Universal

PORKY'S FIVE & TEN (1938) D: Robert [Bob] Clampett.
VOICE: *Mel Blanc.*
Some scheming fish nearly ruin Porky Pig's plan to open a five-and-ten-cent store on a tropic isle; they attack his cargo ship and steal all the merchandise. Blanc stars as Porky. Caricatures of Stan Laurel & Oliver Hardy, Mae West and Greta Garbo. Entry in the LOONEY TUNES series.
SONG: "Happiness Ahead" *(Allie Wrubel; Mort Dixon).*
MUSIC BY Carl W. Stalling.
Released on April 16
(7 min./Vitaphone Sound)
Leon Schlesinger Studios/Warner Bros.

THE PENGUIN PARADE (1938) D: Fred [Tex] Avery.
VOICES: *Cliff Nazarro, Mel Blanc, The Sportsmen Quartet, Fred [Tex] Avery.*
Antarctic animals have a posh nightclub where musical acts perform: Bob Crispy, Fats Walrus and a Ritz Brothers-like trio of penguins. Blanc is various characters. Entry in the MERRIE MELODIES series.
SONG: "Penguin Parade" *(Byron Gay; Richard A. Whiting).*
MUSIC BY Carl W. Stalling.
Released on April 16
(7 min./Vitaphone Sound/Technicolor)
Leon Schlesinger Studios/Warner Bros.

PORKY'S HARE HUNT (1938) D: Ben Hardaway, (Cal Dalton*).*
VOICES: *Mel Blanc.*
Porky Pig takes his dog Zero on a hunt for rabbits and encounters an elusive, zany bunny. Blanc plays Porky, Zero and the rabbit (an early prototype of Bugs Bunny). Entry in the LOONEY TUNES series.
SONGS: "Pop Goes The Weasel" *(traditional, composer unknown)*, "In Caliente" *(Allie Wrubel; Mort Dixon).*
MUSIC BY Carl W. Stalling.
Released on April 30
(7 min./Vitaphone Sound)
Leon Schlesinger Studios/Warner Bros.

NOW THAT SUMMER IS GONE (1938) D: Frank Tashlin.
VOICES: *Mel Blanc, Billy Bletcher.*
Reckless Junior Squirrel gambles away all his acorns and nuts during good weather and has nothing when the cold winter comes. Blanc is Junior and the gambler. Entry in the MERRIE MELODIES series.
SONG: "Who Is My Baby Gonna Love All Winter (Now That Summer Is Gone)" *(Seymour Simons).*
MUSIC BY Carl W. Stalling.
Released on May 14
(7 min./Vitaphone Sound/Technicolor/DVD)
Leon Schlesinger Studios/Warner Bros.

KRAZY'S MAGIC (1938) D: Manny Gould, Ben Harrison.
VOICES: *Mel Blanc, Dave Weber.*
Krazy Kat (Blanc) and friend Kitty take shelter in an old house during a thunderstorm and meet a wacky magician — who gives them a harrowing time.
MUSIC BY Joe DeNat.
Released on May 20
(6 min./RCA Sound/Technicolor)
Charles Mintz Productions/Columbia

INJUN TROUBLE (1938) D: Robert [Bob] Clampett.
VOICES: *Mel Blanc, Billy Bletcher.*
Wagon train scout Porky Pig braves the wrath of deadly Injun Joe and finds help from crazy old westerner Sloppy Moe. Blanc is Porky, Moe and the trail boss. Entry in the LOONEY TUNES series.
MUSIC BY Carl W. Stalling.
Released on May 21
(7 min./Vitaphone Sound)
Leon Schlesinger Studios/Warner Bros.

THE ISLE OF PINGO PONGO (1938) D: Fred [Tex] Avery.
VOICES: *Gil Warren, The Basin Street Boys, The Sons of the Pioneers, Mel Blanc, Fred [Tex] Avery, Robert C. Bruce.*
A parade of animated sight-gags spot this travelogue parody as we sail to a tropical paradise. Blanc is Egghead. Caricature of Fats Waller. Entry in the MERRIE MELODIES series.
MUSIC BY Carl W. Stalling.
Released on May 28
(7 min./Vitaphone Sound/Technicolor)
Leon Schlesinger Studios/Warner Bros.

PORKY THE FIREMAN (1938) D: Frank Tashlin.
VOICES: *Mel Blanc, Tedd Pierce, Elvia Allman.*
Chief Porky Pig has trouble putting out the fire at a theatrical boarding house when his dog assistant, the tenants and a recalcitrant hydrant prove to be obstacles. Blanc is Porky and Slow Dog. Entry in the LOONEY TUNES series.
MUSIC BY Carl W. Stalling.
Released on June 4
(7 min./Vitaphone Sound/DVD)
Leon Schlesinger Studios/Warner Bros.

NELLIE THE INDIAN CHIEF'S DAUGHTER (1938) D: Alex Lovy.
VOICES: *Billy Bletcher, Shirley Reed, Mel Blanc, Dave Weber.*
Swing band musician Bennie Bigwind Gooseskin steps in when Nellie is threatened by Rudolph Ratbone. Blanc provides his vocal talent.
MUSIC BY Frank Churchill.
Released on June 6
(7 min./Western Electric Sound)
Walter Lantz Productions/Universal

KATNIP KOLLEGE (1938) D: Cal Dalton, Cal Howard.
VOICES: *Cliff Nazarro, Johnny 'Scat' Davis, Dave Weber, The Pied Pipers, Mel Blanc, Poley McClintock, George 'Spanky' McFarland, Mabel Todd.*
At college, Johnny the Cat cannot get hep to swing and falls out with his girlfriend Kitty. All is not lost as a ticking clock helps Johnny get some jive. Blanc is various characters. Entry in the MERRIE MELODIES series.
SONGS: "Easy As Rollin' Off A Log" *(M.K. Jerome; Jack Scholl)*, "You're An Education" *(Harry Warren; Al Dubin)*, "Scattin' With Mr. Bear" *(Jerome; Scholl)*.
MUSIC BY Carl W. Stalling.
Released on June 11
(7 min./Vitaphone Sound/Technicolor/DVD)
Leon Schlesinger Studios/Warner Bros.

PORKY'S PARTY (1938) D: Robert [Bob] Clampett.
VOICES: *Mel Blanc.*
Porky Pig celebrates his birthday with a productive silkworm, drunken dog Black Fury, a hungry penguin and cross-eyed Goosey Goose. Blanc is Porky, Black Fury and the penguin. Entry in the LOONEY TUNES series.
SONGS: "Happy Birthday To Me" *(to the tune of "Bei Mir Bist Du Schon" as composed by Sholom Secunda, performed by Blanc as Porky).*
MUSIC BY Carl W. Stalling.
Released on June 25
(7 min./Vitaphone Sound/Video/DVD)
Leon Schlesinger Studios/Warner Bros.

HAVE YOU GOT ANY CASTLES? (1938) D: Frank Tashlin.
VOICES: *Mel Blanc, Tedd Pierce, Delos Jewkes, Georgia Stark.*
Book characters jump off their covers and cavort. Blanc does multiple roles. Caricatures include Alexander Woolcott, Bill 'Bojangles' Robinson, Greta Garbo, Cab Calloway, William Powell, Clark Gable, Paul Muni, Charles Laughton, Stepin Fetchit, W.C. Fields, The Ink Spots, Victor McLaglen, Shirley Temple, Fats Waller and Paul Whiteman. Entry in the MERRIE MELODIES series.
SONGS: "Swing For Sale" *(Saul Chaplin; Sammy Cahn)*, "Have You Got Any Castles, Baby?" *(Richard A. Whiting; Johnny Mercer)*, "You're The Cure For What Ails Me" *(Harold Arlen; E.Y. Harburg)*.
MUSIC BY Carl W. Stalling.
Released on June 25
(7 min./Vitaphone Sound/Technicolor)
Leon Schlesinger Studios/Warner Bros.

LOVE AND CURSES (1938) D: Ben Hardaway, Cal Dalton.
VOICES: *Elmore Vincent, Mel Blanc, The Sportsmen Quartet.*
Dastardly villain Roger St. Clair (Blanc) kidnaps pretty Emily and is tracked down by the resolute Harold. Entry in the MERRIE MELODIES series.
SONG: "All Is Not Gold That Glitters" *(James W. Casey; George A. Norton).*
MUSIC BY Carl W. Stalling.
Released on July 9
(7 min./Vitaphone Sound/Technicolor)
Leon Schlesinger Studios/Warner Bros.

PORKY'S SPRING PLANTING (1938) D: Frank Tashlin.
VOICES: *Mel Blanc, Elvia Allman.*
Porky Pig contends with ravenous fowl which decimate his garden. Blanc is Porky and Streamline the Dog. Entry in the LOONEY TUNES series.
SONGS: "Peckin' With The Penguins" *(Tommy Dorsey; Deane Kincaide),* "Little Man You've Had A Busy Day" *(Mabel Wayne; Maurice Siglar; Al Hoffman),* "April Showers" *(Louis Silvers; B.G. DeSylva).*
MUSIC BY Carl W. Stalling.
Released on July 16
(7 min./Vitaphone Sound)
Leon Schlesinger Studios/Warner Bros.

CINDERELLA MEETS FELLA (1938) D: Fred [Tex] Avery.
VOICES: *Cliff Nazarro, Dave Weber, Elvia Allman, Bernice Hansen, Mel Blanc.*
A stagecoach-riding Cinderella arrives at the ball, where she meets an infatuated Egghead. At the stroke of midnight, she dashes away to attend a theater-showing of this same cartoon. Blanc is the cuckoo clock, Royal Guard and the scream of Cinderella. Entry in the MERRIE MELODIES series.
SONGS: "Please Be Kind" *(Saul Chaplin; Sammy Cahn),* "About A Quarter To Nine" *(Harry Warren; Al Dubin),* "Boy Meets Girl" *(Sammy Fain; Charles Tobias),* "You're An Education" *(Harry Warren; Al Dubin).*
MUSIC BY Carl W. Stalling.
Released on July 23
(7 min./Vitaphone Sound/Technicolor/Rated [TV-G])
Leon Schlesinger Studios/Warner Bros.

BARNYARD ROMEO (1938) D: *Walter Lantz*, Alex Lovy.
VOICES: *Mel Blanc, Sara Berner.*
A romantic triangle develops between a she-goose, a handsome turkey and a female peacock. The goose hatches a plan to win the turkey. Blanc provides his vocal talents. Caricatures of Fanny Brice and Katharine Hepburn.
MUSIC BY Frank Marsales.
Released on August 1
(6 min./Western Electric Sound)
Walter Lantz Productions/Universal

PORKY AND DAFFY (1938) D: Robert [Bob] Clampett.
VOICES: *Mel Blanc.*
Porky Pig manages Daffy Duck as the mad mallard enters the boxing ring against a pugilistic chicken. Blanc is Porky, Daffy, 'The Champ' and the pelican referee. Entry in the LOONEY TUNES series.
SONG: "Singin' In The Bathtub" *(Michael Cleary; Herb Magidson; Ned Washington; sung by Blanc as Daffy).*
MUSIC BY Carl W. Stalling.
Released on August 6
(7 min./Vitaphone Sound/Video/DVD)
Leon Schlesinger Studios/Warner Bros.

THE FROG POND (1938) D: Ub Iwerks.
VOICES: *Billy Bletcher, Elmore Vincent, Mel Blanc.*
A frog community is happy until they are terrorized by a bully frog who wants a home built with slave labor. Blanc is some of the frog citizens. Entry in the COLOR RHAPSODY series.
MUSIC BY Eddie Kilfeather, Joe DeNat.
Released on August 12
(7 min./RCA Sound/Technicolor)
Cartoon Films Limited/Charles Mintz Productions/Columbia

THE MAJOR LIED 'TIL DAWN (1938) D: Frank Tashlin.
VOICES: *Tedd Pierce, Mel Blanc, Tommy Bond.*
A 'veddy British' retired officer tells a young lad (caricature of Freddie Bartholomew, voice of Bond) tall tales of how he bagged his collection of trophies in the African wilds. Blanc is the elephant. Entry in the MERRIE MELODIES series.
MUSIC BY Carl W. Stalling.
Released on August 13
(7 min./Vitaphone Sound/Technicolor)
Leon Schlesinger Studios/Warner Bros.

WHOLLY SMOKE (1938) D: Frank Tashlin.
VOICES: *Mel Blanc, Cliff Nazarro, The Basin Street Boys, Tedd Pierce.*
Porky Pig's experimentation with cigar-smoking knocks him out and causes him to have a nightmare about the evils of tobacco use. Blanc is Porky and the Bully. Caricatures of The Three Stooges, Bing Crosby, Rudy Vallee and Cab Calloway. Entry in the LOONEY TUNES series.
SONGS: "Mysterious Mose" *(with special anti-smoking lyrics; Walter Doyle),* "The Little Old Church In The Valley" *(Egbert Van Alstyne; Gene Arnold; Gus Kahn),* "Sweet Music" *(Harry Warren),* "Daddy's Boy" *(Grady Watts).*
MUSIC BY Carl W. Stalling.
Released on August 27
(7 min./Vitaphone Sound/DVD)
Leon Schlesinger Studios/Warner Bros.

A-LAD-IN BAGDAD (1938) D: Cal Howard, Cal Denton.
VOICES: *Cliff Nazarro, Dave Weber, Bernice Hansen, Mel Blanc.*
Aladdin (alias Egghead) wins a magic lamp and uses it in a competition to win the hand of a sultan's daughter. Blanc is the Villain, the Genie, the Sultan, Beggar and 'Slap-Happy Boy'. Caricatures of Robert Taylor and the Happiness Boys (Billy Jones and Ernie Hare). Entry in the MERRIE MELODIES series.
SONGS: "Half Of Me (Wants To Be Good)" *(Peter DeRose; Sam Lewis),* "Dervisher" *(Theodore Bendix).*
MUSIC BY Carl W. Stalling.
Released on August 27
(7 min./Vitaphone Sound/Technicolor)
Leon Schlesinger Studios/Warner Bros.

GYM JAMS (1938) D: Manny Gould, Ben Harrison.
VOICE: *Mel Blanc.*
Krazy Kat (Blanc) has misadventures at a health resort. Based on the comic strip created by George Herriman.
MUSIC BY Joe DeNat.
Released on September 2
(6 min./RCA Sound/Technicolor)
Charles Mintz Productions/Columbia

CRACKED ICE (1938) D: Frank Tashlin.
VOICES: *Dave Weber, Tedd Pierce, Mel Blanc.*
A pig (who looks suspiciously like W.C. Fields) devises a scheme to steal a barrel of alcohol from a St. Bernard dog. Blanc is the Russian dogs, a drowning bird, a drunken fish and the skating judge. Entry in the MERRIE MELODIES series.
MUSIC BY Carl W. Stalling.
Released on September 10
(7 min./Vitaphone Sound/Technicolor/DVD)
Leon Schlesinger Studios/Warner Bros.

PORKY IN WACKYLAND (1938) D: Robert [Bob] Clampett.
VOICES: *Mel Blanc.*
Screwball cartoon has Porky Pig flying to a surreal setting in search of a valuable rare bird. Blanc is Porky, the Do-Do Bird and various characters. Caricature of the Three Stooges. Entry in the LOONEY TUNES series.
SONG: "Feeling High And Happy" *(Ted Koehler; Rube Bloom).*
MUSIC BY Carl W. Stalling.
Released on September 24
(7 min./Vitaphone Sound/Video/laserdisc/DVD)
Leon Schlesinger Studios/Warner Bros.

A FEUD THERE WAS (1938) D: Fred [Tex] Avery.
VOICES: *Mel Blanc, The Sons of the Pioneers, Billy Bletcher, Dave Weber, Fred [Tex] Avery.*
A well-meaning Egghead/Elmer Fudd decides to end a hillbilly feud, but finds all guns on both sides pointed at him. Blanc is Egghead/Elmer, Non-Stop Corrigan, Old Gray Hair, Cuckoo Bird, Angry McCoy, Peace-Deriding Weaver, Apple-Bonked Weaver. Roy Rogers provided Egghead/Elmer's singing voice! Entry in the MERRIE MELODIES series.
SONG: "Wearing Of The Green" *(composer unknown).*
MUSIC BY Carl W. Stalling.
Released on September 24
(7 min./Vitaphone Sound/Technicolor)
Leon Schlesinger Studios/Warner Bros.

THE WINNING TICKET (1938) D: Isadore [Friz] Freleng.
VOICES: *Billy Bletcher, Mel Blanc, Dave Weber, Jeanne Dunn, Elvia Allman.*
The Captain's winning sweepstakes ticket is coveted by crafty John Silver (Blanc), who disguises himself as a woman in order to steal it. Entry in CAPTAIN AND THE KIDS series, based on the comic strip created by Rudolph Dirks.
SONG: "Ach Du Lieber Augustine" *(traditional, composer unknown).*
MUSIC BY Scott Bradley, Bert Lewis.
Released on October 1
(7 min./Western Electric Sound/sepiatone)
Metro-Goldwyn-Mayer

LITTLE PANCHO VANILLA (1938) D: Frank Tashlin.
VOICES: *Mel Blanc, Shirley Reed.*
Pancho brags that he could be a great bullfighter; he gets his chance to really throw the bull when he is accidentally catapulted into the matador's arena. Blanc provides his vocal talents. Entry in the MERRIE MELODIES series.
SONG: "In Caliente" *(Allie Wrubel; Mort Dixon).*
MUSIC BY Carl W. Stalling.
Released on October 8
(7 min./Vitaphone Sound/Technicolor/DVD)
Leon Schlesinger Studios/Warner Bros.

PORKY'S NAUGHTY NEPHEW (1938) D: Robert [Bob] Clampett.
VOICES: *Mel Blanc, Bernice Hansen.*
Porky Pig (Blanc) and his violence-prone nephew are on the beach when
they compete in a swim race. Caricature of Eddie Cantor. Entry in the
LOONEY TUNES series.
SONGS: "Japanese Sandman" *(Richard A. Whiting; Raymond B. Egan).*
MUSIC BY Carl W. Stalling.
Released on October 15
(7 min./Vitaphone Sound)
Leon Schlesinger Studios/Warner Bros.

THE HONDURAS HURRICANE (1938) D: Robert Allen.
VOICES: *Billy Bletcher, Mel Blanc.*
A cockfight is staged between the Captain's bantam and Pirate John's
robot rooster, but those bratty kids — Hans and Fritz — decide to spoil
the proceedings. Blanc is Pirate John. Entry in the CAPTAIN AND THE
KIDS series, based on the comic strip created by Rudolph Dirks.
MUSIC BY Scott Bradley, *(Bert Lewis).*
Released on October 15
(7 min./Western Electric Sound/sepiatone)
Metro-Goldwyn-Mayer

JOHNNY SMITH AND POKER-HUNTAS (1938) D: Fred [Tex] Avery.
VOICES: *Arthur Q. Bryan, Mel Blanc, Bernice Hansen.*
Pioneer explorer Johnny Smith (aka Egghead) dares the wrath of savage
Coney Island Indians (Blanc) when he takes a Native American maiden
for a bride. Entry in the MERRIE MELODIES series.
MUSIC BY Carl W. Stalling.
Released on October 22
(7 min./Vitaphone Sound/Technicolor)
Leon Schlesinger Studios/Warner Bros.

PORKY IN EGYPT (1938) D: Robert [Bob] Clampett.
VOICES: *Mel Blanc, Dave Weber.*
A journey in the desert turns into a hallucinatory misadventure when the hot sun gets the best of Porky Pig's camel. Blanc is Porky, Humpty-Bumpty (the camel), various Egyptians and 'da voices'. Caricatures of Amos 'n' Andy (Freeman Gosden and Charles Correll) and The Lone Ranger. Entry in the LOONEY TUNES series.
MUSIC BY Carl W. Stalling.
Released on November 5
(7 min./Vitaphone Sound/DVD)
Leon Schlesinger Studios/Warner Bros.

YOU'RE AN EDUCATION (1938) D: Frank Tashlin.
VOICES: *Mel Blanc, Billy Bletcher, Dave Weber.*
Travel office pamphlets come to life in this gag parade spoofing locations around the world, spotlighting the chase to apprehend a globe-trotting thief.
SONGS: "Food's An Education" *(to the tune of "You're An Education", as composed by Harry Warren),* "Let The Rest Of The World Go By" *(Ernest Ball; J. Keirn Brennan),* "Have You Got Any Castles, Baby?" *(Richard A. Whiting; Johnny Mercer),* "Avalon" *(Vincent Rose; Al Jolson; B.G. DeSylva),* "I Love A Parade" *(Harold Arlen; Ted Koehler),* "The Isle Of Capri" *(Will Grosz; Jimmy Kennedy),* "Night Over Shanghai" *(Harry Warren; Johnny Mercer),* "Puppchen" *(Harry Ruby; Bert Kalmar).*
MUSIC BY Carl W. Stalling.
Released on November 5
(7 min./Vitaphone Sound/Technicolor/DVD)
Leon Schlesinger Studios/Warner Bros.

THE NIGHT WATCHMAN (1938) D: Charles M. [Chuck] Jones.
VOICES: *Gay Seabrook, Mel Blanc, The Sportsmen Quartet, Bernice Hansen.*
An ill Thomas Cat has to leave his son in charge of guarding the kitchen, which is good news to a band of raiding mice (Blanc). Entry in the MERRIE MELODIES series.
SONG: "In the Shade of the Old Apple Tree" *(Egbert Van Alstyne; Harry Williams).*
MUSIC BY Carl W. Stalling.
Released on November 19
(7 min./Vitaphone Sound/Technicolor/Rated [TV-G]/DVD)
Leon Schlesinger Studios/Warner Bros.

THE DAFFY DOC (1938) D: Robert [Bob] Clampett.
VOICES: *Mel Blanc, Sara Berner.*
Daffy Duck is a medical assistant who wants to operate on a patient and chooses passerby Porky Pig. A chase around the hospital ensues with axes, mallets and an iron lung as props. Blanc is Daffy and Porky. Entry in the LOONEY TUNES series.
SONGS: "You Go To My Head" *(J. Fred Coots; Haven Gillespie),* "Love Is On The Air Tonight" *(Richard A. Whiting; Johnny Mercer),* "Dramatic Tension" *(John S. Zamecnik).*
MUSIC BY Carl W. Stalling.
Released on November 26
(7 min./Vitaphone Sound/DVD)
Leon Schlesinger Studios/Warner Bros.

THE DISOBEDIENT MOUSE (1938) D: Lester Kline.
VOICES: *Bernice Hansen, Dave Weber, Mel Blanc.*
Baby-Face Mouse falls in with a crime school and ends up in Professor Ratface's milk-stealing and pickpocket gang. Blanc provides his vocal talent. Entry in the CARTUNE COMEDY series.
MUSIC BY Frank Marsales.
Released on November 28
(7 min./Western Electric Sound/2-Strip Technicolor)
Walter Lantz Productions/Universal

DAFFY DUCK IN HOLLYWOOD (1938) D: Fred [Tex] Avery.
VOICES: *Mel Blanc, Dave Weber, Jim Bannon.*
A film director buys trouble when he refuses to let Daffy Duck make a movie; the mad mallard proceeds to wreck the whole production. Blanc is Daffy, I.M. Stupendous, the rooster actor and various assistant directors. Caricature of Katharine Hepburn. Entry in the MERRIE MELODIES series.
MUSIC BY Carl W. Stalling.
Released on December 3
(7 min./Vitaphone Sound/Technicolor/Video/DVD)
Leon Schlesinger Studios/Warner Bros.

THE LONE MOUNTIE (1938) D: Manny Gould, Ben Harrison.
VOICES: *Mel Blanc, Leone LeDoux.*
Krazy Kat becomes a Canadian Mountie to impress his girlfriend, but must pursue villainous Yukon Jake. Blanc is Krazy and Jake. Based on the comic strip created by George Herriman.
MUSIC BY Joe DeNat.
Released on December 10
(6 min./RCA Sound/Technicolor)
Charles Mintz Productions/Columbia

PORKY THE GOB (1938) D: Ben Hardaway, Cal Dalton.
VOICES: *Mel Blanc, The Sportsmen Quartet, Dave Weber.*
Navy man (?) Porky Pig (Blanc) single-handedly defends his ship against pirates in a submarine. Entry in the LOONEY TUNES series.
SONGS: "Song of the Marines (We're Shovin' Right Off Again)" *(Harry Warren; Al Dubin)* "My Bonnie Lies Over The Ocean" *(Lyric: Charles E. Pratt; Music: slight Pratt revision of unknown composer's work),* "Mess Call" *(traditional, composer unknown).*
MUSIC BY Carl W. Stalling.
Released on December 17
(7 min./Vitaphone Sound)
Leon Schlesinger Studios/Warner Bros.

COUNT ME OUT (1938) D: Ben Hardaway, Cal Dalton.
VOICES: *Cliff Nazarro, Dave Weber, Mel Blanc, Fred [Tex] Avery.*
Egghead takes a correspondence course in boxing and immediately gets into the ring to fight the champ. Blanc is the boxing coach (on record). Entry in the MERRIE MELODIES series.
SONGS: "Please Be Kind" *(Saul Chaplin; Sammy Cahn),* "You Go To My Head" *(J. Fred Coots; Haven Gillespie).*
MUSIC BY Carl W. Stalling.
Released on December 17
(7 min./Vitaphone Sound/Technicolor)
Leon Schlesinger Studios/Warner Bros.

MIDNIGHT FROLICS (1938) D: Ub Iwerks.
VOICES: *Mel Blanc, Harry Stanton.*
A mouse and cuckoo bird discuss the existence of ghosts and are promptly visited by six musical spirits. Blanc is undetermined characters. Entry in the COLOR RHAPSODY series.
MUSIC BY Joe DeNat, Eddie Kilfeather.
Released on December 23
(7 min./RCA Sound/Technicolor)
Cartoon Films Limited/Charles Mintz Productions/Columbia

THE MICE WILL PLAY (1938) D: Fred [Tex] Avery.
VOICES: *Bernice Hansen, Mel Blanc, The Sportsmen Quartet.*
In a scientist's laboratory some mice get into trouble fooling with the equipment. Johnny Mouse dashes to save screaming Susie from a cat (Blanc). Entry in the MERRIE MELODIES series.
SONG: "Don't Spare The Rice" *(to the tune of "Here Comes The Bride," Music: Richard Wagner).*
MUSIC BY Carl W. Stalling.
Released on December 31
(7 min./Vitaphone Sound/Technicolor/DVD)
Leon Schlesinger Studios/Warner Bros.

SOUP TO MUTTS (1939) D: Lester Kline.
VOICES: *Mel Blanc.*
A disguised cat crashes a canine amateur talent contest. Blanc is various characters. Entry in the CARTUNE series.
MUSIC BY Frank Marsales.
Released on January 9
(7 min./Western Electric Sound/Technicolor)
Walter Lantz Productions/Universal

SCRAPPY'S ADDED ATTRACTION (1939) D: *(No director credited).*
VOICES: *Mel Blanc, Robert Winkler, Dave Weber.*
Scrappy (Blanc) and Margie run a movie house, but are pestered by Titan the Terrible Twerp. Takes-offs on John Barrymore and Greta Garbo.
MUSIC BY Joe DeNat.
Released on January 13
(6½ min./RCA Sound/Technicolor)
Charles Mintz Productions/Columbia

DOG GONE MODERN (1939) D: Charles M. [Chuck] Jones.
VOICES: *Mel Blanc, The Sportsmen Quartet.*
A big dog and little pup wander into an experimental automated house and are victimized by various devices. Blanc is the curious dogs and the voice of the futuristic home. Entry in the MERRIE MELODIES series.
MUSIC BY Carl W. Stalling.
Released on January 14
(7 min./Vitaphone Sound/Technicolor/Rated [TV-G])
Leon Schlesinger Studios/Warner Bros.

IT'S AN ILL WIND (1939) D: Ben Hardaway, Cal Dalton.
VOICES: *Mel Blanc, Danny Webb.*
Porky Pig (Blanc) and Dippy (a.k.a. Gabby) Goose let their imaginations get the better of them when they use an abandoned yacht club as shelter against a storm. Entry in the LOONEY TUNES series.
MUSIC BY Carl W. Stalling.
Released on January 28
(7 min./Vitaphone Sound)
Leon Schlesinger Studios/Warner Bros.

HAM-ATEUR NIGHT (1939) D: Fred [Tex] Avery.
VOICES: *Phil Kramer, Mel Blanc, Elvia Allman, Fred [Tex] Avery.*
A local theater puts on a talent show with some odd acts. Egghead struts his stuff attempting to sing. Blanc is various characters. Entry in the MERRIE MELODIES series.
SONGS: "She'll Be Comin' Round The Mountain" *(traditional, composer unknown),* "Drink To Me Only With Thine Eyes" *(Music: possibly Colonel R. Mellish; Lyrics: originally an earlier poem by Ben Jonson),* "You Go To My Head" *(J. Fred Coots; Haven Gillespie).*
MUSIC BY Carl W. Stalling.
Released on January 28
(7 min./Vitaphone Sound/Technicolor)
Leon Schlesinger Studios/Warner Bros.

ROBIN HOOD MAKES GOOD (1939) D: Charles M. [Chuck] Jones.
VOICES: *Gay Seabrook, Sara Berner, Mel Blanc, Bernice Hansen.*
When three squirrels play a game of 'Robin Hood', a sly and hungry fox (Blanc) disguises himself as Maid Marian. Entry in the MERRIE MELODIES series.
MUSIC BY Carl W. Stalling.
Released on February 11
(7 min./Vitaphone and RCA Sound/Technicolor)
Leon Schlesinger Studios/Warner Bros.

THE MAGIC BEANS (1939) D: Lester Kline.
VOICES: *Mel Blanc, Sara Berner.*
Baby Face Mouse experiences his version of the 'Jack and the Beanstalk' story, complete with a giant mouse (Blanc). Entry in the NERTZERY RHYME series.
MUSIC BY Frank Marsales.
Released on February 13
(7 min./Western Electric Sound/2-Strip Technicolor)
Walter Lantz Productions/Universal

PORKY'S TIRE TROUBLE (1939) D: Robert [Bob] Clampett.
VOICES: *Mel Blanc, Billy Bletcher.*
Porky Pig's dog follows his master to work at a tire factory, where the mutt falls into a rubberizing solution and becomes a bouncing and stretchable hound. Blanc is Porky. Caricatures of Edward G. Robinson, Edna May Oliver, Clark Gable and Hugh Herbert. Entry in the LOONEY TUNES series.
SONG: "The Panic Is On" *(Thomas "Fats" Waller; Bert Clarke; George Clarke; Winston Collins Tharp).*
MUSIC BY Carl W. Stalling.
Released on February 18
(7 min./Vitaphone Sound)
Leon Schlesinger Studios/Warner Bros.

THE GORILLA HUNT (1939) D: Ub Iwerks.
VOICES: *Mel Blanc.*
Jungle hunters go into the wilds in search of a prize gorilla. Blanc is the various characters. Entry in the COLOR RHAPSODY series.
MUSIC BY Eddie Kilfeather, Joe DeNat.
Released on February 24
(8 min./RCA Sound/Technicolor)
Charles Mintz Productions/Columbia

JITTERBUG FOLLIES (1939) D: Milt Gross.
VOICES: *Mel Blanc, Georgia Stark, Dave Weber.*
Count Screwloose (Blanc) is putting on an amateur talent show, but two tough guys horn in to make sure everything is 'run on the square'. Based on the newspaper comic strip created by Milt Gross.
SONG: "Jitterbug Follies" *(Elbert C. Lewis).*
MUSIC BY Scott Bradley.
Released on February 25
(9 min./Western Electric Sound/sepiatone)
Metro-Goldwyn-Mayer

GOLD RUSH DAZE (1939) D: Ben Hardaway, Cal Dalton.
VOICES: *Joe Twerp, Mel Blanc, The Sportsmen Quartet.*
A gas station owner tells a traveler of his misadventures searching the world for gold. Blanc provides his vocal talents. Entry in the MERRIE MELODIES series.
SONG: "My Sweetheart Needs Gold For Her Teeth" *(composer unknown)*, "Ride, Tenderfoot, Ride" *(Richard A. Whiting; Johnny Mercer).*
MUSIC BY Carl W. Stalling.
Released on February 25
(7 min./Vitaphone Sound/Technicolor)
Leon Schlesinger Studios/Warner Bros.

BIRTH OF A TOOTHPICK (1939) D: Burt Gillett.
VOICES: *Danny Webb, Mel Blanc.*
Big Dan tries to save a beloved tree from being cut down. Blanc provides his vocal talents. Entry in the CARTUNE series.
MUSIC BY Frank Marsales.
Released on February 27
(7½ min./Western Electric Sound/2-Strip Technicolor)
Walter Lantz Productions/Universal

PORKY'S MOVIE MYSTERY (1939) D: Robert [Bob] Clampett.
VOICES: *Mel Blanc, Billy Bletcher, Sara Berner, Danny Webb.*
Porky Pig (Blanc) assumes the role of detective 'Mr. Motto' and pursues the mysterious phantom that is causing havoc at Warner Brothers Studios. Caricature of Hugh Herbert. Entry in the LOONEY TUNES series.
SONG: "Japanese Sandman" *(Richard A. Whiting; Raymond B. Egan).*
MUSIC BY Carl W. Stalling.
Released on March 11
(7 min./Vitaphone Sound)
Leon Schlesinger Studios/Warner Bros.

A DAY AT THE ZOO (1939) D: Fred [Tex] Avery.
VOICES: *Gil Warren, Mel Blanc, Danny Webb.*
At the zoo, Egghead (Blanc) pesters a lion as other animals share their odd characteristics. Entry in the MERRIE MELODIES series.
SONGS: "Mess Call" *(traditional, composer unknown),* "Ten Little Indians" *(traditional, composer unknown).*
MUSIC BY Carl W. Stalling.
Released on March 11
(7 min./Vitaphone Sound/Technicolor)
Leon Schlesinger Studios/Warner Bros.

WANTED: NO MASTER (1939) D: Milt Gross.
VOICE: *Mel Blanc.*
J.R. the Wonder Dog schemes to marry off Count Screwloose to a wealthy widow and finally be rid of his nutty master. Blanc is the Count. Based on the comic strip by Milt Gross.
SONG: "Drink To Me Only With Thine Eyes" *(Music: possibly Colonel R. Mellish; Lyrics: originally an earlier poem by Ben Jonson).*
MUSIC BY Elbert C. Lewis.
Released on March 18
(8 min./Western Electric Sound/sepiatone)
Metro-Goldwyn-Mayer

PREST-O CHANGE-O (1939) D: Charles M. [Chuck] Jones.
VOICE: *Mel Blanc.*
Two dogs, fleeing the dogcatcher, find refuge in a magician's house and encounter a tricky rabbit (Blanc). Entry in the MERRIE MELODIES series.
SONG: "Black Coffee" *(Al Hoffman; Maurice Sigler; Al Goodhart).*
MUSIC BY Carl W. Stalling.
Released on March 25
(7 min./Vitaphone Sound/Technicolor/Rated [TV-G])
Leon Schlesinger Studios/Warner Bros.

THE ONE-ARMED BANDIT (1939) D: Alex Lovy.
VOICES: *Billy Bletcher, Mel Blanc.*
Grandpop's addiction to slot machines causes him to lose the mortgage money, leaving it up to his daughter to save the day. Blanc provides his vocal talents. Entry in the CARTUNE series.
MUSIC BY Frank Marsales.
Released on March 27
(7 min./Western Electric Sound/2-Strip Technicolor)
Walter Lantz Productions/Universal

CHICKEN JITTERS (1939) D: Robert [Bob] Clampett.
VOICES: *Mel Blanc, Danny Webb.*
Porky Pig (Blanc) rallies a formation of farmyard fowl to rescue a duck snatched by a hungry fox. Entry in the LOONEY TUNES series.
MUSIC BY Carl W. Stalling.
Released on April 1
(7 min./Vitaphone Sound)
Leon Schlesinger Studios/Warner Bros.

GOLF CHUMPS (1939) D: Manny Gould, Ben Harrison.
VOICES: *Dave Weber, Mel Blanc.*
Krazy Kat and friend Kitty are given golf tips by the narrator. Blanc provides his vocal talent. Based on the comic strip by George Herriman.
MUSIC BY Joe DeNat.
Released on April 6
(6 min./RCA Sound/Technicolor)
Charles Mintz Productions/Columbia

BARS AND STRIPES FOREVER (1939) D: J.B. [Ben] Hardaway, Cal Dalton.

VOICES: *Mel Blanc, Danny Webb.*

A day at prison turns exciting when a musical jailbreak occurs. Blanc is Warden Paws (an imitation and caricature of Hugh Herbert); Blanc also imitates Jerry Colonna. Entry in the MERRIE MELODIES series.

SONGS: "I'm Going To Scram From Here!" *(composer unknown)*, "Got The South In My Soul" *(Victor Young; Ned Washington; Lee Wiley).*

MUSIC BY Carl W. Stalling.

Released on April 8

(7 min./Vitaphone Sound/Technicolor)

Leon Schlesinger Studios/Warner Bros.

DAFFY DUCK AND THE DINOSAUR (1939) D: Charles M. [Chuck] Jones.

VOICES: *Mel Blanc, Jack Lescoulie.*

Daffy Duck (Blanc) cleverly eludes a mallard-hunting caveman and his pet dinosaur. Caricature of Jack Benny. Entry in the MERRIE MELODIES series.

SONG: "Humoresque, Opus 101/7" *(Antonin Dvorak).*

MUSIC BY Carl W. Stalling.

Released on April 22

(7 min./Vitaphone Sound/Technicolor/Video/DVD)

Leon Schlesinger Studios/Warner Bros.

PORKY AND TEABISCUIT (1939) D: Ben Hardaway, Cal Dalton.

VOICES: *Mel Blanc, Earle Hodgins, Joe Twerp.*

Sent to town by his father on an errand to sell grain, Porky Pig (Blanc) uses the money to buy a broken-down racehorse that likes to listen to slide trombones. Entry in the LOONEY TUNES series.

SONG: "Ride, Tenderfoot, Ride" *(Richard A. Whiting; Johnny Mercer).*

MUSIC BY Carl W. Stalling.

Released on April 22

(7 min./Vitaphone Sound/DVD)

Leon Schlesinger Studios/Warner Bros.

A WORM'S EYE VIEW (1939) D: *(No director credited).*
VOICES: *Dave Weber, Mel Blanc.*
Scrappy goes fishing, but his bait worm (Blanc) tries to convince a fish not to eat him.
MUSIC BY Joe DeNat.
Released on April 28
(7 min./RCA Sound/Technicolor)
Charles Mintz Productions/Columbia

THUGS WITH DIRTY MUGS (1939) D: Fred [Tex] Avery.
VOICES: *John Deering, Mel Blanc, Danny Webb.*
Cops try to nab Killer Diller, who manages to rob 100 banks in one day. Blanc is the tattle-tale bank clerk, annoyed mobster, secret agents and the man in the audience. Caricature of Edward G. Robinson. Entry in the MERRIE MELODIES series.
MUSIC BY Carl W. Stalling
Released on May 6
(7 min./Vitaphone Sound/Technicolor/DVD)
Leon Schlesinger Studios/Warner Bros.

NELLY OF THE CIRCUS (1939) D: Alex Lovy.
VOICES: *Mel Blanc, Dave Weber.*
Our lovely Nelly is abducted by circus talent scout Rascally Ratbone (Blanc), who turns her into a trapeze star. Fear not, for stalwart Dan arrives to save our heroine. Entry in the MELLO-DRAMA series.
MUSIC BY Frank Marsales.
Released on May 8
(7 min./Western Electric Sound/2-Strip Technicolor)
Walter Lantz Productions/Universal

KRISTOPHER KOLUMBUS JR. (1939) D: Robert [Bob] Clampett.
VOICES: *John Deering, Mel Blanc.*
Porky Pig (Blanc) is the famed explorer (name curiously misspelled) who ventures to the new world and discovers jitterbugging Indians. Entry in the LOONEY TUNES series.
SONG: "Minuet, Opus 13 No. 5 in E Major" *(Luigi Boccherini).*
MUSIC BY Carl W. Stalling.
Released on May 13
(7 min./Vitaphone Sound)
Leon Schlesinger Studios/Warner Bros.

LUCKY PIGS (1939) D: Ben Harrison.
VOICES: *Elvia Allman, Dave Weber, Mel Blanc.*
The Pig family think they have it made when they win a sweepstakes jackpot. Blanc provides his vocal talent. Entry in the COLOR RHAPSODY series.
MUSIC BY Joe De Nat.
Released on May 26
(7 min./RCA Sound/Technicolor)
Charles Mintz Productions/Columbia

NAUGHTY BUT MICE (1939) D: Charles M. [Chuck] Jones.
VOICES: *Gay Seabrook, Mel Blanc.*
Sniffles the mouse is in a pharmacy to find a cold remedy and gets intoxicated on an alcoholic medicine. A hungry cat (Blanc) tries to take advantage of the situation. Entry in the MERRIE MELODIES series.
MUSIC BY Carl W. Stalling.
Released on May 30
(6½ min./Vitaphone and RCA Sound/Technicolor)
Leon Schlesinger Studios/Warner Bros.

POLAR PALS (1939) D: Robert [Bob] Clampett.
VOICES: *Mel Blanc, Billy Bletcher.*
When a fur hunter preys on Arctic wildlife, musket-wielding Porky Pig (Blanc) becomes their protector. Entry in the LOONEY TUNES series.
SONGS: "Let's Rub Noses (Like The Eskimoses)" *(Joseph Meyer; Albert Stillman),* "T'Ain't No Sin" *(Walter Donaldson; Edgar Leslie).*
MUSIC BY Carl W. Stalling.
Released on June 3
(7 min./Vitaphone Sound/DVD)
Leon Schlesinger Studios/Warner Bros.

HOBO GADGET BAND (1939) D: Ben Hardaway, Cal Dalton.
VOICES: *Pinto Colvig, Mel Blanc, The Foursome.*
After getting thrown off a train, a batch of hobos use their musical talent to audition for a radio show. Blanc is the hobo at the information booth — Mr. Sneer. Entry in the MERRIE MELODIES series.
SONGS: "Hobo Junktown Gadget Band" *(composer unknown)*, "Corn Pickin'" *(Harry Warren; Johnny Mercer).*
MUSIC BY Carl W. Stalling.
Released on June 17
(7 min./Vitaphone Sound/Technicolor)
Leon Schlesinger Studios/Warner Bros.

SCALP TROUBLE (1939) D: Robert [Bob] Clampett.
VOICES: *Mel Blanc.*
Daffy Duck and Porky Pig, defending a frontier fort, fight off an attack by Sioux Indians. Blanc is Daffy, Porky and the Indian that talks like Jerry Colonna. Entry in the LOONEY TUNES series.
MUSIC BY Carl W. Stalling.
Released on June 24
(7 min./Vitaphone Sound)
Leon Schlesinger Studios/Warner Bros.

BELIEVE IT OR ELSE (1939) D: Fred [Tex] Avery.
VOICES: *Cliff Nazarro, Mel Blanc, Fred [Tex] Avery.*
Egghead (and us) are treated to some odd 'facts', with a disbelieving Egghead allowing himself to be sawed in half to disprove a magician. Blanc is Buck Dodgers showing what life is like on Mars. Entry in the MERRIE MELODIES series.
SONGS: "Sweet Genevieve" *(Henry Tucker; George Cooper)*, "Yoo Hoo" *(Al Jolson; Buddy G. DeSylva).*
MUSIC BY Carl W. Stalling.
Released on June 25
(7 min./Vitaphone Sound/Technicolor)
Leon Schlesinger Studios/Warner Bros.

NELL'S YELLS (1939) D: Ub Iwerks.
VOICE: *Mel Blanc.*
Horatio (Blanc), a hapless hero, goes to the rescue when a villain kidnaps Little Nell. Entry in the COLOR RHAPSODY series. Produced by Ub Iwerks.
MUSIC BY Eddie Kilfeather, Joe De Nat.
Released on June 30
(7 min./RCA Sound/Technicolor)
Cartoon Films Limited/Charles Mintz Productions/Columbia

OLD GLORY (1939) D: Charles M. [Chuck] Jones.
VOICES: *John Deering, Mel Blanc, John Litel.*
Straight-forward, patriotic cartoon about Porky Pig's struggle to learn the Pledge of Allegiance and his dream that has Uncle Sam showing him great moments in American history. Blanc is Porky. Entry in the MERRIE MELODIES series.
SONGS: "The Battle Cry Of Freedom" *(George Frederick Root),* "Battle Hymn Of The Republic" *(William Steffe; Julia Ward Howe),* "America" *(Music: Henry Carey, as "God Save the King"; Later lyrics: Reverend Samuel Francis Smith),* "America The Beautiful" *(Samuel A. Ward; Katherine Lee Bates).*
MUSIC BY Carl W. Stalling, Milton Franklyn.
Released on July 1
(10 min./Vitaphone Sound/Technicolor/Video/DVD)
Leon Schlesinger Studios/Warner Bros.

THE STUBBORN MULE (1939) D: Burt Gillett.
VOICES: *Mel Blanc, Danny Webb.*
Li'l Eightball (Blanc) attempts to move a recalcitrant mule — but fire, hypnotism and pure force do not work.
MUSIC BY Frank Marsales.
Released on July 3
(7 min./Western Electric Sound/2-Strip Technicolor)
Walter Lantz Productions/Universal

PORKY'S PICNIC (1939) D: Robert [Bob]Clampett.
VOICES: *Mel Blanc, Shirley Reed, Bernice Hansen.*
An outing in the park is anything but restful for Porky Pig (Blanc) when his little brat nephew Pinkie wanders into danger at the zoo. Entry in the LOONEY TUNES series.
MUSIC BY Carl W. Stalling.
Released on July 15
(7 min./Vitaphone Sound)
Leon Schlesinger Studios/Warner Bros.

DANGEROUS DAN MCFOO (1939) D: Fred [Tex] Avery.
VOICES: *Robert Cameron Bruce, Arthur Q. Bryan, Mel Blanc, Sara Berner, The Sportsmen Quartet.*
Dan McFoo has to fight off a rival for the hand of 'the girl who's known as Sue'. Blanc is the character who spars with Dan. Caricature of Bette Davis; vocal imitation of Katharine Hepburn. Entry in the MERRIE MELODIES series.
SONG: "When I Saw Sweet Nellie Home (latterly known as "Seeing Nellie Home")" *(John Fletcher; Frances Kyle).*
MUSIC BY Carl W. Stalling.
Released on July 15
(7 min./Vitaphone Sound/Technicolor/DVD)
Leon Schlesinger Studios/Warner Bros.

SNOWMAN'S LAND (1939) D: Charles [Chuck] Jones.
VOICES: *Pinto Colvig, Mel Blanc, The Sportsmen Quartet.*
An inept Canadian Mountie goes after the 'scourge of the North', Dirty Pierre. Blanc is the head Mountie and Pierre. Entry in the MERRIE MELODIES series.
SONG: "Canadian Mounted Police" *(John S. Zamecnik).*
MUSIC BY Carl W. Stalling.
Released on July 29
(7 min./Vitaphone Sound/Technicolor)
Leon Schlesinger Studios/Warner Bros.

WISE QUACKS (1939) D: Robert [Bob] Clampett.
VOICES: *Mel Blanc, Harry E. Lang.*
New father Daffy Duck and pal Porky Pig are horrified when a no-good
buzzard makes off with one of Daffy's brood. Blanc is Daffy, Porky and
Baby Duckling. Entry in the LOONEY TUNES series.
SONG: "Happiness Ahead" *(Allie Wrubel; Mort Dixon).*
MUSIC BY Carl W. Stalling.
Released on August 5
(7 min./Vitaphone Sound/DVD)
Leon Schlesinger Studios/Warner Bros.

SNUFFY'S PARTY (1939) D: Elmer Perkins.
VOICES: *Mel Blanc, Dave Weber.*
There's to be a party in honor of Snuffy Skunk (Blanc), but he gets locked
out of his own celebration. Entry in the CARTUNE series.
MUSIC BY Frank Marsales.
Released on August 7
(7 min./Western Electric Sound/2-Strip Technicolor)
Walter Lantz Productions/Universal

HARE-UM SCARE-UM (1939) D: Ben Hardaway, Cal Dalton.
VOICES: *Mel Blanc.*
An early Bugs Bunny harasses a hunter out to bag some rabbit meat. Blanc
is Bugs, the hunter and the dog. Entry in the MERRIE MELODIES series.
SONG: "Corn Pickin'" *(Harry Warren; Johnny Mercer).*
MUSIC BY Carl W. Stalling.
Released on August 12
(7 min./Vitaphone Sound/Technicolor)
Leon Schlesinger Studios/Warner Bros.

SLAPPHAPPY VALLEY (1939) D: Alex Lovy.
VOICES: *Phil Kramer, Mel Blanc, Danny Webb.*
Punchy takes the train to Death Valley and meets caricatures of Greta
Garbo, Edna May Oliver and Ned Sparks. Blanc is the train announcer.
Entry in the CRACKPOT CRUISE series.
MUSIC BY Frank Marsales.
Released on August 21
*(7 min./Western Electric Mirrophonic Recording/2-Strip Technicolor), Walter
Lantz Productions/Universal*

THE BOOKWORM (1939) D: Isadore [Friz] Freleng, Hugh Harman.
VOICES: *Mel Blanc, Frank Elmquist, Martha Wentworth.*
A witch dispatches her raven to snatch a worm for her potion, but the bird picks on a bookworm whose literary friends come to his defense. Blanc is the raven and the Racket-Buster. Produced by Hugh Harman and Rudolph Ising.
MUSIC BY Scott Bradley.
Released on August 26
(9 min./Western Electric Sound/Technicolor/DVD) Harman-Ising/
Metro-Goldwyn-Mayer

DETOURING AMERICA (1939) D: Fred [Tex] Avery.
VOICES: *Robert C. Bruce, Mel Blanc.*
A spot-gag look at the U.S. involving a geyser, an Indian and a human fly. Blanc is Butterfinger, Cow Puncher and the full-grown Papoose. Caricature of Jerry Colonna. Entry in the MERRIE MELODIES series.
SONG: "The Pilgrim's Chorus" from "Tannheuser" *("Return My Love"; Richard Wagner).*
MUSIC BY Carl W. Stalling.
Academy Award Nomination *(Short Subjects – Cartoon)* Leon Schlesinger
Released on August 26
(9 min./Vitaphone Sound/Technicolor/Video/laserdisc/DVD)
Leon Schlesinger Studios/Warner Bros.

SILLY SUPERSTITION/A HAUNTING WE WILL GO (1939) D: Burt Gillett.
VOICES: *Mel Blanc, Marjorie Tarlton, Dave Weber.*
Li'l Eightball (Blanc) has no use for superstitions until he is visited by a baby ghost. Together, they travel to a haunted mill — where the big ghosts put Eightball to the scare test. Entry in the CARTUNE series.
MUSIC BY Frank Marsales.
Released on August 28
(7 min./Western Electric Mirrophonic Recording/Technicolor)
Walter Lantz Productions/Universal

LITTLE BROTHER RAT (1939) D: Charles M. [Chuck] Jones.
VOICES: *Gay Seabrook, Mel Blanc.*
Sniffles the Mouse participates in a party game of 'scavenger hunt' and goes in search of an owl's egg. Not only does he have to deal with Father Owl, but also with a preying cat. Blanc is Father Owl and the baby owls. Entry in the MERRIE MELODIES series.
SONG: "I'm Happy About The Whole Thing" *(Harry Warren; Johnny Mercer).*
MUSIC BY Carl W. Stalling.
Released on September 2
(7 min./Vitaphone Sound/Technicolor)
Leon Schlesinger Studios/Warner Bros.

PORKY'S HOTEL (1939) D: Robert [Bob] Clampett.
VOICES: *Mel Blanc, Phil Kramer, The Rhythmettes.*
Porky Pig's hostelry remains unoccupied until an old codger goat comes to stay. However, Gabby Goose can't seem to stop pestering the old fellow. Blanc is Porky, Gabby and Gouty Goat. Entry in the LOONEY TUNES series.
SONG: "Honeymoon Hotel" *(Harry Warren; Al Dubin).*
MUSIC BY Carl W. Stalling.
Released on September 2
(7 min./Vitaphone Sound)
Leon Schlesinger Studios/Warner Bros.

SIOUX ME (1939) D: Ben Hardaway, Cal Dalton.
VOICES: *John Deering, Mel Blanc, Billy Bletcher, The Sportsmen Quartet [Bill Days, Maxwell Smith, John Rarig, Thurl Ravenscroft].*
A little papoose secures some rain-making tablets during a drought, but they are eaten by animals and Indians — causing havoc. Blanc is the Indian Chief, Rainmaker, Indian Boy and Baby Turtle. Entry in the MERRIE MELODIES series.
SONGS: "We Want Rain" *(Carl Stalling)*, "April Showers" *(Louis Silvers; B.G. DeSylva).*
MUSIC BY Carl W. Stalling.
Released on September 9
(7 min./Vitaphone Sound/Technicolor)
Leon Schlesinger Studios/Warner Bros.

CROP CHASERS (1939) D: Ub Iwerks.
VOICES: *Mel Blanc, Danny Webb.*
Two scarecrows put an end to a protection racket run by the crows. Blanc is various characters. Entry in the COLOR RHAPSODY series.
MUSIC BY Eddie Kilfeather, Joe De Nat.
Released on September 22
(7 min./RCA Sound/Technicolor)
Cartoon Films Limited/Charles Mintz Productions/Columbia

JEEPERS CREEPERS (1939) D: Robert [Bob] Clampett.
VOICES: *Mel Blanc, Pinto Colvig.*
Police officer Porky Pig investigates a haunted house inhabited by a wacky ghost. Blanc is Porky and the Ghost's singing voice. Entry in the LOONEY TUNES series.
SONGS: "Jeepers Creepers" *(Harry Warren; Johnny Mercer; sung by Blanc as the Ghost),* "A-Haunting We Will Go" *(composer unknown; sung by Blanc as the Ghost).*
MUSIC BY Carl W. Stalling.
Released on September 23
(6 min./Vitaphone Sound)
Leon Schlesinger Studios/Warner Bros.

LAND OF THE MIDNIGHT FUN (1939) D: Fred [Tex] Avery.
VOICES: *Robert C. Bruce, Mel Blanc, Sara Berner, Fred [Tex] Avery.*
An ocean cruise to the South Pole puts the spotlight on silly Eskimo doings. Blanc is various characters. Entry in the MERRIE MELODIES series.
SONG: "Believe Me If All Those Endearing Young Charms" *(Music: possibly Matthew Locke; Lyrics: Sir Willam Davenant.).*
MUSIC BY Carl W. Stalling.
Released on September 23
(7 min./Vitaphone Sound/Technicolor)
Leon Schlesinger Studios/Warner Bros.

NAUGHTY NEIGHBORS (1939) D: Robert [Bob] Clampett.
VOICES: *Mel Blanc, Shirley Reed, The Sons of the Pioneers, Danny Webb.*
Lovebirds Porky and Petunia Pig have a difficult time keeping their respective families from killing each other. Blanc is Porky and McCoy Duck. Entry in the LOONEY TUNES series.
SONGS: "Would You Like To Take A Walk"*(Harry Warren; Mort Dixon; Billy Rose; sung by Blanc and Reed as Porky and Petunia),* "When I'd Yoo-Hoo In The Valley (To My Lulu In The Hills)" *(Henry Russell; Murray Martin).*
MUSIC BY Carl W. Stalling.
Released on October 7
(7 min./Vitaphone Sound)
Leon Schlesinger Studios/Warner Bros.

THE GOOD EGG (1939) D: Charles M. [Chuck] Jones.
VOICES: *Bernice Hansen, Mel Blanc.*
A childless hen adopts a baby turtle who is ostracized by the chickens — until the chicks get into trouble. Blanc is a chicken. Entry in the MERRIE MELODIES series.
SONG: "Military March" *(Franz Schubert).*
MUSIC BY Carl W. Stalling.
Released on October 21
(7 min./Vitaphone Sound/Technicolor)
Leon Schlesinger Studios/Warner Bros.

DREAMS ON ICE (1939) D: Sid Marcus.
VOICES: *Leone LeDoux, Mel Blanc, The Rhythmettes.*
Scrappy employs his toys as he puts on a skating show in his room. Blanc provides his vocal talents. Entry in the COLOR RHAPSODY series.
MUSIC BY Joe De Nat.
Released on November 3
(6 min./RCA Sound/Technicolor)
Charles Mintz Productions/Columbia

FRESH FISH (1939) D: Fred [Tex] Avery.
VOICES: *Robert C. Bruce, Mel Blanc, Danny Webb, Sara Berner.*
Professor Mackerel Fishsticks goes in search of a rare undersea speci-
men and encounters a host of odd creatures. Blanc is the drunken fish.
Caricatures of Ned Sparks, Katharine Hepburn, Robert L. Ripley and
Lionel Barrymore. Entry in the MERRIE MELODIES series.
SONG: "You Must Have Been A Beautiful Baby" *(Harry Warren; Johnny
Mercer; sung by Blanc as the drunken fish),* "Let The Rest Of The World
Go By" *(Ernest Ball; J. Keirn Brennan),* "Ten Little Indians" *(traditional,
composer unknown).*
MUSIC BY Carl W. Stalling.
Released on November 4
(7 min./Vitaphone Sound/Technicolor)
Leon Schlesinger Studios/Warner Bros.

PIED PIPER PORKY (1939) D: Robert [Bob] Clampett.
VOICES: *Mel Blanc, Danny Webb.*
A rat-chasing Porky Pig (Blanc) uses a clumsy cat to root out the last
rodent in Hamelin. Entry in the LOONEY TUNES series.
SONG: "Violin Concerto Allegretto Non Troppo in E Minor" *(Felix
Mendelssohn-Bartholdy).*
MUSIC BY Carl W. Stalling.
Released on November 4
(7 min./Vitaphone Sound)
Leon Schlesinger Studios/Warner Bros.

PORKY THE GIANT KILLER (1939) D: Ben Hardaway, Cal Dalton.
VOICES: *Mel Blanc, Billy Bletcher, Danny Webb.*
Porky Pig is the lone invader of a giant's castle, where he reluctantly
becomes baby-sitter for the behemoth's big infant. Blanc is Porky, Baby
Giant and the Knight. Entry in the LOONEY TUNES series.
MUSIC BY Carl W. Stalling.
Released on November 18
(7 min./Vitaphone Sound)
Leon Schlesinger Studios/Warner Bros.

FAGIN'S FRESHMAN (1939) D: Ben Hardaway, Cal Dalton.
VOICES: *Lionel Stander, Bobbie Winkler, Mel Blanc, The Sportsmen Quartet.*
Blackie is a kitten who desires to be a tough guy. He leaves home to join
with a group of budding gangsters. Blanc provides his vocal talents. Entry
in the MERRIE MELODIES series.
SONGS: "Three Little Kittens" *(traditional, composer unknown)*, "We're
Working Our Way Through College" *(Richard A. Whiting; Johnny Mercer).*
MUSIC BY Carl W. Stalling.
Released on November 18
(7 min./Vitaphone Sound/Technicolor)
Leon Schlesinger Studios/Warner Bros.

THE SLEEPING PRINCESS (1939) D: Burt Gillett.
VOICES: *Sara Berner, Mel Blanc.*
A disgruntled good fairy zaps the Princess with a sleeping spell when
she isn't invited to the girl's christening. Blanc provides his vocal talents.
Entry in the NERTZERY RHYME series.
MUSIC BY Frank Marsales.
Released on November 20
(9½ min./Western Electric Sound/Technicolor)
Walter Lantz Productions/Universal

THE MILLIONAIRE HOBO (1939) D: *(No director credited).*
VOICES: *Mel Blanc, Dave Weber.*
A bum finds out the hard way that when one inherits a 'million', one
must find out a million what? Blanc provides his vocal talent. Entry in
the PHANTASY series.
MUSIC BY Joe De Nat.
Released on November 24
(6½ min./RCA Sound)
Columbia

SNIFFLES AND THE BOOKWORM (1939) D: Charles M. [Chuck] Jones.
VOICES: *Gay Seabrook, Mel Blanc, Cliff Nazarro, The Sportsmen Quartet.*
Sniffles the Mouse scares a book store bookworm, who summons literary characters to get rid of the trespasser; soon, they are all threatened by an awakening Frankenstein's Monster. Blanc is various characters. Entry in the MERRIE MELODIES series.
SONG: "Mutiny In The Nursery" *(Harry Warren; Johnny Mercer).*
MUSIC BY Carl W. Stalling.
Released on December 2
(7 min./Vitaphone Sound/Technicolor)
Leon Schlesinger Studios/Warner Bros.

PEACE ON EARTH (1939) D: Hugh Harman.
VOICES: *Mel Blanc, The Hollywood Choirboys.*
We see a world inhabited only by animals. Old Grampa Squirrel (Blanc) tells the young ones how man once owned the Earth — but destroyed themselves with warfare.
SONGS: "Hark! The Herald Angels Sing" *(Felix Mendelssohn-Bartholdy; Charles Wesley),* "Silent Night, Holy Night" *(Franz Gruber; Joseph Mohr).*
MUSIC BY Scott Bradley.
Academy Award Nomination *(Short Subject – Cartoon)* Hugh Harman.
Released on December 9
(10 min./Western Electric Sound/Technicolor/Rated [TV-G]/Video/DVD),
Hugh Harman/Metro-Goldwyn-Mayer

SCREWBALL FOOTBALL (1939) D: Fred [Tex] Avery.
VOICES: *John Wald, Mel Blanc.*
A wild gridiron 'classic' takes place at the Chili Bowl. Blanc is Coach, football players, cheerleader and 'motivator'. Entry in the MERRIE MELODIES series.
MUSIC BY Carl W. Stalling.
Released on December 16
(7 min./Vitaphone Sound/Technicolor)
Leon Schlesinger Studios/Warner Bros.

THE FILM FAN (1939) D: Robert [Bob] Clampett.
VOICES: *Mel Blanc, Robert C. Bruce, Billy Bletcher.*
Porky Pig goes on an errand to the grocery store, but is lured into a movie show advertising the double feature 'Honeymoon in Bali' with 'The Old Maid'. Blanc is Porky and the theater usher. Entry in the LOONEY TUNES series.
SONG: "Loch Lomond" *(traditional melody; lyrics by Andrew Long).*
MUSIC BY Carl W. Stalling.
Released on December 16
(7 min./Vitaphone Sound/DVD)
Leon Schlesinger Studios/Warner Bros.

MOTHER GOOSE IN SWINGTIME (1939) D: Manny Gould.
VOICES: *Sara Berner, Mel Blanc, Dave Weber.*
A parade of caricatured Hollywood stars populate Daddy Higgins' bedtime story. Blanc is various characters. Entry in the COLOR RHAPSODY series.
MUSIC BY Joe De Nat.
Released on December 19
(7 min./RCA Sound/Technicolor)
Columbia

THE CURIOUS PUPPY (1939) D: Charles [Chuck] Jones.
VOICE: *Mel Blanc.*
A little pup wanders into an amusement park after-hours and gets into mischief, despite the park's watchdog. Blanc provides vocal effects. Entry in the MERRIE MELODIES series.
SONG: "Oh! You Crazy Moon" *(Jimmy Van Heusen; Johnny Burke).*
MUSIC BY Carl W. Stalling.
Released on December 30
(7 min./Vitaphone Sound/Technicolor/Rated [TV-G])
Leon Schlesinger Studios/Warner Bros.

PORKY'S LAST STAND (1940) D: Robert [Bob] Clampett.
VOICES: *Mel Blanc, Danny Webb.*
When a tough customer comes to Porky Pig's and Daffy Duck's out-of-the-way lunch wagon, Daffy looks for hamburger meat and Porky attempts to fry an egg. Complications arise when Daffy runs into a mad bull and Porky's egg hatches a chick. Blanc is Porky and Daffy. Entry in the LOONEY TUNES series.
SONGS: "(Ho-De-Ay) Start The Day Right" *(Maurice Spitalny; Al Lewis; Charles Tobias; sung by Blanc as Porky, along with the chorus),* "With Plenty Of Gravy [Money] And You" *(Harry Warren; Al Dubin; sung by Blanc as Daffy),* "All In Favor Say 'Aye'" *(Cliff Friend),* "I'd Love To Take Orders From You" *(Harry Warren; Al Dubin).*
MUSIC BY Carl W. Stalling.
Released on January 6
(7 min./Vitaphone Sound/DVD)
Leon Schlesinger Studios/Warner Bros.

THE EARLY WORM GETS THE BIRD (1940) D: Fred [Tex] Avery.
VOICES: *Mel Blanc, Bernice Hansen.*
A baby blackbird wakes up early to catch a worm for breakfast, but falls into the clutches of a hungry fox. Blanc is the baby blackbird, the fox and baby's disgruntled brother. Entry in the MERRIE MELODIES series.
SONG: "Mammy's Little Coal Black Rose" *(Richard A. Whiting).*
MUSIC BY Carl W. Stalling.
Released on January 13
(7 min./Vitaphone Sound/Technicolor)
Leon Schlesinger Studios/Warner Bros.

AFRICA SQUEAKS (1940) D: Robert [Bob] Clampett.
VOICES: *Mel Blanc, Kay Kyser.*
Jungle explorer Porky Pig (Blanc) ventures into the African continent to discover its 'secrets' and meets swing bandleader 'Cake Icer' leading a native combo. Caricatures of Kay Kyser and Spencer Tracy. Entry in the LOONEY TUNES series.
SONG: "You're the Greatest Discovery (Since 1492!)" *(Terry Shand; Mack David).*
MUSIC BY Carl W. Stalling.
Released on January 27
(7 min./Vitaphone Sound)
Leon Schlesinger Studios/Warner Bros.

THE HAPPY TOTS' EXPEDITION (1940) D: Ben Harrison.
VOICES: *Mel Blanc, The King's Men.*
The Happy Tots (Blanc) board their rocket-ship to explore the 'lost planet'. Based on characters created by Harrison Cady. Entry in the COLOR RHAPSODY series.
MUSIC BY Joe De Nat.
Released on February 9
(7 min./RCA Sound/Technicolor)
Charles Mintz Productions/Columbia

BUSY BAKERS (1940) D: Ben Hardaway, Cal Dalton.
VOICES: *Mel Blanc, The Sportsmen Quartet.*
A destitute baker's act of charity towards a blind elf is reciprocated when the beggar's friends come to help the baker boost his business. Blanc is Swenson the Baker, Blind Man Elf, Cross-Eyed Elf and the 'Jerry Colonna' Elf. Entry in the MERRIE MELODIES series.
SONG: "The Happy, Slappy Little Baker Man" *(composer unknown).*
MUSIC BY Carl W. Stalling.
Released on February 10
(7 min./Vitaphone Sound/Technicolor/DVD)
Leon Schlesinger Studios/Warner Bros.

ALI-BABA BOUND (1940) D: Robert [Bob] Clampett.
VOICES: *Mel Blanc.*
With the troops gone to a convention in Boston, Porky Pig is the only Foreign Legionnaire left to defend his desert fort from Ali Baba and his 'Dirty Sleeves'. Blanc is Porky, 'Suicide Squad' and the camels 'Baby Dumpling' and 'Humpmobile'. Caricature of George Raft. Entry in the LOONEY TUNES series.
SONG: "Girlfriend Of The Whirling Dervish" *(Harry Warren; Al Dubin; Johnny Mercer; sung by Blanc as Porky).*
MUSIC BY Carl W. Stalling.
Released on February 17
(7 min./Vitaphone Sound)
Leon Schlesinger Studios/Warner Bros.

ELMER'S CANDID CAMERA (1940) D: Charles M. [Chuck] Jones.
VOICES: *Mel Blanc, Arthur Q. Bryan.*
Amateur photographer Elmer Fudd wants to get some wildlife shots and discovers that (an early) Bugs Bunny (Blanc) is the true definition of 'wild'. Entry in the MERRIE MELODIES series.
SONG: "What's New?" *(Bob Haggart; Johnny Burke).*
MUSIC BY Carl W. Stalling.
Released on March 2
(7 min./Vitaphone Sound/Technicolor/Video/DVD)
Leon Schlesinger Studios/Warner Bros.

BLACKBOARD REVUE (1940) D: Ub Iwerks.
VOICES: *Mel Blanc, The Rhythmettes.*
As midnight approaches, the drawings on a school blackboard begin to cavort. Blanc is various characters. Entry in the COLOR RHAPSODY series.
MUSIC BY Eddie Kilfeather, Joe De Nat.
Released on March 15
(6½ min./RCA Sound/Technicolor)
Cartoon Films Limited/Columbia

PILGRIM PORKY (1940) D: Robert [Bob] Clampett.
VOICES: *Mel Blanc, Robert C. Bruce, The Sportsmen Quartet.*
Porky Pig (Blanc) captains the Mayflower on its jerky journey to the new world, where we see the Statue of Liberty (as a toddler) and Chief Sitting Bull as greeter. Entry in the LOONEY TUNES series.
MUSIC BY Carl W. Stalling.
Released on March 16
(7 min./Vitaphone Sound/DVD)
Leon Schlesinger Studios/Warner Bros.

CROSS-COUNTRY DETOURS (1940) D: Fred [Tex] Avery.
VOICES: *Carlton KaDell, Mel Blanc, Sara Berner.*
As an Eskimo dog runs to California, we see a bear admonishing a tourist at Yosemite Park; a shy deer doing an impression of Mae West; a polar bear sensitive to the cold and a phone operator not allowing a tourist to connect with his echo across the Grand Canyon. Blanc is the Yosemite bear, Scoutmaster, polar bear, bobcat, hiker gila monster and the husky. Entry in the MERRIE MELODIES series.
MUSIC BY Carl W. Stalling.
Released on March 16
(7 min./Vitaphone Sound/Technicolor)
Leon Schlesinger Studios/Warner Bros.

CONFEDERATE HONEY (1940) D: I. [Isadore][Friz] Freleng.
VOICES: *Jim Bannon, Arthur Q. Bryan, Sara Berner, Mel Blanc, The Sportsmen Quartet.*
Termite Terrace's version of *Gone With The Wind:* Elmer Fudd, as Ned Cutler, pursues Crimson O'Hairoil while the Civil War rages. Blanc is the lazy slave. Caricature of Hugh Herbert. Entry in the MERRIE MELODIES series.
SONGS: "My Old Kentucky Home" *(Stephen Foster),* "When Johnny Comes Marching Home" *(traditional, composer unknown),* "The Battle Cry Of Freedom" *(George Frederick Root).*
MUSIC BY Carl W. Stalling.
Released on March 30
(7 min./Vitaphone Sound/Technicolor)
Leon Schlesinger Studios/Warner Bros.

THE BEAR'S TALE (1940) D: Fred [Tex] Avery.
VOICES: *Robert C. Bruce, Mel Blanc, Bernice Hansen, Sara Berner, Fred [Tex] Avery.*
As the three bears take a bicycle trip, Red Riding Hood and Goldilocks deal with a hungry wolf (Blanc). Entry in the MERRIE MELODIES series.
SONGS: "My Old Kentucky Home" *(Stephen Foster),* "Mary Had A Little Lamb" *(traditional, composer unknown).*
MUSIC BY Carl W. Stalling.
Released on April 13
(7 min./Vitaphone Sound/Technicolor/DVD)
Leon Schlesinger Studios/Warner Bros.

SLAP HAPPY PAPPY (1940) D: Robert [Bob] Clampett.
VOICES: *Cliff Nazarro, Jack Lescoulie, Mel Blanc, Danny Webb.*
When Eddie Cackler's hen-wife produces nothing but female chicks, he seeks advice from Bing the Rooster — who advises Eddie to croon for a boy. Blanc is Porky Pig. Caricatures of Eddie Cantor, Bing Crosby, Kay Kyser and Ned Sparks. Entry in the LOONEY TUNES series.
SONG: "I've Got A Lot Of Beautiful Babies (And Each And Every One Is A Boy)" *(Harry Warren; Johnny Mercer).*
MUSIC BY Carl W. Stalling.
Released on April 13
(6 min./Vitaphone Sound/DVD)
Leon Schlesinger Studios/Warner Bros.

PORKY'S POOR FISH (1940) D: Robert [Bob] Clampett.
VOICE: *Mel Blanc.*
Porky Pig (Blanc) hopes to do a thriving business with his pet fish emporium, but a hungry cat tries to eat his stock. Entry in the LOONEY TUNES series.
SONG: "I Am Porky The Pig" *(composer unknown).*
MUSIC BY Carl W. Stalling.
Released on April 27
(7 min./Vitaphone Sound/DVD)
Leon Schlesinger Studios/Warner Bros.

THE HARDSHIP OF MILES STANDISH (1940) D: I. [Friz] Freleng.
VOICES: *Robert C. Bruce, Arthur Q. Bryan, Mel Blanc.*
Grandpa tells what 'really happened' during Pilgrim days when John Alden (a.k.a. Elmer Fudd) courted Priscilla. Blanc is Grandpa Miles Standish and the Indians. Caricatures of Edna May Oliver and Hugh Herbert. Entry in the MERRIE MELODIES series.
SONGS: "Drink To Me Only With Thine Eyes" *(Music: probably Colonel R. Mellish; Lyrics: originally an earlier poem by Ben Jonson.),* "Comin' Through The Rye" *(traditional, composer unknown).*
MUSIC BY Carl W. Stalling.
Released on April 27
(7 min./Vitaphone Sound/Technicolor)
Leon Schlesinger Studios/Warner Bros.

FISH FOLLIES (1940) D: *(No director credited).*
VOICES: *Mel Blanc, Robert Winkler.*
A young boy learns about the fish world from a guide (Blanc). Entry in the PHANTASY series.
MUSIC BY Joe De Nat.
Released on May 10
(6 min./RCA Sound)
Columbia

YOU OUGHT TO BE IN PICTURES (1940) D: I. [Friz] Freleng.
VOICES: *Mel Blanc.* WITH: Leon Schlesinger, Michael Maltese.
Combination of live action and animation with Daffy Duck tricking Porky Pig into quitting Warner Brothers, paving the way for Daffy to become his replacement. Blanc is Porky and Daffy; he also dubs the live action Studio Guard (Maltese), the Stagehand and the Animator. Real-life cartoon producer Schlesinger appears as himself. Entry in the LOONEY TUNES series.
SONGS: "I'll Be Famous On The Screen" *(Cliff Friend; Dave Franklin; sung by Blanc as Daffy)*, "You Ought To Be In Pictures" *(Dana Suesse; Edward Heyman).*
MUSIC BY Carl W. Stalling.
Released on May 18
(9 min./Vitaphone Sound/Video/DVD)
Leon Schlesinger Studios/Warner Bros.

A GANDER AT MOTHER GOOSE (1940) D: Fred [Tex] Avery.
VOICES: *Robert C. Bruce, Mel Blanc, Sara Berner.*
Nursery rhymes are sent up in this spoof featuring Contrary Mary's garden, Humpty Dumpty's fall, an amorous Jack & Jill and an ugly Miss Muffet; the Three Little Pigs are ready for the wolf's huffing and puffing — with a bottle of mouthwash! Blanc is Humpty Dumpty, Jack, the Big Bad Wolf, Dog, Eagle and Mouse. Entry in the MERRIE MELODIES series.
SONGS: "Silent Night" *(Franz Gruber; Joseph Mohr)*, "Humpty Dumpty" *(traditional, composer unknown).*
MUSIC BY Carl W. Stalling.
Released on May 25
(7 min./Vitaphone Sound/Technicolor/DVD)
Leon Schlesinger Studios/Warner Bros.

THE EGG HUNT (1940) D: Ub Iwerks.
VOICES: *Mel Blanc, Elvia Allman.*
Professor Crackpot (Blanc) relates the details of his quest for a rare dino-
saur egg in the Gobi Desert. Entry in the COLOR RHAPSODY series.
MUSIC BY Eddie Kilfeather, Joe De Nat.
Released on May 31
(8 min./RCA Sound/Technicolor)
Cartoon Films Limited/Columbia

TOM TURKEY AND HIS HARMONICA HUMDINGERS (1940) D: Hugh
Harman.
VOICE: *Mel Blanc.*
Tom (Blanc) and his mouth-organ aggregation manage to destroy a local
store with their 'harmonizing'.
MUSIC BY Scott Bradley.
Released on June 8
(7 min./Western Electric Sound/Technicolor/DVD)
Hugh Harman/Metro-Goldwyn-Mayer

THE CHEWIN' BRUIN (1940) D: Robert [Bob] Clampett.
VOICES: *Robert C. Bruce, Mel Blanc.*
Porky Pig listens to how an old-time hunter fought down a bear whose
taste ran to chewing tobacco. Blanc is Porky, the Bear and the bear trap.
Entry in the LOONEY TUNES series.
SONG: "The Bear Went Over The Mountain" *(traditional, composer
unknown).*
MUSIC BY Carl W. Stalling.
Released on June 8
(6 min./Vitaphone Sound)
Leon Schlesinger Studios/Warner Bros.

BARNYARD BABIES (1940) D: Sid Marcus.
VOICES: *Robert Winkler, Mel Blanc, Danny Webb.*
A hen has a brood of chicks, one of which wants to be a federal agent.
Blanc provides his vocal talent. Entry in the FABLE series.
MUSIC BY Joe De Nat.
Released on June 14
(7 min./RCA Sound/Technicolor)
Columbia

CIRCUS TODAY (1940) D: Fred [Tex] Avery.
VOICES: *Edward J. Marr, Mel Blanc.*
We see the various acts offered by 'Jingling Bros. Circus', including utensil-eating Gamer the Glutton, lit-coal-walker Hot Foot Hogan and high-jumper Count Morris Leapoff. Blanc is the Narrator, the Balloon Vender, Hogan, a monkey, a stork, a gorilla, an elephant and the Conductor. Entry in the MERRIE MELODIES series.
SONG: "San Antonio" *(Egbert Van Alstyne; Harry Williams).*
MUSIC BY Carl W. Stalling.
Released on June 22
(8 min./Vitaphone Sound/Technicolor)
Leon Schlesinger Studios/Warner Bros.

LITTLE BLABBERMOUSE (1940) D: I. [Friz] Freleng.
VOICES: *Bill Thompson, Mel Blanc, The Sportsmen Quartet.*
A mouse (with the definite flavor of W.C. Fields) gives a spot-gag guided tour of a drug store during its closed hours; he also has to deal with a pesky cat. Blanc is the bothersome title character. Entry in the MERRIE MELODIES series.
SONGS: "Sing While You're Dressing" *(composer unknown),* "I'd Love To Take Orders From You" *(Harry Warren; Al Dubin),* "Shake Your Powder Puff" *(Sammy Fain; Irving Kahal),* "I'm The Cure For What Ails You" *(Harold Arlen; E.Y. Harburg),* "Half Of Me Wants To Be Good" *(Peter DeRose; Sam Lewis),* "All In Favor, Say 'Aye'" *(Cliff Friend).*
MUSIC BY Carl W. Stalling.
Released on July 6
(7 min./Vitaphone Sound/Technicolor)
Leon Schlesinger Studios/Warner Bros.

PORKY'S BASEBALL BROADCAST (1940) D: Isadore [Friz] Freleng.
VOICES: *Mel Blanc.*
Porky Pig (Blanc) is the announcer as we see a wacky game of baseball at 'Yankum Stadium'. Entry in the LOONEY TUNES series.
SONG: "Loch Lomond" *(Traditional melody; Lyrics: Andrew Long).*
MUSIC BY Carl W. Stalling.
Released on July 6
(7 min./Vitaphone Sound/Rated [TV-G]/DVD)
Leon Schlesinger Studios/Warner Bros.

NEWS ODDITIES (1940) D: *(No director credited).*
VOICES: *Mel Blanc, Danny Webb.*
A cartoon newsreel with Blanc doing various characters. Entry in the
PHANTASY series.
MUSIC BY Joe De Nat.
Released on July 19
(6 min./RCA Sound)
Columbia

THE POOCH PARADE (1940) D: *(No director credited).*
VOICES: *Mel Blanc, Billy Bletcher.*
Scrappy enters his mutt Yippy in a dog show, where Yippy disguises
himself as a rabbit to lead the other pups on a chase. Blanc provides his
vocal talent. Entry in the FABLE series.
MUSIC BY Joe De Nat.
Released on July 19
(6 min./RCA Sound/Technicolor)
Columbia

THE EGG COLLECTOR (1940) D: Charles M. [Chuck] Jones.
VOICES: *Gay Seabrook, Mel Blanc.*
Sniffles the Mouse and his bookworm pal go on an expedition to steal
an owl's egg, but are nearly devoured by the big old owl (Blanc). Entry
in the MERRIE MELODIES series.
MUSIC BY Carl W. Stalling.
Released on July 20
(7 min./Vitaphone Sound/Technicolor)
Leon Schlesinger Studios/Warner Bros.

THE BOOKWORM TURNS (1940) D: Hugh Harman.
VOICES: *Mel Blanc, Frank Elmquist.*
Dr. Jekyll switches the brains of a raven and a bookworm. Blanc is various
characters.
MUSIC BY Scott Bradley.
Released on July 20
(8 min./Western Electric Sound/Technicolor)
Hugh Harman/Metro-Goldwyn-Mayer

A WILD HARE (1940) D: Fred [Tex] Avery.
VOICES: *Mel Blanc, Arthur Q. Bryan.*
Elmer Fudd wants to shoot a 'wabbit', but Bugs Bunny just won't go down without a (screwy) fight. Blanc is Bugs and a skunk. Entry in the MERRIE MELODIES series.
MUSIC BY Carl W. Stalling.
Academy Award Nomination *(Short Subject – Cartoon)* Leon Schlesinger.
Released on July 27
(7 min./Vitaphone Sound/Technicolor/Rated [TV-G]/Video/DVD)
Leon Schlesinger Studios/Warner Bros.

PATIENT PORKY (1940) D: Robert [Bob] Clampett.
VOICES: *Mel Blanc, Ben Frommer, Sara Berner.*
Porky Pig is in the hospital suffering a tummy ache and has the misfortune of falling into the clutches of a crazy cat who thinks he's a doctor. Blanc is Porky, Bugs Bunny, Dr. Chilled Air, Elevator Operator, Oliver Owl, Scottish Dog and the Program Seller. Entry in the LOONEY TUNES series.
SONG: "I Want To Be a Surgeon" *(to the tune of "We're Working Our Way Through College"; Richard A. Whiting; Johnny Mercer),* "Devil May Care" *(Harry Warren; Johnny Burke).*
MUSIC BY Carl W. Stalling.
Released on August 24
(7 min./Vitaphone Sound/Video/DVD)
Leon Schlesinger Studios/Warner Bros.

CEILING HERO (1940) D: Fred [Tex] Avery.
VOICES: *Robert C. Bruce, Mel Blanc.*
A parade of gags on the subject of air travel. Blanc is various characters. Entry in the MERRIE MELODIES series.
MUSIC BY Carl W. Stalling.
Released on August 24
(7 min./Vitaphone Sound/Technicolor)
Leon Schlesinger Studios/Warner Bros.

TANGLED TELEVISION (1940) D: Sid Marcus.
VOICES: *Mel Blanc, Danny Webb.*
An early satirical look at TV, with a singer and a travelogue. Blanc is various characters. Entry in the COLOR RHAPSODY series.
MUSIC BY Joe De Nat.
Released on August 30
(7 min./RCA Sound/Technicolor)
Columbia

MALIBU BEACH PARTY (1940) D: I. [Friz] Freleng.
VOICES: *Jack Lescoulie, Mel Blanc, Sara Berner, Danny Webb, Marie Greene.*
A series of spot-gags with animated Hollywood stars occurs at a party given by Jack Bunny (a caricature of Jack Benny). Blanc is Winchester the valet (caricature of Eddie 'Rochester' Anderson). Other caricatures: Don Ameche, Fred Astaire, John Barrymore, Ben Bernie, Fanny Brice, James Cagney, Claudette Colbert, Joan Crawford, Bette Davis, Andy Devine, Robert Donat, Deanna Durbin, Alice Faye, Clark Gable, Greta Garbo, Cary Grant, Phil Harris, Bob Hope, Kay Kyser, Mary Livingstone, Carole Lombard, Fred MacMurray, Robert Montgomery, Adolphe Menjou, George Raft, Ginger Rogers, Cesar Romero, Mickey Rooney, Ned Sparks, Spencer Tracy, Loretta Young. Entry in the MERRIE MELODIES series.
SONGS: "Avalon" *(Vincent Rose; Al Jolson; B.G. DeSylva),* "Love In Bloom" *(Ralph Rainger; Leo Robin),* "God Save The Queen" *(Henry Carey),* "Vienna Blood" *(Johann Strauss),* "Carissima" *(Arthur A. Penn),* "Devil May Care" *(Harry Warren; Johnny Burke).*
MUSIC BY Carl W. Stalling.
Released on September 14
(7 min./Vitaphone Sound/Technicolor/Rated [TV-G])
Leon Schlesinger Studios/Warner Bros.

CALLING DR. PORKY (1940) D: I. [Friz] Freleng.
VOICES: *Mel Blanc, Sara Berner.*
Porky Pig is a doctor treating a drunken patient plagued by pink elephants.
Blanc is Porky, a pink elephant and the dizzy man. Entry in the LOONEY
TUNES series.
SONG: "Parade Of The Animals" *(Justin Ring; Fred Hager).*
MUSIC BY Carl W. Stalling.
Released on September 21
(7 min./Vitaphone Sound)
Leon Schlesinger Studios/Warner Bros.

FARMER TOM THUMB (1940) D: *(No director credited).*
VOICES: *Brooke Temple, Mel Blanc, Sara Berner.*
Tom gets the idea that vitamins will make his father's unimpressive crops
grow. Blanc provides his vocal talents. Entry in the FABLE series.
MUSIC BY Joe De Nat.
Released on September 27
(6 min./RCA Sound/Technicolor)
Columbia

STAGE FRIGHT (1940) D: Charles M. [Chuck] Jones.
VOICE: *Mel Blanc.*
Two pups look for a bone backstage at a vaudeville theater and encounter
a tough bird (Blanc). Entry in the MERRIE MELODIES series.
MUSIC BY Carl W. Stalling.
Released on September 28
(7 min./Vitaphone Sound/Technicolor/DVD)
Leon Schlesinger Studios/Warner Bros.

MR. ELEPHANT GOES TO TOWN (1940) D: Arthur Davis.
VOICES: *Mel Blanc, Danny Webb.*
A circus ringmaster is dismayed to find his performing elephant drunk
on cold medicine. Blanc provides his vocal talents. Entry in the COLOR
RHAPSODY series.
MUSIC BY Joe De Nat.
Released on October 4
(7½ min./RCA Sound/Technicolor)
Columbia

PREHISTORIC PORKY (1940) D: Robert [Bob] Clampett.
VOICES: *Mel Blanc, Sara Berner, The Sportsmen Quartet.*
Cave-pig Porky is out to get a new suit of 'skins' and falls prey to a black panther. Blanc is Porky, the panther, Rover the Dinosaur, a vulture, a Tyrannosaurus Rex and a singing bird. Entry in the LOONEY TUNES series.
SONGS: "Those Were Wonderful Days" *(Murray Mencher; Jack Scholl; Charles Tobias),* "Revolutions Etude" *(Frederic Chopin).*
MUSIC BY Carl W. Stalling.
Released on October 12
(7 min./Vitaphone Sound/DVD)
Leon Schlesinger Studios/Warner Bros.

HOLIDAY HIGHLIGHTS (1940) D: Fred [Tex] Avery.
VOICES: *Gil Warren, Mel Blanc, Sara Berner, Fred [Tex] Avery.*
Animated gag-fest centering on holidays throughout the year. Blanc is the New Year's Baby, Tommy, George Washington, a dog, a fox and a turkey. Entry in the MERRIE MELODIES series.
SONGS: "Shine On, Harvest Moon" *(Nora Bayes; Jack Norworth),* "Moonlight Bay" *(Percy Wenrich; Edward Madden),* "Silent Night, Holy Night" *(Franz Gruber; Joseph Mohr),* "Hail To The Chief" *(James Sanderson).*
MUSIC BY Carl W. Stalling.
Released on October 12
(7 min./Vitaphone Sound/Technicolor)
Leon Schlesinger Studios/Warner Bros.

HAPPY HOLIDAYS (1940) D: *(No director credited).*
VOICES: *Mel Blanc, Leone Le Doux.*
A child acts up when it comes time to go to school. Blanc provides his vocal talents. Entry in the PHANTASY series.
MUSIC BY Joe De Nat.
Released on October 25
(6 min./RCA Sound)
Columbia

THE SOUR PUSS (1940) D: Robert [Bob] Clampett.
VOICES: *Mel Blanc.*
Porky Pig and his cat decide to have fish for dinner, but don't count on the antics of a freaky flying fish. Blanc is Porky, the cat and the flying fish. Entry in the LOONEY TUNES series.
SONGS: "All This And Heaven Too" *(M.K. Jerome; Jack Scholl)*, "All In Favor Say 'Aye'" *(Cliff Friend).*
MUSIC BY Carl W. Stalling.
Released on November 2
(7 min./Vitaphone Sound/DVD)
Leon Schlesinger Studios/Warner Bros.

THE MAD HATTER (1940) D: Sid Marcus.
VOICES: *John Wald, Mel Blanc.*
A cartoon look at how women's hats are created. Blanc is various characters. Entry in the COLOR RHAPSODY series.
MUSIC BY Joe De Nat.
Released on November 3
(6 min./RCA Sound/Technicolor)
Columbia

WACKY WILDLIFE (1940) D: Fred [Tex] Avery.
VOICES: *Robert C. Bruce, Mel Blanc, Bernice Hansen, Tedd Pierce.*
As we tour the jungle, some off-beat animals parade by. Blanc is the bobcat. Entry in the MERRIE MELODIES series.
SONG: "Vienna Blood" *(Johann Strauss).*
MUSIC BY Carl W. Stalling.
Released on November 9
(7 min./Vitaphone Sound/Technicolor)
Leon Schlesinger Studios/Warner Bros.

THE LONESOME STRANGER (1940) D: Hugh Harman.
VOICES: *Mel Blanc.*
A western hero rides into town to get the Killer Diller Boys, who eliminated the sheriff and plan to rob a stagecoach. Blanc is various characters.
MUSIC BY Scott Bradley.
Released on November 23
(9 min./Western Electric Sound/Technicolor/DVD)
Hugh Harman/Metro-Goldwyn-Mayer

KNOCK! KNOCK! (1940) D:Walter Lantz.
VOICES: *Bernice Hansen, Mel Blanc, Sara Berner.*
Woody Woodpecker makes his first appearance as he goes about destroying Andy Panda's house. Blanc is Woody, Papa Panda and the two sanitarium woodpeckers.
MUSIC BY Frank Marsales.
Released on November 25
(6 min./Western Electric Sound/Technicolor)
Walter Lantz/Universal

PORKY'S HIRED HAND (1940) D: I. [Friz] Freleng.
VOICES: *Mel Blanc.*
To protect his chickens from a wily fox, Porky Pig employs a feeble-minded watchman named Gregory Grunt. Blanc is Porky, Gregory and the fox. Entry in the LOONEY TUNES series.
MUSIC BY Carl W. Stalling.
Released on November 30
(7 min./Vitaphone Sound)
Leon Schlesinger Studios/Warner Bros.

OF FOX AND HOUNDS (1940) D: Fred [Tex] Avery, Rich Hogan.
VOICES: *Mel Blanc, Fred [Tex] Avery.*
Willoughby the Dog matches (half-) wits with a clever fox. Blanc is the fox and the bear. Entry in the MERRIE MELODIES series.
SONG: "Let The Rest Of The World Go By" *(Ernest Ball; J. Keirn Brennan).*
MUSIC BY Carl W. Stalling.
Released on December 7
(7 min./Vitaphone Sound/Technicolor)
Leon Schlesinger Studios/Warner Bros.

PAUNCH 'N' JUDY (1940) D: Ben Harrison.
VOICES: *Mel Blanc, Sara Berner, Cliff Nazarro.*
Daddy Higgins (Blanc) takes up photography but fails to reckon with Baby Snooks. Entry in the FABLE series.
MUSIC BY Joe De Nat.
Released on December 13
(6 min./RCA Sound/Technicolor)
Columbia

MRS. LADYBUG (1940) D: Rudolf Ising.
VOICES: *Mel Blanc, Sara Berner, The Rhythmettes.*
Mrs. Ladybug hires a housekeeper — not realizing it is a hungry, bug-eating spider (Blanc) in disguise.
MUSIC BY Scott Bradley.
Released on December 21
(9 min./Western Electric Sound/Technicolor)
Rudolf Ising/*Metro-Goldwyn-Mayer*

SHOP, LOOK AND LISTEN (1940) D: I. [Friz] Freleng.
VOICES: *Bill Thompson, Mel Blanc.*
Sequel to *Little Blabbermouse* reunites the brat (Blanc) with the 'W.C. Fields' mouse as they venture through J.T. Gimlet's department store. Entry in the MERRIE MELODIES series.
MUSIC BY Carl W. Stalling.
Released on December 21
(7 min./Vitaphone Sound/Technicolor/DVD)
Leon Schlesinger Studios/Warner Bros.

THE TIMID TOREADOR (1940) D: Robert [Bob] Clampett, Norman McCabe.
VOICES: *Mel Blanc.*
Porky Pig is working at the bullfight arena as a hot tamale salesman when he ends up in the ring with a nasty bull. Blanc is Porky, Slapsy Maxie Rosenbull, the Announcer, a heckler and various Mexicans. Entry in the LOONEY TUNES series.
SONGS: "The Gaucho Serenade" *(Nat Simon; John Redmond; James Cavanaugh),* "La Cucaracha" *(traditional, composer unknown; sung by Blanc as Porky).*
MUSIC BY Carl W. Stalling.
Released on December 21
(7 min./Vitaphone Sound)
Leon Schlesinger Studios/Warner Bros.

ELMER'S PET RABBIT (1941) D: Charles M. [Chuck] Jones.
VOICES: *Mel Blanc, Arthur Q. Bryan.*
Elmer Fudd buys Bugs Bunny (Blanc) to be his pet rabbit and fixes up an
outdoor pen for Bugs; nothing doing — Bugs immediately moves into the
house with a frustrated Elmer. Entry in the MERRIE MELODIES series.
SONG: "While Strolling Through the Park One Day" *("Ed Haley," prob-*
ably a pseudonym for Robert E. Keiser; hummed by Blanc as Bugs).
MUSIC BY Carl W. Stalling.
Released on January 4
(7 min./Vitaphone Sound/Technicolor/Rated [TV-G]/Video)
Leon Schlesinger Studios/Warner Bros.

A HELPING PAW (1941) D: Sid Marcus.
VOICES: *Mel Blanc.*
When Chester gets new glasses, he is guided home by Tobias, an intoxicated
dog. Blanc is the various characters. Entry in the COLOR RHAPSODY series.
MUSIC BY Joe De Nat.
Released on January 7
(6 min./RCA Sound/Technicolor)
Columbia

WESTERN DAZE (1941) D: George Pal.
VOICES: *Billy Bletcher, Mel Blanc.*
Jim Dandy, new to the West, is tricked into the saddle of a stolen horse.
He pursues the real thieves to set matters right. Blanc provides his vocal
talents. Entry in the MADCAP MODEL series.
MUSIC BY Andre Kostelanetz, David Raksin.
Released on January 7
(7 min./Western Electric Sound/Technicolor)
George Pal Productions/Paramount

PORKY'S SNOOZE REEL (1941) D: Robert [Bob] Clampett, Norman
McCabe.
VOICES: *Robert C. Bruce, Mel Blanc.*
Porky Pig (Blanc) hosts a spot-gag newsreel of 'topical events' and imitates
Lew Lehr. Entry in the LOONEY TUNES series.
MUSIC BY Carl W. Stalling.
Released on January 11
(7 min./Vitaphone Sound/Rated [TV-G])
Leon Schlesinger Studios/Warner Bros.

THE STREAMLINED DONKEY (1941) D: Sid Marcus.
VOICES: *John Wald, Mel Blanc.*
Fearing the worst, Mama Donkey tries to keep her speedy son away from the racing world. Blanc is various characters. Entry in the FABLE series.
MUSIC BY Joe De Nat.
Released on January 17
(6 min./RCA Sound/Technicolor)
Columbia

THE FIGHTING 69½TH (1941) D: I. [Friz] Freleng.
VOICES: *Mel Blanc, The Sportsmen Quartet, Kent Rogers.*
When picnic-goers leave some food behind, red and black ants go to war over the spoils. Blanc is a black ant, the Red Ant Captain and the Black Ant General. Entry in the MERRIE MELODIES series.
SONG: "Garryowen" *(traditional, composer unknown).*
MUSIC BY Carl W. Stalling.
Released on January 18
(7 min./Vitaphone Sound/Technicolor/DVD)
Leon Schlesinger Studios/Warner Bros.

MOUSE TRAPPERS (1941) D: *Walter Lantz*, Alex Lovy.
VOICES: *Dick Nelson, Sara Berner, Mel Blanc.*
Andy Panda's family spots a mouse in their house and Pop is ordered to catch it. Blanc provides his vocal talents.
MUSIC BY Darrell Calker.
Released on January 27
(6 min./Western Electric Sound/Technicolor)
Walter Lantz Productions/Universal

THE CRACKPOT QUAIL (1941) D: Fred [Tex] Avery.
VOICE: *Mel Blanc.*
Willoughby the Dog returns to hunt down a crazy quail (Blanc), but cannot stop crashing into trees. Entry in the MERRIE MELODIES series.
MUSIC BY Carl W. Stalling.
Released on February 15
(7 min./Vitaphone Sound/Technicolor)
Leon Schlesinger Studios/Warner Bros.

THE HAUNTED MOUSE (1941) D: Fred [Tex] Avery.
VOICES: *Walter Tetley, Mel Blanc.*
A cat (Blanc) travels to a ghost town where he is tormented by the spirit of a deceased mouse. Entry in the LOONEY TUNES series.
MUSIC BY Carl W. Stalling.
Released on February 15
(7 min./Vitaphone Sound)
Leon Schlesinger Studios/Warner Bros.

FAIR TODAY (1941) D:*Walter Lantz*, Alex Lovy.
VOICES: *Robert C. Bruce, Mel Blanc, Grace Stafford.*
A tour of the county fair spotlights various gags. Blanc is the myriad people and animals. Entry in the CARTUNE series.
MUSIC BY Darrell Calker.
Released on February 24
(7 min./Western Electric Mirrophonic Recording/Technicolor)
Walter Lantz Productions/Universal

THE WAY OF ALL PESTS (1941) D: Arthur Davis.
VOICES: *Mel Blanc.*
Reaching the limit of their abuse from man, the insects (Blanc) strike back. Entry in the COLOR RHAPSODY series.
MUSIC BY Joe De Nat.
Released on February 28
(7½ min./RCA Sound/Technicolor)
Columbia

THE CAT'S TALE (1941) D: I. [Friz] Freleng.
VOICES: *Mel Blanc.*
With all the chasing around the house, a mouse tries to call a truce between the dog, the cat and himself. Blanc is the various characters. Entry in the MERRIE MELODIES series.
MUSIC BY Carl W. Stalling.
Released on March 1
(7 min./Vitaphone Sound/Technicolor)
Leon Schlesinger Studios/Warner Bros.

JOE GLOW, THE FIREFLY (1941) D: Charles M. [Chuck] Jones.
VOICE: *Mel Blanc.*
Wafting into a camper's tent, Joe (Blanc) goes on an expedition over the sleeping man's body and his table of imposing items. Entry in the LOONEY TUNES series.
MUSIC BY Carl W. Stalling.
Released on March 8
(7 min./Vitaphone Sound)
Leon Schlesinger Studios/Warner Brothers

THE CARPENTERS (1941) D: Paul Fennell.
VOICES: *Mel Blanc.*
A trio of gadget-men (Blanc) attempt to build a house. Entry in the COLOR RHAPSODY series.
MUSIC BY Clarence Wheeler.
Released on March 14
(8 min./RCA Sound/Technicolor)
Cartoon Films Limited/Columbia

IT HAPPENED TO CRUSOE (1941) D: *No director credited.*
VOICES: *Jack Lescoulie, Danny Webb, Mel Blanc.*
A cannibal king banishes his son Westchester from the tribe for being a vegetarian! Crusoe discovers Westchester, hires him as a valet, and takes him along on a tiger hunt in a dilapidated jalopy. Voice imitations: Fred Allen (cannibal king), Jack Benny (Crusoe), and Eddie "Rochester" Anderson (Westchester), none of which are voiced by Blanc. Blanc is the sounds of Crusoe's jalopy. Entry in the Fable series.
MUSIC BY Joe De Nat.
Released on March 14
(6 min./RCA Sound/Technicolor)
Columbia

TORTOISE BEATS HARE (1941) D: Fred [Tex] Avery.
VOICES: *Mel Blanc.*
Bugs Bunny, indignant at this cartoon's title, challenges Cecil Turtle to a race and makes what he thinks is an easy $10 side bet. What Bugs doesn't know is that Cecil has a lot of helpful relatives. Blanc is Bugs, Cecil, Chester Turtle and other turtles. Entry in the MERRIE MELODIES series. MUSIC BY Carl W. Stalling.
Released on March 15
(7 min./Vitaphone Sound/Technicolor/Video/DVD)
Leon Schlesinger Studios/Warner Bros.

PORKY'S BEAR FACTS (1941) D: I. [Friz] Freleng.
VOICES: *Mel Blanc.*
Porky Pig prepares his larder for winter while his shiftless bear-neighbor strums his banjo. When cold weather hits, the hungry bruin comes begging at Porky's door. Blanc is Porky, the bear, a cow, a dog and a mouse. Entry in the LOONEY TUNES series.
SONGS: "As You Sow, So Shall Ye Reap" *(composer unknown; sung by Blanc as Porky),* "Working Can Wait" *(Jimmy Van Heusen; Edgar DeLange).*
MUSIC BY Carl W. Stalling.
Released on March 29
(7 min./Vitaphone Sound)
Leon Schlesinger Studios/Warner Bros.

GOOFY GROCERIES (1941) D: Robert [Bob] Clampett.
VOICES: *Mel Blanc, Bea Benaderet.*
Store products come to life, including a gorilla who escapes from an animal crackers cookie box to wreak havoc among the groceries. Blanc is the 'Ned Sparks' crab, Jack Bunny, Chicken Pie, a dog, the gorilla, black boy and 'Superman'. Caricature of Eddie 'Rochester' Anderson. Entry in the MERRIE MELODIES series.
MUSIC BY Carl W. Stalling.
Released on March 29
(8 min./Vitaphone Sound/Technicolor/DVD)
Leon Schlesinger Studios/Warner Bros.

HYSTERICAL HIGH SPOTS IN AMERICAN HISTORY (1941) D:Walter Lantz.
VOICES: *Mel Blanc, Sara Berner.*
Events in U.S. history are given the gag treatment in this outing. Blanc is various characters. Entry in the CARTUNE series.
MUSIC BY Darrell Calker.
Released on March 31
(6 min./Western Electric Sound/Technicolor)
Walter Lantz Productions/Universal

THE LITTLE MOLE (1941) D: Hugh Harman.
VOICE: *Mel Blanc.*
A short-sighted mole gets a pair of glasses with which to see the world better, but he loses them. Blanc is the mole and Dr. Primrose Skunk. Produced by Hugh Harman.
MUSIC BY Scott Bradley.
Released on April 5
(9 min./Western Electric Sound/Technicolor)
Metro-Goldwyn-Mayer

THE LAND OF FUN (1941) D: Sid Marcus.
VOICES: *John Wald, Mel Blanc.*
The efforts of a little car to pass a large truck punctuate this gag-fest surrounding holidays. Blanc is various characters. Entry in the COLOR RHAPSODY series.
MUSIC BY Joe De Nat.
Released on April 18
(6 min./RCA Sound/Technicolor)
Columbia

SPEAKING OF ANIMALS *(1941 to 1949; Theatrical Shorts Series)*
Live action footage of animals with dubbed voices in numerous settings. Mel Blanc lent his voice talents to a number of these (51 were made in all), but at this time individual information for the shorts is unavailable. Produced by Jerry Fairbanks for Apex Productions and Paramount.

PORKY'S PREVIEW (1941) D: Fred [Tex] Avery.
VOICES: *Mel Blanc, Sara Berner, Cliff Nazarro.*
Porky Pig has made his own animated cartoon and all his animal friends arrive at the makeshift theater to have a look. Blanc is Porky, the kangaroo, the firefly usher and the skunk. Entry in the LOONEY TUNES series.
SONG: "Playmates" *(Saxie Dowell),* "September in the Rain" *(Harry Warren; Al Dubin; using an Al Jolson takeoff, Blanc sings this song as Porky's crudely-drawn animated cartoon of a sunflower.).*
MUSIC BY Carl W. Stalling.
Released on April 19
(7 min./Vitaphone Sound/DVD)
Leon Schlesinger Studios/Warner Bros.

THE TRIAL OF MR. WOLF (1941) D: I. [Friz] Freleng.
VOICES: *Mel Blanc, Sara Berner.*
When the Big Bad Wolf (Blanc) testifies in defense of his various crimes, he manages to shift the blame to a cunning Red Riding Hood and her weapon-wielding Grandma.
SONGS: "The Little Old Church In The Valley" *(Egbert Van Alstyne; Gene Arnold),* "Oh Dear, What Can The Matter Be?" *(traditional, composer unknown).*
MUSIC BY Carl W. Stalling.
Released on April 26
(7 min./Vitaphone Sound/Technicolor/DVD)
Leon Schlesinger Studios/Warner Bros.

THE GOOSE GOES SOUTH (1941) D: Joseph Barbara, William Hanna.
VOICES: *Truman Bradley, Cliff Nazarro, Mel Blanc, Sara Berner, Harry E. Lang.*
Instead of flying, a young goose decides to hitchhike south. Blanc provides his vocal talents.
SONG: "My Old Kentucky Home" *(Stephen Foster).*
MUSIC BY Scott Bradley.
Released on April 26
(9 min./Western Electric Sound/Technicolor/DVD)
Metro-Goldwyn-Mayer

SCRUB ME MAMA WITH A BOOGIE BEAT (1941) D:Walter Lantz.
VOICES: *Nellie Lutcher, Mel Blanc.*
Lazy Town is full of lethargic denizens until a lively gal puts some life into them. Blanc is the Boat Captain, Fighters 1 and 2, 'Mammy' washing clothes and various citizens.
MUSIC BY Darrell Calker.
Released on April 28
(6 min./Western Electric Sound/Technicolor)
Walter Lantz Productions/Universal

PORKY'S ANT (1941) D: Charles M. [Chuck] Jones.
VOICE: *Mel Blanc.*
Porky Pig (Blanc) and his pygmy guide, Inki, ply the African jungle in search of a rare valuable ant. Entry in the LOONEY TUNES series.
MUSIC BY Carl W. Stalling.
Released on May 10
(7 min./Vitaphone Sound)
Leon Schlesinger Studios/Warner Bros.

FARM FROLICS (1941) D: Robert [Bob] Clampett.
VOICES: *Robert C. Bruce, Mel Blanc, Sara Berner, Cliff Nazarro.*
Barnyard antics include a horse doing a canter (a la Eddie Cantor); a dog which is trained to fetch the newspaper, but stops to read the funnies; birds have their house financed by the Federal Housing Administration; and a 'ZaSu Pitts' mama hog with eager and hungry piglets. Blanc is the Farm Dog, Rosebud and Piggy. Entry in the MERRIE MELODIES series.
SONGS: "I'm Happy About The Whole Thing" *(Harry Warren; Johnny Mercer)*, "Rebecca Of Sunnybrook Farm" *(Albert Gumble; Seymour Brown)*, "Mess Call" *(traditional, composer unknown).*
MUSIC BY Carl W. Stalling.
Released on May 10
(7 min./Vitaphone Sound/Technicolor/DVD)
Leon Schlesinger Studios/Warner Bros.

HOLLYWOOD STEPS OUT (1941) D: Fred [Tex] Avery.
VOICES: *Kent Rogers, Sara Berner, Mel Blanc.*
A batch of movie stars enjoy a gag-filled evening at a nightclub. Caricatures include Clark Gable pursuing a blonde; Greta Garbo selling cigarettes and getting a hot-foot from Harpo Marx; a bashful James Stewart struggling over asking Dorothy Lamour to dance; and several stars trying to get a peek behind exotic dancer Sally Rand's 'bubble'. Blanc is 'Jerry Colonna'. Other caricatures: Mischa Auer, Wallace Beery, Leon Schlesinger and Henry Binder (from the Warner Bros. cartoon production unit), Humphrey Bogart, James Cagney, Claudette Colbert, Bing Crosby, Errol Flynn, Henry Fonda, Judy Garland, Cary Grant, Oliver Hardy, Sonja Henie, J. Edgar Hoover, Boris Karloff, Kay Kyser, Buster Keaton, Peter Lorre, Groucho Marx, Adolphe Menjou, David Niven, William Powell, Tyrone Power, George Raft, Sally Rand, Edward G. Robinson, Cesar Romero, Mickey Rooney, Ann Sheridan, C. Aubrey Smith, Ned Sparks, The Three Stooges, Leopold Stokowski, Lewis Stone, Spencer Tracy, Arthur Treacher, Jane Wyman, Johnny Weissmuller. Entry in the MERRIE MELODIES series.
MUSIC BY Carl W. Stalling.
Released on May 24
(7 min./Vitaphone Sound/Technicolor/Rated [TV-G]/DVD)
Leon Schlesinger Studios/Warner Bros.

A COY DECOY (1941) D: Robert [Bob] Clampett.
VOICES: *Mel Blanc.*
A wolf tries to pin down a fast-moving Daffy Duck as their chase occurs among the tomes in a bookstore. Blanc is Daffy, Porky Pig and the decoy duckling. Entry in the LOONEY TUNES series.
SONGS: "Ride, Tenderfoot, Ride" *(Richard A. Whiting; Johnny Mercer; sung by Blanc as Porky)*, "I Can't Along Little Dogie" *(M.K. Jerome; Jack Scholl; sung by Blanc as Porky and Daffy)*, "Moonlight Sonata" *(Ludwig von Beethoven)*.
MUSIC BY Carl W. Stalling.
Released on June 7
(7 min./Vitaphone Sound)
Leon Schlesinger Studios/Warner Bros.

HIAWATHA'S RABBIT HUNT (1941) D: I. [Friz] Freleng.
VOICES: *Mel Blanc.*
A little Indian endeavors to catch Bugs Bunny for his stew. Blanc is Bugs and Hiawatha. Entry in the MERRIE MELODIES series.
SONGS: "By The Waters Of Minnetonka: An Indian Love Song" *(Thurlow Lieurance; J.M. Cavanass),* "When The Swallows Come Back To Capistrano" *(Leon Rene; sung by Blanc as Bugs).*
MUSIC BY Carl W. Stalling.
Academy Award Nomination *(Short Subjects – Cartoon)* Leon Schlesinger.
Released on June 7
(7 min./Vitaphone Sound/Technicolor/Rated [TV-G]/DVD)
Leon Schlesinger Studios/Warner Bros.

SALT WATER DAFFY (1941) D: *Walter Lantz,* Alex Lovy.
VOICES: *Robert C. Bruce, Mel Blanc.*
The Navy gets the gag treatment with a cartoon look at their war games. Blanc is the Navy Captain and sailors. Entry in the CARTUNE series.
MUSIC BY Darrell Calker.
Released on June 9
(7 min./Western Electric Mirrophonic Recording/Technicolor)
Walter Lantz Productions/Universal

KITTY GETS THE BIRD (1941) D: *No director credited.*
VOICES: *Mel Blanc, Sara Berner.*
A cat (Blanc) and mouse spar over a turkey that's meant for the Thanksgiving table. Entry in the FABLE series.
MUSIC BY Eddie Kilfeather.
Released on June 13
(6 min./RCA Sound/Technicolor)
Columbia

THE WACKY WORM (1941) D: I. [Friz] Freleng.
VOICES: *Mel Blanc.*
The chase is on when a crow desires to eat a 'Jerry Colonna' worm. Blanc is both characters. Entry in the MERRIE MELODIES series.
SONG: "Day Dreaming (All Night Long)" *(Harry Warren; Johnny Mercer; sung by Blanc as the worm).*
MUSIC BY Carl W. Stalling.
Released on June 21
(7 min./Vitaphone Sound/Technicolor)
Leon Schlesinger Studios/Warner Bros.

PORKY'S PRIZE PONY (1941) D: Charles M. [Chuck] Jones.
VOICE: *Mel Blanc.*
An inept race-horse tries to impress Porky Pig (Blanc) with his abilities, but makes a clumsy mess of everything. Entry in the LOONEY TUNES series.
"We're In The Money" *(Harry Warren; Al Dubin; sung with substitute lyrics by Blanc as Porky).*
MUSIC BY Carl W. Stalling.
Released on June 21
(7 min./Vitaphone Sound)
Leon Schlesinger Studios/Warner Bros.

HOOLA BOOLA (1941) D: George Pal.
VOICES: *Sam Edwards, Mel Blanc.*
A South Seas tale with Jim Dandy meeting an exotic beauty on a desert isle; both are threatened by cannibals (Blanc). Entry in the MADCAP MODELS series.
MUSIC BY Thurston Knudson.
Released on June 27
(9 min./Western Electric Sound/Technicolor)
George Pal Productions/Paramount

THE WALLFLOWER (1941) D: *(No director credited).*
VOICES: *Danny Webb, Mel Blanc.*
A duck who likes practical jokes is set-upon by an old maid hen at a barn dance. Blanc lends his vocal talents. Entry in the PHANTASY series.
MUSIC BY Joe De Nat.
Released on July 3
(6 min./RCA Sound)
Columbia

THE HECKLING HARE (1941) D: Fred [Tex] Avery.
VOICES: *Mel Blanc, Kent Rogers, Tex Avery.*
Willoughby the Dog chases Bugs Bunny (Blanc) through the woods and both get tripped up by a deep cliff. Entry in the MERRIE MELODIES series.
MUSIC BY Carl W. Stalling.
Released on July 5
(6 min./Vitaphone Sound/Technicolor/Video/DVD)
Leon Schlesinger Studios/Warner Bros.

MEET JOHN DOUGHBOY (1941) D: Robert [Bob] Clampett.
VOICES: *Robert C. Bruce, Mel Blanc, Billy Bletcher, Jack Lescoulie.*
Army private Porky Pig (Blanc) brings us a funny military 'newsreel'. Caricatures of Jack Benny and Eddie 'Rochester' Anderson. Entry in the LOONEY TUNES series.
SONG: "Mess Call" *(traditional; composer unknown).*
MUSIC BY Carl W. Stalling.
Released on July 5
(6 min./Vitaphone Sound/DVD)
Leon Schlesinger Studios/Warner Bros.

WOODY WOODPECKER/THE CRACKED NUT (1941) D: Walter Lantz.
VOICES: *Mel Blanc, Danny Webb, Gay Seabrook.*
Convinced by the other animals that he's crazy, Woody Woodpecker decides to visit a psychiatrist. Blanc is Woody and Dr. Horace N. Buggy. Entry in the CARTUNE series.
MUSIC BY Darrell Calker.
Released on July 7
(7 min./RCA Sound/Technicolor/Video/DVD)
Walter Lantz Productions/Universal

DUMB LIKE A FOX (1941) D: *(No director credited).*
VOICES: *Mel Blanc.*
A fox diverts a hunting dog by putting it on the trail of a skunk. Blanc is the Father Hound, puppy, fox, beaver and skunk. Entry in the FABLE series.
MUSIC BY Eddie Kilfeather, Joe De Nat.
Released on July 18
(6 min./RCA Sound/Technicolor)
Columbia

THE CUCKOO I.Q. (1941) D: Sid Marcus.
VOICES: *Mel Blanc.*
A contestant tries to win on a radio quiz show. Blanc is various characters.
Entry in the COLOR RHAPSODY series.
MUSIC BY Paul Worth.
Released on July 24
(7 min./RCA Sound/Technicolor)
Columbia

ANDY PANDA'S POP (1941) D:*Walter Lantz*, Alex Lovy.
VOICES: *Dick Nelson, Mel Blanc.*
Pop won't pay to have his roof repaired, so he attempts to fix it himself.
Blanc is the man from the 'Acme Roofing Company'. Entry in the CAR-
TUNE series.
MUSIC BY Darrell Calker.
Released on July 28
(7 min./Western Electric Sound/Technicolor)
Walter Lantz Productions/Universal

THE CUTE RECRUIT (1941) D: Arthur Davis.
VOICE: *Mel Blanc.*
Scrappy (Blanc) daydreams he is in the military. Entry in the PHANTASY
series.
MUSIC BY Eddie Kilfeather.
Released on July 31
(6 min./RCA Sound)
Columbia

PLAYING THE PIED PIPER (1941) D: Lou Lilly.
VOICES: *Mel Blanc.*
Music is the bait used by a dumb cat to trap a wiseacre mouse. Blanc
voices the characters. Entry in the FABLE series.
MUSIC BY Eddie Kilfeather.
Released on August 8
(6 min./RCA Sound/Technicolor)
Columbia

AVIATION VACATION (1941) D: Fred [Tex] Avery.
VOICES: *Robert C. Bruce, Mel Blanc.*
We take a trip around the world via airplane — and get a cock-eyed view
of things. Blanc is the Native Chief, Translator, an ostrich and the sick
butterfly. Entry in the MERRIE MELODIES series.
SONG: "April Showers" *(Louis Silvers; B. G. DeSylva).*
MUSIC BY Carl W. Stalling.
Released on August 9
(7 min./Vitaphone Sound/Technicolor)
Leon Schlesinger Studios/Warner Bros.

WE, THE ANIMALS — SQUEAK! (1941) D: Robert [Bob] Clampett.
VOICES: *Sara Berner, Phil Kramer, Mel Blanc, Robert C. Bruce, Billy Bletcher,*
Michael Maltese.
Kansas City Kitty's days of mouse-chasing come back to haunt her when
mice kidnap her kitten. Blanc is Porky Pig, the mice and the crying voice
of Kitty. Entry in the LOONEY TUNES series.
MUSIC BY Carl W. Stalling.
Released on August 9
(6 min./Vitaphone Sound)
Leon Schlesinger Studios/Warner Bros.

THE SCREWDRIVER (1941) D:Walter Lantz.
VOICES: *Mel Blanc.*
A traffic policeman is in for a hard time when he pulls Woody Woodpecker
over for speeding. Blanc is Woody and the policeman. Note: after this
cartoon Ben Hardaway and, later, Grace Stafford voiced Woody while a
recording of Mel Blanc's 'Woody laugh' was used.
MUSIC BY Darrell Calker.
Released on August 11
(6½ min./Western Electric Sound/Technicolor)
Walter Lantz Productions/Universal

SPORT CHUMPIONS (1941) D: I. [Friz] Freleng.
VOICES: *Jim Bannon, Mel Blanc.*
A look at "lowlifes in the world of sports": A 'trick' archer; a new swimming dive, the 'sloppy Joe'; a confusing football maneuver; and a bicycle race at 'Madison Round Garden'. Blanc is the bikers, the catcher, the football players and the referee. Entry in the MERRIE MELODIES series.
MUSIC BY Carl W. Stalling.
Released on August 16
(7 min./Vitaphone Sound/Technicolor)
Leon Schlesinger Studios/Warner Bros.

THE HENPECKED DUCK (1941) D: Robert [Bob] Clampett.
VOICES: *Mel Blanc, Sara Berner.*
Daffy Duck practices his magic tricks on his wife's egg, makes it disappear and fails to bring it back. This lands him in divorce court, presided over by Porky Pig. Blanc is Porky, Daffy, Junior Duck and the divorce court crowd. Entry in the LOONEY TUNES series.
MUSIC BY Carl W. Stalling.
Released on August 30.
(7 min./Vitaphone Sound)
Leon Schlesinger Studios/Warner Bros.

SNOW TIME FOR COMEDY (1941) D: Charles M. [Chuck] Jones.
VOICE: *Mel Blanc.*
Two pups chase a bone in a wintry field and pond, getting in the way of a beaver (Blanc) building his dam. Entry in the MERRIE MELODIES series.
SONG: "Basin Street Blues" *(Spencer Williams).*
MUSIC BY Carl W. Stalling.
Released on August 30
(7 min./Vitaphone Sound/Technicolor/Rated [TV-G]/laserdisc)
Leon Schlesinger Studios/Warner Bros.

ALL THIS AND RABBIT STEW (1941) D: Fred [Tex] Avery.
VOICES: *Mel Blanc, Danny Webb.*
Tiring of being chased by a hunter, Bugs Bunny (Blanc) challenges his
adversary to a game of craps. Entry in the MERRIE MELODIES series.
SONG: "Basin Street Blues" *(Spencer Williams).*
MUSIC BY Carl W. Stalling.
Released on September 13
(7 min./Vitaphone Sound/Technicolor/Video/DVD)
Leon Schlesinger Studios/Warner Bros.

NOTES TO YOU (1941) D: I. [Friz] Freleng.
VOICES: *Mel Blanc.*
When an alley cat sets up a back fence concert during the night, a frus-
trated Porky Pig tries to silence him. Blanc is Porky and the cat. Entry in
the LOONEY TUNES series.
SONGS: "Figaro"
"Make Love With A Guitar" *(Maria Grever; Raymond Leveen),* "Sextet"
from "Lucia di Lammermoor" *(Gaetano Donizetti; Salvatore Cammarano).*
MUSIC BY Carl W. Stalling.
Released on September 20
(7 min./Vitaphone Sound)
Leon Schlesinger Studios/Warner Bros.

THE CRYSTAL GAZER (1941) D: Arthur Davis.
VOICES: *Mel Blanc, Sara Berner.*
The mystic Zaza Raja (Blanc) ventures to a pharaoh's tomb in search of
answers concerning a little girl's future. Entry in the PHANTASY series.
MUSIC BY Eddie Kilfeather.
Released on October 10
(6 min./RCA Sound/Technicolor)
Columbia

THE BUG PARADE (1941) D: Fred [Tex] Avery, Friz Freleng.
VOICES: *Robert C. Bruce, Mel Blanc, Billy Bletcher.*
A closer, and zany, look at insect life that includes a housefly with suction cups on its feet, a firefly who failed to pay his light bill and a cootie excited at the prospect of a camp full of soldiers. Blanc is various bugs. Entry in the MERRIE MELODIES series.
MUSIC BY Carl W. Stalling.
Released on October 21
(7 min./Vitaphone Sound/Technicolor/laserdisc)
Leon Schlesinger Studios/Warner Bros.

ROBINSON CRUSOE JR. (1941) D: Norman McCabe.
VOICES: *Mel Blanc, Robert C. Bruce.*
Shipwrecked on a desert isle, Porky Pig establishes a makeshift home before running into cannibals. Blanc is Porky, Friday, the tortoise, Daddy Rat and the cannibals. Entry in the LOONEY TUNES series.
SONG: "Java Jive" *(Ben Oakland; Milton Drake; sung by Blanc as Porky, Friday and tortoise),* "I Love Coffee, I Love Tea" *(composer unknown).*
MUSIC BY Carl W. Stalling.
Released on October 25
(6 min./Vitaphone Sound)
Leon Schlesinger Studios/Warner Bros.

ROOKIE REVUE (1941) D: I. [Friz] Freleng.
VOICES: *Jackson Wheeler, Mel Blanc, Robert C. Bruce.*
A fractured look at the 'modern' army, which is equipped with oversized pop-guns, a general who cannot read proper gunners' coordinates and a mess hall inhabited by caricatures of WB cartoon producers Tex Avery, Henry Binder and Ray Katz. Blanc is the drill sergeant, soldiers (including one stupid G.I.) and the general. Entry in the MERRIE MELODIES series.
SONGS: "Mess Call" *(traditional, composer unknown),* "All's Fair In Love And War" *(Harry Warren; Al Dubin).*
MUSIC BY Carl W. Stalling.
Released on October 25
(7 min./Vitaphone Sound/Technicolor/laserdisc/DVD)
Leon Schlesinger Studios/Warner Bros.

THE GREAT CHEESE MYSTERY (1941) D: Arthur Davis.
VOICES: *Mel Blanc.*
A cat tries to guard a refrigerator full of goodies from a raid by two scheming mice. Blanc is the various characters. Entry in the FABLE series.
MUSIC BY Paul Worth.
Released on November 1
(6 min./RCA Sound)
Columbia

SADDLE SILLY (1941) D: Charles M. [Chuck] Jones.
VOICES: *Mel Blanc.*
A slate of gags highlight this story of the Pony Express and the runty dude who keeps trying to hitch a ride. Blanc is a Pony Express rider and the dispatcher. Entry in the MERRIE MELODIES series.
MUSIC BY Carl W. Stalling.
Released on November 8
(7 min./Vitaphone Sound/Technicolor)
Leon Schlesinger Studios/Warner Bros.

PORKY'S MIDNIGHT MATINEE (1941) D: Charles M. [Chuck] Jones.
VOICE: *Mel Blanc.*
Night watchman Porky Pig (Blanc) chases a rare pygmy ant through a theater after it gets out of its cage. Entry in the LOONEY TUNES series.
SONG: "I Ought To Be In Pictures" *(Dana Suesse; Edward Heyman; sung by Blanc as Porky).*
MUSIC BY Carl W. Stalling.
Released on November 22
(7 min./Vitaphone Sound)
Leon Schlesinger Studios/Warner Brothers

THE CAGEY CANARY (1941) D: *(Fred [Tex] Avery, Robert [Bob] Clampett).*
VOICES: *Elvia Allman, Mel Blanc.*
A wily cat tries to keep an old woman from rescuing her canary (Blanc) — which the cat plans to devour. Entry in the MERRIE MELODIES series.
SONGS: "Pop Goes The Weasel" *(traditional, composer unknown),* "Voices Of Spring" *(Johann Strauss).*
MUSIC BY Carl W. Stalling.
Released on November 22
(7 min./Vitaphone Sound/Technicolor)
Leon Schlesinger Studios/Warner Bros.

PANTRY PANIC (1941) D: Walter Lantz.
VOICES: *Mel Blanc, Danny Webb, Ben Hardaway.*
Woody Woodpecker (Blanc) finds himself trapped without food and hunted by a hungry cat.
MUSIC BY Darrell Calker.
Released on November 24
(7 min./Western Electric Sound/Technicolor)
Walter Lantz Productions/Universal

THE FOX AND THE GRAPES/FOX AND GRAPES (1941)
D: Frank Tashlin.
VOICES: *Mel Blanc.*
The Crow has a bunch of grapes he wants to swap for Fox's picnic lunch, but the Fox figures he can have both his lunch and the grapes. Blanc is both characters. Entry in the COLOR RHAPSODY series that introduced this cartoon pair.
MUSIC BY Eddie Kilfeather.
Released on December 5
(8 min./RCA Sound/Technicolor)
Columbia

WABBIT TWOUBLE (1941) D: Robert [Bob] Clampett.
VOICES: *Mel Blanc, Arthur Q. Bryan.*
Elmer Fudd cannot get a moment's peace at the same campsite inhabited by Bugs Bunny and a grizzly bear. Blanc is Bugs and the bear. Entry in the MERRIE MELODIES series.
MUSIC BY Carl W. Stalling.
Released on December 20
(7 min./Vitaphone Sound/Technicolor/Video/DVD)
Leon Schlesinger Studios/Warner Bros.

CARTOONS AND SHORT SUBJECTS

PORKY'S POOCH (1941) D: Robert [Bob] Clampett.
VOICES: *Mel Blanc, Sara Berner.*
Rover the Dog tells his pal Sandy how he 'got himself a master' — by pursuing Porky Pig. Blanc is Porky, Rover and Sandy. Entry in the LOONEY TUNES series.
SONGS: "Loch Lomond" *(Traditional melody; Lyrics: Andrew Long)*, "Mi Caballero" *(M.K. Jerome; Jack Scholl).*
MUSIC BY Carl W. Stalling.
Released on December 27
(7 min./Vitaphone Sound/DVD)
Leon Schlesinger Studios/Warner Bros.

THE FIELD MOUSE (1941) D: Hugh Harman.
VOICE: *Mel Blanc.*
The mice in a farm-field 'community' are threatened by the arrival of a new combine harvester. Blanc is Grandpa Mouse.
MUSIC BY Scott Bradley, Baron Keyes.
Released on December 27
(9 min./Western Electric Sound/Technicolor)
Hugh Harman/Metro-Goldwyn-Mayer

CLINK, CLINK, ANOTHER DRINK (1942) D: Reginald LeBorg.
Spike Jones and the City Slickers, Mel Blanc.
Filmed live-action musical rendition of the title novelty song. Blanc slurs and hiccups during the chorus. Entry in the SOUNDIES series.
(1 reel)
Soundies Distributing Corporation of America

HOP, SKIP AND A CHUMP (1942) D: I. [Friz] Freleng.
VOICES: *Mel Blanc.*
A pair of crows (resembling Stan Laurel & Oliver Hardy) set their sights on a 'tasty' grasshopper — one Hopalong Casserole. Blanc is Hopalong and the crows. Entry in the MERRIE MELODIES series.
MUSIC BY Carl W. Stalling.
Released on January 3
(7 min./Vitaphone Sound/Technicolor/laserdisc)
Leon Schlesinger Studios/Warner Bros.

PORKY'S PASTRY PIRATES (1942) D: I. [Friz] Freleng.
VOICES: *Mel Blanc, Kent Rogers.*
A bee and a fly make their way into Porky Pig's bakery shop and start feasting. Blanc is Porky. Entry in the LOONEY TUNES series.
MUSIC BY Carl W. Stalling.
Released on January 17
(7 min./Vitaphone Sound)
Leon Schlesinger Studios/Warner Bros.

THE BIRD CAME C.O.D. (1942) D: Charles M. [Chuck] Jones.
VOICE: *Mel Blanc.*
Conrad Cat (Blanc) discovers the pitfalls and pratfalls of delivering a potted palm backstage at a vaudeville theater. He also finds trouble with a magician's hat. Entry in the MERRIE MELODIES series.
MUSIC BY Carl W. Stalling.
Released on January 17
(7 min./Vitaphone Sound/Technicolor)
Leon Schlesinger Studios/Warner Bros.

ALOHA HOOEY (1942) D: *(Fred [Tex] Avery).*
VOICES: *Mel Blanc, Pinto Colvig, Sara Berner.*
Two love-struck birds try to impress a Hawaiian beauty. Blanc is Sammy Seagull. Entry in the MERRIE MELODIES series.
MUSIC BY Carl W. Stalling.
Released on January 30
(7 min./Vitaphone Sound/Technicolor)
Leon Schlesinger Studios/Warner Bros.

THE HOLLYWOOD MATADOR (1942) D: Walter Lantz.
VOICES: *Mel Blanc, Ben Hardaway.*
Woody Woodpecker enters the bullfight ring with wacky results. Blanc did not actually make this cartoon, but his voice is heard in it. Every time Woody laughs, that's Blanc. The laughs are taken from the soundtracks of earlier cartoons that Blanc made for Walter Lantz while Blanc was still freelancing. It is believed that any actual words spoken by Woody are done by Ben Hardaway.
MUSIC BY Darrell Calker.
Released on February 9
(7 min./Western Electric Sound/Technicolor)
Walter Lantz Productions/Universal

WHO'S WHO IN THE ZOO (1942) D: Norman McCabe.
VOICES: *Robert C. Bruce, Mel Blanc.*
A keeper of the Azuza Zoo, Porky Pig (Blanc) lets us in at the doings of various animals. Entry in the LOONEY TUNES series.
MUSIC BY Carl W. Stalling.
Released on February 14
(8 min./Vitaphone Sound/DVD)
Leon Schlesinger Studios/Warner Bros.

PORKY'S CAFÉ (1942) D: Charles M. [Chuck] Jones.
VOICES: *Mel Blanc.*
Porky Pig waits on a customer with a voracious appetite while Conrad Cat attempts to both cook and cope with a bothersome ant. Blanc is Porky, Conrad and the customer. Entry in the LOONEY TUNES series.
SONGS: "(Ho-Dle-Ay) Start The Day Right" *(Maurice Spitalny; Al Lewis; Charles Tobias; sung with substitute lyrics by Blanc as Porky)*, "As Easy As Rolling Off A Log" *(M.K. Jerome; Jack Scholl).*
MUSIC BY Carl W. Stalling.
Released on February 21
(7 min./Vitaphone Sound)
Leon Schlesinger Studios/Warner Bros.

THE HUNGRY WOLF (1942) D: Robert Allen, Hugh Harman.
VOICE: *Mel Blanc.*
The Wolf (Blanc) may be hungry, but he also has a heart when he cannot bring himself to eat a cute rabbit who's wandered into his den. Produced by Rudolf Ising.
MUSIC BY Scott Bradley.
Released on February 21
(9 min./Western Electric Sound/Technicolor/Video)
Metro-Goldwyn-Mayer

CONRAD THE SAILOR (1942) D: Charles M. [Chuck] Jones.
VOICES: *Mel Blanc, Pinto Colvig, The Sportsmen Quartet.*
Navy cat Conrad goes after Daffy Duck (Blanc) when the manic mallard
heckles him aboard ship. Entry in the MERRIE MELODIES series.
SONG: "We're Shoving Right Off For Home Again" *(composer unknown).*
MUSIC BY Carl W. Stalling.
Released on February 28
(7 min./Vitaphone Sound/Technicolor/Video/DVD)
Leon Schlesinger Studios/Warner Bros.

CRAZY CRUISE (1942) D: *(Fred [Tex] Avery, Robert [Bob] Clampett).*
VOICES: *Robert Cameron Bruce, Mel Blanc.*
A goofy travelogue with the Sphinx having to share space with the
World's Fair Trylon and Perisphere; a tour of 'Veronica Lake' and a band
of rabbits being attacked by a Japanese vulture. Cameo appearance by
Bugs Bunny. Blanc is Bugs and various characters. Entry in the MERRIE
MELODIES series.
MUSIC BY Carl W. Stalling.
Released on March 26
(6 min./Vitaphone Sound/Technicolor/DVD)
Leon Schlesinger Studios/Warner Bros.

THE WABBIT WHO CAME TO SUPPER (1942) D: I. [Friz] Freleng.
VOICES: *Mel Blanc, Arthur Q. Bryan.*
In order to inherit a fortune, Elmer Fudd has to not harm any animals.
Bugs Bunny takes advantage of the situation by moving into Elmer's
home. Blanc is Bugs, the telegram boy and the delivery man. Entry in
the MERRIE MELODIES series.
SONG: "Angel In Disguise" *(Stefan Weiss; Paul Mann; Kim Gannon; sung
by Blanc as Bugs).*
MUSIC BY Carl W. Stalling.
Released on March 28
(7 min./Vitaphone Sound/Technicolor/Video/DVD)
Leon Schlesinger Studios/Warner Bros.

LEON SCHLESINGER PRESENTS BUGS BUNNY/ANY BONDS TODAY?
(1942) D: Robert [Bob] Clampett.
VOICES: *Mel Blanc, Arthur Q. Bryan.*
Cartoon made for the U.S. Government, encouraging patrons to buy War Bonds. Bugs Bunny, Porky Pig and Elmer Fudd sing Irving Berlin's song "Any Bonds Today?" while summoning the Spirit of '76. Blanc is Bugs and Porky.
MUSIC BY Carl W. Stalling.
(3 min./Vitaphone Sound/Technicolor/Video/DVD)
Leon Schlesinger Studios/U.S. Treasury/National Screen/Warner Brothers

SAPS IN CHAPS (1942) D: I. [Friz] Freleng.
VOICES: *Robert C. Bruce, Mel Blanc, Billy Bletcher.*
We see how the wacky west was won: Custer's 'last stand' provides a thirst-quencher for a wanderer; a wagon train consisting of covered loco-motives; bow-legged citizens (including cats and dogs) in frontier towns; and a Pony Express rider having trouble getting on his horse. Blanc is the vulture, a traveler, a cat, a villain and a horse. Entry in the LOONEY TUNES series.
MUSIC BY Carl W. Stalling.
Released on April 11
(7 min./Vitaphone Sound)
Leon Schlesinger Studios/Warner Bros.

HORTON HATCHES THE EGG (1942) D: Robert [Bob] Clampett.
VOICES: *Frank Graham, Kent Rogers, Sara Berner, Mel Blanc, Robert [Bob] Clampett.*
Rhyming cartoon adaptation of the Dr. Seuss story about a faithful ele-phant who protects a fragile bird's egg despite being taken out of the jungle and sold to a circus: "I meant what I said, and I said what I meant; an elephant is faithful, one hundred percent." Blanc is the mouse, the hunters and an audience member. Entry in the MERRIE MELODIES series.
SONG: "The Hut Sut Song" *(Leo Killion; Ted McMichael; Jack Owens).*
MUSIC BY Carl W. Stalling.
Released on April 11
(9 min./Vitaphone Sound/Technicolor/DVD)
Leon Schlesinger Studios/Warner Bros.

MOTHER GOOSE ON THE LOOSE (1942) D:Walter Lantz.
VOICES: *Dick Nelson, Mel Blanc, Sara Berner.*
Blanc voices Little Jack Horner in this gag-parade centered on nursery rhymes. Entry in the CARTUNE series.
MUSIC BY 'Boogie Woogie' [Darrell] Calker.
Released on April 13
(7 min./Western Electric Sound/Technicolor)
Walter Lantz Productions/Universal

DOG TIRED (1942) D: Charles M. [Chuck] Jones.
VOICES: *Mel Blanc.*
Two pups run from an automobile and take refuge in the local zoo. There, they encounter the various funny animals. Blanc is the laughing hyena and the lovebird. Entry in the MERRIE MELODIES series.
MUSIC BY Carl W. Stalling.
Released on April 25
(8 min./Vitaphone Sound/Technicolor)
Leon Schlesinger Studios/Warner Bros.

THE WACKY WABBIT (1942) D: Robert [Bob] Clampett.
VOICES: *Mel Blanc, Arthur Q. Bryan.*
Elmer Fudd is prospecting for gold when Bugs Bunny (Blanc) shows up to pester him. Entry in the MERRIE MELODIES series.
SONGS: "Oh, Susanna" *(Stephen Foster; sung with modified lyrics by Blanc as Bugs),* "The Dying Cowboy (Bury Me Not On The Lone Prairie)" *(traditional, composer unknown; sung by Blanc as Bugs),* "Parade Of The Animals" *(Justin Ring; Fred Hager).*
MUSIC BY Carl W. Stalling.
Released on May 2
(7 min./Vitaphone Sound/Technicolor/Video/DVD)
Leon Schlesinger Studios/Warner Bros.

DAFFY'S SOUTHERN EXPOSURE (1942) D: Norm McCabe.
VOICES: *Mel Blanc, Billy Bletcher.*
Daffy Duck decides not to fly south for the winter and falls prey to a hungry fox and weasel. Blanc is Daffy and the Fox. Caricature of Carmen Miranda. Entry in the LOONEY TUNES series.
SONGS: "The Gaucho Serenade" *(James Cavanaugh; John Redmond; Nat Simon),* "The Blue Tail Fly" *(traditional, composer unknown; sung by Blanc as Daffy).*
MUSIC BY Carl W. Stalling.
Released on May 2
(7 min./Vitaphone Sound)
Leon Schlesinger Studios/Warner Bros.

THE DRAFT HORSE (1942) D: Charles M. [Chuck] Jones.
VOICES: *Mel Blanc.*
A farm horse rushes down to enlist in the Army when he learns the military needs horses for the war effort. Blanc is the horse, the recruiting sergeant and Private Snafu. Entry in the MERRIE MELODIES series.
SONG: "This Is The Way We Plow The Field" *(to the tune of "Here We Go 'Round The Mulberry Bush"; traditional, composer unknown; sung by Blanc as the horse).*
MUSIC BY Carl W. Stalling.
Released on May 9
(7 min./Vitaphone Sound/Technicolor/DVD)
Leon Schlesinger Studios/Warner Bros.

GOODBYE MR. MOTH (1942) D: Walter Lantz.
VOICES: *Sara Berner, Mel Blanc.*
Andy Panda tries to run a successful tailor shop, but a voracious moth (Blanc) eats everything in sight.
MUSIC BY Darrell Calker.
Released on May 11
(7 min./Western Electric Mirrophonic Recording/Technicolor)
Walter Lantz Productions/Universal

LIGHTS FANTASTIC (1942) D: I. [Friz] Freleng.
VOICES: *The Mello Men, Mel Blanc.*
A series of gags based on the neon signs of Times Square in New York City. Blanc is the Eye Test announcer. Entry in the MERRIE MELODIES series.
SONGS: "I Only Have Eyes For You" *(Harry Warren; Al Dubin)*, "My High Polished Nose" *(to the tune of "My Wild Irish Rose"; Chauncey Olcott)*, "Voices Of Spring" *(Johann Strauss)*, "Chinatown, My Chinatown" *(Jean Schwartz; William Jerome)*, "Violin Concerto Allegretto Non Troppo in E Minor" *(Felix Mendelssohn-Bartholdy)*.
MUSIC BY Carl W. Stalling.
Released on May 23
(7 min./Vitaphone Sound/Technicolor/DVD)
Leon Schlesinger Studios/Warner Bros.

NUTTY NEWS (1942) D: Robert [Bob] Clampett.
VOICES: *Arthur Q. Bryan, Mel Blanc.*
Elmer Fudd takes a wacky look at the 'headlines': a mouse turns the tables on a hunter; a barber uses a Hitler jack-in-the-box to scare kid customers into submission; fireflies have an air raid blackout; a parade of battleships sail in a storm, but the USS California defies the weather. Blanc is various characters. Caricatures of WB cartoon creators Leon Schlesinger, Henry Binder and Ray Katz. Entry in the LOONEY TUNES series.
SONGS: "Always In My Heart (Siempre En Mi Corazon)" *(Ernesto Lecuona; Kim Gannon)*, "Loch Lomond" *(Traditional melody; Lyrics: Andrew Long)*, "Tales From The Vienna Woods" *(Johann Strauss)*.
MUSIC BY Carl W. Stalling.
Released on May 23
(6 min./Vitaphone Sound)
Leon Schlesinger Studios/Warner Bros.

NUTTY PINE CABIN (1942) D: Alex Lovy.
VOICES: *Sara Berner, Mel Blanc.*
Andy Panda's construction of a cabin is hindered when beavers (Blanc) steal his wood to build a dam. Entry in the CARTUNE series.
MUSIC BY Darrell Calker.
Released on June 1
(6 min./Western Electric Mirrophonic Recording/Technicolor)
Walter Lantz Productions/Universal

HOBBY HORSE-LAFFS (1942) D: Norman McCabe.
VOICES: *Robert C. Bruce, Mel Blanc, Dick Nelson.*
In a parody of radio's Hobby Lobby, an assortment of 'guests' display their wacky avocations. Blanc is various characters. Entry in the LOONEY TUNES series.
SONGS: "The Merry Peasant" *(Robert Schumann),* "My Bonnie Lies Over The Ocean" *(probably Charles E. Pratt).*
MUSIC BY Carl W. Stalling.
Released on June 6
(6 min./Vitaphone Sound)
Leon Schlesinger Studios/Warner Bros.

HOLD THE LION, PLEASE (1942) D: Charles M. [Chuck] Jones.
VOICES: *Mel Blanc, Harry E. Lang, Fred [Tex] Avery, Tedd Pierce.*
Trying to prove he is truly 'king of the jungle', a lion sets out to capture Bugs Bunny. Blanc is Bugs, the monkey, the giraffe and Mrs. Bugs Bunny. Entry in the MERRIE MELODIES series.
SONG: "When The Swallows Come Back To Capistrano" *(Leon Rene; sung by Blanc as Bugs).*
MUSIC BY Carl W. Stalling.
Released on June 13
(7 min./Vitaphone Sound/Technicolor/Video)
Leon Schlesinger Studios/Warner Bros.

ACE IN THE HOLE (1942) D: Alex Lovy.
VOICES: *Ben Hardaway, Mel Blanc, Dick Nelson.*
A sergeant won't allow Pvt. Woody Woodpecker to fly a plane, but the crazy bird ends in the pilot's seat after some slapstick maneuvers. Blanc provides Woody's laughing and singing voice.
MUSIC BY Darrell Calker.
Released on June 22
(7 min./Western Electric Sound/Technicolor)
Walter Lantz Productions/Universal

GOPHER GOOFY (1942) D: Norman McCabe.
VOICES: *Mel Blanc.*
When a couple of Brooklyn gophers invade his garden, a farmer raises havoc trying to get rid of them. Blanc is the farmer and the gophers. Entry in the LOONEY TUNES series.
MUSIC BY Carl W. Stalling.
Released on June 27
(6 min./Vitaphone Sound)
Leon Schlesinger Studios/Warner Bros.

BUGS BUNNY GETS THE BOID (1942) D: Robert [Bob] Clampett.
VOICES: *Mel Blanc, Kent Rogers, Sara Berner.*
Killer [Beaky] Buzzard is too bashful to hunt his own food, until mama kicks him out of the nest with instructions to bring back a rabbit. Killer's troubles begin when he sets his sights on Bugs Bunny. Blanc is Bugs and the little buzzards. Entry in the MERRIE MELODIES series.
SONG: "Blues In The Night" *(Harold Arlen; Johnny Mercer; sung by Blanc as Bugs).*
MUSIC BY Carl W. Stalling.
Released on July 11
(7 min./Vitaphone Sound/Technicolor/Video/DVD)
Leon Schlesinger Studios/Warner Bros.

WACKY BLACKOUT (1942) D: Robert [Bob] Clampett.
VOICES: *Mel Blanc, Kent Rogers, Bea Benaderet, Danny Webb, The Sportsmen Quartet.*
Wartime blackout conditions have their effect on animals as a woodpecker becomes a riveter at an aircraft plant. Other patriotic critters include a turtle-jeep, a re-treaded caterpillar, a sickly bird who desires to be a dive-bomber and veteran carrier-pigeons. Blanc is various characters. Entry in the LOONEY TUNES series.
SONG: "My Bonnie Lies Over The Ocean" *(probably Charles E. Pratt; sung with substitute lyrics).*
MUSIC BY Carl W. Stalling.
Released on July 11
(7 min./Vitaphone Sound/DVD)
Leon Schlesinger Studios/Warner Bros.

JUKE BOX JAMBOREE (1942) D: Alex Lovy.
VOICE: *Mel Blanc. Vocals by Zedra de la Conde.*
Muzie Mouse (Blanc) is awakened by a blaring juke box and his efforts to shut it down land him in a glass of intoxicating liquor. Entry in the SWING SYMPHONY series.
SONG: "Chi Qui Chiquita" *(composer unknown).*
MUSIC BY Darrell Calker. Academy Award Nomination *(Short Subject – Cartoon) Walter Lantz.*
Released on July 27
(7 min./Western Electric Mirrophonic Recording/Technicolor)
Walter Lantz Productions/Universal

THE DUCKTATORS (1942) D: Norman McCabe.
VOICES: *John McLeish, Mel Blanc, Michael Maltese.*
A fascist duck tries to take over the barnyard until the Dove of Peace gets his dander up. Blanc is the Dove, Hitler-duck, Hirohito-duck, the 'Jerry Colonna' rabbit and the South German duck. Entry in the LOONEY TUNES series.
SONGS: "I'm a Japanese Sap-Man [Sandman]" *(Richard A. Whiting; Ray Egan; sung by Blanc as Hirohito-duck)*, "Dance of The Comedians" from "The Bartered Bride" *(Bedrich Smetana).*
MUSIC BY Carl W. Stalling.
Released on August 1
(7 min./Vitaphone Sound)
Leon Schlesinger Studios/Warner Bros.

FONEY FABLES (1942) D: I. [Friz] Freleng.
VOICES: *Frank Graham, Mel Blanc, Sara Berner.*
Spot-gags on fairy tales, with a wartime slant. Blanc is the baby, the Boy Who Cried Wolf, the Prince, Tom Thumb, the grasshopper, the ant, the giant, Aladdin, the goose and the dog. Entry in the MERRIE MELODIES series.
SONGS: "Sing A Song Of Sixpence" *(traditional, composer unknown)*, "Heaven Can Wait" *(Jimmy Van Heusen; Edgar DeLange)*, "Beautiful Dreamer" *(Stephen Foster)*, "I Dream Of Jeannie With The Light Brown Hair" *(Foster)*, "Symphony No. 5, 1st Movement" *(Ludwig van Beethoven).*
MUSIC BY Carl W. Stalling.
Released on August 1
(7 min./Vitaphone Sound/Technicolor/DVD)
Leon Schlesinger Studios/Warner Bros.

EATIN' ON THE CUFF OR THE MOTH WHO CAME TO DINNER (1942)
D: Robert [Bob] Clampett.
LIVE ACTION: Leo White.
VOICES: *Mel Blanc, Sara Berner.*
A piano-player (live actor White, voice of Blanc) tells us of the love triangle between a hungry moth (also Blanc), a bee and a widow spider. Entry in the LOONEY TUNES series.
SONG: "Frankie And Johnny" *(traditional melody).*
MUSIC BY Carl W. Stalling.
Released on August 22
(7 min./Vitaphone Sound/DVD)
Leon Schlesinger Studios/Warner Bros.

FRESH HARE (1942) D: I. [Friz] Freleng.
VOICES: *Mel Blanc, Arthur Q. Bryan, The Sportsmen Quartet.*
In the snowy wilds, Mountie Elmer Fudd is out to get his rabbit, but a wily Bugs Bunny (Blanc) has other ideas. Entry in the MERRIE MELODIES series.
SONGS: "I Wish I Were In Dixie" *(Daniel Decatur Emmett; sung by Blanc as Bugs),* "Camptown Races" *(Stephen Foster; sung by Blanc as Bugs),* "Canadian Mounted Police" *(J.S. Zamecnik).*
MUSIC BY Carl W. Stalling.
Released on August 22
(7 min./Vitaphone Sound/Technicolor/Video/DVD)
Leon Schlesinger Studios/Warner Bros.

FOX POP (1942) D: Charles M. [Chuck] Jones.
VOICES: *Mel Blanc, Robert C. Bruce, Tedd Pierce.*
A fox relates to a pair of crows his harrowing tale of his stay at a silver fox farm; he thought it meant a life of luxury — but he soon learned he would be skinned for a woman's stole. Blanc is the fox, a crow, the trapper and the dogs. Entry in the MERRIE MELODIES series.
SONGS: "I'll Pray For You" *(Arthur Altman; Kim Gannon),* "Always In My Heart (Siempre En Mi Corazon)" *(Ernesto Lecuona; Kim Gannon).*
MUSIC BY Carl W. Stalling.
Released on September 5
(7 min./Vitaphone Sound/Technicolor/DVD)
Leon Schlesinger Studios/Warner Bros.

THE IMPATIENT PATIENT (1942) D: Norman McCabe, Robert [Bob] Clampett.
VOICES: *Mel Blanc.*
Telegram messenger Daffy Duck gets the hiccups and consults a doctor — who happens to be a mad scientist with a monster formula. Blanc is Daffy, Dr. Jerkyl, Chloe, the cuckoo clock, the voice on the intercom and the radio announcer. Entry in the LOONEY TUNES series.
MUSIC BY Carl W. Stalling.
Released on September 5
(7 min./Vitaphone Sound/Video)
Leon Schlesinger Studios/Warner Bros.

THE DOVER BOYS AT PIMENTO UNIVERSITY OR THE RIVALS OF ROQUEFORT HALL (1942) D: Charles M. [Chuck] Jones.
VOICES: *John McLeish, Mel Blanc, Marjorie Tarlton, Tedd Pierce, The Sportsmen Quartet.*
Tom, Dick and Larry — the three stalwarts of P.U. — come to the rescue of pretty Dora Standpipe when she is kidnapped by dastardly Dan Backslide. Blanc is Dan, Dick, and the telegraph boy. Entry in the MERRIE MELODIES series.
SONGS: "Sweet Genevieve" *(Henry Tucker; George Cooper),* "Far Above Cayuga's Waters (Alma Mater)" *(H.S. Thompson).*
MUSIC BY Carl W. Stalling.
Released on September 10
(7 min./Vitaphone Sound/Technicolor/Video/DVD)
Leon Schlesinger Studios/Warner Bros.

THE LITTLE BROADCAST (1942) D: George Pal.
VOICES: *Billy Bletcher, Sam Edwards, Mel Blanc. Jazz violinist: Joe Venuti.*
Jim Dandy's musical endeavors are sabotaged by a batch of supernatural folk. Blanc provides his vocal talent. Entry in the MADCAP MODELS series.
MUSIC BY David Raksin.
Released on September 25
(7½ min./Western Electric Sound/Technicolor)
George Pal Productions/Paramount

THE HEP CAT (1942) D: Robert [Bob] Clampett.
VOICES: *Mel Blanc, Kent Rogers, Sara Berner.*
A dog uses artificial sex appeal to lure a cat who thinks he's irresistible to females. Blanc is the cat and Rosebud. Notable as the first of the LOONEY TUNES series to be shot in color.
SONGS: "Java Jive" *(Ben Oakland; Milton Drake; sung with substitute lyrics by Blanc as the cat),* "I Love Da Goils And Da Goils Love Me" *(Bob Clampett; Warren Foster).*
MUSIC BY Carl W. Stalling.
Released on October 3
(7 min./Vitaphone Sound/Technicolor/Video/DVD)
Leon Schlesinger Studios/Warner Bros.

THE SHEEPISH WOLF (1942) D: I. [Friz] Freleng.
VOICES: *Mel Blanc.*
A wolf disguises himself as a sheep to infiltrate the flock, but cannot shake the wise dog taking care of them. Blanc is the sheepdog, wolf, black sheep, the herd and wolves. Entry in the MERRIE MELODIES series.
Released on October 17
(7 min./Vitaphone Sound/Technicolor)
Leon Schlesinger Studios/Warner Bros.

THE LOAN STRANGER (1942) D: Alex Lovy.
VOICES: *Kent Rogers, Mel Blanc.*
Woody Woodpecker (re-use of singing voice by Blanc) gets money for his car from a 'loan wolf' who tries to rook Woody for the interest.
MUSIC BY Darrell Calker.
Released on October 19
(6 min./Western Electric Sound/Technicolor)
Walter Lantz Productions/Universal

THE DAFFY DUCKAROO (1942) D: Norman McCabe.
VOICES: *Mel Blanc, Sara Berner.*
Crooner Daffy Duck visits the Wild West, where he falls for an Indian maid — but he must first contend with a jealous 'Little Beaver', an enormous brave. Blanc is Daffy, Little Beaver, the horse and 'tire Indian' Entry in the LOONEY TUNES series.
SONGS: "My Little Buckaroo" *(M.K. Jerome; Jack Scholl; sung by Blanc as Daffy),* "Would You Like To Take A Walk?" *(Harry Warren; Mort Dixon; Billy Rose; sung by Blanc as Daffy).*
MUSIC BY Carl W. Stalling.
Released on October 24
(8 min./Vitaphone Sound)
Leon Schlesinger Studios/Warner Bros.

THE HARE-BRAINED HYPNOTIST (1942) D: I. [Friz] Freleng.
VOICES: *Mel Blanc, Arthur Q. Bryan.*
Elmer Fudd uses hypnosis against Bugs Bunny (Blanc), but the 'wascally wabbit' turns the tables on him. Entry in the MERRIE MELODIES series.
SONG: "Hey, Doc" *(Edgar M. Sampson; Kim Gannon).*
MUSIC BY Carl W. Stalling.
Released on October 31
(7 min./Vitaphone Sound/Technicolor/Video/DVD)
Leon Schlesinger Studios/Warner Bros.

A TALE OF TWO KITTIES (1942) D: Robert [Bob] Clampett.
VOICES: *Mel Blanc, Tedd Pierce.*
A pair of cats (with more than a passing resemblance to the comedy team Abbott & Costello) try to snare Tweety Pie, who states for the first time "I taut I taw a puddy tat!" Blanc is Tweety and 'Catsello'. Entry in the MERRIE MELODIES series.
MUSIC BY Carl W. Stalling.
Released on November 21
(7 min./Vitaphone Sound/Technicolor/Video/DVD)
Leon Schlesinger Studios/Warner Bros.

MY FAVORITE DUCK (1942) D: Charles M. [Chuck] Jones.
VOICES: *Mel Blanc.*
Porky Pig wants to find a campsite to pitch his tent, but they are all taken by Daffy Duck. Blanc is Porky, Daffy, the eagle and baby eagle. Entry in the LOONEY TUNES series.
SONGS: "Moonlight Bay" *(Percy Wenrich; Edward Madden; sung by Blanc as Porky and Daffy),* "Blues In The Night" *(Harold Arlen; Johnny Mercer; sung by Blanc as Porky and Daffy).*
MUSIC BY Carl W. Stalling.
Released on December 5
(7 min./Vitaphone Sound/Technicolor/Video)
Leon Schlesinger Studios/Warner Bros.

CASE OF THE MISSING HARE (1942) D: Charles M. [Chuck] Jones.
VOICES: *Mel Blanc.*
After a stage magician antagonizes Bugs Bunny, the wily rabbit makes sure he shows up at the mage's performance to do some violent upstaging. Blanc is Bugs and Ala Bahma the magician. Entry in the MERRIE MELODIES series.
SONG: "Aloha Oe" *(Queen Liliuokalani; sung by Blanc as Bugs).*
MUSIC BY Carl W. Stalling.
Released on December 12
(8 min./Vitaphone Sound/Technicolor/Video/DVD)
Leon Schlesinger Studios/Warner Bros.

COAL BLACK AND DE SEBBEN DWARFS (1943) D: Robert [Bob] Clampett.
VOICES: *Vivian Dandridge, Leo Watson, Lillian Randolph, Mel Blanc, Danny Webb.*
A stereotyped African American rhyming take on the 'Snow White' fairy tale as So White is targeted for a hit by the wicked queen. In the woods, she receives help from seven little soldiers. Blanc is Dopey Dwarf, worm, the hitman and some other dwarfs. Entry in the MERRIE MELODIES series.
SONG: "You're In The Army Now" *(traditional, composer unknown; sung by Blanc as the Dwarves).*
MUSIC BY Milt Franklyn in collaboration with Eddie Beal. Supervised by Carl Stalling.
Released on January 16
(7 min./Vitaphone and RCA Sound/Technicolor)

Leon Schlesinger Studios/Warner Bros.
CONFUSIONS OF A NUTZY SPY (1943) D: Norman McCabe.
VOICES: *Mel Blanc.*
Constable Porky Pig and his dog Eggbert trail a bomb-carrying spy, the Missing Lynx. Blanc is Porky, Eggbert, Lynx and radio voice. Entry in the LOONEY TUNES series.
MUSIC BY Carl W. Stalling.
Released on January 23
(7 min./Vitaphone Sound)
Leon Schlesinger Studios/Warner Bros.

PIGS IN A POLKA (1943) D: I. [Friz] Freleng.
VOICES: *Mel Blanc, Sara Berner.*
Johannes Brahms'"Hungarian Rhapsody" is used as a motif for this musical re-telling of the 'Three Little Pigs' story. Blanc is the Big Bad Wolf and Pig No. 3. Entry in the MERRIE MELODIES series.
MUSIC BY Carl W. Stalling.
Academy Award Nomination *(Short Subject – Cartoon)* Leon Schlesinger.
Released on February 2
(7 min./Vitaphone Sound/Technicolor/DVD)
Leon Schlesinger Studios/Warner Bros.

TORTOISE WINS BY A HARE (1943) D: Robert [Bob] Clampett.
VOICES: *Mel Blanc, Kent Rogers.*
In a rematch race with Cecil Turtle, Bugs Bunny uses a streamlined tortoise-shell chassis to help him win — but some rabbit gangsters foul things up. Blanc is Bugs, Cecil, Mrs. Turtle, the narrators, the rabbit bookie, second lookout, and rabbit thugs. Entry in the MERRIE MELODIES series.
MUSIC BY Carl W. Stalling.
Released on February 20
(7 min./Vitaphone Sound/Technicolor/Video/DVD)
Leon Schlesinger Studios/Warner Bros.

TO DUCK...OR NOT TO DUCK (1943) D: Charles M. [Chuck] Jones.
VOICES: *Mel Blanc, Arthur Q. Bryan.*
Daffy Duck challenges Elmer Fudd to a boxing match when Fudd declares he's a sportsman. Blanc is Daffy, the duck referee and Laramore the Dog. Entry in the LOONEY TUNES series.
MUSIC BY Carl W. Stalling.
Released on March 6
(6½ min./Vitaphone Sound/Technicolor/Video)
Leon Schlesinger Studios/Warner Bros.

FIFTH COLUMN MOUSE (1943) D: I. [Friz] Freleng.
VOICES: *Mel Blanc, The Sportsmen Quartet, Sherry Allen group, Mike Maltese.*
A cat manages to bribe a mouse to work for him and turn the other mice into slaves. The plan works until he gets too hungry for his own good. Blanc is the cat and various mice. Entry in the MERRIE MELODIES series.
SONG: "Blues In The Night" *(with substitute lyrics; Harold Arlen; Johnny Mercer).*
MUSIC BY Carl W. Stalling.
Released on March 6
(7 min./Vitaphone Sound/Technicolor/laserdisc/DVD)
Leon Schlesinger Studios/Warner Bros.

FLOP GOES THE WEASEL (1943) D: Charles M. [Chuck] Jones.
VOICES: *Mel Blanc, Lillian Randolph.*
A weasel gets more than he bargained for when he steals an egg and hatches a feisty young chicken. Blanc is the baby chick and the weasel. Entry in the MERRIE MELODIES series.
SONG: "Mammy's Little Coal Black Rose" *(Richard A. Whiting; Ray Egan).*
MUSIC BY Carl W. Stalling.
Released on March 20
(8 min./Vitaphone Sound/Technicolor)
Leon Schlesinger Studios/Warner Bros.

HOP AND GO (1943) D: Norman McCabe.
VOICES: *Pinto Colvig, Mel Blanc.*
When Claude Hopper the Kangaroo boasts he's the best jumper in the world, two Scottish rabbits — Andy and Sandy (both voiced by Blanc) — decide to put the marsupial in his place. Blanc also voices a baby bird. Entry in the LOONEY TUNES series.
SONGS: "Singin' In The Shower [Bathtub]" *(Michael Cleary; Ned Washington; Herb Magidson; sung by Blanc as a rabbit),* "Hippety Hop" *(Carl W. Stalling).*
MUSIC BY Carl W. Stalling.
Released on March 27
(6 min./Vitaphone Sound)
Leon Schlesinger Studios/Warner Bros.

SUPER-RABBIT (1943) D: Charles M. [Chuck] Jones.
VOICES: *Mel Blanc, Kent Rogers, Tedd Pierce.*
A scientist feeds Bugs Bunny a mega-vitamin-charged carrot which transforms him into a superhero; he sets out after Cottontail Smith, gun-toting bunny-hater. Blanc is Bugs, Cottontail, the Narrator, the horse, a Texas rabbit and an observer. Entry in the MERRIE MELODIES series.
MUSIC BY Carl W. Stalling.
Released on April 3
(8 min./Vitaphone Sound/Technicolor/Video/DVD)
Leon Schlesinger Studios/Warner Bros.

THE UNBEARABLE BEAR (1943) D: Charles M. [Chuck] Jones.
VOICES: *Mel Blanc, Marjorie Tarlton, June Foray.*
A burglar fox attempts to rifle the home of a police officer bear as Mrs. Bear sleepwalks — and Sniffles the Mouse won't shut up. Blanc is the fox and Officer Bear. Entry in the MERRIE MELODIES series.
MUSIC BY Carl W. Stalling.
Released on April 17
(7 min./Vitaphone Sound/Technicolor)
Leon Schlesinger Studios/Warner Bros.

THE WISE QUACKING DUCK (1943) D: Robert [Bob] Clampett.
VOICES: *Mel Blanc, Darrell Payne.*
Mr. Meek has been ordered to kill a (Daffy) duck for dinner, but has trouble cornering the manic mallard. Blanc is Daffy. Entry in the LOONEY TUNES series.
SONG: "Jeanie With The Light Brown Feathers [Hair]" *(Stephen Foster; sung by Blanc as Daffy).*
MUSIC BY Carl W. Stalling.
Released on May 1
(7 min./Vitaphone Sound/Technicolor/Video/DVD)
Leon Schlesinger Studios/Warner Bros.

GREETINGS BAIT (1943) D: I. [Friz] Freleng.
VOICES: *Mel Blanc.*
Wacky Worm (a Jerry Colonna caricature) goes to work for a fisherman and lures a variety of fish to his hook; Wacky also spars with a pesky crab. Blanc is Wacky, the fish, Dagwood, and the fisherman (also a Jerry Colonna caricature). Entry in the MERRIE MELODIES series.
SONGS: "Make Love With A Guitar" *(Maria Grever; Raymond Leveen; sung by Blanc as Wacky),* "Trade Winds" *(Cliff Friend; Charles Tobias; sung by Blanc as Wacky),* "Memories" *(Egbert Van Alstyne; Gus Kahn; sung by Blanc as Wacky).*
MUSIC BY Carl W. Stalling.
Academy Award Nomination *(Short Subject – Cartoon)* Leon Schlesinger.
Released on May 15
(7 min./Vitaphone Sound/Technicolor/DVD)
Leon Schlesinger Studios/Warner Bros.

TOKIO JOKIO (1943) D: Norman McCabe.
VOICES: *Mel Blanc.*
A 'captured Japanese newsreel' shows the misfires, backfires and total ineptness of the Asian enemy. Blanc is the 'Nippon News' buzzard, Japanese narrator, air raid siren, Professor Tojo, Red Togoson, Admiral Yamamoto, Lord Hee Haw and the human torpedo. Entry in the LOONEY TUNES series.
MUSIC BY Carl W. Stalling.
Released on May 15
(7 min./Vitaphone Sound)
Leon Schlesinger Studios/Warner Bros.

JACK-WABBIT AND THE BEANSTALK (1943) D: I. [Friz] Freleng.
VOICES: *Mel Blanc.*
Trying to purloin some carrots from a giant's victory garden, Bugs Bunny leads his oversize pursuer on a slapstick chase. Blanc is Bugs, the Giant and the Narrator. Entry in the MERRIE MELODIES series.
SONGS: "It Can't Be Wrong" *(Max Steiner),* "Twilight In Turkey" *(Raymond Scott).*
MUSIC BY Carl W. Stalling.
Released on June 12
(7 min./Vitaphone Sound/Technicolor/Video)
Leon Schlesinger Studios/Warner Bros.

THE ARISTO-CAT (1943) D: Charles M. [Chuck] Jones.
VOICES: *Mel Blanc, Tedd Pierce, Michael Maltese.*
Pussy, a spoiled cat in an opulent home, is left to fend for himself but doesn't know what a mouse looks like. Hubie and Bert — two mice out to raid the cheese box — set Pussy straight: a mouse looks just like Rover the Bulldog. Blanc is Pussy, Bert, Madame, the dog, and Meadows. Entry in the MERRIE MELODIES series.
SONG: "Singin' In The Bathtub" *(Michael Cleary; Ned Washington; Herb Magidson; sung by Blanc as Pussy).*
MUSIC BY Carl W. Stalling.
Released on June 19
(7 min./Vitaphone Sound/Technicolor/Video/DVD)
Leon Schlesinger Studios/Warner Bros.

COMING!! SNAFU (1943) D: Chuck Jones.
VOICES: *Mel Blanc, Frank Graham.*
We learn about the goofiest soldier in the Army, Private Snafu (Blanc) and his education in military matters. Entry in the ARMY NAVY SCREEN MAGAZINE series.
SONG: "Strip Polka" *(Johnny Mercer; sung by Blanc as Snafu).*
MUSIC BY Carl W. Stalling.
Released in June
(3 min.)
Warner Bros./United States Army Signal Corps

WACKIKI WABBIT (1943) D: Charles M. [Chuck] Jones.
VOICES: *Mel Blanc, Tedd Pierce, Michael Maltese, Augie Goupil trio.*
Two castaways swim to Bug Bunny's desert isle and proceed to chase him for dinner. Blanc is Bugs. Entry in the MERRIE MELODIES series.
SONG: "Trade Winds" *(Cliff Friend; Charles Tobias; sung by Blanc as Bugs).*
MUSIC BY Carl W. Stalling.
Released on July 3
(7 min./Vitaphone Sound/Technicolor/Video/DVD)
Leon Schlesinger Studios/Warner Bros.

YANKEE DOODLE DAFFY (1943) D: I. [Friz] Freleng.
VOICES: *Mel Blanc, Ken Bennett.*
Talent scout Porky Pig is hoping to go on vacation, but cannot escape agent Daffy Duck — who tries to sell Porky on his new client, Sleepy LaGoof. Blanc is Porky, Daffy and Sleepy's cough. Entry in the LOONEY TUNES series.
SONGS: "I'm Just Wild About Harry" *(Eubie Blake; Noble Sissle; sung by Blanc as Daffy),* "We Watch The Skyways" *(Max Steiner; Gus Kahn; sung by Blanc as Daffy),* "Laugh, Clown, Laugh" *(Ted Fio Rito; Sam Lewis; Joe Young; sung by Blanc as Daffy),* "I'm A Cowboy [Cheyenne]" *(Egbert Van Alstyne; sung by Blanc as Daffy),* "Angel In Disguise" *(Paul Mann; Stefan Weiss; Kim Gannon; sung by Blanc as Daffy),* "William Tell Overture" *(Gioacchino Rossini; sung with substitute lyrics by Blanc as Daffy),* "Can-Can" from "Orpheus in the Underworld" *(Jacques Offenbach),* "In The Garden Of My Heart" *(Ernest Ball; Caro Roma).*
MUSIC BY Carl W. Stalling.
Released on July 3
(7 min./Vitaphone Sound/Technicolor/Video/DVD)
Leon Schlesinger Studios/Warner Bros.

PORKY PIG'S FEAT (1943) D: Frank Tashlin.
VOICES: *Mel Blanc.*
After gambling away their money, Daffy Duck and Porky Pig cannot pay their hotel bill. Both are locked in their room until they come up with the money. Blanc is Porky, Daffy, the hotel manager, elevator gambler and Bugs Bunny. Entry in the LOONEY TUNES series.
SONG: "Perpetual Motion" *(Johann Strauss).*
MUSIC BY Carl W. Stalling.
Released on July 17
(7 min./Vitaphone Sound/Video/DVD)
Leon Schlesinger Studios/Warner Bros.

TIN PAN ALLEY CATS (1943) D: Robert [Bob] Clampett.
VOICES: *Harland Evans, Leo Watson, Clifford Holland, Mel Blanc, Dreamers quartet.*
A jazzy cat visits the Kit Kat Club, where the hot music literally blasts him out of this world. Blanc is the giant lips and the noise of the rubber band.
SONGS: "Nagasaki" *(Harry Warren; Mort Dixon),* "By The Light Of The Silvery Moon" *(Gus Edwards; Edward Madden),* "Give Me That Old Time Religion" *(traditional, composer unknown).*
MUSIC BY Eddie Beal and his band; incidental MUSIC BY Carl Stalling.
Released on July 17
(7 min./Vitaphone Sound/Technicolor)
Leon Schlesinger Studios/Warner Bros.

GRIPES (1943) D: I. [Friz] Freleng.
VOICE: *Mel Blanc.*
Private Snafu (Blanc) is always complaining about the ways of Army life. When he is put in charge, the base becomes susceptible to an enemy attack. Part of the ARMY NAVY SCREEN MAGAZINE series.
MUSIC BY Carl W. Stalling.
Released in July
(3 min./DVD)
Warner Bros./U.S. Army Signal Corps

SCRAP HAPPY DAFFY (1943) D: Frank Tashlin.
VOICES: *Mel Blanc, Dorothy Lloyd, Tedd Pierce.*
Doing his bit for the war effort by collecting scrap metal, Daffy Duck raises the ire of Adolf Hitler — who sends a voracious goat to gobble up the scrap heap. Blanc is Daffy, Hitler, Nazi soldiers, the submarine captain, Billy Goat, Dillingham Duck, Minuteman Duck, Pioneer Duck, Admiral Duck, Lincoln Duck and Daffy's ancestors. Entry in the LOONEY TUNES series.
SONGS: "We're In To Win" *(Morris Orenstein; sung with substitute lyrics by Blanc as Daffy),* "Rienzi" *(Richard Wagner).*
MUSIC BY Carl W. Stalling.
Released on August 21
(7 min./Vitaphone Sound/Video/DVD)
Leon Schlesinger Studios/Warner Bros.

PRIVATE SNAFU: SPIES (1943) D: Chuck Jones.
VOICE: *Mel Blanc.*
When Private Snafu lets slip some military information, enemy agents arrange to have Snafu's ship torpedoed. Blanc is Snafu and Hitler. Part of the ARMY NAVY SCREEN MAGAZINE series.
SONG: "Hand Me Down My Walking Cane" *(composer unknown).*
MUSIC BY Carl W. Stalling.
Released in August
(3 min./Video/DVD)
Warner Bros./U.S. Army Signal Corps

HISS AND MAKE UP (1943) D: I. [Friz] Freleng.
VOICES: *Mel Blanc, Bea Benaderet.*
Before bedtime, Granny lays down an ultimatum to her fighting pets: wake her up and they'll get kicked out into the snow. Blanc is Roscoe the Dog and Wellington. Entry in the MERRIE MELODIES series.
MUSIC BY Carl W. Stalling.
Released on September 11
(7 min./Vitaphone Sound/Technicolor)
Leon Schlesinger Studios/Warner Bros.

A CORNY CONCERTO (1943) D: Robert [Bob] Clampett.
VOICES: *Arthur Q. Bryan, Mel Blanc.*
Elmer Fudd brings us Johann Strauss' classical music set to a pair of comical vignettes: Porky Pig's hunt for Bugs Bunny is underscored by "Tales From The Vienna Woods"; "The Blue Danube" plays through a tale about Daffy Duck wanting to join some swans. Blanc provides vocal effects. Entry in the MERRIE MELODIES series.
MUSIC BY Carl W. Stalling.
Released on September 18
(8 min./Vitaphone Sound/Technicolor/DVD)
Leon Schlesinger Studios/Warner Bros.

THE GOLDBRICK (1943) D: Frank Tashlin.
VOICES: *Mel Blanc.*
Private Snafu decides to goof off while others perform their military tasks. As a result, he ends up in a hospital attacked by the Japanese. Blanc is Snafu, Goldie the Goldbrick, the bird and the Japanese Goldbrick. Part of the ARMY NAVY SCREEN MAGAZINE series.
MUSIC BY Carl W. Stalling.
Released in September
(3 min./DVD)
Warner Bros./U.S. Army Signal Corps

THE INFANTRY BLUES (1943) D: Chuck Jones.
VOICE: *Mel Blanc.*
Private Snafu (Blanc) thinks soldiers in other branches of the armed services have it easy, until he gets a chance to experience them. Part of the ARMY NAVY SCREEN MAGAZINE series.
MUSIC BY Carl W. Stalling.
Released in September
(3 min./DVD)
Warner Bros./U.S. Army Signal Corps

FALLING HARE (1943) D: Robert [Bob] Clampett.
VOICES: *Mel Blanc, Bob Clampett.*
Bugs Bunny tries to stop an orange gremlin from destroying a military plane. Blanc is Bugs and the gremlin. Entry in the MERRIE MELODIES series.
MUSIC BY Carl W. Stalling.
Released on October 30
(7 min./Vitaphone Sound/Technicolor/Video/DVD)
Leon Schlesinger Studios/Warner Bros.

FIGHTING TOOLS (1943) D: Robert [Bob] Clampett.
VOICE: *Mel Blanc.*
The importance of keeping all weapons and equipment well-maintained is illustrated as Private Snafu (Blanc) faces capture by a Nazi soldier; Snafu's guns and jeep malfunction due to his neglect. Part of the ARMY NAVY SCREEN MAGAZINE series.
SONGS: "A Gay Caballero" *(Frank Crumit; Lou Klein),* "The Stars And Stripes" *(John Philip Sousa).*
MUSIC BY Carl W. Stalling.
Released in October
(3 min./DVD)
Warner Bros./U.S. Army Signal Corps

DAFFY — THE COMMANDO (1943) D: I. [Friz] Freleng.
VOICES: *Mel Blanc.*
Daffy Duck parachutes behind enemy lines and spars with Nazi bird General Von Vulture on his way to 'crown' Adolf Hitler. Blanc is Daffy, Von Vulture and Hitler. Entry in the LOONEY TUNES series.
SONG: "She Was Poor But She Was Honest" *(R.P. Weston; Bert Lee; sung by Blanc as Daffy).*
MUSIC BY Carl W. Stalling.
Released on November 28
(7 min./Vitaphone Sound/Technicolor/Video/DVD)
Leon Schlesinger Studios/Warner Bros.

THE HOME FRONT (1943) D: Frank Tashlin.
VOICE: *Mel Blanc.*
Private Snafu (Blanc) is stationed in the Arctic and daydreams of what his family and friends are doing back home — activities that serve the war effort. Part of the ARMY NAVY SCREEN MAGAZINE series.
MUSIC BY Carl W. Stalling.
Released in November
(3 min./DVD)
Warner Bros./U.S. Army Signal Corps

AN ITCH IN TIME (1943) D: Robert [Bob] Clampett.
VOICES: *Arthur Q. Bryan, Mel Blanc, Sara Berner.*
Elmer Fudd and his dog try to get rid of a pesky flea. Blanc is the dog, the cat and the scream of the flea. Entry in the MERRIE MELODIES series.
SONG: "Food Around The Corner" *(Robert Clampett).*
MUSIC BY Carl W. Stalling.
Released on December 4
(7 min./Vitaphone Sound/Technicolor/Video/DVD)
Leon Schlesinger Studios/Warner Bros.

PUSS N' BOOTY (1943) D: Frank Tashlin.
VOICES: *Bea Benaderet, Mel Blanc.*
Rudolph the Cat (Blanc) makes a satisfying habit of eating all the pet canaries introduced into the household — until feisty, feathered Petey comes along. Note: this was the last of the LOONEY TUNES shot in black and white.
MUSIC BY Carl W. Stalling.
Released on December 11
(7 min./Vitaphone Sound/DVD)
Leon Schlesinger Studios/Warner Bros.

RUMORS (1943) D: Friz Freleng.
VOICE: Mel Blanc, Frank Graham.
The danger of spreading rumors among the ranks is illustrated in this cartoon when Private Snafu (Blanc) sets off 'rumor gremlins' that run amok. Part of the ARMY NAVY SCREEN MAGAZINE series.
MUSIC BY Carl W. Stalling.
Released in December
(3 min./DVD)
Warner Bros./U.S. Army Signal Corps

GOING HOME (1944) D: Chuck Jones.
VOICE: *Mel Blanc.*
At home on leave, Private Snafu (Blanc) talks about Army matters and the information leads to his troop getting ambushed.
SONGS: "When Johnny Comes Marching Home" *(traditional, composer unknown)*, "The Band Played On" *(Charles B. Ward)*, "Time Waits For No One" *(Cliff Friend; Charles Tobias)*, "Hail! Hail! The Gang's All Here" *(Theodore Morse; Arthur Sullivan)*.
MUSIC BY Carl W. Stalling.
Unreleased theatrically.
(3 min./DVD)
Warner Bros./U.S. Army Signal Corps

BOOBY TRAPS (1944) D: Robert [Bob] Clampett.
VOICE: Mel Blanc, Robert Bruce.
On desert assignment, Private Snafu (Blanc) discovers an 'oasis' of beautiful women. He tries to show off his musical talent on a piano rigged as a bomb. Part of the ARMY NAVY SCREEN MAGAZINE series.
SONGS: "Those Endearing Young Charms" *(traditional, composer unknown)*, "The Campbells Are Coming" *(traditional, composer unknown)*, "Snake Charmer" *(traditional, composer unknown)*, "Ach, Du Lieber Augustine" *(traditional, composer unknown)*.
MUSIC BY Carl W. Stalling.
Released in January
(3 min./DVD)
Warner Bros./U.S. Army Signal Corps

LITTLE RED RIDING RABBIT (1944) D: I. [Friz] Freleng.
VOICES: *Mel Blanc, Billy Bletcher, Bea Benaderet.*
While Grandma works the night shift at Lockheed, a hungry wolf takes her place as Red Riding Hood and Bugs Bunny (Blanc) arrive. Entry in the MERRIE MELODIES series.
SONGS: "The Five O'Clock Whistle" *(Gene Irwin; Josef Myrow; Kim Gannon)*, "Put On Your Old Gray Bonnet" *(Percy Wenrich; Stanley Murphy; sung by Blanc as Bugs and by Bletcher as the wolf)*.
MUSIC BY Carl W. Stalling.
Released on January 4
(7 min./Vitaphone Sound/Technicolor/Video/DVD)
Leon Schlesinger Studios/Warner Bros.

WHAT'S COOKIN', DOC? (1944) D: Robert [Bob] Clampett.
VOICES: *Mel Blanc, Robert C. Bruce.*
It's Oscar time in Hollywood and Bugs Bunny is sure he'll win an award. When he loses to James Cagney, a riled rabbit puts on a show to prove he's worthy. Blanc is Bugs, the Master of Ceremonies, an audience member and Little Hiawatha in footage from *Hiawatha's Rabbit Hunt* (1941). Also seen is Hollywood location footage from *A Star Is Born* (1937). Entry in the MERRIE MELODIES series.
SONG: "When The Swallows Come Back To Capistrano" *(Leon Rene; sung by Blanc as Bugs).*
MUSIC BY Carl W. Stalling.
Released on January 8
(6 min./Vitaphone Sound/Technicolor/Video/DVD)
Leon Schlesinger Studios/Warner Bros.

MEATLESS FLYDAY (1944) D: I. [Friz] Freleng.
VOICES: *Cy Kendall, Mel Blanc.*
A fly fends off a hungry spider as they flit around the house. Blanc is the military police officer. Entry in the MERRIE MELODIES series.
MUSIC BY Carl W. Stalling.
Released on January 29
(7 min./Vitaphone Sound/Technicolor)
Leon Schlesinger Studios/Warner Bros.

TOM TURK AND DAFFY (1944) D: Charles M. [Chuck] Jones.
VOICES: *Mel Blanc, Billy Bletcher.*
Tom Turk pleads with Daffy Duck to hide him from pilgrim Porky Pig. However, when Daffy learns what kind of delicious dinner Porky hopes to prepare, the manic mallard gives up the turkey. Blanc is Porky and Daffy. Entry in the LOONEY TUNES series.
SONG: "Angel In Disguise" *(Stefan Weiss; Paul Mann; Kim Gannon; sung by Blanc as Daffy).*
MUSIC BY Carl W. Stalling.
Released on February 12
(7 min./Vitaphone Sound/Technicolor/Video)
Leon Schlesinger Studios/Warner Bros.

BUGS BUNNY AND THE THREE BEARS (1944) D: Charles M. [Chuck] Jones.
VOICES: *Mel Blanc, Kent Rogers, Bea Benaderet.*
Mama Bear makes carrot soup instead of porridge to lure Goldilocks into the bears' trap, but Bugs Bunny shows up instead and falls prey to a lovesick Mama. Blanc is Bugs and Henry 'Papa' Bear. Entry in the MERRIE MELODIES series.
SONG: "King For A Day" *(Ted Fio Rito; Sam Lewis; Joe Young).*
MUSIC BY Carl W. Stalling.
Released on February 26
(7 min./Vitaphone Sound/Technicolor/Video/DVD)
Leon Schlesinger Studios/Warner Bros.

JASPER GOES HUNTING (1944) D: George Pal.
VOICES: *Glenn Leedy, Mel Blanc.*
Jasper is out to find some game when he encounters Bugs Bunny (Blanc), who quickly realizes he's in the wrong short. Entry in the MADCAP MODELS series.
MUSIC BY Maurice De Packh.
Released on March 10
(7 min./Western Electric Sound/Technicolor)
George Pal Productions/Paramount

I GOT PLENTY OF MUTTON (1944) D: Frank Tashlin.
VOICES: *Mel Blanc.*
When a wolf learns the sheepdog has joined the military, he scurries down to snatch a lamb — but meets head-on with the flock's new guardian, Killer Diller the Ram. Blanc is the wolf and Killer Diller. Entry in the LOONEY TUNES series.
SONG: "This Is Worth Fighting For" *(Edgar DeLange; Sam H. Stept).*
MUSIC BY Carl W. Stalling.
Released on March 11
(7 min./Vitaphone Sound/Technicolor/Rated [TV-G]/DVD)
Leon Schlesinger Studios/Warner Bros.

THE WEAKLY REPORTER (1944) D: Charles M. [Chuck] Jones.
VOICES: *Frank Graham, Mel Blanc, Bea Benaderet.*
This newsreel spoof spotlights gags built around wartime problems and
activities on the home front, i.e. rationing, citizens' solidarity, etc. Blanc is
the traffic cop, the car share guy, two butchers, the robber, and an official.
Entry in the MERRIE MELODIES series.
MUSIC BY Carl W. Stalling.
Released on March 25
(7 min./Vitaphone Sound/Technicolor/Video/DVD)
Leon Schlesinger Studios/Warner Bros.

PRIVATE SNAFU VS. MALARIA MIKE (1944) D: Chuck Jones.
VOICES: *Mel Blanc, Billy Bletcher.*
Private Snafu (Blanc) fails to take proper precautions and falls victim to
a malaria-carrying mosquito. Part of the ARMY NAVY SCREEN MAGA-
ZINE series.
MUSIC BY Carl W. Stalling.
Released in March
(3 min./DVD)
Warner Bros./U.S. Army Signal Corps

SNAFUPERMAN (1944) D: I. [Friz] Freleng.
VOICES: *Mel Blanc, Tedd Pierce.*
Gaining super powers from a 'Technical Fairy First Class', Private Snafu
(Blanc) fails to use the required manuals and charts — and comes close
to destroying U.S. Forces. Part of the ARMY NAVY SCREEN MAGAZINE
series.
MUSIC BY Carl W. Stalling.
Released in March
(3 min./DVD)
Warner Bros./U.S. Army Signal Corps

TICK TOCK TUCKERED (1944) D: Robert [Bob] Clampett.
VOICES: *Mel Blanc.*
War workers Porky Pig and Daffy Duck are late once too often. Faced with losing their jobs, they try to get a good night's sleep — but are thwarted by wailing cats, bright moonlight and a leaky roof. Blanc is Porky, Daffy, the boss, and cat/dog noises. Entry in the LOONEY TUNES series. A remake of *Porky's Badtime Story* (1937).
MUSIC BY Carl W. Stalling.
Released on April 8
(7 min./Vitaphone Sound/Technicolor/Video)
Leon Schlesinger Studios/Warner Bros.

BUGS BUNNY NIPS THE NIPS (1944) D: I. [Friz] Freleng.
VOICES: *Mel Blanc, Bea Benaderet.*
Bugs Bunny is washed ashore on a South Pacific isle just as the Japanese invade; the rascally rabbit matches wits with enemy soldiers and a massive sumo wrestler. Blanc is Bugs, the Japanese soldiers and the sumo wrestler. Entry in the MERRIE MELODIES series.
MUSIC BY Carl W. Stalling.
Released on April 22
(7 min./Vitaphone Sound/Technicolor)
Leon Schlesinger Studios/Warner Bros.

A LECTURE ON CAMOUFLAGE (1944) D: Chuck Jones.
VOICE: Mel Blanc, Robert Bruce.
Private Snafu (Blanc) is used as a visual aid as the Technical Fairy First Class instructs us on proper military camouflaging techniques. Part of the ARMY NAVY SCREEN MAGAZINE series.
MUSIC BY Carl W. Stalling.
Released in April
(3 min./DVD)
Warner Bros./U.S. Army Signal Corps

THE SWOONER CROONER (1944) D: Frank Tashlin.
VOICES: *Mel Blanc, Richard Bickenbach, Sara Berner, Sam Glaser.*
Porky Pig (Blanc) has turned his farm into a wartime egg-producing factory, but production stops when the chickens become mesmerized by a skinny singing rooster named Frankie. Porky desperately auditions a crooner of his own to keep the hens laying. Includes singing imitations of Frank Sinatra, Nelson Eddy, Al Jolson, Jimmy Durante, Cab Calloway, Vaughn Monroe and Bing Crosby. Entry in the LOONEY TUNES series.
SONGS: "It Can't Be Wrong" *(Max Steiner; Kim Gannon),* "Shortnin' Bread" *(Jacques Wolf),* "As Time Goes By" *(Herman Hupfeld),* "September In The Rain" *(Harry Warren; Al Dubin),* "I'll Pray For You" *(Arthur Altman; Gannon),* "Lullaby Of Broadway" *(Warren; Dubin),* "Always In My Heart" *(Ernesto Lecuona; Gannon),* "Blues In The Night" *(Harold Arlen; Johnny Mercer),* "When My Dreamboat Comes Home" *(Cliff Friend; Dave Franklin),* "Trade Winds" *(Friend; Charles Tobias),* "You Must Have Been A Beautiful Baby" *(Warren; Mercer).*
MUSIC BY Carl W. Stalling.
Academy Award Nomination *(Short Subject – Cartoon)* Warner Brothers.
Released on May 6
(7 min./Vitaphone Sound/Technicolor/Video/DVD)
Leon Schlesinger Studios/Warner Bros.

RUSSIAN RHAPSODY (1944) D: Robert [Bob] Clampett.
VOICES: *Mel Blanc, Robert C. Bruce, Sherry Allen Group.*
Adolf Hitler mans a plane to bomb Russia, but 'Gremlins from the Kremlin' invade his aircraft and destroy it piece-by-piece. Blanc is Hitler, the narrator, the German, some gremlins and the Lew Lehr imitation. Entry in the MERRIE MELODIES series. The gremlins are caricatures of the Schlesinger/WB cartoon production staff: Blanc, Bob Bentley, Henry Binder, Johnny Burton, Lou Cavette, Bob Clampett, Friz Freleng, Ray Katz, Michael Maltese, Melvin Millar, Mike Sasanoff and Rod Scribner.
SONGS: "Song Of The Volga Boatman" *(traditional, composer unknown),* "We Are Gremlins From The Kremlin" "Ach, Du Lieber Augustine" *(traditional, composer unknown).*
MUSIC BY Carl W. Stalling.
Released on May 20
(7 min./Vitaphone Sound/Technicolor/Video)
Leon Schlesinger Studios/Warner Bros.

DUCK SOUP TO NUTS (1944) D: I. [Friz] Freleng.
VOICES: *Mel Blanc.*
A frantic day of hunting occurs when Daffy Duck's buddies fly off, leaving him alone to face rifle-wielding Porky Pig. Blanc is Daffy, Porky and other ducks. Entry in the LOONEY TUNES series.
MUSIC BY Carl W. Stalling.
Released on May 27
(7 min./Vitaphone Sound/Technicolor/Video/DVD)
Leon Schlesinger Studios/Warner Bros.

GAS (1944) D: Chuck Jones.
VOICES: *Mel Blanc, Billy Bletcher.*
Private Snafu is attacked by a deadly vaporous cloud. Bugs Bunny makes a silent cameo appearance. Blanc is Snafu. Part of the ARMY NAVY SCREEN MAGAZINE series.
MUSIC BY Carl W. Stalling.
Released in May
(3 min.)
Warner Bros./U.S. Army Signal Corps

ANGEL PUSS (1944) D: Charles M. [Chuck] Jones.
VOICES: *Mel Blanc.*
When a little boy is paid to drown a cat, the feline escapes and schemes to haunt the boy's conscience as a 'ghost'. Blanc is Li'l Sambo and Angel Puss. Entry in the LOONEY TUNES series.
MUSIC BY Carl W. Stalling.
Released on June 3
(7 min./Vitaphone Sound/Technicolor)
Leon Schlesinger Studios/Warner Bros.

SLIGHTLY DAFFY (1944) D: I. [Friz] Freleng.
VOICES: *Mel Blanc.*
General Daffy Duck and Private Porky Pig defend a frontier fort from some wacky Indians. Blanc is Daffy, Porky, the sentry, the Indians, Rochester and Jerry Colonna. Entry in the MERRIE MELODIES series. A remake of *Scalp Trouble* (1939).
MUSIC BY Carl W. Stalling.
Released on June 17
(7 min./Vitaphone Sound/Technicolor/Video)
Leon Schlesinger Studios/Warner Bros.

HARE RIBBIN' (1944) D: Robert [Bob] Clampett.
VOICES: *Mel Blanc, Sammy Wolfe.*
A Russian dog chases Bugs Bunny (Blanc) into a lake as the pursuit takes place underwater. Entry in the MERRIE MELODIES series.
SONG: "Would It Be Wrong? [It Can't Be Wrong]" *(Max Steiner; Kim Gannon; sung by Blanc as Bugs).*
MUSIC BY Carl W. Stalling.
Released on June 24
(7 min./Vitaphone Sound/Technicolor/Video/DVD)
Leon Schlesinger Studios/Warner Bros.

THE CHOW HOUND (1944) D: Frank Tashlin.
VOICE: Mel Blanc, Frank Graham.
Private Snafu hopes to snag a bull for some fresh beef, but gets butted for his trouble. Blanc is Snafu, the bull and the Army chef. Part of the ARMY NAVY SCREEN MAGAZINE series.
SONGS: "Over There" *(George M. Cohan),* "Rebecca Of Sunnybrook Farm" *(Albert Gumble).*
MUSIC BY Carl W. Stalling.
Released in June
(3 min./DVD)
Warner Bros./U.S. Army Signal Corps

BROTHER BRAT (1944) D: Frank Tashlin.
VOICES: *Mel Blanc, Bea Benaderet, Paul Regan.*
A burly female war worker enlists Porky Pig to baby-sit her violent child. Blanc is Porky, Percy, the cat, and Baby Butch. Entry in the LOONEY TUNES series.
MUSIC BY Carl W. Stalling.
Released on July 15
(7 min./Vitaphone Sound/Technicolor/Video)
Leon Schlesinger Studios/Warner Bros.

HARE FORCE (1944) D: I. [Friz] Freleng.
VOICES: *Mel Blanc, Bea Benaderet, Tedd Pierce.*
When Granny invites a cold Bugs Bunny into her house on a wintry night,
Sylvester the Dog schemes to get rid of him. Blanc is Bugs. Entry in the
MERRIE MELODIES series.
MUSIC BY Carl W. Stalling.
Released on July 22
(7 min./Vitaphone Sound/Technicolor/Video/DVD)
Leon Schlesinger Studios/Warner Bros.

CENSORED (1944) D: Frank Tashlin.
VOICE: *Mel Blanc.*
Private Snafu (Blanc), frustrated that his letters home come back cen-
sored, uses Technical Fairy First Class to get an unaltered missive to his
girlfriend. Unfortunately, the unfiltered message contains information
the enemy uses to ambush American forces. Part of the ARMY NAVY
SCREEN MAGAZINE series.
MUSIC BY Carl W. Stalling.
Released in July
(3 min./DVD)
Warner Bros./U.S. Army Signal Corps

FROM HAND TO MOUSE (1944) D: Charles M.[Chuck] Jones.
VOICES: *Mel Blanc.*
A gullible lion keeps letting himself be outsmarted by a clever mouse. Blanc
is the mouse, the ape, and the lion. Entry in the LOONEY TUNES series.
MUSIC BY Carl W. Stalling.
Released on August 5
(7 min./Vitaphone Sound/Technicolor)
Leon Schlesinger Studios/Warner Bros.

BIRDY AND THE BEAST (1944) D: Robert [Bob] Clampett.
VOICES: *Mel Blanc, Bob Clampett.*
Tweety Pie does his best to violently punish the cat which is after him.
Blanc is Tweety, dog barks, and the cat. Entry in the MERRIE MELODIES
series.
MUSIC BY Carl W. Stalling.
Released on August 19
(7 min./Vitaphone Sound/Technicolor/Video)
Leon Schlesinger Studios/Warner Bros.

BUCKAROO BUGS (1944) D: Robert [Bob] Clampett.
VOICES: *Mel Blanc, Robert Bruce.*
Bugs Bunny's pilfering of carrots from various Victory gardens gets the notice of 'Brooklyn's famous fighting cowboy,' Red Hot Ryder. Blanc is Bugs, Ryder and various villagers. Entry in the LOONEY TUNES series.
SONGS: "My Little Buckaroo" *(M.K. Jerome; Jack Scholl),* "She'll Be Comin' 'Round The Mountain" *(traditional, composer unknown).*
MUSIC BY Carl W. Stalling.
Released on August 26
(7 min./Vitaphone Sound/Technicolor/Video/DVD)
Leon Schlesinger Studios/Warner Bros.

OUTPOST (1944) D: Chuck Jones.
VOICE: *Mel Blanc.*
Private Snafu (Blanc) realizes no detail is too small to defeat the enemy when he finds a discarded Japanese ration can on an island outpost. Part of the ARMY NAVY SCREEN MAGAZINE series.
SONG: "I'm In The Mood For Love" *(Jimmy McHugh; Dorothy Fields).*
MUSIC BY Carl W. Stalling.
Released in August
(3 min.)
Warner Bros./U.S. Army Signal Corps

GOLD IS WHERE YOU LOSE IT (1944) D: Jules White.
Andy Clyde, Emmett Lynn, Gertrude Sutton, Mel Blanc, Hank Mann, Bud Jamison, Eva McKenzie, James C. Morton, Cy Schindell, Frank Mills, Lynton Brent, Eddie Laughton, John Tyrrell.
Live action comedy short with Clyde and Lynn finding stolen bank loot on a prospecting expedition. Blanc plays the stuttering Luke.
Released on September 1
(18 min.)
Columbia

GOLDILOCKS AND THE JIVIN' BEARS (1944) D: I. [Friz] Freleng.
VOICES: *Ernest Whitman, Mel Blanc, Lillian Randolph, H. C. Evans, Sara Berner.*
A jazz jam session leaves their instruments too hot to play, so a bear combo goes for a walk in the woods. They mistake Goldilocks and the Big Bad Wolf as jitterbug dancers, so they start jamming again; the poor wolf gets danced half to death by Goldilocks, Red Riding Hood and Grandma. Blanc is the Wolf, delivery guy and third bear. Entry in the MERRIE MELODIES series.
MUSIC BY Teddy Buckner & his All-Stars. INCIDENTAL MUSIC BY Carl Stalling.
Released on September 2
(7 min./Vitaphone Sound/Technicolor)
Warner Bros.

PLANE DAFFY (1944) D: Frank Tashlin.
VOICES: *Mel Blanc, Sara Berner, Robert C. Bruce.*
When a carrier-pigeon falls into the clutches of a sexy female spy, woman-hater Daffy Duck is assigned to deliver an important message — but he is pursued by 'se-duck-tress' Hatta Mari. Blanc is Daffy, the agent, Adolf Hitler, Hermann Goering and Joseph Goebbels. Entry in the LOONEY TUNES series.
MUSIC BY Carl W. Stalling.
Released on September 16
(7 min./Vitaphone Sound/Technicolor/Video/DVD)
Warner Bros.

PAY DAY (1944) D: I. [Friz] Freleng.
VOICE: *Mel Blanc.*
When Private Snafu (Blanc) squanders his Army pay on trifles, Technical Fairy First Class warns him about saving for the future. Part of the ARMY NAVY SCREEN MAGAZINE series.
SONGS: "The Sorcerer's Apprentice" *(Paul Dukas),* "The Skaters Waltz" *(Emil Waldteufel),* "Espana Waltz" *(Waldteufel),* "Arabian Dance" from "The Nutcracker" *(Pyotr Ilyich Tchaikovsky),* "Russian Dance" from "The Nutcracker" *(Tchaikovsky),* "Winter" *(August Gumble),* "Snafu [Annie] Doesn't Live Here Anymore" *(Harold Spina; Johnny Burke; Joe Young).*
MUSIC BY Carl W. Stalling.
Released in September
(3 min./DVD)
Warner Bros./U.S. Army Signal Corps

LOST AND FOUNDLING (1944) D: Charles M. [Chuck] Jones.
VOICES: *Marjorie Tarlton, Mel Blanc.*
A wayward egg is hatched by Sniffles the Mouse, who discovers the young bird is a rodent-eating hawk. Blanc is Orville the Hawk, birds and snoring. Entry in the MERRIE MELODIES series.
SONG: "Symphony No. 6 in B Minor, Pathetique, Opus 74 (Movement 4)" *(Pyotr Ilyich Tchaikovsky).*
MUSIC BY Carl W. Stalling.
Released on September 30
(7 min./Vitaphone Sound/Technicolor)
Leon Schlesinger Studios/Warner Bros.

THREE BROTHERS (1944) D: I. [Friz] Freleng.
VOICES: *Mel Blanc.*
Private Snafu doesn't want to sort shoes, but when he learns what his brothers Tarfu and Fubar are assigned to perform, he changes his attitude. Blanc is Snafu, Tarfu and Fubar. Part of the ARMY NAVY SCREEN MAGAZINE series. Note: In military parlance, Snafu stands for Situation Normal All Fouled Up; Tarfu is Things Are Really Fouled Up and Fubar is Fouled Up Beyond All Repair.
SONG: "Five O'Clock Whistle" *(Joseph Myrow; Paul Mann).*
MUSIC BY Carl W. Stalling.
Released in September
(3 min./DVD)
Warner Bros./U.S. Army Signal Corps

BOOBY HATCHED (1944) D: Frank Tashlin.
VOICES: *Mel Blanc, Sara Berner.*
A mama duck and a hungry wolf have a tug of war over the half-hatched Robespierre the Duckling. Blanc is Robespierre, the chick, the bear and the wolf. Entry in the LOONEY TUNES series.
MUSIC BY Carl W. Stalling.
Released on October 14
(7 min./Vitaphone Sound/Technicolor/DVD)
Leon Schlesinger Studios/Warner Bros.

THE OLD GREY HARE (1944) D: Robert [Bob] Clampett.
VOICES: *Mel Blanc, Arthur Q. Bryan.*
We flash forward and then backward in time as Elmer Fudd wonders when he'll catch Bugs Bunny, and then reviews memories with the 'wascally wabbit'. Blanc is Bugs and Divine Intervention. Entry in the MERRIE MELODIES series.
MUSIC BY Carl W. Stalling.
Released on October 28
(7 min./Vitaphone Sound/Technicolor/DVD)
Warner Bros.

TARGET SNAFU (1944) D: I. [Friz] Freleng.
VOICE: *Mel Blanc.*
Malaria mosquitoes go through their own brand of basic training and maneuvers before attacking Private Snafu (Blanc). Part of the ARMY NAVY SCREEN MAGAZINE series.
SONG: "Perpetual Motion" *(Johann Strauss).*
MUSIC BY Carl W. Stalling.
Released in October
(3 min./DVD)
Warner Bros./U.S. Army Signal Corps

THE STUPID CUPID (1944) D: Frank Tashlin.
VOICES: *Mel Blanc, Frank Graham.*
Cupid Elmer Fudd gets back at an ungrateful Daffy Duck by arrowing the manic mallard into an affair with a married chicken. Blanc is Daffy, the rooster, dog, cat, bluebird and Emily. Entry in the LOONEY TUNES series.
SONG: "Don't Sweetheart Me" *(Cliff Friend; Charles Tobias; sung by Blanc as Daffy).*
MUSIC BY Carl W. Stalling.
Released on November 25
(7 min./Vitaphone Sound/Technicolor/DVD)
Warner Bros.

STAGE DOOR CARTOON (1944) D: I. [Friz] Freleng.
VOICES: *Mel Blanc, Arthur Q. Bryan.*
When Elmer Fudd chases Bugs Bunny into a vaudeville theater, they continue their pursuit via various acts onstage. Blanc is Bugs and the Southern sheriff. Entry in the MERRIE MELODIES series.
MUSIC BY Carl W. Stalling.
Released on December 30
(7 min./Vitaphone Sound/Technicolor/Video/DVD)
Warner Bros.

SECRETS OF THE CARIBBEAN (1945) D: Chuck Jones.
VOICE: *Mel Blanc.*
Private Snafu (Blanc) is protecting the Panama Canal when he meets beautiful Flora and is battered by giant insects, howler monkeys and carnivorous plants.
MUSIC BY Carl W. Stalling.
Unreleased theatrically.
(3 min.)
Warner Bros./U.S. Army Signal Corps

THE RETURN OF MR. HOOK (1945) D: Robert McKimson.
VOICES: *Mel Blanc, Arthur Lake.*
Sailor Hook wants to get home so he can wed his stateside sweetheart, and learns how to use War Bond savings to his best advantage. Blanc is sailors, sales clerk and the realtor. Written by Hank Ketcham, who later created the comic strip Dennis the Menace.
MUSIC BY Carl W. Stalling.
(2 min./DVD)
Warner Bros./U.S. Navy

TOKYO WOES (1945) D: Robert [Bob] Clampett.
VOICES: *Mel Blanc, Arthur Lake, Sara Berner, Frank Graham.*
After listening to a radio broadcast from Japan, seaman Hook decides to send a bomb at the enemy. Blanc is the Japanese announcer, Sad Sack and the singing bond. Written by Hank Ketcham.
SONGS: "Any Bonds Today?" *(Irving Berlin)*, "The Yankee Doodle Boy" *(George M. Cohan)*, "My Bonnie Lies Over The Ocean" *(traditional, composer unknown)*.
MUSIC BY Carl W. Stalling.
(4 min./DVD)
Warner Bros./U.S. Navy

ENEMY BACTERIA (1945) D: Dick Lundy.
Milburn Stone *(live action)*, VOICE: Thomas Gomez, Mel Blanc.
Combination of live action and animation showing the effects of germ warfare. Blanc is the germs.
(24 min.)
Walter Lantz Productions/U.S. Navy

ODOR-ABLE KITTY (1945) D: Charles M. [Chuck] Jones.
VOICES: *Mel Blanc.*
An alley cat poses as a skunk and immediately garners the amorous attentions of Henry [Pepe LePew]. Blanc is Henry, the cat, dog barks, woman, Bugs, Mrs. Skunk. Entry in the LOONEY TUNES series.
SONG: "Angel In Disguise" *(Stefan Weiss; Paul Mann; Kim Gannon; sung by Blanc as the cat)*.
MUSIC BY Carl W. Stalling.
Released on January 6
(7 min./Vitaphone Sound/Technicolor/DVD)
Warner Bros.

HERR MEETS HARE (1945) D: I. [Friz] Freleng.
VOICES: *Mel Blanc.*
Hermann Goering is taking a hunting trip in the Black Forest when he is accosted by a traveling Bugs Bunny. Blanc is Bugs, Goerring, Adolf Hitler, bird, Stalin, Winchell. Entry in the MERRIE MELODIES series.
MUSIC BY Carl W. Stalling.
Released on January 13
(7 min./Vitaphone Sound/Technicolor/Video)
Warner Bros.

DRAFTEE DAFFY (1945) D: Robert [Bob] Clampett.
VOICES: *Mel Blanc.*
Trying to dodge his military induction, Daffy Duck finds he cannot escape the 'little man from the draft board'. Blanc is Daffy and the 'little man'. Entry in the LOONEY TUNES series.
SONG: "It Had To Be Me [You]" *(Isham Jones; Gus Kahn; sung by Blanc as Daffy).*
MUSIC BY Carl W. Stalling.
Released on January 27
(7 min./Vitaphone Sound/Technicolor/Video/DVD)
Warner Bros.

THE UNRULY HARE (1945) D: Frank Tashlin.
VOICES: *Mel Blanc, Arthur Q. Bryan, The Sportsmen Quartet.*
Elmer Fudd is a surveyor for the railroad, whose tracks will be laid right over a fighting Bugs Bunny's home. Blanc is Bugs and the railroad workers. Entry in the MERRIE MELODIES series.
SONG: "As Time Goes By" *(Herman Hupfeld; sung by Blanc as Bugs).*
MUSIC BY Carl W. Stalling.
Released on February 10
(7 min./Vitaphone Sound/Technicolor/Video/DVD)
Warner Bros.

TRAP HAPPY PORKY (1945) D: Charles M. [Chuck] Jones.
VOICES: *Mel Blanc, The Sportsmen Quartet.*
Bothered by mice, Porky Pig employs a cat to get rid of them. When the cat invites his friends over to party, Porky calls in a bulldog to go after the felines — but the canine would rather party, too. Blanc is Porky, a mouse, the drunken cats and the bulldog. Entry in the LOONEY TUNES series.
SONGS: "Moonlight Bay" *(Percy Wenrich; Edward Madden; sung by Blanc as the cats),* "When Irish Eyes Are Smiling" *(Ernest Ball; George Graff; Chauncey Olcott; sung by Blanc as Porky, the cats and the bulldog).*
MUSIC BY Carl W. Stalling.
Released on February 24
(6½ min./Vitaphone Sound/Technicolor)
Warner Bros.

IN THE ALEUTIANS (1945) D: Chuck Jones.
VOICE: *Mel Blanc.*
Private Snafu (Blanc) is featured in spot gags about the Alaskan islands that are susceptible to Japanese attack. Part of the ARMY NAVY SCREEN MAGAZINE series.
MUSIC BY Carl W. Stalling.
Released in February
(3 min./DVD)
Warner Bros./U.S. Army Signal Corps

LIFE WITH FEATHERS (1945) D: I. [Friz] Freleng.
VOICES: *Mel Blanc, Sara Berner, Dave Barry.*
A spurned male lovebird wants to end it all by giving himself up to Sylvester the Cat. When Sylvester balks, suspecting a trap, the bird has to force himself into the feline's mouth. Blanc is the lovebird, Sylvester, telegram guy. Entry in the MERRIE MELODIES series.
SONG: "They're Either Too Young Or Too Old" *(Arthur Schwartz; Frank Loesser; hummed by Blanc as Sylvester).*
MUSIC BY Carl W. Stalling.
Academy Award Nomination *(Short Subject – Cartoon)* Edward Selzer.
Released on March 24
(7 min./Vitaphone Sound/Technicolor/Rated [TV-G]/Video)
Warner Bros.

BEHIND THE MEAT-BALL (1945) D: *(Frank Tashlin).*
VOICES: *Mel Blanc, Sara Berner.*
Fido (Blanc) is tired of meatless meals and joins a three-way fight with two other dogs over an unclaimed steak. Entry in the LOONEY TUNES series.
MUSIC BY Carl W. Stalling.
Released on April 7
(7 min./Vitaphone Sound/Technicolor)
Warner Bros.

HARE TRIGGER (1945) D: I. [Friz] Freleng.
VOICES: *Mel Blanc.*
Yosemite Sam tries to rob a train, but that's almost impossible with Bugs Bunny aboard. Blanc is the narrator, Bugs, Sam. Entry in the MERRIE MELODIES series.
SONGS: "Go Get The Ax" *(traditional, composer unknown; sung by Blanc as Bugs),* "The Dying Cowboy (Bury Me Not On The Lone Prairie)" *(traditional, composer unknown; sung by Blanc as Bugs),* "Sweet Georgia Brown" *(Maceo Pinkard; Kenneth Casey; sung by Blanc as Bugs).*
MUSIC BY Carl W. Stalling.
Released on May 5
(7 min./Vitaphone Sound/Technicolor/Video)
Warner Bros.

AIN'T THAT DUCKY (1945) D: I. [Friz] Freleng.
VOICES: *Mel Blanc, Victor Moore.*
Daffy Duck protects a sobbing little duckling and his briefcase from a hunter *(caricature of Moore).* Blanc is Daffy and the duckling. Entry in the LOONEY TUNES series.
SONG: "Every Little Movement" *(Karl Hoschna; Otto A. Harbach; sung by Blanc as Daffy).*
MUSIC BY Carl W. Stalling.
Released on May 19
(7 min./Vitaphone Sound/Technicolor/Video)
Warner Bros.

IT'S MURDER SHE SAYS (1945) D: Chuck Jones.
VOICE: Mel Blanc, Marjorie Rambeau, Robert Bruce, Sara Berner.
Anopheles Annie, a malaria mosquito, laments her downfall after the
Army used netting and chemicals against her. However, there's always
hope because of negligent G.I.'s like Private Snafu (Blanc). Part of the
ARMY NAVY SCREEN MAGAZINE series.
MUSIC BY Carl W. Stalling.
Released in May
(3 min./DVD)
Warner Bros./U.S. Army Signal Corps

A GRUESOME TWOSOME (1945) D: Robert [Bob] Clampett.
VOICES: *Mel Blanc, Sara Berner.*
A pair of love-struck cats attempt to catch Tweety Pie in order to win the
affections of a sexy feline. Blanc is Tweety, the 'Jimmy Durante' cat, the
dumb cat, the dog and the bulldog. Entry in the MERRIE MELODIES
series.
SONG: "She Broke My Heart In Three Places" *(Al Hoffman; Jerry
Livingston; Milton Drake).*
MUSIC BY Carl W. Stalling.
Released on June 9
(7 min./Vitaphone Sound/Technicolor/Video/DVD)
Warner Bros.

A TALE OF TWO MICE (1945) D: Frank Tashlin.
VOICES: *Mel Blanc, Tedd Pierce.*
Two mice that resemble the comedy team of Abbott & Costello try to
sneak some cheese past a vicious cat. Blanc is Catsello the Mouse and
the cat. Entry in the LOONEY TUNES series.
SONG: "A Little On The Lonely Side" *(Richard Robertson; Frank Weldon;
James Cavanaugh).*
MUSIC BY Carl W. Stalling.
Released on June 30
(7 min./Vitaphone Sound/Technicolor)
Warner Bros.

WAGON HEELS (1945) D: Robert [Bob] Clampett.
VOICES: *Mel Blanc, Robert C. Bruce, Bob Clampett.*
Frontier scout Porky Pig faces the scourge of redskin territory, Injun Joe. Blanc is Porky, Joe, the bear and the trail boss. Entry in the MERRIE MELODIES series. A remake of *Injun Trouble* (1938).
MUSIC BY Carl W. Stalling.
Released on July 28
(7 min./Vitaphone Sound/Technicolor/Video/DVD)
Warner Bros.

HOT SPOT (1945) D: I. [Friz] Freleng.
VOICE: Mel Blanc, Harold Peary.
The troubles of military operations in Iran conducted under the severe heat. Blanc is Private Snafu. Part of the ARMY NAVY SCREEN MAGAZINE series.
MUSIC BY Carl W. Stalling.
Released in July
(3 min./DVD)
Warner Bros./U.S. Army Signal Corps

HARE CONDITIONED (1945) D: Charles M. [Chuck] Jones.
VOICES: *Mel Blanc, Dave Barry.*
Department store manager Gildersneeze wants to stuff Bugs Bunny and make him part of a store display. Blanc is Bugs and provides one line for Gildersneeze. Entry in the LOONEY TUNES series.
MUSIC BY Carl W. Stalling.
Released on August 11
(7 min./Vitaphone Sound/Technicolor/Video/DVD)
Warner Bros.

FRESH AIREDALE (1945) D: Charles M. [Chuck] Jones.
VOICES: *Frank Graham, Mel Blanc.*
A conniving, blame-shifting dog cheats his way to fame. Blanc is Shep, the cat, the prowler and nightmare voices. Entry in the MERRIE MELODIES series.
MUSIC BY Carl W. Stalling.
Released on August 25
(7 min./Vitaphone Sound/Technicolor)
Warner Bros.

THE BASHFUL BUZZARD (1945) D: Robert [Bob] Clampett.
VOICES: *Mel Blanc, Kent Rogers, Sara Berner.*
Beaky the awkward buzzard has trouble bringing back fresh meat to his mother's nest. Blanc is the farmer, the old rooster, a dragon and the lover in the buggy. Entry in the LOONEY TUNES series.
SONG: "Old MacDonald" *(traditional, composer unknown; sung by Blanc as the farmer).*
MUSIC BY Carl Stalling.
Released on September 5
(7 min./Vitaphone Sound/Technicolor/DVD)
Warner Bros.

SCREEN SNAPSHOTS SERIES 25, NO. 2: RADIO SHOWS (1945) D: Ralph Staub.
Brian Aherne, Barbara Jo Allen, Louise Arthur, Mel Blanc, Judy Canova, Eddie Cantor, Cass Daley, Kay Kyser, Wendell Niles, Ginny Simms, Harry Von Zell, Harlow Wilcox.
The cameras go behind the scenes of some popular radio series of the day, including The Saint, The Pepsodent Show Starring Bob Hope, The Judy Canova Show, The Eddie Cantor Show, The Fitch Bandwagon and Kay Kyser's Kollege of Musical Knowledge. Blanc is Pedro from the Canova program. Entry in the SCREEN SNAPSHOTS series.
Released on October 11
(10 min.)
Columbia

PECK UP YOUR TROUBLES (1945) D: I. [Friz] Freleng.
VOICE: *Mel Blanc.*
Sylvester the Cat has all sorts of pitfalls when he goes after a little woodpecker. Blanc does vocal effects. Entry in the MERRIE MELODIES series.
MUSIC BY Carl W. Stalling.
Released on October 20
(7 min./Vitaphone Sound/Technicolor)
Warner Bros.

OPERATION SNAFU (1945) D: I. [Friz] Freleng.
VOICE: *Mel Blanc.*
Disguised as a geisha girl, Private Snafu (Blanc) sneaks into Japanese military headquarters to snatch a secret document. Part of the ARMY NAVY SCREEN MAGAZINE series.
MUSIC BY Carl W. Stalling.
Released in October
(3 min./DVD)
Warner Bros./U.S. Army Signal Corps

NO BUDDY ATOLL (1945) D: Chuck Jones.
VOICE: *Mel Blanc.*
Private Snafu (Blanc) fights a Japanese general to gain possession of a deserted island. Part of the ARMY NAVY SCREEN MAGAZINE series.
SONG: "All Alone" *(Irving Berlin; sung by Blanc as Snafu).*
MUSIC BY Carl W. Stalling.
Released in October
(3 min./DVD)
Warner Bros./U.S. Army Signal Corps

HARE TONIC (1945) D: Charles M. [Chuck] Jones.
VOICES: *Mel Blanc, Arthur Q. Bryan.*
Bugs Bunny (Blanc) drives Elmer Fudd to panic with a story about the contagious disease 'rabbititus'. Entry in the LOONEY TUNES series.
MUSIC BY Carl W. Stalling.
Released on November 10
(7 min./Vitaphone Sound/Technicolor/Rated [TV-G]/Video/DVD)
Warner Bros.

NASTY QUACKS (1945) D: Frank Tashlin.
VOICES: *Mel Blanc, Robert C. Bruce, Sara Berner.*
A doting daddy gives his little girl a baby duckling — which grows up to be obnoxious houseguest Daffy Duck. Blanc is Daffy, the baby and Daddy. Entry in the MERRIE MELODIES series.
MUSIC BY Carl W. Stalling.
Released on December 1
(7 min./Vitaphone Sound/Tecnicolor/Video)
Warner Bros.

BOOK REVUE (1946) D: Robert [Bob] Clampett.
VOICES: *Mel Blanc, Sara Berner, Dick Bickenbach, Robert Bruce, The Sportsmen Quartet.*
During the night, the characters on book covers come to life, with Daffy Duck cavorting among them. Blanc is Daffy, Big Bad Wolf, Cuckoo Clock, Sea Wolf, Judge, and the cop. Caricatures of Tommy Dorsey, Benny Goodman, Harry James, Gene Krupa and Frank Sinatra. Entry in the LOONEY TUNES series.
SONGS: "Carolina In The Morning" *(Walter Donaldson; Gus Kahn; sung by Blanc as Daffy playing Danny Kaye)*, "La Cucaracha" *(traditional, composer unknown; sung by Blanc as Daffy playing Danny Kaye)*, "Sextet" from "Lucia di Lammermoor" *(Gaetano Donizetti; Salvatore Cammarano; sung with substitute lyrics by Blanc as the Wolf)*.
MUSIC BY Carl W. Stalling.
Released on January 5
(7 min./Vitaphone Sound/Technicolor/Video/DVD)
Warner Bros.

BASEBALL BUGS (1946) D: I. [Friz] Freleng.
VOICES: *Mel Blanc, Frank Graham, Bea Benaderet, The Sportsmen Quartet, Tedd Pierce.*
The Gas-House Gorillas get a lesson in balmy baseball when Bugs Bunny takes on the entire team by himself. Blanc is Bugs, a teetotaler, the umpire, the catcher, left-fielder and the announcer in the final scene. Entry in the LOONEY TUNES series.
SONG: "Sabre And Spurs" *(John Philip Sousa)*.
MUSIC BY Carl W. Stalling.
Released on February 2
(7 min./Vitaphone Sound/Technicolor/Video/DVD)
Warner Bros.

QUENTIN QUAIL (1946) D: Charles M. [Chuck] Jones.
VOICES: *Sara Berner, Tedd Pierce, Mel Blanc.*
Bird Baby Toots wants a worm for supper and Daddy Quentin has
an awful time trying to catch one. Blanc is the crow and Toots' sneeze.
A parody of the then-popular Baby Snooks radio show. Entry in the
MERRIE MELODIES series.
MUSIC BY Carl W. Stalling.
Released on March 2
(7 min./Vitaphone Sound/Technicolor)
Warner Bros.

BABY BOTTLENECK (1946) D: Robert [Bob] Clampett.
VOICES: *Mel Blanc, Sara Berner.*
The post-war baby boom has the stork overworked, so Porky Pig and
Daffy Duck step in to help with an automated infant-delivery service.
Blanc is Porky, Daffy, the narrator, the stork, Scotty Dog, the dog inventor
and various babies. Entry in the LOONEY TUNES series.
SONG: "You Must Have Been A Beautiful Baby" *(Harry Warren; Johnny
Mercer; sung by Blanc as Daffy).*
MUSIC BY Carl W. Stalling.
Released on March 16
(7 min./Vitaphone Sound/Technicolor/Video/DVD)
Warner Bros.

HARE REMOVER (1946) D: Frank Tashlin.
VOICES: *Mel Blanc, Arthur Q. Bryan.*
Scientist Elmer Fudd wants to try out his new potion, but must have a
rabbit to complete his experiment…enter Bugs Bunny. Blanc is Bugs and
Rover. Entry in the MERRIE MELODIES series.
MUSIC BY Carl W. Stalling.
Released on March 23
(7 min./Vitaphone Sound/Technicolor/Video/DVD)
Warner Bros.

DAFFY DOODLES (1946) D: Robert McKimson.
VOICES: *Mel Blanc, Robert C. Bruce.*
Daffy Duck is drawing moustaches on all the posters in town, but cop
Porky Pig is determined to catch him. Blanc is Daffy, Porky, the judge and
the 'Jerry Colonna' jury. Entry in the LOONEY TUNES series.
SONGS: "She Was An Acrobat's Daughter" *(Harry Ruby; Bert Kalmar;
sung by Blanc as Daffy)*, "I'm Just Wild About Harry" *(Eubie Blake; Noble
Sissle; sung by Blanc as Daffy).*
MUSIC BY Carl W. Stalling.
Released on April 16
(7 min./Vitaphone Sound/Technicolor/Video)
Warner Bros.

HOLLYWOOD CANINE CANTEEN (1946) D: Robert McKimson.
VOICES: *Paul Regan, Sara Berner, Mel Blanc, Robert Lyons, Paul Corley.*
The dogs of Tinseltown form their own night spot for 'soldiers' of the
K-9 corps. Blanc is 'Jerry Colonna' dog, 'Lou Costello' dog, 'Joe Besser'
dog, a 'servicedog' and sailor. Other canine caricatures: Bud Abbott,
Blondie & Dagwood, Bing Crosby, Tommy Dorsey, Jimmy Durante,
Benny Goodman, Lionel Hampton, Ish Kabibble, Stan Laurel & Oliver
Hardy, Charlie McCarthy, Carmen Miranda, Edward G. Robinson, Frank
Sinatra, Leopold Stokowski and Monty Woolley. Entry in the MERRIE
MELODIES series.
MUSIC BY Carl W. Stalling.
Released on April 20
(7 min./Vitaphone Sound/Technicolor)
Warner Bros.

HUSH MY MOUSE (1946) D: Charles M. [Chuck] Jones.
VOICES: *Mel Blanc, Marjorie Tarlton, Dick Nelson.*
Cartoon take-off on the popular radio series Duffy's Tavern. When a
tough cat ambles into 'Tuffy's Tavern' to have the 'mouse knuckles' special,
manager Artie sends dumb Filligan to catch Sniffles the Mouse. Blanc is
Artie, Filligan and bulldog. Entry in the LOONEY TUNES series.
MUSIC BY Carl W. Stalling.
Released on May 4
(7 min./Vitaphone Sound/Technicolor)
Warner Bros.

SCREEN SNAPSHOTS SERIES 25, NO. 9: THE JUDY CANOVA RADIO SHOW (1946) D: Ralph Staub.
Judy Canova, Mel Blanc, Ruby Dandridge, Verna Felton, Howard Petrie.
A filmed look at The Judy Canova Show, a Saturday night favorite, and its cast of characters. Blanc is Pedro. Entry in the SCREEN SNAPSHOTS series.
Released on May 23
(11 min.) Columbia

HARE-RAISING HARE (1946) D: Charles M. [Chuck] Jones.
VOICES: *Mel Blanc.*
A mad scientist and his hairy, orange, sneaker-wearing monster lure Bugs Bunny to their castle — where a manic chase occurs. Blanc is Bugs, the 'Peter Lorre' scientist, the monster, and doctor. Entry in the LOONEY TUNES series.
SONGS: "Headin' for My Beddin'" *(sung by Blanc as Bugs),* "Sweet Dreams, Sweetheart" *(M.K. Jerome; Ted Koehler; sung by Blanc as Bugs).*
MUSIC BY Carl W. Stalling.
Released on May 25
(7 min./Vitaphone Sound/Technicolor/Video/DVD)
Warner Bros.

KITTY CORNERED (1946) D: Robert [Bob] Clampett.
VOICES: *Mel Blanc, Bob Clampett.*
Tired of being let out at night, Porky Pig's four cats disguise themselves as Martian invaders to scare their porcine master. Blanc is Porky, Sylvester the Cat, the narrator, small cat, tiny cat, drunk cat, goldfish wife, radio voice, and the moose. Entry in the LOONEY TUNES series.
SONG: "Blues in the Night" *(Harold Arlen; Johnny Mercer; performed by Blanc as four cats).*
MUSIC BY Carl W. Stalling.
Released on June 8
(7 min./Vitaphone Sound/Technicolor/DVD)
Warner Bros.

HOLLYWOOD DAFFY (1946) D: I. [Friz] Freleng.
VOICES: *Mel Blanc, Sara Berner, Dick Bickenbach (re-use).*
Daffy Duck wants to crash into a movie studio, but a stubborn guard is determined to keep him out. Blanc is Daffy, the studio guard, 'Jack Benny', and 'Jimmy Durante'; other caricatures are Bette Davis and Johnny Weissmuller. Entry in the MERRIE MELODIES series.
SONG: "Minute Waltz" *(Frederic Chopin).*
MUSIC BY Carl Stalling.
Released on June 22
(7 min./Vitaphone Sound/Technicolor/Video/DVD)
Warner Bros.

ACROBATTY BUNNY (1946) D: Robert McKimson.
VOICES: *Mel Blanc.*
The circus sets up over Bugs Bunny's rabbit hole and an inquisitive lion learns not to mess with the rascally rabbit. Blanc is Bugs, elephant trumpeting, and Nero the Lion. Entry in the LOONEY TUNES series.
SONG: "Laugh, Clown, Laugh" *(Ted Fio Rito; Sam Lewis; Joe Young; sung by Blanc as Bugs).*
MUSIC BY Carl Stalling.
Released on June 29
(7 min./Vitaphone Sound/Technicolor/Video/DVD)
Warner Bros.

THE EAGER BEAVER (1946) D: Charles M. [Chuck] Jones.
VOICES: *Mel Blanc, Frank Graham.*
A series of gags about tree-cutting beavers culminates in the efforts of one buck-toothed chap to fell a large tree so he can stave off a flood. Blanc is the beaver foreman, first two beavers, a crow, birds and stuttering bird. Entry in the MERRIE MELODIES series.
SONG: "William Tell Overture" *(Gioachino Rossini).*
MUSIC BY Carl Stalling.
Released on July 13
(7 min./Vitaphone Sound/Technicolor)
Warner Bros.

THE GREAT PIGGY BANK ROBBERY (1946) D: Robert [Bob] Clampett, Michael Sasanoff.
VOICES: *Mel Blanc.*
Comic book reader Daffy Duck bangs his head and dreams he is detective 'Duck Twacy', going up against such villains as 88 Teeth, Rubber Head, Pumpkin Head, Neon Noodle, and Juke Box Jaw. Blanc is Daffy, Wolf Man, Rubber Head, Neon Noodle, and a pig.
SONG: "Mysterious Mose" *(Walter Doyle).*
MUSIC BY Carl W. Stalling.
Released on July 20
(7 min./Vitaphone Sound/Technicolor/Video/DVD)
Warner Bros.

BACALL TO ARMS (1946) D: *(Robert [Bob] Clampett, Arthur Davis).*
VOICES: *Robert C. Bruce, Dave Barry, Sara Berner, Mel Blanc.*
A lusty wolf takes in a movie and goes ga-ga over sexy 'Laurie Becool'. Blanc is the fat theater patron, the lion, man in newsreel, a dog, a wolf and a goose. Caricatures of Humphrey Bogart and Lauren Bacall. Entry in the MERRIE MELODIES series.
MUSIC BY Carl Stalling.
Released on August 3
(7 min./Vitaphone Sound/Technicolor/DVD)
Warner Bros.

OF THEE I STING (1946) D: I. [Friz] Freleng.
VOICES: *Robert C. Bruce, Mel Blanc.*
A group of military mosquitoes train to attack their 'target for today': a farmer's hindquarters. Blanc does vocal "calliope" effect. Entry in the LOONEY TUNES series. Re-uses footage from *Target: Snafu* (1944).
MUSIC BY Carl Stalling.
Released on August 17
(7 min./Vitaphone Sound/Technicolor)
Warner Bros.

WALKY TALKY HAWKY (1946) D: Robert McKimson.
VOICES: *Mel Blanc.*
Little Henery Hawk is out to capture a chicken, but doesn't know what one looks like. Enter, I say, enter Foghorn Leghorn the rooster to 'put him straight'. Blanc is Foghorn, Henery, Poppa Hawk, and the dog. Entry in the MERRIE MELODIES series.
MUSIC BY Carl W. Stalling.
Academy Award Nomination *(Short Subject – Cartoon)* Edward Selzer.
MUSIC BY Carl W. Stalling.
Released on August 31
(7 min./Vitaphone Sound/Technicolor/DVD) Warner Bros.

SCREEN SNAPSHOTS NO. 1: RADIO CHARACTERS (1946) D: Ralph Staub.
Jeanine Roos, Pat McGeehan, Dave Willock, Mel Blanc, Jean Eberhart, Dr. Horatio Birdbath. Narrated by Ralph Staub.
Popular radio series 'second bananas' come before the camera, including Blanc as Pedro from The Judy Canova Show. Entry in the SCREEN SNAPSHOTS series.
Released on September 5
(10 min.)
Columbia

RACKETEER RABBIT (1946) D: I. [Friz] Freleng.
VOICES: *Mel Blanc, Dick Nelson.*
Bugs Bunny takes refuge from the rain in an abandoned house used as a hideout by two fleeing gangsters. Blanc is Bugs, gangster voices, and Hugo (a caricature of Peter Lorre). Also caricatured is Edward G. Robinson. Entry in the LOONEY TUNES series.
MUSIC BY Carl Stalling.
Released on September 14
(7 min./Vitaphone Sound/Technicolor/Video)
Warner Bros.

FAIR AND WORM-ER (1946) D: Charles M. [Chuck] Jones.
VOICES: *Robert C. Bruce, Mel Blanc, Sara Berner.*
A wacky chase ensues after a worm searches for a habitable apple: he is set upon by a crow, who is pursued by a cat, followed by a dog which is the quarry of a dog-catcher with a tag-along nagging wife. Blanc is a worm, a dog, a mouse, a dog-catcher and a bird. Entry in the MERRIE MELODIES series.
SONGS: "Freddy the Freshman" *(Cliff Friend; Dave Oppenheim)*, "Home Sweet Home" *(H.R. Bishop)*, "In the Shade of the Old Apple Tree" *(Egbert Van Alstyne)*.
MUSIC BY Carl Stalling.
Released on September 28
(7 min./Vitaphone Sound/Technicolor)
Warner Bros.

THE BIG SNOOZE (1946) D: Robert [Bob] Clampett.
VOICES: *Mel Blanc, Arthur Q. Bryan.*
Fed up with being abused by Bugs Bunny, Elmer Fudd tears up his cartoon contract to go on an extended fishing trip. Bugs follows to make sure Elmer gets no peace. Blanc is Bugs and a Hollywood wolf. Entry in the LOONEY TUNES series.
SONGS: "September in the Rain" *(Harry Warren; Al Dubin; sung by Blanc as Bugs)*, "William Tell Overture" *(Gioachino Rossini)*, "Beautiful Dreamer" *(Stephen Foster; sung by Blanc as Bugs)*, "Someone's Rocking My Dreamboat" *(Leon Rene; Otis Rene; Emerson Scott), (sung by Blanc as Bugs)*, "The Rabbits [Campbells] Are Coming" *(traditional, composer unknown), (sung by Blanc as Bugs)*.
MUSIC BY Carl Stalling.
Released on October 5
(7 min./Vitaphone Sound/Technicolor/Video/DVD)
Warner Bros.

THE MOUSE-MERIZED CAT (1946) D: Robert McKimson.
VOICES: *Mel Blanc, Tedd Pierce, reuse of tracks by Sam Glaser, Dick Bickenbach, Robert Lyons*
Babbit the Mouse plans on using hypnosis to erase Catsello's fear so the fat guy will boldly snatch some food from under the cat's nose. Blanc is Catsello, Jimmy Durante, a cat and dog barks. Entry in the MERRIE MELODIES series.
SONGS: "You Must Have Been a Beautiful Baby" *(Harry Warren; Johnny Mercer),* "Trade Winds" *(Cliff Friend; Charles Tobias),* "The Lullaby of Broadway" *(Warren; Al Dubin).*
MUSIC BY Carl Stalling.
Released on October 19
(7 min./Vitaphone Sound/Technicolor)
Warner Bros.

MOUSE MENACE (1946) D: Arthur Davis.
VOICES: *Mel Blanc.*
Porky Pig builds a robot cat and programs it to go after a wise-guy mouse. Blanc is Porky, the mouse, the lion, the cat, and the mechanical cat. Entry in the LOONEY TUNES series.
MUSIC BY Carl Stalling.
Released on November 2
(7 min./Vitaphone Sound/Technicolor/Video/DVD)
Warner Bros.

RHAPSODY RABBIT (1946) D: I. [Friz] Freleng.
VOICES: *Mel Blanc.*
Bugs Bunny tries to give an urbane piano performance, but a mouse inside the piano takes over the program. Blanc is Bugs and the coughing audience member. Entry in the MERRIE MELODIES series.
SONG: "Second Hungarian Rhapsody" *(Franz Liszt).*
MUSIC BY Carl Stalling.
Released on November 9
(7 min./Vitaphone Sound/Technicolor/Video/DVD)
Warner Bros.

ROUGHLY SQUEAKING (1946) D: Charles M. [Chuck] Jones.
VOICES: *Mel Blanc, Dick Nelson, Stan Freberg.*
Two mice, Hubie and Bertie, play head games with a gullible cat and skeptical dog. Blanc is the cat, the dog, and the bird. Entry in the LOONEY TUNES series.
MUSIC BY Carl Stalling.
Released on November 23
(7 min./Vitaphone Sound/Technicolor/Video)
Warner Bros.

ONE MEAT BRAWL (1947) D: Robert McKimson.
VOICES: *Mel Blanc, Stan Freberg.*
Porky Pig and his dog Mandrake match wits with Grover Groundhog as they try to celebrate the day in his honor. Blanc is Porky, Mandrake, and the singing voice of Grover. Entry in the MERRIE MELODIES series.
SONG: "A Groundhog and His Shadow" *(Carl W. Stalling; Warren Foster).*
MUSIC BY Carl Stalling.
Released on January 18
(7 min./Vitaphone Sound/Technicolor)
Warner Bros.

THE GOOFY GOPHERS (1947) D: Arthur Davis.
VOICES: *Mel Blanc, Stan Freberg.*
Mac and Tosh, two gophers, proceed to raid a lush garden and abuse the watchdog who tries to guard it. Blanc is Mac, the dog, and Bugs Bunny. Entry in the LOONEY TUNES series.
MUSIC BY Carl Stalling.
Released on January 25
(7 min./Vitaphone Sound/Technicolor)
Warner Bros.

BIRTH OF A NOTION (1947) D: Robert McKimson.
VOICES: *Mel Blanc, Stan Freberg.*
Not wanting to fly south for the winter, Daffy Duck chooses to live in the house also occupied by 'Peter Lorre' — who is in search of a duck's wishbone for his mad experiment. Blanc is Daffy, Leopold the Dog, and the 'Joe Besser' goose. Entry in the LOONEY TUNES series.
SONG: "When My Dream Duck [Boat] Comes Home" *(Cliff Friend; Dave Franklin), (sung by Blanc as Daffy).*
MUSIC BY Carl Stalling.
Released on April 12
(7 min./Vitaphone Sound/Technicolor/Video)
Warner Bros.

TWEETIE PIE (1947) D: I. [Friz] Freleng.
VOICES: *Mel Blanc, Bea Benaderet.*
Sylvester the Cat *(called 'Thomas' this time around)* brings Tweety Pie into his master's home, but she warns him not to go after the bird. Blanc is Tweety and Thomas/Sylvester. Entry in the MERRIE MELODIES series.
MUSIC BY Carl Stalling.
Academy Award *(Short Subjects – Cartoon)* Edward Selzer.
Released on May 3
(7 min./Vitaphone Sound/Technicolor/Video/DVD)
Warner Bros.

SCENT-IMENTAL OVER YOU (1947) D: Charles M. [Chuck] Jones.
VOICES: *Mel Blanc, Bea Benaderet, Tedd Pierce.*
A female Mexican hairless dog pastes on a skunk fur and is immediately pursued by that amorous 'stinker' Pepe LePew (Blanc). Entry in the LOONEY TUNES series.
MUSIC BY Carl Stalling.
Released on May 8
(7 min./Vitaphone Sound/Technicolor)
Warner Bros.

RABBIT TRANSIT (1947) D: I. [Friz] Freleng.
VOICES: *Mel Blanc.*
A jet-propelled shell changes hands as Bugs Bunny and Cecil Turtle race each other once again. Blanc is Bugs, Cecil, the delivery man, and telegram boys. Entry in the MERRIE MELODIES series.
MUSIC BY Carl Stalling.
Released on May 10
(7 min./Vitaphone Sound/Technicolor/Video/DVD)
Warner Bros.

HOBO BOBO (1947) D: Robert McKimson.
VOICES: *Robert C. Bruce, Stan Freberg, Mel Blanc.*
Bobo the Elephant wants to join the circus, but first he must hop a ship to America. Blanc is the New Yorkers and the baby. Entry in the MERRIE MELODIES series.
MUSIC BY Carl Stalling.
Released May 17.
(7 min./Vitaphone Sound/Technicolor)
Warner Bros.

A HARE GROWS IN MANHATTAN (1947) D: I. [Friz] Freleng.
VOICES: *Mel Blanc, Bea Benaderet, Tedd Pierce, Mike Maltese.*
Movie star Bugs Bunny tells gossip columnist Lola Beverly how he grew up on the East Side of New York City and had to handle a bunch of tough dogs. Blanc is Bugs, Spike, and various other dogs. Entry in the MERRIE MELODIES series.
SONG: "She's the Daughter of Rosie O'Grady" *(Walter Donaldson; Monty C. Bruce; sung by Blanc as Bugs).*
MUSIC BY Carl Stalling.
Released on May 22
(7 min./Vitaphone Sound/Technicolor/Video/DVD)
Warner Bros.

ALONG CAME DAFFY (1947) D: I. [Friz] Freleng.
VOICES: *Mel Blanc.*
Cookbook salesman Daffy Duck stumbles onto a desolate cabin where
Yosemite Sam and his brother are starving for a duck dinner. Blanc is
Daffy, Yosemite and his brother, and duck decoys. Entry in the LOONEY
TUNES series.
SONG: "Freddy the Freshman" *(Dave Oppenheim; Cliff Friend).*
MUSIC BY Carl Stalling.
Released on June 4
(7 min./Vitaphone Sound/Technicolor/Video)
Warner Bros.

EASTER YEGGS (1947) D: Robert McKimson.
VOICES: *Mel Blanc, Arthur Q. Bryan.*
Bugs Bunny gets more trouble than he bargained for when he takes over
the duty of delivering the Easter Bunny's eggs. A wily Elmer Fudd is
more interested in rabbit stew than eggs. Blanc is Bugs, Easter Rabbit,
and the brat. Entry in the LOONEY TUNES series.
SONG: "I'm the Easter Rabbit, Hooray!"
MUSIC BY Carl Stalling.
Released on June 28
(7 min./Vitaphone Sound/Technicolor/Video/DVD)
Warner Bros.

CROWING PAINS (1947) D: Robert McKimson.
VOICES: *Mel Blanc, Robert Bruce.*
Foghorn Leghorn tells Henery Hawk that if he wants a chicken, then
Sylvester the Cat is his meat. Blanc is Foghorn, Sylvester, Henery, the
chicken and the hen. Entry in the LOONEY TUNES series.
MUSIC BY Carl Stalling.
Released on July 12
(7 min./Vitaphone Sound/Technicolor/Video)
Warner Bros.

A PEST IN THE HOUSE (1947) D: Charles M. [Chuck] Jones.
VOICES: *Mel Blanc, Arthur Q. Bryan.*
A hotel guest just wants some peace and quiet, but bellhop Daffy Duck cannot stop making a racket. Blanc is Daffy, the drunk, and the narrator. Entry in the MERRIE MELODIES series.
SONGS: "How Dry I Am" "Time Waits for No One"
MUSIC BY Carl Stalling.
Released on August 3
(7 min./Vitaphone Sound/Technicolor/Video/DVD)
Warner Bros.

THE FOXY DUCKLING (1947) D: Arthur Davis.
VOICES: *Mel Blanc.*
Insomniac fox chases baby duck. Blanc is the fox, the fish and the duck. Entry in the MERRIE MELODIES series.
MUSIC BY Carl Stalling.
Released on August 23
Warner Bros.

LITTLE ORPHAN AIREDALE (1947) D: Charles M. [Chuck] Jones.
VOICES: *Mel Blanc.*
Charlie Dog tells a runaway mutt how he finagled his way in Porky Pig's 'good graces.' Blanc is Porky, Charlie, Rags McMutt, the cat, and the city geek. Entry in the LOONEY TUNES series. A remake of *Porky's Pooch* (1941*).*
MUSIC BY Carl Stalling.
Released on October 4
(7 min./Vitaphone Sound/Technicolor/Video)
Warner Bros.

DOGGONE CATS (1947) D: Arthur Davis.
VOICES: *Mel Blanc, Bea Benaderet.*
Sylvester and his orange-cat pal beat, batter, and outfox a bulldog trying to deliver a package. Blanc is Wellington, the cat and Uncle Louie. Entry in the MERRIE MELODIES series.
MUSIC BY Carl Stalling.
Released on October 25
(7 min./Vitaphone Sound/Cinecolor)
Warner Bros.

SLICK HARE (1947) D: I. [Friz] Freleng.
VOICES: *Mel Blanc, Arthur Q. Bryan, Dave Barry.*
Elmer Fudd only has twenty minutes to serve fried rabbit to an impatient Humphrey Bogart; the only hare around is a very uncooperative Bugs Bunny. Caricatures of Bogart, Lauren Bacall, Sydney Greenstreet, the Marx Brothers, Ray Milland, Carmen Miranda, Gregory Peck, Frank Sinatra, Leopold Stokowski, and Warner Brothers cartoon staff members Warren Foster and Tedd Pierce. Blanc is Bugs, the waiter, the bartender, and Ray Milland. Entry in the MERRIE MELODIES series.
SONG: "About a Quarter to Nine" *(Harry Warren).*
MUSIC BY Carl Stalling.
Released on November 1
(7 min./Vitaphone Sound/Technicolor/Video/DVD)
Warner Bros.

MEXICAN JOYRIDE (1947) D: Arthur Davis.
VOICES: *Mel Blanc.*
Vacationing in Mexico, Daffy Duck takes in a bullfight and ends up sparring with the bull. Blanc is Daffy, the bull, a Mexican voice, the program guy and a counterman. Entry in the LOONEY TUNES series.
SONGS: "In Caliente" *(Allie Wrubel)*, "Gaucho Serenade" *(Nat Simon; John Redmond; James Cavanaugh)*, "Mexican Hat Dance" *(Felipe A. Partichela)*, "Muchacha" *(Harry Warren).*
MUSIC BY Carl Stalling.
Released on November 29
(7 min./Vitaphone Sound/Technicolor/Video)
Warner Bros.

CATCH AS CATS CAN (1947) D: Arthur Davis.
VOICE: Mel Blanc, Dave Barry.
Sylvester the Cat (Blanc) is caught in the middle of the feud between a 'Bing Crosby' parrot and a 'Frank Sinatra' canary. Entry in the MERRIE MELODIES series.
MUSIC BY Carl Stalling.
Released on December 6
(7 min./Vitaphone Sound/Technicolor)
Warner Bros.

MOUSE WRECKERS (1948) D: Charles M. [Chuck] Jones.
VOICES: *Mel Blanc, Stan Freberg.*
Mice Hubie and Bertie do the 'gaslight' routine on Claude Cat to drive
him crazy and out of the house the two rodents wish to occupy. Blanc is
Bert, Dog and Claude. Entry in the LOONEY TUNES series.
Academy Award Nomination *(Short Subject – Cartoon)* Edward Selzer.
MUSIC BY Carl Stalling.
Released in early 1948
(6 min./Vitaphone Sound/Technicolor/DVD)
Warner Bros.

GORILLA MY DREAMS (1948) D: Robert McKimson.
VOICES: *Mel Blanc.*
Mrs. Gorilla spies Bugs Bunny floating down the river and adopts him
as her own. When they return home, Gruesome Gorilla plots to get rid
of his new 'son.' Blanc is Bugs, Gruesome, Mrs. Gorilla, 'Tarzan,' and the
other gorillas. Entry in the LOONEY TUNES series.
SONGS: "Trade Winds" *(Cliff Friend; Charles Tobias; sung by Blanc as*
Bugs), "Dinner Music for a Pack of Hungry Cannibals" *(Raymond Scott),*
"Goombay Drum" *(Charles Lofthouse; Schuyler Knowlton; Stanley Adams).*
MUSIC BY Carl Stalling.
Released on January 3
(7 min./Vitaphone Sound/Technicolor/Video/DVD)
Warner Bros.

A FEATHER IN HIS HARE (1948) D: Charles M. [Chuck] Jones.
VOICES: *Mel Blanc, Michael Maltese.*
An Indian tries to capture an elusive Bugs Bunny so he can give the
rascally rabbit a 'hare cut and scalp treatment.' Blanc is Bugs, Indian
screaming, and the baby rabbits. Entry in the LOONEY TUNES series.
MUSIC BY Carl Stalling.
Released on February 7
(8 min./Vitaphone Sound/Technicolor/Video)
Warner Bros.

WHAT MAKES DAFFY DUCK? (1948) D: Arthur Davis.
VOICES: *Mel Blanc, Arthur Q. Bryan.*
Daffy Duck is hunted by both Elmer Fudd and a hungry fox. Blanc is
Daffy and the fox. Entry in the LOONEY TUNES series.
SONG: "King for a Day" *(Ted Fio Rito; Sam Lewis; Joe Young; sung by
Blanc as Daffy).*
MUSIC BY Carl Stalling.
Released on February 14
(7 min./Vitaphone Sound/Cinecolor, Technicolor/Video)
Warner Bros.

DAFFY DUCK SLEPT HERE (1948) D: Robert McKimson.
VOICES: *Mel Blanc.*
With a housing crunch in the city, visitor Porky Pig is forced to share a
hotel room with Daffy Duck. Porky cannot get a wink of sleep because the
manic mallard's fidgety doings keep them awake. Blanc is Porky, Daffy, the
hotel clerks, elevator boy, and manager. Entry in the MERRIE MELODIES
series.
SONG: "I'm Just Wild About Hymie [Harry]" *(Eubie Blake; Noble Sissle;
sung by Blanc as Daffy).*
MUSIC BY Carl Stalling.
Released on March 6
(7 min./Vitaphone Sound/Technicolor/Video/DVD)
Warner Bros.

BACK ALLEY OPROAR (1948) D: I. [Friz] Freleng.
VOICES: *Mel Blanc, Arthur Q. Bryan, Gloria Curran, Tudor Williams.*
Sylvester (Blanc) 'entertains' a tired and angry Elmer Fudd with a cat
concerto that turns violent. Entry in the MERRIE MELODIES series. A
remake of *Notes To You* (1941).
SONGS: "Figaro (Largo Al Factotum)" from "The Barber of Seville"
(Gioacchino Rossini; Cesare Sterbing; sung by Blanc as Sylvester), "Second
Hungarian Rhapsody" *(Franz Liszt; sung by Blanc as Sylvester)*, "Some
Sunday Morning" *(M.K. Jerome; Ray Heindorf; Ted Koehler)*, *(sung by
Blanc as Sylvester)*, "You Never Know Where You're Going Until You
Get There" *(Jule Styne; Sammy Cahn; sung by Blanc as Sylvester)*, "Go to
Sleep (Brahms' Lullaby)" *(Johannes Brahms; sung by Blanc as Sylvester)*,
"On Moonlight Bay" *(Percy Wenrich; Edward Madden; sung by Blanc as
Sylvester)*, "Angel in Disguise" *(Stefan Weiss; Paul Mann; Kim Gannon; sung
by Blanc as Sylvester)*, "Sextet" from "Lucia di Lammermoor" *(Gaetano*

Donizetti; Salvatore Cammarano; sung by Blanc as Sylvester's nine lives), "Carissima" *(Arthur A. Penn).*
MUSIC BY Carl Stalling.
Released on March 27
(7 min./Vitaphone Sound/Technicolor/Video/DVD)
Warner Bros.

I TAW A PUTTY TAT (1948) D: I. [Friz] Freleng.
VOICES: *Mel Blanc, Bea Benaderet.*
Tweety Pie is the new arrival in a household that also includes bird-eater Sylvester the Cat. Blanc is Sylvester, Tweety, and the bulldog. Entry in the MERRIE MELODIES series. Partial remake of *Puss N' Booty* (1943).
MUSIC BY Carl Stalling.
Released on April 2
(7 min./Vitaphone Sound/Cinecolor/Video/DVD)
Warner Bros.

RABBIT PUNCH (1948) D: Charles M. [Chuck] Jones.
VOICES: *Mel Blanc, Billy Bletcher.*
Bugs Bunny and a boxer use bricks, boulders, and even a train against each other in their championship fight. Blanc is Bugs and the ring announcer. Entry in the MERRIE MELODIES series.
MUSIC BY Carl Stalling.
Released on April 10
(7 min./Vitaphone Sound/Technicolor/Video/DVD)
Warner Bros.

HOP, LOOK AND LISTEN (1948) D: Robert McKimson.
VOICES: *Mel Blanc.*
Hippity Hopper the Kangaroo escapes the zoo and takes refuge at Sylvester's house — causing the cat to believe Hippity is a giant mouse. Blanc is Sylvester, the bulldog, the hyena, and mother kangaroo. Entry in the LOONEY TUNES series.
MUSIC BY Carl Stalling.
Released on April 17
(6 min./Vitaphone Sound/Technicolor)
Warner Bros.

NOTHING BUT THE TOOTH (1948) D: Arthur Davis.
VOICE: *Mel Blanc.*
Venturing into Indian territory during the Gold Rush, Porky Pig encounters a spectacle-wearing little brave who wants Porky's scalp. Blanc is Porky Pig, Dog, Prospector, Horse, Mohican and Postal Worker. Entry in the MERRIE MELODIES series.
MUSIC BY Carl Stalling.
Released on May 1
(7 min./Vitaphone Sound/Technicolor)
Warner Bros.

BUCCANEER BUNNY (1948) D: I. [Friz] Freleng.
VOICES: *Mel Blanc.*
When Bugs Bunny gets his hands on Yosemite Sam's pirate treasure, the sawed-off villain chases the rabbit aboard his galleon. Blanc is Bugs, Yosemite and the parrot. Entry in the LOONEY TUNES series.
MUSIC BY Carl Stalling.
Released on May 8
(7 min./Vitaphone Sound/Technicolor/Video/DVD)
Warner Bros.

BONE SWEET BONE (1948) D: Arthur Davis.
VOICES: *Mel Blanc.*
Little dog Shep goes up against a big bulldog who has stolen Shep's soup bone. Blanc is Shep, the bulldog, and the museum curator. Entry in the MERRIE MELODIES series.
MUSIC BY Carl Stalling.
Released on May 22
(7 min./Vitaphone Sound/Cinecolor)
Warner Bros.

BUGS BUNNY RIDES AGAIN (1948) D: I. [Friz] Freleng.
VOICES: *Mel Blanc, Robert Bruce.*
Tough hombre Yosemite Sam tries to run Bugs out of a frontier town. Blanc is Bugs, Yosemite, the cowboys, and the skunk. Entry in the MERRIE MELODIES series.
MUSIC BY Carl Stalling.
Released on June 12
(7 min./Vitaphone Sound/Technicolor/DVD)
Warner Bros.

THE RATTLED ROOSTER (1948) D: Arthur Davis.
VOICE: *Mel Blanc.*
A wily worm gets the best of a rooster out for his morning meal. Blanc is both characters. Entry in the LOONEY TUNES series.
SONG: "I'm Forever Blowing Bubbles" *(James Brockman; James Kendis; Nat Vincent; John W. Kellette; sung by Blanc as the worm).*
MUSIC BY Carl Stalling.
Released on June 26
(7 min./Vitaphone Sound/Technicolor)
Warner Bros.

THE UP-STANDING SITTER (1948) D: Robert McKimson.
VOICE: *Mel Blanc.*
Professional babysitter Daffy Duck is hired to mind a newly-hatched chick, but the youngster causes trouble between Daffy and Spike the Bulldog. Blanc is Daffy, I. Squeal, the hen and the chicken. Entry in the LOONEY TUNES series.
MUSIC BY Carl Stalling.
Released on July 3
(7 min./Vitaphone Sound/Cinecolor/Video/DVD)
Warner Bros.

THE SHELL SHOCKED EGG (1948) D: Robert McKimson.
VOICES: *Mel Blanc, Lloyd Turner, The Sportsmen Quartet.*
A half-hatched turtle wanders around the barnyard trying to get out of his shell. Blanc is the mother turtle, Clem, the dog, the rooster and the hen. Entry in the LOONEY TUNES series.
SONG: "Billy Boy" *(traditional, composer unknown).*
MUSIC BY Carl Stalling.
Released on July 10
(7 min./Vitaphone Sound/Technicolor)
Warner Bros.

HAREDEVIL HARE (1948) D: Charles M. [Chuck] Jones.
VOICES: *Mel Blanc, Stan Freberg.*
Bugs Bunny is the test-rabbit on a flight to the moon, but when he lands
there he has company in the form of Marvin Martian. Blanc is Bugs,
Marvin, K-9, the radio jingle singer, and the control center technicians.
Entry in the LOONEY TUNES series.
MUSIC BY Carl Stalling.
Released on July 24
(7 min./Vitaphone Sound/Technicolor/Video/DVD)
Warner Bros.

YOU WERE NEVER DUCKIER (1948) D: Charles M. [Chuck] Jones.
VOICES: *Mel Blanc.*
A poultry show is paying off a $5,000 prize for the best rooster, so Daffy
Duck disguises himself as a Rhode Island Red to win the money. However,
Henery Hawk is at the show to snatch himself a prize bird. Blanc is Daffy,
Henery, the rooster, and George K. Chickenhawk. Entry in the MERRIE
MELODIES series.
MUSIC BY Carl Stalling.
Released on August 7
(7 min./Vitaphone Sound/Technicolor/Video/DVD)
Warner Bros.

DOUGH RAY ME-OW (1948) D: Arthur Davis.
VOICES: *Mel Blanc.*
Heathcliff the dumb cat stands to inherit a fortune from his master, but
scheming Louie the Parrot decides to get rid of Heathcliff permanently.
Blanc is Heathcliff, Louie, and the radio 'music.' Entry in the MERRIE
MELODIES series.
SONG: "On the 5:15" *(Henry I. Marshall).*
MUSIC BY Carl Stalling.
Released on August 14
(7 min./Vitaphone Sound/Cinecolor/DVD)
Warner Bros.

HOT CROSS BUNNY (1948) D: Robert McKimson.
VOICES: *Mel Blanc.*
A doctor wants to experiment on Bugs Bunny by switching his brain with that of a chicken, but the rascally rabbit is having none of that. Blanc is Bugs and the doctor. Entry in the MERRIE MELODIES series.
MUSIC BY Carl Stalling.
Released on August 21
(7 min./Vitaphone Sound/Technicolor/Video/DVD)
Warner Bros.

THE PEST THAT CAME TO DINNER (1948) D: Arthur Davis.
VOICES: *Mel Blanc.*
Porky Pig's home is infested with a single voracious termite named Pierre, who outsmarts the hapless hog at every turn. Blanc is Porky, Pierre, and Sureshot the Dog. Entry in the LOONEY TUNES series.
SONGS: "Mammy's Little Coal Black Rose" *(Richard A. Whiting; Ray Egan), (sung by Blanc as Pierre),* "By a Waterfall" *(Sammy Fain; Irving Kahal; sung by Blanc as Pierre).*
MUSIC BY Carl Stalling.
Released on September 11
(7 min./Vitaphone Sound/Technicolor/Video)
Warner Bros.

HARE SPLITTER (1948) D: I. [Friz] Freleng.
VOICES: *Mel Blanc, Sara Berner.*
Bugs Bunny wants to romance his sweetheart, Daisy Lou, but first he must get rid of Casbah, his rival. Blanc is Bugs and Casbah. Entry in the MERRIE MELODIES series.
MUSIC BY Carl Stalling.
Released on September 25
(7 min./Vitaphone Sound/Technicolor/Video/DVD)
Warner Bros.

ODOR OF THE DAY (1948) D: Arthur Davis.
VOICES: *Mel Blanc.*
A nice, comfy bed becomes the prize sought after by a tired Pepe LePew and a weary dog. Blanc is Pepe, the dog, and the bulldog. Entry in the LOONEY TUNES series.
MUSIC BY Carl Stalling.
Released on October 2
(7 min./Vitaphone Sound/Cinecolor)
Warner Bros.

HOUSE HUNTING MICE (1948) D: Charles M. [Chuck] Jones.
VOICES: *Mel Blanc, Stan Freberg.*
Hubie and Bertie inspect an automated house and run afoul of a robot sweeper. Blanc is Bertie. Entry in the MERRIE MELODIES series.
MUSIC BY Carl Stalling.
Released on October 7
(7 min./Vitaphone Sound/Cinecolor/Video)
Warner Bros.

THE FOGHORN LEGHORN (1948) D: Robert McKimson.
VOICES: *Mel Blanc.*
When Foghorn Leghorn is called a loudmouthed schnook, a confused Henery Hawk tries to determine if he's also a rooster. Blanc is Foghorn, Henery, Charlie the Dog, and Grandpa Hawk. Entry in the MERRIE MELODIES series.
MUSIC BY Carl Stalling.
Released on October 9
(7 min./Vitaphone Sound/Technicolor/Video/DVD)
Warner Bros.

DAFFY DILLY (1948) D: Charles M. [Chuck] Jones.
VOICES: *Mel Blanc.*
Joke-item seller Daffy Duck gets wind of an ailing millionaire who will pay a large sum to anyone who can make him laugh. Daffy goes all out, but a stubborn butler tries to keep him away. Blanc is Daffy, the reporter, the butler, and J.P. Cubish. Entry in the MERRIE MELODIES series.
SONGS: "I'm Looking Over a Four Leaf Clover" *(Harry M. Woods),* "Singin' in the Bathtub" *(Michael Cleary; Herb Magidson; Ned Washington), (sung by Blanc as Daffy).*
MUSIC BY Carl Stalling.
Released on October 21
(7 min./Vitaphone Sound/Cinecolor)
Warner Bros.

A-LAD-IN HIS LAMP (1948) D: Robert McKimson.
VOICES: *Mel Blanc, Jim Backus.*
Bugs Bunny has obtained Aladdin's lamp and follows its genie to Baghdad, where Bugs finds an enemy in caliph Imad Mani Hassan Pheffer — who covets the lamp. Blanc is Bugs, Hassan and the rug's engine. Entry in the LOONEY TUNES series.
SONGS: "Massa's in de Cold Ground" *(Stephen Foster),* "Snake Charmer" *(traditional, composer unknown).*
MUSIC BY Carl W. Stalling.
Released on October 23
(7 min./Vitaphone Sound/Technicolor/Video)
Warner Bros.

KIT FOR CAT (1948) D: I. [Friz] Freleng.
VOICES: *Arthur Q. Bryan, Mel Blanc, Bea Benaderet.*
Elmer Fudd has room for only one cat, so Sylvester tries his best to eliminate his competition — a cute, orange kitten. Blanc is Sylvester, the kitten, Melvin, and the landlord. Entry in the LOONEY TUNES series.
SONG: "They're Either Too Young or Too Old" *(Arthur Schwartz; Frank Loesser), (hummed by Blanc as Sylvester).*
MUSIC BY Carl Stalling.
Released on November 6
(7 min./Vitaphone Sound/Technicolor/DVD)
Warner Bros.

RIFF RAFFY DAFFY (1948) D: Arthur Davis.
VOICES: *Mel Blanc.*
A vagrant Daffy Duck just wants to find a place to sleep in the city, but patrolman Porky Pig keeps evicting him. Blanc is Daffy, Porky, the gopher, and the cuckoo bird. Entry in the LOONEY TUNES series.
MUSIC BY Carl Stalling.
Released on November 7
(7 min./Vitaphone Sound/Cinecolor)
Warner Bros.

THE STUPOR SALESMAN (1948) D: Arthur Davis.
VOICES: *Mel Blanc.*
An escaping bank robber hides out in a country home, where he is visited by persistent appliance salesman Daffy Duck. Blanc is Daffy, Slug McSlug, radio announcer, newsboy, and police radio voice. Entry in the LOONEY TUNES series.
MUSIC BY Carl Stalling.
Released on November 20
(7 min./Vitaphone Sound/Technicolor/Video/DVD)
Warner Bros.

A HORSEFLY FLEAS (1948) D: Robert McKimson.
VOICES: *Mel Blanc.*
A dog's hairy body provides the 'frontier' for a showdown between a settler flea and attacking 'Indian fleas.' Blanc is A. Flea, horsefly, dog, Indian cries, and the engine noise. Entry in the LOONEY TUNES series.
SONGS: "My Old Kentucky Home" *(Stephen Foster)*, "There's a Home Around the Corner" *(composer unknown; ung by Blanc as a flea).*
MUSIC BY Carl Stalling.
Released on December 13
(7 min./Vitaphone Sound/Cinecolor)
Warner Bros.

MY BUNNY LIES OVER THE SEA (1948) D: Charles M. [Chuck] Jones.
VOICES: *Mel Blanc.*
Taking a "wrong turn at Albuquerque" and ending up in Scotland, Bug
Bunny is challenged to a zany game of golf by a belligerent Scotsman.
Blanc is Bugs and MacRory. Entry in the MERRIE MELODIES series.
SONGS: "My Bonnie Lies Over the Ocean" *(traditional folk song, composer
unknown)*, "Loch Lomond" *(traditional, composer unknown).*
MUSIC BY Carl Stalling.
Released on December 14
(7 min./Vitaphone Sound/Technicolor/Video/DVD)
Warner Bros.

SCAREDY CAT (1948) D: Charles M. [Chuck] Jones.
VOICE: *Mel Blanc.*
A gang of sinister mice try to do away with Porky Pig (Blanc) in a dark
mansion, but a terrified *(and mute)* Sylvester keeps watch over his master.
Entry in the MERRIE MELODIES series.
MUSIC BY Carl Stalling.
Released on December 18
(7 min./Vitaphone Sound/Technicolor/Video/DVD)
Warner Bros.

TWO GOPHERS FROM TEXAS (1948) D: Arthur Davis.
VOICES: *Mel Blanc, Stan Freberg.*
A sophisticated dog journeys to the country for a taste of 'raw food,'
namely Goofy Gophers Mac and Tosh. Blanc is Mac and the dog. Entry
in the MERRIE MELODIES series.
MUSIC BY Carl Stalling.
Released on December 27
(7 min./Vitaphone Sound/Cinecolor)
Warner Bros.

A HICK, A SLICK AND A CHICK (1948) D: Arthur Davis.
VOICES: *Mel Blanc, Bea Benaderet.*
Elmo the Mouse competes with Blackie for the affections of Daisy Lou, but first he must bring her an ermine coat. Not knowing what ermine is, Elmo settles on the hide of Herman the Cat. Blanc is Elmo, Herman and Blackie. Entry in the MERRIE MELODIES series.
MUSIC BY Carl Stalling.
Released on December 27
(7 min./Vitaphone Sound/Cinecolor/Rated [TV-G])
Warner Bros.

WILD AND WOODY! (1948) D: Dick Lundy.
VOICES: *Ben Hardaway, Lionel Stander, Jack Mather, Pinto Colvig, Grace Stafford.*
Woody Woodpecker becomes the sheriff in a wild western town inhabited by nasty Buzz Buzzard, whose main occupation is eliminating lawmen. Blanc *(re-used track)* provides Woody's laugh.
MUSIC BY Darrell Calker.
Released on December 31
(6 min./RCA Sound/Technicolor/Video)
Walter Lantz/United Artists

WISE QUACKERS (1949) D: I. [Friz] Freleng.
VOICES: *Mel Blanc, Arthur Q. Bryan.*
Daffy Duck, not wanting to fly south for the winter, arranges to become Elmer Fudd's slave in exchange for lodging and food. Blanc is Daffy, the neighbor, and the dogs. Entry in the LOONEY TUNES series.
SONGS: "Singin' in the Bathtub" *(Michael Cleary; Herb Magidson; Ned Washington),* "The Battle Hymn of the Republic" *(William Steffe; Julia Ward Howe),* "The Battle Cry of Freedom" *(George Frederick Root).*
MUSIC BY Carl Stalling.
Released on January 1
(7 min./Vitaphone Sound/Technicolor/Video)
Warner Bros.

HARE DO (1949) D: I. [Friz] Freleng.
VOICES: *Mel Blanc, Arthur Q. Bryan.*
Elmer Fudd chases Bugs Bunny into a theater where the rascally rabbit outsmarts his bald adversary. Blanc is Bugs, the lion, and the usher. Entry in the MERRIE MELODIES series.
MUSIC BY Carl Stalling.
Released on January 15
(7 min./Vitaphone Sound/Technicolor/Video/DVD)
Warner Bros.

HOLIDAY FOR DRUMSTICKS (1949) D: Arthur Davis.
VOICES: *Mel Blanc.*
Daffy Duck puts Tom Turkey on a diet to keep him from fattening up for a farmer's Thanksgiving table. Blanc is Daffy, Tom, Ma and Pa. Entry in the MERRIE MELODIES series.
SONG: "A Rainy Night in Rio" *(Arthur Schwartz; Leo Robin).*
MUSIC BY Carl Stalling.
Released on January 22
(7 min./Vitaphone Sound/Cinecolor/Video)
Warner Bros.

AWFUL ORPHAN (1949) D: Charles M. [Chuck] Jones.
VOICES: *Mel Blanc.*
Charlie Dog campaigns to be Porky Pig's pet, but Porky steadfastly resists the idea. Blanc is Porky, Charlie, the delivery boy, and the upstairs neighbor. Entry in the MERRIE MELODIES series.
MUSIC BY Carl Stalling.
Released on January 29
(7 min./Vitaphone Sound/Technicolor/Video/DVD)
Warner Bros.

PORKY CHOPS (1949) D: Arthur Davis.
VOICES: *Mel Blanc.*
Woodsman Porky Pig attempts to fell a tree favored by a zoot-suited hipster squirrel. Blanc is Porky, the bear, and the squirrel. Entry in the LOONEY TUNES series.
MUSIC BY Carl Stalling.
Released on February 12
(7 min./Vitaphone Sound/Technicolor/DVD)
Warner Bros.

MISSISSIPPI HARE (1949) D: Charles M. [Chuck] Jones.
VOICES: *Mel Blanc, Billy Bletcher, The Sportsmen Quartet.*
Bugs Bunny is on a riverboat, where he matches wits with a crafty Southern gambler. Blanc is Bugs, the Southern gentleman, and a purser. Entry in the LOONEY TUNES series.
SONGS: "Dixie" *(Daniel Decatur Emmett),* "Camptown Races" *(Stephen Foster; sung by Blanc as Bugs),* "Are You from Dixie?" *(George L. Cobb; Jack Yellen),* "Beautiful Dreamer" *(Foster),* "Jeannie with the Light Brown Hair" *(Foster),* "Minuet, Opus 13 No. 5 in E Major" *(Luigi Boccherini).*
MUSIC BY Carl Stalling.
Released on February 26
(7 min./Vitaphone Sound/Technicolor/DVD)
Warner Bros.

PAYING THE PIPER (1949) D: Robert McKimson.
VOICES: *Mel Blanc.*
The town's cats do not like the idea of Porky Pig chasing the rats away, so the Supreme Cat disguises himself as a rodent to beleaguer Porky. Blanc is Porky, Supreme Cat, the Mayor and three other cats. Entry in the LOONEY TUNES series.
SONGS: "Violin Concerto in E Minor, Opus 64, 3rd Movement" *(Felix Mendelssohn-Bartholdy),* "Octet for Strings, Opus 20, 3rd Movement" *(Mendelssohn).*
MUSIC BY Carl Stalling.
Released on March 12
(7 min./Vitaphone Sound/Technicolor/DVD)
Warner Bros.

DAFFY DUCK HUNT (1949) D: Robert McKimson.
VOICES: *Mel Blanc.*
Porky Pig and his dog bag Daffy Duck and put him in their freezer, but the manic mallard decides on a permanent thaw. Blanc is Daffy, Porky, the dog, the angel and the devil. Entry in the LOONEY TUNES series.
SONGS: "Silent Night, Holy Night" *(Franz Gruber; Joseph Mohr; Al Dubin),* "The Latin Quarter" *(Harry Warren; Dubin; sung by Blanc as Daffy).*
MUSIC BY Carl Stalling.
Released on March 26
(7 min./Vitaphone Sound/Technicolor/Video/DVD)
Warner Bros.

REBEL RABBIT (1949) D: Robert McKimson.
VOICES: *Mel Blanc.*
Insulted at the meager bounty the government pays for rabbits, Bugs Bunny goes on a nationwide rampage to jack up the reward. Blanc is Bugs, the postal employee, game commissioner, the guard, and the Southern senator. Entry in the MERRIE MELODIES series.
MUSIC BY Carl Stalling.
Released on April 9
(7 min./Vitaphone Sound/Technicolor/DVD)
Warner Bros.

HIGH DIVING HARE (1949) D: I. [Friz] Freleng.
VOICES: *Mel Blanc.*
Yosemite Sam wants to see a high-diving act; when the performer doesn't show up, Sam forces carnival barker Bugs Bunny to the platform — but it's Sam who keeps falling into the water. Blanc is Bugs, Yosemite, and a telegram boy. Entry in the LOONEY TUNES series.
MUSIC BY Carl Stalling.
Released on April 30
(7 min./Vitaphone Sound/Technicolor/Video/DVD)
Warner Bros.

CURTAIN RAZOR (1949) D: I. [Friz] Freleng.
VOICES: *Mel Blanc, Dave Barry, Cliff Nazarro, Dorothy Lloyd.*
Porky Pig has the job of auditioning various acts for a talent agency, including an operatic grasshopper, a turtle of 1,000 voices, a flea circus, and a pesky fox who keeps insisting he has the world's greatest act. Blanc is Porky, the grasshopper, the fox, the turtle, Al Jolson, the janitor, the dog and the flea circus dog. Entry in the LOONEY TUNES series.
SONGS: "April Showers" *(Louis Silvers; Buddy G. DeSylva),* "Frat" *(John F. Barth),* "The Blue Danube" *(Johann Strauss),* "Prelude to Act II" from "Lohengrin" *(Richard Wagner).*
MUSIC BY Carl Stalling.
Released on May 21
(7 min./Vitaphone Sound/Technicolor/DVD)
Warner Bros.

BOWERY BUGS (1949) D: Arthur Davis.
VOICES: *Mel Blanc, Billy Bletcher.*
Bugs Bunny (Blanc) spins the yarn of how he caused Steve Brodie to jump off the Brooklyn Bridge in 1886. Entry in the MERRIE MELODIES series.
SONGS: "Frankie and Johnny" *(Frank and Bert Leighton; Ren Shields),* "All That Glitters Is Not Gold" *(James W. Casey; George A. Norton; sung by Blanc as Bugs).*
MUSIC BY Carl Stalling.
Released on June 4
(7 min./Vitaphone Sound/Technicolor/DVD)
Warner Bros.

MOUSE MAZURKA (1949) D: I. [Friz] Freleng.
VOICES: *Mel Blanc.*
A panic-stricken Sylvester the Cat tries to keep a dancing Russian mouse from exploding after it swallows nitroglycerine. Blanc is Sylvester and the narrator. Entry in the MERRIE MELODIES series.
SONGS: "Hungarian Dances No. 7 and 17" *(Johannes Brahms),* "Pizzicato Polka" *(Johann Strauss).*
MUSIC BY Carl Stalling.
Released on June 11
(7 min./Vitaphone Sound/Technicolor)
Warner Bros.

LONG-HAIRED HARE (1949) D: Charles M. [Chuck] Jones.
VOICES: *Mel Blanc, Nicolai Shutorov.*
Giovanni Jones, a rotund opera singer, invites retaliation when he breaks Bugs Bunny's banjo; the rascally rabbit disrupts Jones' concert at the Hollywood Bowl. Blanc is Bugs, the maestro, a delivery boy, the musicians, and the screaming voice of Giovanni. Entry in the LOONEY TUNES series.
SONGS: "A Rainy Night in Rio" *(Arthur Schwartz; Leo Robin; sung by Blanc as Bugs),* "Largo Al Factotum" from "The Barber of Seville" *(Gioacchino Rossini; Cesare Sterbini),* "Beautiful Galathea Overture" *(Franz Von Suppe),* "When Yuba Plays the Rumba on the Tuba" *(Herman Hupfeld),* "Chi Mi Frena in Tal Momento?" from "Lucia di Lammermoor" *(Gaetano Donizetti; Salvatore Cammarano),* "My Gal Is a High-Born Lady" *(Barney Fagan; sung with substitute lyrics by Blanc as Bugs),* "Prelude, 2nd Theme from Act III" of "Lohengrin" *(Richard Wagner).*

MUSIC BY Carl Stalling.
Released on June 25
(7 min./Vitaphone Sound/Technicolor/DVD)
Warner Bros.

HENHOUSE HENERY (1949) D: Robert McKimson.
VOICES: *Mel Blanc.*
Henery Hawk, still after Foghorn Leghorn, teams up with the battered
barnyard dog to get the Southern rooster. Blanc is Foghorn, Henery, and
the dog. Entry in the LOONEY TUNES series.
SONG: "Camptown Races" *(Stephen Foster; sung by Blanc as Foghorn and
Henery).*
MUSIC BY Carl Stalling.
Released on July 2
(7 min./Vitaphone Sound/Technicolor)
Warner Bros.

KNIGHTS MUST FALL (1949) D: I. [Friz] Freleng.
VOICES: *Mel Blanc.*
Bugs Bunny is challenged to a series of jousts by medieval knight Sir
Pantsalot of Drop Seat Manor. Blanc is Bugs, Pantsalot, the announcer,
and the usher. Entry in the MERRIE MELODIES series.
MUSIC BY Carl Stalling.
Released on July 16
(7 min./Vitaphone Sound/Technicolor)
Warner Bros.

BAD OL' PUTTY TAT (1949) D: I. [Friz] Freleng.
VOICES: *Mel Blanc.*
Sylvester the Cat tries a variety of disastrous maneuvers to catch Tweety
Pie, including painting his head to look like a birdcage. Blanc is Sylvester,
Tweety, and the badminton player. Entry in the MERRIE MELODIES
series.
MUSIC BY Carl Stalling.
Released on July 23
(8 min./Vitaphone Sound/Technicolor/DVD)
Warner Bros.

THE GREY HOUNDED HARE (1949) D: Robert McKimson.
VOICES: *Mel Blanc.*
Tunneling into a dog-racing track, Bugs Bunny falls in love with the mechanical rabbit that leads the dogs. Blanc is Bugs, Gnawbone *(a.k.a. Dog #7),* the race announcer, and the other dogs. Entry in the LOONEY TUNES series.
MUSIC BY Carl Stalling.
Released on August 6
(7 min./Vitaphone Sound/Technicolor/DVD)
Warner Bros.

OFTEN AN ORPHAN (1949) D: Charles M. [Chuck] Jones.
VOICES: *Mel Blanc.*
Charlie Dog needs a new master, so he presents his pedigree to impatient farmer Porky Pig. Blanc is Porky, Charlie, the owner and various dogs. Entry in the LOONEY TUNES series.
MUSIC BY Carl Stalling.
Released on August 13
(7 min./Vitaphone Sound/Technicolor)
Warner Bros.

THE WINDBLOWN HARE (1949) D: Robert McKimson.
VOICES: *Mel Blanc, Bea Benaderet.*
New homeowner Bugs Bunny made the mistake of buying from the Three Little Pigs; when the Big Bad Wolf destroys his lodgings, Bugs goes on the warpath. Blanc is Bugs, the three pigs, and the wolf.
SONGS: "Polly Put the Kettle On" *(to the tune of "Who's Afraid of the Big Bad Wolf?"; traditional, composer unknown)* "The Rabbit [Lady] in Red" *(Allie Wrubel; Mort Dixon; sung by Blanc as Bugs).*
MUSIC BY Carl Stalling.
Released on August 27
(7 min./Vitaphone Sound/Technicolor/Video/DVD)
Warner Bros.

DOUGH FOR THE DO-DO (1949) D: No director credited *(Arthur Davis, Friz Freleng)*.
VOICES: *Mel Blanc.*
A combination remake and re-issue of *Porky In Wackyland* (1938), adding new animated footage, re-dubbing, and color. Blanc is Porky Pig, the Mystery Voice, the Red Monster, a cuckoo, a dancer, a prisoner, the 'Rubber Band,' the bird on a wheel, the information clerk and the Do-Do. Entry in the MERRIE MELODIES series.
MUSIC BY Carl Stalling.
Released on September 2
(7 min./Vitaphone Sound/Technicolor/DVD)
Warner Bros.

FAST AND FURRY-OUS (1949) D: Charles M. [Chuck] Jones
VOICES: *Paul Julian, Mel Blanc*
First of the Roadrunner-Coyote cartoons. Blanc does the Coyote effects. Entry in the LOONEY TUNES series.
MUSIC BY Carl Stalling.
Released on September 16.
(7 min./ Vitaphone Sound/ Technicolor/ DVD), Warner Bros.

EACH DAWN I CROW (1949) D: I. [Friz] Freleng.
VOICES: *Frank Graham, Arthur Q. Bryan, Mel Blanc.*
As Elmer Fudd sharpens his ax, our participating narrator encourages John Rooster (Blanc) to 'get' Fudd before Elmer gets him. Entry in the MERRIE MELODIES series.
SONGS: "Carolina in the Morning" *(Walter Donaldson; Gus Kahn)*, "Some Sunday Morning" *(M.K. Jerome; Ray Heindorf; Ted Koehler)*, "William Tell Overture" *(Gioacchino Rossini)*, "Funeral March" *(Frederic Chopin)*, "Great Western Clog" *(traditional, composer unknown)*.
MUSIC BY Carl Stalling.
Released on September 23
(7 min./Vitaphone Sound/Technicolor/DVD)
Warner Bros.

FRIGID HARE (1949) D: Charles M. [Chuck] Jones.
VOICES: *Mel Blanc.*
Bugs Bunny ends up at the South Pole where he becomes the protector of a cute little penguin and rescues it from a hungry Eskimo. Blanc is Bugs and the Eskimo. Entry in the MERRIE MELODIES series.
MUSIC BY Carl Stalling.
Released on October 7
(7 min./Vitaphone Sound/Technicolor/DVD)
Warner Bros.

SWALLOW THE LEADER (1949) D: Robert McKimson.
VOICES: *Robert Bruce, Mel Blanc.*
When the swallows return to Capistrano, a hungry cat (Blanc) is there to greet them — but the leader of the birds is a clever fellow. Entry in the LOONEY TUNES series.
SONG: "When the Swallows Come Back to Capistrano" *(Leon Rene).*
MUSIC BY Carl Stalling.
Released on October 14
(7 min./Vitaphone Sound/Technicolor/DVD)
Warner Bros.

BYE, BYE BLUEBEARD (1949) D: Arthur Davis.
VOICES: *Mel Blanc.*
Porky Pig and a mouse deal with the escaped killer, Bluebeard. Blanc is Porky, the mouse, Bluebeard, the radio workout host, and the radio news reporter. Entry in the MERRIE MELODIES series.
MUSIC BY Carl Stalling.
Released on October 21
(7 min./Vitaphone Sound/Technicolor/Video/DVD)
Warner Bros.

FOR SCENT-IMENTAL REASONS (1949) D: Charles M. [Chuck] Jones.
VOICES: *Mel Blanc.*
The owner of a perfume shop uses a cat to get rid of skunk Pepe LePew, but the romantic polecat falls in love with the female feline. Blanc is Pepe, the gendarme, the cat, and the perfume shop owner. Entry in the LOONEY TUNES series.
SONGS: "The Latin Quarter" *(Harry Warren; Al Dubin),* "Alouette" *(traditional, composer unknown),* "Time Waits for No One" *(Cliff Friend; Charles Tobias;* sung with substitute lyrics by Blanc as Pepe*),* "It's Magic" *(Jule Styne; Sammy Cahn).*
MUSIC BY Carl Stalling.
Academy Award *(Short Subject – Cartoon)* Edward Selzer.
Released on November 12
(7 min./Vitaphone Sound/Technicolor/DVD)
Warner Bros.

HIPPETY HOPPER (1949) D: Robert McKimson.
VOICES: *Mel Blanc.*
A harried mouse, constantly chased by Sylvester the Cat, finds an ally in the form of a baby kangaroo. Blanc is Sylvester, the mouse, and the bulldog. Entry in the MERRIE MELODIES series.
SONG: "Hippety Hop" *(Carl W. Stalling).*
MUSIC BY Carl Stalling.
Released on November 19
(7 min./Vitaphone Sound/Technicolor)
Warner Bros.

WHICH IS WITCH? (1949) D: I. [Friz] Freleng.
VOICES: *Mel Blanc.*
A native witch doctor chases Bugs Bunny with intent to use him in his potion. Blanc is Bugs, the witch doctor and I. C. Spots. Entry in the LOONEY TUNES series.
MUSIC BY Carl Stalling.
Released on December 3
(7 min./Vitaphone Sound/Technicolor)
Warner Bros.

BEAR FEAT (1949) D: Charles M. [Chuck] Jones.
VOICES: *Billy Bletcher, Stan Freberg, Bea Benaderet, Mel Blanc.*
The Bear family spruces up their old vaudeville routines to answer an entertainment ad, but Junior Bear ruins everything. Blanc does Pa yelling, "1928????" Entry in the LOONEY TUNES series.
MUSIC BY Carl Stalling.
Released on December 10
(7 min./Vitaphone Sound/Technicolor)
Warner Bros.

A HAM IN A ROLE (1949) D: Robert McKimson.
VOICES: *Mel Blanc, Stan Freberg.*
The Goofy Gophers get their revenge on a Shakespearean dog when the canine actor evicts them from his home. Blanc is Mac, the dog, and the director. Entry in the LOONEY TUNES series.
MUSIC BY Carl Stalling.
Released on December 13
(7 min./Vitaphone Sound/Technicolor/DVD)
Warner Bros.

RABBIT HOOD (1949) D: Charles M. [Chuck] Jones.
VOICES: *Mel Blanc.*
The Sheriff of Nottingham arrests Bugs Bunny for pilfering some royal carrots, but the rabbit does not go quietly. Blanc is Bugs, the Sheriff, and Little John. Features a live-action sequence of Errol Flynn from *The Adventures of Robin Hood* (1938). Entry in the MERRIE MELODIES series.
SONGS: "London Bridge" *(traditional, composer unknown)*, "Rue Brittania" *(Thomas Augustine Arne).*
MUSIC BY Carl Stalling.
Released on December 24
(8 min./Vitaphone Sound/Technicolor/Video/DVD)
Warner Bros.

HOME, TWEET HOME (1950) D: I. [Friz]Freleng.
VOICES: *Mel Blanc, Bea Benaderet.*
Tweety Pie is trying to take a bath in the park when he is accosted by Sylvester the Cat. Blanc is Sylvester, Tweety and the dog. Entry in the MERRIE MELODIES series.
MUSIC BY Carl Stalling.
Released on January 14
(7 min./Vitaphone Sound/Technicolor/Video)
Warner Bros.

HURDY-GURDY HARE (1950) D: Robert McKimson.
VOICE: *Mel Blanc.*
Bugs Bunny is an organ grinder whose monkey keeps stealing from the take. When Bugs fires him, the crafty chimp recruits a gorilla to put a 'hit' on the rascally rabbit. Blanc is Bugs, the monkey and the gorilla. Entry in the MERRIE MELODIES series.
MUSIC BY Carl W. Stalling.
Released on January 21
(7 min./Vitaphone Sound/Technicolor/DVD)
Warner Bros.

BOOBS IN THE WOODS (1950) D: Robert McKimson.
VOICES: *Mel Blanc.*
Porky Pig is trying to commune with nature while painting a landscape, but Daffy Duck comes along to spoil the reverie. Blanc is Porky, Daffy and the car noises. Entry in the LOONEY TUNES series.
SONGS: "Put 'em in a Box, Tie 'em with a Ribbon, and Throw 'em in the Deep Blue Sea" *(Jule Styne; Sammy Cahn),* "She'll Be Comin' Round the Mountain" *(traditional, composer unknown),* "The Merry-Go-Round Broke Down" *(Cliff Friend; Dave Franklin; sung with substitute lyrics by Blanc as Daffy).*
MUSIC BY Carl Stalling.
Released on January 28
(7 min./Vitaphone Sound/Technicolor/DVD)
Warner Bros.

MUTINY ON THE BUNNY (1950) D: I. [Friz] Freleng.
VOICES: *Mel Blanc.*
Shanghai (Yosemite) Sam tricks Bugs Bunny into becoming his crew-of-one on his galleon; they cannot get anywhere because their antics keep sinking the boat. Blanc is Bugs, Sam, the traumatized sailor, and the mouse. Entry in the LOONEY TUNES series.
SONG: "Yo, Ho, Blow the Man Down" *(traditional, composer unknown).*
MUSIC BY Carl Stalling.
Released on February 11
(7 min./Vitaphone Sound/Technicolor/Video)
Warner Bros.

THE LION'S BUSY (1950) D: I. [Friz] Freleng.
VOICES: *Mel Blanc.*
A ten-year-old lion is presented with information that lions rarely live beyond a decade — and Beaky Buzzard is waiting for his next meal. Blanc plays the lion, Beaky, and vocal effects. Entry in the LOONEY TUNES series.
MUSIC BY Carl Stalling.
Released on February 18
(7 min./Vitaphone Sound/Technicolor)
Warner Bros.

THE SCARLET PUMPERNICKEL (1950) D: Charles M. [Chuck] Jones.
VOICES: *Mel Blanc, Marian Richman.*
Daffy Duck has written a screenplay for J.L. Warner's approval; all about a crusading swashbuckler who attempts to rescue his lady fair from an arranged marriage. The 'all-star' cast features Daffy as the Hero, Porky Pig as the Lord High Chamberlain, Sylvester the Cat as the Grand Duke, and Elmer Fudd as the innkeeper. Blanc is Daffy, Porky, Sylvester, Elmer, the highwayman, and J.L. Entry in the LOONEY TUNES series.
MUSIC BY Carl Stalling.
Released on March 4
(7 min./Vitaphone Sound/Technicolor/Video/DVD)
Warner Bros.

HOMELESS HARE (1950) D: Charles M. [Chuck] Jones.
VOICES: *Mel Blanc, John T. Smith.*
Bugs Bunny (Blanc) puts a roughneck construction worker through his violent paces when the burly builder tries to wipe out Bugs' home. Entry in the MERRIE MELODIES series.
SONG: "Don't Sweetheart Me" *(Cliff Friend; Charles Tobias).*
MUSIC BY Carl W. Stalling.
Released on March 11
(7 min./Vitaphone Sound/Technicolor/Video/DVD)
Warner Bros.

STRIFE WITH FATHER (1950) D: Robert McKimson.
VOICES: *Mel Blanc, Tedd Pierce, Marian Richman*
An English sparrow tries to raise the foundling left on his doorstep — one Beaky Buzzard. Blanc is Beaky and the narrator. Entry in the MERRIE MELODIES series.
MUSIC BY Carl Stalling.
Released on April 1
(7 min./Vitaphone Sound/Technicolor)
Warner Bros.

THE HYPO-CHONDRI-CAT (1950) D: Charles M. [Chuck] Jones.
VOICES: *Mel Blanc, Stan Freberg.*
The mice Hubie and Bertie play on the sick fears of Claude Cat to ensure their stay in a comfortable home. Blanc is Hubie and Claude. Entry in the MERRIE MELODIES series.
MUSIC BY Carl Stalling.
Released on April 15
(7 min./Vitaphone Sound/Technicolor/DVD)
Warner Bros.

BIG HOUSE BUNNY (1950) D: I. [Friz] Freleng.
VOICES: *Mel Blanc.*
Trying to get away from hunters, Bugs Bunny accidentally tunnels into Sing Song Prison — guarded by *(Yosemite)* Sam Schultz. Blanc is Bugs, Sam, and the warden. Entry in the LOONEY TUNES series.
MUSIC BY Carl Stalling.
Released on April 22
(7 min./Vitaphone Sound/Technicolor/Video/DVD)
Warner Bros.

THE LEGHORN BLOWS AT MIDNIGHT (1950) D: Robert McKimson.
VOICES: *Mel Blanc.*
Foghorn Leghorn and the barnyard dog put determined Henery Hawk
on the hunt for each other. Blanc is Foghorn, Henery, and the dog. Entry
in the LOONEY TUNES series.
MUSIC BY Carl Stalling.
Released on May 6
(7 min./Vitaphone Sound/Technicolor)
Warner Bros.

HIS BITTER HALF (1950) D: I. [Friz] Freleng.
VOICES: *Mel Blanc, Martha Wentworth.*
Daffy Duck marries a wealthy widow so he can live on easy street, but
things become rough when she turns out to be a slave-driving harridan
with a mischievous brat. Blanc is Daffy and little Wentworth Duck. Entry
in the MERRIE MELODIES series.
MUSIC BY Carl Stalling.
Released on May 20
(7 min./Vitaphone Sound/Technicolor/DVD)
Warner Bros.

AN EGG SCRAMBLE (1950) D: Robert McKimson.
VOICES: *Mel Blanc, Bea Benaderet.*
Prissy the Chicken goes to extreme lengths to protect her egg when
farmer Porky Pig wants to sell it. Blanc is Porky, Pretty Boy Bagel, the
desk sergeant, the cops and some of Prissy's dialogue. Entry in the
MERRIE MELODIES series.
SONG: "Old MacDonald" *(traditional, composer unknown; sung by Blanc
as Porky).*
MUSIC BY Carl Stalling.
Released on May 27
(7 min./Vitaphone Sound/Technicolor/Video/DVD)
Warner Bros.

WHAT'S UP, DOC? (1950) D: Robert McKimson.
VOICES: *Mel Blanc, Arthur Q. Bryan, The Sportsmen Quartet.*
Bugs Bunny tells how he rose to fame, including the time he took prat-falls for 'star' Elmer Fudd. Blanc is Bugs, 'Eddie Cantor,' and the director. Other caricatures: Jack Benny and Bing Crosby. Entry in the LOONEY TUNES series.
SONGS: "Oh, We're the Boys of the Chorus" *(composer unknown; sung by Blanc as Bugs and the chorus),* "What's Up, Doc?" *(Carl W. Stalling; sung by Blanc as Bugs and Bryan as Elmer),* "Hooray for Hollywood" *(Richard A. Whiting; Johnny Mercer),* "You Must Have Been a Beautiful Baby" *(Harry Warren; Mercer),* "Ain't We Got Fun?" *(Whiting; Ray Egan; Gus Kahn; sung by Blanc as 'Eddie Cantor'),* "Rock-a-Bye Baby" *(Effie I. Canning),* "Are You from Dixie?" *(George L. Cobb; Jack Yellen),* "Voices of Spring" *(Johann Strauss),* "While Strolling Through the Park One Day" *(Ed Haley),* "April Showers" *(Louis Silvers; Buddy G. DeSylva),* "Shuffle Off to Buffalo" *(Warren; Al Dubin),* "Forty-Second Street" *(Warren; Dubin),* "Hungarian Rhapsody No. 2" *(Franz Liszt),* "What's the Matter with Father?" *(Egbert Van Alstyne; Harry H. Williams),* "The Daughter of Rosie O'Grady" *(Walter Donaldson; Monty C. Brice),* "Merrily We Roll Along" *(Michael Carr; Raymond Wallace),* "The Blue Danube" *(Johann Strauss),* "The Irish Washerwoman" *(traditional, composer unknown).*
MUSIC BY Carl Stalling.
Released on June 17
(7 min./Vitaphone Sound/Technicolor/DVD)
Warner Bros.

ALL A BIR-R-R-RD (1950) D: I. [Friz] Freleng.
VOICES: *Mel Blanc, Bea Benaderet.*
Tweety Pie's train ride is far from smooth when he has Sylvester the Cat to contend with. Blanc is Tweety, Sylvester, the dog, and the conductor. Entry in the LOONEY TUNES series.
SONG: "I'm a Tweet Little Bird" *(composer unknown; sung by Blanc as Tweety).*
MUSIC BY Carl Stalling.
Released on June 24
(7 min./Vitaphone Sound/Technicolor/Video/DVD)
Warner Bros.

8 BALL BUNNY (1950) D: Charles M. [Chuck] Jones.
VOICES: *Mel Blanc, Dave Barry.*
Bugs Bunny goes through a series of misadventures while trying to return a top-hatted penguin to the South Pole. Caricature of Humphrey Bogart. Blanc is Bugs, a hobo, a diner and natives. Entry in the LOONEY TUNES series.
SONGS: "Don't Sweetheart Me" *(Cliff Friend; Charles Tobias),* "Calypso Bunny" *(Michael Maltese).*
MUSIC BY Carl Stalling.
Released on July 8
(7 min./Vitaphone Sound/Technicolor/DVD)
Warner Bros.

IT'S HUMMER TIME (1950) D: Robert McKimson.
VOICE: *Mel Blanc.*
A cat's pursuit of a hummingbird disturbs a mean bulldog who metes out a series of punishments to the feline. Blanc is the cat, the dog and the bird. Entry in the LOONEY TUNES series.
MUSIC BY Carl Stalling.
Released on July 22
(7 min./Vitaphone Sound/Technicolor)
Warner Bros.

GOLDEN YEGGS (1950) D: I. [Friz] Freleng.
VOICES: *Mel Blanc.*
Rocky the Gangster makes the mistake of thinking that Daffy Duck is the goose that laid the golden egg. He kidnaps the manic mallard and tells him at gunpoint to produce a gold egg…or else. Blanc is Daffy, Porky Pig, Rocky, Nick, the hotel employee, a goose and the chickens. Entry in the MERRIE MELODIES series.
MUSIC BY Carl Stalling.
Released on August 5
(7 min./Vitaphone Sound/Technicolor/Video/DVD)
Warner Bros.

HILLBILLY HARE (1950) D: Robert McKimson.
VOICES: *Mel Blanc, John T. Smith.*
Bugs Bunny becomes the caller of a violent square dance when the Martin brothers decide to feud with the rascally rabbit. Blanc is Bugs and Curt Martin. Entry in the MERRIE MELODIES series.
SONGS: "I Like Mountain Music" *(Frank Weldon; James Cavanaugh; sung by Blanc as Bugs),* "Skip to My Lou" *(traditional, composer unknown),* "Turkey in the Straw" *(traditional, composer unknown),* "Jesse James" *(traditional, composer unknown).*
MUSIC BY Carl Stalling.
Released on August 12
(7 min./Vitaphone Sound/Technicolor/Video/DVD)
Warner Bros.

DOG GONE SOUTH (1950) D: Charles M. [Chuck] Jones.
VOICES: *Mel Blanc.*
Charlie Dog meets up with a Southern colonel who he wants as his master, but Charlie must first get rid of the colonel's current pet, Belvedere. Blanc is Charlie, the colonel and Belvedere. Entry in the MERRIE MELODIES series.
SONGS: "Yankee Doodle" *(traditional, composer unknown; sung by Blanc as Charlie),* "Dixie" *(Daniel Decatur Emmett),* "Way Down South" *(composer unknown; sung by Blanc as the colonel).*
MUSIC BY Carl Stalling.
Released on August 26
(7 min./Vitaphone Sound/Technicolor)
Warner Bros.

THE DUCKSTERS (1950) D: Charles M. [Chuck] Jones.
VOICES: *Mel Blanc.*
A cascade of pitfalls awaits Porky Pig when he becomes a contestant on a quiz show emceed by Daffy Duck. Blanc is Porky, Daffy, and the audience member. Entry in the LOONEY TUNES series.
MUSIC BY Carl Stalling.
Released on September 2
(7 min./Vitaphone Sound/Technicolor/Video/DVD)
Warner Bros.

A FRACTURED LEGHORN (1950) D: Robert McKimson.
VOICES: *Mel Blanc.*
Foghorn Leghorn and a cat both one-up each other to gain sole posses-
sion of a juicy worm. Blanc is Foghorn, the cat and the worm. Entry in
the MERRIE MELODIES series.
SONGS: "By a Waterfall" *(Sammy Fain; Irving Kahal),* "Got the South in
My Soul" *(Victor Young).*
MUSIC BY Carl Stalling.
Released on September 16
(7 min./Vitaphone Sound/Technicolor/Video)
Warner Bros.

BUNKER HILL BUNNY (1950) D: I. [Friz] Freleng.
VOICES: *Mel Blanc.*
We learn of the little-known Revolutionary War battle of Bagel Heights,
wherein American Bugs Bunny defended his fort against sawed-off
Hessian (Yosemite) Sam Von Schamm. Blanc is Bugs and Sam. Entry
in the MERRIE MELODIES series.
SONG: "Yankee Doodle" *(traditional, composer unknown),* "Hail Columbia"
(Philip Phile; Joseph Hopkinson).
MUSIC BY Carl Stalling.
Released on September 23
(7 min./Vitaphone Sound/Technicolor/DVD)
Warner Bros.

CANARY ROW (1950) D: I. [Friz] Freleng.
VOICES: *Mel Blanc, Bea Benaderet.*
A series of bruising missteps plague Sylvester the Cat when he tries to
snatch Tweety Pie out of a hotel. Blanc is Sylvester, Tweety, the desk clerk,
and the monkey. Entry in the LOONEY TUNES series.
SONGS: "Tweet Little Bird" *(composer unknown; sung by Blanc as Tweety),*
"When Irish Eyes Are Smiling" *(Ernest Ball; Chauncey Olcott; sung by Blanc
as Tweety),* "Organ Grinder's Swing" *(Will Hudson; Irving Mills).*
MUSIC BY Carl Stalling.
Released on October 7
(7 min./Vitaphone Sound/Technicolor/Video/DVD)
Warner Bros.

STOOGE FOR A MOUSE (1950) D: I. [Friz] Freleng.
VOICES: *Mel Blanc.*
A sneaky mouse upsets the friendship between Sylvester the Cat and Mike Bulldog. Blanc is Sylvester, Mike, and the mouse. Entry in the MERRIE MELODIES series.
MUSIC BY Carl Stalling.
Released on October 21
(7 min./Vitaphone Sound/Technicolor)
Warner Bros.

POP 'IM POP! (1950) D: Robert McKimson.
VOICES: *Mel Blanc.*
Sylvester the Cat boasts to Junior about his skill at mouse-catching, until he runs into 'giant rodent' Hippety Hopper the Kangaroo. Blanc is Sylvester, Junior, the carny barker, the stage manager and the puppy. Entry in the LOONEY TUNES series.
MUSIC BY Carl Stalling.
Released on October 28
(7 min./Vitaphone Sound/Technicolor)
Warner Bros.

BUSHY HARE (1950) D: Robert McKimson.
VOICE: *Mel Blanc.*
Bugs Bunny's sojourn in Australia includes adoption by a mother kangaroo and being chased by an Aborigine. Blanc is Bugs, the balloon vendor, 'Nature Boy' *(the Aborigine),* and the kangaroos. Entry in the LOONEY TUNES series.
SONGS: "California, Here I Come" *(Joseph Meyer; Buddy G. DeSylva; Al Jolson), (sung by Blanc as Bugs),* "The Fountain in the Park (While Strolling Through the Park One Day" *(Ed Haley; sung by Blanc as Bugs),* "How Dry I Am" *(traditional, composer unknown; sung by Blanc as Bugs),* "That Wonderful Mother of Mine" *(Walter Goodwin; Clyde Hager).*
MUSIC BY Carl Stalling.
Released on November 11
(7 min./Vitaphone Sound/Technicolor)
Warner Bros.

RABBIT OF SEVILLE (1950) D: Charles M. [Chuck] Jones.
VOICES: *Mel Blanc, Arthur Q. Bryan.*
Bugs Bunny (Blanc) puts his own spin on the Gioacchino Rossini opera "The Barber of Seville" when Elmer Fudd chases him into the Hollywood Bowl. Entry in the LOONEY TUNES series.
SONG: "The Barber of Seville Overture" *(Gioacchino Rossini; Cesare Sterbini), (comedy lyrics by Michael Maltese; sung by Blanc as Bugs).*
MUSIC BY Carl Stalling.
Hugo Award Nomination, 1951 *(Best Dramatic Presentation)* Chuck Jones, director; Michael Maltese, writer *(this was a retro nomination cited in 2001).*
Released on December 16
(7 min./Vitaphone Sound/Technicolor/Rated [TV-G]/DVD)
Warner Bros.

TWO'S A CROWD (1950) D: Charles M. [Chuck] Jones.
VOICES: *Mel Blanc, Bea Benaderet.*
Claude Cat has many comforts in his middle-class home, until his human masters introduce a new pet, Frisky Puppy. Blanc is John, Frisky and Claude. Entry in the LOONEY TUNES series.
MUSIC BY Carl Stalling.
Released on December 30
(7 min./Vitaphone Sound/Technicolor)
Warner Bros.

HARE WE GO (1951) D: Robert McKimson.
VOICES: *Mel Blanc, Grace Lenard.*
Bugs Bunny accompanies Christopher Columbus on his journey to the New World, but bad luck makes Bugs likely to end up in the stew pot. Blanc is Bugs, Columbus, King Ferdinand, the bald sailor, and the crewmen. Entry in the MERRIE MELODIES series.
SONGS: "Santa Lucia" *(Teodoro Cottrau)*, "Let That Be a Lesson to You" *(Richard A. Whiting; Johnny Mercer), (sung by Blanc as Bugs).*
MUSIC BY Carl Stalling.
Released on January 6
(7 min./Vitaphone Sound/Technicolor)
Warner Bros.

A FOX IN A FIX (1951) D: Robert McKimson.
VOICES: *Mel Blanc.*
A fox disguises himself as a dog to get inside a farmyard and make off with some chickens, but the bulldog guard has some 'lessons' for the hapless fox. Blanc is the fox and the bulldog. Entry in the MERRIE MELODIES series.
SONG: "Fiddle Dee Dee" *(Jule Styne; Sammy Cahn).*
MUSIC BY Carl Stalling.
Released on January 20
(7 min./Vitaphone Sound/Technicolor)
Warner Bros.

PUNY EXPRESS (1951) D: No director credited *(Walter Lantz, Dick Lundy).*
VOICES: *Grace Stafford, Mel Blanc (re-use).*
Woody Woodpecker is a Pony Express rider who has to fend off outlaw Buzz Buzzard. Blanc provides Woody's laugh.
MUSIC BY Clarence E. Wheeler.
Released on January 22
(6½ min./RCA Sound/Technicolor)
Walter Lantz Productions/Universal

CANNED FEUD (1951) D: I. [Friz] Freleng.
VOICES: *Mel Blanc, Marian Richman.*
Sylvester the Cat, alone in the house, has plenty of food but needs a can opener. Unfortunately, the only one to be had is in the hands of an elusive mouse. Blanc is Sylvester and Sam. Entry in the LOONEY TUNES series.
MUSIC BY Carl Stalling.
Released on February 3
(7 min./Vitaphone Sound/Technicolor/DVD)
Warner Bros.

RABBIT EVERY MONDAY (1951) D: I. [Friz] Freleng.
VOICES: *Mel Blanc.*
Yosemite Sam stalks and catches Bugs Bunny, but things do not go easily — even when Sam has Bugs in the oven. Blanc is Bugs, Sam, and the audience member. Entry in the LOONEY TUNES series.
SONG: "It's Magic" *(Jule Styne; Sammy Cahn; sung with substitute lyrics by Blanc as Bugs).*
MUSIC BY Carl Stalling.
Released on February 10
(7 min./Vitaphone Sound/Technicolor/Video)
Warner Bros.

PUTTY TAT TROUBLE (1951) D: I. [Friz] Freleng.
VOICES: *Mel Blanc, Bea Benaderet.*
A snow-shoveling Tweety Pie realizes Sylvester the Cat and an orange tabby are both after him, so Tweety resorts to wintertime warfare. Blanc is Tweety, Sylvester, Sam and the first woman's voice. Entry in the LOONEY TUNES series.
SONG: "Tweety Song" *(composer unknown; sung by Blanc as Tweety).*
MUSIC BY Carl Stalling.
Released on February 24
(7 min./Vitaphone Sound/Technicolor/Video/DVD)
Warner Bros.

CORN PLASTERED (1951) D: Robert McKimson.
VOICES: *Mel Blanc, Pat Patrick.*
A farmer (Blanc) does all he can to get rid of a wise-guy crow. Entry in the MERRIE MELODIES series.
SONG: "You Can't Scare a Crow with a Scarecrow" *(composer unknown).*
MUSIC BY Carl Stalling.
Released on March 3
(7 min./Vitaphone Sound/Technicolor)
Warner Bros.

BUNNY HUGGED (1951) D: Charles M. [Chuck] Jones.
VOICES: *Mel Blanc, John T. Smith.*
Bugs Bunny enters the wrestling ring to put his own kind of moves on the Crusher. Blanc is Bugs and the announcer. Entry in the MERRIE MELODIES series.
SONG: "The Washington Post March" *(John Philip Sousa).*
MUSIC BY Carl Stalling.
Released on March 10
(7 min./Vitaphone Sound/Technicolor/DVD)
Warner Bros.

SCENT-IMENTAL ROMEO (1951) D: Charles M. [Chuck] Jones.
VOICES: *Mel Blanc.*
A female cat tries to partake in feeding time at the zoo, but Pepe LePew has an amorous appetite of his own. Blanc is Pepe, Penelope, the zoo-keeper, lion, popcorn cart bird, pigeon feeder, and the poodle. Entry in the MERRIE MELODIES series.
SONGS: "Strolling Though le [the] Park" *(Ed Haley; sung with substitute lyrics by Blanc as Pepe),* "April in Paris" *(Vernon Duke; E.Y. Harburg),* "L'amour, Toujours, L'amour" *(Rudolf Friml),* "The Latin Quarter" *(Harry Warren; Al Dubin),* "Kiss Me Again" *(Victor Herbert),* "Baby Face" *(Harry Akst; Benny Davis; sung by Blanc as Pepe),* La Vie en Rose" *(Louiguy; Edith Piaf; Mack David),* "Cherie, I Love You" *(Lillian Goodman),* "La Marseillaise" *(Claude Joseph Rouget de Lisle).*
MUSIC BY Carl Stalling.
Released on March 24
(7 min./Vitaphone Sound/Technicolor)
Warner Bros.

SLEEP HAPPY (1951) D: No director credited *(Walter Lantz).*
VOICES: *Grace Stafford, Mel Blanc (re-use).*
An exhausted Woody Woodpecker flops as Wally Walrus' boarding house, but causes such a commotion that Wally tries his all to quiet the crazy bird. Blanc provides Woody's laugh.
MUSIC BY Clarence E. Wheeler.
Released on March 26
(7 min./RCA Sound/Technicolor)
Walter Lantz Productions/Universal

A BONE FOR A BONE (1951) D: I. [Friz] Freleng.

VOICES: *Mel Blanc, Stan Freberg.*

A stubborn dog is determined to bury his bone in the Goofy Gophers' den, but the two polite rodents pound some sense into their canine interloper. Blanc is Mac and the dog. Entry in the LOONEY TUNES series.

SONG: "That Was a Big Fat Lie" *(Jule Styne; Sammy Cahn).*

MUSIC BY Carl Stalling.

Released on April 7

(7 min./Vitaphone Sound/Technicolor)

Warner Bros.

THE FAIR HAIRED HARE (1951) D: I. [Friz] Freleng.

VOICES: *Mel Blanc.*

A court rules that Yosemite Sam must share his house with Bugs Bunny because Sam built over his rabbit hole. However, Sam plans to do away with his newfound housemate. Blanc is Bugs, Sam, and the judge. Entry in the LOONEY TUNES series.

SONGS: "Home on the Range" *(Daniel E. Kelly; sung by Blanc as Bugs),* "I Can't Get Along Little Dogie" *(M.K. Jerome; Jack Scholl; sung by Blanc as Sam).*

MUSIC BY Carl Stalling.

Released on April 14

(7 min./Vitaphone Sound/Technicolor/Video)

Warner Bros.

A HOUND FOR TROUBLE (1951) D: Charles M. [Chuck] Jones.

VOICES: *Mel Blanc, Michael Maltese.*

Charlie Dog, still searching for a master, settles on an Italian restaurant owner — who is not receptive to Charlie's charms. The pooch then tries to serve a customer…with disastrous results. Blanc is Charlie, Pasquale, the Captain and some Italians. Entry in the LOONEY TUNES series.

SONGS: "Atsa Matter for You" *(Michael Maltese),* "La Danza" *(Gioacchino Rossini).*

MUSIC BY Carl Stalling.

Released on April 28

(7 min./Vitaphone Sound/Technicolor/DVD)

Warner Bros.

EARLY TO BET (1951) D: Robert McKimson.
VOICES: *Mel Blanc, Stan Freberg.*
A series of penalties await a luckless cat when he loses at gambling. Blanc is the cat, the dog, the customer, Luigi, and the bar patrons. Entry in the MERRIE MELODIES series.
MUSIC BY Carl Stalling.
Released on May 12
(7 min./Vitaphone Sound/Technicolor/DVD)
Warner Bros.

RABBIT FIRE (1951) D: Charles M. [Chuck] Jones.
VOICES: *Mel Blanc, Arthur Q. Bryan.*
Elmer Fudd doesn't know whether to hunt ducks or rabbits when Bugs Bunny and Daffy Duck each insist the other are in season. Blanc is Bugs, Daffy, and the elephant.
MUSIC BY Carl Stalling.
Released on May 19
(7 min./Vitaphone Sound/Technicolor/Video/DVD)
Warner Bros.

WICKET WACKY (1951) D: No director credited *(Walter Lantz).*
VOICES: *Grace Stafford, Mel Blanc (re-use).*
Woody Woodpecker just wants to enjoy his game of croquet, but he is bothered by a persistently pesky gopher. Blanc provides Woody's laugh.
MUSIC BY Clarence E. Wheeler.
Released on May 28
(6 min./RCA Sound/Technicolor)
Walter Lantz Productions/Universal

ROOM AND BIRD (1951) D: I. [Friz] Freleng.
VOICES: *Mel Blanc, Bea Benaderet.*
A hotel dick tries to enforce the 'no pets' rule, but Sylvester the Cat and Tweety Pie evade him while up to their usual antics. Blanc is Sylvester, Tweety, the mouse, the house detective, the dog and the monkey. Entry in the MERRIE MELODIES series.
SONGS: "Tarantella" from "La Boutique Fantasque Suite" *(Gioacchino Rossini; Ottorino Respighi),* "I'm a Tweet Widdle Bird" *(composer unknown; sung by Blanc as Tweety).*
MUSIC BY Eugene Poddany, Milt Franklyn.
Released on June 2
(7 min./Vitaphone Sound/Technicolor/Video/DVD)
Warner Bros.

CHOW HOUND (1951) D: Charles M. [Chuck] Jones.
VOICES: *Mel Blanc, John T. Smith, Bea Benaderet.*
A despicable dog uses a cat and a pet owner's swindling scheme as his meal ticket. Blanc is the cat, the mouse, a doctor, the old man, Timothy and Butch's owner. Entry in the LOONEY TUNES series.
MUSIC BY Carl Stalling.
Released on June 16
(7 min./Vitaphone Sound/Technicolor)
Warner Bros.

FRENCH RAREBIT (1951) D: Robert McKimson.
VOICES: *Mel Blanc, Tedd Pierce.*
Two rival French chefs battle to get Bugs Bunny as their house special, but the rascally rabbit turns the tables. Blanc is Bugs and Francois. Entry in the MERRIE MELODIES series.
SONGS: "A Stranger in Paree" *(Harry Warren),* "Alouette" *(traditional, composer unknown; sung by Blanc as Louis and Antoine),* "On the Rue de la Paix" *(Werner R. Heymann).*
MUSIC BY Eugene Poddany, Milt Franklyn.
Released on June 30
(7 min./Vitaphone Sound/Technicolor/DVD)
Warner Bros.

THE WEARING OF THE GRIN (1951) D: Charles M. [Chuck] Jones.
VOICES: *Mel Blanc, John T. Smith.*
A surreal experience awaits Porky Pig when he stops over at an Irish castle inhabited by two plotting leprechauns. Blanc is Porky and Paddy. Entry in the LOONEY TUNES series.
SONG: "Come Back to Erin" *(Claribel [Charlotte Alington Barnard]).*
MUSIC BY Eugene Poddany, Milt Franklyn.
Released on July 14
(7 min./Vitaphone Sound/Technicolor/DVD)
Warner Bros.

LEGHORN SWOGGLED (1951) D: Robert McKimson.
VOICES: *Mel Blanc.*
Henery Hawk has some complicated deals with the barnyard dog, a cat, and a mouse just to complete the capture of Foghorn Leghorn. Blanc is Foghorn, the dog, a mouse, and Henery. Entry in the MERRIE MELO-DIES series.
SONG: "Some Sunday Morning" *(M.K. Jerome; Ray Heindorf; Ted Koehler).*
MUSIC BY Eugene Poddany, Milt Franklyn.
Released on July 28
(7 min./Vitaphone Sound/Technicolor)
Warner Bros.

HIS HARE RAISING TALE (1951) D: I. [Friz] Freleng.
VOICES: *Mel Blanc.*
Bugs Bunny entertains his nephew by relating his past exploits. Blanc is Bugs, Clyde Rabbit, the umpire, a ball player and a scientist. Includes footage from *Baseball Bugs* (1946), *Rabbit Punch* (1948), *Falling Hare* . (1943), *Hare Devil Hare* (1948), and *Stage Door Cartoon* (1944). Entry in the LOONEY TUNES series.
MUSIC BY Carl Stalling.
Released on August 11
(6 min./Vitaphone Sound/Technicolor)
Warner Bros.

CHEESE CHASERS (1951) D: Charles M. [Chuck] Jones.
VOICES: *Mel Blanc, Stan Freberg.*
After eating their fill of cheese, mice Hubie and Bert feel there is nothing else to live for. They ask Claude Cat to end it all for them, but Claude is dubious. Blanc is Hubie, Claude, and the dog. Entry in the MERRIE MELODIES series.
SONG: "Wintermarchen" *(Alphons Czibulka).*
MUSIC BY Carl Stalling.
Released on August 28
(7 min./Vitaphone Sound/Technicolor/DVD)
Warner Bros.

LOVELORN LEGHORN (1951) D: Robert McKimson.
VOICES: *Mel Blanc, Bea Benaderet.*
Prissy Chicken goes husband-hunting, so Foghorn Leghorn tells her the barnyard dog is just the 'man' for her. Blanc is Foghorn and the dog. Entry in the LOONEY TUNES series.
MUSIC BY Eugene Poddany, Milt Franklyn.
Released on September 8
(7 min./Vitaphone Sound/Technicolor/DVD)
Warner Bros.

TWEETY'S S.O.S. (1951) D: I. [Friz] Freleng.
VOICES: *Mel Blanc, Bea Benaderet.*
Aboard a ship cruise, Sylvester the Cat takes advantage of Granny's near-sightedness to pursue Tweety Pie. Blanc is Tweety, Sylvester, and the ship's captain. Entry in the MERRIE MELODIES series.
SONG: "Stephanie — Gavotte, Opus 312" *(Alphons Czibulka).*
MUSIC BY Carl Stalling.
Released on September 22
(7 min./Vitaphone Sound/Technicolor/DVD)
Warner Bros.

BALLOT BOX BUNNY (1951) D: I. [Friz] Freleng.
VOICES: *Mel Blanc.*
Bugs Bunny and Yosemite Sam run a violent campaign for mayor. Blanc is Bugs, Sam, a man, an ant, a horse, and the women. Entry in the MERRIE MELODIES series.
SONGS: "Those Endearing Young Charms" *(Sir John Stevenson; Thomas Moore).*
MUSIC BY Carl Stalling.
Released on October 6
(7 min./Vitaphone Sound/Technicolor/Video/DVD)
Warner Bros.

WOODY WOODPECKER POLKA (1951) D: No director credited *(Walter Lantz).*
VOICES: *Grace Stafford, Mel Blanc (re-use), the Starlighters.*
Woody thinks dressing up as a gal will gain him admission to a barn dance offering free food. Blanc provides Woody's laugh.
MUSIC BY Clarence E. Wheeler.
Released on October 29
(6 min./RCA Sound/Technicolor)
Walter Lantz Productions/Universal

SLEEPY TIME POSSUM (1951) D: Robert McKimson.
VOICES: *Mel Blanc.*
Paw Possum cannot keep his lazy son from sleeping the day away, despite his most desperate efforts. Blanc is Ma, Pa and Junior. Entry in the MERRIE MELODIES series.
MUSIC BY Carl Stalling.
Released on November 3
(7 min./Vitaphone Sound/Technicolor)
Warner Bros.

DRIP-ALONG DAFFY (1951) D: Charles M. [Chuck] Jones.
VOICES: *Mel Blanc.*
Western hero Daffy Duck and sidekick Porky Pig ride into Snake Bite
Center to have a showdown with the notorious outlaw *(and square dance
caller)* Nasty Canasta. Blanc is Daffy, Porky, Canasta, the bartender and
the scared ice cubes. Entry in the MERRIE MELODIES series.
SONGS: "The Flower of Gower Gulch" *(Michael Maltese),* "Symphonic
Poem No. 3" from "Preludes" *(Franz Liszt).*
MUSIC BY Carl Stalling.
Released on November 17
(7 min./Vitaphone Sound/Technicolor/Video/DVD)
Warner Bros.

DOG COLLARED (1951) D: Robert McKimson.
VOICES: *Mel Blanc.*
A massive mutt's affections have Porky Pig seeking escape from the slob-
bering and bear-hugging hound. Blanc is Porky, the announcer, the old
man, and the butler. Entry in the MERRIE MELODIES series.
SONG: "In My Merry Oldsmobile" *(Gus Edwards; Vincent Bryan; sung
by Blanc as Porky).*
MUSIC BY Carl Stalling.
Released on December 2
(7 min./Vitaphone Sound/Technicolor/Video)
Warner Bros.

BIG TOP BUNNY (1951) D: Robert McKimson.
VOICES: *Mel Blanc.*
When Bruno the performing bear is replaced by Bugs Bunny in the circus,
the scheming bruin sets out to sabotage Bugs' act. Blanc is Bugs, Bruno,
and Colonel Korny. Entry in the MERRIE MELODIES series.
SONG: "She Was an Acrobat's Daughter" *(Harry Ruby).*
MUSIC BY Carl Stalling.
Released on December 12
(7 min./Vitaphone Sound/Technicolor/Video/DVD)
Warner Bros.

TWEET TWEET TWEETY (1951) D: I. [Friz] Freleng.
VOICES: *Mel Blanc.*
A watchful park ranger causes Sylvester the Cat to be cleverer in his pursuit of Tweety Pie. Blanc is Sylvester, Tweety, and the ranger. Entry in the LOONEY TUNES series.
SONG: "Tweety" *(composer unknown; sung by Blanc as Tweety).*
MUSIC BY Carl Stalling.
Released on December 15
(7 min./Vitaphone Sound/Technicolor/Video/DVD)
Warner Bros.

THE PRIZE PEST (1951) D: Robert McKimson.
VOICES: *Mel Blanc, Tedd Pierce.*
Porky Pig wins Daffy Duck in a radio quiz and tries to find ways to get rid of the manic mallard, but there is a complication: Daffy has a Jekyll-Hyde personality; the nasty side emerges when anyone "tries to push me around!" Blanc is Porky, Daffy, Quiz host and Delivery guy. Entry in the MERRIE MELODIES series.
SONGS: "Lucky Day" *(Ray Henderson; Buddy G. DeSylva; Lew Brown),* "King for a Day" *(Ted Fio Rito; Lewis & Young).*
MUSIC BY Carl Stalling.
Released on December 22
(7 min./Vitaphone Sound/Technicolor)
Warner Bros.

DESTINATION MEATBALL (1951) D: No director credited *(Walter Lantz).*
VOICES: *Grace Stafford, Mel Blanc (re-use).*
Supermarket manager Buzz Buzzard tries to swindle Woody Woodpecker, but some invisible ink allows the redbird to retaliate. Blanc provides Woody's laugh.
MUSIC BY Clarence E. Wheeler.
Released on December 24
(6 min./RCA Sound/Technicolor)
Walter Lantz Productions/Universal-International

WHO'S KITTEN WHO? (1952) D: Robert McKimson.
VOICES: *Mel Blanc.*
Sylvester the Cat tries to teach Junior about mouse-catching and once more runs into Hippety Hopper, the baby kangaroo Sylvester mistakes for a giant mouse. Blanc is Sylvester, Junior, Delivery guy. Entry in the LOONEY TUNES series.
SONG: "Meow" *(Saul Chaplin; Sammy Cahn).*
MUSIC BY Carl Stalling.
Released on January 5
(7 min./Vitaphone Sound/Technicolor)
Warner Bros.

OPERATION: RABBIT (1952) D: Charles M. [Chuck] Jones.
VOICES: *Mel Blanc.*
Wile E. Coyote uses many gadgets in his attempts to capture Bugs Bunny. Blanc is Bugs and Wile E. (who talks this time around). Entry in the LOONEY TUNES series.
SONGS: "What's Up, Doc?" *(Carl Stalling),* "I'm Looking Over a Four Leaf Clover" *(Harry M. Woods; Mort Dixon; sung with substitute lyrics by Blanc as Bugs).*
MUSIC BY Carl Stalling.
Released on January 19
(7 min./Vitaphone Sound/Technicolor/Video/DVD)
Warner Bros.

FEED THE KITTY (1952) D: Charles M. [Chuck] Jones.
VOICES: *Bea Benaderet, Mel Blanc.*
Marc Anthony is a bulldog who has a soft spot for the little kitten he has adopted — but he must hide the cat from his stern mistress. Blanc is Marc Anthony. Entry in the MERRIE MELODIES series.
SONG: "Ain't She Sweet?" *(Milton Ager; Jack Yellen).*
MUSIC BY Carl Stalling.
Released on February 2
(7 min./Vitaphone Sound/Technicolor/DVD)
Warner Bros.

GIFT WRAPPED (1952) D: I. [Friz] Freleng.
VOICES: *Mel Blanc, Bea Benaderet, Daws Butler.*
On Christmas morning, Sylvester the Cat is disappointed to get a rubber mouse instead of a real one. When he sees Granny's gift — Tweety Pie in a cage — Sylvester's (mean) spirits brighten. Blanc is Tweety and Sylvester. Entry in the LOONEY TUNES series.
SONGS: "Hark, the Herald Angels Sing" *(Felix Mendelssohn-Bartholdy; Charles Wesley; sung by Blanc as Tweety and Benaderet as Granny)*, "Jingle Bells" *(James Pierpont; sung by Blanc as Tweety)*, "Deck the Halls" *(traditional, composer unknown)*, "The First Noel" *(traditional, composer unknown)*.
MUSIC BY Carl Stalling.
Released on February 16
(7 min./Vitaphone Sound/Technicolor/DVD)
Warner Bros.

14 CARROT RABBIT (1952) D: I. [Friz] Freleng.
VOICES: *Mel Blanc.*
Bugs Bunny's knack for locating gold intrigues Chilicothe (Yosemite) Sam, who forces the rabbit to become his prospecting partner. Blanc is Bugs, Sam, Louie, Pierre, and the Military Police. Entry in the LOONEY TUNES series.
SONG: "Fiddle Dee Dee" *(Jule Styne; Sammy Cahn; sung by Blanc as Bugs)*.
MUSIC BY Carl Stalling.
Released on February 16
(7 min./Vitaphone Sound/Technicolor/Video/DVD)
Warner Bros.

FOXY BY PROXY (1952) D: I. [Friz] Freleng.
VOICES: *Mel Blanc, Stan Freberg.*
Bugs Bunny (Blanc) uses a fox disguise to have some fun with a pack of hunting dogs. Entry in the MERRIE MELODIES series.
MUSIC BY Carl Stalling.
Released on February 23
(7 min./Vitaphone Sound/Technicolor)
Warner Bros.

THUMB FUN (1952) D: Robert McKimson.
VOICES: *Mel Blanc.*
Hitchhiker Daffy Duck gets a ride with Porky Pig and causes all sorts of trouble. Blanc is Daffy, Porky, the obnoxious motorist and the cop. Entry in the LOONEY TUNES series.
SONG: "This Is the Way We Pack Our Bags [Here We Go Round the Mulberry Bush]" *(traditional melody, composer unknown; sung by Blanc as Daffy).*
MUSIC BY Carl Stalling.
Released on March 1
(7 min./Vitaphone Sound/Technicolor/Video)
Warner Bros.

LITTLE BEAU PEPE (1952) D: Charles M. [Chuck] Jones.
VOICES: *Mel Blanc.*
Pepe Le Pew wishes to join the French Foreign Legion, but changes his mind to romantically pursue a reluctant pussycat. Blanc is Pepe, Sergeant, Recruiting Officer, Captain, cat and the Foreign Legion soldiers. Entry in the MERRIE MELODIES series.
SONGS: "La Vie en Rose" *(Louiguy; Edith Piaf; Mack David)*, "A Vision of Salome" *(J. Bodewalt Lampe; sung with added lyrics by Blanc as Pepe).*
MUSIC BY Carl Stalling.
Released on March 29
(7 min./Vitaphone Sound/Technicolor)
Warner Bros.

KIDDIN' THE KITTEN (1952) D: Robert McKimson.
VOICES: *Sheldon Leonard, Bea Benaderet, Mel Blanc.*
Lazy Dodsworth the Cat has been given an ultimatum: "Get rid of those pesky mice or out you go!" Since this is too labor-intensive for Dodsworth, he cons a kitten to do the work. Blanc is the kitten, the mice, and the 'meowing' for Dodsworth. Entry in the MERRIE MELODIES series.
MUSIC BY Carl Stalling.
Released on April 5
(7 min./Vitaphone Sound/Technicolor/DVD)
Warner Bros.

WATER, WATER, EVERY HARE (1952) D: Charles M. [Chuck] Jones.
VOICES: *Mel Blanc, John T. Smith.*
A flood deposits Bugs Bunny at the castle of a mad scientist who needs a brain for his mechanical monster. Blanc is Bugs, Rudolph, and the mouse. Entry in the LOONEY TUNES series.
MUSIC BY Carl Stalling.
Released on April 19
(7 min./Vitaphone Sound/Technicolor/Video/DVD)
Warner Bros.

STAGE HOAX (1952) D: No director credited *(Walter Lantz).*
VOICES: *Grace Stafford, Mel Blanc (re-use).*
Desert traveler Woody Woodpecker wants to get a ride on a passing stagecoach, but a stubborn driver and outlaw Buzz Buzzard cause problems. Blanc provides Woody's laugh.
MUSIC BY Clarence E. Wheeler.
Released on April 21
(7 min./RCA Sound/Technicolor)
Walter Lantz Productions/Universal-International

LITTLE RED RODENT HOOD (1952) D: I. [Friz] Freleng.
VOICES: *Mel Blanc, Bea Benaderet.*
Timmy the Mouse casts himself in the 'Red Riding Hood' role as he encounters the big, bad Sylvester the Cat. Blanc is Sylvester, Teeny, and the two Cats). Entry in the MERRIE MELODIES series.
MUSIC BY Carl Stalling.
Released on May 3
(7 min./Vitaphone Sound/Technicolor/DVD)
Warner Bros.

SOCK A DOODLE DO (1952) D: Robert McKimson.
VOICES: *Mel Blanc, Sheldon Leonard.*
A punch-drunk rooster who lashes out at the sound of a bell becomes Foghorn Leghorn's pawn in his battle with the barnyard dog. Blanc is Foghorn, the dog, and the cow. Entry in the LOONEY TUNES series.
MUSIC BY Carl Stalling.
Released on May 10
(7 min./Vitaphone Sound/Technicolor)
Warner Bros.

ORANGE BLOSSOMS FOR VIOLET (1952) D: *No director credited.*
VOICES: *Mel Blanc, Bea Benaderet, Robert C. Bruce.*
Live-action short melodrama with a cast of trained monkeys. They enact the story of Violet, who has two suitors — rich, but spoiled Harvey and true-blue Fred. When Violet is kidnapped, Fred comes to the rescue. Blanc lends his vocal talents. Entry in the VITAPHONE NOVELTIES series.
MUSIC BY Howard Jackson.
Released on May 24
(9 min./RCA Sound/DVD)
Warner Bros.

THE HASTY HARE (1952) D: Charles M. [Chuck] Jones.
VOICES: *Mel Blanc.*
Labeled a 'typical Earth specimen,' Bugs Bunny is captured by Marvin Martian and put aboard his spaceship. Blanc is Bugs, Marvin, I. Frisby and the trumpet sound. Entry in the LOONEY TUNES series.
SONG: "Fiddle Dee Dee" *(Jule Styne; Sammy Cahn; sung by Blanc as Bugs).*
MUSIC BY Carl Stalling.
Released on June 7
(7 min./Vitaphone Sound/Technicolor/Video/DVD)
Warner Bros.

WOODPECKER IN THE ROUGH (1952) D: No director credited *(Walter Lantz).*
VOICES: *Grace Stafford, Dick Nelson, Ted Von Eltz, Mel Blanc (re-use).*
Woody Woodpecker takes to the golf links where a bully challenges him to a game — at ten dollars a hole. Blanc provides Woody's laugh.
MUSIC BY Clarence E. Wheeler.
Released on June 16
(6 min./RCA Sound/Technicolor)
Walter Lantz Productions/Universal-International

AIN'T SHE TWEET (1952) D: I. [Friz] Freleng.
VOICES: *Mel Blanc, Bea Benaderet.*
One problem separates Sylvester the Cat and his intended meal, Tweety Pie: a yard full of vicious bulldogs. Blanc is Sylvester and Tweety. Entry in the LOONEY TUNES series.
SONG: "Fiddle Dee Dee" *(Jule Styne; Sammy Cahn; sung by Blanc as Tweety).*
MUSIC BY Carl Stalling.
Released on June 21
(7 min./Vitaphone Sound/Technicolor/DVD)
Warner Bros.

THE TURN-TALE WOLF (1952) D: Robert McKimson.
VOICES: *Mel Blanc.*
The Big Bad Wolf tells his nephew how it was he who was victimized by the Three Little Pigs, not the other way around. Blanc is the wolf, his nephew and the pigs. Entry in the MERRIE MELODIES series.
MUSIC BY Carl Stalling.
Released on June 28
(7 min./Vitaphone Sound/Technicolor/DVD)
Warner Bros.

CRACKED QUACK (1952) D: I. [Friz] Freleng.
VOICES: *Mel Blanc.*
Daffy Duck seeks the warmth of Porky Pig's home during the winter, and figures to pose as a stuffed duck so he can remain inside. Blanc is Porky, Daffy, Rover, the fly, and a duck. Entry in the MERRIE MELODIES series.
MUSIC BY Carl Stalling.
Released on June 5
(7 min./Vitaphone Sound/Technicolor)
Warner Bros.

OILY HARE (1952) D: Robert McKimson.
VOICES: *Mel Blanc, Bea Benaderet.*
Bugs Bunny spars with a Texas millionaire who wants to put an oil derrick above the rascally rabbit's hole. Blanc is Bugs and the millionaire. Entry in the MERRIE MELODIES series.
SONGS: "Home on the Range" *(Daniel E. Kelly; Brewster M. Higley; sung with substitute lyrics by Blanc as Bugs),* "Deep in the Heart of Texas" *(Don Swander; June Hershey),* "Red River Valley" *(traditional, composer unknown).*
MUSIC BY Carl Stalling.
Released on June 26
(7 min./Vitaphone Sound/Technicolor/DVD)
Warner Bros.

HOPPY-GO-LUCKY (1952) D: Robert McKimson.
VOICES: *Mel Blanc, Stan Freberg.*
Sylvester the Cat and his empty-headed feline sidekick Benny go mouse-hunting and encounter Hippety Hopper the Baby Kangaroo. Blanc is Sylvester and the mouse. Entry in the LOONEY TUNES series.
MUSIC BY Carl Stalling.
Released on August 9
(7 min./Vitaphone Sound/Technicolor)
Warner Bros.

A BIRD IN A GUILTY CAGE (1952) D: I. [Friz] Freleng.
VOICES: *Mel Blanc.*
Sylvester the Cat sneaks into a closed department store to go after Tweety Pie. Blanc is Tweety and Sylvester. Entry in the LOONEY TUNES series.
SONGS: "Ain't She Sweet?" *(Milton Ager; Jack Yellen; sung by Blanc as Tweety),* "Oh, You Beautiful Doll" *(Nat D. Ayer; Seymour Brown),* "Tip Toe Through the Tulips" *(Joseph Burke; Al Dubin).*
MUSIC BY Carl Stalling.
Released on August 30
(7 min./Vitaphone Sound/Technicolor/Video/DVD)
Warner Bros.

SCALP TREATMENT (1952) D: No director credited *(Walter Lantz)*.
VOICES: *Grace Stafford, Dick Nelson, Mel Blanc (re-use)*.
Buzz Buzzard hopes to win the affections of an Indian maid by presenting her with a headdress…made from Woody Woodpecker's scalped feathers. Blanc provides Woody's laugh.
MUSIC BY Clarence E. Wheeler.
Released on September 8
(7 min./RCA Sound/Technicolor)
Walter Lantz Productions/Universal-International

MOUSE-WARMING (1952) D: Charles M. [Chuck] Jones.
VOICE: *Mel Blanc*.
A love-struck mouse becomes the target of hungry Claude Cat. Blanc does vocal effects. Entry in the LOONEY TUNES series.
SONGS: "Three Blind Mice" *(traditional, composer unknown)*, "Sweethearts" *(Victor Herbert)*, "My Buddy" *(Walter Donaldson; Gus Kahn)*, "About a Quarter to Nine" *(Harry Warren; Al Dubin)*, "My Lucky Day" *(Silvio Hein; Edward Clark)*.
MUSIC BY Carl Stalling, Milt Franklyn.
Released on September 8
(7 min./Vitaphone Sound/Technicolor)
Warner Bros.

RABBIT SEASONING (1952) D: Charles M. [Chuck] Jones.
VOICES: *Mel Blanc, Arthur Q. Bryan*.
Elmer Fudd cannot decide who to shoot, Bugs Bunny or Daffy Duck — thanks to some verbal one-upmanship between the two targets. Blanc is Bugs and Daffy. Entry in the MERRIE MELODIES series.
SONG: "What's Up, Doc?" *(Carl Stalling)*.
MUSIC BY Carl Stalling.
Released on September 20
(7 min./Vitaphone Sound/Technicolor/DVD)
Warner Bros.

TREE FOR TWO (1952) D: I. [Friz] Freleng.
VOICES: *Mel Blanc, Stan Freberg.*
Just as Spike the Bulldog is about to thrash Sylvester the Cat, an escaped panther tears up the mutt — a pattern that repeats itself every time Spike goes after the lisping cat. Blanc is Sylvester and Spike. Entry in the MERRIE MELODIES series.
SONG: "Charleston" *(James P. Johnson; Cecil Mack; sung by Blanc as Sylvester).*
MUSIC BY Carl Stalling.
Released on October 4
(7 min./Vitaphone Sound/Technicolor)
Warner Bros.

THE EGGCITED ROOSTER (1952) D: Robert McKimson.
VOICES: *Mel Blanc, Marian Richman.*
Foghorn Leghorn is baby-sitting his wife's egg when Henery Hawk and the barnyard dog show up to complicate matters. Blanc is Foghorn, Henery, and the dog. Entry in the MERRIE MELODIES series.
MUSIC BY Carl Stalling.
Released on October 4
(7 min./Vitaphone Sound/Technicolor)
Warner Bros.

THE SUPER SNOOPER (1952) D: Robert McKimson.
VOICES: *Mel Blanc, Grace Lenard.*
Private eye Duck Drake, alias Daffy Duck, is summoned to a posh mansion to solve a mystery and meets a seductive female duck. Blanc is Daffy, the Butler and a phone voice. Entry in the LOONEY TUNES series.
MUSIC BY Carl Stalling.
Released on November 11
(7 min./Vitaphone Sound/Technicolor/Video/DVD)
Warner Bros.

RABBIT'S KIN (1952) D: Robert McKimson.
VOICES: *Mel Blanc, Stan Freberg.*
When Pete Puma sets out after Shorty Rabbit, Bugs Bunny enters into
a battle of wits with the 'unarmed' Pete. Blanc is Bugs and Shorty. Entry
in the MERRIE MELODIES series.
MUSIC BY Carl Stalling.
Released on November 15
(7 min./Vitaphone Sound/Technicolor/DVD)
Warner Bros.

TERRIER STRICKEN (1952) D: Charles M. [Chuck] Jones.
VOICES: *Bea Benaderet, Mel Blanc.*
Frisky Puppy needs a bath, but it's Claude Cat who ends up all wet. Blanc
is Claude and Frisky. Entry in the MERRIE MELODIES series.
MUSIC BY Carl Stalling.
Released on November 29
(7 min./Vitaphone Sound/Technicolor)
Warner Bros.

FOOL COVERAGE (1952) D: Robert McKimson.
VOICES: *Mel Blanc.*
High-pressure insurance salesman Daffy Duck tries to sell Porky Pig an
accident policy by setting up a series of violent mishaps in Porky's home.
Blanc is Daffy and Porky. Entry in the LOONEY TUNES series.
MUSIC BY Carl Stalling.
Released on December 13
(7 min./Vitaphone Sound/Technicolor/Video)
Warner Bros.

HARE LIFT (1952) D: I. [Friz] Freleng.
VOICES: *Mel Blanc.*
A curious Bugs Bunny is touring a large airplane when bank robber Yosemite Sam rushes in; he forces the rascally rabbit at gunpoint to pilot the craft for a getaway. Blanc is Bugs and Sam. Entry in the LOONEY TUNES series.
SONG: "Captains of the Clouds" *(Harold Arlen; Johnny Mercer; sung by Blanc as Bugs).*
MUSIC BY Carl Stalling.
Released on December 20
(7 min./Vitaphone Sound/Technicolor)
Warner Bros.

DON'T GIVE UP THE SHEEP (1953) D: Charles M. [Chuck] Jones.
VOICES: *Mel Blanc.*
Ralph Wolf would like to carry off some lambs, but Sam Sheepdog steadfastly guards the flock. Blanc is Ralph, Sam and the wildcat. Entry in the LOONEY TUNES series.
MUSIC BY Carl Stalling.
Released on January 3
(7 min./Vitaphone Sound/Technicolor/DVD)
Warner Bros.

SNOW BUSINESS (1953) D: I. [Friz] Freleng.
VOICES: *Mel Blanc, Bea Benaderet.*
Snowbound in a mountain cabin, Sylvester the Cat and Tweety Pie need food. There is birdseed, however, so Tweety won't starve…and neither will Sylvester, if he can get his paws on the elusive little bird. Blanc is Tweety, Sylvester, the mouse, the man, and the radio reporter. Entry in the LOONEY TUNES series.
SONG: "Song of the Marines (We're Shovin' Right Off Again)" *(Harry Warren; Al Dubin; sung by Blanc as Tweety).*
MUSIC BY Carl Stalling.
Released on January 17
(7 min./Vitaphone Sound/Technicolor/Video/DVD)
Warner Bros.

A MOUSE DIVIDED (1953) D: I. [Friz] Freleng.
VOICES: *Mel Blanc, Bea Benaderet.*
The stork gets drunk and delivers a baby mouse to Sylvester the Cat's home. His paternal instincts take over his predatory ones when other cats try to abduct the youngster. Blanc is Sylvester, the Stork, some cats and a mouse. Entry in the MERRIE MELODIES series.
MUSIC BY Carl Stalling.
Released on January 31
(6½ min./Vitaphone Sound/Technicolor)
Warner Bros.

FORWARD MARCH HARE (1953) D: Charles M. [Chuck] Jones.
VOICES: *Mel Blanc, John T. Smith.*
Bugs Bunny is accidentally drafted into the army and causes trouble for a harried sergeant. Blanc is Bugs, a draftee, a doctor, an optometrist, a colonel, and a general. Entry in the LOONEY TUNES series.
SONG: "Singin' in the Bathtub" *(Michael Cleary; Herb Magidson; Ned Washington, sung by Blanc as Bugs).*
MUSIC BY Carl Stalling, Milt Franklyn.
Released on February 4
(7 min./Vitaphone Sound/Technicolor/Video/DVD)
Warner Bros.

KISS ME CAT (1953) D: Charles M. [Chuck] Jones.
VOICES: *Mel Blanc, Bea Benaderet.*
Marc Antony the Bulldog realizes his kitten-ward Pussyfoot must catch mice in order to remain in the household. Marc takes up teaching the cute cat how to hunt rodents through a series of mishaps. Blanc is Marc Antony, Pussyfoot, Tom, and the mouse. Entry in the LOONEY TUNES series.
MUSIC BY Carl Stalling.
Released on February 21
(6½ min./Vitaphone Sound/Technicolor/DVD)
Warner Bros.

DUCK AMUCK (1953) D: Charles M. [Chuck] Jones.
VOICES: *Mel Blanc.*
Daffy Duck argues with the cartoonist who keeps drawing him into offbeat situations. Blanc is Daffy and (in a cameo) Bugs Bunny. Entry in the MERRIE MELODIES series.
SONGS: "Jingle Bells" *(James Pierpont; sung by Blanc as Daffy)*, "The Song of the Marines" *(Harry Warren; Al Dubin; sung by Blanc as Daffy)*, "Aloha Oe *(Farewell to Thee)*" *(Queen Liliuokalani; sung by Blanc as Daffy)*, "Daffy Duck He Had a Farm [Old MacDonald]" *(traditional, composer unknown; sung by Blanc as Daffy)*.
MUSIC BY Carl Stalling.
Released on February 28
(7 min./Vitaphone Sound/Technicolor/DVD)
Warner Bros.

UPSWEPT HARE (1953) D: Robert McKimson.
VOICES: *Mel Blanc, Arthur Q. Bryan.*
Elmer Fudd wants Bugs Bunny (Blanc) to vacate his penthouse apartment and ends up in an 'anything-you-can-do-I-can-do-better' contest. Entry in the MERRIE MELODIES series.
SONG: "There's No Place Like Home (Home Sweet Home)" *(H.R. Bishop; John Howard Payne; sung with substitute lyrics by Blanc as Bugs).*
MUSIC BY Carl Stalling.
Released on March 14
(6½ min./Vitaphone Sound/Technicolor/Video)
Warner Bros.

A PECK O' TROUBLE (1953) D: Robert McKimson.
VOICES: *Sheldon Leonard, Mel Blanc.*
Lazy cat Dodsworth recruits a kitten to do the 'dirty work' of catching a woodpecker for his meal. Blanc does some vocal effects. Entry in the LOONEY TUNES series.
MUSIC BY Carl Stalling.
Released on March 28
(7 min./Vitaphone Sound/Technicolor/DVD)
Warner Bros.

FOWL WEATHER (1953) D: I. [Friz] Freleng.
VOICES: *Mel Blanc, Bea Benaderet.*
On the farm, Sylvester the Cat chases Tweety Pie — who is protected by Hector the Bulldog and a rooster. Blanc is Tweety, Sylvester, Hector, the rooster, and the hen. Entry in the MERRIE MELODIES series.
SONGS: "Kiss Me, Sweet" *(Milton Drake; sung by Blanc as Tweety),* "Down in Nashville, Tennessee" *(David Mann; Bob Hilliard).*
MUSIC BY Carl Stalling.
Released on April 4
(7 min./Vitaphone Sound/Technicolor/Video)
Warner Bros.

MUSCLE TUSSLE (1953) D: Robert McKimson.
VOICES: *Mel Blanc, Gladys Holland.*
When Daffy Duck loses his girl to muscular Hunky, the manic mallard beefs up his courage and takes on his rival in a series of strength competitions. Blanc is Daffy, Hunky and salesman. Entry in the MERRIE MELODIES series.
MUSIC BY Carl Stalling.
Released on April 18
(7 min./Vitaphone Sound/Technicolor)
Warner Bros.

SOUTHERN FRIED RABBIT (1953) D: I. [Friz] Freleng.
VOICES: *Mel Blanc.*
Colonel Yosemite Sam is a one-man defender of the South, trying to keep out "fur-bearin' Yankee" Bugs Bunny. Blanc is Bugs and Sam. Entry in the LOONEY TUNES series.
SONGS: "Dixie" *(Daniel Decatur Emmett; sung by Blanc as Bugs),* "Old Black Joe" *(Stephen Foster; sung by Blanc as Bugs),* "My Old Kentucky Home" *(Foster; sung by Blanc as Bugs),* "Yankee Doodle" *(traditional, composer unknown; sung by Blanc as Bugs).*
MUSIC BY Carl Stalling.
Released on May 2
(7 min./Vitaphone Sound/Technicolor/DVD)
Warner Bros.

ANT PASTED (1953) D: I. [Friz] Freleng.
VOICES: *Arthur Q. Bryan, Mel Blanc.*
When Elmer Fudd noisily celebrates the Fourth of July, a colony of angry
ants declares war. Blanc is the ants. Entry in the LOONEY TUNES series.
MUSIC BY Carl Stalling.
Released on May 9
(7 min./Vitaphone Sound/Technicolor/Video)
Warner Bros.

THERE AUTO BE A LAW (1953) D: Robert McKimson.
VOICES: *John T. Smith, Bea Benaderet, Mel Blanc.*
A timid motorist (Blanc) continually tries to get off a clover-leaf highway
amid gags concerning automobiles. Entry in the LOONEY TUNES series.
MUSIC BY Carl Stalling.
Released on June 6
(7 min./Vitaphone Sound/Technicolor)
Warner Bros.

HARE TRIMMED (1953) D: I. [Friz] Freleng.
VOICES: *Mel Blanc, Bea Benaderet.*
Bugs Bunny steps in to protect wealthy Granny when fortune-hunting
Yosemite Sam tries to marry her. Blanc is Bugs, Sam, and the minister.
Entry in the MERRIE MELODIES series.
MUSIC BY Carl Stalling.
Released on June 20
(7 min./Vitaphone Sound/Technicolor)
Warner Bros.

TOM TOM TOMCAT (1953) D: I. [Friz] Freleng.
VOICES: *Mel Blanc, Bea Benaderet.*
It's a frontier setting for Tweety Pie and Granny as their covered wagon
is attacked by 'Indians' that look suspiciously like Sylvester the Cat. Blanc
is Tweety, Sylvester, and the cat chief. Entry in the MERRIE MELODIES
series.
MUSIC BY Carl Stalling.
Released on June 27
(6 min./Vitaphone Sound/Technicolor)
Warner Bros.

WILD OVER YOU (1953) D: Charles M. [Chuck] Jones.
VOICES: *Mel Blanc.*
An escaped wildcat from the Paris Exhibition thinks she has it made, until she contends with the persistent amorous (and odorous) advances of skunk Pepe LePew. Blanc is Pepe, the wildcat, the zookeeper, 'Le Hyena,' the newsboy, 'Le Policier,' and a dog. Entry in the LOONEY TUNES series.
SONGS: "Billy Boy" *(traditional, composer unknown; sung with substitute lyrics by Blanc as Pepe),* "Oh, Dear, What Can the Matter Be?" *(traditional, composer unknown; sung by Blanc as Pepe).*
MUSIC BY Carl Stalling.
Released on July 11
(7 min./Vitaphone Sound/Technicolor)
Warner Bros.

DUCK DODGERS IN THE 24½TH CENTURY (1953) D: Charles M. [Chuck] Jones.
VOICES: *Mel Blanc.*
Duck Dodgers (a.k.a. Daffy Duck) and space cadet Porky Pig blast off for Planet X on a mission to procure a needed compound. However, when they arrive, Marvin Martian has claimed the planet for Mars. Blanc is Daffy, Porky, Marvin and Dr. I. Q. Hi. Entry in the MERRIE MELODIES series.
MUSIC BY Carl Stalling.
Released on July 25
(7 min./Vitaphone Sound/Technicolor/Video/DVD)
Warner Bros.

BULLY FOR BUGS (1953) D: Charles M. [Chuck] Jones.
VOICES: *Mel Blanc.*
Bugs Bunny (sorely in need of a compass) burrows into the middle of a Mexican bullring and does battle with a snorting, terrible toro. Blanc is Bugs and the gulping sound of the bull. Entry in the LOONEY TUNES series.
SONGS: "La Cucaracha" *(Mexican traditional, composer unknown),* "Mexican Hat Dance" *(Felipe A. Partichela),* "Las Chiapanecas" *(Mexican traditional, composer unknown).*
MUSIC BY Carl Stalling.
Released on August 8
(7 min./Vitaphone Sound/Technicolor/Video/DVD)
Warner Bros.

PLOP GOES THE WEASEL (1953) D: Robert McKimson.
VOICES: *Mel Blanc.*
The latest round in the on-going war between Foghorn Leghorn and Barnyard Dog sees a hungry weasel added to the proceedings. Blanc is Foghorn, Dog and the weasel. Entry in the LOONEY TUNES series.
MUSIC BY Carl Stalling.
Released on August 22
(7 min./Vitaphone Sound/Technicolor)
Warner Bros.

CAT-TAILS FOR TWO (1953) D: Robert McKimson.
VOICES: *Mel Blanc, Stan Freberg.*
Fast-moving Mexican mouse Speedy Gonzales makes his first appearance as two cats attempt to catch the rapid rodent. Blanc is Speedy and George the Cat. Entry in the MERRIE MELODIES series.
MUSIC BY Carl Stalling.
Released on August 29
(7 min./Vitaphone Sound/Technicolor/DVD)
Warner Bros.

A STREET CAT NAMED SYLVESTER (1953) D: I. [Friz] Freleng.
VOICES: *Mel Blanc, Bea Benaderet.*
Sylvester the Cat lets Tweety Pie in from the cold, but his chase is complicated by interference from Granny and a laid-up Hector Bulldog. Blanc is Tweety, Sylvester, and Hector. Entry in the LOONEY TUNES series.
MUSIC BY Carl Stalling.
Released on September 5
(7 min./Vitaphone Sound/Technicolor)
Warner Bros.

DUCK! RABBIT! DUCK! (1953) D: Charles M. [Chuck] Jones.
VOICES: *Mel Blanc, Arthur Q. Bryan.*
Crafty Daffy Duck puts hunter Elmer Fudd on the trail of Bugs Bunny when he removes all the 'duck season' signs, but Bugs has a few tricks of his own. Blanc is Bugs and Daffy. Entry in the MERRIE MELODIES series.
MUSIC BY Carl Stalling.
Released on October 3
(7 min./Vitaphone Sound/Technicolor/DVD)
Warner Bros.

EASY PECKIN'S (1953) D: Robert McKimson.
VOICES: *Mel Blanc, Gladys Holland.*
A fox eyes a poultry farm full of hens, but runs into tough George the Rooster. Blanc is the fox, hens, and George. Entry in the LOONEY TUNES series.
MUSIC BY Carl Stalling.
Released on October 17
(7 min./Vitaphone Sound/Technicolor)
Warner Bros.

CATTY CORNERED (1953) D: I. [Friz] Freleng.
VOICES: *Mel Blanc.*
Sylvester the Cat's hungry pursuit of Tweety Pie is hampered by a gang of kidnappers who are holding the little yellow bird for ransom. Blanc is Sylvester, Tweety, Rocky, Nick, the newsboy, the news reporter, a police officer, a photographer, and the mayor. Entry in the MERRIE MELODIES series.
MUSIC BY Carl Stalling.
Released on October 31
(7 min./Vitaphone Sound/Technicolor/Video)
Warner Bros.

OF RICE AND HEN (1953) D: Robert McKimson.
VOICES: *Mel Blanc, Bea Benaderet.*
Old maid hen Miss Prissy sets her sights on Foghorn Leghorn, but he likes the bachelor life — until a disguised Barnyard Dog becomes an attentive suitor to her. Blanc is Foghorn, Dog, and the rooster minister. Entry in the LOONEY TUNES series.
SONGS: "Lady of Spain" *(Tolchard Evans; Erell Reaves),* "Frankie and Johnny" *(Leighton Brothers; Ren Shields).*
MUSIC BY Carl Stalling.
Released on November 14
(7 min./Vitaphone Sound/Technicolor)
Warner Bros.

CATS A-WEIGH! (1953) D: Robert McKimson.
VOICES: *Mel Blanc.*
Sylvester the Cat and Junior are official 'ship's cats,' charged with the duty of recapturing baby kangaroo Hippety Hopper when the lad escapes his cage. Blanc is Sylvester, Junior and the roaring mouse. Entry in the MERRIE MELODIES series.
MUSIC BY Carl Stalling.
Released on November 28
(7 min./Vitaphone Sound/Technicolor)
Warner Bros.

ROBOT RABBIT (1953) D: I. [Friz] Freleng.
VOICES: *Mel Blanc, Arthur Q. Bryan.*
Elmer Fudd employs a robot rabbit-hunter to kick Bugs Bunny out of his carrot patch. Blanc is Bugs and the horse. Entry in the LOONEY TUNES series.
SONGS: "It's Magic" *(Jule Styne; Sammy Cahn; sung by Blanc as Bugs),* "In a Little Red Barn (On a Farm in Indiana)" *(Milton Ager; Joe Young), (sung by Blanc as Bugs and Bryan as Elmer).*
MUSIC BY Carl Stalling.
Released on December 12
(7 min./Vitaphone Sound/Technicolor/Video)
Warner Bros.

PUNCH TRUNK (1953) D: Charles M. [Chuck] Jones.
VOICES: *Robert C. Bruce, Mel Blanc, Marian Richman.*
A miniature elephant receives a wide array of goofy reactions from the people who see it. Blanc is the birdbath owner, asylum collector, John, a drunk, a circus cat, and Dr. Robert Bruce Cameron *(an in-joke parodying the name of Blanc's co-actor Robert C. Bruce).* Entry in the LOONEY TUNES series.
MUSIC BY Carl Stalling.
Released on December 19
(7 min./Vitaphone Sound/Technicolor)
Warner Bros.

DOG POUNDED (1954) D: I. [Friz] Freleng.
VOICES: *Mel Blanc.*
Tweety Pie has found a secure place away from Sylvester the Cat: in a nest located in the middle of a dog pound…but do you thinks that will stop persistent (and glutton for punishment) Sylvester? Blanc is Tweety, Sylvester, the dogs, the dogcatcher, and Pepe LePew. Entry in the LOONEY TUNES series.
SONG: "Moonlight Bay" *(Percy Wenrich; Edward Madden; sung by Blanc as Tweety).*
MUSIC BY Carl Stalling.
Released on January 2
(7 min./Vitaphone Sound/Technicolor)
Warner Bros.

I GOPHER YOU (1954) D: I. [Friz] Freleng.
VOICES: *Mel Blanc, Stan Freberg.*
The Goofy Gophers spar with the mechanical workings of a food-processing plant. Blanc is Mac. Entry in the MERRIE MELODIES series.
MUSIC BY Carl Stalling, Milt Franklyn.
Released on January 30
(7 min./Vitaphone Sound/Technicolor)
Warner Bros.

FELINE FRAME-UP (1954) D: Charles M. [Chuck] Jones.
VOICES: *Robert C. Bruce, Mel Blanc.*
Claude Cat successfully gets Marc Antony the Bulldog booted out of the house, leaving little kitten Pussyfoot at the mercy of jealous Claude. Blanc is Claude and dog effects. Entry in the LOONEY TUNES series.
MUSIC BY Carl Stalling.
Released on February 13
(7 min./Vitaphone Sound/Technicolor/Video)
Warner Bros.

CAPTAIN HAREBLOWER (1954) D: I. [Friz] Freleng.
VOICES: *Mel Blanc.*
Pirate (Yosemite) Sam has an explosive time trying to capture Bugs
Bunny's ship. Blanc is Bugs, Sam, the captain, and the crewmen. Entry
in the MERRIE MELODIES series.
MUSIC BY Carl Stalling.
Released on February 16
(7 min./Vitaphone Sound/Technicolor/Video)
Warner Bros.

WILD WIFE (1954) D: Robert McKimson.
VOICES: *Bea Benaderet, Mel Blanc.*
A harried housewife tries to explain to her unsympathetic husband how
she spent her unlucky day. Blanc is John, Son, the mailman, the bank
teller, Red Cross nurse, Casper J. Fragile, a soda jerk, a pedestrian, and
the officer. Entry in the MERRIE MELODIES series.
SONG: "Can't We Talk It Over" *(Victor Young).*
MUSIC BY Carl Stalling.
Released on February 20
(7 min./Vitaphone Sound/Technicolor)
Warner Bros.

NO BARKING (1954) D: Charles M. [Chuck] Jones.
VOICES: *Mel Blanc.*
Claude Cat just wants to catch a bird for breakfast, but a barking puppy
makes him too jumpy. Blanc is Tweety, and various cat and dog effects.
Entry in the MERRIE MELODIES series.
MUSIC BY Carl Stalling, Milt Franklyn.
Released on February 27
(7 min./Vitaphone Sound/Technicolor/DVD)
Warner Bros.

BUGS AND THUGS (1954) D: I. [Friz] Freleng.
VOICES: *Mel Blanc.*
Bugs Bunny, in the city bank to make a carrot withdrawal, hails a taxi and winds up in the getaway car of robbers Rocky and Mugsy. The hoods proceed to take the rabbit 'for a ride,' but Bugs has other thoughts. Blanc is Bugs, Rocky, Mugsy, and the two policemen. Entry in the LOONEY TUNES series.
SONG: "Please Be Kind" *(Saul Chaplin; Sammy Cahn).*
MUSIC BY Milt Franklyn.
Released on March 2
(7 min./Vitaphone Sound/Technicolor/DVD)
Warner Bros.

THE CATS BAH (1954) D: Charles M. [Chuck] Jones.
VOICES: *Mel Blanc, Bea Benaderet.*
Pepe LePew tells of how he 'liberated' a female cat from its owner for an interlude of amorous misadventure. Blanc is Pepe and the camel. Entry in the LOONEY TUNES series.
SONGS: "Cherie, I Love You *(Cherie, Je T'aime)" (Lillian Goodman; sung by Blanc as Pepe),* "As Time Goes By" *(Herman Hupfeld; sung by Blanc as Pepe).*
MUSIC BY Carl Stalling.
Released on March 20
(7 min./Vitaphone Sound/Technicolor)
Warner Bros.

DESIGN FOR LEAVING (1954) D: Robert McKimson.
VOICES: *Mel Blanc, Arthur Q. Bryan.*
Daffy Duck barges in on Elmer Fudd, demonstrating his line of super-modern household accessories — which turn the home into a shambles. Blanc is Daffy, the delivery guy and the mechanical dog. Entry in the LOONEY TUNES series.
MUSIC BY Carl Stalling.
Released on March 27
(7 min./Vitaphone Sound/Technicolor/Video)
Warner Bros.

BELL HOPPY (1954) D: Robert McKimson.
VOICES: *Mel Blanc, Tedd Pierce.*
Sylvester the Cat wants to join an alley-cat club, but the fraternity refuses
to admit him until he catches a giant mouse…enter Hippety Hopper the
Baby Kangaroo. Blanc is Sylvester, the second cat and two men. Entry in
the MERRIE MELODIES series.
MUSIC BY Carl Stalling.
Released on April 17
(7 min./Vitaphone Sound/Technicolor)
Warner Bros.

NO PARKING HARE (1954) D: Robert McKimson.
VOICES: *Mel Blanc, John T. Smith.*
A tough construction worker gets himself battered trying to build a
freeway through Bugs Bunny's rabbit hole. Blanc is Bugs. Entry in the
LOONEY TUNES series.
MUSIC BY Carl Stalling.
Released on May 1
(7 min./Vitaphone Sound/Technicolor)
Warner Bros.

DR. JERKYL'S HIDE (1954) D: I. [Friz] Freleng.
VOICES: *Mel Blanc, Stan Freberg.*
Alfie (a.k.a. Spike) the Bulldog thinks he will have a good time thrashing
Sylvester the Cat, not realizing Sylvester has consumed a mad doctor's
monster formula. Blanc is Sylvester and Alfie. Entry in the LOONEY
TUNES series.
MUSIC BY Carl Stalling.
Released on May 8
(7 min./Vitaphone Sound/Technicolor)
Warner Bros.

CLAWS FOR ALARM (1954) D: Charles M. [Chuck] Jones.
VOICES: *Mel Blanc.*
Porky Pig (Blanc) and a mute Sylvester the Cat stay at a ghost town hotel, where murderous mice wish to do them harm. Entry in the MERRIE MELODIES series.
SONG: "Home on the Range" *(Daniel E. Kelly; Brewster M. Higley; sung by Blanc as Porky).*
MUSIC BY Carl Stalling.
Released on May 22
(7 min./Vitaphone Sound/Technicolor/DVD)
Warner Bros.

LITTLE BOY BOO (1954) D: Robert McKimson.
VOICES: *Mel Blanc, Gladys Holland.*
Foghorn Leghorn's bid to charm his way into Widow Hen's cozy roost leaves him playing ersatz father to the chicken's super-smart son. Blanc is Foghorn and the son. Entry in the LOONEY TUNES series.
MUSIC BY Carl Stalling.
Released on June 5
(7 min./Vitaphone Sound/Technicolor)
Warner Bros.

DEVIL MAY HARE (1954) D: Robert McKimson.
VOICES: *Mel Blanc.*
Bugs Bunny stalls off a hungry Tasmanian Devil by trying to interest the beast in a variety of other booby-trapped 'animals.' Blanc is Bugs, Devil, female devil noises, and the turtle. Entry in the LOONEY TUNES series.
MUSIC BY Carl Stalling.
Released on June 19
(7 min./Vitaphone Sound/Technicolor/Video/DVD)
Warner Bros.

MUZZLE TOUGH (1954) D: I. [Friz] Freleng.
VOICES: *Mel Blanc, Bea Benaderet.*
Sylvester the Cat's new neighbors are moving in: Granny, Tweety Pie, and Hector Bulldog. Sylvester uses various ploys to sneak in and get Tweety. Blanc is Sylvester, Tweety, Hector, and the other dogs. Entry in the MERRIE MELODIES series.
SONG: "It Had to Be You" *(Isham Jones; Gus Kahn).*
MUSIC BY Carl Stalling.
Released on June 26
(7 min./Vitaphone Sound/Technicolor)
Warner Bros.

THE OILY AMERICAN (1954) D: Robert McKimson.
VOICES: *Mel Blanc.*
Moe Hican, a wealthy Indian, and his butler go hunting a resourceful midget moose. Blanc is Moe Hican, the butler and the delivery guy. Entry in the MERRIE MELODIES series.
MUSIC BY Carl Stalling.
Released on July 10
(7 min./Vitaphone Sound/Technicolor)
Warner Bros.

BEWITCHED BUNNY (1954) D: Charles M. [Chuck] Jones.
VOICES: *Mel Blanc, Bea Benaderet.*
Bugs Bunny snatches Hansel and Gretel from the clutches of Witch Hazel, who vents her nefarious frustration on the rascally rabbit. Blanc is Bugs, Hansel, Prince Charming and the broom noises. Entry in the LOONEY TUNES series.
SONGS: "Rock-a-Bye Rabbit [Baby]" *(Effie I. Canning),* "Quizas, Quizas, Quizas" *(Osvaldo Farres).*
MUSIC BY Carl Stalling.
Released on July 24
(7 min./Vitaphone Sound/Technicolor/DVD)
Warner Bros.

SATAN'S WAITIN' (1954) D: I. [Friz] Freleng.
VOICES: *Mel Blanc.*
Devil Dog wants to claim Sylvester the Cat's soul, but the lisping feline has nine lives. The canine Satan isn't worried — if Sylvester keeps violently chasing after Tweety Pie, he'll soon use them up. Blanc is Sylvester, Tweety, Mugsy, Robber and Devil Dog. Entry in the LOONEY TUNES series.
MUSIC BY Carl Stalling.
Released on August 7
(7 min./Vitaphone Sound/Technicolor)
Warner Bros.

STOP! LOOK! AND HASTEN! (1954) D: Charles M. [Chuck] Jones.
VOICES: *Paul Julian, Mel Blanc.*
Tired of licking empty cans, Wile E. Coyote uses a Burmese tiger trap, a spring-up road wall, and leg vitamins to catch the Road Runner. Blanc provides the tiger's vocal effects. Entry in the MERRIE MELODIES series.
MUSIC BY Carl Stalling.
Released on August 14
(7 min./Vitaphone Sound/Technicolor/Video/DVD)
Warner Bros.

YANKEE DOODLE BUGS (1954) D: I. [Friz] Freleng.
VOICES: *Mel Blanc, Bea Benaderet.*
Bugs Bunny teaches his nephew Clyde about how rabbits made American history. Blanc is Bugs, Clyde, Indian, Ben Franklin, Man, King, George Washington. Entry in the LOONEY TUNES series.
MUSIC BY Milt Franklyn.
Released on August 28
(6 min./Vitaphone Sound/Technicolor/DVD)
Warner Bros.

GONE BATTY (1954) D: Robert McKimson.
VOICES: *Robert C. Bruce, Mel Blanc.*
Bobo the Elephant helps the Sweetwater Schnooks in their baseball game against the cheating Greenville Goons. Blanc is the baseball players, the umpire and the second heckler. Entry in the LOONEY TUNES series.
MUSIC BY Carl Stalling.
Released on September 4
(7 min./Vitaphone Sound/Technicolor)
Warner Bros.

GOO GOO GOLIATH (1954) D: I. [Friz] Freleng.
VOICES: *Norman Nesbitt, Mel Blanc, Marian Richman.*
A drunken stork delivers Mrs. Giant's baby to a normal suburban couple by mistake; when the stinko bird returns to fix his mix-up, the titanic toddler has already tried on the Brown Derby and fallen asleep in the Statue of Liberty's arms. Blanc is the Stork, John, Intercom voice and Captain O'Brien. Entry in the MERRIE MELODIES series.
MUSIC BY Carl Stalling.
Released on September 18
(7 min./Vitaphone Sound/Technicolor)
Warner Bros.

BY WORD OF MOUSE (1954) D: I. [Friz] Freleng.
VOICES: *Mel Blanc, Stan Freberg, Walker Edmiston.*
An explanation of America's economic system is the backdrop of this cartoon that sees Sylvester the Cat chasing after a professor mouse. Blanc is Sylvester, Hans, Uncle, Aunt, the elevator operator, and the mice children. Entry in the LOONEY TUNES series.
MUSIC BY Milt Franklyn.
Released on October 2
(7 min./Vitaphone Sound/Technicolor)
Alfred P. Sloane Foundation/Warner Bros.

FROM A TO Z-Z-Z-Z (1954) D: Charles M. [Chuck] Jones.
VOICES: *Dick Beals, Marian Richman, Norman Nesbitt, Mel Blanc.*
The mundane goings-on at school are embellished by little Ralph Phillips' adventurous imagination. Blanc is the numbers, Indians, and the shark. Entry in the LOONEY TUNES series.
MUSIC BY Carl Stalling.
Academy Award Nomination *(Short Subject – Cartoon)* Edward Selzer.
Released on October 16
(7 min./Vitaphone Sound/Technicolor/DVD)
Warner Bros.

QUACK SHOT (1954) D: Robert McKimson.
VOICES: *Mel Blanc, Arthur Q. Bryan.*
Daffy Duck uses booby-trapped decoys, a boatful of explosives, and other devices to deter Elmer Fudd from duck-hunting. Blanc is Daffy and the large fish. Entry in the MERRIE MELODIES series.
MUSIC BY Carl Stalling.
Released on October 30
(7 min./Vitaphone Sound/Technicolor)
Warner Bros.

LUMBER JACK-RABBIT (1954) D: Charles M. [Chuck] Jones.
VOICES: *Mel Blanc, Norman Nesbitt.*
Bugs Bunny finds himself in Paul Bunyan country, where the carrots are gigantic. They are also guarded by Bunyan's enormous puppy 'Smidgen.' Blanc is Bugs and Smidgen. Entry in the LOONEY TUNES series.
SONG: "The Blue-Tail Fly" *(traditional folk song, composer unknown; sung by Blanc as Bugs).*
MUSIC BY Carl Stalling.
Released on November 13
(7 min./Vitaphone Sound/Technicolor/3-D/Video)
Warner Bros.

MY LITTLE DUCKAROO (1954) D: Charles M. [Chuck] Jones.
VOICES: *Mel Blanc.*
Western hero the Masked Avenger (a.k.a. Daffy Duck) and sidekick Porky Pig pursue outlaw Nasty Canasta, who committed the unspeakable crime of square-dancing in a roundhouse. Blanc is Daffy, Porky and Nasty Canasta. Entry in the MERRIE MELODIES series.
SONG: "Lazy Will" *(Michael Maltese; sung by Blanc as Porky).*
MUSIC BY Milt Franklyn.
Released on November 27
(7 min./Vitaphone Sound/Technicolor/Video)
Warner Bros.

SHEEP AHOY (1954) D: Charles M. [Chuck] Jones.
VOICES: *Mel Blanc.*
George *(Ralph)* Wolf uses pole-vaulting, a smoke-screen bomb, and a
bicycle-powered submarine to get to the flock guarded by Fred (Sam)
Sheepdog. Blanc is all the characters. Entry in the MERRIE MELODIES
series.
MUSIC BY Carl Stalling, Milt Franklyn.
Released on December 11
(7 min./Vitaphone Sound/Technicolor)
Warner Bros.

BABY BUGGY BUNNY (1954) D: Charles M. [Chuck] Jones.
VOICES: *Mel Blanc.*
Finster, a bank-robbing midget, disguises himself as a baby and ends up
on Bugs Bunny's doorstep. Getting wise, the rascally rabbit indulges in
some punishing parenting to keep the little gangster at bay. Blanc is Bugs,
Finster, the TV reporter, the sergeant, and Clancy. Entry in the MERRIE
MELODIES series.
SONG: "We're in the Money" *(Harry Warren; Al Dubin; sung by Blanc as
Bugs).*
MUSIC BY Milt Franklyn.
Released on December 18
(7 min./Vitaphone Sound/Technicolor/DVD)
Warner Bros.

SANDY CLAWS (1954) D: I. [Friz] Freleng.
VOICES: *Mel Blanc, Bea Benaderet.*
A day at the beach leaves Tweety Pie stranded on a rock in the sea.
Sylvester the Cat attempts a 'rescue,' but he has to be clever to stay ahead
of the sharks. Blanc is Tweety and Sylvester. Entry in the LOONEY TUNES
series.
SONG: "Love Ya" *(Peter DeRose; Charles Tobias).*
MUSIC BY Carl Stalling, Milt Franklyn.
Academy Award Nomination *(Short Subjects – Cartoon)* Edward Selzer.
Released in December, 1954
(7 min./Vitaphone Sound/Technicolor/Video/DVD)
Warner Bros.

PIZZICATO PUSSYCAT (1955) D: I. [Friz] Freleng.
VOICES: *Norman Nesbitt, Mel Blanc, Marian Richman.*
Mistaken identity leads a cat to the stage of Carnegie Hall to give a piano concert. Blanc is the first doctor, two voices, the third critic, John, the mouse and the cat. Entry in the MERRIE MELODIES series.
SONGS: "The Minute Waltz" *(Frederic Chopin),* "Crazy Rhythm" *(Joseph Meyer; Roger Wolfe Kahn),* "Liebestraum — No. 3" *(Franz Liszt).*
MUSIC BY Milt Franklyn.
Released on January 1
(7 min./Vitaphone Sound/Technicolor/DVD)
Warner Bros.

A HITCH IN TIME (1955) D: Chuck Jones.
VOICE: *Mel Blanc.*
About to leave the Air Force, John McRogers meets 'technical gremlin first class' Grogan (Blanc) — who also says he is departing the service. However, before they go, the pair is shown a comparison of monetary benefits between civilian and military life. A special production for the United States Air Force.
MUSIC BY Milt Franklyn.
(6 min./color)
The United States Air Force/Warner Bros.

FEATHER DUSTED (1955) D: Robert McKimson.
VOICES: *Mel Blanc, Bea Benaderet.*
Foghorn Leghorn decides to make a he-boy-chicken out of Miss Prissy's bookworm son, but the Southern rooster ends up arrested, blasted, and shot full of holes. Blanc is Foghorn and a cop. Entry in the MERRIE MELODIES series.
MUSIC BY Milt Franklyn.
Released on January 15
(7 min./Vitaphones Sound/Technicolor)
Warner Bros.

PESTS FOR GUESTS (1955) D: I. [Friz] Freleng.
VOICES: *Arthur Q. Bryan, Mel Blanc, Stan Freberg.*
A cascade of nuts fouls Elmer Fudd's pursuit of the Goofy Gophers. Blanc
is Mac and the salesman. Entry in the MERRIE MELODIES series.
MUSIC BY Milt Franklyn.
Released on January 29
(7 min./Vitaphone Sound/Technicolor/Video)
Warner Bros.

BEANSTALK BUNNY (1955) D: Charles M. [Chuck] Jones.
VOICES: *Mel Blanc, Arthur Q. Bryan.*
Bugs Bunny and Daffy Duck climb the fabled beanstalk, where they come
face-to-face with a gigantic Elmer Fudd. Blanc is Bugs, Daffy and Jack.
Entry in the MERRIE MELODIES series.
MUSIC BY Carl Stalling.
Released on February 12
(7 min./Vitaphone Sound/Technicolor)
Warner Bros.

ALL FOWLED UP (1955) D: Robert McKimson.
VOICES: *Mel Blanc.*
Getting himself in shape to badger Barnyard Dog, Foghorn Leghorn
also has to deal with chicken-hunting Henery Hawk. Blanc is Foghorn,
Henery, and the Dog. Entry in the LOONEY TUNES series.
MUSIC BY Carl Stalling.
Released on February 19
(7 min./Vitaphone Sound/Technicolor/Video)
Warner Bros.

STORK NAKED (1955) D: I. [Friz] Freleng.
VOICES: *Mel Blanc.*
Daffy Duck sets up a bunch of obstacles to keep a delivery away from
the drunken stork. Blanc is Daffy, the stork, Mr. Pierce, the Frenchman,
Indianb, Daffy's wife and the baby stork. Entry in the MERRIE MELO-
DIES series.
MUSIC BY Milt Franklyn.
Released on February 26
(7 min./Vitaphone Sound/Technicolor/Video)
Warner Bros.

LIGHTHOUSE MOUSE (1955) D: Robert McKimson.
VOICES: *Mel Blanc.*
A pesky mouse has turned off the lighthouse beacon, causing a ship to run aground and free baby kangaroo Hippety Hopper. Sylvester the Cat must catch the mouse or receive a thrashing from the keeper, but the lisping feline runs into Hippety. Blanc is Sylvester, the lighthouse keeper, the captain and the parrot. Entry in the MERRIE MELODIES series.
SONG: "I Cover the Waterfront" *(Johnny Green; Edward Heyman).*
MUSIC BY Milt Franklyn.
Released on March 12
(7 min./Vitaphone Sound/Technicolor)
Warner Bros.

SAHARA HARE (1955) D: I. [Friz] Freleng.
VOICES: *Mel Blanc.*
Bugs Bunny thinks it's Miami Beach, but that 'wrong turn at Albuquerque' has landed him in the Sahara Desert — angering Arab troublemaker Riff-Raff (Yosemite) Sam. Bugs takes refuge in a Foreign Legion fort, but Sam is close behind. Blanc is Bugs, Sam, and Daffy Duck. Entry in the LOONEY TUNES series.
SONG: "Singin' in the Bathtub" *(Michael Cleary; Herb Magidson; Ned Washington; sung by Blanc as Bugs).*
MUSIC BY Milt Franklyn.
Released on March 26
(7 min./Vitaphone Sound/Technicolor/Video/DVD)
Warner Bros.

THE HOLE IDEA (1955) D: Robert McKimson.
VOICES: *Mel Blanc, Robert C. Bruce, Bea Benaderet.*
Professor Calvin Q. Calculus (Blanc) invents the portable hole, which is used by golfers, bone-burying dogs, and a clever crook. Blanc is the Professor, the newsreader, the newsboy and the devil. Entry in the LOONEY TUNES series.
MUSIC BY Milt Franklyn.
Released on April 16
(7 min./Vitaphone Sound/Technicolor/Video)
Warner Bros.

HARE BRUSH (1955) D: I. [Friz] Freleng.
VOICES: *Mel Blanc, Arthur Q. Bryan.*
A psychological mix-up has Bugs Bunny and Elmer Fudd exchanging roles when Bugs visits Mr. Fudd in a sanitarium. Blanc is Bugs, the chairman of the board, the board members, Dr. Oro Myicin, the driver, a bear, and the revenue agent. Entry in the MERRIE MELODIES series.
MUSIC BY Milt Franklyn.
Released on May 7
(7 min./Vitaphone Sound/Technicolor)
Warner Bros.

PAST PERFUMANCE (1955) D: Charles M. [Chuck] Jones.
VOICES: *Mel Blanc, Arthur Q. Bryan, Michael Maltese.*
A silent movie needs a skunk, so a prop man paints a white stripe on a cat — which catches the eye of polecat 'lovair' Pepe LePew. Blanc is Pepe, the director, the assistant, the guard and the second director. Entry in the MERRIE MELODIES series.
MUSIC BY Milt Franklyn.
Released on May 21
(7 min./Vitaphone Sound/Technicolor)
Warner Bros.

TWEETY'S CIRCUS (1955) D: I. [Friz] Freleng.
VOICES: *Mel Blanc.*
While chasing Tweety Pie at the circus, Sylvester the Cat antagonizes a lion and an elephant. Blanc is Sylvester and Tweety. Entry in the MERRIE MELODIES series.
SONG: "Meow" *(Saul Chaplin; Sammy Cahn; sung by Blanc as Sylvester).*
MUSIC BY Milt Franklyn.
Released on June 4
(7 min./Vitaphone Sound/Technicolor/Video)
Warner Bros.

RABBIT RAMPAGE (1955) D: Charles M. [Chuck] Jones.
VOICES: *Mel Blanc, Arthur Q. Bryan.*
A troublesome animator takes out his ire on an increasingly irritated Bugs
Bunny (Blanc). Entry in the LOONEY TUNES series.
MUSIC BY Milt Franklyn.
Released on June 11
(6½ min./Vitaphone Sound/Technicolor/Video)
Warner Bros.

LUMBER JERKS (1955) D: I. [Friz] Freleng.
VOICES: *Mel Blanc, Stan Freberg.*
The Goofy Gophers' new tree-home is uprooted and brought to a furniture
factory, but the two rodents are determined to rebuild their abode — one
piece of furniture at a time. Blanc is Mac and the second driver. Entry in
the LOONEY TUNES series.
MUSIC BY Milt Franklyn.
Released on June 25
(7 min./Vitaphone Sound/Technicolor/DVD)
Warner Bros.

THIS IS A LIFE? (1955) D: I. [Friz] Freleng.
VOICES: *Mel Blanc, Arthur Q. Bryan, June Foray.*
Television host Elmer Fudd has Bugs Bunny give a rundown of his cel-
ebrated life as Daffy Duck and Yosemite Sam begin to fume. Blanc is
Bugs, Daffy, Sam and an announcer. Includes footage from *A Hare Grows
In Manhattan* (1947), *Hare Do* (1949), and *Buccaneer Bunny* (1948). Entry
in the MERRIE MELODIES series.
MUSIC BY Milt Franklyn.
Released on July 9
(6 min./Vitaphone Sound/Technicolor)
Warner Bros.

DOUBLE OR MUTTON (1955) D: Charles M. [Chuck] Jones.
VOICES: *Mel Blanc.*
Ralph Wolf clocks in to begin work stealing sheep, but Sam Sheepdog is one step ahead of the cagey lamb-napper — who uses a high wire and a 'Little Bo Peep' costume as ploys. Blanc is Sam and Ralph. Entry in the LOONEY TUNES series.
SONG: "Mary Had a Little Lamb" *(traditional, composer unknown).*
MUSIC BY Milt Franklyn.
Released on July 13
(7 min./Vitaphone Sound/Technicolor/Video)
Warner Bros.

JUMPIN' JUPITER (1955) D: Charles M. [Chuck] Jones.
VOICE: *Mel Blanc.*
Porky Pig doesn't seem to notice his entire campsite has been abducted by a Jupiterian vulture. However, a frantic *(and mute)* Sylvester the Cat tries desperately to alert his porcine master. Blanc is Porky, coyote howl and vocal effects for Sylvester. Entry in the MERRIE MELODIES series.
MUSIC BY Carl Stalling.
Released on August 6
(7 min./Vitaphone Sound/Technicolor/Video)
Warner Bros.

A KIDDIE'S KITTY (1955) D: I. [Friz] Freleng.
VOICES: *Mel Blanc, June Foray, Lucille Bliss.*
A rough-handed little girl 'adopts' a fleeing Sylvester the Cat *(who doesn't talk)* and puts him through several abusive games. Blanc is cat sounds, the TV announcer, and the bulldog. Entry in the MERRIE MELODIES series.
MUSIC BY Milt Franklyn.
Released on August 20
(7 min./Vitaphone Sound/Technicolor)
Warner Bros.

HYDE AND HARE (1955) D: I. [Friz] Freleng.
VOICES: *Mel Blanc, Jack Edwards.*
A kindly doctor has taken Bugs Bunny in as a pet…Dr. Jekyll, that is. The evil, ax-wielding Mr. Hyde is not too far away. Blanc is Bugs and Jekyll. Entry in the LOONEY TUNES series.
SONG: "Minute Waltz" *(Frederic Chopin).*
MUSIC BY Carl Stalling.
Released on August 27
(7 min./RCA Sound/Technicolor/DVD)
Warner Bros.

DIME TO RETIRE (1955) D: Robert McKimson.
VOICES: *Mel Blanc.*
Daffy Duck's hotel has rooms for only ten cents, but charges customer Porky Pig over $600 to get rid of an increasing number of bothersome pests. Blanc is Daffy, Porky, and cat/dog effects. Entry in the LOONEY TUNES series.
MUSIC BY Milt Franklyn.
Released on September 3
(7 min./Vitaphone Sound/Technicolor/Video)
Warner Bros.

SPEEDY GONZALES (1955) D: I. [Friz] Freleng.
VOICES: *Mel Blanc, Jack Edwards.*
The local mice cannot get any cheese because it is guarded by Sylvester the Cat. The rodents call in Speedy Gonzales to take on Sylvester. Blanc is Speedy and Sylvester, and the second and third mice. Entry in the MERRIE MELODIES series.
MUSIC BY Carl Stalling.
Academy Award *(Short Subjects – Cartoon)* Edward Selzer.
Released on September 17
(7 min./Vitaphone Sound/Technicolor/DVD)
Warner Bros.

KNIGHT-MARE HARE (1955) D: Chuck Jones.
VOICES: *Mel Blanc.*
Bugs Bunny gets a knock on the head, sending him back to medieval times — where he thwarts a knight, extinguishes a fire-breathing dragon, and out-duels Merlin the Magician. Blanc is Bugs, Sir Osis, King, Merlin, and the donkey owner. Entry in the MERRIE MELODIES series.
MUSIC BY Milt Franklyn.
Released on October 1
(7 min./Vitaphone Sound/Technicolor/Video/DVD)
Warner Bros.

TWO SCENT'S WORTH (1955) D: Charles M. [Chuck] Jones.
VOICE: *Mel Blanc.*
A French bank-robber gives himself up after encountering Pepe LePew (Blanc), leaving his cat-accomplice to fend off the amorous skunk. Blanc is Pepe, the robber, the cat and three bank customers. Entry in the MERRIE MELODIES series.
MUSIC BY Milt Franklyn.
Released on October 15
(7 min./Vitaphone Sound/Technicolor/Video)
Warner Bros.

RED RIDING HOODWINKED (1955) D: I. [Friz] Freleng.
VOICES: *Mel Blanc, June Foray.*
When Red Riding Hood takes the bus to Granny's house with Tweety Pie as a gift, Sylvester the Cat and a vacant-headed wolf vie for the yellow morsel. Blanc is Tweety, Sylvester, and the wolf. Entry in the LOONEY TUNES series.
MUSIC BY Milt Franklyn.
Released on October 29
(7 min./Vitaphone Sound/Technicolor/Video/DVD)
Warner Bros.

ROMAN LEGION-HARE (1955) D: Friz Freleng.
VOICES: *Mel Blanc.*
In Rome, 54 AD, Emperor Nero demands a victim for the arena of lions
and charges Captain (Yosemite) Sam of the Roman Guard to find one.
Sam settles on Bugs Bunny. Blanc is Bugs, Sam, Nero, a guard, and the
commentator. Entry in the LOONEY TUNES series.
SONG: "Taps" *(General Daniel Butterfield).*
MUSIC BY Milt Franklyn.
Released on November 12
(7 min./Vitaphone Sound/Technicolor/DVD)
Warner Bros.

HEIR CONDITIONED (1955) D: Friz Freleng.
VOICES: *Mel Blanc, Arthur Q. Bryan, Daws Butler.*
Sylvester the Cat inherits a fortune and wants to live high with his alley-
cat buddies, but lawyer Elmer Fudd shows him (and us) why investing
the money would help the economy. Educational cartoon with Blanc as
Sylvester, Tweety, and Johnny. Entry in the LOONEY TUNES series.
MUSIC BY Milt Franklyn.
Released on November 26
(7 min./Vitaphone Sound/Technicolor)
Sloane Foundation/Warner Bros.

PAPPY'S PUPPY (1955) D: Friz Freleng.
VOICE: *Mel Blanc.*
Sylvester the Cat tries to rid himself of the attack-pup offspring of his
neighbor, Butch J. Bulldog. Blanc is the stork and vocal effects. Entry in
the MERRIE MELODIES series.
MUSIC BY Carl Stalling.
Released on December 17
(7 min./Vitaphone Sound/Technicolor)
Warner Bros.

90 DAY WONDERING (1956) D: Chuck Jones.
VOICES: *Mel Blanc, Daws Butler.*
Ralph Phillips' hitch in the military is over and he is eager to return to
civilian life. When he finds things have changed in his hometown, two
characters — Pete and Re-Pete — argue the pros and cons of re-enlisting.
Blanc provides his vocal talents.
SONGS: "Happy Days Are Here Again" *(Milton Ager; Jack Yellen),* "A Hot
Time in the Old Town Tonight" *(Theo A. Metz; Joe Hayden),* "The Caisson
Song" *(Edmund L. Gruber),* "By the Beautiful Sea" *(Harry Carroll; Harold
R. Atteridge),* "Reveille" *(traditional, composer unknown).*
MUSIC BY Milt Franklyn.
(6 min./color/DVD)
The United States Air Force/Warner Bros.

BUGS' BONNETS (1956) D: Chuck Jones.
VOICES: *Mel Blanc, Arthur Q. Bryan, Robert C. Bruce.*
A variety of hats has a mood-changing effect on the personalities of Bugs
Bunny (Blanc) and Elmer Fudd during one of their chases. Entry in the
MERRIE MELODIES series.
MUSIC BY Milt Franklyn.
Released on January 14
(7 min./Vitaphone Sound/Technicolor/DVD)
Warner Bros.

TOO HOP TO HANDLE (1956) D: Robert McKimson.
VOICES: *Mel Blanc.*
Sylvester the Cat complains there are no mice around, so Junior does
the 'pied piper' bit to attract some rodents. However, Hippety Hopper
the Baby Kangaroo becomes curious about the music. Blanc is Sylvester,
Junior, the zoo official, the man in the park and sounds for a dog, a pig
and a cow. Entry in the LOONEY TUNES series.
MUSIC BY Milt Franklyn.
Released on January 28
(6 min./Vitaphone Sound/Technicolor)
Warner Bros.

WEASEL STOP (1956) D: Robert McKimson.
VOICES: *Mel Blanc, Lloyd Perryman.*
Foghorn Leghorn and Willy the Weasel team up to haze a Southern guard dog who likes to whittle. Blanc is Foghorn, Willy, the barking of the dog, and a hen. Entry in the MERRIE MELODIES series.
MUSIC BY Milt Franklyn.
Released on February 11
(7 min./Vitaphone Sound/Technicolor)
Warner Bros.

THE HIGH AND THE FLIGHTY (1956) D: Robert McKimson.
VOICES: *Mel Blanc.*
Salesman Daffy Duck ramps up the feud between Foghorn Leghorn and Barnyard Dog when he sells them a batch of joke-playing novelties. Blanc is Daffy, Foghorn, and Dog. Entry in the MERRIE MELODIES series.
SONG: "This Is the Way We Bounce the Ball [Here We Go Round the Mulberry Bush]" *(traditional, composer unknown; sung by Blanc as Foghorn).*
MUSIC BY Carl Stalling.
Released on February 18
(7 min./Vitaphone Sound/Technicolor/Video)
Warner Bros.

BROOM-STICK BUNNY (1956) D: Chuck Jones.
VOICES: *Mel Blanc, June Foray.*
Witch Hazel, jealous of Bugs Bunny's ugly Halloween costume, plots to make the rascally rabbit an ingredient in her brew. Blanc is Bugs and the genie. Entry in the LOONEY TUNES series.
MUSIC BY Milt Franklyn.
Released on February 25
(7 min./Vitaphone Sound/Technicolor/DVD)
Warner Bros.

ROCKET SQUAD (1956) D: Chuck Jones.
VOICES: *Mel Blanc.*
Space Age cops Daffy Duck and Porky Pig (a.k.a. Sergeant Joe Monday and Detective Shmoe Tuesday) deadpan their way through their pursuit of the flying saucer bandit. Blanc is Daffy, Porky, George 'Mother' Machree, the chief, and the narrator. Entry in the MERRIE MELODIES series.
SONG: "Mother Machree" *(Ernest Ball; Chauncey Olcott).*
MUSIC BY Milt Franklyn.
Released on March 10
(7 min./Vitaphone Sound/Technicolor/Video/DVD)
Warner Bros.

TWEET AND SOUR (1956) D: Friz Freleng.
VOICES: *Mel Blanc, June Foray.*
Under threat of his life, Sylvester the Cat is charged with protecting Tweety Pie from an orange, one-eyed alley feline. Blanc is Sylvester and Tweety. Entry in the LOONEY TUNES series.
MUSIC BY Milt Franklyn.
Released on March 24
(7 min./Vitaphone Sound/Technicolor/Video)
Warner Bros.

HEAVEN SCENT (1956) D: Chuck Jones.
VOICE: *Mel Blanc.*
A female cat poses as a skunk to ward off a pack of dogs, but has trouble doing the same to love-struck Pepe LePew. Blanc is Pepe, the Cat, dog barks and the fisherman. Entry in the MERRIE MELODIES series.
SONG: "The Band Played On" *(Charles B. Ward; John F. Palmer; sung by Blanc as Pepe).*
MUSIC BY Milt Franklyn.
Released on March 31
(6 min./Vitaphone Sound/Technicolor)
Warner Bros.

MIXED MASTER (1956) D: Robert McKimson.
VOICES: *Mel Blanc, June Foray.*
A mutt in a new household tries to prove to the master that he is a pedigreed pooch. Blanc is Harry and dog sounds. Entry in the LOONEY TUNES series.
MUSIC BY Milt Franklyn.
Released on April 14
(7 min./Vitaphone Sound/Technicolor)
Warner Bros.

RABBITSON CRUSOE (1956) D: Friz Freleng.
VOICES: *Mel Blanc.*
Island castaway Yosemite Sam spies Bugs Bunny washed ashore and quickly attempts to get the rabbit in his stew pot. However, a pesky shark complicates matters. Blanc is Bugs, Sam and Dopey Dick. Entry in the LOONEY TUNES series.
SONGS: "Trade Winds" *(Cliff Friend; Charles Tobias; sung by Blanc as Bugs),* "Secret Love" *(Sammy Fain; Paul Francis Webster; sung by Blanc as Bugs).*
MUSIC BY Milt Franklyn.
Released on April 28
(7 min./Vitaphone Sound/Technicolor/Video)
Warner Bros.

TREE CORNERED TWEETY (1956) D: Friz Freleng.
VOICES: *Mel Blanc, June Foray.*
Ala Dragnet's Jack Webb, Tweety Pie relates his encounters with "a bwack puddy tat, wed nose, white chest, name: Sylvester." Blanc is Tweety and the fisherman. Entry in the MERRIE MELODIES series.
MUSIC BY Milt Franklyn.
Released on May 19
(6½ min./Vitaphone Sound/Technicolor/Video)
Warner Bros.

THE UNEXPECTED PEST (1956) D: Robert McKimson.
VOICES: *Mel Blanc, June Foray.*
A shortage of mice threatens Sylvester the Cat's posh position in a household, so he imports a lone mouse to make it look like a rodent infestation. Blanc is Sylvester, the mouse, and John. Entry in the MERRIE MELODIES series.
MUSIC BY Carl Stalling.
Released on June 2
(6 min./Vitaphone Sound/Technicolor/DVD)
Warner Bros.

NAPOLEON BUNNY-PART (1956) D: Friz Freleng.
VOICES: *Mel Blanc.*
Bugs Bunny tunnels into France and heckles the little emperor Napoleon, who thinks the rabbit should be executed as a spy. Blanc is Bugs, Napoleon, the guard, two men in white coats. Entry in the MERRIE MELODIES series.
SONG: "Le Marseillaise" *(Claude Joseph Rouget de Lisle).*
MUSIC BY Carl Stalling.
Released on June 16
(7 min./Vitaphone Sound/Technicolor)
Warner Bros.

TUGBOAT GRANNY (1956) D: Friz Freleng.
VOICES: *Mel Blanc, June Foray.*
Sylvester the Cat sees Tweety Pie aboard a tugboat and utilizes a variety of watercraft in his thwarted attempts to board the tug. Blanc is Sylvester, Tweety, the fisherman, the fish, and engine effects. Entry in the MERRIE MELODIES series.
MUSIC BY Milt Franklyn.
Released on June 23
(7 min./Vitaphone Sound/Technicolor)
Warner Bros.

STUPOR DUCK (1956) D: Robert McKimson.
VOICES: *Mel Blanc, Daws Butler.*
Mild-mannered reporter Cluck Trent (a.k.a. Daffy Duck) dons the heroic mantle of Stupor Duck to battle the evil Aardvark Ratnick's scheme to destroy the world. Blanc is Daffy, Aardvark, second voice and first climber. Entry in the LOONEY TUNES series.
MUSIC BY Carl Stalling.
Released on July 17
(7 min./Vitaphone Sound/Technicolor/Video/DVD)
Warner Bros.

BARBARY-COAST BUNNY (1956) D: Chuck Jones.
VOICES: *Mel Blanc, Daws Butler.*
When Nasty Canasta steals Bugs Bunny's solid gold boulder, the rascally rabbit ventures into Canasta's casino and wittily cleans him out. Blanc is Bugs. Entry in the LOONEY TUNES series.
SONG: "My Darlin' Clementine" *(Percy Montrose).*
MUSIC BY Carl Stalling.
Released on July 21
(7 min./Vitaphone Sound/Technicolor/Video/DVD)
Warner Bros.

HALF-FARE HARE (1956) D: Robert McKimson.
VOICES: *Mel Blanc, Daws Butler.*
A Tennessee-bound train is the setting for a chase between Bugs Bunny and a pair of hungry hobos, who are cartoon clones of The Honeymooners' Ralph Kramden and Ed Norton. Blanc is Bugs, train caller and detective. Entry in the MERRIE MELODIES series.
MUSIC BY Carl Stalling.
Released on August 18
(7 min./Vitaphone Sound/Technicolor)
Warner Bros.

RAW! RAW! ROOSTER (1956) D: Robert McKimson.
VOICES: *Mel Blanc, Daws Butler.*
Foghorn Leghorn's old college nemesis, Rhode Island Red, visits the
farm — spurring the Southern rooster's efforts to get rid of him. Blanc is
Foghorn and the dazed voice of Red. Entry in the LOONEY TUNES series.
MUSIC BY Carl Stalling.
Released on August 25
(7 min./Vitaphone Sound/Technicolor) Warner Bros.

THE SLAP-HOPPY MOUSE (1956) D: Robert McKimson.
VOICES: *Mel Blanc.*
It is rumored that Sylvester the Cat is past his prime as a mouse-catcher.
To prove the contrary to Junior, Sylvester goes to a rundown house —
where escaped baby kangaroo Hippety Hopper is hiding. Blanc is
Sylvester and Junior. Entry in the MERRIE MELODIES series.
MUSIC BY Carl Stalling.
Released on September 1
(7 min./Vitaphone Sound/Technicolor)
Warner Bros.

A STAR IS BORED (1956) D: Friz Freleng.
VOICES: *Mel Blanc, Arthur Q. Bryan, June Foray.*
Daffy Duck lands a job as Bugs Bunny's stunt-double as they shoot a
motion picture. Daffy has thoughts of elevating his importance at the
studio by sabotaging Bugs, but the violent stunts curtail his enthusiasm.
Blanc is Bugs, Daffy, Yosemite Sam, the producer, the German director
and the assistant. Entry in the LOONEY TUNES series.
MUSIC BY Carl Stalling.
Released on September 15
(7 min./Vitaphone Sound/Technicolor/Video/DVD)
Warner Bros.

DEDUCE, YOU SAY (1956) D: Chuck Jones.
VOICES: *Mel Blanc, June Foray.*
Dorlock Holmes and aide Watkins (a.k.a. Daffy Duck and Porky Pig) get on the trail of the Shropshire Slasher, but run afoul of his flower-peddling 'mum.' Blanc is Daffy, Porky, the Slasher, a telegram boy, Alfie, and the bartender. Entry in the LOONEY TUNES series.
MUSIC BY Milt Franklyn.
Released on September 29
(7 min./Vitaphone Sound/Technicolor/DVD)
Warner Bros.

YANKEE DOOD IT (1956) D: Friz Freleng.
VOICES: *Arthur Q. Bryan, Daws Butler, Mel Blanc.*
Elf king Elmer Fudd recalls his workers from the shop of a shoemaker who needs a lesson in economics and productivity. Educational cartoon with Blanc as Sylvester the Cat. Entry in the MERRIE MELODIES series.
MUSIC BY Milt Franklyn.
Released on October 13
(7 min./Vitaphone Sound/Technicolor)
Sloan Foundation/Warner Bros.

WIDEO WABBIT (1956) D: Robert McKimson.
VOICES: *Mel Blanc, Arthur Q. Bryan, Daws Butler.*
Conned into becoming a target on Elmer Fudd's hunting show, Bugs Bunny escapes and eludes Elmer in the TV studio by visiting the sets of 'You Beat Your Wife,' 'You're Asking for It,' 'Liverace,' and 'You Were There.' Blanc is Bugs, the TV producer, Liverace, and the yelping voice of Elmer. Entry in the MERRIE MELODIES series.
SONG: "Lucky Day" *(Ray Henderson; Lew Brown; Buddy G. DeSylva; sung by Blanc as Bugs).*
MUSIC BY Carl Stalling.
Released on October 27
(6½ min./Vitaphone Sound/Technicolor/Video/DVD)
Warner Bros.

TO HARE IS HUMAN (1956) D: Chuck Jones.
VOICES: *Mel Blanc.*
As a change of pace, Wile E. Coyote uses an elaborate computer to help him catch not the Road Runner, but Bugs Bunny. Blanc is Bugs and a talkative Wile E. Entry in the MERRIE MELODIES series.
SONGS: "Sweet Georgia Brown" *(Maceo Pinkard; Kenneth Casey; sung by Blanc as Bugs)*, "Time Waits for No One" *(Cliff Friend; Charles Tobias; sung with substitute lyrics by Blanc as Bugs)*, "(Ho–dle–Ay) Start the Day Right" *(Maurice Spitalny; Al Lewis; Charles Tobias; sung by Blanc as Bugs)*.
MUSIC BY Milt Franklyn.
Released on December 15
(6½ min./Vitaphone Sound/Technicolor/DVD)
Warner Bros.

TWEET ZOO (1957) D: Friz Freleng.
VOICES: *Mel Blanc.*
Sylvester the Cat joins a tour through the zoo and sets his sights on capturing Tweety Pie…but he must also contend with bears, lions, crocodiles, and elephants. Blanc is Sylvester, Tweety, the zoo tour conductor, the rhino, the lion, Cedric and Terry Tiger. Entry in the MERRIE MELODIES series.
MUSIC BY Milt Franklyn.
Released on January 12
(7 min./Vitaphone Sound/Technicolor/Video)
Warner Bros.

ALI BABA BUNNY (1957) D: Chuck Jones.
VOICES: *Mel Blanc.*
Burrowing into a Middle Eastern treasure cave, Bugs Bunny and Daffy Duck also discover it is guarded by giant, sword-wielding Hassan. Blanc is Bugs, Daffy, Hassan, the sultan, and the genie. Entry in the MERRIE MELODIES series.
MUSIC BY Carl Stalling, Milt Franklyn.
Released on February 9
(7 min./Vitaphone Sound/Technicolor/DVD)
Warner Bros.

GO FLY A KIT (1957) D: Chuck Jones.
VOICES: *Daws Butler, Mel Blanc.*
The tale of a flying cat and how he saved his lady-love from the clutches of a nasty bulldog. Blanc is the customer, and cat/dog effects. Entry in the LOONEY TUNES series.
MUSIC BY Milt Franklyn.
Released on February 23
(7 min./Vitaphone Sound/Technicolor/DVD)
Warner Bros.

BEDEVILLED RABBIT (1957) D: Robert McKimson.
VOICES: *Mel Blanc.*
Bugs Bunny, trying to keep off the dinner menu, shows the Tasmanian Devil how to make wild turkey surprise — a powder keg with ruffled decorations. Blanc is Bugs, Tasmanian Devil, the she-devil, and the crocodile. Entry in the MERRIE MELODIES series.
SONG: "Attsa Matter for You" *(Michael Maltese; sung by Blanc as Bugs).*
MUSIC BY Milt Franklyn.
Released on April 13
(6 min./Vitaphone Sound/Technicolor/Video)
Warner Bros.

CHEESE IT, THE CAT! (1957) D: Robert McKimson.
VOICES: *Daws Butler, June Foray, Mel Blanc.*
Mice Ralph Crumbden and Ned Morton set out to steal food from the refrigerator for Alice's surprise party, but cannot get past the cat (Blanc). This is LOONEY TUNES' version of TV's popular *Honeymooners* (here called 'The Honeymousers').
MUSIC BY Carl Stalling, Milt Franklyn.
Released on May 4
(7 min./Vitaphone Sound/Technicolor)
Warner Bros.

FOX-TERROR (1957) D: Robert McKimson.
VOICES: *Mel Blanc.*
A slick, hen-hungry fox tricks Foghorn Leghorn and Barnyard Dog out of the chicken coop, but Foggy and Dog turn the tables on him. Blanc is Foghorn, the dog, the fox and the small rooster. Entry in the MERRIE MELODIES series.
MUSIC BY Carl Stalling, Milt Franklyn.
Released on May 11
(7 min./Vitaphone Sound/Technicolor)
Warner Bros.

TWEETY AND THE BEANSTALK (1957) D: Friz Freleng.
VOICES: *Mel Blanc, June Foray.*
Sylvester the Cat has a towering beanstalk grow under his bed, depositing him in giant-land. He can hardly believe his eyes when he spots an oversized Tweety Pie…but there is also an enormous bulldog around. Blanc is Sylvester, Tweety, the mouse, and the giant. Entry in the MERRIE MELODIES series.
MUSIC BY Milt Franklyn.
Released on May 16
(7 min./Vitaphone Sound/Technicolor/DVD)
Warner Bros.

PIKER'S PEAK (1957) D: Friz Freleng.
VOICES: *Mel Blanc.*
There is a prize of 50,000 'cronkites' for climbing the Schmatterhorn and Yosemite Sam aims to win it. When Bugs Bunny becomes his competition, the red-haired runt plots to get rid of the rabbit. Blanc is Bugs and Sam. Entry in the LOONEY TUNES series.
SONG: "When I Yoo Hoo" *(Henry Russell; Murray Martin).*
MUSIC BY Carl Stalling, Milt Franklyn.
Released on May 25
(7 min./Vitaphone Sound/Technicolor)
Warner Bros.

STEAL WOOL (1957) D: Chuck Jones.
VOICES: *Mel Blanc.*
The 9-to-5 antics of lamb-stealing Ralph Wolf and flock-guard Sam Sheepdog include an explosive mishap on a dynamite bridge and a misfiring giant rubber band. Blanc is Ralph and Sam. Entry in the LOONEY TUNES series.
MUSIC BY Milt Franklyn.
Released on June 8
(7 min./Vitaphone Sound/Technicolor/DVD)
Warner Bros.

BOSTON QUACKIE (1957) D: Robert McKimson.
VOICES: *Mel Blanc, June Foray.*
The 'man in the green hat' steals a valuable attaché case, setting Quackie (i.e. Daffy Duck) on his trail as a train speeds through Europe. Blanc is Daffy, Porky Pig, Waiter, cabbie, Salesman, Narrator, Consulate, Green Hat and dog noises. Entry in the LOONEY TUNES series.
MUSIC BY Milt Franklyn.
Released on June 22
(7 min./Vitaphone Sound/Technicolor/Video)
Warner Bros.

WHAT'S OPERA, DOC? (1957) D: Chuck Jones.
VOICES: *Mel Blanc, Arthur Q. Bryan.*
An adaptation of Richard Wagner's 'ring cycle' opera to a one-reel cartoon. Hunter Elmer Fudd pursues Bugs Bunny, who transforms into a Brunhilde-like rabbit-Valkyrie. Blanc is Bugs and the screaming voice of Elmer. Entry in the MERRIE MELODIES series.
Richard Wagner songs:
"Return My Love" *(with alternate lyrics by Michael Maltese)*, "The Pilgrim's Chorus" from "Tannhauser"
"Overture" and "The Flying Dutchman" from "The Flying Dutchman"
"Overture" from "Tannhauser"
"Rienzi"
"Ride of the Valkyries" from "Die Walkure"
"Horn Call" from "Siegfried"
MUSIC BY Milt Franklyn.
Released on July 6
(7 min./Vitaphone Sound/Technicolor/National Film Registry 1992/DVD)
Warner Bros.

TABASCO ROAD (1957) D: Robert McKimson.
VOICES: *Mel Blanc, Tom Holland.*
Speedy Gonzales has his little paws full trying to keep his drunken mice friends from the clutches of Sylvester the Cat. Blanc is Speedy, Manuel, Pablo, the cat and mice. Entry in the LOONEY TUNES series.
MUSIC BY Carl Stalling, Milt Franklyn.
Academy Award Nomination *(Short Subject – Cartoon)* Edward Selzer.
Released on July 20
(7 min./Vitaphone Sound/Technicolor/DVD)
Warner Bros.

BIRDS ANONYMOUS (1957) D: Friz Freleng.
VOICES: *Mel Blanc.*
Realizing he needs help with his bird-eating addiction, Sylvester the Cat joins a support group to aid him in keeping away from Tweety Pie. Blanc is Sylvester, Tweety, Clarence, Sam, other cats, TV Chef and radio announcer. Entry in the MERRIE MELODIES series.
SONGS: "Bye Bye, Blackbird" *(Ray Henderson; Mort Dixon)*, "When the Red, Red Robin Comes Bob, Bob-Bobbin' Along" *(Harry M. Woods)*, "Tip-Toe Through the Tulips" *(Joseph Burke; Al Dubin).*
MUSIC BY Milt Franklyn.
Academy Award *(Short Subject – Cartoon)* Edward Selzer.
Released on August 10
(7 min./Vitaphone Sound/Technicolor/DVD)
Warner Bros.

DUCKING THE DEVIL (1957) D: Robert McKimson.
VOICES: *Mel Blanc.*
Daffy Duck is after a $5,000 reward for the Tasmanian Devil and learns that music keeps the beast from going on a rampage. Blanc is Daffy, Tasmanian Devil, Zookeeper, Delivery guy, postman, and the announcer. Entry in the MERRIE MELODIES series.
SONGS: "Toujours, L'Amour" *(Rudolf Friml; Catherine Chisholm Cushing), (sung by Blanc as Daffy)*, "I'm Looking Over a Four-Leaf Clover" *(Harry M. Woods; Mort Dixon), (sung by Blanc as Daffy)*, "Carolina in the Morning" *(Walter Donaldson; Gus Kahn; sung by Blanc as Daffy)*, "When Irish Eyes Are Smiling" *(Ernest Ball; George Graff; Chauncey Olcott; sung by Blanc as Daffy)*, "On Moonlight Bay" *(Percy Wenrich; Edward Madden; sung by Blanc as Daffy)*.
MUSIC BY Milt Franklyn.
Released on August 17
(7 min./Vitaphone Sound/Technicolor/Video)
Warner Bros.

BUGSY AND MUGSY (1957) D: Friz Freleng.
VOICES: *Mel Blanc.*
Bugs Bunny sets two gangsters against each other when they hide out in an abandoned house. Blanc is Bugs, Mugsy, Rocky and radio voice. Entry in the LOONEY TUNES series.
MUSIC BY Carl Stalling, Milt Franklyn.
Released on August 31
(7 min./Vitaphone Sound/Technicolor)
Warner Bros.

GREEDY FOR TWEETY (1957) D: Friz Freleng.
VOICES: *Mel Blanc, June Foray.*
Even though laid-up in the hospital, our players (Sylvester the Cat, Tweety Pie, and the bulldog) manage an awkward chase with cumbersome casts and nurse Granny. Blanc is Sylvester, Tweety and dog. Entry in the LOONEY TUNES series.
MUSIC BY Milt Franklyn.
Released on September 28
(7 min./Vitaphone Sound/Technicolor/Video)
Warner Bros.

TOUCHE AND GO (1957) D: Chuck Jones.
VOICES: *Mel Blanc.*
Pepe Le Pew pursues his lady-cat fair underwater, aboard a ship, and on a desert isle. Blanc is Pepe, Penelope, the street painter, the dog, the boat captain, and a shark. Entry in the MERRIE MELODIES series.
MUSIC BY Milt Franklyn.
Released on October 12
(7 min./Vitaphone Sound/Technicolor)
Warner Bros.

SHOW BIZ BUGS (1957) D: Friz Freleng.
VOICES: *Mel Blanc.*
A jealous Daffy Duck attempts to outdo Bugs Bunny and win applause during a vaudeville show. Blanc is Bugs, Daffy, cab driver and manager. Entry in the LOONEY TUNES series.
SONGS: "I'm Looking Over a Four-Leaf Clover" *(Harry M. Woods; Mort Dixon)*, "Tea for Two" *(Vincent Youmans; Otto Harbach; Irving Caesar)*, "Jeepers Creepers" *(Harry Warren; Johnny Mercer)*, "Believe Me If All Those Endearing Young Charms" *(traditional Irish melody; lyrics by Thomas Moore)*, "Shave and a Haircut" *(traditional; composer unknown)*.
MUSIC BY Milt Franklyn.
Released on November 2
(7 min./Vitaphone Sound/Technicolor/Video/DVD)
Warner Bros.

MOUSE-TAKEN IDENTITY (1957) D: Robert McKimson.
VOICES: *Mel Blanc.*
Escaped baby kangaroo Hippety Hopper takes refuge in the county museum, where Sylvester the Cat and Junior are mouse-catchers. Blanc is Sylvester, Junior and the Zoo delivery guy. Entry in the MERRIE MELO-DIES series.
MUSIC BY Carl Stalling, Milt Franklyn.
Released on November 16
(7 min./Vitaphone Sound/Technicolor)
Warner Bros.

GONZALES' TAMALES (1957) D: Friz Freleng.
VOICES: *Mel Blanc, Jack Edwards, June Foray.*
All the male mice in the village are fed up with Speedy Gonzales stealing their girls, so they trick Sylvester the Cat into chasing the rapid rodent. Blanc is Speedy, Sylvester, Pedro, a mouse and the friend of Jose. Entry in the MERRIE MELODIES series.
MUSIC BY Carl Stalling, Milt Franklyn.
Released on November 30
(7 min./Vitaphone Sound/Technicolor/DVD)
Warner Bros.

RABBIT ROMEO (1957) D: Robert McKimson.
VOICES: *Mel Blanc, Arthur Q. Bryan, June Foray.*
Elmer Fudd's houseguest is a homely, lovesick female rabbit, who instantly falls for Bugs Bunny (Blanc) when Elmer tricks him into a visit. Entry in the MERRIE MELODIES series.
MUSIC BY Milt Franklyn.
Released on December 14
(6 min./Vitaphone Sound/Technicolor/DVD)
Warner Bros.

DON'T AXE ME (1958) D: Robert McKimson.
VOICES: *Mel Blanc, Arthur Q. Bryan, June Foray.*
Elmer Fudd's wife wants duck for dinner, so Elmer ventures out with an axe to do in Daffy Duck. However, the fast-talking mallard does what he can to keep off the chopping block. Blanc is Daffy and the Barnyard Dog. Entry in the MERRIE MELODIES series.
MUSIC BY Milt Franklyn.
Released on January 4
(7 min./Vitaphone Sound/Technicolor/Video)
Warner Bros.

TORTILLA FLAPS (1958) D: Robert McKimson.
VOICES: *Mel Blanc, Tom Holland.*
When a big crow crashes a mice fiesta, Speedy Gonzales handles the dumb bird in his own fashion. Blanc is Speedy, mice, and the crow. Entry in the LOONEY TUNES series.
MUSIC BY Milt Franklyn.
Released on January 18
(7 min./Vitaphone Sound/Technicolor/DVD)
Warner Bros.

HARE-LESS WOLF (1958) D: Friz Freleng.
VOICES: *Mel Blanc, June Foray.*
A forgetful Charles M. Wolf is nagged by his wife to get a rabbit for supper, but quarry Bugs Bunny has to keep reminding Charlie who he is supposed to be hunting. Blanc is Bugs and Charles. Entry in the MERRIE MELODIES series.
MUSIC BY Milt Franklyn.
Released on February 1
(7 min./Vitaphone Sound/Technicolor)
Warner Bros.

A PIZZA TWEETY-PIE (1958) D: Friz Freleng.
VOICES: *Mel Blanc, June Foray.*
Sylvester the Cat adopts an Italian accent as he pursues Tweety Pie on a holiday in Venice. Blanc is Sylvester, Tweety, and the spaghetti bird. Entry in the LOONEY TUNES series.
SONG: "Santa Lucia" *(Teodoro Cottrau; sung by Blanc as Tweety).*
MUSIC BY Milt Franklyn.
Released on February 22
(7 min./Vitaphone Sound/Technicolor/Video/DVD)
Warner Bros.

ROBIN HOOD DAFFY (1958) D: Chuck Jones.
VOICES: *Mel Blanc.*
Friar Tuck (a.k.a. Porky Pig) is seeking to join Robin Hood's merry men. However, when he meets inept 'Robin' Daffy Duck, the friar has a hard time believing Daffy is truly the stalwart hero. Blanc is Daffy and Porky. Entry in the MERRIE MELODIES series.
SONGS: "Barbara Allen" *(traditional English tune, composer unknown; sung by Blanc as Porky),* "Come Lasses and Lads" *(traditional, composer unknown; sung with substitute lyrics by Blanc as Daffy).*
MUSIC BY Milt Franklyn.
Released on March 8
(7 min./Vitaphone Sound/Technicolor/Rated [G]/DVD)
Warner Bros.

HARE-WAY TO THE STARS (1958) D: Chuck Jones.
VOICES: *Mel Blanc.*
Accidentally climbing into a rocket ship, Bugs Bunny is blasted into space. There he meets Marvin Martian, who has plans to blow up Earth because "it obstructs my view of Venus." Blanc is Bugs, Marvin and the countdown voice. Entry in the LOONEY TUNES series.
MUSIC BY Milt Franklyn.
Released on March 29
(7 min./Vitaphone Sound/Technicolor/Video)
Warner Bros.

FEATHER BLUSTER (1958) D: Robert McKimson.
VOICES: *Mel Blanc.*
An aged Foghorn Leghorn and Barnyard Dog look back fondly (?) on their long-running feud. Blanc is Foghorn and Dog. Includes footage from *Henhouse Henery* (1949) and *The High And The Flighty* (1956). Entry in the MERRIE MELODIES series.
MUSIC BY Milt Franklyn, Carl Stalling.
Released on May 10
(7 min./Vitaphone Sound/Technicolor)
Warner Bros.

NOW, HARE THIS (1958) D: Robert McKimson.
VOICES: *Mel Blanc.*
Bugs Bunny advises the Big Bad Wolf on how to properly snare a rabbit —
which includes tendering a dinner invitation. Blanc is Bugs, the Wolf and
Nephew. Entry in the LOONEY TUNES series.
MUSIC BY Milt Franklyn.
Released on May 31
(7 min./Vitaphone Sound/Technicolor)
Warner Bros.

TO ITCH HIS OWN (1958) D: Chuck Jones.
VOICE: *Mel Blanc.*
A peaceful dog gets in the middle of the conflict between a strong-man
flea and a bullying bulldog. Blanc is the bulldog, a dog catcher, a butcher,
and the tv voice. Entry in the MERRIE MELODIES series.
SONG: "Lullaby (Cradle Song)" *(Johannes Brahms).*
MUSIC BY Carl Stalling.
Released on June 28
(7 min./Vitaphone Sound/Technicolor)
Warner Bros.

DOG TALES (1958) D: Robert McKimson.
VOICES: *Robert C. Bruce, Mel Blanc, Mary Jane Croft.*
A series of canine gags punctuate this funny look at dogs of all kinds.
Blanc is the Chihuahua, French poodle, Doberman, Elvis Dog, Victor
Barky, Charlie Dog, a cat, St. Bernard, the coach dog, and Laddie. Entry
in the LOONEY TUNES series.
MUSIC BY Milt Franklyn.
Released on July 26
(7 min./Vitaphone Sound/Technicolor)
Warner Bros.

WEASEL WHILE YOU WORK (1958) D: Robert McKimson.
VOICES: *Mel Blanc.*
Foghorn Leghorn and Barnyard Dog are pounding each other in a wintertime setting when a hungry Willy Weasel appears. Blanc is Foghorn, Dog, and Willy. Entry in the MERRIE MELODIES series.
MUSIC BY John Seeley.
Released on August 6
(7 min./Vitaphone Sound/Technicolor)
Warner Bros.

KNIGHTY KNIGHT BUGS (1958) D: Friz Freleng.
VOICES: *Mel Blanc.*
Court jester Bugs Bunny is on a quest to retrieve King Arthur's Singing Sword and must take it from the Black Knight *(Yosemite Sam)* and his fire-sneezing dragon. Blanc is Bugs, Sam, King Arthur, Sir Osis of Liver, Sir Loin of Beef, knights, and the dragon. Entry in the LOONEY TUNES series.
MUSIC BY Milt Franklyn.
Academy Award *(Short Subjects – Cartoons)* John W. Burton.
Released on August 23
(7 min./Vitaphone Sound/Technicolor/DVD)
Warner Bros.

A BIRD IN A BONNET (1958) D: Friz Freleng.
VOICES: *Mel Blanc, June Foray, Daws Butler.*
Getting away from Sylvester the Cat, Tweety Pie perches on Granny's new hat. Sylvester follows Granny all over town, seeking a chance to snatch the chapeau and Tweety. Blanc is Sylvester, Tweety and man in street. Entry in the MERRIE MELODIES series.
MUSIC BY John Seeley.
Released on September 27
(6 min./Vitaphone Sound/Technicolor)
Warner Bros.

PRE-HYSTERICAL HARE (1958) D: Robert McKimson.
VOICES: *Mel Blanc, Dave Barry.*
Bugs Bunny learns that his ancestor, circa 10,000 B.C., also had to put up with the hunting urge of a pre-historic Elmer Fudd. Blanc is Bugs, a saber-tooth rabbit, the narrator, dinosaurs, and a saber-tooth tiger. Entry in the LOONEY TUNES series.
MUSIC BY John Seeley.
Released on November 1
(7 min./Vitaphone Sound/Technicolor)
Warner Bros.

GOPHER BROKE (1958) D: Robert McKimson.
VOICES: *Mel Blanc, Stan Freberg.*
The Goofy Gophers conspire to get Barnyard Dog out of the way so they can get at some harvested vegetables. Blanc is Mac, the dog and the psychiatrist. Entry in the LOONEY TUNES series.
MUSIC BY John Seeley.
Released on November 15
(7 min./Vitaphone Sound/Technicolor)
Warner Bros.

CAT FEUD (1958) D: Chuck Jones.
VOICES: *Mel Blanc.*
Cute kitten Pussyfoot is abandoned at a construction site where guard-bulldog Marc Antony takes pity on him. When Claude Cat appears to steal Pussyfoot's meal, Marc goes into action against the interloper. Blanc is Marc and Pussyfoot. Entry in the MERRIE MELODIES series.
MUSIC BY Milt Franklyn.
Released on December 20
(7 min./Vitaphone Sound/Technicolor/DVD)
Warner Bros.

BATON BUNNY (1959) D: Chuck Jones, Abe Levitow.
VOICE: *Mel Blanc.*
Bugs Bunny (mute this outing) conducts the Warner Brothers Symphony Orchestra in a rendition of Franz Von Suppe's "Morning, Noon and Night in Vienna," until a pesky fly threatens to disrupt the concert. Blanc is a coughing bum. Entry in the LOONEY TUNES series.
MUSIC BY Milt Franklyn.
Released on January 10
(6 min./Vitaphone Sound/Technicolor/Video/DVD)
Warner Bros.

MOUSE-PLACED KITTEN (1959) D: Robert McKimson.
VOICES: *Mel Blanc, June Foray.*
Clyde and Matilda Mouse's adopted 'son' Junior Cat gets a job as mouser in a lady's home, putting Junior in an odd position when 'mom' and 'pop' come to visit. Blanc is Clyde and Junior. Entry in the MERRIE MELO-DIES series.
MUSIC BY Milt Franklyn.
Released on January 24
(7 min./Vitaphone Sound/Technicolor)
Warner Bros.

CHINA JONES (1959) D: Robert McKimson.
VOICES: *Mel Blanc, June Foray.*
An adventurer in the Far East, China Jones *(a.k.a. Daffy Duck),* hopes to rescue a prisoner being held by Limey Louie. Blanc is Daffy, Charlie Chung *(a.k.a. Porky Pig),* a Chinese man and Limey Louie. Entry in the LOONEY TUNES series.
MUSIC BY Milt Franklyn.
Released on February 14
(7 min./Vitaphone Sound/Technicolor/Video)
Warner Bros.

HARE-ABIAN NIGHTS (1959) D: Ken Harris, Michael Maltese.
VOICES: *Mel Blanc.*
Bugs Bunny attempts to entertain Sultan *(Yosemite)* Sam by telling of his adventures, *a la* sequences from *Bully For Bugs* (1953), *Water, Water Every Hare* (1952), and *Sahara Hare* (1955). Blanc is Bugs and Sam. Entry in the MERRIE MELODIES series.
MUSIC BY Milt Franklyn.
Released on February 28
(7 min./Vitaphone Sound/Technicolor)
Warner Bros.

TRICK OR TWEET (1959) D: Friz Freleng.
VOICES: *Mel Blanc, Daws Butler.*
Sylvester the Cat has competition in his Tweety Pie chase — an orange tabby named Sam. Blanc is Sylvester and Tweety. Entry in the MERRIE MELODIES series.
MUSIC BY Milt Franklyn.
Released on March 21
(7 min./Vitaphone Sound/Technicolor)
Warner Bros.

THE MOUSE THAT JACK BUILT (1959) D: Robert McKimson.
LIVE ACTION: Jack Benny. VOICES: *Benny, Mary Livingstone, Eddie Anderson, Don Wilson, Mel Blanc.*
The mice equivalents of Benny and his associates want to go out on the town, so a cagey cat disguises himself as a cheap nightclub (!) with his mouth as the entrance. Blanc is Ed (the vault guard), and Benny's sputtering Maxwell automobile. Entry in the MERRIE MELODIES series.
MUSIC BY Milt Franklyn.
Released on April 4
(6 min./Vitaphone Sound/Technicolor/DVD)
Warner Bros.

APES OF WRATH (1959) D: Friz Freleng.
VOICES: *Mel Blanc, June Foray.*
An inebriated stork captures Bugs Bunny (Blanc) and delivers him on the doorstep of Mr. and Mrs. Elvis Gorilla — where a disgusted Papa Elvis plots to do away with Bugs. Blanc is Bugs, The Stork, Elvis Gorilla and Daffy Duck. Entry in the MERRIE MELODIES series.
MUSIC BY Milt Franklyn.
Released on April 18
(7 min./Vitaphone Sound/Technicolor/Video)
Warner Bros.

A MUTT IN A RUT (1959) D: Robert McKimson.
VOICES: *Mel Blanc, Arthur Q. Bryan, Daws Butler.*
Rover the Dog believes his master, Elmer Fudd, plans to take him out in the woods and shoot him...so Rover plans to turn the tables. Blanc is Carlton Canine, Rover and the cat sounds. Entry in the LOONEY TUNES series.
MUSIC BY Milt Franklyn.
Released on May 23
(6 min./Vitaphone Sound/Technicolor)
Warner Bros.

BACKWOODS BUNNY (1959) D: Robert McKimson.
VOICES: *Mel Blanc, Daws Butler.*
Bugs Bunny (Blanc) burrows into the Ozarks, where he becomes the meal plan for B.O. Buzzard and his son, Elvis. Entry in the MERRIE MELODIES series.
MUSIC BY Milt Franklyn.
Released on June 13
(7 min./Vitaphone Sound/Technicolor)
Warner Bros.

REALLY SCENT (1959) D: Abe Levitow.
VOICES: *Mel Blanc, June Foray.*
Fabrette the New Orleans Cat spots Pepe Le Pew and is immediately smitten — but what to do about his odor? Blanc is Pepe, the crewmen, shoppers, and 'seweur rat.' Entry in the MERRIE MELODIES series.
SONG: "Blow the Man Down" *(traditional, composer unknown; sung with substitute lyrics by Blanc as Pepe).*
MUSIC BY *Milt Franklyn.*
Released on June 27
(7 min./Vitaphone Sound/Technicolor)
Warner Bros.

MEXICALI SHMOES (1959) D: Friz Freleng.
VOICES: *Mel Blanc, Dal McKennon.*
Two guitar-playing amigo cats forsake music for mice and set out after Speedy Gonzales. Blanc is Speedy and Jose cat. Entry in the LOONEY TUNES series.
MUSIC BY Milt Franklyn.
Academy Award Nomination *(Short Subjects – Cartoons)* John W. Burton.
Released on July 4
(7 min./Vitaphone Sound/Technicolor/Video/DVD)
Warner Bros.

TWEET AND LOVELY (1959) D: Friz Freleng.
VOICES: *Mel Blanc.*
Sylvester the Cat uses various destructive devices to keep Spike the Bulldog from protecting Tweety Pie; however, they all seem to backfire. Blanc is Sylvester and Tweety. Entry in the MERRIE MELODIES series.
SONG: "Singin' in the Bathtub" *(Michael Cleary; Herb Magidson; Ned Washington; sung by Blanc as Tweety).*
MUSIC BY Milt Franklyn.
Released on July 18
(7 min./Vitaphone Sound/Technicolor/Video)
Warner Bros.

WILD AND WOOLLY HARE (1959) D: Friz Freleng.
VOICES: *Mel Blanc.*
Western stalwart Bugs Bunny vows to keep the 5:15 train from being robbed by Yosemite Sam. Blanc is Bugs, Sam, two Cowboys, Injun Joe, Gambler, Old Timer, and the old man. Entry in the LOONEY TUNES series.
MUSIC BY Milt Franklyn.
Released on August 1
(7 min./Vitaphone Sound/Technicolor/Video)
Warner Bros.

CAT'S PAW (1959) D: Robert McKimson.
VOICES: *Mel Blanc.*
Sylvester the Cat and his son, Junior *(both voiced by Blanc),* encounter a tough little eagle when they go bird-stalking in the mountains. Entry in the LOONEY TUNES series.
MUSIC BY Milt Franklyn.
Released on August 15
(7 min./Vitaphone Sound/Technicolor)
Warner Bros.

HERE TODAY, GONE TAMALE (1959) D: Friz Freleng.
VOICES: *Mel Blanc, Tom Holland.*
Sylvester the Cat is in a Mexican port guarding a cheese boat when Speedy Gonzales races in to steal some. Blanc is Speedy, Sylvester and three mice. Entry in the LOONEY TUNES series.
MUSIC BY Milt Franklyn.
Released on August 29
(7 min./Vitaphone Sound/Technicolor/DVD)
Warner Bros.

BONANZA BUNNY (1959) D: Robert McKimson.
VOICES: *Mel Blanc, Robert C. Bruce.*
Bugs Bunny takes his gold strike into a Klondike saloon, where greedy Blacque Jacques Shellacque schemes to take it from him. Blanc is Bugs, Blacque Jacques, the bartender and dog. Entry in the MERRIE MELO-DIES series.
SONG: "A Bicycle Built for Two (Daisy Bell)" *(Harry Dacre).*
MUSIC BY Milt Franklyn.
Released on September 5
(7 min./Vitaphone Sound/Technicolor)
Warner Bros.

A BROKEN LEGHORN (1959) D: Robert McKimson.
VOICES: *Mel Blanc, June Foray.*
A young upstart rooster wants to take over Foghorn Leghorn's job in the farmyard, so Foggy whips up some schemes to rid himself of the little pest. Blanc is Foghorn and Junior Rooster. Entry in the LOONEY TUNES series.
MUSIC BY Milt Franklyn.
Released on September 26
(7 min./Vitaphone Sound/Technicolor/DVD)
Warner Bros.

A WITCH'S TANGLED HARE (1959) D: Abe Levitow.
VOICES: *Mel Blanc, June Foray.*
Bugs Bunny and Witch Hazel's antics during their chase at Castle Macbeth inspire a writer — one William Shakespeare. Blanc is Bugs and Sam Krubish. Entry in the LOONEY TUNES series.
MUSIC BY Milt Franklyn.
Released on October 31
(7 min./Vitaphone Sound/Technicolor/Video)
Warner Bros.

UNNATURAL HISTORY (1959) D: Abe Levitow.
VOICES: *Ed Prentiss, Mel Blanc, June Foray.*
An offbeat look at animal behavior with Blanc voicing various characters. Entry in the LOONEY TUNES series.
MUSIC BY Milt Franklyn.
Released on November 14
(6 min./Vitaphone Sound/Technicolor)
Warner Bros.

TWEET DREAMS (1959) D: Friz Freleng.
VOICES: *Mel Blanc, June Foray, Bea Benaderet (re-use).*
Sylvester the Cat's failures in catching Tweety Pie land him on the psychi-
atrist's couch, where he recounts various episodes from *Too Hop To Handle*
(1956), *Tweety's Circus* (1955), *A Street Cat Named Sylvester* (1953), *Sandy*
Claws (1955), and *Gift Wrapped* (1952). Blanc is Sylvester, Tweety, Doctor
Milt Towne, a dog, and Junior. Entry in the LOONEY TUNES series.
MUSIC BY Milt Franklyn.
Released on December 5
(6 min./Vitaphone Sound/Technicolor)
Warner Bros.

PEOPLE ARE BUNNY (1959) D: Robert McKimson.
VOICES: *Mel Blanc, Daws Butler, June Foray.*
Bugs Bunny and Daffy Duck raise Cain at the TV studio as they violently
participate in various game shows. Blanc is Bugs, Daffy, and a TV host.
Entry in the MERRIE MELODIES series.
MUSIC BY Milt Franklyn.
Released on December 19
(6 min./Vitaphone Sound/Technicolor)
Warner Bros.

WEST OF THE PESOS (1960) D: Robert McKimson.
VOICES: *Mel Blanc, Tom Holland, Merrie Virginia.*
Mexican mice are being held in a research laboratory, guarded by Sylvester
the Cat. Speedy Gonzales outraces the "pussy-gato" to save his friends.
Blanc is Speedy, Sylvester and Mice. Entry in the MERRIE MELODIES
series.
MUSIC BY Milt Franklyn.
Released on January 23
(7 min./Vitaphone Sound/Technicolor/DVD)
Warner Brothers

HORSE HARE (1960) D: Friz Freleng.
VOICES: *Mel Blanc.*
Cavalry soldier Bugs Bunny protects Fort Lariat from an Indian attack spearheaded by Renegade (Yosemite) Sam. Blanc is Bugs, Sam, Geronimo, Chief, Colonel, and Mule. Entry in the LOONEY TUNES series.
MUSIC BY Milt Franklyn.
Released on February 13
(7 min./Vitaphone Sound/Technicolor)
Warner Brothers

WILD WILD WORLD (1960) D: Robert McKimson.
VOICES: *Daws Butler, Mel Blanc.*
A long-lost piece of film shows us the 'actual' history of cavemen, including the real reason behind the discovery of fire — to give each other hot-foots! Blanc does cavemen sounds. Entry in the MERRIE MELODIES series.
MUSIC BY Milt Franklyn.
Released on February 27
(7 min./Vitaphone Sound/Technicolor)
Warner Brothers

GOLDIMOUSE AND THE THREE CATS (1960) D: Friz Freleng.
VOICES: *Mel Blanc, June Foray.*
Sylvester the Cat attempts to catch the blonde-haired mouse who walks into his family's home, eats their porridge, and makes herself comfortable in their beds. Blanc is Sylvester and Junior. Entry in the LOONEY TUNES series.
MUSIC BY Milt Franklyn.
Released on March 15
(7 min./Vitaphone Sound/Technicolor/DVD)
Warner Brothers

PERSON TO BUNNY (1960) D: Friz Freleng.
VOICES: *Mel Blanc, Daws Butler, Arthur Q. Bryan.*
When Bugs Bunny is the subject of a TV interview, Daffy Duck and Elmer Fudd show up to hog the spotlight. Blanc is Bugs and Daffy. Entry in the MERRIE MELODIES series.
MUSIC BY Milt Franklyn.
Released on April 1
(7 min./Vitaphone Sound/Technicolor/Video)
Warner Brothers

WHO SCENT YOU? (1960) D: Chuck Jones.
VOICES: *Mel Blanc.*
A deserted luxury ocean liner provides romance for Pepe Le Pew when he pursues a female cat who snuck aboard. Blanc is Pepe, Penelope, Le Capitaine, the first mate, and the crewmen. Entry in the LOONEY TUNES series.
SONGS: "How Dry I Am" *(traditional, composer unknown; sung by Blanc as Pepe),* "The Band Played On" *(Charles B. Ward; John F. Palmer; sung by Blanc as Pepe).*
MUSIC BY Milt Franklyn.
Released on April 23
(7 min./Vitaphone Sound/Technicolor)
Warner Brothers

HYDE AND GO TWEET (1960) D: Friz Freleng.
VOICES: *Mel Blanc.*
Sylvester the Cat recklessly chases Tweety Pie into Dr. Jekyll's lab, where the little yellow bird gets a dose of an elixir that turns him into a giant, cat-bashing monster. Blanc is Sylvester, Tweety, Mr. Hyde and two cats. Entry in the MERRIE MELODIES series.
MUSIC BY Milt Franklyn.
Released on May 14
(7 min./Vitaphone Sound/Technicolor/Video)
Warner Brothers

RABBIT'S FEAT (1960) D: Chuck Jones.
VOICES: *Mel Blanc.*
Wile E. Coyote advises us of his plan to catch ad eat Bugs Bunny — who thwarts the canine at every turn. Blanc is Bugs and Wile E. Entry in the LOONEY TUNES series.
MUSIC BY Milt Franklyn.
Released on June 4
(7 min./Vitaphone Sound/Technicolor/Video)
Warner Brothers

CROCKETT DOODLE DO (1960) D: Robert McKimson.
VOICES: *Mel Blanc.*
Foghorn Leghorn (Blanc) wants to teach little Egghead Jr. how to survive in the great outdoors, but 'Eggy' outsmarts the rooster with science. Entry in the MERRIE MELODIES series.
MUSIC BY Milt Franklyn.
Released on June 25
(7 min./Vitaphone Sound/Technicolor)
Warner Brothers

MOUSE AND GARDEN (1960) D: Friz Freleng.
VOICES: *Mel Blanc, Daws Butler.*
Cats Sylvester and Sam find they cannot trust each other when it comes to sharing a mouse they have captured. Blanc is Sylvester and the mouse. Entry in the LOONEY TUNES series.
SONG: "On Moonlight Bay" *(Percy Wenrich; Edward Madden)*
MUSIC BY Milt Franklyn.
Academy Award Nomination *(Short Subjects – Cartoons)* Warner Brothers.
Released on July 15
(7 min./Vitaphone Sound/Technicolor/DVD)
Warner Brothers

READY, WOOLEN AND ABLE (1960) D: Chuck Jones.
VOICES: *Mel Blanc.*
Multiple Sam Sheepdogs bedevil an increasingly frustrated Ralph Wolf when he tries to steal lambs from Sam's flock. Blanc is Sam and Ralph. Entry in the MERRIE MELODIES series.
MUSIC BY Milt Franklyn.
Released on July 30
(7 min./Vitaphone Sound/Technicolor/Video)
Warner Brothers

FROM HARE TO HEIR (1960) D: Friz Freleng.
VOICES: *Mel Blanc.*
Bugs Bunny, representing a benevolent foundation, is ready to present a penniless Yosemite Sam with a fortune — but only if the red-haired runt refrains from losing his temper. Blanc is Bugs, Sam and accountant. Entry in the MERRIE MELODIES series.
MUSIC BY Milt Franklyn.
Released on September 3
(7 min./Vitaphone Sound/Technicolor)
Warner Brothers

THE DIXIE FRYER (1960) D: Robert McKimson.
VOICES: *Mel Blanc, Daws Butler.*
Foghorn Leghorn's trip South for the winter takes a harrowing turn when he almost lands in the stewpot of B.O. Buzzard and son Elvis. Blanc is Foghorn. Entry in the MERRIE MELODIES series.
SONG: "Camptown Races" *(Stephen Foster; sung with substitute lyrics by Blanc as Foghorn).*
MUSIC BY Milt Franklyn.
Released on September 24
(7 min./Vitaphone Sound/Technicolor)
Warner Brothers

HOPALONG CASUALTY (1960) D: Chuck Jones.
VOICES: *Mel Blanc.*
Wile E. Coyote gets into trouble when he swallows a bottle of earthquake pills. Blanc is Wile E. Coyote's vocal effects. Entry in the MERRIE MELODIES series.
MUSIC BY Milt Franklyn.
Released on October 8
(7 min./Vitaphone Sound/Technicolor/Video)
Warner Brothers

TRIP FOR TAT (1960) D: Friz Freleng.
VOICES: *Mel Blanc, June Foray.*
Sylvester the Cat embarks on a global chase for Tweety Pie when Granny takes the bird along on a world cruise. Blanc is Sylvester, Tweety, Tattoo Artist and Japanese voice. Entry in the MERRIE MELODIES series.
MUSIC BY Milt Franklyn.
Released on October 29
(7 min./Vitaphone Sound/Technicolor)
Warner Brothers

DOG GONE PEOPLE (1960) D: Robert McKimson.
VOICES: *Hal Smith, Mel Blanc, Noel Blanc.*
Elmer Fudd is charged with caring for Rupert, a dog who chooses to live — and raise havoc — like a real person. Blanc is Rupert, Mr. Crabtree and the traffic cop. Entry in the MERRIE MELODIES series.
SONGS: "Cheerful Little Earful" *(Harry Warren; Ira Gershwin; Billy Rose),* "Please Don't Talk About Me When I'm Gone" *(Sam H. Stept; Sidney Clare).*
MUSIC BY Milt Franklyn.
Released on November 12
(7 min./Vitaphone Sound/Technicolor)
Warner Brothers

HIGH NOTE (1960) D: Chuck Jones.
VOICE: *Mel Blanc.*
A stylish cartoon about one of the musical notes (Blanc) for "The Blue Danube" *(composed by Johann Strauss)* getting drunk after sampling "The Little Brown Jug" *(composed by Joseph Winner).* Entry in the LOONEY TUNES series.
OTHER SONGS: "How Dry I Am" *(traditional, composer unknown),* "Lullaby" *(Johannes Brahms),* "Where, Oh Where, Has My Little Dog Gone?" *(traditional German folk song, composer unknown)*
MUSIC BY Milt Franklyn.
Academy Award Nomination *(Short Subject – Cartoon)* David H. DePatie.
Released on December 3
(7 min./Vitaphone Sound/Technicolor)
Warner Brothers

LIGHTER THAN HARE (1960) D: Friz Freleng.
VOICES: *Mel Blanc.*
Yosemite Sam of outer space attempts to capture 'Earth specimen' Bugs
Bunny, but the rascally rabbit decimates Sam's robot henchmen. Blanc is
Bugs, Sam, Robot ZX29-B, robot ferret, Bugs Robot, and the alien king.
Entry in the MERRIE MELODIES series.
MUSIC BY Milt Franklyn.
Released on December 17
(6 min./Vitaphone Sound/Technicolor)
Warner Brothers

CANNERY WOE (1961) D: Robert McKimson.
VOICES: *Mel Blanc, Tom Holland.*
Speedy Gonzales saves the cheese festival for the mice by stealing the
fromage despite Sylvester the Cat's various traps. Blanc is Speedy, Jose,
Mayor and Sylvester. Entry in the LOONEY TUNES series.
MUSIC BY Milt Franklyn.
Released on January 7
(7 min./Vitaphone Sound/Technicolor/DVD)
Warner Brothers

ZIP 'N' SNORT (1961) D: Chuck Jones.
VOICES: *Paul Julian, Mel Blanc.*
Wile E. Coyote's Road Runner-catching gambits include a grenade in
a model plane; iron pellets mixed with bird seed; and Acme brand axle
grease on his feet. Blanc provides the Coyote's vocal effects. Entry in the
MERRIE MELODIES series.
MUSIC BY Milt Franklyn.
Released on January 21
(7 min./Vitaphone Sound/Technicolor/Video)
Warner Brothers

HOPPY DAZE (1961) D: Robert McKimson.
VOICES: *Mel Blanc.*
A waterfront tough-cat acts as a trainer for Sylvester as he is recruited to become a champion mouser. Sylvester's first 'opponent' is Hippety Hopper the Baby Kangaroo. Blanc is Sylvester and the tough cat. Entry in the LOONEY TUNES series.
MUSIC BY Milt Franklyn.
Released on February 11
(7 min./Vitaphone Sound/Technicolor)
Warner Brothers

THE MOUSE ON 57TH STREET (1961) D: Chuck Jones.
VOICES: *Mel Blanc, Merrie Virginia.*
A mouse steals a valuable diamond from a jewelry store and is pursued by a red-mustached cop and his dumb partner. Blanc is the cops, Spiffany's man, Mouse, Muldoon. Entry in the MERRIE MELODIES series.
MUSIC BY Milt Franklyn.
Released on February 25
(6 min./Vitaphone Sound/Technicolor)
Warner Brothers

STRANGLED EGGS (1961) D: Robert McKimson.
VOICES: *Mel Blanc, Julie Bennett.*
A starving Foghorn Leghorn is close to marrying Miss Prissy the Hen, but first he must look after her foundling — Henery Hawk. Blanc is Foghorn and Henery. Entry in the MERRIE MELODIES series.
MUSIC BY Milt Franklyn.
Released on March 18
(7 min./Vitaphone Sound/Technicolor)
Warner Brothers

BIRDS OF A FATHER (1961) D: Robert McKimson.
VOICES: *Mel Blanc.*
When Junior begins making friends with birds, a shocked Sylvester the Cat is determined to make his son a bird-hunter. Blanc is Sylvester and Junior. Entry in the LOONEY TUNES series.
MUSIC BY Milt Franklyn.
Released on April 1
(6 min./Vitaphone Sound/Technicolor/Video)
Warner Brothers

D' FIGHTIN' ONES (1961) D: Friz Freleng.
VOICES: *Mel Blanc.*
On the way to the city pound, Sylvester the Cat and a bulldog manage to escape — but they are handcuffed together. MERRIE MELODIES' version of the motion picture *The Defiant Ones* with Blanc as Sylvester and the bulldog.
MUSIC BY Milt Franklyn.
Released on April 22
(7 min./Vitaphone Sound/Technicolor)
Warner Brothers

THE ABOMINABLE SNOW RABBIT (1961) D: Chuck Jones.
VOICES: *Mel Blanc.*
Traveling (i.e. burrowing) together, Bugs Bunny and Daffy Duck are on their way to Palm Springs when a wrong turn lands them in the Himalayan Mountains. While there, the gigantic (and dumb) Abominable Snowman makes pets of our heroes. Blanc is Bugs, Daffy, and Hugo the Snowman. Entry in the LOONEY TUNES series.
MUSIC BY Milt Franklyn.
Released on May 20
(7 min./Vitaphone Sound/Technicolor/Video/DVD)
Warner Brothers

LICKETY-SPLAT (1961) D: Chuck Jones.
VOICES: *Mel Blanc.*
Wile E. Coyote uses dynamite darts in his latest bid to capture the Road Runner, but their wayward flight proves to be hazardous to the coyote. Blanc provides the Coyote's vocal effects. Entry in the LOONEY TUNES series.
MUSIC BY Milt Franklyn.
Released on June 3
(7 min./Vitaphone Sound/Technicolor)
Warner Brothers

A SCENT OF THE MATTERHORN (1961) D: Chuck Jones.
VOICES: *Mel Blanc, Adolf Hartenstein.*
Amorous skunk Pepe Le Pew pursues a female cat in the Swiss Mountains.
Blanc is Pepe, Penelope, the cow, chickens, pig, dog, and a frog. Entry in
the LOONEY TUNES series.
SONG: "Tip-Toe Through the Tulips with Me" *(Joseph Burke; Al Dubin),*
(sung by Blanc ad Pepe).
MUSIC BY Milt Franklyn.
Released on June 24
(7 min./Vitaphone Sound/Technicolor)
Warner Brothers

THE REBEL WITHOUT CLAWS (1961) D: Friz Freleng.
VOICES: *Mel Blanc.*
During the Civil War, Tweety Pie is a dispatch bird for Confederate
forces and must elude Yankee cat Sylvester. Blanc is Tweety, Sylvester, the
Sergeant and two Generals. Entry in the LOONEY TUNES series.
MUSIC BY Milt Franklyn.
Released on July 15
(7 min./Vitaphone Sound/Technicolor/Video)
Warner Brothers

COMPRESSED HARE (1961) D: Chuck Jones.
VOICES: *Mel Blanc.*
Bugs Bunny's new neighbor is Wile E. Coyote, who wants to make an
impression by having Bugs for dinner — literally! Various traps backfire,
including a super-powerful electromagnet. Blanc is Bugs and Wile E.
Entry in the MERRIE MELODIES series.
SONG: "Singin' in the Bathtub" *(Michael Cleary; Herb Magidson; Ned*
Washington; sung by Blanc as Bugs).
MUSIC BY Milt Franklyn.
Released on July 29
(7 min./RCA Sound/Technicolor)
Warner Brothers

THE PIED PIPER OF GUADALUPE (1961) D: Friz Freleng.
VOICES: *Mel Blanc.*
Speedy Gonzales rescues his mice friends when Sylvester the Cat lures
them into his jug with hypnotic flute music. Blanc is Speedy and Sylvester.
Entry in the LOONEY TUNES series.
MUSIC BY Milt Franklyn.
Academy Award Nomination *(Short Subjects – Cartoon)* Friz Freleng.
Released on August 19
(7 min./Vitaphone Sound/Technicolor/DVD)
Warner Brothers

PRINCE VIOLENT/PRINCE VARMINT (1961) D: Friz Freleng.
VOICES: *Mel Blanc.*
(Yosemite) Sam the Terrible is a Viking out to storm a castle protected
by peasant Bugs Bunny. Blanc is Bugs, Sam, the elephant, guard, and the
peasants. Entry in the LOONEY TUNES series.
MUSIC BY Milt Franklyn.
Released on September 2
(7 min./Vitaphone Sound/Technicolor)
Warner Brothers

DAFFY'S INN TROUBLE (1961) D: Robert McKimson.
VOICES: *Mel Blanc, Merrie Virginia.*
Tired of working for hotel owner Porky Pig, Daffy Duck opens his own
place of business and attempts to sabotage Porky. Blanc is Daffy, Porky,
and the robber. Entry in the LOONEY TUNES series.
SONG: "The Latin Quarter" *(Harry Warren; Al Dubin; sung by Blanc as
Daffy).*
MUSIC BY Milt Franklyn.
Released on September 23
(7 min./Vitaphone Sound/Technicolor)
Warner Brothers

WHAT'S MY LION? (1961) D: Robert McKimson.
VOICES: *Hal Smith, Herb Vigran, Mel Blanc.*
Rocky the Mountain Lion figures he has the perfect plan to escape the hunter: sneak into Elmer Fudd's cabin and pose as one of his trophies. Blanc is Delivery boy and Rocky. Entry in the LOONEY TUNES series.
MUSIC BY Milt Franklyn.
Released on October 21
(6 min./Vitaphone Sound/Technicolor)
Warner Brothers

THE LAST HUNGRY CAT (1961) D: Friz Freleng.
VOICES: *Mel Blanc, June Foray, Ben Frommer.*
Sylvester the Cat begins to break down under the guilt when an Alfred Hitchcock-like bear convinces him he has murdered Tweety Pie. Blanc is Sylvester, Tweety and Radio Voice. Entry in the MERRIE MELODIES series.
MUSIC BY Milt Franklyn.
Released on December 2
(7 min./Vitaphone Sound/Technicolor/DVD)
Warner Brothers

NELLY'S FOLLY (1961) D: Chuck Jones.
VOICES: *Ed Prentiss, Gloria Wood, John A. Ford, Mel Blanc.*
Nelly, a singing giraffe, is taken out of the jungle to become an American entertainment star until she falls in love with a married giraffe. Blanc is the tortoise, giraffe and bird. Entry in the MERRIE MELODIES series.
SONGS: "Auld Lang Syne" *(traditional, composer unknown),* "I'm the Flower of Gower Gulch" *(Michael Maltese).*
MUSIC BY Milt Franklyn.
Academy Award Nominee *(Short Subjects – Cartoons)* Chuck Jones.
Released on December 30
(7 min./Vitaphone Sound/Technicolor)
Warner Brothers

WET HARE (1962) D: Robert McKimson.
VOICES: *Mel Blanc.*
When nefarious Blacque Jacques Shellacque dams up Bugs Bunny's water supply, the rascally rabbit goes into action against the nasty lumberjack. Blanc is Bugs and Blacque Jacques. Entry in the LOONEY TUNES series.
SONG: "April Showers" *(Louis Silvers; B.G. DeSylva).*
MUSIC BY Milt Franklyn.
Released on January 20
(7 min./Vitaphone Sound/Technicolor)
Warner Brothers

A SHEEP IN THE DEEP (1962) D: Chuck Jones.
VOICES: *Mel Blanc.*
The 'blue collar' meadow inhabitants, Sam Sheepdog and Ralph Wolf, spar over a flock of lambs…with each ending up in a multitude of sheep costumes. Blanc is Sam and Ralph. Entry in the MERRIE MELODIES series.
MUSIC BY Milt Franklyn.
Released on February 10
(7 min./Vitaphone Sound/Technicolor)
Warner Brothers

NOW HEAR THIS (1962) D: Chuck Jones.
VOICES: *Mel Blanc.*
An elderly man discards his old hearing-aid horn for a new one, leading to exaggerated adventures with sound effects. Blanc provides vocal effects. Entry in the LOONEY TUNES series.
SONG: "Rue Brittania" *(Thomas Augustine Arne).*
MUSIC BY Bill [William] Lava.
Academy Award Nomination *(Short Subjects – Cartoons)* Warner Brothers. Release date unknown.
(6 min./Vitaphone Sound/Technicolor)
Warner Brothers

FISH AND SLIPS (1962) D: Robert McKimson.
VOICES: *Mel Blanc.*
Sylvester the Cat has more than a few mishaps when he and Junior go fishing at the public aquarium. Blanc is Sylvester and Junior. Entry in the LOONEY TUNES series.
MUSIC BY Milt Franklyn.
Released on March 10
(6 min./Vitaphone Sound/Technicolor)
Warner Brothers

QUACKODILE TEARS (1962) D: Art Davis.
VOICES: *Mel Blanc, June Foray.*
Daffy Duck (Blanc) loses his wife's egg in a litter of crocodile eggs; when he tries to take his back, Mrs. Crocodile thinks he is stealing one of hers. Blanc is Daffy and George Crocodile. Entry in the MERRIE MELODIES series.
MUSIC BY Milt Franklyn.
Released on March 31
(6 min./Vitaphone Sound/Technicolor/Video)
Warner Brothers

CROWS' FEAT (1962) D: Friz Freleng, Hawley Pratt.
VOICES: *Mel Blanc, Tom Holland.*
Two Mexican crows stop at a cornfield and spar with a scarecrow (who looks like Elmer Fudd) determined to chase them out. Blanc is Jose and Count-down. Entry in the MERRIE MELODIES series.
SONG: "La Paloma" *(Sebastian Yradier).*
MUSIC BY Milt Franklyn.
Released on April 21
(6 min./Vitaphone Sound/Technicolor)
Warner Brothers

MEXICAN BOARDERS (1962) D: Friz Freleng.
VOICES: *Mel Blanc, Tom Holland.*
Speedy Gonzales' visiting cousin, Slowpoke Rodriguez, causes more work for the rapid rodent when he must continually save Slowpoke from the clutches of Sylvester the Cat. Blanc is Speedy and Sylvester. Entry in the LOONEY TUNES series.
MUSIC BY Milt Franklyn.
Released on May 12
(7 min./Vitaphone Sound/Technicolor/DVD)
Warner Brothers

ADVENTURES OF THE ROAD RUNNER (1962) D: Chuck Jones, Maurice Noble, Tom Ray.
VOICES: *Mel Blanc, Dick Beals, Nancy Wible, Richard [Dick] Tufeld, The Rhythmaires.*
Two little boys watch the Road Runner and Wile E. Coyote (Blanc) on TV as Wile E. explains why his attempts at catching the bulleting bird always fail; and why he wants to eat him in the first place. Note: this featurette was culled from a failed pilot for a proposed television series, *The Road Runner Show;* it contains footage from *From A to Z-Z-Z-Z* (1954) and *To Beep Or Not To Beep* (not released until 1963). The always economically-minded Warner Brothers Studio later re-edited this featurette into two shorts, "Zip Zip Hooray" and "Roadrunner a Go Go" (never released in theaters, but shown on television).
SONG: "Out on the Desert" *(Milt Franklyn).*
MUSIC BY Milt Franklyn.
Released on June 2
(26 min./RCA Sound/Technicolor/DVD)
Warner Brothers

BILL OF HARE (1962) D: Robert McKimson.
VOICES: *Mel Blanc.*
Bugs Bunny attempts to dissuade the Tasmanian Devil from having a
rabbit dinner by sending him after succulent moose (actually a speeding
train) and giving him indigestion with a dynamite shish-ka-bob. Blanc is
Bugs, Captain, Shark and Tas. Entry in the MERRIE MELODIES series.
SONG: "L'Amour, Toujours, L'Amour" *(Rudolf Friml; Catherine Chisholm
Cushing; sung by Blanc as Bugs).*
MUSIC BY Milt Franklyn.
Released on June 9
(7 min./Vitaphone Sound/Technicolor/Video)
Warner Brothers

ZOOM AT THE TOP (1962) D: Chuck Jones, Maurice Noble.
VOICES: *Paul Julian, Mel Blanc.*
Wile E. Coyote falls prey to a stubborn bear trap and a glue-soaked boo-
merang in his latest attempts to catch the Road Runner. Blanc provides
the Coyote's vocal effects. Entry in the MERRIE MELODIES series.
MUSIC BY Milt Franklyn.
Released on June 30
(7 min./Vitaphone Sound/Technicolor)
Warner Brothers

THE SLICK CHICK (1962) D: Robert McKimson.
VOICES: *Mel Blanc, Julie Bennett.*
Foghorn Leghorn doesn't know what he is letting himself in for when he
agrees to babysit Widow Hen's destructive little brat. Blanc is Foghorn,
Junior, and Mr. Cackle. Entry in the LOONEY TUNES series.
MUSIC BY Milt Franklyn.
Released on July 21
(7 min./Vitaphone Sound/Technicolor)
Warner Brothers

LOUVRE COME BACK TO ME! (1962) D: Chuck Jones, Maurice Noble.
VOICES: *Mel Blanc, Julie Bennett.*
The amorous skunk Pepe Le Pew (Blanc) pursues his latest romantic 'conquest' among the artworks of Paris' Louvre Museum and fends off her alley cat lover. Blanc is Pepe, the Cat and the bird. Entry in the LOONEY TUNES series.
SONG: "Aupres de ma Blonde" *(French traditional, composer unknown), (sung by Blanc as Pepe).*
MUSIC BY Milt Franklyn.
Released on August 18
(7 min./Vitaphone Sound/Technicolor/Video)
Warner Brothers

HONEY'S MONEY (1962) D: Friz Freleng.
VOICES: *Mel Blanc, June Foray, Billy Booth.*
An overbearing widow has a fortune, so Yosemite Sam (Blanc) marries her — and is forced to 'play' with her behemoth son Wentworth. Entry in the MERRIE MELODIES series.
MUSIC BY Milt Franklyn.
Released on September 1
(7 min./Vitaphone Sound/Technicolor/Video)
Warner Brothers

THE JET CAGE (1962) D: Friz Freleng.
VOICES: *Mel Blanc, June Foray.*
Tweety Pie becomes a pilot when his birdcage is outfitted with a flying engine and wings. Sylvester the Cat awaits his chance to ambush the bird. Blanc is Tweety, Sylvester, and the blackbird. Entry in the LOONEY TUNES series.
SONG: "Sonata No. 16 in C Major" *(Wolfgang Amadeus Mozart).*
MUSIC BY Milt Franklyn, William Lava.
Released on September 22
(7 min./Vitaphone Sound/Technicolor)
Warner Brothers

MOTHER WAS A ROOSTER (1962) D: Robert McKimson.
VOICES: *Mel Blanc.*
When Barnyard Dog slips an ostrich egg underneath a sleeping Foghorn
Leghorn, Foggy wakes up to think he has hatched offspring and immedi-
ately sets out to make the boy a proud chicken. Blanc is Foghorn, Ostrich
and Dog.
MUSIC BY Milt Franklyn.
Released on October 20
(6 min./Vitaphone Sound/Technicolor)
Warner Brothers

GOOD NOOSE (1962) D: Robert McKimson.
VOICES: *Mel Blanc.*
Daffy Duck is caught as a stowaway aboard a ship helmed by a Charles
Laughton-like captain. He orders Daffy to be hanged unless the duck can
put on a good magic show. Blanc is Daffy, the captain, Mr. Tristan the
Parrot, and the islander. Entry in the LOONEY TUNES series.
MUSIC BY William Lava.
Released on November 10
(7 min./Vitaphone/Technicolor)
Warner Brothers

SHISHKABUGS (1962) D: Friz Freleng.
VOICES: *Mel Blanc.*
Royal cook Yosemite Sam is ordered by the king to prepare hasenpfeffer,
but Sam doesn't know where he will get the special ingredient — rabbit.
Then, Bugs Bunny shows up wanting to borrow a cup of carrots. Blanc is
Bugs, Sam, and the king. Entry in the LOONEY TUNES series.
MUSIC BY Bill [William] Lava.
Released on December 8
(7 min./Vitaphone Sound/Technicolor)
Warner Brothers

MARTIAN THROUGH GEORGIA (1962) D: Chuck Jones, Abe Levitow.
VOICES: *Ed Prentiss, Mel Blanc.*
A Martian travels to Earth, where he thinks life is better — until he is regarded as a monster. Blanc is the warden, a businessman, an old man, the little boy, a taunting voice, and scared citizens. Entry in the LOONEY TUNES series.
MUSIC BY Bill [William] Lava.
Released on December 29
(6 min./Vitaphone Sound/Technicolor)
Warner Brothers

PENT-HOUSE MOUSE (1963) D: Chuck Jones, Maurice Noble.
VOICES: *Mel Blanc.*
Tom the Cat's posh penthouse lifestyle is upset when Jerry the Mouse arrives. Blanc provides vocal effects for the characters.
MUSIC BY Eugene Poddany.
Released in January
(7 min./Western Electric Sound/Metrocolor)
SIB-Tower 12/Metro-Goldwyn-Mayer

I WAS A TEENAGE THUMB (1963) D: Chuck Jones.
VOICES: *Mel Blanc, Richard Peel, Ben Frommer, Julie Bennett.*
A couple's newborn miniature baby is kidnapped by a bird and goes through several adventures, leading up to his heroic deeds that win him the hand of a princess. Blanc is Ralph K. Merlin, and King Arthur. Entry in the MERRIE MELODIES series.
MUSIC BY Bill [William] Lava.
Released on January 19
(6 min./Vitaphone Sound/Technicolor)
Warner Brothers

DEVIL'S FEUD CAKE (1963) D: Friz Freleng.
VOICES: *Mel Blanc, Jerry Hausner.*
Yosemite Sam ends up in Hades, but he can get out if he successfully lures Bugs Bunny into taking his place. Blanc is Bugs, Sam, and the Devil. Includes re-dubbed and re-scored footage from *Hare Lift* (1952), as well as sequences from *Roman Legion Hare* (1955) and *Sahara Hare* (1955). Entry in the MERRIE MELODIES series.
MUSIC BY Bill [William] Lava.
Released on February 9
(6 min./Vitaphone Sound/Technicolor)
Warner Brothers

FAST BUCK DUCK (1963) D: Robert McKimson.
VOICES: *Mel Blanc.*
A destitute Daffy Duck (Blanc) figures there is easy money in becoming a companion to a millionaire. However, a persistent guard dog gets in Daffy's way. Blanc is Daffy, dog, cat and millionaire. Entry in the MERRIE MELODIES series.
MUSIC BY Bill [William] Lava.
Released on March 9
(7 min./Vitaphone Sound/Technicolor)
Warner Brothers

THE MILLION-HARE (1963) D: Robert McKimson.
VOICES: *Mel Blanc.*
As part of a TV competition, Bugs Bunny races Daffy Duck to the studio — where a million dollars awaits the winner. Blanc is Bugs, Daffy and TV announcer. Entry in the LOONEY TUNES series.
SONG: "The Blue Danube" *(Johann Strauss).*
MUSIC BY Bill [William] Lava.
Released on April 6
(7 min./Vitaphone Sound/Technicolor)
Warner Brothers

MEXICAN CAT DANCE (1963) D: Friz Freleng.
VOICES: *Mel Blanc.*
The mice stage a bullfight-style match between Speedy Gonzales and Sylvester the Cat. Blanc is Speedy and Sylvester. Includes footage from Bully For Bugs (1950). Entry in the LOONEY TUNES series.
MUSIC BY Bill [William] Lava.
Released on April 20
(6 min./Vitaphone Sound/Technicolor)
Warner Brothers

WOOLEN UNDER WHERE (1963) D: Phil Monroe, Richard Thompson.
VOICES: *Mel Blanc.*
Ralph Wolf is back to attempt stealing lambs from Sam Sheepdog's flock. Ralph uses such devices as a suit of armor, a cannon, dynamite, and a skin-diving outfit. Blanc is Sam and Ralph. Entry in the MERRIE MELODIES series.
MUSIC BY Bill [William] Lava.
Released on May 11
(7 min./Vitaphone Sound/Technicolor)
Warner Brothers

HARE-BREADTH HURRY (1963) D: Chuck Jones, Maurice Noble.
VOICES: *Mel Blanc.*
Since the Road Runner 'sprained a giblet' and cannot appear in this cartoon, Bugs Bunny (Blanc) stands in for his buddy and leads Wile E. Coyote on a mishap-laden chase. Entry in the LOONEY TUNES series.
MUSIC BY Bill [William] Lava.
Released on June 8
(7 min./Vitaphone Sound/Technicolor)
Warner Brothers

BANTY-RAIDS (1963) D: Robert McKimson.
VOICES: *Mel Blanc.*
A beatnik rooster infiltrates Foghorn Leghorn's farm and tries to make time with Foggy's hen friends. Blanc is Foghorn, Barnyard Dog, Banty Rooster, a tough rooster, and the giggling chicken. Entry in the MERRIE MELODIES series.
MUSIC BY Bill [William] Lava.
Released on June 29
(6 min./Vitaphone Sound/Technicolor)
Warner Brothers

CHILI WEATHER (1963) D: Friz Freleng.
VOICES: *Mel Blanc.*
Sylvester the Cat unsuccessfully tries to keep Speedy Gonzales from stealing food out of a processing plant. Blanc is Speedy, Sylvester, and the mice. Entry in the MERRIE MELODIES series.
MUSIC BY Bill [William] Lava.
Released on August 17
(7 min./Vitaphone Sound/Technicolor/DVD)
Warner Brothers

THE UNMENTIONABLES (1963) D: Friz Freleng.
VOICES: *Mel Blanc, Ralph James, Julie Bennett.*
This cartoon take-off on TV's popular The Untouchables has agent Elegant Mess (a.k.a. Bugs Bunny) using his resources to chase down gangsters Rocky and Mugsy. Blanc is Bugs, Rocky, Mugsy, Snitch, and the agency director. Entry in the MERRIE MELODIES series.
MUSIC BY Bill [William] Lava.
Released on September 7
(7 min./Vitaphone Sound/Technicolor)
Warner Brothers

THE THREE STOOGES SCRAPBOOK (1963) D: Sam Nicholson.
VOICES: *Moe Howard, Larry Fine, Joe de Rita, Mel Blanc.*
The Three Stooges and their parrot Feathers (Blanc) aid Christopher Columbus in discovering America. Animated short which was originally part of an unaired television pilot.
Released in Septembe
(9 min./Glenn Glenn Sound/color)
Normandy/TV Spots/Columbia

AQUA DUCK (1963) D: Robert McKimson.
VOICES: *Mel Blanc.*
Daffy Duck strikes it rich in the desert, but his need for water about does him in — until a pack rat offers to trade water to Daffy in exchange for his big gold nugget. Blanc is Daffy and Pack Rat. Entry in the MERRIE MELODIES series.
MUSIC BY Bill [William] Lava.
Released on September 28
(7 min./Vitaphone Sound/Technicolor)
Warner Brothers

MAD AS A MARS HARE (1963) D: Chuck Jones, Maurice Noble.
VOICES: *Mel Blanc.*
Bugs Bunny rockets to Mars, where he aggravates nasty little Marvin Martian. Blanc is Bugs, Marvin, and the Cape Canaveral controller. Entry in the MERRIE MELODIES series.
MUSIC BY Bill [William] Lava.
Released on October 19
(7 min./Vitaphone Sound/Technicolor/DVD)
Warner Brothers

CLAWS IN THE LEASE (1963) D: Robert McKimson.
VOICES: *Mel Blanc, Nancy Wible.*
A hillbilly lady becomes smitten with Junior and takes the kitten into her home. Then Sylvester the Cat tries to follow his son's lead, but is promptly ejected. Blanc is Sylvester and Junior. Entry in the MERRIE MELODIES series.
MUSIC BY Bill [William] Lava.
Released on November 9
(7 min./Vitaphone Sound/Technicolor)
Warner Brothers

TRANSYLVANIA 6-5000 (1963) D: Chuck Jones, Maurice Noble.
VOICES: *Mel Blanc, Ben Frommer, Julie Bennett.*
Burrowing into Transylvania, Bugs Bunny (Blanc) meets thirsty vampire Count Bloodcount. Bugs defends himself by using a pair of magic words that continually switch the attacking Count from human to bat — at the most inopportune times for the vampire. Entry in the MERRIE MELODIES series.
SONG: "It's Magic" *(Jule Styne; Sammy Cahn; sung with substitute lyrics by Blanc as Bugs).*
MUSIC BY Bill [William] Lava.
Released on November 30
(7 min./Vitaphone Sound/Technicolor/DVD)
Warner Brothers

IS THERE A DOCTOR IN THE MOUSE? (1964) D: Chuck Jones, Maurice Noble.
VOICES: *Mel Blanc.*
Jerry Mouse finds it easier to get away from Tom Cat after he develops a super-speed elixir. Blanc is Tom, Jerry, and various sound effects.
MUSIC BY Eugene Poddany.
No release date available
(7 min./Westrex Sound/Metrocolor)
SIB Tower 12/Metro-Goldwyn-Mayer

THE UNSHRINKABLE JERRY MOUSE (1964) D: Chuck Jones, Maurice Noble.
VOICES: *Mel Blanc.*
Tom Cat has to contend not only with Jerry, but also a new kitten in the house. Blanc provides vocal effects.
MUSIC BY Eugene Poddany.
No release date available
(7 min./Westrex Sound/Metrocolor)
SIB Tower 12/Metro-Goldwyn-Mayer

SNOWBODY LOVES ME (1964) D: Chuck Jones, Maurice Noble.
VOICES: *Mel Blanc.*
A frozen Jerry Mouse finds refuge at a Swiss chalet — and also a quantity of Swiss cheese. Tom Cat does his best to keep Jerry from *le fromage.* Blanc is Tom and Jerry.
MUSIC BY Eugene Poddany.
No release date available
(8 min./Western Electric Sound/Metrocolor)
SIB Tower 12/Metro-Goldwyn-Mayer

MUCH ADO ABOUT MOUSING (1964) D: Chuck Jones, Maurice Noble.
VOICES: *Mel Blanc.*
Jerry Mouse has an ally in a wharf bulldog who messes up Tom Cat every time Jerry blows a whistle. Blanc is Tom, Jerry, the bulldog, and the puppy.
MUSIC BY Eugene Poddany.
No release date available
(7 min./Westrex Sound/Metrocolor)
Metro-Goldwyn-Mayer

DUMB PATROL (1964) D: Gerry Chiniquy.
VOICES: *Mel Blanc.*
In the skies of World War 1, Allied pilot Bugs Bunny engages the dread German flyer Baron (Yosemite) Sam Von Shamm. Their aerial dogfight sees Sam fall out of his plane and getting blasted. Blanc is Bugs, Sam, the French officer, and the German officer. Entry in the LOONEY TUNES series.
SONGS: "There's a Long, Long Trail" *(Zo Elliott),* "Mademoiselle from Armentieres" *(French traditional; composer unknown).*
MUSIC BY Bill [William] Lava.
Released on January 18
(6 min./Vitaphone Sound/Technicolor)
DePatie-Freleng Enterprises/Warner Brothers

A MESSAGE TO GRACIAS (1964) D: Robert McKimson.
VOICES: *Mel Blanc, Roger Green.*
El Supremo the Mouse needs to get a dispatch to General Gracias, but all
his carriers are ambushed by Sylvester the Cat. El Supremo then engages
the services of Speedy Gonzales. Blanc is Speedy, a mouse, El Supremo
and Sylvester. Entry in the LOONEY TUNES series.
MUSIC BY Bill [William] Lava.
Released on February 8
(6 min./Vitaphone Sound/Technicolor/DVD)
DePatie-Freleng Enterprises/Warner Brothers

BARTHOLOMEW VERSUS THE WHEEL (1964) D: Robert McKimson.
VOICES: *Leslie Barringer, Mel Blanc.*
A wheel-chasing dog gets himself into trouble when he latches onto
an airplane wheel and is dispatched to the Sahara Desert. Blanc is
Bartholomew, the cat, an Egyptian, and an Egyptian dog. Entry in the
MERRIE MELODIES series.
MUSIC BY Bill [William] Lava.
Released on February 29
(6 min./Vitaphone Sound/Technicolor)
Warner Brothers

BEAR HUG (1964) D: William Hanna, Joseph Barbera.
VOICES: *Daws Butler, Mel Blanc, Janet Waldo.*
Loopy de Loop tries to broker a romance between Braxton Bear (Blanc)
and Emmy-Lou, but things get fouled up.
MUSIC BY Hoyt Curtin.
Released on March 5
(6½ min./RCA Sound/Eastmancolor, Technicolor)
Hanna-Barbera/Columbia

FREUDY CAT (1964) D: Robert McKimson.
VOICES: *Mel Blanc.*
Sylvester the Cat still has not realized that Hippety Hopper is a baby kangaroo, so he visits a psychiatrist to help him with his visions of 'giant mice.' Blanc is Sylvester and Junior. Includes footage from *The Slap Hoppy Mouse* (1950), *Cats A-Weigh* (1953),, and *Who's Kitten Who?* (1952). Entry in the LOONEY TUNES series.
MUSIC BY Bill [William] Lava.
Released on March 14
(6 min./Vitaphone Sound/Technicolor)
DePatie-Freleng Enterprises/Warner Brothers

DR. DEVIL AND MR. HARE (1964) D: Robert McKimson.
VOICES: *Mel Blanc.*
Bothered by the slobbering Tasmanian Devil, Bugs Bunny assumes the role of a doctor and gives Tas some real treatments. Blanc is Bugs and Tas. Entry in the MERRIE MELODIES series.
SONGS: "By a Waterfall" *(Sammy Fain; Irving Kahal; sung by Blanc as Bugs)*, "London Bridge Is Falling Down" *(traditional, composer unknown)*.
MUSIC BY Bill [William] Lava.
Released on March 28
(7 min./Vitaphone Sound/Technicolor/DVD)
DePatie-Freleng Enterprises/Warner Brothers

NUTS AND VOLTS (1964) D: Friz Freleng.
VOICES: *Mel Blanc.*
Sylvester the Cat employs electronic devices, including a robot, to chase down Speedy Gonzales. Blanc is Speedy and Sylvester. Entry in the LOONEY TUNES series.
MUSIC BY Bill [William] Lava.
Released on April 25
(6 min./Vitaphone Sound/Technicolor/DVD)
DePatie-Freleng Enterprises/Warner Brothers

THE ICEMAN DUCKETH (1964) D: Phil Monroe, Maurice Noble.
VOICES: *Mel Blanc.*
Daffy Duck plans on making big bucks by selling Bugs Bunny's fur, but
first Daffy must trap the rascally rabbit in the frozen North. Blanc is Bugs,
Daffy, Frenchman, Indian, and clerk. Entry in the LOONEY TUNES series.
SONG: "Baby Face" *(Harry Akst; Benny Davis; sung by Blanc as Bugs).*
MUSIC BY Bill [William] Lava.
Released on May 16
(6 min./Vitaphone Sound/Technicolor)
Warner Brothers

HAWAIIAN AYE AYE (1964) D: Gerry Chiniquy.
VOICES: *Mel Blanc, June Foray.*
An island holiday for Granny and Tweety Pie has the little bird pro-
tected by a shark, but this doesn't stop Sylvester the Cat from attempting
to snatch Tweety. Blanc is Tweety and Sylvester. Entry in the MERRIE
MELODIES series.
SONG: "Hula Lou" *(Milton Charles; Wayne King; Jack Yellen; sung by Blanc
as Tweety).*
MUSIC BY Bill [William] Lava.
Released on June 27
(7 min./Vitaphone Sound/Technicolor/DVD)
Warner Brothers

FALSE HARE (1964) D: Robert McKimson.
VOICES: *Mel Blanc.*
The Big Bad Wolf wants to initiate Bugs Bunny into his club, but it is all
a ruse to make Bugs his supper. Blanc is Bugs, Big Bad Wolf, Nephew
Wolf, and Foghorn Leghorn. Entry in the LOONEY TUNES series.
MUSIC BY Bill [William] Lava.
Released on July 16
(6 min./Vitaphone Sound/Technicolor)
Warner Brothers

SENORELLA AND THE GLASS HUARACHE (1964) D: Hawley Pratt.
VOICES: *Mel Blanc, Tom Holland.*
A re-do of the Cinderella story with Mexican characters and setting.
Blanc is the second Mexican who narrates the cartoon. Entry in the
LOONEY TUNES series.
MUSIC BY Bill [William] Lava.
Released on August 1
(6 min./Vitaphone Sound/Technicolor/DVD)
Warner Brothers

TROUBLE BRUIN (1964) D: William Hanna, Joseph Barbera.
VOICES: *Daws Butler, Mel Blanc, Nancy Wible.*
Loopy de Loop's French accent gets him in 'Dutch' with a bear (Blanc*).*
MUSIC BY Hoyt Curtin.
Released on September 17
(6 min./RCA Sound/Eastmancolor, Technicolor)
Hanna-Barbera/Columbia

BEAR KNUCKLES (1964) D: William Hanna, Joseph Barbera.
VOICES: *Daws Butler, Mel Blanc, Janet Waldo.*
Braxton Bear (Blanc) gets rid of Emmy-Lou's latest beau, who quickly
employs Loopy de Loop to help him get her back.
MUSIC BY Hoyt Curtin.
Released on October 15
(6 min./RCA Sound/Eastmancolor, Technicolor)
Hanna-Barbera/Columbia

PANCHO'S HIDEAWAY (1964) D: Friz Freleng, Hawley Pratt.
VOICES: *Mel Blanc, Ralph James.*
Speedy Gonzales faces bandit Pancho Vanilla in order to retrieve the
loot he has stolen. Blanc is Speedy, Pancho and citizens. Entry in the
LOONEY TUNES series.
MUSIC BY Bill [William] Lava.
Released on October 24
(6 min./Vitaphone Sound/Technicolor/DVD)
DePatie-Freleng Enterprises/Warner Brothers

ROAD TO ANDALAY (1964) D: Friz Freleng, Hawley Pratt.
VOICES: *Mel Blanc.*
Sylvester the Cat employs a falcon to get the rapid rodent Speedy Gonzales.
Blanc is Speedy and Sylvester. Entry in the MERRIE MELODIES series.
MUSIC BY Bill [William] Lava.
Released on December 26
(6 min./Vitaphone Sound/Technicolor)
DePatie-Freleng Enterprises/Warner Brothers

DUEL PERSONALITY (1965) D: Chuck Jones, Maurice Noble.
VOICES: *June Foray, Mel Blanc.*
Tom and Jerry agree to engage in a classic duel at dawn. Blanc is a scream-
ing Tom and a laughing Jerry.
MUSIC BY Dean Elliot.
No Release date available
(6 min./Western Electric Sound/Metrocolor/Rated [G])
Metro-Goldwyn-Mayer

THE YEAR OF THE MOUSE (1965) D: Chuck Jones, Maurice Noble.
VOICES: *June Foray, Mel Blanc.*
Is Tom Cat trying to kill himself in his sleep? That is what Jerry Mouse
wants him to think. Blanc provides the characters' vocal effects.
MUSIC BY Eugene Poddany.
No release date available
(7 min./Westrex Sound/Metrocolor)
Metro-Goldwyn-Mayer

HAUNTED MOUSE (1965) D: Chuck Jones, Maurice Noble.
VOICES: *Mel Blanc.*
Tom Cat meets a mouse who possesses magic powers — including hyp-
nosis. Blanc provides the characters' vocal effects.
MUSIC BY Eugene Poddany.
No release date available
(7 min./Westrex Sound/Metrocolor/DVD)
Metro-Goldwyn-Mayer

TOM-IC ENERGY (1965) D: Chuck Jones, Maurice Noble.
VOICES: *Mel Blanc, June Foray.*
Tom Cat tries to acquire perpetual motion in his chase with Jerry Mouse.
Blanc provides the characters' vocal effects.
MUSIC BY Eugene Poddany.
No release date available
(6 min./Westrex Sound/Metrocolor)
Metro-Goldwyn-Mayer

AH, SWEET MOUSE-STORY OF LIFE (1965) D: Chuck Jones, Maurice
Noble.
VOICES: *June Foray, Mel Blanc.*
Jerry uses a blaring horn to dissuade Tom from chasing him around the
ledge of a high-rise building. Blanc provides the characters' vocal effects.
MUSIC BY Eugen Poddany.
No release date available
(7 min./Westrex Sound/Metrocolor)
Metro-Goldwyn-Mayer

OF FELINE BONDAGE (1965) D: Chuck Jones, Maurice Noble.
VOICES: *June Foray, Mel Blanc.*
Jerry Mouse finds aid in eluding Tom Cat (Blanc) with an invisibility
elixir provided by a fairy godmouse.
MUSIC BY Eugene Poddany.
No release date available
(6 min./Westrex Sound/Metrocolor) Metro-Goldwyn-Mayer

THE CAT'S ME-OUCH (1965) D: Chuck Jones, Maurice Noble.
VOICES: *June Foray, Mel Blanc.*
Jerry Mouse's latest ally against Tom Cat is a small bulldog. Blanc pro-
vides vocal effects.
MUSIC BY Eugene Poddany.
No release date available
(7 min./Westrex Sound/Metrocolor)
Metro-Goldwyn-Mayer

BAD DAY AT CAT ROCK (1965) D: Chuck Jones.
VOICES: *Mel Blanc.*
Tom Cat and Jerry Mouse's violent chase continues, this time atop a skyscraper. Blanc provides vocal effects for Tom and Jerry.
MUSIC BY Eugene Poddany.
Release date unavailable.
(7 min./Western Electric Sound/Metrocolor)
Metro-Goldwyn-Mayer

JERRY-GO-ROUND (1965) D: Abe Levitow.
VOICE: *Mel Blanc.*
Tom Cat may have to think twice when Jerry Mouse becomes the buddy of a circus elephant. Blanc provides vocal effects. Produced by Chuck Jones.
SONG: "O Cara Mamma Mia" *(traditional, composer unknown).*
MUSIC BY Eugene Poddany.
Release date unavailable.
(6 min./Western Electric Sound/Metrocolor)
Metro-Goldwyn-Mayer

IT'S NICE TO HAVE A MOUSE AROUND THE HOUSE (1965) D: Friz Freleng, Hawley Pratt.
VOICES: *Mel Blanc, GeGe Pearson.*
Granny decides to give Sylvester the Cat a rest and hires pest exterminator Daffy Duck to get rid of Speedy Gonzales. Blanc is Daffy and Speedy. Entry in the LOONEY TUNES series.
MUSIC BY Bill [William] Lava.
Released on January 16
(6 min./Vitaphone Sound/Technicolor)
DePatie-Freleng Enterprises/Warner Brothers

CATS AND BRUISES (1965) D: Friz Freleng, Hawley Pratt.
VOICES: *Mel Blanc.*
Sylvester the Cat disrupts the mice's Cinco de Mayo fiesta, but Speedy Gonzales takes care of him. Blanc is Speedy, Sylvester and mice. Entry in the MERRIE MELODIES series.
SONG: "Cielito Lindo" *(traditional, composer unknown; sung by Blanc as Speedy).*
MUSIC BY Bill [William] Lava.
Released on January 30
(6 min./Vitaphone Sound/Technicolor/DVD)
DePatie-Freleng Enterprises/Warner Brothers

THE WILD CHASE (1965) D: Friz Freleng, Hawley Pratt.
VOICES: *Mel Blanc, Paul Julian.*
The Road Runner and Speedy Gonzales are holding a race to see which is the fastest, as Wile E. Coyote and Sylvester the Cat team to catch them. Blanc is Speedy, Sylvester, Race caller, Starter. Entry in the MERRIE MELODIES series.
MUSIC BY Bill [William] Lava.
Released on February 27
(6 min./Vitaphone Sound/Technicolor/DVD),
DePatie-Freleng Enterprises/Warner Brothers

MOBY DUCK (1965) D: Robert McKimson.
VOICES: *Mel Blanc.*
Daffy Duck and Speedy Gonzales are washed ashore on a desert isle with a crate of canned food. Daffy quickly hogs all the cans, but Speedy has the can opener. Blanc is Daffy, Speedy and Robinson Crusoe. Entry in the LOONEY TUNES series.
MUSIC BY Bill [William] Lava.
Released on March 27
(6 min./Vitaphone Sound/Technicolor)
DePatie-Freleng Enterprises/Warner Brothers

CROW'S FEAT (1965) D: Joseph Barbera, William Hanna.
VOICES: *Daws Butler, Mel Blanc.*
Loopy de Loop has trouble when he takes over a scarecrow's duties. Blanc is the crow.
MUSIC BY Hoyt Curtin.
Released on April 14
(6 min./RCA Sound/Eastmancolor, Technicolor) Hanna-Barbera/Columbia

ASSAULT AND PEPPERED (1965) D: Robert McKimson.
VOICES: *Mel Blanc.*
A battle with cannons and land mines takes place between rancho baron Daffy Duck and peon mouse Speedy Gonzales. Blanc is Daffy, Speedy and mice. Entry in the MERRIE MELODIES series.
MUSIC BY Bill [William] Lava.
Released on April 24
(6 min./Vitaphone Sound/Technicolor)
DePatie-Freleng Enterprises/Warner Brothers

PICKLED PINK (1965) D: Friz Freleng, Hawley Pratt.
VOICE: *Mel Blanc.*
A drunk (Blanc) takes the Pink Panther home to his less-than-enchanted wife.
MUSIC BY Henry Mancini, Bill [William] Lava.
Released on May 12
(6 min./RCA Sound/DeLuxe Color/DVD)
Mirisch/Geoffrey/DePatie-Freleng Enterprises/United Artists

WELL WORN DAFFY (1965) D: Robert McKimson.
VOICES: *Mel Blanc.*
Speedy Gonzales and his two mice *companeros* are thirsting in the desert when they spot Daffy Duck's oasis, but Daffy won't let them drink. Blanc is Speedy, Daffy, Pedro, Jose, and Camel. Entry in the LOONEY TUNES series.
MUSIC BY Bill [William] Lava.
Released on May 22
(6 min./Vitaphone Sound/Technicolor)
DePatie-Freleng Enterprises/Warner Brothers

SUPPRESSED DUCK (1965) D: Robert McKimson.
VOICES: *Mel Blanc.*
A forest ranger's boundary line creates obstacles for Daffy Duck's bear hunt. Blanc is Daffy, the ranger, and the bear. Entry in the LOONEY TUNES series.
MUSIC BY Bill [William] Lava.
Released on June 26
(6 min./Vitaphone Sound/Technicolor)
DePatie-Freleng Enterprises/Warner Brothers

CORN ON THE COP (1965) D: Irv Spector.
VOICES: *Mel Blanc, Joanie Gerber.*
Policemen Daffy Duck and Porky Pig mistake Granny for a supermarket thief and suffer an umbrella-beating for their trouble. Blanc is Daffy, Porky, the robber, the pirate trick-or-treater, clerk, police dispatcher, and Officer Flaherty. Entry in the MERRIE MELODIES series.
MUSIC BY Bill [William] Lava.
Released on July 24
(6 min./Vitaphone Sound/Technicolor)
DePatie-Freleng Enterprises/Warner Brothers

TEASE FOR TWO (1965) D: Robert McKimson.
VOICES: *Mel Blanc.*
Daffy Duck is prospecting for gold when he encounters the Goofy Gophers, who lay claim to the spot on which Daffy wants to dig. Blanc is Daffy, Mac, Tosh, and the cosmonaut. Entry in the LOONEY TUNES series.
MUSIC BY Bill [William] Lava.
Released on August 28
(6 min./Vitaphone Sound/Technicolor)
DePatie-Freleng Enterprises/Warner Brothers

CHILI CORN CORNY (1965) D: Robert McKimson.
VOICES: *Mel Blanc, [Pedro] Gonzales-Gonzales.*
Speedy Gonzales and Loco Crow want to sample the corn in Daffy Duck's field, but the manic mallard has other ideas. Blanc is Daffy and Speedy. Entry in the LOONEY TUNES series.
MUSIC BY Bill [William] Lava.
Released on October 23
(6 min./Vitaphone Sound/Technicolor)
DePatie-Freleng Enterprises/Warner Brothers

GO GO AMIGO (1965) D: Robert McKimson.
VOICES: *Mel Blanc, [Pedro] Gonzales-Gonzales.*
Speedy Gonzales and some mice are having a party in Daffy Duck's TV
& radio shop; Daffy is determined to stop them. Blanc is Speedy, Daffy,
mice and radio voice. Entry in the MERRIE MELODIES series.
MUSIC BY Bill [William] Lava.
Released on November 20
(7 min./Vitaphone Sound/Technicolor) DePatie-Freleng Enterprises

MATINEE MOUSE (1966) D: Tom Ray.
VOICES: *Mel Blanc.*
Tom Cat and Jerry Mouse (both voiced by Blanc) set aside their chase
to view some scenes from old 'Tom & Jerry' cartoons. Includes footage
from *Love That Pup* (1949), *The Flying Cat* (1952), *Jerry's Diary* (1949),
The Flying Sorceress (1956), and *The Truce Hurts* (1948).
MUSIC BY Dean Elliot.
No release date available
(6 min./Western Electric Sound/Metrocolor)
Metro-Goldwyn-Mayer

JERRY, JERRY, QUITE CONTRARY (1966) D: Chuck Jones, Maurice
Noble.
VOICES: *Mel Blanc.*
Jerry Mouse's sleepwalking endangers Tom Cat. Blanc is Tom and Jerry.
MUSIC BY Dean Elliot.
No release date available
(7 min./Western Electric Sound/Metrocolor/Rated [G])
Metro-Goldwyn-Mayer

CATTY-CORNERED (1966) D: Abe Levitow.
VOICES: *Mel Blanc, June Foray.*
Jerry Mouse uses connecting doors in his mouse-hole to pit Tom against
a rival cat. Blanc provides vocal effects. Produced by Chuck Jones.
MUSIC BY Carl Bandt.
No release date available
(7 min./Western Electric Sound/Metrocolor)
SIB-Tower 12/Metro-Goldwyn-Mayer

LOVE ME, LOVE MY MOUSE (1966) D: Chuck Jones, Ben Washam.
VOICES: *June Foray, Mel Blanc.*
Tom Cat's girlfriend meets Jerry Mouse and immediately becomes Jerry's protector. Blanc provides vocal effects for Tom and Jerry. Produced by Chuck Jones.
SONG: "Lullaby" *(Johannes Brahms).*
MUSIC BY Eugene Poddany.
No release date available
(6 min./Westrex Sound/Metrocolor/Rated [G])
SIB-Tower 12/Metro-Goldwyn-Mayer

THE ASTRODUCK (1966) D: Robert McKimson.
VOICES: *Mel Blanc.*
Daffy Duck hopes to enjoy a summer holiday in a rented Mexican hacienda, but Speedy Gonzales is already there — and eager to heckle the irate duck. Blanc is Daffy, Speedy, and the realtor. Entry in the LOONEY TUNES series.
MUSIC BY Bill [William] Lava.
Released on January 1
(7 min./Vitaphone Sound/Technicolor)
DePatie-Freleng Enterprises/Warner Brothers

MUCHO LOCOS (1966) D: Robert McKimson.
VOICES: *Mel Blanc.*
A broken TV set does not provide much entertainment for a little mouse until Speedy Gonzales helps him conjure up images of 'El Stupido' Daffy Duck. Blanc is Speedy, Daffy, crow, cat, mice. Includes footage from *China Jones* (1959), *Deduce You Say* (1956), *Mexicali Shmoes* (1959), *Robin Hood Daffy* (1958), and *Tortilla Flaps* (1958). Entry in the MERRIE MELODIES series.
MUSIC BY Herman Stein.
Released on February 5
(6 min./Vitaphone Sound/Technicolor)
DePatie-Freleng Enterprises/Warner Brothers

PINK PUNCH (1966) D: Hawley Pratt.
VOICE: *Mel Blanc.*
The Pink Panther is hawking his new product, Pink Punch, when a pesky green asterisk gets in the way. Blanc provides vocal effects.
MUSIC BY William Lava, Henry Mancini.
Released on February 21
(6 min./RCA Sound/DeLuxe Color)
Mirisch/Geoffrey/DePatie-Freleng Enterprises/United Artists

MEXICAN MOUSE-PIECE (1966) D: Robert McKimson.
VOICES: *Mel Blanc, Ralph James.*
Daffy Duck hopes to ship some captured mice to starving cats overseas, but Speedy Gonzales attempts to save his compadres. Blanc is Daffy and Speedy. Entry in the MERRIE MELODIES series.
MUSIC BY Bill [William] Lava.
Released on February 26
(6 min./Vitaphone Sound/Technicolor)
DePatie-Freleng Enterprises/Warner Brothers

DAFFY RENTS (1966) D: Robert McKimson.
VOICES: *Mel Blanc, [Pedro] Gonzales-Gonzales.*
When Daffy Duck's robot mouse-catcher double-crosses him, Daffy must capture Speedy Gonzales on his own. Blanc is Daffy, Speedy, Herman, First nurse, Cats. Entry in the LOONEY TUNES series.
MUSIC BY Irving Gertz.
Released on March 26
(6 min./Vitaphone Sound/Technicolor)
DePatie-Freleng Enterprises/Warner Brothers

A-HAUNTING WE WILL GO (1966) D: Robert McKimson.
VOICES: *Mel Blanc, June Foray.*
Daffy Duck investigates when his nephew says he has seen a real witch. It turns out that Speedy Gonzales has been transformed into a duplicate of Witch Hazel (who cannot shake the Mexican accent). Blanc is Daffy, Speedy and nephew. Entry in the LOONEY TUNES series. Uses re-worked footage from *Duck Amuck* (1953) and *Broomstick Bunny* (1956).
SONG: "Aloha Oe" *(Queen Lilioukalani).*
MUSIC BY Bill [William] Lava.
Released on April 16
(7 min./Vitaphone Sound/Technicolor/DVD)
DePatie-Freleng Enterprises/Warner Brothers

SNOW EXCUSE (1966) D: Robert McKimson.
VOICES: *Mel Blanc.*
In a cold, wintry mountain cabin, Daffy Duck figures he has got plenty of firewood to keep warm — until a frozen Speedy Gonzales pilfers it. Blanc is Daffy, Speedy and mailman. Entry in the MERRIE MELODIES series.
MUSIC BY Bill [William] Lava.
Released on May 21
(6 min./Vitaphone Sound/Technicolor)
DePatie-Freleng Enterprises/Warner Brothers

A SQUEAK IN THE DEEP (1966) D: Robert McKimson.
VOICES: *Mel Blanc.*
Daffy Duck races against Speedy Gonzales in the Guadalajara-to-Hawaii yacht club competition. Blanc is Daffy, Speedy and PA voice. Entry in the LOONEY TUNES series.
SONGS: "Hula Lou" *(Edward Grossmith; Ted D. Wood; sung by Blanc as Speedy),* "Alo-Ahe" *(Lothar Olias; Gunnter Loose; sung by Blanc as Daffy).*
MUSIC BY Walter Greene.
Released on July 19
(6 min./Vitaphone Sound/Technicolor)
DePatie-Freleng Enterprises/Warner Brothers

FEATHER FINGER (1966) D: Robert McKimson.
VOICES: *Mel Blanc.*
Daffy Duck hires himself out as a gunfighter to get rid of Speedy Gonzales, the pest of Hangtree, Texas. Blanc is Daffy, Speedy, and Mayor Phur E. Katt. Entry in the MERRIE MELODIES series.
MUSIC BY Walter Greene.
Released on August 20
(6 min./Vitaphone Sound/Technicolor/Rated [G])
DePatie-Freleng Enterprises/Warner Brothers

SWING DING AMIGO (1966) D: Robert McKimson.
VOICES: *Mel Blanc.*
Speedy Gonzales' rock 'n' roll performance at the Go Go Club is keeping Daffy Duck awake, so the mallard tries to silence the party. Blanc is Speedy, Daffy and mice. Entry in the LOONEY TUNES series.
MUSIC BY Walter Greene.
Released on September 17
(6 min./Vitaphone Sound/Technicolor)
DePatie-Freleng Enterprises/Warner Brothers

A TASTE OF CATNIP (1966) D: Robert McKimson.
VOICES: *Mel Blanc, [Pedro] Gonzales-Gonzales.*
Daffy Duck seeks psychiatric help when he fears he is turning into a cat and is obsessed with eating Speedy Gonzales. Blanc is Daffy, Speedy and cat effects. Entry in the MERRIE MELODIES series.
MUSIC BY Walter Greene.
Released on December 3
(6 min./Vitaphone Sound/Technicolor)
DePatie-Freleng Enterprises/Warner Brothers

BUSCH ADVERTISEMENT (1967) D: Joseph Barbera, William Hanna.
VOICES: *Alan Reed, Mel Blanc, Jean Vander Pyl, Gerry Johnson, John Stephenson.*
The Flintstone characters appear in this featurette for Busch beer. Blanc is Barney Rubble.
(25 min./color)
Hanna-Barbera/Garoner Advertising

THE MOUSE FROM H.U.N.G.E.R. (1967) D: Abe Levitow.
VOICES: *Mel Blanc.*
Secret agent Jerry Mouse's assignment is to steal the cheese supply guarded by Tom Cat. Blanc is Tom and the cigar store Indian.
MUSIC BY Dean Elliot.
No release date available
(6 min./Westrex Sound/Metrocolor/Rated [G])
SIB-Tower 12/Metro-Goldwyn-Mayer

CAT AND DUPLI-CAT (1967) D: Chuck Jones, Maurice Noble.
VOICES: *Mel Blanc, Dal McKennon, Terence Monck.*
Tom Cat discovers he has a rival who also wants to capture Jerry Mouse. Blanc is Tom, Jerry, and the rival cat.
MUSIC BY Eugene Poddany.
No release date available
(7 min./Western Electric Sound/Metrocolor)
SIB-Tower 12/Metro-Goldwyn-Mayer

DAFFY'S DINER (1967) D: Robert McKimson.
VOICES: *Mel Blanc.*
Daffy Duck runs a roadside eatery specializing in 'mouseburgers,' but he is fresh out of mice — until Speedy Gonzales shows up. Blanc is Daffy, Speedy, El Supremo, and the garbage man. Entry in the MERRIE MELODIES series.
MUSIC BY Walter Greene.
Released on January 21
(6 min./Vitaphone Sound/Technicolor/Rated [G])
DePatie-Freleng Enterprises/Warner Bros.

O-SOLAR-MEOW (1967) D: Abe Levitow.
VOICES: *Mel Blanc.*
Tom & Jerry (vocal effects by Blanc) go space-age as they conduct their latest chase aboard an orbiting rest station. Jerry wants some cheese from a supply satellite and Tom uses various gadgets to stop him. Produced by Chuck Jones.
MUSIC BY Eugene Poddany.
Released on January 29
(6 min./Westrex Sound/Metrocolor)
SIB-Tower 12/Metro-Goldwyn-Mayer

QUACKER TRACKER (1967) D: Rudy Larriva.
VOICES: *Mel Blanc.*
A hunting club offers a lifetime membership to the 'ignoramus' who is willing to capture Speedy Gonzales. In walks Daffy Duck to accept the challenge. Blanc is Speedy, Daffy, Mouse, Hunter and Club President. Entry in the LOONEY TUNES series.
MUSIC BY Frank Perkins, William Lava.
Released on April 29
(5 min./Vitaphone Sound/Technicolor/DVD)
Format/Warner Bros.

THE MUSIC MICE-TRO (1967) D: Rudy Larriva.
VOICES: *Mel Blanc.*
Speedy Gonzales and his mariachi band follow Daffy Duck to his Balmy Springs retreat and drive the manic mallard crazy with their insistence on auditioning. Blanc is Daffy and Speedy. Entry in the MERRIE MELODIES series.
MUSIC BY William Lava.
Released on May 27
(7 min./Vitaphone Sound/Technicolor)
Format/Warner Bros.

THE SPY SWATTER (1967) D: Rudy Larriva.
VOICES: *Mel Blanc.*
Secret agent Speedy Gonzales is entrusted with a strength formula and must keep it out of the hands of enemy spy Daffy Duck. Blanc is Speedy, Daffy, Mr. Sam Brown, the professor, and Hugo the Robot.
MUSIC BY William Lava.
Released on June 24
(6 min./Vitaphone Sound/Technicolor)
Format/Warner Bros.

SPEEDY GHOST TO TOWN (1967) D: Alex Lovy.
VOICES: *Mel Blanc.*
Daffy Duck takes a lot of punishment to steal Speedy Gonzales' 'gold' mine map. Blanc is Daffy, Speedy and Miguel. Entry in the MERRIE MELODIES series.
MUSIC BY William Lava.
Released on July 29
(6 min./Vitaphone Sound/Technicolor/Rated [G])
Warner Brothers

RODENT TO STARDOM (1967) D: Alex Lovy.
VOICES: *Mel Blanc.*
While in Hollywood, Daffy Duck is discovered by a film director who wants to put the mallard in movies — as a stunt double for Speedy Gonzales. Blanc is Daffy, Speedy, Hassenpfeffer, Assistant, and Ducky Lamour. Entry in the LOONEY TUNES series.
MUSIC BY William Lava.
Released on September 23
(6 min./Vitaphone Sound/Technicolor/Rated [G])
Warner Bros.-Seven Arts

GO AWAY STOWAWAY (1967) D: Alex Lovy.
VOICES: *Mel Blanc.*
Daffy Duck has to put up with pesky Speedy Gonzales while on an ocean voyage. Blanc is Daffy and Speedy. Entry in the MERRIE MELODIES series.
SONGS: "La Cucaracha" *(Mexican traditional, composer unknown)*, "You Oughta Be in Pictures" *(Dana Suesse)*, "Rock-a-Bye Baby" *(Effie I. Canning)*.
MUSIC BY William Lava.
Released on September 30
(6 min./Vitaphone Sound/Technicolor/Rated [G])
Warner Bros.-Seven Arts

FIESTA FIASCO (1967) D: Alex Lovy.
VOICES: *Mel Blanc.*
Daffy Duck sets out to ruin Speedy Gonzales' party plans by employing
a rain-making device. Blanc is Speedy, Daffy, Pancho, Mouse, Rudolfo,
Pedro. Entry in the LOONEY TUNES series.
MUSIC BY William Lava.
Released on December 9
(6 min./Vitaphone Sound/Technicolor)
Warner Bros.-Seven Arts

SKY SCRAPER CAPER (1968) D: Alex Lovy.
VOICES: *Mel Blanc.*
When Daffy Duck goes sleepwalking around a construction site, amigo
Speedy Gonzales sees to it that Daffy is not hurt. Blanc is Daffy, Speedy
and Ice Cream man. Entry in the LOONEY TUNES series.
MUSIC BY William Lava.
Released on March 9
(6 min./Vitaphone Sound/Technicolor)
Warner Bros.-Seven Arts

SEE YA LATER, GLADIATOR (1968) D: Alex Lovy.
VOICES: *Mel Blanc.*
Sent back in time to Ancient Rome, Daffy Duck and Speedy Gonzales
end up in the gladiators' ring to face an angry lion. Blanc is Speedy, Daffy,
the scientist, 'fathead' Roman, the lion, and Emperor Nero. Entry in the
LOONEY TUNES series.
MUSIC BY William Lava.
Released on June 29
(6 min./Vitaphone Sound/Technicolor/Rated [G])
Warner Bros.-Seven Arts

CHIMP & ZEE (1968) D: Alex Lovy.
VOICES: *Mel Blanc.*
A hunter in the jungle is after a blue-tailed monkey, but has trouble catch-
ing one — until he dresses as a female simian. Blanc is the Professor and
chimp sounds. Entry in the MERRIE MELODIES series.
MUSIC BY William Lava.
Released on October 12
(5 min./Vitaphone Sound/Technicolor/Rated [G])
Warner Bros.-Seven Arts

BUNNY AND CLAUDE: WE ROB CARROT PATCHES (1968)
D: Bob [Robert] McKimson.
VOICES: *Mel Blanc, Pat Woodell. Vocals by Billy Strange.*
Two rabbit bandits elude the sheriff as they go on a carrot-robbing spree.
Parody of the film *Bonnie and Clyde* with Blanc as Claude, the sheriff and
the storekeeper. Entry in the LOONEY TUNES series.
SONG: "The Ballad of Bunny and Claude" *(composer unknown).*
MUSIC BY William Lava.
Released on November 9
(6 min./Vitaphone Sound/Technicolor/Rated [G])
Warner Bros.-Seven Arts

THE GREAT CARROT-TRAIN ROBBERY (1969)
D: Bob [Robert] McKimson.
VOICES: *Mel Blanc, Pat Woodell. Vocals by Billy Strange.*
Rabbit-bandits Bunny and Claude are at it again, this time heisting a
trainload of carrots. Blanc is Claude, the sheriff and the station agent.
Entry in the MERRIE MELODIES series.
MUSIC BY William Lava.
Released on January 25
(6 min./Vitaphone Sound/Technicolor/Rated [G])
Warner Bros.

A POLITICAL CARTOON (1974) D: Joe [Joseph] Adamson, Jim Morrow.
LIVE ACTION: *Alex Krakower, Liam Smith, Joseph Adamson, Lindsay
Doran, Jim Morrow*
VOICE: *Mel Blanc*
Mixture of live action and animation about two men who scheme to run
a cartoon character for president. Blanc voices Bugs Bunny.
Released in October
(22 min./color/Video/DVD)
Produced by Joe [Joseph] Adamson and Jim Morrow

THE DUXORCIST (1987) D: Greg Ford, Terry Lennon.
VOICES: *Mel Blanc, B.J. Ward.*
Paranormal investigator Daffy Duck (Blanc) attempts to exorcise a sexy
female duck. Entry in the LOONEY TUNES series.
MUSIC BY Hal Willner, Carl Stalling, Milt Franklyn.
Released on November 20
(8 min./color/Rated [G]/DVD)
Warner Bros.

THE NIGHT OF THE LIVING DUCK (1988) D: Greg Ford, Terry Lennon.
VOICES: *Mel Blanc, Mel Torme.*
Daffy Duck (Blanc) reads monster comic books and dreams he is a singer
in a nightclub full of famous creatures, such as Dracula, Frankenstein's
Monster, and the Mummy. Entry in the MERRIE MELODIES series.
SONG: "Monsters Lead Such Interesting Lives" *(Virg Dzurinko; Greg
Ford).*
MUSIC BY Hal Willner, Carl Stalling, Milt Franklyn.
Released on September 23
(7 min./stereo sound/color/Rated [G]/DVD)
Warner Bros.

FIFTY YEARS OF BUGS BUNNY IN 3½ MINUTES (1989) D: Chuck
Workman.
VOICES: *Mel Blanc, Noel Blanc.*
A look at classic cartoon clips with Mel Blanc as Bugs Bunny, Daffy Duck,
and Wile E. Coyote.
MUSIC BY Hummie Mann.
Released on December 1
(4 min./color)
Calliope/Warner Bros.

Feature Films
Contributed by Randy Bonneville

PINOCCHIO (1940) D: Ben Sharpsteen, Hamilton Luske, Bill Roberts, Jack Kinney, Norman Ferguson, Wilfred Jackson, T. Hee.
VOICES: *Dickie Jones, Cliff Edwards, Christian Rub, Evelyn Venable, Walter Catlett, Charles Judels, Frankie Darro, Don Brodie, Jack Bailey, Linsay MacHarrie, John McLeish, Stuart Buchanan, Patricia Page, Jack Mercer, Virginia Davis, Clarence Nash, Mel Blanc, The King's Men, Marion Darlington.*
An elderly puppeteer (Rub) fashions a wooden boy that comes to life. However, in order to become a real boy, Pinocchio (Jones) has to prove he is worthy. Blanc is the hiccupping Gideon the Cat. Charles Judels' performance as Stromboli garnered an AFI Villains Nomination. SOURCE: story by Carlo Collodi.

SONGS: "When You Wish Upon A Star" *(Academy Award Winner; AFI Song 7),* "Little Wooden Head", "Give A Little Whistle", "Turn On The Old Music Box" *(instrumental),* "Hi-Diddle-Dee-Dee *(An Actor's Life For Me)*", "I've Got No Strings" *(all by Leigh Harline–Ned Washington).*

Additional Academy Award *(Music – Original Score)* Leigh Harline, Paul J. Smith, Ned Washington.

"A lie keeps growing and growing until it's as clear as the nose on your face" — The Blue Fairy *(Evelyn Venable; AFI Movie Quote Nominee).*
National Film Registry 1994
AFI Greatest Movies Nominee
AFI Thrills Nominee
AFI Cheers 38
AFI Top Ten Animation 2

Box Office: $3,600,000

Released on February 7
(88 min./RCA Sound/Technicolor/Rated [G]/Video/Laserdisc/DVD)
Walt Disney Productions/RKO Radio

BROADWAY MELODY OF 1940 (1940) D: Norman Taurog.
Fred Astaire, Eleanor Powell, George Murphy, Frank Morgan, Ian Hunter, Florence Rice, Lynne Carver, Ann Morriss, Trixie Frischke, Douglas McPhail, Herman Bing, Jack Mulhall, Barbara Jo Allen [Vera Vague], Joe Yule, Irving Bacon, Mel Blanc, Charlotte Arren, Gladys Blake, Johnny Broderick, Don Brodie, Paul E. Burns, George Chandler, Joseph Crehan, Hal K. Dawson, Edgar Dearing, James Flavin, The Music Maids, Mel[ville] Ruick, William Tannen, Russell Wade.
After getting his star break, hoofer Murphy's success goes to his head and causes a strain in his partnership with Astaire. Blanc plays a panhandler.

CHOREOGRAPHY BY Bobby Connelly.
SONGS: "Please Don't Monkey With Broadway" *(Cole Porter),* "All Ashore" *(Roger Edens),* "Between You And Me" *(Porter),* "I've Got My Eyes On You" *(Porter),* "I Concentrate On You" *(Porter),* "Begin The Beguine" *(Porter; AFI Song Nominee),* "Jukebox Dance" *(Walter Ruick).*
MUSIC BY Roger Edens, Walter Ruick, Alfred Newman.
Released on February 9.
(102 min./Western Electric Sound/Video/Laserdisc/DVD)
Metro-Goldwyn-Mayer

APRIL SHOWERS (1948) D: James V. Kern.
Jack Carson, Ann Sothern, Robert Alda, S.Z. Sakall, Robert [Bobby] Ellis, Richard Rober, Joseph Crehan, Billy Curtis, John Gallaudet, Philip Van Zandt, Ray Walker, William Haade, Mel Blanc (voice), Barbara Bates, Penny Edwards, Richard Erdman, Pat Flaherty, Lila Leeds, Weaver Levy, Paul Maxey, Mary Stuart, Minerva Urecal.
A family vaudeville act headed by dad Carson splits up when he hits the bottle. Blanc's voice is heard as Ellis' midget impersonation.

SOURCE: "Barbary Host" *(story)* by Joe Laurie Jr.
CHOREOGRAPHY BY LeRoy Prinz.
SONGS: "The Stars And Stripes Forever" *(John Philip Sousa),* "Mr. Lovejoy And Mr. Gay" *(Ray Heindorf-Jack Scholl),* "Cuddle Up A Little Closer" *(Karl Hoschna-Otto A. Harbach),* "The World's Most Beautiful Girl" *(Kim Gannon-Ted Fetter),* "Little Trouper" *(Gannon-Walter Kent),* "Moonlight Bay" *(Percy Wenrich-Edward Madden),* "April Showers" *(Louis Silvers-B.G. DeSylva),* "Are You From Dixie" *(George L. Cobb-Jack Yellen),* "Put On Your Old Grey Bonnet" *(Wenrich-Stanley Murphy),* "While Strolling Through

The Park One Day" *(Ed Haley)*, "Every Little Movement" *(Hoschna-Harbach)*, "Pretty Baby" *(Tony Jackson-Egbert Van Alstyne-Harbach)*, "Carolina In The Morning" *(Walter Donaldson-Gus Kahn)*, "Mary, You're A Little Bit Old-Fashioned" *(Henry Marshall-Marion Sunshine)*, "It's Tulip Time In Holland" *(Richard A. Whiting-Dave Radford)*
MUSIC BY Max Steiner, Ray Heindorf.
Released on March 27.
(94 min./RCA Sound)
Warner Brothers

TWO GUYS FROM TEXAS (1948) D: David Butler, (I. [Friz] Freleng).
Dennis Morgan, Jack Carson, Dorothy Malone, Penny Edwards, Forrest Tucker, Fred Clark, Gerald Mohr, John Alvin, Andrew Tombes, Monte Blue, The Philharmonica Trio, Mel Blanc (voice), Lane Chandler, Brandon Hurst, Clifton Young.
Morgan and Carson are a pair of vaudeville troupers who have to go on the lam after crossing some crooks. They take refuge on a Texas ranch, where they meet Malone and Edwards. Blanc is the voice of Bugs Bunny during an animated sequence featuring caricatures of Morgan and Carson.

SOURCE: "Howdy Stranger" *(play)* by Louis Pelletier Jr. and Robert Sloane.
FILMED AT the Thunderbird Ranch in Palm Springs, CA.
CHOREOGRAPHY BY LeRoy Prinz.
SONGS: "There's Music In The Land", "I Don't Care If It Rains All Night", "I Never Met A Texan", "Ev'ry Day I Love You (Just A Little Bit More)", "I Wanna Be A Cowboy In The Movies", "Hankerin'", "At The Rodeo" *(all by Jule Styne-Sammy Cahn)*.
MUSIC BY Frederick Hollander, Ray Heindorf, Leo F. Forbstein.
Released on September 4.
(86 min./Vitaphone and RCA Sound/Technicolor)
Warner Brothers

MY DREAM IS YOURS (1949) D: Michael Curtiz, (Friz Freleng).
Jack Carson, Doris Day, Lee Bowman, Adolphe Menjou, Eve Arden, S.Z. Sakall, Selena Royle, Edgar Kennedy, Sheldon Leonard, Franklin Pangborn, John Berkes, Ada Leonard, Frankie Carle, 'Bugs Bunny & Tweety Bird [Pie]' [voice of Mel Blanc], Iris Adrian, Sandra Gould, Bob Carson, Lennie Bremen,

Marion Martin, Frank Scannell, Chili Williams, Art Gilmore, James Flavin, Rudy Friml Jr., Paul Maxey, Don Brodie, Tristram Coffin, Chester Clute, George Neise, Joan Vohs, Eve Whitney.
A talent scout (Carson) discovers a new singing star in a 'girl-next-door' type (Day). Blanc voices Bugs and Tweety in a dream sequence.

SOURCE: "Hot Air" *(story)* by Jerry Wald and Paul Finder Moss.
FILMED AT Iverson Ranch, Chatsworth, CA.
CHOREOGRAPHY BY LeRoy Prinz.
SONGS: "Hooray For Hollywood" *(Richard A. Whiting-Johnny Mercer)*, "Love Finds A Way" *(Harry Warren-Ralph Blane)*, "Canadian Capers" *(Guy Chandler-Bert White-Henry Cohen-Earle Burtnett) (adapted as "Cuttin' Capers" by Warren-Blane)*, "My Dream Is Yours" *(Warren-Blane)*, "Tick-Tick-Tick" *(Warren-Blane)*, "The Merry-Go-Round Broke Down" *(Cliff Friend-Dave Franklin)*, "Someone Like You" *(Warren-Blane)*, "Five O'Clock Whistle" *(Gene Irwin-Joseph Myrow)*, "Freddie, Get Ready" *(Warren-Blane) (based on "Hungarian Rhapsody No. 2" by Franz Liszt)*, "Vienna Blood" *(Johann Strauss)*, "With Plenty Of Money And You" *(Warren-Al Dubin)*, "Lullaby Of Broadway" *(Warren-Dubin)*, "I'll String Along With You" *(Warren-Dubin)*, "What's Up Doc?" *(Carl Stalling)*, "Nagasaki" *(Warren-Mort Dixon)*, "I Wanna Go Back To Bali" *(Warren-Dubin)*, "You Must Have Been A Beautiful Baby" *(Warren-Mercer)*, "Avalon" *(Vincent Rose)(based on "E Lucevan Le Stelle" from "Tosca" by Giacomo Puccini)*, "Jeepers Creepers" *(Warren-Mercer)*, "I Only Have Eyes For You" *(Warren-Dubin)*, "Bull Dog" *(Cole Porter)*
MUSIC BY Howard Jackson, Ray Heindorf.
Released on April 16.
(101 min./RCA and Vitaphone Sound/Technicolor/Video/Laserdisc/DVD)
Michael Curtiz Productions/Warner Brothers

NEPTUNE'S DAUGHTER (1949) D: Edward Buzzell.
Esther Williams, Red Skelton, Ricardo Montalban, Betty Garrett, Keenan Wynn, Xavier Cugat and His Orchestra, Ted de Corsia, Mike Mazurki, Mel Blanc, George Mann, Frank Mitchell, Joi Lansing, Theresa Harris, Elaine Sterling, Dick Simmons, Pierre Watkin, Juan Duval, Harold S. Kruger, Carl Saxe, Matt Moore, Dewey Robinson, Dorothy Abbott, Del Henderson, Kay Mansfield, Heinie Conklin.
Lady bathing-suit designer Williams finds romance south of the border with handsome Latin Montalban. Blanc plays Julio Pancho.

FILMED AT Weeki Wachee Springs, FL.
CHOREOGRAPHY BY Jack Donohue.
SONGS: "I Love Those Men" *(Frank Loesser),* My Heart Beats Faster"
(Loesser), On A Slow Boat To China" *(Loesser),* Baby, It's Cold Outside"
(Loesser; Academy Award Winner; AFI Song Nominee), Jungle Rhumba"
(Toni Beaulieu), Carnivales De Oriente" *(Hechavarria Rafael Cueto),*
Cachita" *(Rafael Hernandez-Bernardo San Cristobal),* "Jungle Fantasy"
(Esy Morales)
MUSIC BY George E. Stoll.

One of the 29 top-grossing films of 1948-49 *(Box Office: $3,500,000).*

Released in June.
(93 min./Western Electric Sound/Technicolor/Video/Laserdisc/DVD)
Metro-Goldwyn-Mayer

IT'S A GREAT FEELING (1949) D: David Butler.
*Dennis Morgan, Doris Day, Jack Carson, Bill Goodwin, Irving Bacon, Claire
Carleton, The Famous Mazzone-Abbott Dancers, Harlan Warde, Jacqueline
De Wit, Errol Flynn, David Butler, Michael Curtiz, King Vidor, Raoul
Walsh, Gary Cooper, Joan Crawford, Sydney Greenstreet, Danny Kaye,
Patricia Neal, Eleanor Parker, Ronald Reagan, Edward G. Robinson, Jane
Wyman, Maureen Reagan, Mel Blanc (voice), Sandra Gould, James Holden,
Olan Soule. Narrated by Douglas Kennedy.*
Hollywood story about Morgan and Carson searching for a director to
helm their next picture, but Carson's enormous ego gets in the way. Blanc
voices Bugs Bunny in an animated cameo.

SOURCE: "Two Guys and a Girl" *(story)* by I.A.L. Diamond.
SONGS: "It's A Great Feeling" *(Academy Award Nominee),* "Give Me A
Song With A Beautiful Melody", "Blame My Absent-Minded Heart",
"That Was A Big, Fat Lie", "Fiddle Dee Dee", "At The Café Rendezvous"
"There's Nothing Rougher Than Love" *(all by Jule Styne-Sammy Cahn).*
MUSIC BY Ray Heindorf, (Howard Jackson).
Released on August 1.
*(85 min./RCA and Vitaphone Sound/Technicolor/Video/Laserdisc) Warner
Brothers*

CHAMPAGNE FOR CAESAR (1950) D: Richard B. Whorf.
Ronald Colman, Celeste Holm, Vincent Price, Barbara Britton, Art Linkletter, Gabriel Heatter, George Fisher, Byron Foulger, Ellye Marshall, Vicki Raaf, John Eldredge, Lyle Talbot, George Leigh, John Hart, Mel Blanc (voice), Peter Brocco, Brian O'Hara, Jack Daly, Gordon Nelson, Herbert Lytton, George Meader, Robert Clarke, Caesar (a parrot).
When an intellectual with a photographic memory begins to win big on a radio quiz show, the program's sponsor sends a vamp to break the smart man's concentration. Blanc is the voice of Caesar the parrot, who has a fondness for expensive wine. Produced by Harry M. Popkin.

MUSIC BY Dmitri Tiomkin.

AFI Laughs Nominee

Released on May 11.
(99 min./RCA Sound/Video/Laserdisc/DVD)
Cardinal/United Artists

THE FULLER BRUSH GIRL (1950) D: Lloyd Bacon.
Lucille Ball, Eddie Albert, Carl Benton Reid, Gale Robbins, Jeff Donnell, Jerome Cowan, John Litel, Fred Graham, Lee Patrick, Arthur Space, Jack Perrin, Sid Tomack, Billy Vincent, Lorin Raker, Lelah Tyler, Sarah Edwards, Emil Sitka, Lois Austin, Isabel Randolph, Isabel Withers, Red Skelton, Gail Bonney, Mary Treen, John Doucette, Barbara Pepper, Myron Healey, Bud Osborne, Joseph Crehan, Jean Willes, Val Avery, Syd Saylor, Frank Wilcox, Mel Blanc (voice).
Door-to-door saleslady Ball and boyfriend Albert run afoul of killers, cops and smugglers when they stumble onto a murder. Blanc is the voice of the parrot.

SONG: "Put The Blame On Mame" *(Allan Roberts-Doris Fisher)*
MUSIC BY Heinz Roemheld, Morris Stoloff.
Released on September 15.
(85 min./Video/Laserdisc)
Columbia

SCANDAL SHEET (1952) D: Phil Karlson.
Broderick Crawford, Donna Reed, John Derek, Rosemary DeCamp, Henry O'Neill, Henry [Harry] Morgan, James Millican, Griff Barnett, Jonathan Hale, Pierre Watkin, Ida Moore, Ralph Reed, Luther Crockett, Charles Cane, Jay Adler, Don Beddoe, Kathryn Card, Victoria Horne, Peter Virgo, Matt Willis, Ric Roman, Eugene Baxter, Katherine Warren, Helen Brown, Charles Coleman, Ralph Volkie, John 'Skins' Miller, Garry Owen, Guy Wilkerson, Mel Blanc, Gertrude Astor.
A ruthless newspaper editor finds himself the target of investigative reporters when he accidentally kills his former wife. Blanc is the drunken witness.

SOURCE: Adapted from the 1944 novel *The Dark Page* by Samuel Fuller.
PRODUCED BY Edward Small.
MUSIC BY George Duning, Morris Stoloff.
Released on January 16.
(82 min.)
Motion Pictures Investors Productions/Columbia

JACK AND THE BEANSTALK (1952) D: Jean Yarbrough.
Bud Abbott & Lou Costello, Buddy Baer, Shaye Cogan, James Alexander, Dorothy Ford, Barbara Brown, David Stollery, William Farnum, Johnny Conrad & Dancers, Joe Kirk, Hank Mann, Patrick the Harp (voice of Arthur Shields), Mel Blanc (voice), Charles Perry, Almira Sessions.
Comic turn on the classic fairy tale with Costello dreaming he's being menaced by a huge giant. Blanc voices the farm animals.

CHOREOGRAPHY BY Johnny Conrad.
SONGS: "Jack And The Beanstalk", "I Fear Nothing", "Darlene", "Dreamer's Cloth", "He Never Looked Better In His Life" *(all by Lester Lee–Bob Russell).*
MUSIC BY Heinz Roemheld, Raoul Kraushaar.
Released on April 12.
(78 min., 82 min. versions/Western Electric Recording/Sepiatone, SuperCinecolor/Video/Laserdisc/DVD)
Exclusive/Warner Brothers

BREAKFAST AT TIFFANY'S (1961) D: Blake Edwards.
Audrey Hepburn, George Peppard, Patricia Neal, Buddy Ebsen, Martin Balsam, Vilallonga, John McGiver, Alan Reed Sr., Dorothy Whitney, Miss Beverly Hills [Powers], Stanley Adams, Claude Stroud, Mickey Rooney, Elvia Allman, Henry Beckman, Mel Blanc (voice), Tommy Farrell, Gil Lamb, Glen Vernon, Putney [Orangey, a cat].
An offbeat, small-town goodtime girl (Hepburn) travels to New York City and captivates a young writer (Peppard), but their romance does not progress smoothly. Blanc is the voice of Hepburn's drunken visitor.

SOURCE: Based on a novella by Truman Capote.
FILMED IN Manhattan, NY.
SONGS: "Moon River" *(Henry Mancini-Johnny Mercer; Academy Award Winner, Golden Laurel Award Winner, AFI Song 4)*, "Lovers In The Park" *(Mancini-Jay Livingston-Ray Evans)*, "Something For Cat" *(Mancini)*, "Moon River Cha Cha" *(Mancini-Mercer)*.

Academy Award *(Music – Scoring of a Dramatic or Comedy Picture)* Henry Mancini.

Academy Award Nominations: *(Actress)* Audrey Hepburn. *(Writing – Screenplay – Based on Material from Another Medium)* George Axelrod. *(Art Direction – Set Decoration – Color)* Hal Pereira, Roland Anderson; Sam Comer, Ray Moyer.

Directors Guild of America Award Nomination: *(Best Director)* Blake Edwards.

Golden Globe Award Nominations: *(Best Comedy Picture)* Martin Jurow, Richard Shepherd. *(Best Actress, Comedy or Musical)* Audrey Hepburn.

Writers Guild of America Award: *(Best Written Comedy)* George Axelrod, based on the novella by Truman Capote.

Grammy Award: *(Best Soundtrack Album or Recording or Score from Motion Pictures or Television)* Henry Mancini.

Golden Laurel Award Nominations: *(Top Comedy)* Martin Jurow, Richard Shepherd *(3rd place)*. *(Top Female Comedy Performance)* Audrey Hepburn *(3rd place)*. *(Top Musical Score)* Henry Mancini *(3rd place)*.

Satellite Award Nomination *(2006): (Best Classic DVD)* For the Anniversary Edition.

"How do I look?" — Holly Golightly *(Audrey Hepburn; AFI Movie Quote Nominee)*
AFI Greatest Movie Nominee
AFI Laughs Nominee
AFI Passions 61

Released on October 5.
(115 min./Technicolor/Rated [TV-G]/Video/Laserdisc/DVD)
Jurow-Shepherd/Paramount

SNOW WHITE AND THE THREE STOOGES (1961) D: Walter Lang.
Carol Heiss, The Three Stooges [Moe Howard, Larry Fine, Joe DeRita], Edson Stroll, Patricia Medina, Guy Rolfe, Michael David, Buddy Baer, Edgar Barrier, Peter Coe, Chuck Lacy, Lisa Mitchell, Blossom Rock, Sam Flint, Owen McGiveney, Gloria Doggett, Leon McNabb, Leslie Farrell, Craig Cooke, Burt Mustin, Richard Collier, Herbie Faye, Edward Innes, Mel Blanc (voice).
Snow White finds help against the wicked queen not from the seven dwarves, but from the Three Stooges. Comedy-fantasy with Blanc as the voice of Quinto.

CHOREOGRAPHY BY Ron Fletcher and Ivan Lane.
SONGS: "Lookin' For People, Lookin' For Fun" *(Harry Harris),* "A Place Called Happiness" *(Harris),* "Birthday Part III" *(Lyn Murray-Harris),* "Birthday Part IV" *(Ivan Lane-Earl K. Brent),* "A Day Like This" *(Brent),* "Because I'm In Love" *(Harris) (Sung by Blanc as ventriloquist's dummy "Quinto," briefly assisted near the end by Edson Stroll),* "I Said It Then, I Say It Now" *(Harris).*
MUSIC BY Lyn Murray, Arthur Morton, Edward B. Powell.

Writers Guild of America Award Nomination: *(Best Written Musical)* Noel Langley, Elwood Ullman; story by Charles Wick.

Released on December 29.
(107 min./Westrex Recording/DeLuxe Color/CinemaScope/
Rated [G]/Video/DVD)
Chanford/20th Century-Fox

GAY PURR-EE (1962) D: Abe Levitow.
VOICES: *Judy Garland, Robert Goulet, Red Buttons, Paul Frees, Hermione Gingold, Mel Blanc, Julie Bennett, Joan Gardner, June Foray.* NARRATED BY *Morey Amsterdam.* VOCALS BY *Thurl Ravenscroft.*
Mewsette (Garland) is a French farm cat who journeys to Paris to experience life and love, but she falls into the paws of a moneyed cad who plans on selling her to a bride-seeking American tomcat. Animated feature with Blanc as the Bartender, the Driver, the Bulldog and mice sounds.

SONGS: "Gay Purr-ee Overture", "Take My Hand, Paree", "Mewsette", "Little Drops Of Rain", "Paris Is A Lonely Town", "Roses Red, Violets Blue", "The Money Cat", "Portraits Of Mewsette", "The Horse Won't Talk", "Bubbles", "The Mewsette Finale" *(all by Harold Arlen-E.Y. Harburg).* MUSIC BY Mort Lindsey, Joseph J. Lilley.
Released on October 24.
(86 min./RCA Sound/Technicolor/Video/Laserdisc/DVD)
United Productions of America/Warner Brothers

DAYS OF WINE AND ROSES (1962) D: Blake Edwards.
Jack Lemmon, Lee Remick, Charles Bickford, Jack Klugman, Alan Hewitt, Tom Palmer, Debbie Megowan, Maxine Stuart, Jack Albertson, Ken Lynch, Katherine Squire, Gail Bonney, Mary Benoit, Ella Ethridge, Rita Kenaston, J. Pat O'Malley, Robert 'Buddy' Shaw, Al Paige, Doc Stortt, Rus Bennett, Dick Crockett, Roger Barrett, Jack Railey, Lisa Guiraut, Carl Arnold, Tom Rosqui, Barbara Hines, Charlene Holt, Olan Soule, Mel Blanc (voice).
A couple's marriage descends into alcoholism when his work stresses and insecurities prove too great; their battle against the disease is not without tragedy. Blanc provides the voices of some cartoon characters.

SOURCE: Adapted from the teleplay by JP Miller.
SONG: "Days Of Wine And Roses" *(Henry Mancini-Johnny Mercer; Academy Award Winner, Golden Laurel Award Nominee [4th place], AFI Song 39)*
MUSIC BY Henry Mancini.

Academy Award Nominations:
(Actor) Jack Lemmon. *(Actress)* Lee Remick. *(Art Direction – Set Decoration – Black & White)* Joseph Wright; George James Hopkins. *(Costume Design—Black & White)* Don Feld.

Golden Globes Award Nominations:
(Best Drama Picture) Martin Manulis. *(Best Director)* Blake Edwards. *(Best Actor, Drama)* Jack Lemmon. *(Best Actress, Drama)* Lee Remick.

Golden Laurel Awards:
(Top Drama) Martin Manulis. *(Top Female Dramatic Performance)* Lee Remick. *(Top Male Dramatic Performance)* Jack Lemmon.

Additional Golden Laurel Award Nomination:
(Top Male Supporting Performance) Charles Bickford *(3rd place)*.

San Sebastian [Spain] International Film Festival Awards:
(OCIC Award) Blake Edwards. *(Prize San Sebastian—Best Actor)* Jack Lemmon. *(Prize San Sebastian—Best Actress)* Lee Remick.

Fotogramas de Plata Award [Spain]:
(Best Foreign Performer) Jack Lemmon *(USA)*.

British Academy of Film and Television Arts Award Nominations:
(Best Film from Any Source) Martin Manulis. *(Best Foreign Actor)* Jack Lemmon *(USA)*. *(Best Foreign Actress)* Lee Remick *(USA)*.

AFI Greatest Movies Nominee

Released on December 26.
(117 min./Video/Laserdisc/DVD)
Manulis-Jalem/Warner Brothers

PALM SPRINGS WEEKEND (1963) D: Norman Taurog.
Troy Donahue, Connie Stevens, Ty Hardin, Stefanie Powers, Robert Conrad, Andrew Duggan, Jack Weston, Carole Cook, Jerry Van Dyke, Zeme North, Billy Mumy, Dorothy Green, Robert Gothie, Greg Benedict, Gary Kincaid, Mark Dempsey, Jim Shane, Tina Cole, Sandy Kevin, Roger Bacon, Dabbs Greer, Margo Spinker, Dorothy Abbott, The Modern Folk Quartet, Bess Flowers, Mike Henry, Dawn Wells, Red West, Linda Gray, Mel Blanc (voice).
A teen holiday at a California resort results in romance when boy athletes arrive at a hotel housing a bevy of pretty girls. Blanc is the voice of the Bugs Bunny doll. Filmed on location.

SONGS: "Live Young" *(Paul Evans-Larry Kusik)*, "Go Go Devil" *(Frank Perkins)*, "Hurricane Twist" *(Perkins)*, "Roll With The Punch Bowl Rock" *(Perkins)*, "I Was Born In East Virginia" *(Paul Deacon-Fred Thompson-Sonny Sean-Bob Casteaux)*
MUSIC BY Frank Perkins.
Released on November 5.
(100 min./RCA Sound/Technicolor/Video/Laserdisc/DVD)
Warner Brothers

HEY THERE, IT'S YOGI BEAR (1964) D: William Hanna, Joseph Barbera.
VOICES: *Daws Butler, Don Messick, Julie Bennett, Mel Blanc, Hal Smith, J. Pat O'Malley, Jean Vander Pyl, Howard Morris, Allen Melvin. Vocals by James Darren, Jonah & The Wailers, Bill Lee, Ernest Newton, Jackie Ward.*
Yogi Bear's antics finally get him shipped out of Jellystone Park. Searching for him, Cindy Bear falls into the clutches of an evil circus-master and his dog. Animated feature with Blanc voicing the Grifter.

SONGS: "Hey There It's Yogi Bear" *(David Gates)*, "Ven-e, Ven-e, Ven-a"
MUSIC BY Marty Paich.
Released on June 3.
(89 min./RCA Sound/Eastmancolor/Rated [G]/Video/Laserdisc/DVD)
Hanna-Barbera/Columbia

KISS ME, STUPID (1964) D: Billy Wilder.
Dean Martin, Kim Novak, Ray Walston, Felicia Farr, Cliff Osmond, Barbara Pepper, James [Skip] Ward, Doro Merande, Bobo Lewis, Tommy Nolan, Alice Pearce, John Fiedler, Arlen Stuart, Howard McNear, Cliff Norton, Mel Blanc, Eileen O'Neill, Susan Wedell, Bern Hoffman, Alan Dexter, Henry Beckman, Henry Gibson, Gene Darfler, Laurie Fontaine, Mary Jane Saunders, Kathy Garber, Richard Reeves. VOCALS BY *Ian Freebairn-Smith.*
Martin is a successful singer who takes an interest in struggling songwriter Walston so he can get closer to the man's wife — but Walston has a trick of his own. Blanc plays Dr. Sheldrake.

SOURCE: "L'ora Della Fantasia" *(play)* by Anna Bonacci.
PRODUCED BY Billy Wilder.

SONGS: "'Swonderful", "I'm A Poached Egg", "Sophia" *(revision of "Wake Up Brother")*, "All The Live Long Day" *(incorporating fragments of "Phoebe")* *(all by George & Ira Gershwin).*
MUSIC BY Andre Previn.
Released on December 22.
(126 min./Westrex Sound/Panavision/Rated [PG-13]/Video/Laserdisc/DVD)
Mirisch/Phalanx/Lopert/United Artists

THE MAN CALLED FLINTSTONE (1966) D: Joseph Barbera, William Hanna.
VOICES: *Alan Reed, Mel Blanc, Jean Vander Pyl, Gerry Johnson, Don Messick, Janet Waldo, Paul Frees, Harvey Korman, John Stephenson, June Foray, Henry Corden, Russi Taylor.* VOCALS BY *Louis Prima.*
Bedrock's favorite citizen, Fred Flintstone, is mistaken for a secret agent and must thwart the plans of the evil Green Goose. Animated feature with Blanc as Barney Rubble, the helicopter pilot, the Mayor, Turtle and Scales.
SONGS: "Think Love (Pensate Amore)" *(Doug Goodwin)*, "Spy Type Guy" *(Goodwin)*, "The Man Called Flintstone" *(John McCarthy)*, "Team Mates" *(John McCarthy; performed by Blanc and Reed)*, "Happy Sounds Of Paree" *(Goodwin)*, "When We Are Grown Up"
MUSIC BY Marty Paich, Ted Nichols.
Released on August 3.
(87 min./RCA Sound/Eastmancolor, Columbia Color/Video/Laserdisc/DVD)
Hanna-Barbera/Columbia

THE PHANTOM TOLLBOOTH (1969) D: Chuck Jones, Abe Levitow, David Monahan.
Butch Patrick, Michael Earl.
VOICES: *Mel Blanc, Daws Butler, Candy Candido, Hans Conried, June Foray, Patti Gilbert, Shep Menken, Cliff Norton, Larry Thor, Les Tremayne, The Jack Halloran Group, Thurl Ravenscroft, Herg Vigran.*
Mixture of live action and animation with Patrick as a boy who enters a fantasy land besieged by a war between letters and numbers. Blanc is Officer Short Shrift, the Word Speller, the Dodecahedron, a Lethargian and a king's advisor.

SOURCE: Adaptation of the novel by Norton Juster.

SONGS: "Milo's Song" *(Lee Pockriss-Norman Gimbel),* "Don't Say There's Nothing To Do In The Doldrums" *(Pockriss-Paul Vance, sung by Blanc and Patrick),* "Time Is A Gift" *(Pockriss-Gimbel),* "Noise, Beautiful Noise" *(Pockriss-Vance),* "Word Market *(Words In A Word)*" *(Pockriss-Gimbel),* "Numbers Are The Only Thing That Count" *(Pockriss-Gimbel),* "Rhyme And Reason Reign" *(Pockriss-Gimbel)*
MUSIC BY Dean Elliott.
Released on November 7.
(90 min./Western Electric Sound/Metrocolor/Rated [G]/video/DVD)
Animation Visual Arts/Educational Film Centre/Metro-Goldwyn-Mayer

HOW'S YOUR LOVE LIFE? (1971) D: Russ [Russel] Vincent.
John Agar, Vera Allen, Mel Blanc, Eve Brent, Leslie Brooks, William Hudson, Mary Beth Hughes, Sean Kenney, Grant Williams, John Armond, Babette, Doris Barton, Joe Castagna, Regina Champlin, Rick Cooper, Dixie Daugherty, Dana Diamond, Sonja Dunson, Stuart Gardner, Linda Susan Hill, Sahara Jones, Rigg Kennedy, Sheri Lohr, Rosalind Miles, Sherry Mills, Nitchka Newell, Floyd Schenk, Lois Ursoni, Russel Vincent, Steve Vincent, Vincene Wallace, Michael West, Alicio Balsa, Jack Angelo, Jack Gonzales.
Exploitation film featuring Blanc as Blackie.

MUSIC BY Robert 'Bumps' Blackwell.
(111 min./color)
Sportsfilm/Cal-Tex

SCALAWAG/JAMIE'S TREASURE HUNT (1973) D: Kirk Douglas, Zoran Calic.
Kirk Douglas, Mark Lester, Neville Brand, George Eastman, Don Stroud, Lesley-Anne Down, Danny DeVito, Mel Blanc (voice), Phil Brown, Shaft Douglas.
A hunt for buried loot in 1840s Mexico involves a boy, a one-legged rogue and hostile Indians. Blanc voices Barfly the Parrot.

SOURCE: Loose adaptation of *Treasure Island* by Robert Louis Stevenson.
FILMED IN Yugoslavia.
SONGS: "When Your Number's Up You Go" *(John Cameron-Lionel Bart),* "The Scalawag Song" *(Cameron),* "Silver Fishes" *(Cameron)*
MUSIC BY John Cameron.

Released on November 14.
(93 min./Technicolor/Rated [G])
Bryna/Ibex/Inex-Oceania/Paramount

JOURNEY BACK TO OZ (1974) D: Hal Sutherland.
VOICES: *Liza Minnelli, Milton Berle, Herschel Bernardi, Paul Ford, Margaret Hamilton, Jack E. Leonard, Paul Lynde, Ethel Merman, Mickey Rooney, Rise Stevens, Danny Thomas, Mel Blanc, Larry Storch, Dallas McKennon.*
Another tornado appears to whisk Dorothy Gale (Minnelli) back to the land of Oz, where she must aid her old friend the Scarecrow (Rooney) in saving the kingdom from evil witch Mombi (Merman). Animated sequel to the live-action *Wizard Of Oz* (1939), with Blanc as the Crow. Based on characters created by L. Frank Baum. *Note: Production on this film began in 1970 using audio tracks recorded for an aborted 1962 project.*

SONGS: "A Faraway Land", "Signpost Song", "Keep A Happy Thought", "The Horse On The Carousel", "B-R-A-N-E", "An Elephant Never Forgets", "You Have Only You", "If You're Gonna Be A Witch — Be A Witch", "H-E-A-R-T", "N-E-R-V-E", "Return To The Land Of Oz March", "That Feeling For Home" *(all by Jimmy Van Heusen-Sammy Cahn).*
MUSIC BY Walter Scharf.
Released on June 19.
(90 min./color/Rated [G]/video/DVD)
Filmation/Warner Brothers

BUCK ROGERS IN THE 25TH CENTURY (1979) D: Daniel Haller.
Gil Gerard, Pamela Hensley, Erin Gray, Henry Silva, Tim O'Connor, Joseph Wiseman, Duke Butler, Felix Silla, Mel Blanc (voice), Caroline Smith, John Dewey-Carter, H.B. Haggerty, Kevin Coates, David Cadiente, Gil Serna, Larry Duran, Kenny Endoso, Eric Lawrence.
A 20th Century man falls into suspended animation and is awakened 500 years later in a future society at the brink of war, due to the machinations of a sexy but villainous princess. Blanc is the voice of Twiki the Robot. Adapted from the comic strip by Philip Knowlan and Dick Calkins. Theatrical film which served as the pilot for a later TV series.

SONG: "Suspension" *(Stu Phillips-Glen A. Larson).*
MUSIC BY Stu Phillips.

Academy of Science Fiction, Fantasy & Horror Films [Saturn] Award: *(Best Costumes)* Jean-Pierre Dorleac.

Academy of Science Fiction, Fantasy & Horror Films [Saturn] Award Nomination: *(Best Supporting Actress)* Pamela Hensley.

Released on March 30 (Box Office: $12,010,000).
(89 min./Technicolor/Rated [PG]/DVD)
Universal

BUGS BUNNY SUPERSTAR (1975) D: Larry Jackson.
Friz Freleng, Tex Avery, Bob Clampett, Mel Blanc (voice). NARRATED BY *Orson Welles.*
Documentary and 'home movies' about the 1940s Warner Brothers cartoons and the men who made them. Blanc voices the various characters. Cartoons shown are *What's Cooking Doc?* (1944), *A Wild Hare* (1940), *I Taw A Putty Tat* (1948), *Rhapsody Rabbit* (1946), *Corny Concerto* (1943), *Walky Talky Hawky* (1946), *The Old Grey Hare* (1944), *My Favorite Duck* (1942), *Hair-Raising Hare* (1946) and *The Unmentionables* (1963).

MUSIC BY Ian Whitcomb.
Released on December 19.
(91 min./Technicolor/Video/Laserdisc/DVD)
Hair-Raising Films/United Artists

THE GREAT AMERICAN CHASE (1979) D: Chuck Jones, Phil Monroe. VOICES: Mel Blanc, June Foray.
Bugs Bunny (Blanc) tours his mansion and thinks back on his film career, giving us his insights on humor and movie chases. Five complete cartoons from the Warner Brothers library are presented: *Hareway To The Stars* (1958); *What's Opera, Doc?* (1957); *Duck Amuck* (1953); *Bully For Bugs* (1953) and *Rabbit Fire* (1951). Also, excerpts are shown from *Duck Dodgers In The 24 ½Th Century* (1953); *Robin Hood Daffy* (1958); *Ali Baba Bunny* (1957); *For Scent-Imental Reasons* (1949); *Longhaired Hare* (1949) and *Operation: Rabbit* (1952). In addition, there are clips from *Road Runner* cartoons. Produced by Chuck Jones. Also known as *The Bugs Bunny/Road Runner Movie.*

MUSIC BY Carl Stalling, Milt Franklyn, Dean Elliott.
Released on September 30.
(97 min./Vitaphone Sound/Technicolor/Rated [G]/DVD)
Warner Brothers

FRIZ FRELENG'S LOONEY, LOONEY, LOONEY BUGS BUNNY MOVIE (1981) D: Friz Freleng.
VOICES: *Mel Blanc, June Foray, Stan Freberg, Frank Welker, Frank Nelson.*
NARRATED BY *Ralph James.*
Bugs Bunny is a busy rabbit as he runs afoul of a devilish Yosemite Sam; saves Tweety Pie from a couple of gangsters and hosts a wacky awards show. Blanc is Bugs, Sam, Daffy Duck, Sylvester the Cat, Tweety, Porky Pig, Speedy Gonzales, Pepe LePew, King Arthur, Sir Osis of Liver, Sir Loin of Beef, Gerry the Idjit Dragon, Satan, Treasury Director, Rocky, Mugsy, Judge, Clancy, O'Hara, Policemen and Clarence B.A. Bird. Blend of new animated footage with classic Warner Brothers cartoons *Knighty Knight Bugs* (1958), *Sahara Hare* (1955), *Roman Legion Hare* (1955), *High Diving Hare* (1949), *Hare Trimmed* (1953), *Wild And Wooly Hare* (1959), *Catty Cornered* (1953), *Golden Yeggs* (1950), *The Unmentionables* (1963), *Three Little Bops* (1957) and *Show Biz Bugs* (1957).

MUSIC BY Rob Walsh, Don McGinnis, Milt Franklyn, Bill [William] Lava, Shorty Rogers, Carl Stalling.
Released on November 20.
(80 min./Technicolor/Rated [G]/video/DVD)
DePatie-Freleng Enterprises/Warner Brothers

BUGS BUNNY'S 3RD MOVIE: 1001 RABBIT TALES (1982) D: Friz Freleng, Chuck Jones, Dave Detiege, Art Davis, Bill Perez.
VOICES: *Mel Blanc, Lennie Weinrib, Shep Menken.*
When publishing reps Bugs Bunny and Daffy Duck travel to the Far East, they meet a sultan and his bratty nephew—who demands to be entertained. Blanc is Bugs, Daffy, Porky Pig, Sultan Yosemite Sam, Sylvester the Cat, Junior, Speedy Gonzales, Tweety Pie, Genie, Hassan, Big Bad Wolf, Beanstalk Giant, Elvis Gorilla and the Stork. New animation frames classic Warner Brothers cartoons: *Ali Baba Bunny* (1957), *Apes Of Wrath* (1959), *Bewitched Bunny* (1954), *Cracked Quack* (1952), *Goldimouse And The Three Cats* (1960), *Mexican Boarders* (1962), *One Froggy Evening*

608   MEL BLANC: THE MAN OF A THOUSAND VOICES

(1955), *Pied Piper Of Guadalupe* (1961), *Red Riding Hoodwinked* (1955), *Tweety And The Beanstalk* (1957) and *Wise Quackers* (1949).

MUSIC BY Rob Walsh, Bill [William] Lava, Milt Franklyn, Carl Stalling.
Released on November 19.
(76 min./Technicolor/Rated [G]/video/DVD)
Warner Brothers

DAFFY DUCK'S MOVIE: FANTASTIC ISLAND (1983) D: Friz Freleng, Phil Monroe.
VOICES: *Mel Blanc, June Foray, Les Tremayne.*
Daffy Duck and Speedy Gonzales find a treasure map and a magical well on a desert isle. They soon discover that rivals Yosemite Sam and the Tasmanian Devil are also looking for the loot. Blanc is Daffy, Speedy, Sam, Tas, Bugs Bunny, Porky Pig, Tweety Pie, Sylvester the Cat and Foghorn Leghorn. Compilation of new animation and classic Warner Brothers cartoons: *Buccaneer Bunny* (1948), *Stupor Duck* (1956), *Greedy For Tweety* (1957), *Banty Raids* (1963), *Louvre Come Back To Me* (1962), *Tree For Two* (1952), *Curtain Razor* (1949), *A Mouse Divided* (1953), *Of Rice And Hen* (1953) and *From Hare To Heir* (1960).

MUSIC BY Milt Franklyn, Carl Stalling.
Released on August 5.
(78 min./Technicolor/Rated [G]/Video/Laserdisc/DVD)
Warner Brothers

STRANGE BREW (1983) D: Dave Thomas, Rick Moranis.
Dave Thomas, Rick Moranis, Max Von Sydow, Paul Dooley, Lynne Griffin, Mel Blanc (voice), Angus MacInness, Brian McConnachie, Tom Harvey, Douglas Campbell, Len Doncheff, Jill Frappier, David Beard, Thick Wilson, Robert Windsor, Buddy (a dog).
The beer-loving Canadian brothers, Bob and Doug McKenzie (Moranis, Thomas), go to extreme lengths to quaff some suds and end up at a castle/brewery run by megalomaniac Von Sydow. Blanc is the voice of Mr. McKenzie. Based on characters from the television series *SCTV*.

SONG: "Strange Brew" *(Ian Thomas)*
MUSIC BY Charles Fox.

Genie Award: *(Golden Reel)* Louis M. Silverstein, Jack Grossberg.

Released on August 26.
(90 min./Metrocolor/Rated [PG]/Video/Laserdisc/DVD)
Metro-Goldwyn-Mayer/United Artists

HEATHCLIFF: THE MOVIE (1986) D: Bruno Bianchi.
VOICES: *Mel Blanc, Donna Christie, Peter Cullen, Jeannie Elias, Stan Jones, Marilyn Lightstone, Danny Mann, Derek McGrath, Marilyn Schreffler, Danny Wells, Ted Zeigler.*
Heathcliff the Cat tells his nephews of his exploits in a cat-food commercial, taking on the neighborhood bulldog and going head-to-head with feline gangsters. Blanc is Heathcliff and Spike. Mixture of new animation and excerpts from the *Heathcliff* television series. Adapted from the comic strip by George Gately.

MUSIC BY Shuki Levy, Haim Saban.
Released on January 17.
(73 min./color/Rated [G]/DVD)
Clubhouse Pictures/Atlantic

WHO FRAMED ROGER RABBIT (1988) D: Robert Zemeckis.
Bob Hoskins, Christopher Lloyd, Joanna Cassidy, Stubby Kaye, Alan Tilvern, Richard Le Parmentier, Joel Silver, Morgan Deare, Laura Frances, Paul Springer, Richard Ridings, Ed Herlihy.
VOICES: *Charles Fleischer, Lou Hirsch, April Winchell, Mae Questel, Mel Blanc, Morgan Deare, Tony Anselmo, Joe Alaskey, Richard Williams, Mary T. Radford, Tony Pope, David Lander, June Foray, Fred Newman, Russi Taylor, Wayne Allwine, Les Perkins, Peter Westy, Pat Buttram, Jim Gallant, Jim Cummings, Cherry Davis, Frank Sinatra, Kathleen Turner, Amy Irving, Jack Angel, Nancy Cartwright, Frank Welker.*
A cartoon-hating private eye (Hoskins) ventures in Toontown to clear animated-shorts star Roger Rabbit, who is suspected of murdering a human. Blanc is Bugs Bunny, Daffy Duck, Porky Pig, Sylvester the Cat and Tweety Pie. Seamless blend of live-action and animation pays homage to both the great cartoon shorts and film noir genres of the 1940s. Highlights include the brief on-screen pairing of Mickey Mouse and Bugs Bunny, plus a piano-playing duel between Donald and Daffy Duck(s).

SOURCE: *Who Censored Roger Rabbit* (1981 book) by Gary K. Wolf. PRO-
DUCED BY Steven Spielberg.
SONGS: "Why Don't You Do Right?" *(Joe McCoy)*, "The Merry-Go-
Round Broke Down" *(Cliff Friend-Dave Franklin)*, "Smile, Darn Ya,
Smile" *(Jack Meskill-Charles O'Flynn-Max Rich)*, "Witchcraft" *(Cy
Coleman; Carolyn Leigh)*, "Hungarian Rhapsody No. 2" *(Franz Liszt)*.
MUSIC BY Alan Silvestri.

Academy Awards:
(Film Editing) Arthur Schmidt. *(Sound Effects Editing)* Charles L.
Campbell, Louis L. Edemann. *(Visual Effects)* Ken Ralston, Richard
Williams, Edward Jones, George Gibbs.

(Special Achievement Award – Animation Direction) Roger Williams.

Academy Award Nominations:
(Cinematography) Dean Cundey. *(Art Direction; Set Decoration)* Elliott
Scott; Peter Howitt. *(Sound)* Robert Knudson, John Boyd, Don
Digirolamo, Tony Dawe.

Los Angeles Film Critics Association Award:
(Special – Technical Achievement) Steven Spielberg, Kathleen Kennedy.

Golden Globe Award Nominations:
(Best Comedy or Musical Picture) Steven Spielberg. *(Best Actor, Comedy or
Musical)* Bob Hoskins.

Directors Guild of America Award Nomination:
(Best Director) Robert Zemeckis.

Writers Guild of America Award Nomination:
(Best Adapted Screenplay) Jeffrey Price, Peter Seaman, based on the book
Who Censored Roger Rabbit by Gary K. Wolf.

"I'm not bad. I'm just drawn that way." — Jessica Rabbit *(voice of Kathleen
Turner; AFI Movie Quote Nominee)*

Released on June 22.
(103 min./color/Rated [PG]/AFI Laughs Nominee/Video/Laserdisc/DVD)
Amblin/Touchstone/Buena Vista

DAFFY DUCK'S QUACKBUSTERS (1988) D: Greg Ford, Terry Lennon. VOICES: *Mel Blanc, Roy Firestone, B.J. Ward, Mel Torme, Ben Frommer, Julie Bennett.*
New millionaire Daffy Duck decides to sink his wealth in the ghostbusting business and enlists his pals Bugs Bunny and Porky Pig as his aides. Daffy is really scheming to eradicate the ghost of J.B. Cubish, who left him the money — and now wants it back. Blanc is Daffy, Bugs, Porky, Sylvester the Cat, Tweety Pie, J.B. Cubish and the monsters. Mix of old and new animation with classic Warner Brothers cartoons: *Daffy Dilly* (1948), *The Prize Pest* (1951), *Water Water Every Hare* (1952), *Hyde And Go Tweet* (1960), *Claws For Alarm* (1954), *The Duxorcist* (1987), *The Abominable Snow Rabbit* (1961), *Transylvania 6-5000* (1963), *Punch Trunk* (1953) and *Jumpin' Jupiter* (1955).

MUSIC BY Hal Willner, Carl Stalling, Milt Franklyn, Bill [William] Lava.
Released on September 24.
(72 min./Technicolor/Rated [G]/video)
Warner Brothers

JETSONS: THE MOVIE (1990) D: William Hanna, Joseph Barbera. VOICES: *George O'Hanlon, Mel Blanc, Penny Singleton, Tiffany, Patric Zimmerman, Don Messick, Jean Vander Pyl, Ronnie Schell, Patty Deutsch, Dana Hill, Russi Taylor, Paul Kreppel, Rick Dees, Jeff Bergman, Brad Garrett, Frank Welker.*
George Jetson (O'Hanlon) is sent on a business assignment to find out why a Spacely Industries asteroid is not providing its required ore quota. He relocates the family, sets to work at the factory site, discovers a sabotage plot...and promptly disappears. Can Elroy and the gang save George and straighten out the situation? Animated comedy-adventure with Blanc as Mr. Spacely. Based on *The Jetsons* television series. *Note: Both George O'Hanlon and Mel Blanc passed away before the film's release and it is dedicated in their memory.*

SONGS: "We're The Jetsons *(Jetsons' Rap)*, "With You All The Way", "Stayin' Together", "You And Me", "I Always Thought I'd See You Again", "Home", "Maybe Love" *(Tim James-Steve Kempster-Steve McClintock)*, "Through The Blue", "Mall Theme" *(John Duarte)*.
MUSIC BY George Tobin, John Debney, Brad Dechter, Ira Hearshen.

Released on July 6.
(81 min./Dolby Sound/color/Rated [G]/Video/Laserdisc)
Hanna-Barbera/Wang Film Productions/Cuckoo's Nest Studios/Universal

Video Release

SPARKY'S MAGIC PIANO (1987) D: Lee Mishkin.
VOICES: *Josh Rodine, Alan W. Livingston, Vincent Price, Coral Browne, Mel Blanc, Tony Curtis, Peter Gerald, Cloris Leachman, Nancy Olson, Heidi Sorenson.* NARRATED BY *William Schallert.*
Sparky is a boy who befriends a very special piano, and together they become a music sensation. When Sparky's virtuosity goes to his head, the piano gives him a life lesson. Blanc lends his vocal talents to this direct-to-video feature co-produced by Blanc's son Noel. Piano solos by Leonard Pennario.

MUSIC BY Lalo Schifrin.

(47 min/color/video/DVD)
SMP Associates

Television

The Jack Benny Program CBS/NBC
October 28, 1950-September 10, 1965.
The comic misadventures of a vain and miserly TV star, along with skits and sketches.

Cast

Jack Benny . . . . *Himself*
Mary Livingstone. . . . . *Herself (1950-59)*
Rochester. . . . .*Eddie Anderson*
Dennis Day, vocalist. . . . . *Himself*
Friend, Announcer . . . . *Don Wilson*
Floorwalker, Various Roles . . . . *Frank Nelson*
Mr. Kitzel, Various Roles . . . .*Artie Auerbach*
Professor LeBlanc, Sound of the Maxwell auto,
Various Roles. . . . . .Mel Blanc
Vocalists . . . . .The Sportsmen Quartet
Orchestra . . . . Mahlon Merrick

Produced by Irving Fein, Hilliard Marks, Ralph Levy, Norman Abbott, Fred DeCordova
J & M Entertainment/McCadden Productions/Revue [Universal TV]
Approx. 343 episodes.

The Colgate Comedy Hour NBC May 10, 1953.
STAR: *Eddie Cantor.* ANNOUNCER: *John Cannon. The Al Goodman Orchestra.*
Eddie introduces several young entertainers. In a filmed skit, Maxie the Taxi *(Cantor)* picks up Bonzo the Chimp *(voice of Mel Blanc)* as his fare. Other guests are opera tenor Jan Peerce, singers Connie Russell and Sid Milano, dancer Billy Daniels, ballerina Nancy Crompton and pianist John Robertson. Also: Hari Kari.

The Colgate Comedy Hour NBC June 7, 1953.
STAR: *Eddie Cantor.* ANNOUNCER: *John Cannon. The Al Goodman Orchestra.*
Eddie and Ida Cantor celebrate their 39th wedding anniversary amid guests Dinah Shore, George Jessel, Ralph Edwards, Billy Daniels, Dave Rubinoff and his violin, Jimmy Wallington, Lita Baron, Ciro's owner Herman Hover, pianist Ticker Freeman and vocal group The Notables.
Voice of Chimp: Mel Blanc.

Musical Chairs NBC July 9-September 17, 1955.
Panel-quiz show wherein musical performers are faced with viewer-submitted questions about pop tunes.

> Host . . . . *Bill Leyden (7, 9 to 7, 30)*
> *Gene Rayburn (8, 6 to 9, 17)*
> Regulars . . . . *Johnny Mercer, Bobby Troup, Mel Blanc*
> Vocal Group. . . . . *The Cheerleaders*
> Orchestra. . . . . *Bobby Troup (The Troup Group)*

Produced by Bob Masson, Frank Dawzig, Bart Ross.
Approx. 11 episodes.

The People's Choice NBC "Sock vs. Crutcher" November 3, 1955.
STARS: *Jackie Cooper, Pat Breslin, Paul Maxey, Margaret Irving, Cleo (a dog; voice of Mary Jane Croft).*
Sock Miller (Cooper) learns that his dog Cleo is in the pound charged with snapping at Sock's political and romantic rival, Roger Crutcher (John Stephenson).
Miguel: Jose Gonzales Gonzales. Greentree: Mel Blanc. Sanchez: Carlos Vera.

Private Secretary CBS "Two and Two Make Five" March 3, 1957.
STARS: *Ann Sothern, Don Porter, Ann Tyrrell, Jesse White, Joan Banks.*
A harassed investigator from the Department of Internal Revenue tries to make some sense out of Susie McNamara's convoluted filing system when she undergoes an audit. Meanwhile, Peter Sands (Porter) is searching for the perfect voice to cast in a cartoon commercial.
Mr. Bascom: Mel Blanc. Fritz Kaslo: Tommy Vize.

Bell Science Series NBC; SPECIAL "Hemo the Magnificent" March 20, 1957. Documentary on blood and circulation in the human body presented with dramatic photography and animation. Produced and directed by Frank Capra.
Dr. Research: Dr. Frank Baxter. Fiction Writer: Richard Carlson. Voice of Squirrel: Mel Blanc. Voice of Deer: June Foray. Hemo: Marvin Miller. Lab Assistant: Sterling Holloway.
(Video/DVD)

Bell Science Series NBC; SPECIAL "The Unchained Goddess"
February 12, 1958.
With the help of animated characters, the Fiction Writer (Richard Carlson) and Dr. Research (Dr. Frank Baxter) talk about the weather and describe what scientists are doing about it. They illustrate the origins of such weather elements as winds, clouds, rain, snow, hail and lightning; show how these elements combine to produce weather; and depict scientific attempts to predict and control weather. Produced by Frank Capra.
VOICES: *Mel Blanc, Hans Conried, Lurene Tuttle, Franklin Pangborn, Jay Novello, Ken Peters.*
(Video/DVD)

Shower of Stars CBS "Jack Benny's 40th Birthday Celebration"
February 13, 1958.
HOST: *Bill Lundigan.*
Jack Benny has promised to admit to turning 40 today (he steadfastly 'remained' at 39 since entering radio in 1932) and there's a big party. Jack and Rochester (Eddie Anderson) are at home preparing for the festivities. Jack is concentrating on the speeches he's sure he will be called upon to make on how it feels to turn 40. Scheduled to visit are colleagues, former and current, including wife Mary Livingstone, Van Johnson, Jo Stafford, Bob Crosby, Dennis Day, Phil Harris, Paul Douglas, Don Wilson, The Sportsmen, Andy Devine, Frank Parker, Larry Stevens, Mel Blanc, Sam Hearn, Johnny Green, Don Bestor, Frank Nelson, Mahlon Merrick, Ted Weems, Joe [Joseph] Kearns and George Olson. Mayor Robert Sabonjian of Waukegan, IL, Jack's home town, is also a guest.
SONGS: Singers and Dancers: "What A Day This Has Been"
Jo: "Life Begins At 40"
Van, Don Wilson, Andy: "Bennies From Heaven"
Note: Jack Benny's actual birth date is February 14, 1894.

The Garry Moore Show CBS October 14, 1958.
STARS: *Garry Moore, Durward Kirby, Marion Lorne. The Paul Godkin Dancers. The Howard Smith Orchestra.*
Garry's guests are vocalists Tommy Sands and Louise O'Brien; comedienne Audrey Meadows and comic actor Andy Devine. In a western sketch, Andy sings "Dear Horse"…with multi-voiced Mel Blanc as the equine's front end.

Perry Mason CBS "The Case of the Perjured Parrot" December 20, 1958.
STARS: *Raymond Burr, Barbara Hale, William Hopper, William Talman, Ray Collins.*
Perry (Burr) is retained by Ellen Monteith (Jody Lawrence), who has been accused of murdering Fremont Sabin. Mason finds himself in the unusual position of requesting that the slain man's parrot, Casanova (voice of Mel Blanc), be brought to the inquest.
Fred Bascomb: Robert E. Griffin. Sheriff Barnes: Frank Ferguson. Andy Templet: Edgar Buchanan. Mr. Langley: Joe [Joseph] Kearns. District Attorney R. Sprague: Jason Johnson. Stephanie Sabin: Fay Baker. Richard Wald: Dan Barton. Charles Sabin: Maurice Manson. Helen Watkins: Pamela Branch. Court Clerk: Jesslyn Fax. Rufus Bolding: Howard Culver.
(DVD)

77 Sunset Strip ABC "The Fifth Stair" March 6, 1959.
STARS: *Efrem Zimbalist Jr., Roger Smith, Edd Byrnes, Louis Quinn, Jacqueline Beer, Byron Keith.*
Stuart Bailey and partner Jeff Spencer (Zimbalist, Smith) are involved in a blackmail scheme after Jeff writes a letter to beautiful Margo Wendice. Margo's husband hires a killer after assuming Jeff is having an affair with his wife. When Margo kills the assassin in self-defense, she is accused of murder — along with Jeff. Mel Blanc is the voice of Kookie (Byrnes) imitating Bugs Bunny.
Margo: Julie Adams. Tony Wendice: Richard Long. Detective: Joe Partridge. Homicide Lieutenant: Patrick McVey. Killer: Richard Devon. Singer: Betsy Duncan. Also: The Frankie Ortega Trio.

The Many Loves of Dobie Gillis CBS "The Best Dressed Man"
October 6, 1959.
STARS: *Dwayne Hickman, Bob Denver, Frank Faylen, Florida Friebus, Sheila James.*
Pretty Thalia Menninger, the apple of Dobie's eye, seems to be much impressed by well-dressed Milton Armitage *(Warren Beatty).* Dobie *(Hickman)* decides to get back into the picture by making a deal with a local clothier to model some of his fashions at school.
Thalia: Tuesday Weld. Mr. Ziegler, the tailor: Mel Blanc. Linda Sue Faversham: Yvonne Craig. Mr. Pomfritt: William Schallert.

General Electric Theater CBS "Mr. O'Malley" December 20, 1959.
HOST: *Ronald Reagan.* ANNOUNCER: *Don Morrow.*
A small boy wishes on a star for a fairy godmother who can make his dream of a puppy for Christmas come true, and is answered by a cigar-smoking, pink-winged fairy godfather named O'Malley. Based on the comic strip *Barnaby* by Crockett Johnson. *Unsuccessful pilot for a proposed series.*
Mr. O'Malley: Bert Lahr. Barnaby Baxter: Ronny [Ron] Howard. Voice of Leprechaun: Mel Blanc. Alice Baxter: June Dayton. George Baxter: William Redfield. Dr. Harvey: Don Beddoe. Janie: Debbie Megowan.

The Shirley Temple Show NBC "The Land of Oz" September 18, 1960.
STAR: *Shirley Temple. The Vic Schoen Orchestra.*
First show of the season. Lord Nikidik, wickedest denizen of Oz, hits upon a scheme to take over the kingdom; his assistant — Mombi the witch. Temple plays the dual role of Princess Ozma and Tip in this adaptation of L. Frank Baum's story. *Broadcast in color.*
Mombi: Agnes Moorehead. Nikidik: Jonathan Winters. Scarecrow: Ben Blue. Jack Pumpkinhead: Sterling Holloway. Tin Woodman: Gil Lamb. Graves: Arthur Treacher. Glinda the Good: Frances Bergen. Colonel: Charles Boaz. Jellia Jamb: Mari Lynn. Lightning Bug Repairman: Norman Leavitt. Royal Army of Oz: William Keene. Court Doctor: Lou Merrill. Voices of Sawhorse and Book: Mel Blanc. The Gump: Maurice Dallimore.
(DVD)

Mister Magoo SYNDICATED 1960-62.
The animated exploits of a near-sighted old gentleman whose inability to see anything for what it really is gets him into trouble.

Voice Cast

Quincy Magoo, Mother Magoo . . . .*Jim Backus*
Millie . . . . *Julie Bennett*
Tycoon Magoo, Various Characters . . . . *Paul Frees*
Hamlet . . . .*Richard Crenna*
Waldo, Prezley . . . . *Jerry Hausner*
Prezley . . . . *Daws Butler*
Various Characters. . . . . *Henny Backus, Mel Blanc,*
June Foray, Joan Gardner, Barney Phillips

Produced by Henry G. Saperstein, Steve Bosustow
(United Productions of America)
33 episodes (130 five-minute cartoons @ four per half-hour).

The Flintstones ABC September 30, 1960-September 2, 1966.
Animated situation comedy about the humorous events in the 'suburban' lives of two Stone Age families.

Voice Cast

Fred Flintstone . . . . *Alan Reed*
Barney Rubble, Dino the Dinosaur. . . . . *Mel Blanc*
Daws Butler (1961)
Wilma Flintstone, Pebbles Flintstone . . . .*Jean Vander Pyl*
Betty Rubble . . . . *Bea Benaderet (1960-64)*
Gerry Johnson (1964-66)
Bamm Bamm Rubble . . . . *Don Messick (1963-66)*
The Great Gazoo. . . . . *Harvey Korman (1965-66)*
Various Roles. . . . . *Daws Butler, Howard Morris,*
Hal Smith, John Stephenson
Announcer. . . . . *Bill Baldwin*

Produced by William Hanna, Joseph Barbera
(Hanna-Barbera/Screen Gems [Columbia TV])
167 episodes.

The Bugs Bunny Show ABC October 11, 1960-September 25, 1962.
The adventures of the rascally rabbit and many of his zany compatri-
ots. Classic Warner Brothers cartoons presented with new introductory
sequences.

Voice Cast

Host . . . . Dick Coughlin
Bugs Bunny, Pepe LePew, Speedy Gonzales, Daffy Duck, Yosemite
Sam, Tasmanian Devil, Tweety Pie, Elmer Fudd (only in the footage
created for this program), Porky Pig, Charlie Dog, Foghorn Leghorn,
George P. Dog, Sylvester the Cat, Junior . . . . Mel Blanc

Produced by Chuck Jones, Friz Freleng
(Warner Brothers TV)
52 episodes.

Angel CBS "The Argument" November 10, 1960.
STARS: *Annie Farge, Marshall Thompson, Doris Singleton, Don Keefer.*
ANNOUNCER: *Roy Rowan.*
Suzie, George and the Smiths are having a friendly poker game. Then
Angel (Farge) calls George's bluff, followed by George's comment about
Angel's antique clock — and tempers flare.
Gardener: Bob Ozakazi. Salesman: Mel Blanc. Danby: Max Mellinger.

Bell Science Series NBC; SPECIAL "The Thread of Life" December 9, 1960.
HOST: *Dr. Frank Baxter.*
Why do things taste different to different people? Why are there more
color-blind men than women? What determines whether a baby will be a
boy or a girl? Scientists offer answers to these questions, and to more basic
ones, such as why no two living things are exactly alike. They explain that
heredity is ruled by unseen units called genes. Tonight's animated film
illustrates the mathematics that 'proves' the existence of genes. Motion
pictures shot through a microscope show the tiny parts of a cell which
carry the genes. A scale model represents the chemical structure of DNA,
a substance which may be the unit of heredity itself — the 'thread of life.'
Ship's Voice: Mel Blanc.
(Video)

Dennis the Menace CBS "Miss Cathcart's Best Friend" January 22, 1961.
STARS: *Jay North, Herbert Anderson, Gloria Henry, Joseph Kearns, Jeannie Russell.*
Dennis (North) overhears his mother say that lonely Miss Cathcart (Mary Wickes) needs a good friend. Since a dog is considered man's best friend, Dennis decides Miss Cathcart needs a dog.
Mr. Trinkle: Mel Blanc. Arthur: John Zaremba. Tommy Anderson: Billy Booth. Maurice: Paul Barselow.

Here's Hollywood NBC 1961.
Daytime interview show with guest Mel Blanc.

The Dick Tracy Show SYNDICATED September 1961-1962.
Animated exploits of detective Dick Tracy and his assistants pitting their wits against an assortment of foes. Loosely based on the comic strip by Chester Gould.

Voice Cast

Dick Tracy	Everett Sloane
Heap O'Calorie	Johnny Coons
Go Go Gomez	Mel Blanc
Hemlock Holmes	Jerry Hausner
Joe Jitsu	Benny Rubin
Various Roles	June Foray, Paul Frees, Joan Gardner, Howard Morris

Produced by Henry G. Saperstein, Peter DeMet, Glan Heisch
(United Productions of America)
33 episodes (130 five-minute cartoons @ four per show).

The Hanna-Barbera New Cartoons SYNDICATED 1962-63.
Animated animals cavort in three segments: *Lippy the Lion* (a tale-spinning jungle cat cannot follow through on his boasts), *Touché Turtle* (a sword-wielding terrapin fights evil-doers), and *Wally Gator* (a plotting alligator hopes to one day escape from the zoo).

Voice Cast

Lippy the Lion, Wally Gator, Various Characters	Daws Butler
Hardy Har Har	Mel Blanc
Touché Turtle	Bill Thompson
Dum Dum	Alan Reed
Mr. Twiddles, Various Characters	Don Messick

Produced by William Hanna, Joseph Barbera
(Hanna-Barbera/Screen Gems [Columbia TV])
52 episodes.

The Jetsons ABC September 23, 1962-September 8, 1963.
Animated situation comedy about a family living in the 'super-electronic age' of a future century.

Voice Cast

George Jetson. . . . . *George O'Hanlon*
Jane Jetson. . . . . *Penny Singleton*
Judy Jetson . . . . *Janet Waldo*
Elroy Jetson. . . . . *Daws Butler*
Astro . . . . *Don Messick*
Rosie the Robot . . . . *Jean Vander Pyl*
Cosmo G. Spacely, Various Characters. . . . . *Mel Blanc*
Various Characters. . . . . *Herschel Bernardi, Howard McNear,*
Howard Morris, Frank Nelson, John Stephenson

Produced by William Hanna, Joseph Barbera
(Hanna-Barbera/Screen Gems [Columbia TV])
24 episodes.

The Many Loves of Dobie Gillis CBS "Strictly for the Birds" November 28, 1962.
STARS: *Dwayne Hickman, Bob Denver, Frank Faylen, Florida Friebus, Sheila James.*
Dobie and Maynard's knowledge of American history isn't so hot. For their upcoming exam, they seek the aid of a talking mynah bird (voice of Mel Blanc).
Dr. Imogene Burkhart: Jean Byron. Bird Shop Owner: Pat Goldin. Betsy Dolly Martha Trueblood: Julie Parrish.

"Arthur Godfrey Loves Animals" CBS; SPECIAL March 18, 1963.
Arthur Godfrey believes that animals are the most misunderstood 'people'. In comedy and song, he tries to enhance our appreciation of our finned, feathered and four-footed friends. A series of stills show us Arthur's Virginia farm and some of its strange denizens: a llama and an elephant. In a sequence filmed at Marineland of the Pacific, we see trained porpoises perform.
Shari Lewis & 'Lamb Chop' & 'Hush Puppy', Mel Blanc, Paul Lynde.

Burke's Law ABC "Who Killed Mr. X?" September 27, 1963.
STARS: *Gene Barry, Gary Conway, Regis Toomey, Leon Lontoc.*
To some people, life is a merry-go-round, but it ends for one man beside a carousel. At the scene, Captain Burke (Barry) finds a matchbook — which leads him to the home of actress Stacy Owens (Elizabeth Montgomery).
Annabelle Rogers: Ann Harding. Barrie Coleman: Dina Merrill. Gregory: Charlie [Charles] Ruggles. Harold Mason: Jim Backus. Alison Grahame: Barrie Chase. Voice of Edward the Mynah Bird: Mel Blanc. Henry Geller: Soupy Sales. 1st Attorney: Hank [Harvey] Grant. 2nd Attorney: Cecil Smith. 3rd Attorney: Vernon Scott. 4th Attorney: Dan Jenkins. Little Boy: Fred Barry. Blonde Southern Girl: Allyson Ames.
(DVD)

Magilla Gorilla SYNDICATED/ABC January 14, 1964-September 2, 1967.
Animated cartoon. A good-natured ape resides at Peebles Pet Shop, where the owner hopes to sell the monkey to someone better able to afford his food bill. Two mountain critters, Punkin Puss and Mush Mouse, carry on a feud. Sheriff Ricochet Rabbit and his drawling deputy chase outlaws. A polar bear and seal bedevil an Arctic army colonel.

Voice Cast

Magilla Gorilla, Punkin Puss	*Allan Melvin*
Mr. Peebles, Mush Mouse, Breezly	*Howard Morris*
Ogee	*Jean Vander Pyl*
Ricochet Rabbit	*Daws Butler*
Deputy Droopalong Coyote, Sneezly	*Mel Blanc*
Colonel Fusby	*John Stephenson*

Produced by William Hanna, Joseph Barbera
(Hanna-Barbera/Screen Gems [Columbia TV])
58 episodes.

The Peter Potamus Show SYNDICATED/ABC
January 14, 1964-January 24, 1967.
Animated cartoon. A hippo explorer travels the globe and through time in his flying magic balloon. A polar bear and seal bedevil an Arctic army colonel. A trio of canine 'goofy guards' (Yippee, Yappee, Yahooey) serve a pint-sized king. Sheriff Ricochet Rabbit and his drawling deputy chase outlaws.

Voice Cast

Peter Potamus, Yahooey, Ricochet Rabbit . . . . *Daws Butler*
So-So the Monkey. . . . . *Don Messick*
Breezly the Polar Bear . . . . *Howard Morris*
Sneezly, Deputy Droopalong Coyote. . . . . *Mel Blanc*
Colonel Fusby . . . .*John Stephenson*
Yippee. . . . . *Doug Young*
Yappee, King. . . . . *Hal Smith*

Produced by William Hanna, Joseph Barbera
(Hanna-Barbera/Screen Gems [Columbia TV])
42 episodes.

The Object Is… ABC March 16 thru 20, 1964.
HOST: *Dick Clark.*
Six panelists, consisting of three celebrities and three studio-audience members, try to identify famous personalities from 'object' clues associated with that person. This week's guests are singer-actress Eartha Kitt, voice artist Mel Blanc and Rod Serling of TV's *Twilight Zone.*

The Mike Douglas Show SYNDICATED April 16, 1964.
HOST: *Mike Douglas. The Ellie Frankel Quartet.*
Co-host this week is Della Reese. Guests today are comic Jerry Lester, cartoon voice Mel Blanc and bandleader Cab Calloway.

The Beverly Hillbillies CBS "Granny Learns to Drive" May 20, 1964.
STARS: *Buddy Ebsen, Irene Ryan, Donna Douglas, Max Baer Jr., Raymond Bailey, Nancy Kulp.* ANNOUNCER: *Bill Baldwin.*
Granny *(Ryan)* decides to learn how to operate a car after a stranger demands money for giving her a lift — in his cab.
Richard Burten: Mel Blanc. Motorcycle Cop: Harry Lauter.

The Porky Pig Show ABC September 20, 1964-September 2, 1967.
Weekly network compilation of selected Warner Bros. theatrical cartoons with Mel Blanc's voice characterizations.

The Munsters CBS "Munster Masquerade" September 24, 1964.
STARS: *Fred Gwynne, Yvonne De Carlo, Al Lewis, Butch Patrick, Beverly Owen.*
Debut show of the series. Marilyn Munster (Owen) has been dating Tom Daly, who's a bit reticent about meeting her folks. He suggests that both families meet at the masquerade party to be held soon at his parents' residence.
Tom: Linden Chiles. Agnes Daly: Mabel Albertson. Albert Daly: Frank Wilcox. Mrs. Morton: Lurene Tuttle. Voice of the Raven: Mel Blanc.

The Lucy Show CBS "Lucy Gets the Bird" December 7, 1964.
STARS: *Lucille Ball, Vivian Vance, Gale Gordon, Candy Moore, Jimmy Garrett, Ralph Hart.* ANNOUNCER: *Roy Rowan. The Wilbur Hatch Orchestra.*
Mr. Mooney (Gordon) is boarding his pet parakeet, Greenback (voice of Mel Blanc), at the Carmichael household. When Lucy accidentally lets the bird fly away, she and Viv buy a replacement and hope to pass it off as Greenback.
Tim Herbert, John Fox, Ginny Tyler.

Gilligan's Island CBS "Angel on the Island" December 12, 1964.
STARS: *Bob Denver, Alan Hale Jr., Jim Backus, Natalie Schafer, Tina Louise, Russell Johnson, Dawn Wells.*
Ginger (Louise) is miserable over not being able to appear on Broadway, so wealthy Mr. Howell (Backus) agrees to back her in a very 'off-Broadway' production of "Cleopatra".
Voice of Parrot: Mel Blanc.
(DVD)

The Munsters CBS "Grandpa Leaves Home" December 24, 1964.
STARS: *Fred Gwynne, Yvonne De Carlo, Al Lewis, Butch Patrick, Pat Priest.*
Grandpa (Lewis) decides it's best to go away for good when he begins feeling unloved, unwanted and — worst of all — unnoticed.
Nightclub Manager: Robert Strauss. Fellow: Bill Dugan. Woman: Iris Adrian. Voice of the Raven: Mel Blanc.

Sinbad Jr. SYNDICATED 1965.
Animated cartoon. A young sailor finds adventure and thwarts evil, gaining strength from his magic belt.
Voice Cast
Sinbad Jr. . . . . Tim Matthieson [Matheson]
Salty the Parrot. . . . . Mel Blanc

Produced by William Hanna, Joseph Barbera
(Hanna-Barbera/American International TV)
25 episodes (100 five-minute cartoons @ four per show).

Gilligan's Island CBS "Water, Water Everywhere" January 2, 1965.
STARS: *Bob Denver, Alan Hale Jr., Jim Backus, Natalie Schafer, Tina Louise, Russell Johnson, Dawn Wells.*
Hope springs eternal, but water doesn't — the island's spring has gone dry, leaving the castaways without fresh water. To make matters worse, Gilligan (Denver) manages to waste all the water that was saved before the drought.
Voice of Ribbit the Frog: Mel Blanc. (DVD)

The Munsters CBS "Herman's Child Psychology" September 16, 1965.
STARS: *Fred Gwynne, Yvonne De Carlo, Al Lewis, Butch Patrick, Pat Priest. First show of the season.* Eddie (Patrick) announces that he's going to run away from home. Herman (Gwynne) decides to use a little psychology and let the youngster go.
Leo: Gene Blakely. Charlie Pike: Michel Petit. Voice of the Raven: Mel Blanc.

The Atom Ant/Secret Squirrel Show NBC
October 2, 1965-September 7, 1968.
Animated cartoon. Insect-sized superhero Atom Ant fights nefarious villains. Secret Squirrel carries out his spy assignments for the Double Q Agency. Squiddly Diddly the Squid wishes to escape his Marineland cage and see the world. The lazy Hillbilly Bears attempt to avoid steady work. Granny Sweet overlooks Precious Pupp's mischievous hi-jinks. A sorceress eschews black magic and instead strives to do good deeds.

Voice Cast

Atom Ant	*Howard Morris, Don Messick*
Secret Squirrel	*Mel Blanc*
Morocco Mole, Squiddly Diddly	*Paul Frees*
Chief Winchley	*John Stephenson*
Paw Rugg	*Henry Corden*
Ma Rugg, Floral Rugg, Winsome Witch	*Jean Vander Pyl*
Precious Pupp	*Don Messick*
Granny Sweet	*Janet Waldo*

Produced by William Hanna, Joseph Barbera
(Hanna-Barbera/Screen Gems [Columbia TV])
26 episodes.

The Munsters CBS "Herman's Driving Test" November 25, 1965.
STARS: *Fred Gwynne, Yvonne De Carlo, Al Lewis, Butch Patrick, Pat Priest.*
Herman (Gwynne) has been promised a raise in salary and a more important post at the funeral parlor — if he can pass a driving test.
Charles Wiggins: Charlie [Charles] Ruggles. Voice of the Raven: Mel Blanc.

Abbott & Costello SYNDICATED 1966.
The cartoon adventures of comedians Bud Abbott and Lou Costello.

Voice Cast

Bud Abbott	*Himself*
Lou Costello	*Stan Irwin*
Various Characters.	*Mel Blanc, Don Messick,*
Hal Smith, John Stephenson, Janet Waldo	

Produced by William Hanna, Joseph Barbera
(Hanna-Barbera/RKO General-Jomar TV)
39 episodes (156 five-minute cartoons @ four per episode).

"Alice in Wonderland or What's a Nice Kid Like You Doing in a Place Like This" ABC; SPECIAL March 30, 1966.
In this way-out spoof of Lewis Carroll's children's classic, Alice tumbles through her TV set after her dog Fluff — and falls into Wonderland. There are two voices for Alice: Janet Waldo *(speaking)* and Doris Drew Allen *(singing)*.

Voice Cast

White Rabbit	*Howard Morris*
Cheshire Cat	*Sammy Davis Jr.*
Hedda Hatter	*Hedda Hopper*
March Hare, King of Hearts.	*Daws Butler*
Mad Hatter	*Harvey Korman*
Dormouse	*Don Messick.*
The Talking Caterpillar a.k.a.	
Fred Flintstone and Barney Rubble	*Alan Reed, Mel Blanc.*
White Knight	*Bill Dana*
Queen of Hearts	*Zsa Zsa Gabor.*
Humphrey Dumpty, Father	*Allan Melvin.*

SONGS: Howard, Doris: "Life's A Game". Sammy: "What's A Nice Kid Like You Doing In A Place Like This?" Alan, Mel: "They'll Never Split

Us Apart". Bill, Doris: "Today's A Wonderful Day". Doris: "I'm Home".
(Lee Adams-Charles Strouse).

The Munsters CBS "Herman's Lawsuit" April 21, 1966.
STARS: *Fred Gwynne, Yvonne De Carlo, Al Lewis, Butch Patrick, Pat Priest.*
Herman has been hit by a woman motorist who wants to make a $10,000
cash settlement, but the big lug thinks he's being sued — for damages
to the lady's auto.
*Mrs. Kingsley: Dorothy Green. Ted: Jerome Cowan. Voice of the Raven: Mel
Blanc.*

The Munsters CBS "A Visit From the Teacher" May 12, 1966.
STARS: *Fred Gwynne, Yvonne De Carlo, Al Lewis, Butch Patrick, Pat Priest.*
Herman helps Eddie write a school essay — about Eddie's "average
American parents."
Miss Thompson: Pat Woodell. Voice of the Raven: Mel Blanc.

The Road Runner Show CBS/ABC
September 10, 1966-September 2, 1972.
Weekly network compilation of Warner Brothers theatrical cartoons with
voice characterizations by Mel Blanc.

The Monkees NBC "Monkees in a Ghost Town" October 24, 1966.
STARS: *Davy Jones, Peter Tork, Micky Dolenz, Mike Nesmith.*
Stranded in a ghost town after the Monkeemobile *(vocals by Mel Blanc)*
runs out of gas, the cool quartet find themselves held prisoner.
*Bessie Kowalski: Rose Marie. Lenny: Lon Chaney [Jr.]. George: Len Lesser.
1st Cop: Hollis Morrison.*
SONGS: "Tomorrow's Gonna Be Another Day" *(Tommy Boyce-Steve
Venet),* "Papa Gene's Blues" *(Michael Nesmith),* "Everybody Loves My
Baby (But My Baby Don't Love Nobody But Me)" *(Jack Palmer; Spencer
Williams),* "Hi, Neighbor" *(Jack Owens)*

"The Jack Benny Hour" NBC; SPECIAL December 1, 1966.
Jack does a reprise of his famous "Si" routine, with sidekick Mel Blanc as Sy, the leader of a misfit Mariachi band. The Smothers Brothers do "I Talk To The Trees." Jack also asks guest Trini Lopez for a guitar lesson and presents his very own beauty pageant — a parody of every beauty contest ever seen — with Phyllis Diller. Jack Elliott conducts the orchestra.

SONGS: Trini: "Fly Me To The Moon" *(Bart Howard)*; "This Train" *(Traditional gospel song; new words and music by Woody Guthrie).* Band: "Spanish Flea" *(Music : Julius Wechter; lyrics: Cissy Wechter).* Jack: "Here She Is, Miss Northern and Southern Hemisphere".

"Crusade 67" *(Syndicated; Special)(KPHO-TV, Phoenix, AZ)* April 30, 1967. The 1967 Cancer Crusade presents a variety program with Sammy Davis Jr., Jack Benny, Lorne Greene, Joan Crawford, Mel Blanc and Myron Cohen.

Wacky Races CBS September 14, 1968-September 5, 1970.
Animated cartoon. A group of auto daredevils compete in slapstick races.

Voice Cast

Dick Dastardly, Clyde, Red Max	*Paul Winchell*
Penelope Pitstop	*Janet Waldo*
Muttley, Professor Pat Pending, Sawtooth	
Ring-a-Ding, Little Gruesome.	*Don Messick*
Peter Perfect, Rufus Ruffcat, Sergeant Blast,	
Rock Slag, Gravel Slag, Big Gruesome	*Daws Butler*
The General, Luke Bear, Blubber Bear.	*John Stephenson*
The Anthill Mob	*Mel Blanc*
Narrator	*Dave Willock*

Produced by William Hanna, Joseph Barbera, Iwao Takamoto *(Hanna-Barbera/Heatter-Quigley)*
13 episodes.

"The Fabulous Shorts" NBC; SPECIAL October 17, 1968.
Jim Backus hosts a cartoon roundup featuring many Oscar-winners. Walt Disney's achievements are traced from *Steamboat Willie* (which intro-duced Mickey Mouse in 1928) to the Academy Award winner *Flowers And Trees* (1932), *The Old Mill* (1937) and *Der Fuehrer's Face*, a 1942 war cartoon with Donald Duck. Contemporary efforts include *Munro*, Jules

Feiffer's sly tale of a 4-year-old draftee; John and Faith Hubley's *Moonbird*, narrated by the artists' sons; Yugoslavia's *Ersatz*, the first foreign Oscar winner; two illustrated Tijuana Brass tunes "Tijuana Taxi" and "Spanish Flea"; and *The Critic*, a Mel Brooks-Ernest Pintoff creation. Voice artist Mel Blanc shows how a 'Bugs Bunny' cartoon is made, and Jim Backus says a few words about 'Mr. Magoo'.

The Mothers-in-Law NBC "The Birth of Everything But the Blues" December 1, 1968.
STARS: *Eve Arden, Kaye Ballard, Richard Deacon, Herbert Rudley, Jerry Fogel, Deborah Walley.*
Eve and Kaye tackle the care and feeding of a motley menagerie when they take over Suzie's job as a pet-sitter. The ladies' problems are increasing rapidly — most of the critters are expecting.
Dr. Butler: Herbert Voland. Man: Del Moore. Voice of the Mynah Bird: Mel Blanc.

The Perils of Penelope Pitstop CBS
September 13, 1969-September 5, 1971.
Animated cartoon. A sweet Southern gal and a sextet of reformed gangsters foil the plots of the Hooded Claw, who is after Penelope's inheritance.

Voice Cast

Penelope Pitstop . . . . *Janet Waldo*
Sylvester Sneakly, the Hooded Claw . . . . *Paul Lynde*
Chug-a-Boom, Yak Yak, Bully Brothers . . . . *Mel Blanc*
Clyde, Softie . . . . *Paul Winchell*
Zippy, Pockets, Dum Dum, Snoozy. . . . . *Don Messick*
Narrator . . . . *Gary Owens*

Produced by William Hanna, Joseph Barbera, Alex Lovy
(Hanna-Barbera)
17 episodes.

Here's Lucy C B S "Lucy Goes to the Air Force Academy" part 2. September 29, 1969.
S T A R S : *Lucille Ball, Gale Gordon, Lucie Arnaz, Desi Arnaz Jr., Mary Jane Croft.* A N N O U N C E R : *Roy Rowan. The Marl Young Orchestra.*
Lucy's efforts to get Craig (Desi Arnaz Jr.) enrolled at the academy result in being dragged along the halls behind a floor-polisher, an unscheduled performance on closed-circuit TV and disruption of a mock battle maneuver. *Filmed on location.*
Superintendent: Roy Roberts. Voice of Red Company and Woodward: Mel Blanc.

Pat Paulsen's Half a Comedy Hour A B C January 22, 1970.
S T A R S : Pat Paulsen, Hal Smith, Bob Einstein, Sherry Miles, Jean Byron, George Spell, Joan Gerber, Pepe Brown, Pedro Regas, Vanetta Rogers. The Denny Vaughn Orchestra.
Debut show of the series. In his comedy acting debut, former Vice President Hubert Humphrey aids a distressed motorist (Pat). Debbie Reynolds plays an unruly prisoner causing problems for warden Pat. An interview with cartoon character Daffy Duck (voice of Mel Blanc). Pat shows viewers how to assemble a TV set and parodies a TV leading man.

Where's Huddles? C B S July 1-September 9, 1970.
Animated cartoon. Pro football serves as the backdrop for this comedy about the antics of two players for the Rhinos team.

Voice Cast

Ed Huddles	Cliff Norton
Bubba McCoy	Mel Blanc
Marge Huddles	Jean Vander Pyl
Claude Pertwee	Paul Lynde
Penny McCoy	Marie Wilson
Freight Train	Herb Jeffries
Mad Dog Maloney	Alan Reed
Fumbles	Don Messick
Sports Announcer	Dick Enberg

Produced by William Hanna, Joseph Barbera, Alex Lovy
(Hanna-Barbera)
10 episodes.

Lancelot Link, Secret Chimp ABC
September 12, 1970-September 4, 1971.
Simian operatives of A.P.E. (Agency to Prevent Evil) thwart the no-good monkeyshines perpetrated by agents of C.H.U.M.P. (Criminal Headquarters for Underworld Master Plan). Also, Daffy Duck cartoons.
Voice Cast
(dubbing live-action chimps 'acting' the various roles)
Lancelot Link . . . . *Dayton Allen*
Mata Hairi. . . . . *Joan Gerber*
Daffy Duck . . . . *Mel Blanc*
Various Characters. . . . . *Steven Hoffman, Bernie Kopell*
Narrator, Various Characters. . . . . *Malachi Throne*

Produced by Allan Sandler, Stan Burns, Mike Marmer
(Sandler–Burns–Marmer Productions)
26 episodes.

Sabrina and the Groovie Goolies/Sabrina the Teen-Age Witch CBS
September 12, 1970-September 1, 1973.
Animated cartoon. An adolescent sorceress tries, sometimes unsuccessfully, to keep her powers from affecting unsuspecting humans.
Voice Cast
Sabrina, Aunt Hilda, Aunt Zelda . . . . *Jane Webb*
Salem Spellman . . . . *Mel Blanc*

Produced by Norm Prescott, Lou Scheimer
(Filmation)
35 episodes.

"Tales of Washington Irving" SYNDICATED; SPECIAL *(WLFI-TV, Channel 8, Terre Haute, IN)* November 1, 1970.
1. "The Legend of Sleepy Hollow" — The story of gawky schoolteacher Ichabod Crane, who was last seen one moonless autumn night fleeing from a headless horseman.
2. "Rip Van Winkle" — Tale of a good-natured, henpecked ne'er-do-well who joins a group of Dutch elves in a game of ninepins, takes a sip from their keg…and falls asleep for twenty years.
Voices: Mel Blanc, George Firth, Joan Gerber, Byron Kane, Julie McWhirter [Dees], Don Messick, Ken Samson, Lennie Weinrib, Brian Zax, Larraine Zax.

"Jack Benny's 20th Anniversary Special" NBC; SPECIAL November 16, 1970.
STARS: *Jack Benny, Mary Livingstone, Phil Harris, Dennis Day, Eddie 'Rochester' Anderson, Don Wilson.*
Jack and his famous cast of cohorts celebrate two decades in television. Featured are excerpts from past shows and a skit depicting the 'Benny cast' in the future. Also appearing are familiar Benny sidemen Mel Blanc, Benny Rubin, Artie Auerbach and Frank Nelson. Guests include Lucille Ball, Bob Hope, George Burns, Dean Martin, Dinah Shore, Frank Sinatra and Red Skelton.

Curiosity Shop ABC September 11, 1971-September 2, 1972.
Children's show set in a magical place designed to stimulate young imaginations and prompt questions.

Cast

Pam	*Pamelyn Ferdin*
Cindy	*Jerrelyn Fields*
Gerrard	*John Levin*
Ralph	*Kerry MacLane*
Gittel the Bumbling Witch	*Barbara Minkus*
Mr. Jones' Answering Service	*Chuck Jones*
Animation Voices	*Mel Blanc, June Foray,*
Bob Holt, Don Messick, Les Tremayne	
Puppets	*The Bob Baker Marionettes*

Produced by Chuck Jones, Herbert Klynn, Abe Levitow
(Format Films/Sandler-Burns-Marmer Productions)

Juvenile Jury SYNDICATED *(WPIX-TV, Channel 11, New York City)* October 24, 1971.
HOST: *Jack Barry.*
A panel of youngsters gives advice to viewers' submitted questions. Today's guest is the voice of Bugs Bunny — Mel Blanc — who demonstrates his knack for creating special voices.

The Tonight Show Starring Johnny Carson NBC November 4, 1971.
HOST: *Johnny Carson.* ANNOUNCER: *Ed McMahon. The Doc Severinsen Orchestra.*
Among Johnny's guests are country singer Roy Clark, comic actor Billy DeWolfe, actress Barbara Feldon, actor Jack Lemmon and the voice cast of The Flintstones — Alan Reed, Mel Blanc and Jean Vander Pyl.

Night Gallery NBC "Cool Air"/"Camera Obscura"/"Quoth the Raven"
December 8, 1971.
HOST: *Rod Serling.*
1. A doctor has discovered a way to prolong life by using a refrigeration device.
Agatha Howard: Barbara Rush. Dr. Juan Munos: Henry Darrow. Mrs. Gibbons: Beatrice Kay. Charles Crowley: Larry Blake. Iceman: Karl Lukas.
2. A ruthless moneylender encounters a camera which is also a time-traveling machine.
Mr. Gingold: Ross Martin. William Sharsted: Rene Auberjonois. Abel Joyce: Arthur Malet. Lamplighter: Milton Parsons. Sanderson: Philip Kenneally. Amos Drucker: Brendan Dillon. Sharsted Sr.: John Barclay.
3. In a vignette, writer Edgar Allan Poe (Marty Allen) receives inspiration from a black bird.
Voice of Raven: Mel Blanc.

The Flintstones Comedy Hour/The Flintstones Show CBS
September 9, 1972-January 26, 1974.
Animated cartoon. The Flintstones and Rubbles return to involve themselves in the doings of their children and friends.

Voice Cast

Fred Flintstone	Alan Reed
Barney Rubble, Zonk, Stub	Mel Blanc
Wilma Flintstone	Jean Vander Pyl
Betty Rubble, Wiggy, Cindy	Gay Hartwig
Pebbles Flintstone	Mickey Stevens
Bamm Bamm Rubble	Jay North
Moonrock, Bronto	Lennie Weinrib
Penny	Mitzi McCall
Fabian	Carl Esser
Noodles, Mr. Slate	John Stephenson
Schleprock	Don Messick

Produced by William Hanna, Joseph Barbera, Iwao Takamoto
(Hanna-Barbera)

The ABC Saturday Superstar Movie ABC "Yogi's Ark Lark"
September 16, 1972.
Yogi Bear and his animal friends sail away from Jellystone National Park to find a new, unpolluted habitat.

Voice Cast

Yogi Bear, Huckleberry Hound,
Quick Draw McGraw . . . . *Daws Butler*
Boo Boo, Ranger Smith. . . . . *Don Messick*
Secret Squirrel. . . . . *Mel Blanc*
Top Cat. . . . .*Arnold Stang*
Magilla Gorilla . . . .*Allan Melvin*

The ABC Saturday Superstar Movie ABC "Daffy Duck and Porky Pig Meet the Groovie Goolies" December 16, 1972.
It is a comic tale of sabotage at a movie studio when the classic funny animals run into that band of wacky musical monsters.

Voice Cast

Daffy Duck, Porky Pig, Elmer Fudd, Yosemite Sam, Tweetie Pie,
Road Runner, Wile E. Coyote, Pepe LePew, Foghorn Leghorn,
Sylvester the Cat, Charlie Dog . . . . *Mel Blanc*
The Goolies . . . .*Howard Morris.*
The Phantom. . . . . *Larry Storch.*

"The Cricket in Times Square" ABC; SPECIAL April 24, 1973.
How does a Connecticut cricket wind up in Times Square? Chester C. Cricket hops a ride at a picnic on a leftover liverwurst sandwich. Now the little guy is taking the big city by storm with a special talent: while most of his ilk merely chirp, Chester can make a tune — any tune — sound like a violin solo. Animated adaptation of a children's story written by George Selden.

Voice Cast

Chester, Cat, Father, Music Teacher . . . . *Les Tremayne*
Tucker Mouse . . . . *Mel Blanc*
Mother . . . .*June Foray*
Mario. . . . .*Kerry MacLane.*

The Merv Griffin Show SYNDICATED August 2, 1973.
HOST: *Merv Griffin.*
Merv shines his spotlight on the days of old-time radio and welcomes guests Edgar Bergen, Harold Peary, Mel Blanc and Arch Oboler.

Yogi's Gang ABC September 8, 1973-August 30, 1975.
Animated cartoon. Yogi Bear and his pals take on enemies of nature and man.

Voice Cast

Yogi Bear, Quick Draw McGraw, Huckleberry Hound, Snagglepuss,
Augie Doggie, Wally Gator, Peter Potamus . . . . *Daws Butler*
Boo Boo, Ranger John Smith, Touche Turtle,
Squiddly Diddly, Atom Ant, So-So . . . . *Don Messick*
Doggie Daddy . . . .*John Stephenson*
Secret Squirrel . . . . *Mel Blanc*
Magilla Gorilla . . . .*Allan Melvin*
Paw Rugg . . . . *Henry Corden*

Produced by William Hanna, Joseph Barbera, Iwao Takamoto
(Hanna-Barbera)
15 episodes.

Speed Buggy CBS September 8, 1973-August 30, 1975.
Animated cartoon. A talking dune buggy with a sputtering personality helps his teen pals solve crimes and catch crooks.

Voice Cast

Speed Buggy . . . . *Mel Blanc*
Tinker . . . . *Phil Luther Jr.*
Debbie . . . . *Arlene Golonka*
Mark . . . .*Mike Bell*

Produced by William Hanna, Joseph Barbera, Iwao Takamoto
(Hanna-Barbera)
16 episodes.

The New Scooby-Doo Movies CBS "The Weird Winds on Winona"
October 13, 1973.
VOICES: *Don Messick, Frank Welker, Heather North, Casey Kasem, Nichole Jaffe.*
Scooby-Doo (Messick) and the gang make a stopover in Winona, MS, after the Mystery Machine breaks down. Also there is Speed Buggy (Mel Blanc) and his cohorts, investigating the strange midnight winds that are scaring the locals. Together, the two mystery-solving teams get to the bottom of the matter — a plot to raze the old town and build a new one.
Debbie: Arlene Golonka. Tinker: Phil Luther Jr. Mark: Mike Bell. Also: Sherry

Alberoni, Joe Besser, Jerry Dexter, Richard Elkins, Stu Gilliam, Mark Hamill, Jackie Joseph, Julie McWhirter [Dees], Barbara Pariot, Janet Waldo, Johnny Williams, Scatman Crothers, Robert DoQui, Jamie Farr, Bob Hastings, Alan Oppenheimer, John Stephenson, Jonathan Walmsley.

"A Very Merry Cricket" ABC; SPECIAL December 14, 1973.
Harry the Cat and Tucker the Mouse are bemoaning the lack of real Christmas spirit around them. They search out Chester C. Cricket so he can provide some of his magical music for the holiday.
Voice Cast
Chester, Harry . . . . *Les Tremayne*
Tucker, Alley Cat. . . . . *Mel Blanc*

The Tonight Show Starring Johnny Carson NBC January 23, 1974.
HOST: *Johnny Carson.* ANNOUNCER: *Ed McMahon. The Doc Severinsen Orchestra.*
Guests: comedian Jack Benny and his sideman, voice artist Mel Blanc; 'Muppeteer' Jim Henson; Maria Muldaur; and Dr. Irwin Maxwell Stillman.

"Jack Benny" NBC; SPECIAL December 28, 1974.
HOST: *Tom Snyder.*
Broadcast from Waukegan, IL. Memories of beloved comedian Jack Benny, aired one day following his passing. Johnny Green, Mel Blanc, Dennis Day, Sheldon Leonard, Jack Paar, Isaac Stern, Herb Schlusser.

"A Tribute to Jack Benny" CBS; SPECIAL December 29, 1974.
HOST: *Charles Kuralt.* REPORTERS: *Richard Threlkeld, David Culhane.*
Coverage of the late comedian's funeral, plus interviews and clips from Benny's TV and radio series and appearances. Bob Hope gives a eulogy. Eddie Anderson, Mel Blanc, Ronald Reagan, William S. Paley, Johnny Carson, Carol Burnett, Jimmy [James] Stewart.

"Yankee Doodle Cricket" ABC; SPECIAL January 16, 1975.
Chester C. Cricket, Harry the Cat and Tucker the Mouse relate their ancestors' contributions to the struggle for American independence.
Chester: Les Tremayne. Harry: Mel Blanc. Tucker: June Foray.

Camera Three CBS "The Boys From Termite Terrace" 1975.
HOST: *John Canemaker.*
A look back at 'Termite Terrace', the nickname for Warner Brothers' cartoon studio, which produced hundreds of *Looney Tunes* and *Merrie Melodies* from the 1930s through the 1960s. The cartoons starred the likes of Bugs Bunny, Daffy Duck, Porky Pig, Sylvester & Tweety, The Road Runner and many others. Seen are interviews with the prime-movers of the unit, including animation director-producers Robert [Bob] Clampett, Friz Freleng and Chuck Jones, as well as voice artist Mel Blanc.

"The Good Old Days of Radio" PBS; SPECIAL 1976.
HOST: *Steve Allen. The Les Brown Orchestra.*
Steve presides over this history of radio entertainment during the 1930s and '40s. Orchestra leader Lawrence Welk; Bill Hay (announcer for Amos 'n' Andy); Norman Corwin (writer-producer of The Columbia Workshop and related series); Helen O'Connell (vocalist for Jimmy Dorsey); Lurene Tuttle (Adventures of Sam Spade and many other series); Janet Waldo (Meet Corliss Archer); Dennis Day, Mel Blanc (both of The Jack Benny Program) and Edgar Bergen. Cyril Ritchard in a fund appeal for support of public television stations.

The Merv Griffin Show SYNDICATED *(WNEW-TV, Channel 5, New York City)* January 28, 1976.
HOST: *Merv Griffin.*
Memories of Jack Benny as offered by fellow comedian and friend George Burns; Jack's former manager Irving Fein; singer and friend Gisele MacKenzie; and Benny cohorts Mel Blanc and Don Wilson.

"Carnival of the Animals" CBS; SPECIAL November 22, 1976.
All new animation of Bugs Bunny, Porky Pig and Daffy Duck combine with live action of musician Michael Tilson Thomas in a performance of material taken from the compositions of Camille Saint-Saens and the poetry of Ogden Nash.
Voice of Bugs Bunny, Porky Pig, Daffy Duck: Mel Blanc.

"Bugs Bunny's Easter Special" CBS; SPECIAL April 7, 1977.
With the Easter Bunny out sick, Granny calls on Bugs to help deliver the holiday egg baskets. Features the classic Warner Brothers cartoons *For Scent-Imental Reasons* (1949), *Knighty Knight Bugs* (1958), *Robin Hood Daffy* (1958), *Sahara Hare* (1955) and *Birds Anonymous* (1957).

Voice Cast

Bugs Bunny, Daffy Duck . . . . *Mel Blanc*
Granny. . . . .*June Foray*

Scooby's All-Star Laff-a-Lympics/Scooby's All-Stars ABC
September 10, 1977-September 8, 1979.
Animated cartoon. A whole passel of characters divide into three teams to compete in various comedic sporting contests.

Voice Cast

Scooby-Doo, Boo Boo, Pixie, Dastardly Dalton, Mumbly,
Mr. Creepley, Announcer . . . . *Don Messick*
Snagglepuss, Yogi Bear, Huckleberry Hound, Hokey Wolf,
Snooper & Blabber, Wally Gator, Quick Draw McGraw,
Augie Doggie, Jinks, Scooby-Dum, Dirty Dalton . . . *Daws Butler*
Doggie Daddy, Dread Baron,
The Great Fondoo . . . .*John Stephenson*
Grape Ape, Orful Octopus, Dinky Dalton. . . . . *Bob Holt*
Mildew Wolf, Yakky Doodle, Dynomutt, Tinker, Sooey Pig,
Magic Rabbit . . . . *Frank Welker*
Cindy Bear . . . . *Julie Bennett*
Shaggy . . . . *Casey Kasem*
Hong Kong Phooey . . . . *Scatman Crothers*
Jeannie . . . .*Julie McWhirter [Dees]*
Babu. . . . .*Joe Besser*
Blue Falcon. . . . . *Gary Owens*
Captain Caveman, Speed Buggy . . . . *Mel Blanc*
Brenda Chance, Daisy Mayhem . . . . *Marilyn Schreffler*
Dee Dee Sykes. . . . . *Vernee Watson*
Taffy Dare, Mrs. Creepley. . . . .*Laurel Page*
Also . . . .*Alan Reed*

Produced by William Hanna, Joseph Barbera, Art Scott, Alex Lovy, Don Jurwich, Iwao Takamoto
(Hanna–Barbera)
13 episodes.

"A Flintstone Christmas" NBC; SPECIAL December 7, 1977.
The holiday is in jeopardy when Santa Claus falls off Fred Flintstone's roof and sprains his ankle. Fearing he cannot make his timely Christmas Eve deliveries, Santa asks Fred and Barney to complete his gift run. They agree and set off on their joyful mission — despite some difficulties.

Voice Cast

Fred Flintstone . . . . Henry Corden
Barney Rubble . . . . Mel Blanc
Santa Claus . . . . Hal Smith
Wilma & Pebbles Flintstone . . . . Jean Vander Pyl
Betty Rubble . . . . B.J. Ward
Bamm Bamm Rubble . . . . Lucille Bliss
Mr. Slate . . . . John Stephenson
Also . . . . Virginia Gregg, Gay Hartwig

"A Connecticut Rabbit in King Arthur's Court" CBS; SPECIAL February 23, 1978.
A Looney Tunes version of the Mark Twain story of a 'modern' rabbit (Bugs Bunny) transplanted in time to the days of Camelot, meeting King Arthur (Daffy Duck) and varlet Porky Pig. They are confronted by villainous Elmer Fudd and Yosemite Sam. Mel Blanc provides the voice characterizations.

"The Flintstones Little Big League" NBC; SPECIAL April 6, 1978.
Fred gets jealous when Barney becomes a success managing a Little League baseball team. Fred immediately agrees to helm a similar team for Mr. Slate. When the championship approaches, it looks like Fred's team will go head-to-head with Barney's.

Voice Cast

Fred Flintstone . . . . Henry Corden
Barney Rubble . . . . Mel Blanc.
Wilma Flintstone . . . . Jean Vander Pyl
Betty Rubble . . . . Gay Hartwig.
Pebbles Flintstone . . . . Pamela Anderson.
Bamm Bamm Rubble . . . . Frank Welker.
Mr. Slate . . . . John Stephenson
Officer . . . . Ted Cassidy.
Judge Shale . . . . Herb Vigran
Dusty . . . . Lucille Bliss.
Lefty . . . . Randy Gray
Also . . . . Don Messick.

Yogi's Space Race NBC September 9, 1978-January 27, 1979.
Animated cartoon. Yogi Bear and pals compete in a series of races
throughout the galaxy.

Voice Cast

Yogi Bear, Huckleberry Hound . . . . *Daws Butler*
Scare Bear. . . . .*Joe Besser*
Jabberjaw, Buford, Nugget Nose, Captain Good, Kleen Cat,
Phantom Phink, Sludge . . . . *Frank Welker*
Rita . . . . *Pat Parris*
Wendy. . . . . *Marilyn Schreffler*
Quack-Up. . . . . *Mel Blanc*
Announcer. . . . . *Gary Owens*

Produced by William Hanna, Joseph Barbera, Iwao Takamoto, Art Scott,
Ray Patterson
(Hanna-Barbera)
13 episodes.

"Bugs Bunny's Howl-oween Special" CBS; SPECIAL October 26, 1978.
Mel Blanc provides voice characterizations for new animation surrounding the classic Warner Brothers cartoon *A-Haunting We Will Go (1966)*
and clips from *Broomstick Bunny* (1956), *Transylvania 6-5000* (1963),
Scaredy Cat (1948) and *Claws For Alarm* (1954).

The Galaxy Goof-Ups NBC November 4, 1978-March 3, 1979.
Animated cartoon. A band of funny animals police the spaceways as part
of a futuristic law-enforcement unit. A spin-off from *Yogi's Space Race.*

Voice Cast

Yogi Bear, Huckleberry Hound . . . . *Daws Butler*
The General, Captain Snerdley . . . .*John Stephenson*
Scare Bear. . . . .*Joe Besser*
Quack-Up. . . . . *Mel Blanc*

Produced by William Hanna, Joseph Barbera, Art Scott
(Hanna-Barbera)

"How Bugs Bunny Won the West" CBS; SPECIAL November 15, 1978. Denver Pyle *(in a live-action sequence)* tells how the 'rascally rabbit' tamed the wild frontier. Mel Blanc provides voice characterizations for new animation surrounding clips from these classic Warner Brothers cartoons: *Bonanza Bunny* (1959), *Wild And Wooly Hare* (1959), *Dripalong Daffy* (1951), *Barbary Coast Bunny* (1956) and two others.

The Merv Griffin Show SYNDICATED 1978.
HOST: *Merv Griffin.*
Voice artist Mel Blanc is a guest.

The New Fred and Barney Show/Fred and Barney Meet the Thing/Fred and Barney Meet the Shmoo NBC February 3, 1979-November 15, 1980. Animated cartoon. The comedic misadventures of everyone's favorite Stone Age families, the Flintstones and the Rubbles. A teenager uses his special rings to turn into a massive, rock-skinned hero. A shape-changing pear-like creature aids three teens in probing weird phenomena.

Voice Cast

Fred Flintstone . . . . *Henry Corden*
Barney Rubble . . . . *Mel Blanc*
Wilma & Pebbles Flintstone . . . .*Jean Vander Pyl*
Betty Rubble . . . .*Janet Waldo, Gay Autterson*
Bamm Bamm Rubble . . . . *Don Messick*
Dino the Dinosaur . . *Don Messick (1979), Mel Blanc (1979-80)*
George Slate, Stretch, Dr. Harkness. . . . .*John Stephenson*
Benjy Grimm . . . . *Wayne Morton (1979)*
The Thing . . . . *Joe Baker (1979)*
Kelly . . . . *Noelle North (1979)*
Betty, Benjy's friend, Miss Twilly . . . . . *Marilyn Schreffler (1979)*
Spike . . . . *Art Metrano (1979)*
Ronald Radford . . . .*John Erwin (1979)*
Turkey. . . . . *Michael Sheehan (1979)*
The Shmoo . . . . *Frank Welker (1979-80)*
Nita . . . . *Dolores Cantu-Primo (1979-80)*
Billie Joe . . . . *Chuck McCann (1979-80)*
Mickey . . . .*Bill Idelson (1979-80)*

Produced by William Hanna, Joseph Barbera, Iwao Takamoto, Art Scott, Alex Lovy
(Hanna-Barbera)

"Bugs Bunny's Valentine" CBS; SPECIAL February 14, 1979.
A 'stupid Cupid' (Elmer Fudd) gives Bugs Bunny the 'love bug'. Mel Blanc provides voice characterizations for new animation surrounding the classic Warner Brothers cartoon *Hare Trimmed* (1953). Also, clips from *The Grey Hounded Hare* (1949), *Hare Splitter* (1948), *Little Beau Pepe* (1952), *The Super Snooper* (1952) and four others.

"You're the Greatest, Charlie Brown" CBS; SPECIAL March 19, 1979.
Charlie Brown strives to win the decathlon event in the Junior Olympics. Written by *Peanuts* creator Charles Schulz.
Charlie Brown: Arrin Skelly. Linus: Daniel Anderson. Snoopy: Bill Melendez. Peppermint Patty: Patricia Ann Patts. Lucy: Michelle Muller. Paula: Casey Carlson. Sally: Scott Beach. Schroeder: Tim Hall. Mel Blanc provides Charlie Brown's grunts.

"The Bugs Bunny Mother's Day Special" CBS; SPECIAL May 12, 1979.
Bugs Bunny encounters a pickled stork as they honor mothers. Mel Blanc provides voice characterizations for new animation bridging these abridged classic Warner Brothers cartoons: *Stork Naked* (1955) and *Apes Of Wrath (1959)*. Also, clips from *Bushy Hare* (1950), *Goo Goo Goliath* (1954), *Mother Was A Rooster* (1962) and *Quackodile Tears* (1962).

Buck Rogers in the 25th Century NBC
September 20, 1979-April 16, 1981.
A 20th century astronaut falls into suspended animation, awakening 500 years later to aid his newfound friends in battling evil forces on Earth. He later joins the crew of a starship to search for displaced humans in the galaxy. Adapted from the comic strip created by Phil Knowlan and Dick Calkins.

Cast
Captain William 'Buck' Rogers . . . . *Gil Gerard*
Colonel Wilma Deering . . . . *Erin Gray*
Dr. Huer . . . . *Tim O'Connor (1979–80)*
Twiki . . . . *Felix Silla*
Mel Blanc (voice)
 Bob Eyea (voice, 1981)
Dr. Theopolis . . . . *Eric Server (voice, 1979–80)*
Princess Ardala . . . . *Pamela Hensley (1979–80)*
Kane . . . . *Henry Silva (1979)*
 . . . . *Michael Ansara (1979–80)*

Hawk . . . . *Thom Christopher (1981)*
Dr. Goodfellow . . . . *Wilfred Hyde-White (1981)*
Admiral Asimov . . . . *Jay Garner (1981)*
Crichton . . . . *Jeff David (voice, 1981)*
Lieutenant Devlin . . . . *Paul Carr (1981)*
Narrator . . . . *William Conrad (1979-80)*
. . . .*Hank Sims (1981)*

Produced by Bruce Lansbury, David O'Connell, John Gaynor *(1979-80)*;
John Mantley, John Stephens, Calvin Clements *(1981)*
(Universal TV)
35 episodes.

"Bugs Bunny's Thanksgiving Diet" C B S; S P E C I A L November 15, 1979.
Diet doctor Bugs Bunny 'prescribes' two classic Warner Brothers cartoons —
Bedevilled Rabbit (1957) and *Rabbit Every Monday* (1951). Also, clips from
Beep Beep (1952), *Canned Feud* (1951), *Trip For Tat* (1960) and five others.
Mel Blanc provides voice characterizations for the new animation.

"Bugs Bunny's Looney Christmas Tales" C B S; S P E C I A L November 27, 1979.
All-new animation makes up this trio of holiday shorts: "Bugs Bunny's
Christmas Carol" — Bugs tries to teach Scrooge (Yosemite Sam) the
meaning of Christmas; Porky Pig is Bob Cratchet. "Freeze Frame" —
Wile E. Coyote discovers the Road Runner's weakness is cold weather,
so he consults his Acme catalogue to find a winter-making snow-cloud
seeder. "Fright Before Christmas" — An escaping Tasmanian Devil
comes upon a Santa Claus suit and, in his disguise, takes refuge with
Bugs and his nephew Clyde.
*Mel Blanc voices Bugs, Yosemite, Porky, Foghorn Leghorn, Pepe LePew, Tweety
Pie, Sylvester the Cat, Tasmanian Devil, the light-company man, airplane
pilots, Santa Claus, Elmer Fudd and the Road Runner.*

"Scooby-Doo Goes Hollywood" S Y N D I C A T E D; S P E C I A L
December 23, 1979.
Scooby is getting a chance to star in his first film, but first the timid mutt
and his pals must uncover the identity of the mysterious figure sabotaging
the production.
Voice Cast
Scooby-Doo . . . . *Don Messick*
Freddy Jones . . . . *Frank Welker*

Daphne Blake . . . . Heather North Kenney
Velma Dinkley. . . . . Patricia Stevens
Norville 'Shaggy' Rogers . . . . Casey Kasem
C.J. . . . . Rip Torn
Film Director, First Vice President, Terrier . . . . Stan Jones
Jesse Rotten, Vice President Jackie Carlson . . . . .Michael Bell
Cherie, Sis, Receptionist . . . . Marilyn Schreffler
Lavonne, Second Woman, Waitress . . . . Joan Gerber
Man at Roller Rink . . . . Mel Blanc
Brother, Guard, Announcer's Voice. . . . . Patrick Fraley
Kerry, Girl Fan, Executive Secretary . . . . Ginny McSwain

3-2-1 Contact PBS "Near/Far: Space Travel" March 6, 1980.
STARS: *Liz Moses, Ginny Ortiz, Leon W. Grant.*
Science program for children. Dr. Huer (Tim O'Connor) and Twiki the
Robot (voice of Mel Blanc) visit from TV's *Buck Rogers in the 25th Century.*
Soapy Suds: Michael Vale.

Captain Caveman and the Teen Angels ABC March 8 to June 12, 1980.
Animated cartoon. A hairy runt from the Stone Age finds himself in
modern times, helping a trio of girls to fight crime.

Voice Cast

Captain Caveman . . . . Mel Blanc
Dee Dee Sykes. . . . . Vernee Watson
Brenda Chance . . . . Marilyn Schreffler
Taffy Dare. . . . . Laurel Page

Produced by William Hanna, Joseph Barbera, Alex Lovy
(Hanna-Barbera)
16 episodes.

"Daffy Duck's Easter Special" NBC; SPECIAL April 1, 1980.
More all-new cartoons: "The Yolks on You" — Daffy and Sylvester the
Cat fight over a golden egg discarded by Miss Prissy; Foghorn Leghorn
also appears. "The Chocolate Chase" — Factory guard Daffy ...cheats
some Mexican mice out of money they've saved to buy chocolate for their
children; they call in Speedy Gonzales to right the wrong. "Daffy Flies
North" — Daffy suffers a series of pratfalls when he tries to hitchhike
north without flying.
Mel Blanc voices Daffy, Sylvester, Foghorn, Speedy and the duck flock leader.

"*Bugs Bunny's Busting Out All Over*" CBS; SPECIAL May 21, 1980.
The third presentation of all-new cartoons. "Portrait of the Artist as a Young Bunny" — Bugs traces his eternal chase with Elmer Fudd all the way back to his youth. "Soup or Sonic" — Wile E. Coyote goes after the Road Runner with a firecracker, giant flypaper and Acme tennis-ball bombs, but winds up reduced to tiny size. "Spaced Out Bunny" — Marvin Martian has teamed up with Hugo the Abominable Snowman to capture Bugs, but the rascally rabbit outfoxes them.
Mel Blanc voices Bugs, Elmer, Wile E., the 'enlarged' Road Runner, Marvin, Hugo and Grouchy Butterfly.

"*Murder Can Hurt You!*" ABC; TV-MOVIE May 21, 1980.
In this spoof of TV detectives, eight gumshoes get together to battle a criminal mastermind. Narrated by Don Adams. Directed by Roger Duchowny for Aaron Spelling Productions.
Ironbottom: Victor Buono. Hatch: John Byner. Pony Lambretta: Tony Danza. Studsky: Jamie Farr. Nojak: Gavin McLeod. Jim MacSkye: Buck Owens. Salty Sanderson: Connie Stevens. Parks the Pusher: Jimmie Walker. Palumbo: Burt Young. Starkos: Marty Allen. Mr. Bernice: Richard Deacon. Raquel: Gunilla Hutton. Virginia Trickwood: Roz Kelly. Serafina Palumbo: Liz Torres. Man in White: Mitchell Kreindel. Thug: Michael DeLano. Sophia: Tessa Richarde. Marilyn: E. Wetta Little. Purse-Snatch Victim: Iris Adrian. Hooker: Muffi Durham. Willie the Wino: Mason Adams. Voice of Chickie Baby: Mel Blanc.

"*The Flintstones' New Neighbors*" NBC; SPECIAL September 26, 1980.
A new family is moving in next door to the Flintstones and Rubbles — a clan of grotesques called the Frankenstones.

Voice Cast

Fred Flintstone	*Henry Corden*
Barney Rubble	*Mel Blanc*
Wilma and Pebbles Flintstone	*Jean Vander Pyl*
Betty Rubble	*Gay Autterson*
Bamm Bamm Rubble, Vulture	*Don Messick*
Frank Frankenstone	*John Stephenson*
Hidea Frankenstone	*Julie McWhirter [Dees]*
Oblivia Frankenstone	*Pat Parris*
Stubby Frankenstone	*Jim MacGeorge*
Creeply, Mother Pterodactyl	*Frank Welker*

Heathcliff and Dingbat/Heathcliff and Marmaduke/Heathcliff and the Catillac Cats ABC/SYNDICATED October 4, 19800-1984.
Animated cartoon. An attitudinal cat has rough-and-tumble adventures in his neighborhood, antagonizing the milkman and dodging the dog-catcher. A vampire mutt and his creepy pals work out of the office of Odd Jobs Inc. A large Great Dane with the temperament of a youngster gets into mischief. Some neighborhood cats join Heathcliff to thwart junkyard dog Leroy.

Voice Cast

Heathcliff, Spike, Muggsy, Iggy, Mr. Schultz,
The Milkman . . . . *Mel Blanc*
Sonja. . . . . *Julie McWhirter [Dees], Marilyn Schreffler,*
. . . . *June Foray, Marilyn Lightstone (1984)*
Clem, Digby, Dogsnatcher. . . . . *Henry Corden (1980-82)*
Crazy Shirley, Grandma, Marcy. . . . . *June Foray (1980-82)*
Dingbat . . . . *Frank Welker (1980-82)*
Nobody, Sparerib. . . . . *Don Messick (1980-82)*
Marmaduke, Phil Winslow. . . . .*Paul Winchell (1981-82)*
Dottie Winslow, Barbie Winslow, Billy Winslow,
Missy . . . .*Russi Taylor (1981-82)*
Barbie's Sister . . . . *Marilyn Schreffler (1981-82)*
Cleo, Iggy . . . . *Donna Christie (1984)*
Riffraff, Wordsworth, Milkman . . . . *Stanley Jones (1984)*
Hector, Fish Market Proprietor. . . . . *Danny Mann (1984)*
Spike, Muggsy, Knuckles. . . . .*Derek McGrath (1984)*
Bush, Raul . . . . *Danny Wells (1984)*
Leroy, Mungo, Grandpa . . . . *Ted Ziegler (1984)*
Various Characters: Joe Baker (1980-82), Michael Bell (1980-82), Rachel Blake (1980-82), Melendy Britt (1980-82), Alan Dinehart (1980-82), Shep Menken (1980-82), Alan Oppenheimer (1980-82), Hal Smith (1980-82), Joan Van Ark (1980-82), Peter Cullen (1984), Jeannie Elias (1984)
Vocals. . . . .*Scatman Crothers (1981-82)*

Produced by Joe Ruby, Ken Spears, Jerry Eisenberg *(1980-82)*; Gordon Kent *(1981-82)*; Jean Chalopin, Andy Heyward, Tom Katayan *(1984)* *(Ruby-Spears; DIC/McNaught Syndicate/LBS)*
92 episodes.

"The Bugs Bunny Mystery Special" CBS; SPECIAL October 26, 1980.
Porky Pig, ala Alfred Hitchcock, hosts the classic Warner Brothers cartoon *Big House Bunny* (1950). Also, clips from *Bugs And Thugs* (1954), *Hare Lift* (1952), *Operation: Rabbit* (1952), *Catty Cornered* (1953) and three others. Mel Blanc voices the new animation.

"The Flintstones Meet Rockula and Frankenstone" NBC; SPECIAL October 30, 1980.
When the Flintstones and Rubbles win a trip on a game show, they end up in 'Rocksylvania' — home of the vampire Count Rockula and his servant-monster Frankenstone. Things get complicated when Rockula wants to make Wilma his bride.

Voice Cast

Fred Flintstone	*Henry Corden*
Barney Rubble, Dino the Dinosaur	*Mel Blanc*
Wilma Flintstone, Frau G	*Jean Vander Pyl*
Count Rockula	*John Stephenson*
Betty Rubble	*Gay Autterson*
Monty Marble	*Casey Kasem*
Frankenstone	*Ted Cassidy*
Igor, Wolf	*Don Messick*
Mr. Silica, Bat	*Lennie Weinrib*

"The Flintstones: Fred's Final Fling" NBC; SPECIAL November 7, 1980.
Does Fred have only 24 hours left to live? That's what he thinks and he plans to go out with a bang.

Voice Cast

Fred Flintstone	*Henry Corden*
Barney Rubble, Dino the Dinosaur	*Mel Blanc*
Wilma and Pebbles Flintstone	*Jean Vander Pyl*
Betty Rubble	*Gay Autterson*
Frank Frankenstone	*John Stephenson*
Also	*Don Messick*

The Flintstones Comedy Show NBC
November 22, 1980-September 5, 1981.
Animated cartoon. The Flintstones and Rubbles in new adventures of Stone Age takes on modern lifestyles. Also, "Captain Caveman" — A copy boy at the Bedrock Daily Granite transforms himself into a superhero; "Bedrock Cops" — Fred and Barney are reserve police officers bumbling their way through cases with the help of the Shmoos; "Pebbles, Dino and Bamm Bamm" — The teen offspring of Fred, Wilma, Barney and Betty solve mysteries along with their pet dinosaur; "Dino and the Cave Mouse" — The Flintstones' pet chases a pesky rodent; and "The Frankenstones" — A family of monsters live next to Fred and Wilma.

Voice Cast

Fred Flintstone. . . . . *Henry Corden*
Barney Rubble, Dino the Dinosaur. . . . . *Mel Blanc*
Wilma Flintstone . . . .*Jean Vander Pyl*
Betty Rubble, Wiggy. . . . . *Gay Autterson*
Pebbles Flintstone, Cave Mouse . . . .*Russi Taylor*
Bamm Bamm . . . . *Michael Sheehan*
Lou Granite . . . . *Ken Mars*
Sergeant Boulder, Moonrock . . . . *Lennie Weinrib*
Mr. Slate. . . . .*John Stephenson*
Penny . . . . *Mitzi McCall*
Schleprock . . . . *Don Messick*
Frank Frankenstone . . . .*Charles Nelson Reilly*
Hidea Frankenstone . . . . *Ruta Lee*
Oblivia Frankenstone. . . . . *Pat Parris*
Atrocia Frankenstone . . . .*Zelda Rubenstein*
Freaky Frankenstone. . . . .*Paul Reubens [Pee Wee Herman]*
Rockjaw . . . . *Frank Welker*
Captain Caveman . . . . *Joe Baker*
Various Characters: Frank Nelson, Marilyn Schreffler, Lurene Tuttle, Paul Winchell

Produced by William Hanna, Joseph Barbera, Jayne Barbera, Margaret Loesch, Alex Lovy, Carl Urbano
(Hanna-Barbera)
18 episodes.

"Bugs Bunny: All-American Hero" CBS; SPECIAL May 21, 1981.
Bugs tells nephew Clyde Rabbit his exploits in shaping the U.S.A. via the classic Warner Brothers cartoons *Bunker Hill Bunny* (1950), *Dumb Patrol* (1964), *Rebel Without Claws* (1961) and clips from *Ballot Box Bunny* (1951), *Southern Fried Rabbit* (1953) and *Yankee Doodle Bugs* (1954). Mel Blanc voices Bugs and Clyde in the new animation.

The Trollkins CBS September 12, 1981-September 4, 1982.
Animated cartoon. The tiny denizens of a hollow tree-trunk put up with the ineptitude of their mayor and clumsy police force.

Voice Cast

Mayor Lumpkin . . . . *Paul Winchell*
Sheriff Pudge Trollson. . . . .*Alan Oppenheimer*
Pixlee Trollson, Deputroll Dotty. . . . . *Jennifer Darling*
Blitz Plumkin. . . . .*Steve Spears*
Flooky, Bogg, Top Troll. . . . . *Frank Welker*
Grubb Trollmaine. . . . .*Michael Bell*
Deputroll Flake. . . . . *Marshall Efron*
Afid. . . . . *Hank Saroyan*
Slug. . . . . *Bill Callaway*
Various Characters: *Jered Barclay, Mel Blanc, Scatman Crothers, Peter Cullen, Billie Hayes, Ken Mars, Don Messick, Robert Allan Ogle, Bob Sarlatte, Marilyn Schreffler, Rick Segal, Hal Smith, John Stephenson, Lennie Weinrib, Alan Young*

Produced by William Hanna, Joseph Barbera, Kay Wright
(Hanna-Barbera)
13 episodes.

The Flintstones NBC October 4-October 18, 1981.
Animated cartoon. The Flintstones and Rubbles interact with their monstrous neighbors the Frankenstones.

Voice Cast

Fred Flintstone, Scorpion . . . . *Henry Corden*
Barney Rubble, Dino the Dinosaur,
Pterodactyl Chicks. . . . . *Mel Blanc*
Wilma and Pebbles Flintstone. . . . .*Jean Vander Pyl*
Betty Rubble. . . . . *Gay Autterson*
Bamm Bamm Rubble, Vulture . . . . *Don Messick*
Frank Frankenstone, Rockelle . . . .*John Stephenson*

Oblivia Frankenstone . . . . *Pat Parris*
Hidea Frankenstone . . . . *Julie McWhirter [Dees]*
Stubby Frankenstone. . . . . *Jim MacGeorge*
Creeply, Mother Pterodactyl, Pterodactyl Chicks . . . . *Frank Welker*

Produced by William Hanna, Joseph Barbera, Alex Lovy
(Hanna–Barbera)
4 episodes.

"*Daffy Duck's Thanks-for-Giving Special*" NBC; SPECIAL
November 24, 1981.
A new cartoon: "Duck Dodgers and the Return of the 24½th Century" —
Dodgers (Daffy Duck) and his sidekick attempt to protect a yo-yo
polishing molecule as Marvin Martian plots to solve Earth's fuel prob-
lems…by blowing up the planet. Also, the classic Warner Brothers cartoon
His Bitter Half (1950) and clips from *The Scarlet Pumpernickel* (1950),
Robin Hood Daffy (1958) and *Dripalong Daffy* (1951). Mel Blanc voices
Daffy, Porky Pig, Marvin, Gossamer and the computer in the new cartoon.

"*Bugs Bunny's Mad World of Television*" CBS; SPECIAL January 11, 1982.
Bugs takes over as head of QTTV and programs the classic Warner
Brothers cartoon *This Is A Life?* (1955). Also, clips from *The Ducksters*
(1950), *Wideo Wabbit* (1956), *What's Up Doc?* (1950), *Past Perfumance*
(1955) and others. Mel Blanc voices the new animation.

"*An Ounce of Prevention*" ABC; SPECIAL 1982.
Mel Blanc and cartoon friends Bugs Bunny, Daffy Duck, Sylvester the
Cat and Tweety Pie demonstrate ways to avoid burn hazards in the
home. Public service featurette made for the Shriners Burn Institute in
Cincinnati, OH. Mel Blanc voices the characters.
Jennifer: Erin Robert.

Too Close for Comfort ABC "A Thanksgiving Tale" November 25, 1982.
STARS: *Ted Knight, Nancy Dussault, Deborah Van Valkenburgh, Lydia
Cornell, JM J. Bullock.*
Iris' disappearance on Thanksgiving adds excitement to a family gather-
ing already enlivened by the presence of Grandpa and the thoughts of
Baby Andrew.
*Iris: Audrey Meadows. Grandpa Huey Rush: Ray Middleton. Voice of Andrew
Rush: Mel Blanc.*

The Tonight Show Starring Johnny Carson NBC May 26, 1983.
HOST: *Johnny Carson.* ANNOUNCER: *Ed McMahon. The Doc Severinsen Orchestra.*
Among the guests is Mel Blanc.

This Is Your Life SYNDICATED "Mel Blanc" February 11, 1984.
HOST: *Joseph Campanella.*
Comedian-impressionist Rich Little helps Joseph to spring the surprise on Mel Blanc as the voice artist behind such characters as Bugs Bunny, Daffy Duck, Porky Pig and Barney Rubble is honored. Guests include Estelle Blanc, Mel's wife of some 50 years; son Noel, Mel's partner in his voice business; Dr. Louis Conway, the physician who treated Mel after a life-threatening car crash (he brought Mel out of his coma by asking how Bugs Bunny was doing); Harry Jackson, a friend of 65 years...who was ordered to report to the principal office for something Mel did...Chuck Jones, friend and animation director at Warner Bros. Pictures; and Milt Josefsberg, writer for *The Jack Benny Program.* At the end of the show, a group of 13 children from Wilshire United Methodist Church enter with a giant, carrot-shaped cake.

The Jetsons SYNDICATED September 15, 1985-1987.
Animated cartoon. The further adventures of the space age family living in the future.

Voice Cast

George Jetson. . . . .*George O'Hanlon*
Jane Jetson. . . . .*Penny Singleton*
Judy Jetson . . . .*Janet Waldo*
Elroy Jetson. . . . . *Daws Butler*
Rosie the Robot. . . . .*Jean Vander Pyl*
Astro . . . . *Don Messick*
Cosmo G. Spacely . . . . *Mel Blanc*
Cogswell. . . . .*John Stephenson*
Orbity. . . . . *Frank Welker*
Various Characters: Bob Arbogast, Rene Auberjonois, Gay Autterson, Jered Barclay, Dick Beals, Michael Bell, Susan Blu, Victoria Carroll, Didi Conn, Henry Corden, Dave Coulier, Peter Cullen, Brian Cummings, Julie Dees, Jerry Dexter, June Foray, Pat Fraley, Joan Gardner, Joan Gerber, Ralph James, Stanley Jones, Peter Leeds, Jim MacGeorge, Kenneth Mars, Chuck McCann, Edie McClure, Allan Melvin, Howard Morris, Frank Nelson, Cliff Norton, Bob Ridgley,

Marilyn Schreffler, Avery Schreiber, Fred Travalena, B.J. Ward,
Lennie Weinrib, Paul Winchell, Bill [William] Woodson

Produced by William Hanna, Joseph Barbera, Bob Hathcock, Jeff Hall,
Alex Lovy, Jayne Barbera, Jean MacCurdy, Joe Taritero
(Hanna-Barbera)
51 episodes.

"The Jetsons Christmas Carol" SYNDICATED; SPECIAL December 1985.
When George Jetson asks his boss Cosmo Spacely for a raise at Christmas,
the penny-pinching industrialist refuses. This action prompts a visit by
three holiday spirits.

Voice Cast

George Jetson . . . . *George O'Hanlon*
Jane Jetson . . . .*Penny Singleton*
Judy Jetson . . . . *Janet Waldo*
Elroy Jetson . . . . *Daws Butler*
Rosie the Robot . . . . *Jean Vander Pyl*
Astro . . . . *Don Messick*
Cosmo G. Spacely, Jacob Marsley . . . . *Mel Blanc*
Cogswell . . . .*John Stephenson*
Ghost of Christmas Present, Orbity,
Young Spacelys . . . . *Frank Welker*

"Bugs Bunny/Looney Tunes 50th Anniversary Special" NBC; SPECIAL
January 14, 1986.
A half-century of cartoon zaniness is paid tribute by various guests.
Interviews with Mel Blanc (who voices new animation), Friz Freleng
and Chuck Jones. Also seen are rare pencil tests and cartoon footage.
David Bowie, Steve Martin, Kirk Douglas, Cher, George Burns.

The Flintstone Kids ABC September 13, 1986-May 26, 1990.
Animated cartoon. A look at the Flintstones and Rubbles as children.
Also, life from Dino the Dinosaur's point of view and the adventures of
Captain Caveman.

Voice Cast

Freddy Flintstone . . . . *Scott Menville (1986-88)*
. . . . *Lennie Weinrib (1990)*
Barney Rubble, Flab Slab . . . . *Hamilton Camp*

Wilma Slaghoople . . . .*Elizabeth Lyn Fraser (1986–88)*
. . . . *Julie Dees (1990)*
Betty, Miss Rockbottom. . . . .*B.J. Ward*
Dino, Captain Caveman, Robert Rubble . . . . *Mel Blanc*
Ed and Edna Flintstone. *Henry Corden*
Doris Slaghoople . . . .*Jean Vander Pyl*
Flo Rubble, Rocky Ratrock . . . . *Marilyn Schreffler*
Commissioner . . . . *Lennie Weinrib*
Mickey, Mica, Tarpit Tommy . . . .*Julie Dees*
Dreamchip Gemstone, Granite Janet. . . . . *Susan Blu*
Nate Slate, Stalagbite . . . . *Frank Welker*
Philo Quartz. . . . . *Bumper Robinson*
Officer Quartz . . . . *Rene Levant*
Cavey Jr . . . .*Charles Adler*
Narrator . . . . *Ken Mars*
Various Characters: Bever-Leigh Banfield, Jon Bauman, Michael
Bell, Jim Cummings, Rick Dees, Dick [Richard] Erdman, Takayo
Fisher, Pat Fraley, June Foray, Arte Johnson, Buster Jones, Aron
Kincaid, Allan Lurie, Tress MacNeille, Janet May, Howard Morris,
George O'Hanlon, Rob Paulsen, Michael Rye [Rye Billsbury], John
Stephenson, Beau Weaver, Patric Zimmerman

Produced by Kay Wright
(Hanna-Barbera)
22 episodes.

"The Jetsons Meet the Flintstones" SYNDICATED; SPECIAL
November 9, 1987.
Elroy Jetson's school science project, a time machine, transports his
family to prehistoric Bedrock — where they meet the Flintstones and
Rubbles. Then, the Flintstones are sent into the future. How will these
time switches affect our favorite cartoon families?
Voice Cast

Fred Flintstone, Knight . . . . *Henry Corden*
Barney Rubble, Dino the Dinosaur,
Cosmo Spacely. . . . . *Mel Blanc*
Wilma Flintstone, Rosie the Robot,
Mrs. Spacely . . . .*Jean Vander Pyl*
Betty Rubble, Jet Rivers, Investor,
Panelist, Harem Girl . . . .*Julie Dees*

George Jetson. . . . .*George O'Hanlon*
Jane Jetson. . . . .*Penny Singleton*
Judy Jetson, Female Computer. . . . .*Janet Waldo.*
Henry Orbit, Elroy Jetson, Cogswell. . . . . *Daws Butler*
Astro, R.U.D.I., Mac, Announcer,
Store Manager, Robot. . . . . *Don Messick*
Didi . . . . *Brenda Vaccaro*
Nate Slate, Moderator, Investor, Poker Player. . . . .*John Stephenson*
Turk Tarpit. . . . . *Hamilton Camp*
Iggy, Second Announcer. . . . .*Jon Bauman*
Dan Rathroom, Johnny, Mr. Goldbrick . . . . *Frank Welker*
Also . . . . *Patric Zimmerman*

"Rockin' With Judy Jetson" SYNDICATED; SPECIAL 1988.

Judy Jetson writes a song to give to her favorite music star, Sky Rocker. She gets the chance to see him at a concert, but a music-hating witch kidnaps Rocker — with Judy determined to help him escape. George Jetson follows his daughter, but gets tossed in jail. Now it's up to Elroy and Astro to affect a rescue — but who do they save first, Judy or George?

Voice Cast

Judy Jetson . . . .*Janet Waldo*
George Jetson. . . . .*George O'Hanlon*
Jane Jetson. . . . .*Penny Singleton*
Elroy Jetson. . . . . *Daws Butler*
Astro . . . . *Don Messick.*
Rosie. . . . .*Jean Vander Pyl*
Cosmo Spacely. . . . . *Mel Blanc*
Mr. Microchips, Manny . . . . *Hamilton Camp*
Nicky. . . . .*Eric Suter*
Ramm, Dee-Jay . . . . *Beau Weaver*
Starr, Fan Club President, Zowie: Pat Musick. Felonia*Ruth Buzzi*
Quark, Zappy. . . . .*Charles Adler*
High Loopy Zoomy. . . . . *P.L. Brown*
Rhoda Starlet . . . . *Selette Cole*
Gruff, Commander Comsat, Bouncer . . . .*Peter Cullen*
Iona . . . .*Cindy McGee*
Sky Rocker, Zany . . . .*Rob Paulsen*
Zippy . . . .*B.J. Ward*
Zilchy . . . . *Pat Fraley.*

"Roger Rabbit and the Secrets of Toon Town" CBS; SPECIAL
September 13, 1988.
HOST: *Joanna Cassidy.*
This documentary shows what went into the making of *Who Framed Roger Rabbit* (1988), with interviews and insights. Mel Blanc and his son, Noel, have a back-and-forth discussion — both doing the Bugs Bunny voice. *Tony Anselmo, Charles Fleischer, Lou Hirsch, Bob Hoskins, Gene Kelly, Christopher Lloyd, Mae Questel, Kathleen Turner, Dick Van Dyke, Friz Freleng, Chuck Jones, Ward Kimball, George Gibbs, Robert Watts, Ken Ralston, Robert Zemeckis, Steven Spielberg, Richard Williams.*

"Bugs vs. Daffy: Battle of the Music Video Stars" CBS; SPECIAL
October 21, 1988.
Bugs Bunny and Daffy Duck are rival video disc jockeys who compete in presenting various song sequences from classic Warner Brothers cartoons. Mel Blanc voices the new animation. Clips are shown from *Leon Schlesinger Presents Bugs Bunny/Any Bonds Today?* (1942), *Porky's Papa* (1938), *Porky's Poor Fish* (1940), *Shake Your Powder Puff* (1934), *Scrap Happy Daffy* (1943), *Boobs In The Woods* (1950), *Fifth Column Mouse* (1943), *Wearing Of The Grin* (1951) and others.

"Bugs Bunny's Wild World of Sports" SYNDICATED; SPECIAL
February 15, 1989.
Who will win the Sportsman of the Year award? Classic Warner Brothers cartoons showcase the sporting achievements of Bugs Bunny, Daffy Duck, Porky Pig, Foghorn Leghorn, Tweety Pie, et. al. Mel Blanc voices the new animation. Clips are shown from *Raw! Raw! Rooster* (1956), *Sports Chumpions* (1941), *To Duck Or Not To Duck* (1943), *Bunny Hugged* (1951), *High Diving Hare* (1949), *My Bunny Lies Over The Sea* (1948), *The Leghorn Blows At Midnight* (1950), *Frigid Hare* (1949), *Lovelorn Leghorn* (1951), *Bad Ol' Puddy Tat* (1949) and *Little Boy Boo* (1954).
Sportscaster: Roy Firestone. Maggie: Randi Rosenholtz. Also: Paul Kuhn.

Television Commercials

American Express
Clark Bar (as Porky Pig)
Milky Way
Nine Lives

Recordings
Contributed by Walt Mitchell

The following is a list of all known recordings that Mel Blanc made for record companies, including, when known, the characters he voiced. Sometimes the exact year that a record was released is not currently known, therefore an educated guess with a "?" is used.

I want to express two debts of gratitude for the Bozo information in my discography chapter. A special thank you *to Tom Holbrook of Illinois. He is writing a book about Bozo, and likes to be known as the Bozologist! Another special* thank you *goes to Jack Mirtle, a Canadian musician, author and record collector who has just completed a book about all Capitol children's records. Some additional discographical data in this book is from his research and his kind cooperation in this regard is greatly appreciated.*

Also, thanks to Peter Muldavin and Fred DeHut for information about Little Golden Records. — Walt Mitchell

Promotional and Demonstration Records

These records were not intended to be sold to the public, so they were never assigned catalog nor, in most cases, disc numbers. The first eight records are Capitol pressings. Many of the others were manufactured by or for Mel Blanc Associates (later Blanc Communications Corp.).

MASTER NUMBER: 2242-2D *(cardboard picture disc)*
Greetings and here's good wishes for a 14 carrot Christmas from Capitol
    Records
DISC SIZE: 8"
SPEED: 78
YEAR: 1947

MASTER NUMBER: 5221-Y/5223-Z
Season's Greetings from Capitol, 1949 / Part 2
DISC SIZE: 7"
SPEED: 78
YEAR: 1949

MASTER NUMBER: 5223-Y/5224-Z

Bugs Bunny "Star of Capitol Records and Warner Bros. Cartoons Campaigning for the March of Dimes" / Part 2

DISC SIZE: 7"

SPEED: 78

YEAR: 1950

MASTER NUMBER: 6301-Y/6302-Z

Any Friend of Bozo is a Friend of Mine! / Part 2 *(Note: Although the disc itself is a 7-inch 45, it was distributed as part of a 10-inch Record-Reader book.)*

DISC SIZE: 7"

SPEED: 45

YEAR: 1950

MASTER NUMBER: 6303-Y/6304-Z

Sneak Preview / Part 2

DISC SIZE: 7"

SPEED: 45

YEAR: 1950

MASTER NUMBER: PRO-15/PRO-16

I Taut I Taw a Record Dealer / Part 2

DISC SIZE: 7"

SPEED: 45

YEAR: 1950

MASTER NUMBER: PRO-104

Capitol Cavalcade Commorating the Tenth Anniversary of Capitol Records, Inc. *(Note: Mel's bit is in Part 2, being one chorus of "I Taut I Taw a Puddy Tat")*

DISC SIZE: 10"

SPEED: 33

YEAR: 1952

MASTER NUMBER: PRO-162/PRO-163

The Woody Woodpecker (Radio) Show / Part 2

DISC SIZE: 10"

SPEED: 78

YEAR: 1953

MASTER NUMBER: CO 1029 A
Hollywood Flashback
DISC SIZE: 12"
SPEED: 33
YEAR: 1962

MASTER NUMBER: TAD 2403
Oregon Holiday *(Part 1 only)*
DISC SIZE: 7"
SPEED: 33
YEAR: 1965?

MASTER NUMBER: TAD 2698 and TAD 2985 *(each is a one-sided record)*
Mel Blanc Takes a Humorous Look at Commercials: Past, Present
    & Future... *(at the 1966 Annual Awards Luncheon of the Station
    Representatives Association. Note: Several packaging variations — and at
    least two audio edit versions — of this promotional LP are known to exist)*
DISC SIZE: 12"
SPEED: 33
YEAR: 1966

MASTER NUMBER: TAD 2749-RE
Superfun *(1-sided record)*
DISC SIZE: 12"
SPEED: 33
YEAR: 1966

MASTER NUMBER: TAD 2830/TAD 2831
Superfun *(Return to Paper Plates-#1)*
DISC SIZE: 12"
SPEED: 33
YEAR: 1967

MASTER NUMBER: TAD 2832/TAD 2833
Superfun *(Return to Paper Plates-#2)*
DISC SIZE: 12"
SPEED: 33
YEAR: 1967

MASTER NUMBER: TAD 2834/TAD 2835
Superfun *(Return to Paper Plates-#3)*
DISC SIZE: 12"
SPEED: 33
YEAR: 1967

MASTER NUMBER: TAD 2932/TAD 2866
Superfun *(sample comedy material)*
DISC SIZE: 12"
SPEED: 33
YEAR: 1967

MASTER NUMBER: TAD 2960/TAD 2961
Superfun
DISC SIZE: 10"
SPEED: 33
YEAR: 1967

MASTER NUMBER: TAD 3036/TAD 3037
Superfun *(cover same as 2960; gags vary)*
DISC SIZE: 10"
SPEED: 33
YEAR: 1967

MASTER NUMBER: MBA 101A/MBA 101B
Superfun — Stick It In Your Format
DISC SIZE: 10"
SPEED: 33
YEAR: 1968

MASTER NUMBER: War.Bro. WBE-100
"Happy Birthday Call" from Bugs Bunny
DISC SIZE: 7"
SPEED: 45
YEAR: 1973

MASTER NUMBER: United 8550 (K-10857)
Beverly Hills Federal Savings Presents Mel Blanc. The voice of Bugs
    Bunny.
DISC SIZE: 7"
SPEED: 33
YEAR: 1980?
(The two above are one-sided records.)

MASTER NUMBER: FFP-480
Remember, You're Among Friends. *(Side A only. Among several celebrities
    speaking for forest fire prevention, Mel does one 60-second track.)*
DISC SIZE: 7"
SPEED: 33
YEAR: 1980

Original Issues

78 RPM (Adult Series) Album Sets

Top Ten Set 2
The Jack Benny Album
YEAR: 1947

Top Ten Set 4
The Burns and Allen Album
YEAR: 1947

78 RPM (Adult Series) Album Singles

MASTER NUMBER: Bluebird B-11466
Clink, Clink, Another Drink *(by Spike Jones and His City Slickers, hiccups
    by Mel Blanc)*
YEAR: 1942

MASTER NUMBER: Capitol 15145
Woody Woodpecker *(by The Sportsmen and Mel Blanc and his original
    Woody Woodpecker voice)*
YEAR: 1948

MASTER NUMBER: Capitol 57-560
I'm Just Wild About Animal Crackers / Big Bear Lake
YEAR: 1949

MASTER NUMBER: Capitol 57-780
Toot, Toot, Tootsie (Goodbye) / I've Got a Lovely Bunch of Coconuts
YEAR: 1949

MASTER NUMBER: 57-790
Take It Easy, Take It Light (The Regal Rhumba)
YEAR: 1949
(Note: This Latin-genre track was recorded by Chuy Reyes and his Orchestra. Mel was added to the session to sing the vocal chorus, which he did in his Mexican accent, of course. Mel's participation was anonymous, as he is credited on the label only as "Pedro.")

MASTER NUMBER: Capitol 869
There's a Hole in the Iron Curtain *(by Mickey Katz and His Orchestra, vocal by Mel Blanc)*
YEAR: 1950

MASTER NUMBER: Varsity 8054
Maw and Paw *(by Judy Canova and Mel Blanc. Note: Recorded early in 1947 by Majestic Records, which went bankrupt before it could issue the selection. Issued by Issued by Varsity/Royale on 78 rpm circa 1950 and on 45 rpm probably in 1951.)*
YEAR: 1950

MASTER NUMBER: Capitol 1441
K-K-K-Katy / Flying Saucers *(Note: Actually, the "K-K-K-Katy" side was cut in 1949 at the "Big Bear Lake" session. Capitol withheld it until now, for reasons unknown.)*
YEAR: 1950

MASTER NUMBER: Capitol 1727
Ten Little Bottles in the Sink / Okmnx
YEAR: 1951

MASTER NUMBER: Capitol 1853
Christmas Chopsticks / I Tant Wait Till Quithmuth
YEAR: 1951

MASTER NUMBER: Capitol 1948
That's All Folks! / Won't You Ever Get Together With Me
YEAR: 1951

MASTER NUMBER: Capitol 2048
Morris / Lord Bless His Soul
YEAR: 1952

MASTER NUMBER: Capitol 2261
I Tell My Troubles to Joe / The Missus Wouldn't Approve
YEAR: 1952

MASTER NUMBER: Capitol 2430
Little Red Monkey / Tia Juana (sic)
YEAR: 1953

MASTER NUMBER: Capitol 2470
I Love Me / Somebody Stole My Gal
YEAR: 1953

MASTER NUMBER: Capitol 2619
Yah, Das Ist Ein Christmas Tree* / I Tant Wait Till Quithmuth
YEAR: 1953
(Longer version in children's section as # CAS 3191)*

MASTER NUMBER: Capitol 2635
I'm in the Mood for Love / My Kinda Love *(as by "Le Blanc")*
YEAR: 1953

MASTER NUMBER: Capitol 2718
The Lady Bird Song / I Dess I Dotta Doe
YEAR: 1954

MASTER NUMBER: Capitol 2764
Money / Polly, Pretty Polly
YEAR: 1954

MASTER NUMBER: Decca 30482
Jimminy Christmas *(by The Woodyettes, Grace Stafford as Woody Woodpecker,
    Mel Blanc as Santa Claus. Probably issued as 78 rpm.)*
YEAR: 1957

Capitol 78 RPM Multiple Record Children's Album Sets

*(Note: story parts are not in consecutive order, but cross-coupled on each disc so
that performances could be played in proper sequence on an automatic record
changer.)*

Prefix codes:
CC — 3 shellac discs in hard-cover album; no book
DC — Same, but discs made of "unbreakable" tougher shellac compound
DCN — Same, but hinged box set instead of album; plastic or vinyl discs
DBX — Record-Reader storybook with two records in hard-cover album
DBS — Gatefold heavy paper cover with two records and no book

First Edition:

MASTER NUMBER: Capitol CC 64
Bugs Bunny
Bugs Bunny Meets Elmer Fudd – Part 1 / Porky Pig in Africa – Part 2
    (C10089)
Bugs Bunny Meets Elmer Fudd – Part 2 / Porky Pig in Africa – Part 1
    (C10090)
Daffy Duck Flies South – Part 1 / Part 2 (C10091)
YEAR: 1947

Second Edition:

MASTER NUMBER: Capitol DC 117
Bugs Bunny
Bugs Bunny Meets Elmer Fudd – Part 1 / Porky Pig in Africa – Part 2
    (7-25031)
Bugs Bunny Meets Elmer Fudd – Part 2 / Porky Pig in Africa – Part 1
    (7-25032)
Daffy Duck Flies South – Part 1 / Part 2 (7-25033)
YEAR: 1948

Third Edition:

MASTER NUMBER: Capitol DCN 117
Bugs Bunny
(Same numbers/titles as DC 117. "N" denotes hinged box set in place of
     pocket-style album.)
YEAR: 1954?

MASTER NUMBER: Capitol DBX 93
Bugs Bunny and the Tortoise — Part 1 / Part 4 (25017)
Part 2 / Part 3 (25018)
YEAR: 1948

MASTER NUMBER: Capitol DBX 3021
Bugs Bunny in Storyland — Part 1 / Part 4 (7-30056)
Part 2 / Part 3 (7-30057)
YEAR: 1949

MASTER NUMBER: Capitol DBX 3032
Woody Woodpecker and His Talent Show — Part 1 / Part 4 (77-30075)
Part 2 / Part 3 (77-30076)
YEAR: 1949

MASTER NUMBER: Capitol DBS 3077
Bugs Bunny Sings (by Bugs and friends)
I'm Glad That I'm Bugs Bunny / Daffy Duck's Rhapsody (7-32018)
I Taut I Taw a Puddy Tat / Yosemite Sam (7-32019)
YEAR: 1950

MASTER NUMBER: Capitol DBS 3091
Woody Woodpecker's Picnic — Part 1 / Part 4 (7-32036)
Part 2 / Part 3 (7-32037)
YEAR: 1951

MASTER NUMBER: Capitol DBX 3102
Tweety's Puddy Tat Twouble — Part 1 / Part 4 (7-32049)
Part 2 / Part 3 (7-32050)
YEAR: 1951

Capitol 78 RPM Children's Single-Record Albums

(Note: Sold in heavy paper jackets containing colorful illustrations.)

MASTER NUMBER: Capitol CAS 3072
Bugs Bunny Meets Hiawatha / Part 2 (32011)
YEAR: 1950

MASTER NUMBER: Capitol CAS 3073
Daffy Duck Meets Yosemite Sam / Part 2 (32012)
YEAR: 1950

MASTER NUMBER: Capitol CAS 3074
Tweety Pie / Part 2 (32013)
YEAR: 1950

MASTER NUMBER: Capitol CAS 3098
Henery Hawk / Part 2 (32045)
YEAR: 1951

MASTER NUMBER: Capitol CAS 3104
I Taut I Taw a Puddy Tat / Yosemite Sam (32052)*
YEAR: 1952

MASTER NUMBER: Capitol CAS 3111
Bugs Bunny Meets Elmer Fudd / Part 2 (32059)*
YEAR: 1952

MASTER NUMBER: Capitol CAS 3112
Daffy Duck Flies South / Part 2 (32060)*
YEAR: 1952

MASTER NUMBER: Capitol CAS 3113
Porky Pig in Africa / Part 2 (32061)*
YEAR: 1952

MASTER NUMBER: Capitol 3118
Tweet, Tweet, Tweety / Part 2 (32066)
YEAR: 1952

MASTER NUMBER: Capitol CAS 3119
Bugs Bunny and the Grow-Small Juice / Part 2 (32067)
YEAR: 1952

MASTER NUMBER: Capitol CAS 3137
Henery Hawk's Chicken Hunt / Part 2 (32086)
YEAR: 1952

MASTER NUMBER: Capitol CAS 3139
Bugs Bunny and Aladdin's Lamp / Part 2 (32089)
YEAR: 1952

MASTER NUMBER: Capitol CAS 3140
Woody Woodpecker and the Scarecrow / Part 2 (32090)
YEAR: 1952

MASTER NUMBER: Capitol CAS 3147
Daffy Duck's Feathered Friend / Part 2 (32097)
YEAR: 1952

MASTER NUMBER: Capitol CAS 3148
Sylvester and Hippety Hopper / Part 2 (32098)
YEAR: 1952

MASTER NUMBER: Capitol CAS 3149
Woody Woodpecker and the Animal Crackers / Part 2 (32099)
YEAR: 1953

MASTER NUMBER: Capitol CAS 3155
Tweet and Toot / The E. I. O. Song (32105)
YEAR: 1953

MASTER NUMBER: Capitol CAS 3161
Woody Woodpecker and the Lost Monkey / Part 2 (32111)
YEAR: 1953

MASTER NUMBER: Capitol CAS 3168
Bugs Bunny and Rabbit Seasoning / Part 2 (32119)
YEAR: 1953

MASTER NUMBER: Capitol CAS 3169
Snowbound Tweety / Part 2 (32120)
YEAR: 1953

MASTER NUMBER: Capitol CAS 3170
Little Red Monkey / The Pussy Cat Parade (32121)
YEAR: 1953

MASTER NUMBER: Capitol CAS 3171
Woody Woodpecker and His Space Ship / Part 2 (32122)
YEAR: 1953

MASTER NUMBER: Capitol CAS 3172
Wild West Henery Hawk / Part 2 (32123)
YEAR: 1953

MASTER NUMBER: Capitol CAS 3188
Pied Piper Pussycat / Part 2 (32127)
YEAR: 1953

MASTER NUMBER: Capitol CAS 3191
Yah, Dis Ist Ein Christmas Tree / I Tant Wait Til Quithmuth Day (32130)
YEAR: 1953

MASTER NUMBER: Capitol CAS 3199
Daffy Duck's Duck Inn / Part 2 (32138)
YEAR: 1954

MASTER NUMBER: Capitol CAS 3200
Bugs Bunny and the Pirate / Part 2 (32139)
YEAR: 1954

MASTER NUMBER: Capitol CAS 3212
Tweety's Good Deed / Part 2 (32157)
YEAR: 1954

MASTER NUMBER: Capitol CAS 3213
It's Lots of Fun to Share / The Party Song (32158)
YEAR: 1954

MASTER NUMBER: Capitol CAS 3218
Woody Woodpecker's Fairy Godmother / Part 2 (32163)
YEAR: 1955

MASTER NUMBER: Capitol CAS 3219
D-O-G Spells Dog, D-O-G / Part 2 (32164)
YEAR: 1955

MASTER NUMBER: Capitol CAS 3225
It's Fun to be Generous / Wheezy Woozy Whatomobile (32169)
YEAR: 1955

MASTER NUMBER: Capitol CAS 3227
Mrs. Hazard's House / Part 2 (32171)
YEAR: 1955

MASTER NUMBER: Capitol CAS 3230
Woody Woodpecker in Mixed-Up Land / Part 2 (32174)
YEAR: 1955

MASTER NUMBER: Capitol CAS 3236
Woody Woodpecker Meets Davy Crockett / Part 2 (32180)
YEAR: 1955

MASTER NUMBER: Capitol CAS 3240
Save Up Your Pennies / Day Dreaming Danny (32184)
YEAR: 1956
(Note: Originally part of a multi-disc set, this new single-disc version was released while the multi-disc original was still available. New cover art was created for the new issue.)

Alternate-Number Standard 45 RPM Capitol Children's Album Sets

MASTER NUMBER: Capitol CCF 3004
Bugs Bunny
(Box set. Same couplings as the three 78 RPM set issues. Disc numbers: 54-30022, 54-30023 and 54-30024)
YEAR: 1949

MASTER NUMBER: Capitol CBXF 3022
Bugs Bunny in Storyland
(Record-Reader. Disc numbers: 54-30058 and 54-30059)
YEAR: 1949

MASTER NUMBER: Capitol CBXF 3036
Bugs Bunny and the Tortoise
(Record-Reader. Disc numbers: 54-30090 and 54-30091)
YEAR: 1949

Capitol 45 RPM Extended Play (EP) Children's Albums & Record-Readers

MASTER NUMBER: Capitol EAXF 3022
Bugs Bunny in Storyland
YEAR: 1953

MASTER NUMBER: Capitol EAXF 3032
Woody Woodpecker and His Talent Show
YEAR: 1953

MASTER NUMBER: Capitol EAXF 3036
Bugs Bunny and the Tortoise
YEAR: 1953

MASTER NUMBER: Capitol EAXF 3102
Tweety's Puddy Tat Twouble
YEAR: 1953

MASTER NUMBER: Capitol EAP 3175
Bugs Bunny Meets Hiawatha / Daffy Duck's Feathered Friend
YEAR: 1953

MASTER NUMBER: Capitol EAP 3176
Bugs Bunny and the Grow-Small Juice / Sylvester and Hippety Hopper
YEAR: 1953

MASTER NUMBER: Capitol EAP 3177
Bugs Bunny and Aladdin's Lamp / Henery Hawk
YEAR: 1953

MASTER NUMBER: Capitol EAP 3178
Daffy Duck Meets Yosemite Sam / Porky Pig in Africa
YEAR: 1953

MASTER NUMBER: Capitol EAP 3179
Tweet, Tweet, Tweety / Henery Hawk's Chicken Hunt
YEAR: 1953

MASTER NUMBER: Capitol EAP 3181
Woody Woodpecker and the Scarecrow
YEAR: 1953

MASTER NUMBER: Capitol EAP 3182
Woody Woodpecker and the Animal Crackers
YEAR: 1953

MASTER NUMBER: Capitol EBF 436
Party Panic!
(Big Bear Lake, Ten Little Bottles in the Sink, K-K-K-Katy, Morris, I
    Taut I Taw a Puddy Tat, Toot, Toot, Tootsie Goodbye, Lord Bless 'Is
    Soul, I'm Just Wild About Animal Crackers)
YEAR: 1953

10-Inch LPs

MASTER NUMBER: Capitol HX 3060
Woody Woodpecker and His Talent Show
YEAR: 1950

MASTER NUMBER: Capitol HX 3063
Bugs Bunny In Storyland / Bugs Bunny Meets Elmer Fudd; Daffy Duck
    Flies South
YEAR: 1950

MASTER NUMBER: Capitol HX 3065
Bozo Under the Sea *(does not include Mel, but "Pinto" Colvig)* / I'm Just
    Wild About Animal Crackers
YEAR: 1950

MASTER NUMBER: Capitol HX 3067
Bugs Bunny and the Tortoise
YEAR: 1950

MASTER NUMBER: Capitol H 436
Party Panic! *(Same song sequence as 45 EP issue)*
YEAR: 1953

Non-Capitol-Contract Children or Adult Single Issues

MASTER NUMBER: Royale 54 (45225)
Maw and Paw *(as by Judy Canova)* / *(not by Mel)*
DISC SIZE: 7"
SPEED: 45
YEAR: 1951?

MASTER NUMBER: Tribute 501
A Tribute to Elvis Presley *(Part 1 only. An all-star tribute in which Mel
    speaks a sound-bite-length bit praising Presley's platters)*
DISC SIZE: 7"
SPEED: 45
YEAR: 1956

MASTER NUMBER: Golden R366
Daffy Duck — *(Birthday song for kids born in)* March / *(not by Mel, though
    he is given label credit)*
DISC SIZE: 6"
SPEED: 78
YEAR: 1957

MASTER NUMBER: Warner Bros 5129
Tweety's Twistmas Twouble / I Keep Hearing Those Bells
DISC SIZE: 7"
SPEED: 45
YEAR: 1959

MASTER NUMBER: Warner Bros. 5156
Blimey / I Can't Fool My Heart
DISC SIZE: 7"
SPEED: 45
YEAR: 1960

MASTER NUMBER: Warner Bros. 5369
Tia Juana Ball *(as by The Ralke-Talkies with Speedy Gonzales; Mel's name is in very small print under Speedy's) / (not by Mel)*
DISC SIZE: 7"
SPEED: 45
YEAR: 1961

MASTER NUMBER: Golden EP 653
Songs of The Flintstones
DISC SIZE: 7"
SPEED: 45
YEAR: 1961

MASTER NUMBER: Dot 45-16368
Speedy Gonzales *(as by Pat Boone; no Mel credit. Mel speaks as Speedy during song) / (not by Mel)*
DISC SIZE: 7"
SPEED: 45
YEAR: 1962

MASTER NUMBER: Golden R680
Meet the Flintstones *(no Mel credit; cover reads Songs of The Flintstones) / (not by Mel)*
DISC SIZE: 6"
SPEED: 78
YEAR: 1962?

MASTER NUMBER: Golden R739
Dino the Dino / Part 2
DISC SIZE: 6"
SPEED: 78
YEAR: 1963

MASTER NUMBER: HBR CS 7021
Goldirocks and the Three Bearosauruses / Part 2 *(Flintstones record)*
DISC SIZE: 7"
SPEED: 45
YEAR: 1965

MASTER NUMBER: HBR CS 7059
Hansel & Gretel / Part 2 *(Flintstones record; no Mel credit)*
DISC SIZE: 7"
SPEED: 45
YEAR: 1965

MASTER NUMBER: HBR CS 70??
Treasure Island *(Sinbad, Jr. record; no Mel credit)*
DISC SIZE: 7"
SPEED: 45
YEAR: 1965

MASTER NUMBER: Talking Show Projector 223-236
Bugs Bunny in "Buccaneer Bugs"; Tweety & Sylvester in "Tweet Bird"
    / *(not by Mel)*
DISC SIZE: 7"
SPEED: 45
YEAR: 1971
*(Meant to accompany a filmstrip showing the cartoon pictures. A bell signal
interrupts the stories as a cue to go to the next picture. The two stories are
short — combined, they total just 3 minutes. Manufactured by Kenner.)*

MASTER NUMBER: Peter Pan 1972
Get That Pet *(Starring Bugs Bunny, with Tweety and Sylvester. Record and
    softcover coordinated book)*
DISC SIZE: 7"
SPEED: 45
YEAR: 1973
*(Peter Pan Records produced 63 known book-and-record issues in this series,
but Mel is not on any of The Flintstones titles)*

Talking/Singing Greeting Cards

MASTER NUMBER: American Telecard BDL2001
Hi There *(Cast: Bugs Bunny, Road Runner, Wile E. Coyote)*
DISC SIZE: 6"
SPEED: 33
YEAR: 1964

MASTER NUMBER: American Telecard BDL2002
Happy Birthday *(Cast: Tweety and Sylvester)*
DISC SIZE: 6"
SPEED: 33
YEAR: 1964

MASTER NUMBER: Record Cards 50B9027
Happy Birthday *(Cast: Tweety and Sylvester. Same content as BDL2002)*
DISC SIZE: 6"
SPEED: 33
YEAR: 1964

MASTER NUMBER: Record Cards 50B9028
Happy Birthday *(Cast: Bugs Bunny, Porky Pig, Tweety and Sylvester)*
DISC SIZE: 6"
SPEED: 33
YEAR: 1964

MASTER NUMBER: Record Cards 50B9029
Happy Birthday *(Cast: Bugs Bunny and Elmer Fudd; Fudd voice: Hal Smith)*
DISC SIZE: 6"
SPEED: 33
YEAR: 1964

MASTER NUMBER: Record Cards 50B9034
Happy Birthday *(Cast: Count Dracula, Frankenstein's Monster, the Wolf
    Man and the Mummy; voices by Mel Blanc and Lennie Weinrib)*
DISC SIZE: 6"
SPEED: 33
YEAR: 1964

MASTER NUMBER: Record Cards 50R9041
I Love You *(Cast: Count Dracula and the Wolf Man; voices by Mel Blanc and Lennie Weinrib)*
DISC SIZE: 6"
SPEED: 33
YEAR: 1964

MASTER NUMBER: Record Cards 50R9042
Wish You Were Here *(Cast: Count Dracula, others uncertain; voices by Mel Blanc and Lennie Weinrib)*
DISC SIZE: 6"
SPEED: 33
YEAR: 1964

MASTER NUMBER: Record Cards 50C9043
Get Well Soon!! *(Cast: Bugs Bunny and Elmer Fudd; Fudd voice: Hal Smith)*
DISC SIZE: 6"
SPEED: 33
YEAR: 1964
(The above Record Cards are credited to "Buzza/Cardozo," but American Telecard is also referenced. This suggests the former might be a subsidiary of the latter. Certainly the two card series look identical in manufacture. The recording aspect was done by Columbia Records. Mel recorded others in this group, but the content of those is unknown at present.)

12-Inch 33 1/3 RPM Children or Adult Original Issues

MASTER NUMBER: Capitol T 3241
Jack Benny Plays The Bee ably assisted by Isaac Stern *(Mel speaks two brief roles near the beginning of this long LP.)*
YEAR: 1956

MASTER NUMBER: Decca DL 8659
Woody Woodpecker's Family Album *(Mel voices the male characters, but Grace Stafford is Woody.)*
YEAR: 1957

MASTER NUMBER: Warner Bros. B 1323

Drink Along With Irving *(Sketch: Separate Bar Stools, with Bea Benedaret and Key Howard. Monologue: Liquor Is Our Business)*

YEAR: 1959

MASTER NUMBER: Warner Bros. W 1352

The Whimsical World of Irving Taylor *(Sketch: Separate Bar Stools, with Bea Benedaret and Key Howard. Contains some of Warner Bros. B 1323)*

YEAR: 1959

MASTER NUMBER: RCA Camden CAL 662

Judy Canova *(LP title. Mel performs as Paw in Maw and Paw sketches, and as Tex, an old cowpoke in Two Gun Judy sketches)*

YEAR: 1960

MASTER NUMBER: Columbia CL 1950 & (Stereo) CS 8450

Snow White and The Three Stooges *(Mel speaks and sings anonymously on the soundtrack and lp as ventriloquist dummy Quinto. Song: "Because I'm In Love.")*

YEAR: 1961

MASTER NUMBER: Golden LP 66

Songs of The Flintstones

YEAR: 1961

MASTER NUMBER: Colpix LP 302

The Flintstones *(Original TV Soundtracks)*

YEAR: 1961

MASTER NUMBER: Dot DLP 3455 & (Stereo) DLP 25455

Pat Boone's Golden Hits featuring Speedy Gonzales *(Mel is heard speaking as Speedy only on that track; no Mel credit)*

YEAR: 1962

MASTER NUMBER: Warner Bros. W 1472 & (Stereo) WS 1472
La Dolce Henke *(Mel Blanc is heard on only one track of this LP, which is
     humorous orchestra arrangements created by Mel Henke. Song: "Farmer
     John." Mel Blanc does barnyard animal sounds — no singing nor speech.)*
YEAR: 1962
*(Note: The only copy of this record that is known to me is the stereo pressing.
Because mono LPs were also issued this far back, I believe that it is safe to
assume that a mono pressing with this catalog number was also released.)*

MASTER NUMBER: Colpix CP 213
The Jetsons *(Original TV Soundtracks)*
YEAR: 1964

MASTER NUMBER: Golden LP 120
Magilla Gorilla and His Pals
YEAR: 1964

MASTER NUMBER: HBR HLP 2021
Goldirocks and the Three Bearosauruses *(Flintstones record)*
YEAR: 1965

MASTER NUMBER: HBR HLP 2038
Hansel & Gretel *(Flintstones record)*
YEAR: 1965

MASTER NUMBER: HBR HLP 2039
Treasure Island *(Sinbad, Jr. record)*
YEAR: 1965

MASTER NUMBER: HBR HLP 2051
The New Alice in Wonderland or What's a Nice Kid Like You Doing in
     a Place Like This?
YEAR: 1966

MASTER NUMBER: HBR HLP 2055
The Man Called Flintstone *(Song: Team Mates. The only track with Mel's
     voice on the whole LP)*
YEAR: 1966

MASTER NUMBER: Peter Pan 8132
The New Adventures of Bugs Bunny *(Stories: Hunger Pains, The Carrot Kid, What's Up MacDoc?, Getting the Bugs Out)*
YEAR: 1973

MASTER NUMBER: Peter Pan 8134
Four More Adventures of Bugs Bunny *(Stories: Get That Pet, Porky's Picnic, Moon Bunny, Maestro Bugs)*
YEAR: 1974

MASTER NUMBER: Peter Pan 8137
Holly-Daze *(Stories: Bugs the Red-Nose Bunny, Santa Claustrophobia, Holly-Daze, 'Twas a Sight Before Christmas)*
YEAR: 1974

MASTER NUMBER: ABC Dunhill DSD 50191
Earle Doud Presents Kenneth Mars as Henry the First
YEAR: 1974
(Mars stars in this comedy LP as a dead-on Henry Kissinger. A large supporting cast is with him, but Mel is only heard on three tracks, including the showstopping Disneyland sketch.)

Reissues

(Year refers to catalog issue, not year recorded)

MASTER NUMBER: RCA Victor 20-3338
The Clink Clink Polka *(reissue of "Clink, Clink, Another Drink")*
DISC SIZE: 10"
SPEED: 78
YEAR: 1949

MASTER NUMBER: Capitol F4185
There's a Hole in the Iron Curtain
DISC SIZE: 7"
SPEED: 45
YEAR: 1959
(Different from the original. This novelty, which Mel co-wrote with Mickey Katz in 1950, was kidding the growing Russian menace. With the Cold War

heating up again as the decade neared its end, Capitol decided to dust it off and put it out again. But first, it had to be updated. Near the beginning of the record, Mel, using his Russian accent, announces a "Special message from Uncle Joe." This referred to Russian premier, Joseph Stalin. To update the newer issue, "Joe" was changed to "Nik" to make a sarcastic nod to Stalin's successor, Nikita Khruschev.)

MASTER NUMBER: Ju-Dee *(no number)*
Judy Canova *(LP title. Mel performs as Paw in Maw and Paw sketches, and as Tex, an old cowpoke in the Two Gun Judy sketches.)*
DISC SIZE: 12"
SPEED: 33
YEAR: 1961

MASTER NUMBER: Golden LP 71
Bugs Bunny Songfest
DISC SIZE: 12"
SPEED: 33
YEAR: 1962
(This is the LP which contains a birthday song for children born in a given month of the year. Each song was sung by a different Warner Bros. cartoon character, with no Mel credit. Ollie Owl's song for children born in April was not Mel's track; it was done by an anonymous imitator. The remaining 11 tracks and voices which Mel did record are:

Sylvester — January	*Speedy Gonzales — August*
Tweety Bird — February	*Bugs Bunny — September*
Daffy Duck — March	*Hippety Hopper — October*
Porky Pig — May	*Foghorn Leghorn — November*
Henery Hawk — June	*Cicero Pig — December)*
Pepe Le Pepe (sic) — July	

MASTER NUMBER: Capitol J 3257
Bugs Bunny and His Friends *(Stories: Bugs Bunny Meets Elmer Fudd, Porky Pig in Africa, Daffy Duck's Duck Inn, Bugs Bunny and the Grow-Small Juice, Happy Hippety Hopper, and Bugs Bunny Meets Hiawatha)*
DISC SIZE: 12"
SPEED: 33
YEAR: 1963
(This LP contains what is apparently the first release of the 1953 story, Happy Hippety Hopper)

MASTER NUMBER: Capitol J 3261
Tweety Pie (Stories: Tweety Pie, Sylvester and Hippety Hopper, Tweet
    Tweet Tweety, and Pied Piper Pussy Cat)
DISC SIZE: 12"
SPEED: 33
YEAR: 1963

MASTER NUMBER: Capitol J 3263
Woody Woodpecker's Picnic
DISC SIZE: 12"
SPEED: 33
YEAR: 1963

MASTER NUMBER: Capitol JAO 3251
Woody Woodpecker and his Talent Show

MASTER NUMBER: Capitol J 3266
Bugs Bunny in Storyland *(Contains title story plus songs: "I'm Glad That
    I'm Bugs Bunny," "Daffy Duck's Rhapsody," "I Taut I Taw a Puddy Tat,"
    and "Yosemite Sam")*
DISC SIZE: 12"
SPEED: 33
YEAR: 1963
*(Note: This release does not have the storybook pages with Record-Reader
artwork. When this story was a Record-Reader, the page-turning intro and
narration were spoken by Arthur Q. Bryan as Elmer Fudd. On these LP
issues, the picture configuration was different, so Record-Reader narrators
had to be called back into Capitol studios to record the corresponding slight
variation to fit the new format. But Mr. Bryan had died in 1959, and Mel
was not yet comfortable replacing him as Elmer Fudd. The result was that this
story was re-mastered for this issue and a subsequent one. On this release and
the other, all references to the pictures and page-turning cues were eliminated
so that the story could be reissued without the additional pictures beyond the
front cover.)*

MASTER NUMBER: Capitol L-6686
Bozo and His Pals *(Songs: "Little Red Monkey" and "Pussy Cat Parade")*
DISC SIZE: 12"
SPEED: 33
YEAR: 1970?
(The cover bears Capitol's CP — Creative Products — logo, while the record labels have Capitol's SM — Special Markets — logo. The LP's contents were programmed by Dave Dexter, Jr.)

MASTER NUMBER: Capitol L 6818-RR
(Bozo Under the Sea) / Bugs Bunny and the Tortoise
DISC SIZE: 12"
SPEED: 33
YEAR: 1972
(This issue contains the Record-Reader format for both stories. Both corresponding booklets are bound inside a gatefold cover. They are placed one on top of the other, and are somewhat reduced in size in order to fit into limited space. This series is titled "The Capitol Children's Book & Record Library." Evidence shows that other LPs which did not include Record-Reader booklets were also part of this group, despite the word "Book" in the series title.)

MASTER NUMBER: RCA LPV-580
The Golden Age of Comedy *(Sketch: Ma and Pa — Judy Canova and Mel Blanc)*
DISC SIZE: 12"
SPEED: 33
YEAR: 1972

MASTER NUMBER: Wonderland/Golden LP-285
T. V. Cartoons *(Song: "Meet the Flintstones." Of course, Mel sings as Barney Rubble.)*
YEAR: 1973

MASTER NUMBER: RCA (Germany) RCS 3217-1-2 (AKA 26.28019)
Spike Jones Murders Again *(Song: "Clink, Clink, Another Drink" Vol. 2 of 3 two-disc sets)*
DISC SIZE: 12"
SPEED: 33
YEAR: 1973

MASTER NUMBER: RCA (England) HY 1006 (Starcall series)
That Old Black Magic — Spike Jones *(Song: "Clink, Clink, Another Drink"*
    No Mel credit)
DISC SIZE: 12"
SPEED: 33
YEAR: 1975

MASTER NUMBER: Capitol L-6957
Bugs Bunny and His Friends *(Stories: Bugs Bunny Meets Elmer Fudd, Daffy*
    Duck Flies South, and Porky Pig in Africa)
DISC SIZE: 12"
SPEED: 33
YEAR: 1975

MASTER NUMBER: Capitol L-6958
Tweety Pie (Stories: Tweety Pie, and Sylvester and Hippety Hopper)
DISC SIZE: 12"
SPEED: 33
YEAR: 1975

MASTER NUMBER: Capitol L-6959
(Bozo on the Farm) *(Stories: Henery Hawk's Chicken Hunt, and an earlier*
    story simply titled Henery Hawk)
DISC SIZE: 12"
SPEED: 33
YEAR: 1975

MASTER NUMBER: Capitol L-6961
Woody Woodpecker's Picnic
DISC SIZE: 12"
SPEED: 33
YEAR: 1975

MASTER NUMBER: Capitol L-6962
Bugs Bunny and the Tortoise
DISC SIZE: 12"
SPEED: 33
YEAR: 1975

MASTER NUMBER: Capitol L-6963
I Taut I Taw a Puddy Tat *(Songs: title song, plus Daffy Duck's Rhapsody, Yosemite Sam, and That's All Folks; no Bonnie Baker credit on the last title)*
disc size: 12"
SPEED: 33
YEAR: 1975

MASTER NUMBER: Capitol L-6988
Bugs Bunny in Storyland
DISC SIZE: 12"
SPEED: 33
YEAR: 1975

MASTER NUMBER: Capitol L-6989
Woody Woodpecker and His Talent Show
DISC SIZE: 12"
SPEED: 33
YEAR: 1975
(The L-prefix issues listed above were part of a series commissioned by Ziv International. Though Ziv's logo appears on all covers and labels, the dominant company name is still Capitol. None of Ziv's releases were released in the Record-Reader format with the gatefold cover. As a result, Bugs Bunny and the Tortoise, Bugs Bunny in Storyland *and* Woody Woodpecker and His Talent Show *were all remastered in order to edit out the on-disc references to turning the pages.)*

MASTER NUMBER: Peter Pan BR 511
Bugs Bunny — 3 Funny Stories *(Stories: Moon Bunny, Maestro Bugs, and Getting the Bugs Out; extra illustrations show scenes in each story.)*
DISC SIZE: 12"
SPEED: 33
YEAR: 1975

MASTER NUMBER: Peter Pan 2312
Moon Bunny *(starring Bugs Bunny)*
DISC SIZE: 7"
SPEED: 33
YEAR: 1976

MASTER NUMBER: Peter Pan 2313
Hunger Pains *(starring Daffy Duck)*
DISC SIZE: 7"
SPEED: 33
YEAR: 1976

MASTER NUMBER: Peter Pan 2314
The Carrot Kid *(starring Speedy Gonzales)*
DISC SIZE: 7"
SPEED: 33
YEAR: 1976

MASTER NUMBER: Peter Pan 2315
What's Up, MacDoc? *(starring Elmer Fudd)*
DISC SIZE: 7"
SPEED: 33
YEAR: 1976

MASTER NUMBER: Peter Pan 2316
Porky's Picnic *(starring Porky Pig)*
DISC SIZE: 7"
SPEED: 33
YEAR: 1976
(Columbia Records reissued a number of Hanna-Barbera LPs from the mid-1960s beginning in 1977 through one of Columbia's subsideries, Columbia Special Products [CSP]. Mel was on some of these, but was never credited.)

MASTER NUMBER: Capitol SL-8084
Baby Snooks & Friends *(Mel's stories are on Side 2: Bugs Bunny and Aladdin's Lamp, Tweety's Good Deed, and Daffy Duck Meets Yosemite Sam)*
DISC SIZE: 12"
SPEED: 33
YEAR: 1977
(This is a Capitol Special Markets issue, with SM logo on the cover and labels, while the back cover reads: "Re-issued by Children's Treasure Club.")

MASTER NUMBER: Capitol L-8108
Jack Benny Fiddles With The Classics *(Reissue of "Jack Benny Plays The Bee, ably assisted by Isaac Stern")*
DISC SIZE: 12"
SPEED: 33
YEAR: 1978

MASTER NUMBER: Peter Pan 2603
Bugs Bunny in 'Twas a Sight Before Christmas
DISC SIZE: 7"
SPEED: 33
YEAR: 1978

MASTER NUMBER: CSP (Columbia Special Products) ACS 8450
Snow White and The Three Stooges *(Song: "Because I'm In Love," plus dialogue as off-screen voice of ventriloquist dummy Quinto.)*
YEAR: 1983

MASTER NUMBER: PRI SL-9306
Christmas Comedy Classics *(Songs: I Tan't Wait Till Quithmuth Day, and The Hat I Got For Christmas is Too Beeg)*
DISC SIZE: 12"
SPEED: 33
YEAR: 1985
(This is also a CSM pressing.)

Songwriting Credits

Big Bear Lake *(Mel J. Blanc)*
I Keep Hearing Those Bells *(Mel J. Blanc, Alan W. Livingston)*
O K M N X *(Mel J. Blanc)*
Pancho's Christmas *(Mel J. Blanc, Marve A. Fisher)*
There's a Hole in the Iron Curtain *(Mel J. Blanc, Mickey Katz)*
Tia Juana *(sic)* *(Mel J. Blanc, ? Clark, ? Blue)*
Tweety's Twistmas Twouble *(Mel J. Blanc, Alan W. Livingston)*
Ugga Ugga Boo Ugga Boo Boo Ugga *(Mel J. Blanc, with additional words and music by Eddie Maxwell, Irving Miller, Mac Benoff)*
Wheezy Woozy Whatomobile (Mel J. Blanc, Phil Boutelje)

Endnotes

Cartoons and Short Subjects

The Animated Film Encyclopedia, A Complete Guide to American Shorts, Features, and Sequences, 1900-1979 by Graham Webb, McFarland, 2000.

The Animated Movie Guide by Jerry Beck, Chicago Review Press/A Cappella, 2005.

The Big Cartoon Database, Internet website at *www.bcdb.com*

The Columbia Comedy Shorts, Two-Reel Hollywood Film Comedies, 1933-1958 by Ted Okuda with Edward Watz, McFarland Classics, 1986.

The Columbia Story by Clive Hirschhorn, Crown, 1989.

The Encyclopedia of Animated Cartoon Series by Jeff Lenburg, Arlington House, 1981.

Feature Films, 1940-1949, A United States Filmography by Alan G. Fetrow, McFarland, 1994.

Feature Films, 1950-1959, A United States Filmography by Alan G. Fetrow, McFarland, 1999.

Feature Films, 1960-1969, A Filmography of English-Language and Major Foreign-Language United States Releases by Harris M. Lentz III, McFarland, 2001.

Film Noir, An Encyclopedic Reference to the American Style, Edited by Alan Silver and Elizabeth Ward, The Overlook Press, 1979.

The Films of the Seventies by Marc Sigoloff, McFarland Classics, 1984.

The Films of 20th Century-Fox, A Pictorial History by Tony Thomas & Aubrey Solomon, Citadel Press, 1979.

Halliwell's Film and Video Guide, 6th Edition, by Leslie Halliwell, Charles Scribner's Sons, 1987.

Hollywood Song, The Complete Film & Musical Companion (3 volumes) by Ken Bloom, Facts on File, 1995.

Internet Movie Database, website at *www.imdb.com.*

Leonard Maltin's Classic Movie Guide edited by Leonard Maltin, Plume, 2005, 2010.

Leonard Maltin's 1996 Movie & Video Guide, Edited by Leonard Maltin, Plume/Penguin, 1995.

Looney Tunes and Merrie Melodies, A Complete Illustrated Guide to the Warner Bros. Cartoons by Jerry Beck & Will Friedwald, Owl/Donald Hutter/Henry Holt, 1989.

The MGM Story by John Douglas Eames, Crown, 1979.

Movie Awards, The Ultimate, Unofficial Guide to the Oscars, Golden Globes, Critics, Guild & Indie Honors by Tom O'Neil, Perigee, 2001.

The Paramount Story by John Douglas Eames, Crown, 1985.

The RKO Story by Richard B. Jewell with Vernon Harbin, Arlington House, 1982.

70 Years of the Oscar, The Official History of the Academy Awards by Robert Osborne, Abbeville Press, 1999.

Spike Jones Off the Record, The Man Who Murdered music by Jordan R. Young, Past Times, 1994.

That's Not All Folks! by Mel Blanc and Philip Bashe, Warner Books, 1988.

The Three Stooges Scrapbook by Jeff Lenburg, Joan Howard Maurer, Greg Lenburg; Citadel Press, 1982.

The United Artists Story by Ronald Bergan, Crown, 1986.

Videohound's Cult Flicks & Trash Pics, Edited by Carol Schwartz with Jim Olenski, Visible Ink Press, 2002.

Vintage Movies Radio Television Magazine, "Lucille Ball Special", Edited by Randy Bonneville, October, 2006.

Vitaphone Films, A Catalogue of the Features and Shorts by Roy Liebman, McFarland, 2003.

The Warner Bros. Story by Clive Hirschhorn, Crown, 1979.

Television

The Big Cartoon Database, website @ www.bcdb.com.

The Complete Directory to Prime Time Network and Cable TV Shows, 1946-Present, 9th Edition, by Tim Brooks and Earle Marsh, Ballantine, 2007.

The Encyclopedia of Animated Cartoon Series by Jeff Lenburg, Arlington House, 1981.

The Encyclopedia of Daytime Television by Wesley Hyatt, Billboard/Watson-Guptill, 1997.

Encyclopedia of Television, Series, Pilots and Specials, 1937-1973, 1974-1984 (2 volumes) by Vincent Terrace, New York Zoetrope, 1986.

The Encyclopedia of TV Game Shows by David Schwartz, Steve Ryan and Fred Wostbrock, New York Zoetrope, 1987.

Internet Movie Database, www.imdb.com.

Jim Davidson's Classic TV Info, www.classictvinfo.com.

Movies Made for Television, 1964-2004, Volume 2, by Alvin H. Marill, Scarecrow Press, 2005.

Raymond Burr, a Film, Radio and Television Biography by Ona L. Hill, McFarland, 1994.

Science Fiction Television Series, Episode Guides, Histories, and Cast Credits for 62 Prime Time Shows, 1959 through 1989 by Mark Phillips and Frank Garcia, McFarland, 1996.

Television Cartoon Shows, An Illustrated Encyclopedia, 1949 through 1993 by Hal Erickson, McFarland, 1995.

Television Chronicles magazine, No. 12, January 1998 issue, Rubber Chicken Publications.

Television Specials, 3201 Entertainment Spectaculars, 1939-1993 by Vincent Terrace, McFarland, 1995.

Television Variety Shows by David M. Inman, McFarland, 2006.

This Is Your Life The Ultimate Collection, website @ www.tvdepot.com/tiyl/home.jsp.

Total Television, The Comprehensive Guide to Programming From 1948 to the Present, 4th Edition, by Alex McNeil, Penguin, 1996.

TV Guide magazine, various issues 1953-1978, Televiews News/Triangle Publications.

Vintage Movies Radio Television magazine, "Lucille Ball Special", edited by Randy Bonneville, October 2006 issue.

Song List
Compiled by Randy Bonneville

(Note: For many of the Looney Tunes and Merrie Melodies a number of songs were used repeatedly, often as background music. They are listed below.)

"The Merry-Go-Round Broke Down" *(Cliff Friend; Dave Franklin; The Looney Tunes theme)* "Merrily We Roll Along" *(Eddie Cantor; Charlie Tobias; Murray Mencher; Merrie Melodies theme)*, "A-Hunting We Will Go" *(traditional, composer unknown)*, "Ain't We Got Fun?" *(Richard A. Whiting; Gus Kahn; Raymond B. Egan)*, "All This And Heaven Too" *(James Van Heusen; Edgar DeLange)*, "Aloha Oe *(Farewell To Thee)*" *(Queen Liliuokalani)*, "Alouette" *(traditional, composer unknown)*, "The Alphabet Song" *(Music: Monsieur Bouin; Lyricist: Unknown)*, "Am I Blue?" *(Harry Akst; Grant Clarke)*, "Angel In Disguise" *(Stefan Weiss; Paul Mann; Kim Gannon)*, "Animal Fair" *(traditional, composer unknown)*, "April In Paris" *(Vernon Duke; E.Y. Harburg)*, "Are You From Dixie?" *(George L. Cobb; Jack Yellen)*, "Arkansas Traveler" *(Sanford Faulkner)*, "The Army Air Corps Song" *(Robert Crawford)*, "Artist's Life" *(Johann Strauss)*, "As Time Goes By" *(Herman Hupfeld)*, "Athalie Overture" *(Felix Mendelssohn-Bartholdy)*, "At Your Service, Madame" *(Harry Warren; Al Dubin)*, "Auld Lang Syne" *(traditional, composer unknown)*, "Baa, Baa Black Sheep" *(Music: Variation on above theme by Monsieur Bouin; Lyricist: Unknown)*, "Baby Face" *(Harry Akst; Benny Davis)*, "Beautiful Dreamer" *(Stephen Foster)*, "Bei Mir Bist Du Schoen" *(Sholom Secunda; Jacob Jacobs; Saul Chaplin; Sammy Cahn)*, "Blow The Man Down" *(traditional, composer unknown)*, "The Blue Danube" *(Johann Strauss)*, "Blues In The Night" *(Harold Arlen; Johnny Mercer)*, "Bob White *(Whatcha Gonna Swing Tonight?)*" *(Bernard Hanighen; Johnny Mercer)*, "Boulevardier From The Bronx" *(Harry Warren; Al Dubin)*, "Boy Scout In Switzerland" *(Raymond Scott)*, "Brahms' Lullaby *(Cradle Song)*" *(Johannes Brahms)*, "Bridal Chorus" from "Lohengrin" *(Richard Wagner)*, "By A Waterfall" *(Sammy Fain; Irving Kahal)*, "Bye, Bye Blackbird" *(Ray Henderson; Mort Dixon)*, "California, Here I Come" *(Joseph Meyer; Al Jolson; B.G. DeSylva)*, "The Campbells Are Coming" *(traditional, composer unknown)*, "Camptown Races"

(Stephen Foster), "Captains Of The Clouds" *(Harold Arlen; Johnny Mercer),* "Carolina In The Morning" *(Walter Donaldson; Gus Kahn),* "Carry Me Back To Old Virginny" *(James Allen Bland),* "Charleston" *(James P. Johnson; Cecil Mack),* "Cheerful Little Earful" *(Harry Warren),* "Cherie, I Love You" *(Lillian Goodman),* "Cheyenne" *(Egbert Van Alstyne; Harry Williams),* "Las Chiapanecas" *(traditional, composer unknown),* "Chicken Reel" *(Joseph M. Daly),* "Chopsticks" *(Euphemia Allen),* "Columbia, The Gem Of The Ocean *(The Red, White And Blue)*" *(David T. Shaw; Thomas A. Beckett),* "Concert In The Park" *(Cliff Friend; Dave Franklin),* "Confidentially" *(Harry Warren; Al Dubin; Johnny Mercer),* "Congo" *(M.K. Jerome),* "La Cucaracha" *(traditional, composer unknown),* "Cuddle Up A Little Closer" *(Karl Hoschna; Otto Harbach),* "A Cup Of Coffee, A Sandwich And You" *(Joseph Meyer; Billy Rose; Al Dubin),* "The Daughter Of Rosie O'Grady" *(Walter Donaldson; Monty C. Brice),* "Day Dreaming All Night Long" *(Harry Warren; Johnny Mercer),* "Dear Little Boy Of Mine" *(Ernest Ball; J. Keirn Brennan),* "Deep In A Dream" *(Jimmy Van Heusen; Eddie De Lange),* "Dinner Music For A Pack Of Hungry Cannibals" *(Raymond Scott),* "Dixie" *(Daniel Decatur Emmett),* "Don't Give Up The Ship" *(Harry Warren; Al Dubin),* "Don't Sweetheart Me" *(Cliff Friend; Charles Tobias),* "Down In Nashville, Tennessee" *(David Mann; Bob Hilliard),* "Down In The Valley" *(traditional, composer unknown),* "The Dying Cowboy *(Bury Me Not On The Lone Prairie)*" *(traditional, composer unknown)* "Egyptian Barn Dance" *(Raymond Scott),* "Der Erlkonig" *(Franz Schubert),* "Every Little Movement" *(Karl Hoschna; Otto Harbach),* "Far Above Cayuga's Waters *(Alma Mater; Annie Lisle)*" *(H.S. Thompson),* "Fiddle-Dee-Dee" *(Jule Styne; Sammy Cahn),* "Fingal's Cave Overture" *(Felix Mendelssohn-Bartholdy),* "Five O' Clock Whistle" *(Gene Irwin; Joseph Myrow),* "For He's A Jolly Good Fellow" *(traditional, composer unknown),* "42nd Street" *(Harry Warren; Al Dubin),* "Frankie And Johnny" *(Bert Leighton; Jack Brooks),* "Frat" *(John F. Barth),* "Freddy The Freshman" *(Cliff Friend; Dave Oppenheim),* "Fruhlingslied *(Spring Song)*" *(Felix Mendelssohn-Bartholdy),* "Funeral March" *(Frederic Chopin),* "Garden Of The Moon" *(Harry Warren; Al Dubin; Johnny Mercer),* "Gavotte In D" *(Francois-Joseph Gossec),* "Gee, But You're Swell" *(Abel Baer; Charles Tobias),* "The Girl Friend Of The Whirling Dervish" *(Harry Warren; Al Dubin; Johnny Mercer),* "The Girl I Left Behind Me" *(traditional, composer unknown),* "Goodnight, Ladies" *(traditional, composer unknown),* "Gotta Be This Or That" *(Sunny Skylar),* "Happy Days Are Here Again" *(Milton Ager; Jack Yellen),* "The Happy Farmer" *(Raymond Scott),* "Heaven Can Wait" *(Jimmy Van Heusen),* "Here We Go 'Round The Mulberry Bush" *(traditional, composer unknown),* "Hickory Dickory Dock" *(traditional, composer unknown),* "Hippety Hop" *(Carl W. Stalling),* "(Ho-Dle-Ay) Start The Day Right" *(Maurice Spitalny; Al Lewis; Charles Tobias),* "Home On The Range" *(Daniel E. Kelly),* "Home, Sweet Home" *(Sir Henry R. Bishop; John Howard Payne),* "Hooray For Hollywood" *(Richard A. Whiting; Johnny Mercer),* "How Dry I Am" *(Music, Dr. Edward F. Rimboult; Lyricist: Unknown),* "How Many Hearts Have You Broken *(With Those Great Big Beautiful Eyes)*" *(Al Kaufman),* "Huckleberry Duck" *(Raymond Scott),* "Hungarian Dance No. 5 and 7" *(Johannes Brahms),* "Hungarian Rhapsody No. 2" *(Franz Liszt),* "I Can't Get Along Little Dogie" *(M.K. Jerome),* "If I Could Be With You One Hour Tonight" *(James P. Johnson; Henry Creamer),* "I'll Pray For You" *(Arthur Altman; Kim Gannon),* "I'm Forever Blowing Bubbles" *(James Brockman; James Kendis; Nat Vincent; John W. Kellette),* "I'm Just Wild About Harry" *(Eubie Blake; Noble Sissle),* "I'm Looking Over A Four Leaf Clover" *(Harry M. Woods; Mort Dixon),* "In A Little Red Barn *(On A Farm Down In Indiana)*" *(Milton Ager; Joe Young),* "In An 18th Century Drawing Room" *(Raymond Scott),* "Indian Dawn" *(John S. Zamecnik),* "Indian War Dance" *(John S. Zamecnik),* "In My Merry Oldsmobile" *(Gus Edwards; Vincent Bryan),* "In The Good Old Summertime" *(George Evans; Ren Shields),* "In The Shade Of The Old Apple Tree" *(Egbert Van Alstyne; Harry Williams),* "In The Stirrups" *(John S. Zamecnik),* "The Irish Washerwoman" *(traditional, composer unknown),* "It Can't Be Wrong" *(Max Steiner; Kim Gannon),* "It Had To Be You" *(Isham Jones; Gus Kahn),* "It Looks Like A Big Night Tonight" *(Egbert Van Alstyne; Harry Williams),* "It's Magic" *(Jule Styne; Sammy Cahn),* "I've Been Working On The Railroad" *(traditional, composer unknown),* "Java Jive" *(Ben Oakland; Milton Drake),* "Jeanie With The Light Brown Hair" *(Stephen Foster),* "Jeepers Creepers" *(Harry*

Warren; Johnny Mercer), "Jingle Bells" *(James Pierpont)*, "Jolly Robbers Overture" *(Franz von Suppe)*, "Jubilo" *(traditional, composer unknown)*, "Kiss Me, Sweet" *(Milton Drake)*, "The Kiss Waltz" *(Joseph Burke; Al Dubin)*, "The Lady In Red" *(Allie Wrubel; Mort Dixon)*, "Lady Of Spain" *(Tolchard Evans; Erell Reaves)*, "L'Amour, Toujours, L'Amour" *(Rudolf Friml)*, "Largo Al Factotum" from "The Barber of Seville" *(Gioacchino Rossini; Cesare Sterbini)*, "The Latin Quarter" *(Harry Warren; Al Dubin)*, "Laugh, Clown, Laugh" *(Ted Fio Rito; Sam Lewis; Joe Young)*, "Let That Be A Lesson To You" *(Richard A. Whiting; Johnny Mercer)*, "A Life On The Ocean Wave" *(Henry Russell; Epes Sargent)*, "Light Cavalry Overture" *(Franz Von Suppe)*, "Listen To The Mockingbird" *(Septimus Winner, under the pseudonym "Alice Hawthorne," his mother's maiden name)*, "Little Brown Jug" *(Joseph Winner)*, "Little Old Fashioned Music Box" *(George W. Meyer; Pete Wendling; Mack David)*, "A Little On The Lonely Side" *(Richard Robertson; Frank Weldon; James Cavanaugh)*, "Loch Lomond" *(traditional, composer unknown)*, "London Bridge Is Falling Down" *(traditional, composer unknown)*, "Long, Long Ago" *(Thomas Haynes Bayley)*, "Love Me And The World Is Mine" *(Ernest Ball; Dave Reed Jr.)*, "Love Ya" *(Peter DeRose; Charles Tobias)*, "Lucky Day" *(Ray Henderson; B.G. DeSylva; Lew Brown)*, "Lullaby Of Broadway" *(Harry Warren; Al Dubin)*, "Marine Hymn" *(Jacques Offenbach; L.Z. Phillips)*, "Massa's In De Cold, Cold Ground" *(Stephen Foster)*, "Melancholy Mood" *(Walter Schumann)*, "Memories" *(Egbert Van Alstyne; Gus Kahn)*, "Meow" *(Saul Chaplin; Sammy Cahn)*, "Mexican Hat Dance *(El Jarabe Tapatio)*" *(Felipe A. Partichela)*, "Minuet In G" *(Ludwig van Beethoven)*, "Mutiny In the Nursery" *(Harry Warren; Johnny Mercer)*, "My Buddy" *(Walter Donaldson; Gus Kahn)*, "My Country 'Tis Of Thee *(America)*" *(traditional, composer unknown)*, "My Grandfather's Clock" *(Henry Clay Work)*, "My Isle Of Golden Dreams" *(Walter Blaufuss; Gus Kahn)*, "My Little Buckaroo" *(M.K. Jerome; Jack Scholl)*, "Mysterious Mose" *(Walter Doyle; Ted Weems)*, "Nagasaki" *(Harry Warren; Mort Dixon)*, "Oh, Susanna" *(Stephen Foster)*, "Oh, You Beautiful Doll" *(Nat D. Ayer; A. Seymour Brown)*, "Old Black Joe" *(Stephen Foster)*, "The Old Folks At Home" *(Stephen Foster)*, "The Old Grey Mare" *(traditional, composer unknown)*, "Old Hound Dog" *(composer unknown)*, "Old King Cole" *(Richard A. Whiting; Johnny Mercer)*, "Old MacDonald" *(traditional, composer unknown)*, "On The 5:15" *(Henry I. Marshall; Stanley Murphy)*, "On The Rue De La Paix" *(Werner R. Heymann; Ted Koehler)*, "The Organ Grinder's Swing" *(Will Hudson; Irving Mills)*, "The Penguin" *(Raymond Scott)*, "Perpetual Motion" *(Johann Strauss)*, "Pilgrim's Chorus" from "Tannhauser" *(Richard Wagner)*, "Poet And Peasant Overture" *(Franz Von Suppe)*, "Powerhouse" *(Raymond Scott)*, "Pretty Baby" *(Tony Jackson; Egbert Van Alstyne; Otto Harbach)*, "Puddin' Head Jones" *(Lou Handman; Alfred Bryan)*, "Put 'Em In Box, Tie 'Em With a Ribbon, Throw 'Em In the Deep Blue Sea" *(Jule Styne; Sammy Cahn)*, "Put On Your Old Grey Bonnet" *(Percy Wenrich; Stanley Murphy)*, "Reckless Night Aboard An Ocean Liner" *(Raymond Scott)*, "Ride Of The Valkyries" from "Die Walkure" *(Richard Wagner)*, "Ride, Tenderfoot, Ride" *(Richard A. Whiting; Johnny Mercer)*, "Rock-A-Bye Baby" *(Effie I. Canning; Robert Burdette)*, "The Sailor's Hornpipe" *(traditional, composer unknown)*, "Santa Lucia" *(Teodoro Cottrau)*, "Says Who? Says You, Says I!" *(Harold Arlen; Johnny Mercer)*, "September In The Rain" *(Harry Warren; Al Dubin)*, "She Broke My Heart In Three Places" *(Al Hoffman; Jerry Livingston; Milton Drake)*, "She'll Be Comin' Round The Mountain" *(traditional, composer unknown)*, "She Was An Acrobat's Daughter" *(Harry Ruby; Bert Kalmar)*, "Short'nin' Bread" *(Jacques Wolf)*, "Shuffle Off To Buffalo" *(Harry Warren; Al Dubin)*, "Sing A Song Of Sixpence" *(J. W. Elliott)*, "Singing Down The Road" *(Raymond Scott)*, "Singin' In The Bathtub" *(Michael Cleary; Herb Magidson; Ned Washington)* "Sing, You Son Of A Gun" *(Richard A. Whiting; Johnny Mercer)*, "Sleep, Baby, Sleep" *(traditional, composer unknown)*, "Snake Charmer" *(traditional, composer unknown)*, "Sobre Las Olas *(Over The Waves)*" *(Juventino Rosas)*, "Someone's Rocking My Dream Boat" *(Leon Rene; Otis Rene; Emerson Scott)*, "Some Sunday Morning" *(M.K. Jerome; Ray Heindorf; Ted Koehler)*, "Something Tells Me" *(Harry Warren)*, "The Song Of The Marines" *(Harry Warren; Al Dubin)*, "Strip Polka" *(Johnny Mercer)*, "Sweet Dreams, Sweetheart" *(M.K. Jerome; Ted Koehler)*, "Sweet Georgia Brown" *(Ben Bernie; Maceo Pinkard; Bernie Casey)*, "Sweethearts" *(Victor Herbert)*, "Symphony No. 5, First Movement" *(Ludwig van Beethoven)*

"Tango Muchacha" *(Harry Warren; Al Dubin)*, "Taps" *(General Daniel Butterfield)*, "The Teddy Bear's Picnic" *(John W. Bratton; Jimmy Kennedy)*, "Tenting Tonight On The Old Camp Ground" *(Walter Kitteridge)*, "That Wonderful Mother Of Mine" *(Walter Goodwin)*, "There's A Brand New Picture In My Picture Frame" *(Cliff Friend; Dave Franklin)*, "They're Either Too Young Or Too Old" *(Arthur Schwartz; Frank Loesser)*, "Three Blind Mice" *(traditional, composer unknown)*, "Time Waits For No One" *(Cliff Friend; Charles Tobias)*, "A Tisket, A Tasket" *(traditional, composer unknown)*, "The Toy Trumpet" *(Raymond Scott)*, "Trade Winds" *(Cliff Friend; Charles Tobias)*, "Traffic" *(John S. Zamecnik)*, "Traumerei" *(Robert Schumann)*, "Turkey In The Straw" *(traditional, composer unknown)*, "Twilight In Turkey" *(Raymond Scott)*, "Twinkle, Twinkle Little Star" *(Music: Monsieur Bouin in 1761; Lyrics: Jane Taylor, added in 1806)*, "The Umbrella Man" *(Vincent Rose; Larry Stock; James Cavanaugh)*, "La Vie En Rose" *(Louis "Louiguy" Guglielmi; Edith Piaf; English lyrics: Mack David)*, "Vieni, Vieni" *(Vincent Scotto)*, "A Vision Of Salome" *(J. Bodewalt Lampe)*, "War Dance For Wooden Indians" *(Raymond Scott)*, "The Washington Post" *(John Philip Sousa)*, "Wedding March" *(Felix Mendelssohn-Bartholdy)*, "We Did It Before And We Can Do it Again" *(Cliff Friend; Charles Tobias)*, "We're In The Money" *(Harry Warren; Al Dubin)*, "We're In To Win" *(Morris Orenstein)*, "We're Working Our Way Through College" *(Richard A. Whiting; Johnny Mercer)*, "What's The Matter With Father (He's All Right)" *(Egbert Van Alstyne; Harry Williams)*, "What's Up, Doc?" *(Carl W. Stalling)*, "When Irish Eyes Are Smiling" *(Ernest Ball; George Graff; Chauncey Olcott)*, "When My Dream Boat Comes Home" *(Cliff Friend; Dave Franklin)*, "When The Swallows Come Back To Capistrano" *(Leon Rene)*, "When Yuba Plays The Rumba On The Tuba" *(Herman Hupfeld)*, "Where, Oh Where Has My Little Dog Gone?" *(composer unknown)*, "While Strolling Through The Park One Day" *(Ed Haley)*, "William Tell Overture" *(Gioacchino Rossini)*, "Winter" *(Albert Gumble; Alfred Bryan)*, "Wintermarchen" *(Alphons Czibulka)*, "With Plenty Of Money And You" *(Harry Warren; Al Dubin)*, "The Woods Are Full Of Cuckoos *(And My Heart Is Full Of Love)*" *(J. Fred Coots; Charles Newman)*, "Yankee Doodle" *(traditional, composer unknown)*, "Yo, Ho, Ho And A Bottle Of Rum" *(traditional, composer unknown)*, "You Must Have Been A Beautiful Baby" *(Harry Warren; Johnny Mercer)*, "You Never Know Where You're Goin' Till You Get There" *(Jule Styne; Sammy Cahn)*, "You Ought To Be In Pictures" *(Dana Suesse; Edward Heyman)*, "You're In The Army Now" *(traditional, composer unknown)*.

Discography

Mel Blanc did the bulk of his best phonograph record work during his years as an exclusive Capitol artist. What follows is an overview of which voices were used on which records. Following the voices used for each performance, I have included the names of the people who did voice work in support of Mel, and which characters each person voiced. Finally (where the recording is a story), I tell you who narrated it. If it was Mel in character, I give the character's name as the narrator. "Narration by Mel Blanc" means that he is narrating the story in his normal speaking voice. Not quite all of Mel's Capitol titles will be found here, but most of them are present. And we'll start with a few tracks that he cut before he made those best-selling Capitol Records. Enjoy, Folks!

"Clink, Clink, Another Drink" (Standard drunk voice.) Mel sings a chorus, but gets label credit on the Bluebird issue only for his hiccups. This credit is in turn omitted from the RCA reissue ("The Clink Clink Polka") which does give him a vocal refrain credit.

"The Violin Lesson" Parts 1 and 2. "Getting a Shave" (All three sides as Professor LeBlanc.) With Jack Benny as himself on all sides. Eddie Anderson as Rochester added on "Getting a Shave." All from *The Jack Benny Album*.

"What Every Old Husband Should Know" Part 1. (The Happy Postman.) From *The Burns and Allen*

Album. With George, Gracie and announcer Bill Goodwin. "There's a Hole in the Iron Curtain" (Russian accent.)

"Woody Woodpecker" (Woody's voice only.) With The Sportsmen. "Greetings and Here's Good Wishes for a 14 Carrot (sic) Christmas from Capitol Records" (Bugs Bunny.) With Alan Livingston as record dealer and Johnny Mercer as himself. This was Mel's only 78 that was pressed on cardboard. Disc is 8" in diameter. "Season's Greetings from Capitol 1949" (Bugs Bunny, Yosemite Sam, Woody Woodpecker, the Vice-President in Charge of Speeds, and possibly, the classical artist. With Big Red Alton, Marvin Ash, Nappy Lamare, Zutty Singleton, Country Washburne and The Starlighters. All provide music bits, except Bugs. He serves as emcee.

"I'm Just Wild About Animal Crackers" (Animal sounds, several unnamed speaking voices, plus Bugs Bunny and Tweety Pie.) With The Sportsmen. "Big Bear Lake" (Meek-little-man voice and motorboat sounds.) With The Sportsmen. Song written by Mel Blanc. "Toot, Toot, Tootsie (Goodbye)" (Al Jolson takeoff, complete with whistling; Porky Pig tag.) "I've Got a Lovely Bunch of Cocoanuts" (English accent.) "I Taut I Taw a Puddy Tat" (Tweety Pie and Sylvester, including duet chorus.) "Yosemite Sam" (Sam's voice only.)

"K-K-Katy" (Same voice as used for Porky Pig.) Although Mel uses his Porky Pig voice, he is referred to during the song as "Mel Blanc." Recorded at the same session as "Big Bear Lake" and "I'm Just Wild About Animal Crackers" in 1949, it was not released by Capitol until 1951. With The Sportsmen.

"Flying Saucers" (Meek hillbilly voice.) "Ten Little Bottles in the Sink" (Own voice, getting progressively intoxicated, plus a few bars of whistling.) "Okmnx" (Two unnamed voices.) Written by Mel Blanc. "Christmas Chopsticks" (Kid voice, with animal sounds and vocal sound effects.) "I Tant Wait Till Quitmuth" (Kid voice.) "That's All Folks!" (Porky Pig.) With Bonnie Baker. "Won't You Ever Get Together With Me" (Tweety and Sylvester.) "Morris" (Own voice.) Uncredited backup vocal group sounds like The Starlighters. "Lord Bless His Soul" (English accent.) Same backup group as "Morris."

"I Tell My Troubles to Joe" (Meek little man voice.) "The Missus Wouldn't Approve" (Meek little man voice.) Both written by Harry Stewart, a Capitol Records comedian who sang songs in a Japanese dialect as Harry Kari and in a Swedish dialect as Yogi Yorgesson.

"Yah, Das Ist Ein Christmas Tree" (German accent.) Based on the old song, "Schnitzelbank," the gimmick of this song is that new phrases are added to each chorus, sung in reverse sequence from the order in which the phrase groups are introduced, something akin to "Old MacDonald Had a Farm." "I'm in the Mood for Love" (French accent.) "My Kinda Love" (French accent.)

"I Love Me" (Unnamed voice once used for a mouse, somewhat like Marvin the Martian.) "Somebody Stole My Gal" (Rich Texan voice, speeded up.) "Little Red Monkey" (Unnamed voice, to represent monkey) "Tia Juana" (Mexican accent.) Written by Mel Blanc. "The Woody Woodpecker Polka" (Woody's voice only.) With The Starlighters. "Trixie, the Piano Playing Pixie" (Unnamed voice, speeded up.) With The Starlighters. "The Lady Bird Song" (Kid voice, with whistling.) "I Dess I Dotta Doe" (Kid voice.) "Money" (Rich Texan voice.) Satirist Stan Freberg helped write this one. "Polly, Pretty Polly" (Own voice and parrot voice.) "Pancho's Christmas" (Mexican accent.) Mel Blanc collaborated with another songwriter to write this one. "The Hat I Got for Christmas Is Too Beeg" (Mexican accent.)

"Any Friend of Bozo is a Friend of Mine!" (Bugs Bunny, in support of "Pinto" Colvig as Bozo the Clown.) With June Foray doing additional voices. "Sneak Preview" (Bugs Bunny, Woody Woodpecker, record dealer.) With "Pinto" Colvig as Bozo the Clown. "I Taut I Taw a Record

Dealer" (Tweety, Sylvester, brief Bugs Bunny.) With Fanny Brice as Baby Snooks, Hanley Stafford as Daddy, "Pinto" Colvig briefly as Bozo the Clown, and an unidentified female voice as the record clerk. "The Woody Woodpecker Show" (Woody's voice, with Mel also speaking as himself on this radio program demo.)

"Bugs Bunny Meets Elmer Fudd" (Bugs Bunny, owl, turtle, mockingbird, narrator.) With Arthur Q. Bryan as Elmer Fudd (Bryan receives label credit). "Daffy Duck Flies South" (Daffy, duck leader, Backwardsland native.) "Porky Pig in Africa" (Porky Pig, elephant, crane, leopard, parrots, ape, rhino, "baby" bird, possibly ant chorus.)

"Bugs Bunny and the Tortoise" (Bugs Bunny, Daffy Duck, Henery Hawk, tortoise, cab driver, postal clerk.) Narrated by Elmer Fudd (always Arthur Q. Bryan on Capitol Records). With Dave Barry as the sneezing duck.

"Bugs Bunny in Storyland" (Bugs Bunny, Daffy Duck, Porky Pig, Old King Cole, Fiddlers Three, Mary's lamb, Bo-Peep's sheep, Beaky Buzzard, Little Red Riding Hood's wolf.) Narrated by Elmer Fudd. With June Foray as Little Miss Muffet, the spider, Mary (Had a Little Lamb), Little Boy Blue, Little Bo-Peep, Little Red Riding Hood, Cicero Pig, the Good Fairy. "Woody Woodpecker and His Talent Show" (Woody Woodpecker, Happy Hedgehog, Happy's Little Shaver, Billy Goat. It is believed that Harry "Yogi Yorgesson" Stewart was the voice of Wally Walrus for this story. This is based on aural identification; no proof of the statement exists in writing.) There are other characters in this story which may or may not have been done by Mel. Evidence indicates that "Pinto" Colvig was at this recording session and some or all of the remaining voices may have been done by him. He was known to be able to do animal sound effects with his voice. "Tweety's Puddy Tat Twouble" (Tweety, Sylvester, Merry-Go-Round operator, zookeeper, plus monkey and lion sounds.) Narrated by Mel Blanc. With June Foray as Granny.

"I'm Glad That I'm Bugs Bunny" (Bugs voice only.) "Daffy Duck's Rhapsody" (Daffy voice only.) "Woody Woodpecker's Picnic" (Woody Woodpecker, Tommy Turtle, Mr. Opossum, English Bulldog, Irish Setter, German Shepherd, Scotch Terrier, ant chorus.) Narrated by Knox Manning. With June Foray as Sammy Squirrel, Mrs. Opossum and French Poodle. "Bugs Bunny Meets Hiawatha" (Bugs Bunny, Indian.) Narrated by Elmer Fudd. With June Foray as Hiawatha. "Daffy Duck Meets Yosemite Sam" (Daffy Duck, Yosemite Sam.) Mel probably also did some of the animal sounds. With Pinto Colvig as Uncle Ulysses. "Tweety Pie" (Tweety Pie, Sylvester, sputtering electric fan sound effect.) Narrated by Tom Reddy. With June Foray as Mistress (female owner of Tweety, more familiarly known as Granny.)

"Henery Hawk" (Henery Hawk, Foghorn Leghorn, Daffy Duck, barnyard dog, other animal sounds.) With June Foray as Henery's mother. "Tweet, Tweet, Tweety" (Tweety, Sylvester.) Narrated by Tweety. With June Foray as Granny. "Bugs Bunny and the Grow-Small Juice" (Bugs Bunny, Daffy Duck.) Narration by Bugs Bunny. With June Foray as Mr. Bee and the Queen Bee. "Henery Hawk's Chicken Hunt" (Henery Hawk, Foghorn Leghorn, Henery's father, barnyard dog, field mouse.) Narrated by Elmer Fudd. Henery's father's voice is Mel's regular speaking voice, and the voice of the field mouse is the same as he used in "I Love Me." "Bugs Bunny and Aladdin's Lamp" (Bugs Bunny, horse race announcer.) Narrated by Mel Blanc. With Billy Bletcher as the Genie.

"Woody Woodpecker and the Scarecrow" (Woody Woodpecker, scarecrows, farmer, crows.) Narrated by Mel Blanc. "Daffy Duck's Feathered Friend" (Daffy Duck, Elmer Fudd's hunting dog.) With Arthur Q. Bryan (Bryan label credit) as Elmer Fudd. "Tweet and Toot" (Kid voice, bird and dog sounds.) ""The E. I. O. Song" (Six unnamed voices.) "Woody Woodpecker and the Lost Monkey" (Woody Woodpecker, elephant, angry homeowner, bass drummer with German accent, monkey.) "Snowbound Tweety" (Tweety, Sylvester.) Narrated by Mel Blanc. With June Foray as

Granny. "Woody Woodpecker and the Animal Crackers" (Woody Woodpecker, animal crackers, cakes, other bake shop foods.)

"The Pussycat Parade" (Kid watching parade, Persian cat, Siamese cat, tomcat.) "Woody Woodpecker and His Space Ship" (Woody Woodpecker, Wally Walrus, two-headed space creature.) Narrated by Mel Blanc. "Wild West Henery Hawk" (Henery Hawk, Foghorn Leghorn, bantam chickens, turtle.) Narrated by Mel Blanc.

"Bugs Bunny and Rabbit Seasoning" (Bugs Bunny, Elmer Fudd's hunting dog.) Narrated by Mel Blanc. With Arthur Q. Bryan as Elmer Fudd. "Happy Hippety Hopper" (Hippety Hopper, little mouse, tough cat, incredulous dog.) Narrated by Mel Blanc. "Pied Piper Pussycat" (Sylvester, Teeny — who is usually known as Sylvester, Jr. — mouse chorus.) Narrated by Elmer Fudd. "Daffy Duck's Duck Inn" (Daffy Duck, dog and cat sounds.) Narrated by Mel Blanc. With Arthur Q. Bryan as Elmer Fudd. "Bugs Bunny and the Pirate" (Bugs Bunny, Yosemite Sam.) Narrated by Mel Blanc.

"Tweety's Good Deed" (Tweety, Sylvester, dog, dog catchers, mayor.) Narrated by Mel Blanc. "Woody Woodpecker and the Truth Tonic" (Woody Woodpecker, Wally Walrus, bus patron.) Narrated by Mel Blanc. With June Foray as boy. "It's Lots of Fun to Share" (Own voice.) "The Party Song" (Own voice.) With June Foray. "D-O-G Spells Dog, D-O-G" (Several unnamed voices as Mel displays his versatility in this two-part song.) With June Foray. "Woody Woodpecker's Fairy Godmother" (Woody Woodpecker, homeowner, dog.) With June Foray as Fairy Godmother. "It's Fun to be Generous" (Kid voice.) "Wheezy Woozy Whatomobile." (Own voice plus antique car vocal sound effect.) Mel wrote this with another songwriter. "Mrs. Hazard's House" (A ladder, an electric cord, a medicine bottle, and a match.) Narrated by Mel Blanc. With June Foray as boy, boy's mother and Mrs. Hazard. She received label credit this time.

"Woody Woodpecker in Mixed-Up Land" (Woody Woodpecker, mayor.) Narrated by Mel Blanc. With June Foray as mixed-up boy and girl. "Woody Woodpecker Meets Davy Crockett" (Woody Woodpecker.) Narrated by Mel Blanc. With Daws Butler as Davy Crockett and Billy Bletcher as Indian. "Save Up Your Pennies" (Kid voice.) "Day Dreaming Danny" (Own voice, but pleasantly aggressive tone, plus a few animal sounds.)

Index

Numbers in *italics* indicate photographs.

About The Author

BEN OHMART runs BearManor Media, a small press publishing *big* books in the entertainment field. He has written books on Don Ameche, The Bickersons, Judy Canova, Paul Frees, Daws Butler, Alan Reed, and Walter Tetley. He lives in Kyoto, Japan with his wife, Mayumi.

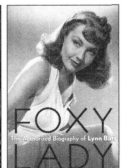

Printed in Great Britain
by Amazon